Transitions to Democracy

The International Library of Politics and Comparative Government

General Editor: David Arter
Associate Editor: Gordon Smith

Titles in the Series:

France
David S. Bell

Italy
Mark Donovan

Germany
Klaus H. Goetz

Revolution and Political Change
Alexander J. Groth

New Politics
Ferdinand Müller-Rommel
and Thomas Poguntke

Legislatures and Legislators
Philip Norton

European Union
Neill Nugent

Nationalism
Brendan O'Leary

Transitions to Democracy
Geoffrey Pridham

The Media
Margaret Scammell and
Holli Semetko

Parties and Party Systems
Steven B. Wolinetz

Transitions to Democracy

Comparative Perspectives from Southern Europe,
Latin America and Eastern Europe

Edited by

Geoffrey Pridham

In Association with the Centre for Mediterranean Studies
University of Bristol

Dartmouth

Aldershot • Brookfield USA • Singapore • Sydney

Published by
Dartmouth Publishing Company Limited
Gower House
Croft Road
Aldershot
Hants GU11 3HR
England

Dartmouth Publishing Company
Old Post Road
Brookfield
Vermont 05036
USA

British Library Cataloguing in Publication Data
Transitions to Democracy: Comparative
Perspectives from Southern Europe, Latin
America and Eastern Europe. –
(International Library of Politics &
Comparative Government)
 I. Pridham, Geoffrey II. Series
 321.8

Library of Congress Cataloging-in-Publication Data
Transitions to democracy: comparative perspectives from Southern
    Europe, Latin America and Eastern Europe / edited by Geoffrey Pridham.
            p. cm.— (The International library of politics and
    comparative government)
        Includes bibliographical references and index.
        ISBN 1–85521–424–5
            1. Democracy—Case studies. 2. Democracy—Europe, Southern.
    3. Democracy—Latin America. 4. Democracy—Europe, Eastern.
    5. Authoritarianism. 6. Post–communism. 7. Representative
    government and representation—Case studies. I. Pridham, Geoffrey.
    1942– . II. Series.
    JC423.T664 1995
    321.8'09'045—dc20
                                                                    94–47359
                                                                         CIP

ISBN 1 85521 424 5

Printed in Great Britain at the University Press, Cambridge

Contents

Acknowledgements

The editors and publishers wish to thank the following for permission to use copyright material.

Blackwell Publishers for the essays: Alan Ware (1992), 'Liberal Democracy: One Form or Many?', *Political Studies*, XL, pp. 130-45; Laurence Whitehead (1992), 'The Alternatives to "Liberal Democracy": a Latin American Perspective', *Political Studies*, XL, pp. 146-59; Jean Grugel (1991), 'Transitions from Authoritarian Rule: Lessons from Latin America', *Political Studies*, XXXIX, pp. 363-68; Zoltan D. Barany (1993), 'Civil-Military Relations in Comparative Perspective: East-Central and Southeastern Europe', *Political Studies*, XLI, pp. 594-610.

Cambridge University Press for the essays: Grzegorz Ekiert (1991), 'Democratization Processes in East Central Europe: A Theoretical Reconsideration', *British Journal of Political Science*, 21, pp. 285-313; Attila Ágh (1991), 'The Transition to Democracy in Central Europe: A Comparative View', *Journal of Public Policy*, 11, pp. 133-51.

Frank Cass & Company Limited for the essays: Giuseppe Di Palma (1984), 'Government Performance: An Issue and Three Cases in Search of Theory', *West European Politics*, 7, pp. 172-87; Constantine P. Danopoulos (1991), 'Democratising the Military: Lessons from Mediterranean Europe', *West European Politics*, 14, pp. 25-41; Alfred Tovias (1984), 'The International Context of Democratic Transition', *West European Politics*, 7, pp. 158-71; Geoffrey Pridham (1990), 'Political Actors, Linkages and Interactions: Democratic Consolidation in Southern Europe', *West European Politics*, 13, pp. 103-17. Copyright © Frank Cass & Company Limited.

Comparative Politics for the essays: Stephanie Lawson (1993), 'Conceptual Issues in the Comparative Study of Regime Change and Democratization', *Comparative Politics*, 26, pp. 183-205; Dankwart A. Rustow (1970), 'Transitions to Democracy: Toward a Dynamic Model', *Comparative Politics*, 3, pp. 337-63; Terry Lynn Karl (1990), 'Dilemmas of Democratization in Latin America', *Comparative Politics*, 23, pp. 1-21.

Government and Opposition for the essay: Arend Lijphart (1990), 'The Southern European Examples of Democratization: Six Lessons for Latin America', *Government and Opposition*, 25, pp. 68-84.

International Social Science Journal for the essay: Terry Lynn Karl and Philippe C. Schmitter (1991), 'Modes of Transition in Latin America, Southern and Eastern Europe', *International Social Science Journal*, 128, pp. 269-84.

The Johns Hopkins University Press for the essay: Philippe C. Schmitter and Terry Lynn Karl

(1991), 'What Democracy Is . . . And Is Not', *Journal of Democracy*, **2**, pp. 75-88; Samuel P. Huntington (1991), 'Democracy's Third Wave', *Journal of Democracy*, **2**, pp. 12-34; Robert M. Fishman (1990), 'Rethinking State and Regime: Southern Europe's Transition to Democracy', *World Politics*, **42**, pp. 422-40; Peter Hakim and Abraham F. Lowenthal (1991), 'Latin America's Fragile Democracies', *Journal of Democracy*, **2**, pp. 16-29.

Kluwer Academic Publishers for the essay: Paul G. Lewis (1990), 'Democratization in Eastern Europe', *Coexistence*, **27**, pp. 245-67.

The MIT Press for the essay: Juan J. Linz (1990), 'Transitions to Democracy', *The Washington Quarterly*, **13**, pp. 143-64.

Leonardo Morlino (1994), 'Democratic Consolidation: Definition and Models', Revised English version. (Published in *Rivista Italiana di Scienza Politica*, **XVI** (1986), pp. 197-238.) Copyright © Leonardo Morlino.

Sage Publications Inc for the essay: Philippe C. Schmitter (1992), 'The Consolidation of Democracy and Representation of Social Groups', *American Behavioral Scientist*, **35**, pp. 422-49. Copyright © 1991 by Sage Publications Inc. Donald Share (1987), 'Transitions to Democracy and Transition through Transaction', *Comparative Political Studies*, **19**, pp. 525-48. Copyright © 1987 by Sage Publications Inc.

Sage Publications Limited for the essay: Attila Ágh (1993), 'The "Comparative Revolution" and the Transition in Central and Southern Europe', *Journal of Theoretical Politics*, **5**, pp. 231-52.

Philippe C. Schmitter (1994), 'The Consolidation of Political Democracies'. Revised version. Unpublished paper. Copyright © Philippe C. Schmitter.

Every effort has been made to trace all the copyright holders, but if any have been inadvertently overlooked the publishers will be pleased to make the necessary arrangements at the first opportunity.

Series Preface

The International Library of Politics and Comparative Government brings together in one series the most significant journal articles to appear in the field of comparative politics in the last twenty-five years or so. The aim is to render readily accessible to teachers, researchers and students an extensive range of essays which, together, provide an indispensable basis for understanding both the established conceptual terrain and the new ground being broken in the fast changing field of comparative political analysis.

The series is divided into three major sections: *Institutional Studies, Thematic Studies* and *Country Studies*. The *Institutional* volumes focus on the comparative investigation of the basic processes and components of the modern pluralist polity, including electoral behaviour, parties and party systems, interest groups, constitutions, legislatures and executives. There are also collections dealing with such major international actors as the European Union and United Nations.

The *Thematic* volumes address those contemporary problems, processes and issues which have assumed a particular salience for politics and policy-making in the late twentieth century. Such themes include: democratization, revolution and political change, 'New Politics', nationalism, terrorism, the military, the media, human rights, consociationalism and the challenges to mainstream party political ideologies.

The *Country* volumes are particularly innovative in applying a comparative perspective to a consideration of the political science tradition in individual states, both large and small. The distinctive features of the national literature are highlighted and the wider significance of developments is evaluated.

A number of acknowledged experts have been invited to act as editors for the series; they preface each volume with an introductory essay in which they review the basis for the selection of articles, and suggest future directions of research and investigation in the subject area.

The series is an invaluable resource for all those working in the field of comparative government and politics.

DAVID ARTER
Professor of European Integration
Leeds Metropolitan University

GORDON SMITH
Emeritus Professor of Government
London School of Economics and Political Science

Introduction

The phenomenon of transitions to liberal democracy has become a major concern for political scientists in recent decades, especially in the last few years. The problems of democratic transition and consolidation have increasingly come to exercise the attentions of comparativists in particular, with their interest in how far a common regional environment might be conducive to such a systemic trend. There are even some journals now devoted to the subject of democratization. Regime transition has thus become a growth area in its own right, while also of course relating to such broader concerns as political change and democratic theory.

This expansion of regime transition studies clearly reflects recent and current trends. Most dramatically, it responds to the collapse of Communist regimes in Eastern Europe and the former Soviet Union. Such a change, unexpected by common admission among experts and political leaders alike, was quickly recognized as one of the principal historical occurrences of the 20th century. The transitions which have followed in the East have since become very difficult – much more so than the previous and successful ones in Southern Europe – not least because they are really a dual process of economic as well as political change. Being difficult transitions, they have been that much more challenging to political scientists, even calling into question some earlier theoretical assumptions about democratic transition. Meanwhile, this phenomenon has recently spread to other continents, including Africa; the prospects also seem better for stable democracies in Latin America which has previously undergone not only transitions to, but also inversions from, democracy.

Serious academic work on democratic transition began in the mid-1970s just as the authoritarian regimes in Southern Europe (Iberia and Greece) were disintegrating, so allowing these countries to embark on democratization. Much of the research on this theme was inspired by the opportunity to compare simultaneous regime changes in states that had long been under authoritarian rule.[1] Quite apart from the encouragement to research on the countries concerned – made possible by much improved access to sources on contemporary and earlier political events – this fresh interest in democratic transition produced some fruitful comparative work and stimulated new thinking on the subject. This included looking back in time and drawing contrasts as well as comparisons with the postwar returns to democracy in Western Europe, such as in Italy and West Germany. A few ambitious projects also attempted inter-regional comparisons by analysing the transitions in Southern Europe with those in Latin America.[2]

It is small wonder that some works on transition have referred to 'waves' of democratization. The chief proponent of this view is Samuel Huntington, who has spoken of a current 'third wave' following a first one that commenced in the last century and continued until the 1920s. The second wave began after the defeat of fascism in the Second World War; the third he saw as starting in the mid-1970s and as having led, by the 1990s, to a doubling of the number of democratic governments in the world.[3] However, as Huntington points out, there have also been reverse tendencies with the collapse of some new democracies, such as in Latin America, following the second wave of transitions. Also, judging by current predictions, it is conceivable that some of the new democracies in Eastern Europe and, more probably, in the ex-USSR will not succeed. Despite such negative trends, the evidence for democracy becoming ever more popular over the past two decades is overwhelming. According to one recent survey, the number of formally democratic states in the world rose from 25 per cent in 1973 to 45 per cent in 1990; while by 1993, 126 (or 68 per cent) of the 183 states in the world are democratic or are in the course of becoming democratic, compared with 44 in 1972 and 56 in 1980.[4]

The term 'waves' suggests historical cycles of democratization involving significant transnational influences affecting different countries in the same region. However, as Huntington indicates and the literature on transitions emphasizes, there is a fragility common to new democracies for reasons that lie to a large degree within the countries themselves. This cautions strongly against the kind of triumphalist views about democracy that surfaced in some Western official circles after the regime changes in Eastern Europe. What happened in 1989 was only the beginning of a long and complicated process. Within a year, it was noted that 'the East Europeans are discovering that there is a large, dangerous chasm between grabbing freedom and establishing democracy; there is no natural progression'.[5] Given the confusion that may arise in looking at present regime changes, it is therefore necessary at this point to clarify the key terms used in this volume.

'Democratization' is a loose expression describing the overall process of regime change from start to completion; namely, from the end of the previous authoritarian system to the stabilization and rooting of new democracies. It therefore includes both stages of what are referred to in the comparative literature as 'transition' to a liberal or constitutional democracy and its subsequent 'consolidation'. The outcome is a system that should meet certain procedural requirements, such as the provision of regular elections and institutional mechanisms that check executive power, as well as the guarantee of human rights and evolution towards a remaking of political culture that is supportive of democratic political life.

By 'democratic transition', we refer to a stage of regime change that is decisive. It commences at the point when a previous totalitarian or authoritarian system begins to collapse or disintegrate leading to the situation when, with a new constitution in place, the democratic structures become routinized and the political elites adjust their behaviour to liberal democratic norms. Transition tasks involve, above all, negotiating the constitutional settlement and finalizing the rules of procedure for political competition, but also dismantling authoritarian agencies and abolishing laws unsuitable for democratic politics. In comparison, 'democratic consolidation' is usually a lengthier process, but also one with wider and possibly deeper effects. It involves, in the first instance, the gradual removal of the uncertainties that invariably surround transition, followed by the full institutionalization of the new democracy, the internalization of its rules and institutional procedures and the dissemination of democratic values.

It is thus an opportune moment to look afresh at the state of the art in the literature on transitions to liberal democracy, given the challenges posed by recent regime change and the widespread, albeit uncertain, progress of democratization in various regions of the world. With this literature now abundant, the selection of examples has necessarily been strict. The principal bias has been towards essays which are comparative in approach or perspective. Any inclusion of country-specific studies, however excellent, would have made selection virtually impossible considering the obvious constraints on space. It was also felt that comparative work would provide a suitable context for the most recent and still incomplete transitions in Eastern Europe. Otherwise, preference has been given to essays of quality which are both stimulating and are likely to have some long-term relevance to the study of democratic transition. Some are more accessible than others to the general reader, but availability has remained a criterion very secondary to the above considerations.

The volume consists of five parts, with the third sub-divided into the three area studies of Southern Europe, Latin America and Eastern Europe. The fourth part has been devoted to international aspects of transition, since this has for long remained a neglected, if not underrated, dimension in the literature. A final part on democratic consolidation is included to round off this survey, not least as there has been a lack of clarity in some writing as to when transition ends and consolidation begins. We now turn briefly to each part in turn for a summary of the essays selected and a consideration of their thematic context.

Part I: Liberal Democracy: Conceptual Issues for Regime Change

Early theoretical essays on transition referred blandly to 'liberal democracy' as the outcome, but with little definitional precision. Over time, however, comparative studies have come to recognize the obvious – that liberal democracies comprise a fairly wide range of possible structures. For instance, the transitions in Southern Europe occasioned some debate about whether there was any 'Mediterranean model' of democracy that might be different from the systems in Western Europe.[6] Furthermore, it is now acknowledged that there is a need for stricter attention to what really is a 'liberal democracy'. There has, for instance, been some division between those looking for what is called 'procedural democracy' (satisfying certain formal requirements such as free elections) and a more ample or qualitative version sometimes called 'substantive democracy'.

This basic question about the nature of liberal democracy has acquired more urgency following the changes in Eastern Europe. As Paul Lewis has commented, the situation there is not 'particularly clearcut in terms of the idea of democracy and conceptions of the basis for its development in the area'. For many in the region, democracy remains an ill-defined objective with diverse associations, while for others it is synonymous with material wealth (as in the West) rather than political values.[7] Furthermore, some basic differences concerning the nature of democracy have surfaced between elite circles in Western and Eastern Europe – with preferences veering respectively towards standard or procedural democracy (drawing on liberal ideas of conflicting interests) as against expansive or participatory democracy, emphasizing the importance of civil society and influenced by communitarian views.[8] The predominance of procedural requirements in official Western circles has been evident in the doctrine of 'democratic conditionality' in return for economic aid. It has surfaced too in the prospect of eventual membership of the European Union, although in this case respect for human rights has come to be stressed more.

For the above reasons, Part I is an important prelude to our more direct handling of theoretical and empirical aspects of the transition process. In Chapter 1, Philippe Schmitter and Terry Karl usefully set out relevant criteria of what is and is not a liberal democracy, their preference being for the procedural version. On the latter count, they identify various criteria which in effect serve to caution against inflated expectations of performance by new democracies. The emergence of a distinction on the part of the public between 'system' (the new democracy) and 'government' (the party elite(s) in power at a particular moment) is fair evidence of progress in transition towards the prospect of consolidation. As Huntington notes laconically, 'democracy does not mean that problems will be solved; it does mean that rulers can be removed; and the essence of democratic behaviour is doing the latter because it is impossible to do the former'.[9]

Using key features of liberal democracies, Alan Ware differentiates between forms of the system in Chapter 2. He notes a tendency among liberal democracies to 'borrow' institutional or procedural ideas from other countries, a tendency all the more pronounced among new democracies, as was evident in Southern Europe and is certainly present in Eastern Europe. On the general question of 'exporting' liberal democracy as such, he rightly warns that the cultural context in which such a system is implanted is crucial to its survival prospects.

Stephanie Lawson's approach is similar in its attention to definitional questions, but takes the discussion forward by emphasizing the need to distinguish between 'regime' and the 'state'. This theme, absent in the earlier literature on transitions, is discussed again in Chapter 11 by Fishman in the section on Southern Europe. The relationship, indeed confusion, between the two under authoritarianism is one that can have implications for the course of transition, a problem particularly pertinent after four decades of Communist rule in Eastern Europe.

Part II Theoretical and Comparative Interpretations of Transition and Authoritarian Collapse

Theoretical approaches to democratic transition have not as a whole represented any coherent work. Broadly seen, they have tended to diverge between two schools of thinking, known as the functionalist or macro-oriented and the genetic or micro-oriented approaches.

The former, concerned with long-term developments of a socioeconomic kind, has given paramount attention to structural or environmental determinants of political system change. It has inclined to the view that regime changes are preconditioned by certain phenomena like economic development, cultural patterns or simply modernization. On the other hand, the genetic school has given priority to conjunctural factors and strategic choice, and especially to political determinants of regime change. It has preferred to emphasize the importance of political choice and strategy by actors during the actual transition process.[10] Genetic approaches have tended to be more influential in empirical research from the time of the transitions in Southern Europe onwards.

Their basic difference is one of outlook. While functionalist views have been criticized for being too deterministic, genetic interpretations have dwelt on the uncertainties of transition and the scope for mistaken and perhaps fateful decisions. Nevertheless, when applied to empirical research, there is more compatibility between these two approaches than is commonly recognized. In effect, the functionalists focus on a different time scale than the geneticists, namely on longer-term processes prior to the occurrence of transition, but also conceivably following its achievement. Socioeconomic change of the kind highlighted by functionalists cannot of course be telescoped into the relatively short time span of democratic transition. The two schools are perhaps most compatible when looking at the subsequent process of democratic consolidation, which is longer-lasting and is determined by interactions between politics, society and the economy.

Our concern in this volume is primarily with the transition process proper. For this reason, the authors selected in Part II sympathize more with the genetic approach. Chapter 4 by Dankwart Rustow is one of the most cited in comparative work on transitions, and is included here because of its influence on later work. It does not represent any grand theory and is hardly the last word on transition, but it emphasizes the dynamics of that process, sets out a framework for analysis and throws out some useful notions. It should be pointed out, however, that his final 'habituation phase' is one that effectively leads into the subsequent process of consolidation.

Philippe Schmitter next takes us back in time in 'speculating' about the demise of authoritarian regimes. This is relevent since what has been called the 'pre-transition' stage may well have a formative effect on the course and duration of transition problems. In this period the dictatorship's weaknesses become terminal; the system begins to disintegrate and the path is set for eventual regime change. In particular, we are interested here in the causes of authoritarian regimes 'opening up' and subsequently breaking down. Such change may arise from a variety of developments, such as military defeat, basic economic failure, socioeconomic transformation and its political repercussions, as well as from the disintegration of the dominant coalition between elite groups supporting the authoritarian regime.[11] These developments are not mutually exclusive and may interact to produce a negative dynamic. For instance, a basic policy failure (especially economic) may provoke strategic divisions between hard and softliners in the ruling coalition. Schmitter takes a rather lofty stance on these matters, but provides a necessary context to our primary concern with the actual commencement of democratization.

The 'pre-transition' stage is invariably marked by some form of liberalization of the authoritarian regime, which makes limited concessions to domestic or international pressures for change. Juan Linz argues in Chapter 6 that liberalization is no guarantee of democratization, disagreeing with those who see an essential link between the nature of authoritarian collapse and the form of transition. His essay should be noted for its discussion of non-democratic regime types and of different paths to democracy (in reference to Alfred Stepan).

Whatever the link between the two, a basic distinction should be drawn between liberalization and democratization. The former is largely a defensive response, being an attempt by a dictatorship to control change. According to Leonardo Morlino, however, democratization is marked by 'the real recognition of civil and political rights and, where necessary, by a complete transformation' that favours the reconstruction of civil society. He continues:

> Political parties and a party system emerge. The organisation of interest groups, such as labour unions, takes place. The elaboration, or adoption, of the principal democratic institutions and procedures that will characterise the regime, such as electoral laws and a specified relationship between executive and legislative powers, occurs.[12]

It is democratization proper that is the subject of Samuel Huntington's thesis of 'waves'.

Chapter 7 – a grand historical survey of events on different continents – encapsulates the arguments presented in his book, *The Third Wave*.[13] Such change may benefit from a 'demonstration effect' or from 'snowballing' that may occur among countries geographically proximate and culturally similar. Huntington identifies various obstacles to democratization which are more applicable to some regions than others. And he touches in passing on the relationship between economic and political change: 'economic development makes democracy possible; political leadership makes it real'.

Terry Karl and Philippe Schmitter take a broad comparative look at transition, combining the three regions which are the subject of the next part of this volume. They are concerned with the question of how such similar outcomes (demise of authoritarian rule, advent of democracy) could emerge from such diverse national and regional situations and what they may have in common. Given the different modes of transition and different types of democracy which result, it is difficult to generalize across regions, but the authors explore a number of hypotheses. In particular, they look at the mode of transition from autocratic rule as a principal determinant of what kind of democracy will emerge and at the preconditions (or rather, sets of preconditions) for democratization. While prone to genetic thinking on regime change, they nevertheless argue that the conditioning effect of structures on strategy during transition must be considered.

The successive regional waves of democratization covered by this volume have undoubtedly influenced comparative approaches in transition studies. This is particularly true of the first of these in Southern Europe. Focal points of this work have been the phases of transition (as in Rustow), the different paths to democracy or how transition starts (such as Stepan's categories, summarized above by Linz), but more particularly the types of transition. These are sometimes broadly distinguished as evolutionary or revolutionary, although such a simple typology distracts from the complexities of the transition process. For it is conceivable that a national case may veer towards different 'models' of transition during different phases of the process.

Variations in the style and scope of transition have conventionally ranged from reform (or transaction) to rupture, with the course of transition varying between the incremental and protracted struggle. There have as well been cases of democratic restoration, notably when authoritarian interludes have been brief. Furthermore, there is the familiar distinction between 'top-down' and 'bottom-up' progressions in the scope of transition. Much of the comparative literature, and especially that specializing in Southern Europe, has also explicitly stressed the importance of pacts among transition actors as a means for introducting stability in a new and fragile democracy.

Part III National Case-Studies of Transition: Three Area Studies

Southern Europe

Some 'middle-range theory' on regime change has shown an interest in inter-regional observations, stressing differencs of transition environments, but also deriving specific lessons from one set of cases for another. Arend Lijphart illustrates this approach in Chapter 9: 'Six Lessons for Latin America'. His focus, however, is only on institutional factors which tend to underplay national variations within Southern Europe. But his conclusions are useful, both on crucial differences between the two regions (such as socioeconomic) and on the role of the military and the geographical proximity of the superpower.

Giuseppe Di Palma focuses on an issue commonly raised in transition studies: how much the prospects for new democracies hinge on the performance by their first governments. It is commonly assumed that these systems face a legitimacy problem which is connected in some way with their early success or failure in satisfying (especially economic) policy demands. Di Palma views this problem sceptically arguing, in the spirit of Rustow, that transferring allegiance to a new democracy is largely a matter of calculation and interest. Moreover, such a system benefits from a 'coalition of consent' through the compromises that prompted the democratic settlement in the first place. He applies this hypothesis to the cases of Southern Europe.

Di Palma further underlines the importance of a country's institutional history in determining how far the state may extricate itself from the shadow of the outgoing dictatorship. This theme is central to Robert Fishman in Chapter 11 where he claims that the transitions literature has not adequately explored the distinction between state and regime. In Fishman's view, this is necessary not only for identifying the source which initiated democratization – such as from within the authoritarian regime or not – but, more importantly, for understanding the subsequent trajectory of transition. This is more likely to be successful when state and regime can be distinguished from one another. Where this is not the case, 'special problems are likely to emerge in the process of democratisation'.

Donald Share is concerned, on the other hand, with the actual process of transition – its start, duration and end point, but especially its nature. Introducing four major types of transition, he concentrates on transition by transaction, examining this model in the light of the Spanish experience of the late 1970s which has often been viewed as an archetype. From this example he draws lessons about the crucial role of elite attitudes and skill in conducting transition through transaction. This included the ability to gather support for democratization from a wide range of forces, including the cooperation of the opposition in bringing about system change. Also evident in the Spanish case was the government's control over the process, allowing for rapid and orderly transition.

There was one major threat to the success of the Spanish transition, namely from the military. This problem is explored by Constantine Danopoulos in Chapter 13 who considers all three countries in Southern Europe. The author examines ways in which the military was transformed from supporting authoritarianism to actually defending a democratic system. This he does by discussing in turn societal and organizational factors, the latter referring to military professionalism (concentrating on and improving their professional role rather than intervening in politics) as a possible stimulus to democratization.

Latin America

Responding to Rustow's original question about what conditions make democracy possible, Terry Karl takes issue with the once-dominant concern with prerequisites or preconditions for democracy, referring to economic performance, political culture and historical conditions. Reviewing the literature on this approach in Chapter 14, the author argues that the Latin American experience disproves any generalizations on such a basis. Instead, it is better not to look for single or clear causes of democratization, but rather to focus on the process itself.

Karl argues in favour of 'structured contingency' (already mentioned in Chapter 8) whereby social structures present both limits on and opportunities for contingent choice (decisions by transition actors). Different types of transition in Latin America are then examined to illustrate this theme.

Such a 'path-dependent' approach, stressing the actual course of transition, may clarify how far structural changes facilitate or hinder democratization. In comparison, Peter Hakim and Abraham Lowenthal examine more descriptively the problems facing democratization in Latin America. Noting the trend towards democracy in the region, they find that the new systems there nevertheless remain 'fragile'. The real problem is not so much achieving transition, but rather developing conditions that favour eventual democratic consolidation. 'It will take years of struggle to secure democratic stability in most countries of Latin America' where democratic institutions are likely to 'remain vulnerable for decades to come'.

Laurence Whitehead sees Latin America generally as an example of 'democracy by default', whereby anti-democratic ideologies and systems of government are in retreat (see Chapter 16). This he identifies as the key explanation of the return to democratic regimes during the 1980s. Compared with earlier transitions in the region, this recent wave is different in several significant ways. These include less sympathy for authoritarian rule on the part of economic interests, the end of the Cold War (which had encouraged strategic imperatives to the detriment of democratization) and the weakened appeal of the Cuban model. While dwelling on the obstacles to consolidation in the region, he identifies factors that may eventually assist its progress, such as secure frontiers and the widespread preference for 'pactism' in bringing about returns to democracy. Combined with the fact that Latin America is already operating (albeit poorly functioning) market economies, these factors lead Whitehead to conclude that 'it is difficult to find good arguments that the prospects for consolidated and participatory democracy are better in Eastern Europe than in the Latin subcontinent'.

Jean Grugel's short essay makes the pertinent point that theories of transition have been limited by their 'top-down bias'. This inhibits a full explanation of the factors leading to democratization, ignoring the role of opposition to authoritarian regimes and, more generally, the role of popular organizations in the transition process. This wider perspective is present in other work on regime change in Latin America.[14] Although Grugel applies this approach to the case of Chile, the argument has a vital relevance to the more recent cases of Eastern Europe.

Eastern Europe

The collapse of Communist systems in Eastern Europe and the former USSR opened the way for a whole new set of regime transitions. We look here at Eastern Europe, having already examined two other regions where the process of democratic transition occurred earlier and is largely completed. Research on the current transitions in Eastern Europe has, among other things, been conscious of inter-regional parallels, the 'Spanish model' of evolutionary transition in particular having an appeal. Inter-regional comparisons also appear in some of the essays selected here. Our concern is primarily with the political transition, in line with the basic focus of this volume, although notice is taken of how this might be affected by the parallel process of economic transformation from state to market economies.

A thoughtful early comparative view of the Eastern European transitions is that by Grzegorz Ekiert (Chapter 18). His chief concern is with the prospects for, or rather limits to, democratization in the region. These he sees as considerable, given the rapid collapse of state power, combined with serious economic decline and social crisis. His sober assessment is still pertinent today and is more typical of the present difficulties surrounding transition than of the euphoria or optimism of the first year of 'freedom'. Ekiert argues the need for new frameworks for approaching the transitions in the East. This is most evident when dealing with relations between the party-state and society across time, given the survival capacity of 'domestic society' even under Stalinism. This dimension is ignored by Western scholars because of their 'narrow preoccupation with political elites and the political decision-making process'. Such rethinking of theoretical concerns in regime transition is compelling after the reconstruction of 'political society' and its crucial role in the events of 1989.

This same need for new frames of reference similarly colours Attila Agh's view of the transitions in Central Europe, although he tends to adopt a more upbeat view. Agh's approach is very much linked to Western comparative concepts and the lessons to be learned from previous waves of democratization, especially in Southern Europe. Global factors are increasingly influential in moves to democratization, which 'are first of all a function of the world system and not an exclusively domestic political formation'. Agh believes that European 'substantive' conceptions of democracies are more relevant to Central Europe than American formalistic ones because of the former's attention to social and economic participation. He believes this dichotomy helps to explain the successful transitions in Southern Europe and the continuing fragility of democracies in Latin America.

Paul Lewis also sees some virtue in comparisons with Southern Europe, but not to the extent of ignoring significant differences. The economic context is very different and the limited previous experience of political democracy in Eastern Europe warns against any talk there of 'redemocratisation'. In Chapter 20, Lewis argues for relating this current democratization to the broad context of modernization, since this draws attention to relations between the political process and social forces on the one hand, and the global economic context on the other. He identifies various tensions in Eastern European transitions relating to the role of the state, political culture, weak institutional development and political participation.

Attila Agh's second, more recent, essay is again inspired by inter-regional comparisons. In his view, parallels between Southern and Central Europe draw strength from common historical traditions and cultural similarities, from failures to adapt structurally to world economic crises and from an inclination towards parliamentary models and negotiated transitions. Agh introduces four scenarios for the transitions in the East, ranging from 'easy Westernisation' to a Third World-type of outcome or 'Latin Americanisation' (populism or possibly authoritarian rule). While most analyses of Eastern European transitions are cautious if not somewhat pessimistic about their chances of success, one surprising aspect has been the general absence of any military threat. With the dramatic exceptions of the former Yugoslavia and parts of the ex-USSR, in most of Eastern Europe the military has remained restrained, unlike in the Southern European transitions. Zoltan Barany provides an early assessment of the reasons for this, and relates these to civil-military relations under the Communist systems.

Part IV The International Context of Transition

This dimension has previously been disregarded or underplayed in transition studies, which is surprising given historical examples of (re)democratizations which occurred after the Second World War under Allied occupation. For a long time, work on 'third wave' cases tended to consider international factors as at best secondary, and usually as variables dependent on domestic processes of regime change. Thus Schmitter attributed the greater likelihood of new democracies persisting in Southern Europe than in Latin America in part to a more supportive international framework in Europe.[15]

Some writers such as Huntington and Linz have paid attention to both domestic and external factors in democratization, while being primarily concerned with the former. Proponents of dependency theory argued, on the other hand, for the primary importance of external factors, although their work had little influence on studies of the European democratizations. It has been assumed that, in their case, international factors have been more relevant to democratic consolidation than to democratic transition.[16]

The regime changes in Eastern Europe have finally challenged the neglect of the international dimension in democratic transitions. This is because of the very salience there of external actors like the Soviet Union and later the European Union, as well as those influences deriving from the East's 'return to Europe'. These events have forced comparativists working in this area to confront the relative weight of external and domestic determinants of regime change. Huntington, for instance, recognizes Eastern Europe as presenting the most dramatic version of the 'snowballing' or 'demonstration effect' in transitions.[17]

The international context thus deserves special attention in this volume. It is of course a collective term for a variety of different external actors or pressures, including national governments and regional or international organizations, as well as non-governmental or non-state actors and some less tangible transnational influences such as telecommunications and cultural trends. Geoffrey Pridham's research agenda establishes a broad framework for analysing interactions between political system change and such external factors (Chapter 23). Recognizing that this aspect of transition is a complex one, he argues for disaggregating both international and domestic environments and for focusing on different linkages between them (inner-directed as well as outer-directed).

Alfred Tovias examines the international context with respect to the Southern European transitions of the 1970s. He argues that the economic environment of these transitions was at first sight unfavourable for their prospects of success, but that in practice various conditions eventually assisted them. These included the existence of integrative international organizations and supportive networks for economic stabilization, the commitment of West European governments (for strategic reasons) to democratic stability in the Mediterranean, and the absence of hostile foreign intervention as witnessed in the 1930s.

Philippe Schmitter recognizes the general need to question the paramount importance of domestic factors in democratization in the light of events in Eastern Europe. Admitting that the 'international context' is difficult to identify exactly, he looks at various sub-contexts. His main contribution to the debate in Chapter 25 is to present four thematic approaches called trends, events, waves and stages. This is intended to highlight more clearly than before the constraints on and opportunities for transitions deriving from outside. He still concludes, however, that international factors have more lasting effects on democratic consolidation than on democratic transition.

Part V Towards Democratic Consolidation

The consolidation of new democracies is a much less studied theme than their transitions. This is partly due to the fact that there have been many more transitions in the three regions than subsequent consolidations. Several countries in Latin America have managed the first but not (yet) the second, while in earlier decades some have even reverted to dictatorship. And, of course, it is too soon to start talking of possible consolidation in Eastern Europe when, by comparative criteria, most countries there have by and large not yet completed the transition process. On the other hand, the democracies of Southern Europe are now generally seen as having not only achieved transition (invariably by the early 1980s), but also as having subsequently worked through consolidation. It comes as no surprise, then, that most comparative work and theorizing about democratic consolidation has been with respect to Southern European cases.[18]

There is another and more complicated reason for this dearth of work on consolidation. The process of democratic consolidation is much less easy to define precisely than is transition. Indeed, there is some difference among experts as to how long the process lasts (some favouring roughly a decade, others arguing for anything up to a generation). But democratic consolidation not only takes longer than transition (which in Southern Europe required on average about half a decade); it is also a process involving many more levels of activity and hence many more actors, including societal as well as political-institutional ones. This question of levels of consolidation is explored in the essays selected in this section.

The end point of consolidation may be said to have been reached when a (no longer new) democracy has become rooted in a country and been reinforced by significant evolution of its political culture – which may be called the democratization of values. Therefore, not merely have the prospects for rival system alternatives been removed ('negative consolidation'), but affective links with that democracy have also developed on the part of elites and public alike ('positive consolidation'). Such a system then acquires legitimacy.

This process takes us well beyond the terms of reference of this volume. However, Part V on consolidation is included by way of completing this review of transition, for clearly there must be a relationship between the two successive processes. Some of the literature has debated how much a particular type of transition may help to determine the nature and perhaps length of consolidation in a country. Huntington, for instance, has argued that 'a peaceful, consensual transition favours democratic consolidation' and that, conversely, a violent one is likely to raise problems for generating a deeper commitment to democratic institutions and values.[19] At the same time, the qualitative differences between transition and consolidation noted above mean that the latter is not simply an extension of the former.

Philippe Schmitter's long review of the subject in Chapter 26 is not only useful definitionally, but enlightening on precisely the different levels of the process of consolidation and on its differences from transition. According to him, it is even possible for some areas of consolidation to begin to develop before transition is fully achieved. An advocate of the view that the mode of transition is the primary determinant of the type of consolidation achieved, Schmitter sees the latter as in many ways involving a 'structuration' of political behaviour and as having moved significantly beyond the high-risk situation that often marks transition. Consolidation may, however, proceed at different paces at different levels. Schmitter also considers 'partial regimes' and their consolidation with reference to different sites where new system legitimation occurs.

Leonardo Morlino's essay on consolidation clarifies some further definitional problems, as well as different aspects of the process. It is broadly similar to Schmitter in its interpretation of that process, but draws on cross-regional experiences by including Latin America as well as Southern Europe. It also dwells more specifically on some of the different levels and actors involved in consolidation.

One of these is political parties, the subject of Geoffrey Pridham's analysis of linkages and interactions in the process of consolidation (Chapter 28). This study considers their role systemically by examining in turn three relationships: between parties and the state; between different parties; and between parties and society. In general, he argues that the progress of the different levels of consolidation should be measured in conjunction, while noting how they may interact. This is preferable to judging consolidation with reference to isolated variables, such as the existence of 'anti-system' parties. There is an obvious relationship between the consolidation of new democracies and the consolidation of their party systems, although the two – while parallel – may not always proceed at exactly the same pace or have the same duration.

While Pridham argues for the centrality of parties in the process of democratic consolidation, Schmitter tends to take issue with this idea when discussing social groups as an example of a 'partial regime' (Chapter 29). As elsewhere, he makes a link with the nature of the previous regime: 'the more a departing autocracy was characterised by extensive state corporatism or monistic control by the governing party, the greater will be the probable difficulty of adjusting to voluntarism and "official" indifference'. He also sees the role of groups as having less relevance for the survival or persistence of a new democracy than for the type of democracy that is consolidated.

Conclusion: The Future of Democratic Transition Studies

What has the literature on transitions to democracy taught us about the nature of this process, and what future directions of research are likely to develop in the field? Most of all, this survey and the essays that follow emphatically counter the triumphalist outlook that surfaced in 1989. This reaction trumpeted the simplistic notion that 'democracy' had won the contest between systems, without carefully examining the form of systems that were emerging following the collapse of Communist rule in the East. As Vaclav Havel put it succinctly, 'we have done away with the totalitarian system, but we have yet to win democracy'.

Democratic transition is a fairly delicate process, and a successful outcome cannot be guaranteed. As the literature shows, much depends on the process itself – how it is handled by political actors, what favourable or unfavourable circumstances impinge and, significantly, how memories and inheritances from the past are transmitted to the new game of democratic politics.

Southern Europe has clearly led the way in comparative and empirical research on democratic transitions by virtue of comprising a regional set of opportune cases that worked through transition and led to the consolidation of new democracies in the European mould. Nevertheless, the Latin American and Eastern European examples have presented a rich field for students of democratization, if only because there have been so many more of them. Already, the experience of change in Eastern Europe has not only begun to inform comparative approaches, but also to challenge some existing hypotheses. While established transition theory still provides viable directions for assessing what is now happening in that region, it needs to adapt, develop and broaden its scope.

For instance, with respect to key moments of decision making, theories of transition have given prominence to the role of elites – especially, though not exclusively, to political elites. It is this aspect of the literature that has probably been most heavily criticized by those working on the current transitions. As David Ost maintained in an early response to the change: 'Until we place the concept of civil society in the forefront, we will not be able to theoretically address developments in Eastern Europe'.[20] And as so many of the publications on the events of 1989 underline, the role of the masses proved decisive in the collapse of the Communist regimes, which was invariably described as a 'revolution'.[21] It is important, nevertheless, to consider the transition process as a series of different and sometimes fluctuating phases that allow varying opportunities for both elite action and mass influence. In particular, we need to give more attention to interactions between both spheres, especially at key moments of regime change.

Another deficiency of transition theory has been its common neglect of historical explanations. As Ian Roxborough has noted, the transitions literature has often been ahistorical, whereas it is important to put waves of democratization into historical or time contexts.[22] There is generally a need to root the study of transitions more firmly within the frame of historical sequence (such as national history). No transition, however radical, can break completely with the past because of inheritances (including negative ones) from the previous regime and the impact of historical memory and national culture. This need has been highlighted by the transitions in Eastern Europe and by the related 'rebirth of history' thesis.

A third deficiency in the literature is the tendency discussed above to under-emphasize, if not ignore, the importance of the international context of democratization. Recent work has begun to rectify this problem,[23] with events in Eastern Europe dramatizing the need to incorporate external factors in analysing transition. Those working in the field have thus been compelled to broaden their perspectives.

Empirical studies of earlier transitions have as a rule illustrated the various directions set out in theoretical work. At the same time, research on transitions in Southern Europe and Latin America has in effect moved thematic concerns somewhat beyond the rather narrow confines of the theory. This has painted a richer and more complex picture of transition processes, while (not surprisingly) identifying significant differences between simultaneous cases.

Altogether, the study of transitions to democracy – now an area in its own right – is likely to have a promising future. The questions posed by those processes taking place in Eastern Europe (if not elsewhere) and the difficulties they face will continue to provide stimulation and challenge. We also need reminding that the eventual outcomes in that region may not, in some cases, be comparable to the established democracies in Western Europe. Indeed, there has been a certain 'culture-bound' attitude present in expectations about system change in the

East, most evident on the part of Western governments but also sometimes in academic research.

Notes

1. For example, J. Herz (1982), *From Dictatorship to Democracy*, Westport: Greenwood Press; G. Pridham (ed.) (1984), *The New Mediterranean Democracies: Regime Transition in Spain, Greece and Portugal*, London: Frank Cass.
2. Notably, G. O'Donnell, P. Schmitter and L. Whitehead (eds) (1986), *Transitions from Authoritarian Rule: Prospects for Democracy*, Baltimore: Johns Hopkins University Press. See also, D. Ethier (ed.) (1990), *Democratic Transition and Consolidation in Southern Europe, Latin America and South-East Asia*, Houndmills: Macmillan.
3. For Huntington, see Chapter 7 in this volume; also, his (1991) book, *The Third Wave: Democratisation in the Late 20th Century*, London: University of Oklahoma Press.
4. Quoted by A. Leftwich (1993), 'Voting can damage your wealth', in *The Times Higher Education Supplement*, 13 August.
5. *The Times*, 19 January 1991.
6. See A. Lijphart et al. (1988), 'A Mediterranean model of democracy? The Southern European democracies in comparative perspective' in *West European Politics*, January; cf. chapter 1 in Pridham, *New Mediterranean Democracies*.
7. P. Lewis (1993), 'Democracy and its future in Eastern Europe' in D. Held (ed.), *Prospects for Democracy*, Cambridge: Polity Press, pp. 293, 296.
8. N. Rengger (1994), 'Towards a culture of democracy?: democratic theory and democratisation in Eastern and Central Europe' in G. Pridham, E. Herring and G. Sanford (eds), *Building Democracy?: The International Dimension of Democratisation in Eastern Europe*, London: Pinter.
9. Huntington, *Third Wave*, pp. 262–3.
10. See Pridham, chapter 1 in *New Mediterranean Democracies*, for a summary of these different approaches.
11. L. Morlino (1987), 'Democratic establishments: a dimensional analysis' in E. Baloyra (ed.), *Comparing New Democracies: Transition and Consolidation in Mediterranean Europe and the Southern Cone*, Boulder: Westview Press, p. 74.
12. Ibid, p. 55.
13. See Huntington, *Third Wave*.
14. E.g. P. Cammack (1991), 'Democracy and development in Latin America', review article in *Journal of International Development*, 3; also his 'Democratisation and citizenship in Latin America' in M. Moran and G. Parry (eds) (1993), *Democracy and Democratisation*, Macmillan.
15. Schmitter, introduction to *Transitions from Authoritarian Rule*. See also in the same book L. Whitehead, 'International aspects of democratisation' as an early example of a comparative approach to this subject.
16. However on international factors in transition, see G. Pridham (ed.) (1991), *Encouraging Democracy: The International Context of Regime Transition in Southern Europe*, Leicester: Leicester University Press.
17. Huntington, *Third Wave*, p. 104.
18. Especially the major project on 'The Nature and Consequences of Democracy in the New Southern Europe', funded by the SSRC (New York) and directed by Nikiforos Diamandouros and Richard Gunther. This work will result in five edited volumes on the process and achievement of consolidation in the region. On consolidation, see G. Pridham (ed.) (1990), *Securing Democracy: Political Parties and Democratic Consolidation in Southern Europe*, London: Routledge; also J. Higley and R. Gunther (eds) (1992), *Elites and Democratic Consolidation in Latin America and Southern Europe*, Cambridge: Cambridge University Press.
19. Huntington, *Third Wave*, p. 276.

20. D. Ost (1990), 'Transition theory and Eastern Europe', paper for the conference on Democratization in Latin America and Eastern Europe, Pultusk (Poland), May.
21. D. McSweeney and C. Tempest (1993), 'The political science of democratic transition in Eastern Europe', *Political Studies*, September.
22. I. Roxborough (1988), 'The dilemmas of redemocratisation', *Government and Opposition*, Summer, pp. 363–4.
23. See Geoffrey Pridham, Eric Herring and George Sanford (1994) (eds), *Building Democracy?: The International Dimension of Democratisation in Eastern Europe*, London: Leicester University Press.

Part I
Liberal Democracy:
Conceptual Issues for Regime Change

[1]

WHAT DEMOCRACY IS
. . . AND IS NOT

Philippe C. Schmitter & Terry Lynn Karl

Philippe C. Schmitter *is professor of political science and director of the Center for European Studies at Stanford University.* **Terry Lynn Karl** *is associate professor of political science and director of the Center for Latin American Studies at the same institution. The original, longer version of this essay was written at the request of the United States Agency for International Development, which is not responsible for its content.*

For some time, the word democracy has been circulating as a debased currency in the political marketplace. Politicians with a wide range of convictions and practices strove to appropriate the label and attach it to their actions. Scholars, conversely, hesitated to use it—without adding qualifying adjectives—because of the ambiguity that surrounds it. The distinguished American political theorist Robert Dahl even tried to introduce a new term, "polyarchy," in its stead in the (vain) hope of gaining a greater measure of conceptual precision. But for better or worse, we are "stuck" with democracy as the catchword of contemporary political discourse. It is the word that resonates in people's minds and springs from their lips as they struggle for freedom and a better way of life; it is the word whose meaning we must discern if it is to be of any use in guiding political analysis and practice.

The wave of transitions away from autocratic rule that began with Portugal's "Revolution of the Carnations" in 1974 and seems to have crested with the collapse of communist regimes across Eastern Europe in 1989 has produced a welcome convergence towards a common definition of democracy.[1] Everywhere there has been a silent abandonment of dubious adjectives like "popular," "guided," "bourgeois," and "formal" to modify "democracy." At the same time, a remarkable consensus has emerged concerning the minimal conditions that polities must meet in order to merit the prestigious appellation of "democratic." Moreover, a number of international organizations now monitor how well these standards are met; indeed, some countries even consider them when formulating foreign policy.[2]

What Democracy Is

Let us begin by broadly defining democracy and the generic *concepts* that distinguish it as a unique system for organizing relations between rulers and the ruled. We will then briefly review *procedures*, the rules and arrangements that are needed if democracy is to endure. Finally, we will discuss two operative *principles* that make democracy work. They are not expressly included among the generic concepts or formal procedures, but the prospect for democracy is grim if their underlying conditioning effects are not present.

One of the major themes of this essay is that democracy does not consist of a single unique set of institutions. There are many types of democracy, and their diverse practices produce a similarly varied set of effects. The specific form democracy takes is contingent upon a country's socioeconomic conditions as well as its entrenched state structures and policy practices.

Modern political democracy is a system of governance in which rulers are held accountable for their actions in the public realm by citizens, acting indirectly through the competition and cooperation of their elected representatives.[3]

A *regime or system of governance* is an ensemble of patterns that determines the methods of access to the principal public offices; the characteristics of the actors admitted to or excluded from such access; the strategies that actors may use to gain access; and the rules that are followed in the making of publicly binding decisions. To work properly, the ensemble must be institutionalized—that is to say, the various patterns must be habitually known, practiced, and accepted by most, if not all, actors. Increasingly, the preferred mechanism of institutionalization is a written body of laws undergirded by a written constitution, though many enduring political norms can have an informal, prudential, or traditional basis.[4]

For the sake of economy and comparison, these forms, characteristics, and rules are usually bundled together and given a generic label. Democratic is one; others are autocratic, authoritarian, despotic, dictatorial, tyrannical, totalitarian, absolutist, traditional, monarchic, oligarchic, plutocratic, aristocratic, and sultanistic.[5] Each of these regime forms may in turn be broken down into subtypes.

Like all regimes, democracies depend upon the presence of *rulers*, persons who occupy specialized authority roles and can give legitimate commands to others. What distinguishes democratic rulers from nondemocratic ones are the norms that condition how the former come to power and the practices that hold them accountable for their actions.

The *public realm* encompasses the making of collective norms and choices that are binding on the society and backed by state coercion. Its content can vary a great deal across democracies, depending upon preexisting distinctions between the public and the private, state and society, legitimate coercion and voluntary exchange, and collective needs and individual preferences. The liberal conception of democracy advocates circumscribing the public realm as narrowly as possible, while the socialist or social-democratic approach would extend that realm through regulation, subsidization, and, in some cases, collective ownership of property. Neither is intrinsically more democratic than the other—just *differently* democratic. This implies that measures aimed at "developing the private sector" are no more democratic than those aimed at "developing the public sector." Both, if carried to extremes, could undermine the practice of democracy, the former by destroying the basis for satisfying collective needs and exercising legitimate authority; the latter by destroying the basis for satisfying individual preferences and controlling illegitimate government actions. Differences of opinion over the optimal mix of the two provide much of the substantive content of political conflict within established democracies.

Citizens are the most distinctive element in democracies. All regimes have rulers and a public realm, but only to the extent that they are democratic do they have citizens. Historically, severe restrictions on citizenship were imposed in most emerging or partial democracies according to criteria of age, gender, class, race, literacy, property ownership, tax-paying status, and so on. Only a small part of the total population was eligible to vote or run for office. Only restricted social categories were allowed to form, join, or support political associations. After protracted struggle—in some cases involving violent domestic upheaval or international war—most of these restrictions were lifted. Today, the criteria for inclusion are fairly standard. All native-born adults are eligible, although somewhat higher age limits may still be imposed upon candidates for certain offices. Unlike the early American and European democracies of the nineteenth century, none of the recent democracies in southern Europe, Latin America, Asia, or Eastern Europe has even attempted to impose formal restrictions on the franchise or eligibility to office. When it comes to informal restrictions on the effective exercise of citizenship rights, however, the story can be quite different. This explains the central importance (discussed below) of procedures.

Competition has not always been considered an essential defining condition of democracy. "Classic" democracies presumed decision making based on direct participation leading to consensus. The assembled citizenry was expected to agree on a common course of action after listening to the alternatives and weighing their respective merits and demerits. A tradition of hostility to "faction," and "particular interests" persists in democratic thought, but at least since *The Federalist Papers* it has become widely accepted that competition among factions is a necessary evil in democracies that operate on a more-than-local scale. Since, as James Madison argued, "the latent causes of faction are sown into the nature of man," and the possible remedies for "the mischief of faction" are worse than the disease, the best course is to recognize them and to attempt to control their effects.[6] Yet while democrats may agree on the inevitability of factions, they tend to disagree about the best forms and rules for governing factional competition. Indeed, differences over the preferred modes and boundaries of competition contribute most to distinguishing one subtype of democracy from another.

> "However central to democracy, elections occur intermittently and only allow citizens to choose between the highly aggregated alternatives offered by political parties..."

The most popular definition of democracy equates it with regular *elections*, fairly conducted and honestly counted. Some even consider the mere fact of elections—even ones from which specific parties or candidates are excluded, or in which substantial portions of the population cannot freely participate—as a sufficient condition for the existence of democracy. This fallacy has been called "electoralism" or "the faith that merely holding elections will channel political action into peaceful contests among elites and accord public legitimacy to the winners"—no matter how they are conducted or what else constrains those who win them.[7] However central to democracy, elections occur intermittently and only allow citizens to choose between the highly aggregated alternatives offered by political parties, which can, especially in the early stages of a democratic transition, proliferate in a bewildering variety. During the intervals between elections, citizens can seek to influence public policy through a wide variety of other intermediaries: interest associations, social movements, locality groupings, clientelistic arrangements, and so forth. *Modern democracy, in other words, offers a variety of competitive processes and channels for the expression of interests and values—associational as well as partisan, functional as well as territorial, collective as well as individual. All are integral to its practice.*

Another commonly accepted image of democracy identifies it with *majority rule*. Any governing body that makes decisions by combining the votes of more than half of those eligible and present is said to be democratic, whether that majority emerges within an electorate, a parliament, a committee, a city council, or a party caucus. For exceptional purposes (e.g., amending the constitution or expelling a member), "qualified majorities" of more than 50 percent may be required, but few would deny that democracy must involve some means of aggregating the equal preferences of individuals.

A problem arises, however, when *numbers* meet *intensities*. What happens when a properly assembled majority (especially a stable, self-perpetuating one) regularly makes decisions that harm some minority (especially a threatened cultural or ethnic group)? In these circumstances, successful democracies tend to qualify the central principle of majority rule in order to protect minority rights. Such qualifications can take the form of constitutional provisions that place certain matters beyond the reach of majorities (bills of rights); requirements for concurrent majorities in several different constituencies (confederalism); guarantees securing the autonomy of local or regional governments against the demands of the central authority (federalism); grand coalition governments that incorporate all parties (consociationalism); or the negotiation of social pacts between major social groups like business and labor (neocorporatism). The most common and effective way of protecting minorities, however, lies in the everyday operation of interest associations and social movements. These reflect (some would say, amplify) the different intensities of preference that exist in the population and bring them to bear on democratically elected decision makers. Another way of putting this intrinsic tension between numbers and intensities would be to say that "in modern democracies, votes may be counted, but influences alone are weighted."

Cooperation has always been a central feature of democracy. Actors must voluntarily make collective decisions binding on the polity as a whole. They must cooperate in order to compete. They must be capable of acting collectively through parties, associations, and movements in order to select candidates, articulate preferences, petition authorities, and influence policies.

But democracy's freedoms should also encourage citizens to deliberate among themselves, to discover their common needs, and to resolve their differences without relying on some supreme central authority. Classical democracy emphasized these qualities, and they are by no means extinct, despite repeated efforts by contemporary theorists to stress the analogy with behavior in the economic marketplace and to reduce all of democracy's operations to competitive interest maximization. Alexis de Tocqueville best described the importance of independent groups for democracy in his *Democracy in America*, a work which remains a major source of inspiration for all those who persist in viewing democracy as something more than a struggle for election and re-election among competing candidates.[8]

In contemporary political discourse, this phenomenon of cooperation and deliberation via autonomous group activity goes under the rubric of "civil society." The diverse units of social identity and interest, by remaining independent of the state (and perhaps even of parties), not

only can restrain the arbitrary actions of rulers, but can also contribute
to forming better citizens who are more aware of the preferences of
others, more self-confident in their actions, and more civic-minded in
their willingness to sacrifice for the common good. At its best, civil
society provides an intermediate layer of governance between the
individual and the state that is capable of resolving conflicts and
controlling the behavior of members without public coercion. Rather
than overloading decision makers with increased demands and making
the system ungovernable,[9] a viable civil society can mitigate conflicts
and improve the quality of citizenship—without relying exclusively on
the privatism of the marketplace.

Representatives—whether directly or indirectly elected—do most of the
real work in modern democracies. Most are professional politicians who
orient their careers around the desire to fill key offices. It is doubtful
that any democracy could survive without such people. The central
question, therefore, is not whether or not there will be a political elite
or even a professional political class, but how these representatives are
chosen and then held accountable for their actions.

As noted above, there are many channels of representation in modern
democracy. The electoral one, based on territorial constituencies, is the
most visible and public. It culminates in a parliament or a presidency
that is periodically accountable to the citizenry as a whole. Yet the sheer
growth of government (in large part as a byproduct of popular demand)
has increased the number, variety, and power of agencies charged with
making public decisions and not subject to elections. Around these
agencies there has developed a vast apparatus of specialized
representation based largely on functional interests, not territorial
constituencies. These interest associations, and not political parties, have
become the primary expression of civil society in most stable
democracies, supplemented by the more sporadic interventions of social
movements.

The new and fragile democracies that have sprung up since 1974
must live in "compressed time." They will not resemble the European
democracies of the nineteenth and early twentieth centuries, and they
cannot expect to acquire the multiple channels of representation in
gradual historical progression as did most of their predecessors. A
bewildering array of parties, interests, and movements will all
simultaneously seek political influence in them, creating challenges to the
polity that did not exist in earlier processes of democratization.

Procedures that Make Democracy Possible

The defining components of democracy are necessarily abstract, and
may give rise to a considerable variety of institutions and subtypes of
democracy. For democracy to thrive, however, specific procedural norms

must be followed and civic rights must be respected. Any polity that fails to impose such restrictions upon itself, that fails to follow the "rule of law" with regard to its own procedures, should not be considered democratic. These procedures alone do not define democracy, but their presence is indispensable to its persistence. In essence, they are necessary but not sufficient conditions for its existence.

Robert Dahl has offered the most generally accepted listing of what he terms the "procedural minimal" conditions that must be present for modern political democracy (or as he puts it, "polyarchy") to exist:

> 1) Control over government decisions about policy is constitutionally vested in elected officials.
>
> 2) Elected officials are chosen in frequent and fairly conducted elections in which coercion is comparatively uncommon.
>
> 3) Practically all adults have the right to vote in the election of officials.
>
> 4) Practically all adults have the right to run for elective offices in the government. . . .
>
> 5) Citizens have a right to express themselves without the danger of severe punishment on political matters broadly defined. . . .
>
> 6) Citizens have a right to seek out alternative sources of information. Moreover, alternative sources of information exist and are protected by law.
>
> 7) . . . Citizens also have the right to form relatively independent associations or organizations, including independent political parties and interest groups.[10]

These seven conditions seem to capture the essence of procedural democracy for many theorists, but we propose to add two others. The first might be thought of as a further refinement of item (1), while the second might be called an implicit prior condition to all seven of the above.

8) Popularly elected officials must be able to exercise their constitutional powers without being subjected to overriding (albeit informal) opposition from unelected officials. Democracy is in jeopardy if military officers, entrenched civil servants, or state managers retain the capacity to act independently of elected civilians or even veto decisions made by the people's representatives. Without this additional caveat, the militarized polities of contemporary Central America, where civilian control over the military does not exist, might be classified by many scholars as democracies, just as they have been (with the exception of Sandinista Nicaragua) by U.S. policy makers. The caveat thus guards against what we earlier called "electoralism"—the tendency to focus on the holding of elections while ignoring other political realities.

9) The polity must be self-governing; it must be able to act independently of constraints imposed by some other overarching political system. Dahl and other contemporary democratic theorists probably took

this condition for granted since they referred to formally sovereign nation-states. However, with the development of blocs, alliances, spheres of influence, and a variety of "neocolonial" arrangements, the question of autonomy has been a salient one. Is a system really democratic if its elected officials are unable to make binding decisions without the approval of actors outside their territorial domain? This is significant even if the outsiders are themselves democratically constituted and if the insiders are relatively free to alter or even end the encompassing arrangement (as in Puerto Rico), but it becomes especially critical if neither condition obtains (as in the Baltic states).

Principles that Make Democracy Feasible

Lists of component processes and procedural norms help us to specify what democracy is, but they do not tell us much about how it actually functions. The simplest answer is "by the consent of the people"; the more complex one is "by the contingent consent of politicians acting under conditions of bounded uncertainty."

In a democracy, representatives must at least informally agree that those who win greater electoral support or influence over policy will not use their temporary superiority to bar the losers from taking office or exerting influence in the future, and that in exchange for this opportunity to keep competing for power and place, momentary losers will respect the winners' right to make binding decisions. Citizens are expected to obey the decisions ensuing from such a process of competition, provided its outcome remains contingent upon their collective preferences as expressed through fair and regular elections or open and repeated negotiations.

The challenge is not so much to find a set of goals that command widespread consensus as to find a set of rules that embody contingent consent. The precise shape of this "democratic bargain," to use Dahl's expression,[11] can vary a good deal from society to society. It depends on social cleavages and such subjective factors as mutual trust, the standard of fairness, and the willingness to compromise. It may even be compatible with a great deal of dissensus on substantive policy issues.

All democracies involve a degree of uncertainty about who will be elected and what policies they will pursue. Even in those polities where one party persists in winning elections or one policy is consistently implemented, the possibility of change through independent collective action still exists, as in Italy, Japan, and the Scandinavian social democracies. If it does not, the system is not democratic, as in Mexico, Senegal, or Indonesia.

But the uncertainty embedded in the core of all democracies is bounded. Not just any actor can get into the competition and raise any issue he or she pleases—there are previously established rules that must be respected. Not just any policy can be adopted—there are conditions that must be met. Democracy institutionalizes "normal," limited political uncertainty. These boundaries vary from country to country. Constitutional guarantees of property, privacy, expression, and other rights are a part of this, but the most effective boundaries are generated by competition among interest groups and cooperation within civil society. Whatever the rhetoric (and some polities appear to offer their citizens more dramatic alternatives than others), once the rules of contingent consent have been agreed upon, the actual variation is likely to stay within a predictable and generally accepted range.

This emphasis on operative guidelines contrasts with a highly persistent, but misleading theme in recent literature on democracy—namely, the emphasis upon "civic culture." The principles we have suggested here rest on rules of prudence, not on deeply ingrained habits of tolerance, moderation, mutual respect, fair play, readiness to compromise, or trust in public authorities. Waiting for such habits to sink deep and lasting roots implies a very slow process of regime consolidation—one that takes generations—and it would probably condemn most contemporary experiences *ex hypothesi* to failure. Our assertion is that contingent consent and bounded uncertainty can emerge from the interaction between antagonistic and mutually suspicious actors and that the far more benevolent and ingrained norms of a civic culture are better thought of as a *product* and not a producer of democracy.

How Democracies Differ

Several concepts have been deliberately excluded from our generic definition of democracy, despite the fact that they have been frequently associated with it in both everyday practice and scholarly work. They are, nevertheless, especially important when it comes to distinguishing subtypes of democracy. Since no single set of actual institutions, practices, or values embodies democracy, polities moving away from authoritarian rule can mix different components to produce different democracies. It is important to recognize that these do not define points along a single continuum of improving performance, but a matrix of potential combinations that are *differently* democratic.

1) *Consensus*: All citizens may not agree on the substantive goals of political action or on the role of the state (although if they did, it would certainly make governing democracies much easier).

2) *Participation*: All citizens may not take an active and equal part in politics, although it must be legally possible for them to do so.

3) *Access*: Rulers may not weigh equally the preferences of all who come before them, although citizenship implies that individuals and groups should have an equal opportunity to express their preferences if they choose to do so.

4) *Responsiveness*: Rulers may not always follow the course of action preferred by the citizenry. But when they deviate from such a policy, say on grounds of "reason of state" or "overriding national interest," they must ultimately be held accountable for their actions through regular and fair processes.

5) *Majority rule*: Positions may not be allocated or rules may not be decided solely on the basis of assembling the most votes, although deviations from this principle usually must be explicitly defended and previously approved.

6) *Parliamentary sovereignty*: The legislature may not be the only body that can make rules or even the one with final authority in deciding which laws are binding, although where executive, judicial, or other public bodies make that ultimate choice, they too must be accountable for their actions.

7) *Party government*: Rulers may not be nominated, promoted, and disciplined in their activities by well-organized and programmatically coherent political parties, although where they are not, it may prove more difficult to form an effective government.

8) *Pluralism*: The political process may not be based on a multiplicity of overlapping, voluntaristic, and autonomous private groups. However, where there are monopolies of representation, hierarchies of association, and obligatory memberships, it is likely that the interests involved will be more closely linked to the state and the separation between the public and private spheres of action will be much less distinct.

9) *Federalism*: The territorial division of authority may not involve multiple levels and local autonomies, least of all ones enshrined in a constitutional document, although some dispersal of power across territorial and/or functional units is characteristic of all democracies.

10) *Presidentialism*: The chief executive officer may not be a single person and he or she may not be directly elected by the citizenry as a whole, although some concentration of authority is present in all democracies, even if it is exercised collectively and only held indirectly accountable to the electorate.

11) *Checks and Balances*: It is not necessary that the different branches of government be systematically pitted against one another, although governments by assembly, by executive concentration, by judicial command, or even by dictatorial fiat (as in time of war) must be ultimately accountable to the citizenry as a whole.

While each of the above has been named as an essential component of democracy, they should instead be seen either as indicators of this or that type of democracy, or else as useful standards for evaluating the performance of particular regimes. To include them as part of the generic definition of democracy itself would be to mistake the American polity for the universal model of democratic governance. Indeed, the parliamentary, consociational, unitary, corporatist, and concentrated arrangements of continental Europe may have some unique virtues for guiding polities through the uncertain transition from autocratic to democratic rule.[12]

What Democracy Is Not

We have attempted to convey the general meaning of modern democracy without identifying it with some particular set of rules and institutions or restricting it to some specific culture or level of development. We have also argued that it cannot be reduced to the regular holding of elections or equated with a particular notion of the role of the state, but we have not said much more about what democracy is not or about what democracy may not be capable of producing.

There is an understandable temptation to load too many expectations on this concept and to imagine that by attaining democracy, a society will have resolved all of its political, social, economic, administrative, and cultural problems. Unfortunately, "all good things do not necessarily go together."

First, democracies are not necessarily more efficient economically than other forms of government. Their rates of aggregate growth, savings, and investment may be no better than those of nondemocracies. This is especially likely during the transition, when propertied groups and administrative elites may respond to real or imagined threats to the "rights" they enjoyed under authoritarian rule by initiating capital flight, disinvestment, or sabotage. In time, depending upon the type of democracy, benevolent long-term effects upon income distribution, aggregate demand, education, productivity, and creativity may eventually combine to improve economic and social performance, but it is certainly too much to expect that these improvements will occur immediately—much less that they will be defining characteristics of democratization.

Second, democracies are not necessarily more efficient administratively. Their capacity to make decisions may even be slower than that of the regimes they replace, if only because more actors must be consulted. The costs of getting things done may be higher, if only because "payoffs" have to be made to a wider and more resourceful set of clients (although one should never underestimate the degree of corruption to be found within autocracies). Popular satisfaction with the new democratic government's performance may not even seem greater, if only because necessary compromises often please no one completely, and because the losers are free to complain.

Third, democracies are not likely to appear more orderly, consensual, stable, or governable than the autocracies they replace. This is partly a byproduct of democratic freedom of expression, but it is also a reflection of the likelihood of continuing disagreement over new rules and institutions. These products of imposition or compromise are often initially quite ambiguous in nature and uncertain in effect until actors have learned how to use them. What is more, they come in the aftermath of serious struggles motivated by high ideals. Groups and individuals with recently acquired autonomy will test certain rules, protest against the actions of certain institutions, and insist on renegotiating their part of the bargain. Thus the presence of antisystem parties should be neither surprising nor seen as a failure of democratic consolidation. What counts is whether such parties are willing, however reluctantly, to play by the general rules of bounded uncertainty and contingent consent.

> *"...democracies will have more open societies and polities than the autocracies they replace, but not necessarily more open economies."*

Governability is a challenge for all regimes, not just democratic ones. Given the political exhaustion and loss of legitimacy that have befallen autocracies from sultanistic Paraguay to totalitarian Albania, it may seem that only democracies can now be expected to govern effectively and legitimately. Experience has shown, however, that democracies too can lose the ability to govern. Mass publics can become disenchanted with their performance. Even more threatening is the temptation for leaders to fiddle with procedures and ultimately undermine the principles of contingent consent and bounded uncertainty. Perhaps the most critical moment comes once the politicians begin to settle into the more predictable roles and relations of a consolidated democracy. Many will find their expectations frustrated; some will discover that the new rules of competition put them at a disadvantage; a few may even feel that their vital interests are threatened by popular majorities.

Finally, democracies will have more open societies and polities than the autocracies they replace, but not necessarily more open economies. Many of today's most successful and well-established democracies have historically resorted to protectionism and closed borders, and have relied extensively upon public institutions to promote economic development. While the long-term compatibility between democracy and capitalism does not seem to be in doubt, despite their continuous tension, it is not clear whether the promotion of such liberal economic goals as the right of individuals to own property and retain profits, the clearing function of markets, the private settlement of disputes, the freedom to produce without government regulation, or the privatization of state-owned enterprises necessarily furthers the consolidation of democracy. After all, democracies do need to levy taxes and regulate certain transactions, especially where private monopolies and oligopolies exist. Citizens or their representatives may decide that it is desirable to protect the rights of collectivities from encroachment by individuals, especially propertied ones, and they may choose to set aside certain forms of property for public or cooperative ownership. In short, notions of economic liberty that are currently put forward in neoliberal economic models are not synonymous with political freedom—and may even impede it.

Democratization will not necessarily bring in its wake economic growth, social peace, administrative efficiency, political harmony, free markets, or "the end of ideology." Least of all will it bring about "the end of history." No doubt some of these qualities could make the consolidation of democracy easier, but they are neither prerequisites for it nor immediate products of it. Instead, what we should be hoping for is the emergence of political institutions that can peacefully compete to form governments and influence public policy, that can channel social and economic conflicts through regular procedures, and that have sufficient linkages to civil society to represent their constituencies and commit them to collective courses of action. Some types of democracies, especially in developing countries, have been unable to fulfill this promise, perhaps due to the circumstances of their transition from authoritarian rule.[13] The democratic wager is that such a regime, once established, will not only persist by reproducing itself within its initial confining conditions, but will eventually expand beyond them.[14] Unlike authoritarian regimes, democracies have the capacity to modify their rules and institutions consensually in response to changing circumstances. They may not immediately produce all the goods mentioned above, but they stand a better chance of eventually doing so than do autocracies.

NOTES

1. For a comparative analysis of the recent regime changes in southern Europe and Latin America, see Guillermo O'Donnell, Philippe C. Schmitter, and Laurence Whitehead, eds., *Transitions from Authoritarian Rule*, 4 vols. (Baltimore: Johns Hopkins University Press, 1986). For another compilation that adopts a more structural approach see Larry Diamond, Juan Linz, and Seymour Martin Lipset, eds., *Democracy in Developing Countries*, vols. 2, 3, and 4 (Boulder, Colo.: Lynne Rienner, 1989).

2. Numerous attempts have been made to codify and quantify the existence of democracy across political systems. The best known is probably Freedom House's *Freedom in the World: Political Rights and Civil Liberties*, published since 1973 by Greenwood Press and since 1988 by University Press of America. Also see Charles Humana, *World Human Rights Guide* (New York: Facts on File, 1986).

3. The definition most commonly used by American social scientists is that of Joseph Schumpeter: "that institutional arrangement for arriving at political decisions in which individuals acquire the power to decide by means of a competitive struggle for the people's vote." *Capitalism, Socialism and Democracy* (London: George Allen and Unwin, 1943), 269. We accept certain aspects of the classical procedural approach to modern democracy, but differ primarily in our emphasis on the accountability of rulers to citizens and the relevance of mechanisms of competition other than elections.

4. Not only do some countries practice a stable form of democracy without a formal constitution (e.g., Great Britain and Israel), but even more countries have constitutions and

legal codes that offer no guarantee of reliable practice. On paper, Stalin's 1936 constitution for the USSR was a virtual model of democratic rights and entitlements.

5. For the most valiant attempt to make some sense out of this thicket of distinctions, see Juan Linz, "Totalitarian and Authoritarian Regimes" in *Handbook of Political Science*, eds. Fred I. Greenstein and Nelson W. Polsby (Reading, Mass.: Addision Wesley, 1975), 175-411.

6. "Publius" (Alexander Hamilton, John Jay, and James Madison), *The Federalist Papers* (New York: Anchor Books, 1961). The quote is from Number 10.

7. See Terry Karl, "Imposing Consent? Electoralism versus Democratization in El Salvador," in *Elections and Democratization in Latin America, 1980-1985*, eds. Paul Drake and Eduardo Silva (San Diego: Center for Iberian and Latin American Studies, Center for US/Mexican Studies, University of California, San Diego, 1986), 9-36.

8. Alexis de Tocqueville, *Democracy in America*, 2 vols. (New York: Vintage Books, 1945).

9. This fear of overloaded government and the imminent collapse of democracy is well reflected in the work of Samuel P. Huntington during the 1970s. See especially Michel Crozier, Samuel P. Huntington, and Joji Watanuki, *The Crisis of Democracy* (New York: New York University Press, 1975). For Huntington's (revised) thoughts about the prospects for democracy, see his "Will More Countries Become Democratic?," *Political Science Quarterly* 99 (Summer 1984): 193-218.

10. Robert Dahl, *Dilemmas of Pluralist Democracy* (New Haven: Yale University Press, 1982), 11.

11. Robert Dahl, *After the Revolution: Authority in a Good Society* (New Haven: Yale University Press, 1970).

12. See Juan Linz, "The Perils of Presidentialism," *Journal of Democracy* 1 (Winter 1990): 51-69, and the ensuing discussion by Donald Horowitz, Seymour Martin Lipset, and Juan Linz in *Journal of Democracy* 1 (Fall 1990): 73-91.

13. Terry Lynn Karl, "Dilemmas of Democratization in Latin America," *Comparative Politics* 23 (October 1990): 1-23.

14. Otto Kirchheimer, "Confining Conditions and Revolutionary Breakthroughs," *American Political Science Review* 59 (1965): 964-974.

[2]

Political Studies (1992), XL, Special Issue, 130–145

Liberal Democracy: One Form or Many?

ALAN WARE*

This article examines whether there are significant differences between liberal democracies which warrant them being classified as different forms of democracy. The article begins by outlining six features of liberal democracy which are crucial in understanding how this type of government works. The subsequent section examines the origins of liberal democracy and considers the relevance of arguments derived from American 'exceptionalism'. Attention is then focused on liberal democratic governments today – by reference to Lijphart's distinction between 'majoritarian' and 'consensus' democracies. Finally, the article looks at whether the form of liberal democracy is changed substantially when it is transplanted into a cultural context different from the one in which it originated. The general conclusion is that there is no case for identifying different forms of liberal democracy.

I

For Macpherson they are instances of *liberal democracy*, for Miliband they are exemplars of *capitalist democracy*, for Epstein they are the *western democracies*, for Dahl they are *polyarchies*, while for Lijphart they are simply *democracies*.[1] Despite the disagreement about what they should be called, there is little disagreement that today they include among their number Britain, France, Germany, the US and more than 40 other regimes. For the sake of brevity, I refer to these liberal/capitalist/western democracies from now on as, simply, liberal democracies. At the outset I want to make two related points about the political systems to which I am referring, to prevent the entire thrust of the subsequent argument from being misunderstood.

First, liberal democracies are only one kind of logically possible system of representative democracy – liberal democracy is not synonymous with representative democracy. Indeed, I refer later to one such variant, 'elected dictatorships', in which there are virtually no constraints on the use of power by an elected president. To explicate the second point I will begin by stating Holden's definition of liberal democracy. This is a definition which I believe to be incomplete, and in some respects misleading, but it does have the virtue of explicating part of the liberal character of liberal democracy:

* I am very grateful to David Held for his comments on an earlier draft and for passing on to me the comments made at the special conference by the other participants. I would also like to thank Laurence Whitehead and Joni Lovenduski for their advice.
    ¹ C. B. Macpherson, *The Life and Times of Liberal Democracy* (Oxford, Oxford University Press, 1977); R. Miliband, *Capitalist Democracy in Britain* (Oxford, Oxford University Press, 1982); L. D. Epstein, *Political Parties in Western Democracies* (London, Pall Mall, 1967); R. A. Dahl, *Polyarchy* (New Haven and London, Yale University Press, 1971); A. Lijphart, *Democracies* (New Haven and London, Yale University Press, 1984).

0032–3217/92/Special Issue/130–16/$03.00 © 1992 *Political Studies*

> A political system in which (a) the whole people positively or negatively, make, and are entitled to make the basic determining decisions on important matters of public policy; and (b) they make, and are only entitled to make, such decisions in a restricted sphere since the legitimate sphere of public authority is limited.[2]

It is quite clear that, given such a definition, there are many conceivable types of *liberal* democracy other than those which have actually developed. For example, a world of 'liberal democracies' can be imagined in which economic production and distribution is conducted entirely by small producer and consumer cooperatives, which are themselves democratically run, and in which the political system contains several levels of decision-making, the lowest of which involves extensive mass participation. Undoubtedly, the conduct of political life would be very different in such a world than the present one. The regimes we know as liberal democracies are only one form of government in which the people 'take basic determining decisions' and in which the power of 'public authority is limited'.

It might be an interesting exercise to discuss which of these other forms of 'liberal democracy' were not merely conceivable but could be sustained as stable political systems. Indeed, given the title of my article, it might be thought that this is the sort of exercise in which I am engaged here. It is not. I am concerned only with liberal democracy as it emerged in Western Europe and North America and was later 'exported' (through conquest, colonization and imitation) to some other parts of the world. These liberal democracies are the product of a particular historical experience which has moulded key features of these democracies. The aim of this article is to consider that experience. Was there, in fact, a single form of liberal democracy that emerged in certain advanced commercial/industrial societies? Does the contemporary liberal democratic world contain not one, but two, forms of liberal democracy? Does the 'exporting' of the liberal democratic model tend to create mutations, which are 'liberal democracies' according to Holden's definition, but which are transformed into radically different regimes from those in the areas where liberal democracy originated? These questions are especially important given the possibility of both continuing democratization in Eastern Europe and democratization in the states that formerly comprised the Soviet Union.

II

Before turning to these issues, however, it is necessary first to outline the key features of liberal democracy as it developed. There are six features to which particular attention should be given – features to which I shall refer later in this article. These are: the link between liberal democracy and nationalism; its development from capitalism; its claims to protect the civil liberties of the individual; the crucial role assigned to the election of key public officials; institutionalization in the political system; and the cooperation between liberal democracies for the greater part of their existence.

---

[2] B. Holden, *Understanding Liberal Democracy* (Oxford, Philip Allan, 1988), pp. 12–13.

Democracy within Nation-states

Holden's definition of 'liberal democracy' makes no reference to the unit in which the people make their determining decisions. Conceivably this could be within units no bigger than small cities or, equally, it could be within the framework of a political system embracing the entire planet. However, it is the nation-state which has been the arena where liberal democracy has operated since it first emerged. As Smith observes: ' . . . the world is divided, first and foremost, into "nation-states" – states claiming to be nations – and national identity everywhere underpins the recurrent drive for popular sovereignty and democracy, as well as the exclusive tyranny that it sometimes breeds'.[3] Until recently, at least, defenders of liberal democracy have accepted as given a world divided into nation-states, and liberal democratic theory is directed towards the nation-state as being the fundamental unit of politics and government.

A Capitalist Economy

All liberal democracies have a large part of their economic activity conducted by individuals or privately owned firms operating on a for-profit basis. As a number of democratic theorists have pointed out, there is no *logical* connection between the distribution of political power in a regime and its form of economic organization; in Dahl's formulation both democracy and dictatorship are compatible with either capitalism or socialism.[4] Yet among the liberal democracies we do not find regimes in which representative government is practised in an economic system dominated, for example, by either worker-owned and controlled cooperatives or by state-owned and run enterprises. If we leave aside those countries on which liberal democratic regimes have been imposed by colonization or conquest, there can be no doubt that the growth of liberal democratic practices is associated with the emergence of private-enterprise commercial or industrial societies. In the US liberal democratic political institutions were established in a commercial but pre-industrial society; in Britain the growth of a liberal democratic state began in commercial society but the transformation to a recognizably full version of such a state was not completed until after industrialization.

Liberal democracy grew out of a particular historical experience. It did not, and could not, emerge in conditions where the vast majority of persons were organized in families that were wholly self-sufficient. It was a product of economic interdependence through commerce. Commercialization and then industrial-ization proliferated the range of interests in the post-medieval western states – interests that demanded constraints on how these states were governed. Of course, the precise relationship between commercialization, the proliferation of interests and the sustenance of representative government has been difficult for social scientists to establish. Barrington Moore, for example, argued that it was the switch by the aristocracy in Britain to commercial agriculture (unlike the behaviour of their counterparts in France, Russia or much of Germany) that was a crucial determinant in the evolution towards democracy in this country.[5] Even

---

[3] A. D. Smith, *National Identity* (London, Penguin, 1991), p. 143.

[4] Robert A. Dahl, *Modern Political Analysis* (Englewood Cliff, NJ, Prentice-Hall, 1963), pp. 8–9.

[5] Barrington Moore, Jr, *Social Origins of Dictatorship and Democracy* (Boston, Beacon Press, 1966), p. 419.

ALAN WARE   133

though Moore's precise account of the origins of liberal democracy is rejected by most political scientists today, there are still few satisfactory accounts of the link between commercialization and liberal democracy.

But that there is such a connection is not in doubt. Liberal democracy did not arise immediately after the fall of the Roman empire, for example, nor during the Reformation. It was the product of the interplay of particular socioeconomic and political forces. Thus, even though, like Holden, we might define 'liberal democracy' without reference to the link between the form of government and the nature of the economic system, liberal democracies cannot be understood except in the context of a particular range of economic institutions and practices.

The Protection of Civil Liberties

The claim of the liberal democracies to be *liberal* democracies rests on the claim that they have both well-established and also accessible procedures for protecting the liberties of individual citizens. It is such procedures which ensure that, to use Holden's phrase, public authority is limited. Obviously, there is no necessary connection between the protection of such freedoms and the existence of a capitalist economy. For example, with a community-owned and run economy (or one run by the state), individuals might have a whole range of liberties protected by courts and other bodies whilst still being prohibited from owning the means of production. If it is to be contended that such liberties cannot be adequately protected under non-capitalist economic conditions, then it would have to be shown, for example, that only privately owned economies could generate the kind of intermediate organizations which would prevent the abuse of state power. Since many of the intermediate organizations (including families, cooperatives and others) which are held to act as buffers between the individual and the state in liberal democracies do not seem to owe their vitality to the private enterprise system, such a case would be difficult to construct.

Nevertheless, of course, there is a connection between the private enterprise economy and the freedom of individuals in liberal democracies. The demand for rights of *habeas corpus* and a whole series of other rights in the seventeenth and eighteenth centuries emanated primarily from independent farmers and traders who feared the uncertainties deriving from unlimited state power. The demand for limited government, for constitutional government, had its origins in the transformation of economic life. It was only later that the demands for protecting the rights of individuals were linked to the demand for popular input into the governing processes.

The Election of Major Public Officials

The fourth feature of liberal democracy is that, at the very least, key public officials are subject to regular election – though in some countries (as in the US after the Jacksonian era) many more officials have been subject to election. It is through the election of representatives – usually, at least in part, on a territorial basis – that liberal democracies provide for the people making (in Holden's words) 'the basic determining decisions on important matters of public policy'. Other devices for popular input into decision-making – such as referendums or town meetings – are not found in all liberal democracies and cover smaller areas of decision-making than those for which elected representatives are (at least formally) responsible. Moreover, liberal democracy does not provide for the popular election of officials outside the *public* arena – for example, in economic institutions.

But who does the electing in liberal democracies? Just as the ideology of liberal democracy today posits that all within the state should have their freedoms protected, so that ideology also posits that all should be able to vote – one person, one vote. In both respects what happens in liberal democracies has departed, and continues to depart, quite considerably from the ideal.

At various times and in various countries women, the poor, non-citizens and others have been excluded from the ballot. The fact is that states that are quite recognizable as liberal democracies have functioned with only a minority of people resident within their boundaries having the vote. For example, at the time of the 1929 election (when nearly all adults were entitled to vote) the character of the British political system was little different from 1910, when the electorate was very much smaller, with all women and a significant minority of men not having an entitlement to vote. It is only if we offer a stipulative definition of liberal democracy that includes a near-universal franchise (such as Holden's which refers to the 'whole people') that those 19 years can be seen as embracing a regime change. In reality, there was little change in these years – that is, in terms of how Britain was governed.[6] Obviously, this is not to deny that exclusion from the ballot denies a potentially valuable resource to excluded groups, but to insist that liberal democracy requires universal suffrage is to introduce a wholly artificial distinction between types of regime. It is the election of public officials – elections in which a broad range of, but not necessarily all, interests within the state have the vote – that is the distinctive feature of liberal democracy.[7]

Institutionalization in the Political System

In theory periodic elections place checks on political leaders; in practice these checks may be weak, so that other means are needed to prevent an elected leader (especially in a presidential system) from governing arbitrarily and without restraint. Such an outcome would be a threat to both civil liberties and the stability of the regime. In liberal democracies there are a number of institutions which have developed to restrict the abuse of power. Even in Westminster-model democracies, where unrestricted parliamentary sovereignty seems to open up that possibility, a variety of devices has reduced the autonomy of the majority party. Indeed, it was precisely the availability of such institutions (including local government) to its opponents that led to the Thatcher government's attempts to reduce their powers and to increase its own autonomy; the result has been a partial de-institutionalization of British democracy.

The United World of Liberal Democracy

For much of their existence liberal democracies have been *in opposition to* other kinds of regimes. Unlike, say, the case of military regimes, there has been close

---

[6] However, the size of the UK decreased with the creation of the Irish Free State.

[7] However, this conception of liberal democracy is not the same as Schumpeter's idea of democracy; for Schumpeter it was the availability of elections, even if there was a very small electorate, which was the crucial democratic device. J. A. Schumpeter, 'Two concepts of democracy', in A. Quinton (ed.), *Political Philosophy* (Oxford, Oxford University Press, 1967), pp. 153–88.

ALAN WARE   135

association between most of the liberal democracies which has prompted the perception that there is a liberal democratic 'world of politics'. For seven decades after the 1914–18 war the international political environment led many liberal democracies to cooperate and to define themselves as constituting a distinct 'world of politics'. In the 1920s and 1930s there was a fear that 'non-democratic' forms of government would exploit their internal weaknesses, although military alliances between them remained suspect long after the experience of 1914–18. Between 1939 and 1941 the alliance between most of the liberal democracies prompted the growth of cooperation between the right-wing dictatorships of Germany, Italy and Japan. After the second world war many of the liberal democratic regimes became linked to each other through a series of military alliances designed to contain the influence of the Soviet Union.

Because so much of the lifetime of liberal democracy has been spent in such collaboration, it has encouraged a tendency to view liberal democracies as constituting a single type of regime. But is such an assumption warranted?

III

Contemporary political (and other social) scientists view the emergence of liberal democracies as forming a common pattern. There were pressures to disperse political power in regimes which had similar socioeconomic structures. Where such conditions pertained liberal democracy was possible and could be sustained. This point has been made well by Dahl:

> Historically, polyarchy has been strongly associated with a society marked by a host of interrelated characteristics . . . [which] are so highly intercorrelated as to justify the conclusion – if further justification of a rather obvious historical judgement were necessary – that they are all indicators of a more or less distinguishable type of social system . . . In the extensive and growing body of research on the conditions of democracy, probably nothing is more firmly established than the correlations between any of these societal measures and indicators of democracy or polyarchy.[8]

Of course, there has been intense disagreement on the question of what these conditions are (compare Dahl with Barrington Moore, for example) and on the impact on democratization of civil wars, external wars and so on. Nevertheless, most contemporary social scientists regard the democratization process in the US, Britain, Scandinavia and elsewhere as being largely explicable in terms of similar factors. This is not the perspective of all scholars, however.

In particular, there are those historians and social scientists who view American political development as 'exceptional'. The notion of American exceptionalism originates with Tocqueville:

> The position of the Americans is . . . quite exceptional and it may be believed that no democratic people will ever be placed in a similar one . . . Let us cease, then, to view all democratic nations under the example of the American people, and attempt to survey them at length with their own features.[9]

The 'exceptionalism' argument proceeds as follows. The American political system is different from any other; it is a 'republican' form of government in

---

[8] R. A. Dahl, *Democracy and Its Critics* (New Haven and London, Yale University Press, 1989) p. 251.

[9] A. de Tocqueville, *Democracy in America, Vol. II* (New York, Vintage Books, 1990), pp. 36–7.

which popular input into the political system is balanced by a series of devices which limit the likely use of power – federalism, the separation of powers, and various checks and balances. The US came to have these institutions because it had unique socio-political origins. This is a point which has been developed most famously by the historian Daniel Boorstin.[10] In Foley's words, Boorstin

> explicitly condemns the very idea that the American revolution or the American constitution can in any way be characterized as part of the undifferentiated international movement known as the Enlightenment . . . [He] claims unequivocally that America is special because it is divinely ordained . . . The result of this mystical exceptionalism (what Boorstin calls 'giveness') is that American history, to Boorstin, can be understood only in terms of working itself out from an original seed which had already determined all subsequent developments in a predefined manner . . . [11]

According to this kind of view, the similar experiences of the European states, with respect to feudalism and so on, *might* make it possible to speak of the emergence of liberal democracy in general in Europe, but the US cannot be assimilated with that experience. Whatever the similarities between these democracies and the American republic, they are merely superficial. They have different origins and the two kinds of political system work quite differently.

For my purposes it is possible to identify a 'radical' and a 'moderate' version of the exceptionalism argument. The radical version is Boorstin's – it rejects comparisons between democratization in America and elsewhere. If Boorstin were correct, political science would have no alternative but to recognize that there are (at least) two quite distinct forms of liberal democracy; they have their origins in very different social structures. However, the Boorstin version can be dismissed quite easily. It pays no attention to the connection between changes in economic structures and forms of government, and the impact of the former on the latter. In brief, the evidence he considers is much too limited.

Perhaps the leading exponent of the 'moderate' version is Seymour Martin Lipset,[12] who traces significant developments in American politics – the absence of a large social democratic movement, hostility to the role of the state and so on – to the values originating from the founding of the state:

> The revolutionary ideology which became the American creed is liberalism in its eighteenth- and nineteenth-century meanings which stressed anti-statism. The United States is unique in that it started from a revolutionary event and defined its *raison d'être* ideologically. Other countries' sense of themselves is derived from a common history, not an ideology. And if they have a historic conservative set of values, it is Toryism, statist communitarianism, *noblesse oblige*.[13]

---

[10] D. J. Boorstin, *The Genius of American Politics* (Chicago, University of Chicago Press, 1953).

[11] M. Foley, *Laws, Men and Machines: Modern American Government and the Appeal of Newtonian Mechanics* (London and New York, Routledge, 1990), pp. 22 and 23.

[12] The most recent statement of these arguments is S. M. Lipset, 'American exceptionalism reaffirmed', in B. E. Shafer (ed.), *Is America Different?* (Oxford, Clarendon Press, 1991); but see also *The First New Nation* (New York, W. W. Norton, 1979), *Continental Divide* (New York, Routledge, 1990) and 'Why no socialism in the United States?', in S. Bialer and S. Sluzar (eds), *Sources of Contemporary Radicalism* (Boulder, CO, Westview, 1977).

[13] Lipset, 'American exceptionalism reaffirmed', pp. 6–7.

Yet there are several reasons for being sceptical about any claim that Lipset's argument provides the basis for a classification between different kinds of liberal democracies.

First, and for reasons which I have sketched out elsewhere, Lipset's account of exceptionalism gives too little weight to the institutional factors which have contributed to the differences between, for example, American and Canadian political development.[14] It is far from clear that the absence of socialism in the US should be attributed to values established in the late eighteenth century rather than to institutional constraints on the growth of mass movements in America. Secondly, while Lipset sees American political development as having followed a unique path, he also argues that European social structure is becoming Americanized, so that there is now a partial convergence of European and American democracies.[15] Thirdly, Lipset's version of the 'exceptionalism' argument, unlike Boorstin's, does leave open the question of whether, despite the obvious differences between American democracy and democracy elsewhere, we can identify two (or more) distinct forms of liberal democracy.

There is not the space here to develop an adequate account of why I do not think we should regard the US as a separate kind of liberal democracy, but some of the points I would make can be outlined. In particular, the case for American 'exceptionalism' always looks strongest when the US is contrasted with a mythical composite parliamentary democracy – one containing such diverse elements as the strong French central state, British parliamentary practices (with their lack of powers for individual legislators), German party organizations, and Scandinavian-type welfare states. Put up against such a model the US does look different! But, of course, no liberal democracy comes close to resembling this model. There are federal parliamentary systems (Australia, Canada, Germany); there are legislatures which play an important role in legislative initiation (the Swedish *Rikstag*); a number of European parties have weak, decentralized party organizations which place power largely in the hands of elected politicians (the French centre-right parties); and there are states with relatively modest state welfare programmes (Ireland). Once we start to disaggregate the 'model' the US does not look quite such an unusual case.

That the US is a rather distinctive member of the liberal democracy 'family' cannot be doubted. What is being denied here is that it constitutes an entirely separate branch of that family, whose origins and subsequent development are so different that it must be classified all by itself. With respect to the general factors that prompted the growth of liberal democracy, and with respect to the sorts of government that first emerged in these states, what unites all the liberal democracies is more striking than the particular differences in their paths to democratization.

IV

The second argument to be considered is that, even if liberal democracies have a common origin, there are today quite distinct types of liberal democracy. In this section attention will be focused on countries in those areas of the world in which liberal democracy emerged and has been sustained continuously since the post-

---

[14] A. Ware, 'Patronage and federalism', *Government and Opposition*, 26 (1991), 115–19.
[15] Lipset, 'American exceptionalism reaffirmed', p. 39.

1945 political settlement. In the next section I will consider liberal democracy elsewhere.[16]

Since the 1950s political scientists have attempted to develop classifications of liberal democratic regimes. In that decade it was commonplace to distinguish between Anglo-American and Continental European political systems. Supposedly, the former were characterized by homogeneous, secular political cultures while the latter were marked by fragmentation. The supposed Continental European political culture embraced France, Germany and Italy, whilst Scandinavia and the Low Countries were seen as intermediate cases.[17] The failure of this typology to take account of the rather different cultures in several continental European countries led Lijphart to a very different analysis. In what he called 'consociational democracies' (and he had in mind Switzerland, the Netherlands, Belgium and Austria), elite accommodation made for highly stable political systems, compared with, say, Italy or the French Fourth Republic.[18] Nevertheless, the coherence of the concept of 'consociational democracy' and its empirical validity were much debated subsequently, and in the 1980s Lijphart produced a new typology of liberal democracies in which he drew a distinction between 'majoritarian' and 'consensus' governments.

Lijphart identifies two dimensions on which regimes may be majoritarian or consensual, and this yields four categories of liberal democratic state. The one dimension consists of what can be described as socio-political factors whilst the other dimension consists of constitutional factors.[19] Dimension I embraces (a) whether cabinets are minimal winning ones, (b) executive dominance, (c) the effective number of parties in the polity, (d) the number of issue dimensions, and (e) electoral disproportionality.[20] Dimension II is the 'constitutional' dimension and embraces (i) unicameralism, (ii) centralization – measured in terms of the central government's share of tax receipts and (iii) constitutional flexibility.[21] These dimensions yield four possible types of liberal democratic regime:

1 *majoritarian*: these are the pure majoritarian states,[22] majoritarian on both dimensions;
2 *majoritarian-federal*: these are majoritarian on dimension I but consensual on dimension II;[23]
3 *consensual-unitary*: these are consensual with respect to dimension I but majoritarian with respect to dimension II;[24]
4 *consensual*: these are the pure consensual cases,[25] consensual on both dimensions.

---

[16] In fact, Japan is included in both sections; liberal democracy did not develop autonomously in East Asia, but Japan has had a liberal democratic regime since it regained its independence in 1952.

[17] G. A. Almond, 'Comparative political systems', *Journal of Politics*, 18 (1956), pp. 398 and 405.

[18] A. Lijphart, *The Politics of Accommodation* (Berkeley, University of California Press, 1968).

[19] Lijphart, *Democracies*, pp. 215–20.

[20] The 'majoritarian' democracy on this dimension is of the 'ideal' Westminster type – it has minimum winning cabinets, dominance by the political executive, two parties, a single-issue dimension dividing the parties and electoral disproportionality. The 'consensus' democracy has the opposite of these features.

[21] The 'majoritarian' democracy is unicameral, centralized and has a flexible constitution – again, the 'consensus' democracy is the opposite of this.

[22] New Zealand (the best exemplar), the UK, Ireland, Luxembourg, Sweden and Norway.

[23] The US (the best exemplar), Canada, Germany, Austria, Australia and Japan.

[24] Israel (the best exemplar), Denmark, Finland, French Fourth Republic and Iceland.

[25] Switzerland (the best exemplar), Belgium, Netherlands, Italy and the French Fifth Republic.

ALAN WARE   139

Unlike Boorstin, Lijphart does not regard the US as 'exceptional'. His findings
suggest that it is frequently a deviant case but, in terms of his continuum, it 'is
somewhere in the middle'.[26] Indeed, he regards it as prototypical of the
majoritarian-federal type.

Lijphart's classification is the most subtle attempt thus far to distinguish
between types of mature liberal democracies. But do the regimes in each category
have that much in common with each other? Consider first some key aspects of
political institutions other than those specified in Lijphart's classification – a
classification in which, for example, Sweden is grouped with the UK
('majoritarian'), Austria with the US ('majoritarian-federal'), and Belgium and
Italy with the French Fifth Republic ('consensual'). In traditional liberal
democratic theory legislatures are supposed to provide a vital link between voters
and elected public officials. We might assume that the majoritarian systems would
tend to break this form of linkage while consensual democracies would sustain
them. Certainly the weak legislature is evident in the Westminster-style
democracies, but these regimes are not the only examples of majoritarian
democracies. Sweden is in this category and yet it provides for considerable input
by the legislature into the policy-making process. On the other hand, the
'consensual' Fifth Republic created one of the weakest legislatures among the
liberal democracies.

Then there is party penetration of society and state – that is, the extent to which
parties have institutionalized links with their electorates and are able to exercise
control over state bureaucracies.[27] Party penetration of the state is relatively high
in Sweden but (until the 1980s) was very low in Britain; again penetration of
society was high in the former but low in the latter. Austria and the US are at the
two extremes in relation to both – party penetration is probably higher in Austria
than in any other regime while during the twentieth century it has become very
low in the US. Again, both Italy and Belgium would rank fairly high in this
regard while the Fifth Republic has only moderate party penetration of state and
society. Here too there is no pattern corresponding to the 'majoritarian'/
'consensual' categories.

Finally, consider interest groups. Liberal corporatist patterns of interest
intermediation are most usually associated with Sweden and Norway (both
'majoritarian'), Denmark and Finland (both 'consensual-unitary') and Austria
('majoritarian-federal'). In neither the UK ('majoritarian') nor France ('consensual') have corporatist tendencies been strong, and in the US ('majoritarian-
federal') they have been especially weak. Once again, there is no correspondence
between the majoritarian/consensual distinction and patterns of institutional
behaviour. Whilst Lijphart has produced a useful analytic framework, it does not
seem to help us identify wholly different forms of government within liberal
democracy.[28]

[26] Lijphart, *Democracies*, p. 32.
[27] See A. Ware, *Citizens, Parties and the State* (Cambridge, Polity Press, 1987), pp. 188–203.
[28] And, it must be stressed it *is* a useful typology. His categories of liberal democracies do
correlate, though, as we might expect, with other significant variables in liberal democratic states –
including, for example, density of trade union membership. Generally unitary liberal democracies
have much higher union densities than non-unitary ones; there is a greater incentive for unions to
mobilize and for members to join when political power is constitutionally centralized. Thus the mean
union density in majoritarian democracies is 63.4 per cent and in the consensual-unitary states it is
74.4 per cent; it is only 40.6 per cent in majoritarian-federal states and 44.8 per cent in consensual
states. Data on union density is for the late 1970s and is taken from M. Wallerstein, 'Union
organization in advanced industrial democracies', *American Political Science Review*, 83 (1989), p. 482.

To check whether this judgement is correct we should consider the policy output of the different categories of liberal democracy; we can examine the share of GNP formed by expenditures on social security – that is, government-sponsored schemes of welfare. Wilensky's data cover the 21 countries embraced by Lijphart's typology (obviously excluding the French Fourth Republic) for 1966 – that is, in the middle of the post-war era on which the Lijphart typology is founded.[29] The proportion of GNP devoted to social security varies from 6.2 per cent in Japan to 21 per cent in Austria. The mean share of GNP devoted to social security in the pure 'majoritarian' states is 14.2 per cent while in the pure 'consensual' democracies it is 16.4 per cent. (In the 'majoritarian-federal' states the proportion is 12.3 per cent and in the 'consensual-unitary' states 10.9 per cent.) In other words, it is not possible to show differences of such a scale that it is clear that we are faced with two radically different forms of government.

Nevertheless, these same data do show that political structures in liberal democracies affect policy outcomes. For example, they confirm the long-established point that federal systems devote a smaller proportion of their GNP to social security than most other states. Excluding the 'administrative-federal' states, such as Germany, there are four truly federal states on Lijphart's list – Australia, Canada, Switzerland and the US. Respectively they spend 9.0, 10.1, 9.5 and 7.9 per cent on social security. Only Iceland (8.7), Israel (8.0) and Japan (6.2) spend a similarly low proportion of GNP on welfare.

Clearly, there are differences among liberal democratic regimes both with regard to their institutional arrangements and their policy outputs. However, these differences are not so great that they indicate the existence of quite distinct types of governmental system. Moreover, and this is an argument I do not have space to develop here, the mature liberal democracies resemble each other far more than they do any other political systems. The general conclusion to be drawn from this is that there is no evidence of two or more distinct forms of liberal democracy developing among the mature democracies.

There remains one possibility to consider. Perhaps the 'exporting' of liberal democracy to ex-colonies (such as India) or to regimes which were conquered militarily, but which had no previous history of liberal democracy (such as Japan), transforms liberal democracy. In other words, might not introducing liberal democratic institutions onto societies that are very different from those in which liberal democracy emerged originally produce a 'mutation' – a form of government that is not the same as in the older democratic regimes.

V

Before examining this issue it is necessary first to classify liberal democracies with respect to their origin. Obviously, any list of liberal democracies is likely to have controversial inclusions and exclusions and to become out of date very soon after it has been compiled. The one used here is derived from the *Economist World Atlas of Elections* (published in 1987) which identified 39 countries in which there were free elections;[30] to these 39 countries are added a further ten countries which were fully independent liberal democracies in 1987, but which had populations of less than 200,000 – the cut-off point for inclusion in the *Atlas*.[31] These 49

[29] H. L. Wilensky, *The Welfare State and Equality* (Berkeley, University of California Press, 1975), p. 122.
[30] This list includes Fiji – the *Atlas* being published before the *coup* in that country.
[31] Antigua and Barbuda, Dominica, Grenada (restored to liberal democracy after the 1985

ALAN WARE   141

countries may then be classified as follows, the number in each category being identified in parentheses:

1 *European* (19)
2 *Established as liberal democracies by European settlers* (5)[32]
3 *Liberal democracy imposed on non-European country* (1)[33]
4 *'Ex-British' colonies* (19)[34]
5 *Other states in the Caribbean, and Central and South America* (5)

For my purpose, of course, it is the contrast between the first two categories and the remaining three on which attention is focused.

Clearly, these categories conceal important similarities between individual members of different categories. For example, within Europe there are several instances of liberal democracy being imposed on countries after military conquest (Germany, Italy, Austria) as well as 'ex-British' colonies (Cyprus). Again, in both the newly democratic southern European countries and in Latin America external pressures have been important in establishing liberal democracy. In the former case the European Community has reinforced domestic demands for this form of government,[35] while in the latter case the recognition that foreign investors usually have confidence in this kind of regime can aid democratization. Moreover, it could be argued that the distinction between the 'settler' states identified in category (2) and at least some of the states in category (5) is somewhat artificial. Yet, despite its many limitations, this classification is of some value when considering what happens to liberal democracy when it is transposed to a cultural and economic context very different from that in which it arose originally. Not least, it highlights the fact that a significant number of liberal democracies, admittedly some of which are very small, have survived outside the original areas of development.

Nevertheless, an obvious point to make about the 'exporting' of liberal democracy is that there are many instances in which it failed. British decolonization in Africa, in particular, showed the unworkability of the Westminster model in some contexts. The African states were not nation-states – they were artificially defined territories; they were not fully commercial or industrial societies; and, in addition, they lacked the intermediate institutions which prevent the ruthless exploitation of power. The liberal democratic constitutions collapsed very quickly. Then, in most of Central and South America, there is a long history of regime change, democratic regimes of one kind or another being formed and then collapsing. In this area, especially, there have been instances of

invasion), Kiribati, Nauru, St Christopher and Nevis, St Lucia, St Vincent, Tuvalu and Western Samoa.

   [32] Australia, Canada, Israel, New Zealand, US.

   [33] Japan.

   [34] Of these 19 states, ten are the very small island states in the Caribbean and the Pacific Ocean omitted from the *Atlas* list; there are a further four, larger states in the Caribbean and a further three larger states in the Pacific; the remaining two countries are India and Botswana. [One of the problems in classifying the newly independent countries in the Pacific region is that some of them were previously administered by Australia and New Zealand rather than by Britain. For my purposes it is the imposition of the Westminster-model on independence that is the interesting aspect of their political structures. For convenience, I use the (admittedly misleading) expression 'ex-British' to describe them.]

   [35] L. Whitehead, 'Democracy for convergence in Southern Europe: a comparative politics perspective', in G. Pridham (ed.), *Encouraging Democracy* (Leicester, Leicester University Press, 1991), pp. 59–60.

non-liberal democracies – regimes in which elected rulers have been able to govern without the checking power provided by institutionalization in the liberal democracies; relatively unresponsive leaders have handed on to equally unresponsive elected successors ('elected dictatorships'). In other words, copying the *electoral* institutions of liberal democracies does not ensure that liberal democracy will result.

When the 'national question' has been resolved and when there is a sufficiently high level of institutionalization, liberal democracy might be introduced successfully. But just as there are pressures, emanating from the liberal democratic world, on other regimes to democratize, so too are there even stronger pressures for liberal democracies to operate capitalist economies. Liberal democracy not only emerged from capitalism originally but today it helps to sustain capitalism. Obviously, greater economic interdependence in the late twentieth century precludes any one liberal democracy from adopting policies which might be effective in a more closed economy. For example, the Mitterrand government's expansionist economic policies in the early 1980s benefited the German and other economies as much as France's whilst, at the same time, creating inflationary pressures in France itself.

But this argument can be pushed further – some international business corporations and liberal democratic governments actually help to destabilize particular liberal democratic regimes if their policies depart from those compatible with capitalism. The best example of this is Chile, where US firms in the early 1970s (and covertly the US government itself) preferred the Allende government to be overthrown by military *coup* rather than for it to remain in office; assistance was given to the opponents of the government. It was because the social and economic policies of Allende's government were held to work against the interests of the international market economy, and American enterprises in particular, that this intervention occurred. Both indirectly and directly, then, the world system of liberal democracy tends to restrict the range of liberal democracies that actually develop.[36] This facilitates the reproduction of forms of government broadly similar to those found in Europe and in the liberal democracies founded by European settlers.

But if there is a tendency for the liberal democratic world to reproduce regimes in its own likeness elsewhere, might not the values and social structures in these newer democracies transform the practices of liberal democracy? In doing this might there not have been created new forms of liberal democracy? Might not the power of landlords in Latin America, attitudes to social hierarchy in Japan, or social structure in India have produced very different kinds of liberal democracy than that found in the European and settler states?

Certainly, post-war Japan was characterized by rather different public policy priorities than those in the older liberal democracies. As was noted earlier, Wilensky's data for the mid-1960s show Japan as devoting the lowest proportion of GNP to expenditures on social security. This reflected a policy of building a welfare society rather a welfare state:

[36] Of course, the Allende example might be disputed on the ground that the nationalization programmes of that government resulted in such a concentration of power in the hands of the state that it amounted to a significant dismantling of key intermediate institutions, and hence to the dismantling of liberal democracy itself. But nationalization without compensation is not, of itself, incompatible with the practice of liberal democracy, and whether it amounts to de-institutionalization can only be determined by examining the overall configuration of intermediate institutions.

ALAN WARE   143

> A welfare society implies a combination of governmental intervention and
> welfare functions performed by nongovernmental institutions such as the
> family, the community and enterprises. In the 1970s, however, governmental
> expenditure for social security expanded considerably. The impetus for this
> change came from the emerging demographic pressures of an aging society
> and the weakening of family ties that accompanied urbanization.[37]

Two points seem obvious about this aspect of Japanese public policy: the
Japanese approach to social welfare differs from European approaches, but in
many respects the American approach has been just as exceptional. Moreover,
even in Japan pressures for greater governmental involvement developed.

Nor does the political process indicate the establishment of a radically different
form of liberal democracy. Political parties long predate the post-war political
system – the first party cabinet being formed in 1898.[38] The close (and sometimes
corrupt) links between leading party officials and industrialists are not unique to
Japan; they have been evident elsewhere, particularly in Germany. Moreover, the
connections that individual legislators seek to establish with voters through their
koenkai can be seen as a peculiar combination of patron–client relations and the
kind of personal campaign organization established by American politicians. The
differences between the Japanese political process and those of other liberal
democracies is not so great, then, that it seems to constitute a wholly different
family of liberal democracies.

Yet, it might be asked whether this results from Japan being a wealthy,
industrial society. What of the poorer states, such as Jamaica; should their forms
of government be seen as a different *family* of liberal democracies? Certainly, their
relative poverty means that the pattern of public policies is rather different in
these liberal democracies. The poorest states (for example, India) spend relatively
little on social security, and even those with higher GNPs, but still not as high as
the poorest liberal democracies in Europe or North America, spend much less on
social security. For example, Venezuela, Trinidad and Tobago, Cyprus and
Jamaica all spent less than 4 per cent of GNP on social security in 1966, whilst
Ireland (the poorest of the European/North American democracies) spent 11.1
per cent of its GNP on welfare.[39]

And what about the cultural context in which democracy is practised? Might
not patterns of dependence between the powerful and the powerless be radically
different in the 'poorer' democracies. Undoubtedly, clientelism is far more
prevalent in the latter than in, for example, northern Europe or North America
today. But if we compare the 'poorer' liberal democracies with the US in the
1870s or France in 1900 our judgement is very different. Indeed, in some ways, the
distribution of patronage and the rewarding of supporters with privileged
positions in contemporary Jamaica is remarkably similar in many respects to
American politics in the nineteenth century. Moreover, aspects of this style of
politics survive in many liberal democracies today – the Italian Christian
Democrats, for example, consolidated their hold on the Italian state through
appointments of their supporters to a variety of positions.

It is true, of course, that some features of democratic politics in Latin America
or India, for example, are far less prevalent in Europe or the settler states. The

[37] S. Verba et al., *Elites and the Idea of Equality* (Cambridge, MA, Harvard University Press,
1987), p. 275.
[38] J. A. A. Stockwin, 'Japan: the leader–follower relationship in parties', in A. Ware (ed.),
Political Parties (Oxford, Basil Blackwell, 1987), p. 100.
[39] Wilensky, *The Welfare State and Equality*, p. 123.

power exercised by local landlords in rural communities was probably always much less in the latter, and the violence which often erupts in Indian elections is generally absent. It is also true that in the era of the state of emergency Mrs Gandhi was able to overcome what institutional opposition there was to move India towards 'elected dictatorship'. For a variety of reasons, India is more likely than most of the European and settler liberal democracies to move away from liberal democratic practices from time to time – and it is not inconceivable that liberal democracy could collapse there. But I suggest that none of this amounts to a case for saying that how government works in India, when it is functioning as a liberal democracy, is *so* different from how it worked in many European democracies 70 years ago – or even today. Power is not evenly distributed in European societies – some groups have virtually no power; nor have the 'national' questions been resolved – Northern Ireland being one instance. In short, even in its heartland, liberal democracy rarely corresponds to the image it seeks to project for itself – in the past, and often today, liberal democratic practices often diverge from those specified in liberal democratic theory. And it is not just in the 'poorer' states that this occurs.

VI

To the arguments already presented in accounting for the similarity between the various liberal democracies may be added another. Liberal democracies tend to 'borrow' from elsewhere institutions that seem to work. For example, some of the Westminster-model countries have taken the idea of the ombudsman from Scandinavia and have utilized it in their own regimes. Or again, electoral systems are often copied from existing models rather than wholly new systems introduced.[40] However, it is not just at the level of individual institutions that the seemingly successful is transplanted and apparent failures rejected. Entire structures of institutions are rejected. The American system of the separation of powers is the governmental equivalent of the Betamax video system – it was the model no one else wanted, largely because of the enormous problems in coordinating policy-making that such a system creates. Consequently, the first fully developed liberal democracy has an institutional structure that, from one perspective, is unique – even though each of the American states has itself copied the model set up at the federal level in 1787.[41]

All this suggests is that *if* liberal democracies are established in, for example, Eastern Europe within the next few years they are likely to resemble rather closely liberal democracies elsewhere – except, obviously, the US. We might reasonably expect that these democracies will not copy the American model simply because of the problems of political coordination that it poses. Of course, it is far from clear whether the democratization process in Eastern Europe will collapse or lead to 'elected dictatorships' rather than liberal democracy. To a large extent success will depend on solving 'national questions' and on decentralizing economic power and, given the dominance of the capitalist economies in the west, that will involve a switch to capitalism rather than to some other form of economic organization. However, as important in making liberal democracy possible will be the construction of a variety of institutions to prevent the untramelled use of

[40] See A. Reeve and A. Ware, *Electoral Systems* (London, Routledge, 1992), pp. 4–6.
[41] The one minor departure from the standard is of comparatively recent origin: Nebraska adopted its unicameral legislature in 1937.

ALAN WARE   145

state power. What is most unlikely to occur, though, is the emergence of liberal democracies which differ markedly in their *modus operandi* from the existing liberal democracies.

[3]

Conceptual Issues in the Comparative Study of Regime Change and Democratization

Stephanie Lawson

There is no richer field of enquiry in contemporary comparative politics than the study of regime change and especially "democratization." Throughout the last two decades, and especially in the 1980s, many authoritarian regimes around the world, while perhaps not succumbing altogether, have certainly withered. The most extensive changes have come about in eastern Europe. In southern Europe and parts of Latin America, too, democratization has gained in strength, while in Asia the Philippines and South Korea have experienced similar movement. But in Asia the repression of some democratization movements has also been severe, China and Burma providing notable examples. Another exception to the democratization trend was the coup in Fiji, the first in the Pacific. But in some neighboring countries such as Tonga and Western Samoa, resistance to traditional rule (although it is relatively benign) is growing, and more democratic institutions may emerge. South Africa is still undergoing a significant transformation. Elsewhere in Africa authoritarian regimes continue to predominate and are likely to do so for some time. There is, nonetheless, a growing dissatisfaction with single-party rule which has generated a "wave of demands for more pluralistic political institutions."[1]

Much of the recent scholarly work devoted to the process of democratization has been empirical, although there has been concern also with constructing general explanations for the breakdown of authoritarianism and the processes through which democratization has taken place. Amongst the most comprehensive works of this kind is the four volume collection edited by Diamond, Linz, and Lipset.[2] Other significant collections of studies have been edited by Enrique A. Baloyra[3] and by O'Donnell, Schmitter, and Whitehead.[4] The case studies in these works provide a very substantial resource from which cognate studies in regime change (and maintenance) can draw. Earlier studies, like that edited by John Herz,[5] have provided similar resources, again largely through case study analysis. Other writers have been concerned to provide explanatory models with particular emphasis on those conditions most amenable to the growth and consolidation of democratic politics.[6]

Despite the extensive scope of some of these works, there are several important subjects which receive very much less attention than they deserve but which are central to the issue of regime transformation. There is little attempt, for example, to examine the concept of "regime" as distinct from "state" or "government." It seems that each of these is, very largely, taken as given. Yet it is by no means clear that these terms convey, as a matter of course, a level of conceptualization appropriate to the scope or nature of regime change studies. If the relationships between these concepts are to be characterized with any precision, then, a clearer conceptual framework is an essential starting point.

Another problem involves the question of basic regime types, since a regime change necessarily implies a shift from one type to another. This, too, is central to the issue. The

183

Comparative Politics   January 1993

construction of elaborate, formal typologies is not necessary for the purpose of describing basic regime types, although these typologies may be important complements to the broader categories in terms of identifying distinctive modes of regime change and the varying ways in which democracy is institutionalized.[7] But a meaningful distinction between democratic and nondemocratic regimes is essential when dealing with regime change in terms of "democratization." This may involve taking a stand on "essentially contested concepts" like "democracy,"[8] and it is certain to attract some virulent accusations about ethnocentric bias. But this is better than having nothing to say at all, for, as Daniel Levine points out, without an adequate concept of democracy the entire effort of attempting to understand regime change "stalls virtually at the starting point."[9] Also, although there may be "an evolving consensus on what democracy means," this is no cause for complacence.[10] The word "democracy" has suffered too many abuses in its application for its meaning to be taken for granted. For the purpose of this discussion, my elaboration of democracy and its antithesis is one which sets up a dichotomous classification rather than a continuum on which more or less democratic (or authoritarian) regimes can be placed. This is not to deny the analytic utility of a continuum model for regime change studies, especially in empirical evaluations of actual regimes. But an adequate conceptualization—and an adequate continuum for that matter—requires the opposing types to be clearly delineated, and it is against such a delineation that "real world" regimes can be judged.

A third problem concerns the limited attention that has been paid to the role of some important institutional factors and/or agents in the process of democratization. Levine discerns, for example, that political parties in the volumes by O'Donnell et al. are notable "mostly by their absence."[11] Nancy Bermeo makes a similar point and urges that parties be brought back in to the analysis of regime change and the processes of legitimation.[12] In terms of democratic consolidation, Gillespie also emphasizes the importance, not only of political parties, but of party systems as well.[13] An area of even greater neglect in regime change analysis concerns the question of constitutional political opposition, which is linked closely to the role of political parties and party systems. Although the importance of this kind of opposition is supported implicitly in democratization studies, it is rarely treated explicitly. Yet, as I shall argue later, constitutional opposition is crucial in the establishment and maintenance of democratic regimes and is therefore one of the most important indicators of democratization.

State, Regime, and Government

It is difficult to avoid engaging in the debate about the nature of the state when attempting to set up definitions, but the immediate conceptual or definitional problem can not be resolved at this stage unless reference to the vast literature on the state is kept to a minimum. It is important nonetheless to emphasize that the conception of the state should not be too narrowly construed, which it is if we view it only in terms of the capitalist-socialist dichotomization. As Sklar points out, the implications of this dichotomy is that the mode of economic production determines the nature and form of political power, thereby relegating to secondary rank such issues as the constitutional status of citizens and all that this carries with it.[14] This is especially important when considering the notion of regime in relation to

Stephanie Lawson

constitutionalism, which will be dealt with shortly. First, however, we shall look at some characterizations of "regime."

> A regime may be thought of as the formal and informal organization of the centre of political power, and of its relations with the broader society. A regime determines who has access to political power, and how those who are in power deal with those who are not.[15]

Fishman notes that this has implications for the question of regime type, which involves making distinctions among concepts such as democracy, totalitarianism, and authoritarianism (which will be addressed later). At a more basic structural level, he points out also that "regimes are more permanent forms of political organization than specific governments."[16] In other words, governments may come and go, while the regime remains more or less in place.

Another definition is given by Calvert, who says that "'a regime is the name usually given to a government or sequence of governments in which power remains essentially in the hands of the same social group."[17] This is consonant with the idea that a change of government does not (normally or necessarily) involve a change in regime. But it implies also that governments formed within or under a particular regime are all essentially of the same character. To the extent that these governments share a commitment, or at least conform to the broad rules and norms of the regime, this is a valid formulation. But it does not necessarily follow that the same "social group" is thereby accorded a continuous monopoly of power. This seems to imply that successive governments are virtually identical in terms of the interests that they represent. Although this may be true in some cases, an unqualified universal claim to this effect suggests a very static view of political activity at the level of government. It certainly accords little or no significance, for example, to the dynamics or effects of party competition.

Although the notion of "regime" in international relations theory is obviously situated in a different context of relationships, the formulation of definitions there provides some further insights relevant to the domestic arena. Stephen D. Krasner first defines international regimes as "principles, norms, rules and decision-making procedures around which actors converge in a given issue area."[18] This obviously can not be applied *in toto* to domestic regimes since the actors within these are not restricted to given issue areas. The idea that regimes embody—or are an embodiment of—particular norms and procedures is the key point, and this is applicable in a general way to the notion of "regime" in both international and domestic contexts.

Of particular interest is the distinction Krasner makes between principles and norms, on the one hand, and rules and procedures, on the other, and the implications that this distinction has in detecting instances of regime change.

> Principles and norms provide the basic defining characteristics of a regime. There may be many rules and decision-making procedures that are consistent with the same principles and norms. *Changes in rules and decision-making procedures are changes within regimes*, provided that principles and norms are unaltered.[19]

The key to the definition of "regime" here is clearly related to the values embodied in the

185

Comparative Politics   January 1993

principles and norms and implies that rules and procedures (which can take various forms and still be consistent with the character of the regime) derive from and are secondary to these values. A case of regime change, on this account, is therefore indicated primarily by a change in (or abandonment of) the principles and norms governing the nature of the regime. This accords with the view put forward by Budge and Farlie that political stability is predicated on "the continuity of basic features of a regime . . . while their non-continuance constitutes regime change."[20]

Krasner also considers the case of "regime weakening," which may constitute a phase in regime change. This occurs where the relationships between norms, principles, and rules become less coherent or where actual practice becomes increasingly inconsistent with the values or rules of the regime. Thus, Krasner concludes, in general, that:

> [C]hange within a regime involves alterations of rules and decision-making procedures, but not of norms or principles; change of regime involves alteration of norms and principles; and weakening of a regime involves incoherence among the components of the regime or inconsistency between the regime and related behavior.[21]

We have so far identified some key characteristics of a "regime" and have discerned as well certain important factors in relation to regime type and regime change. But we need to consider further the distinction among state, regime, and government.

The state is frequently characterized as "an inclusive concept that covers all aspects of policymaking and enforcement of legal sanctions" while government "is simply the agency through which the state acts in the political community."[22] Following this general line, Calvert says that:

> The state is the community organized for political purposes; the government is the individual or team of individuals that takes decisions which affect the lives of their fellow citizens. Governments succeed one another; the state endures. . . . [23]

Although these statements are helpful to a point, they do not give an adequate account of the state/regime/government distinction because they do not consider the notion of regime. The analyses of Chazan et al. and Fishman, however, do at least address all three concepts.[24] As noted earlier, Fishman says that a regime is a more permanent form of political organization than a specific government. To be more precise, it should be added that a regime may endure—like the state—while the process in which political control of the state alternates between parties of government (and opposition) is much more fluid. To be more specific still, there may be a succession of different governments, but state and regime usually remain constant by virtue of the fact that the different governments exercise power within the framework of the established regime and without disturbing the fundamental structure of the state. This is clearly applicable to those political systems in which there is a firm tradition of constitutional rule and provision is made for peaceful succession of government, normally by means of popular elections governed by the rules and procedures of the regime.[25] In these cases a change in government does not in any way signify a change in the constitutional order. Here, then, the notion of regime is linked very closely to the ideas associated with constitutionalism and the rule of law, which in turn derive from a

186

Stephanie Lawson

stream of thought which has its ancestry in Aristotle's conception of *politeia* and Cicero's *constitutio*.[26] The idea of "constitution" as developed from this stream encapsulates both the "total establishment of a state system" as well as the "more restricting notions of the limitations on government power by the 'power of the people.' "[27] The doctrine of constitutionalism that emerged emphasizes the importance of prescribing the specific limits of (constitutional) government, as well as the way in which politics and the affairs of the state are conducted generally. By prescribing such limits and establishing the rules of political conduct, constitutionalism underscores the norms of democratic politics and gives rise to a much clearer distinction among state, regime, and government.

Constitutionalism is now a common tradition in the West but is much less in evidence elsewhere. In nonwestern states it is often much more difficult to distinguish among state, regime, and government, and in some cases there may be no discernible distinction. Fishman notes, for example, that a defining characteristic of a totalitarian regime is the significant extent to which it penetrates the apparatus of the state.[28] It may be added that "government" in this case would be virtually synonymous with "regime." This is obviously an important point when it comes to sorting out the essential differences between democratic and authoritarian regimes, which we shall come to shortly. For the moment, there is one further issue to be considered in relation to the state/regime distinction.

While Fishman says that a regime is more permanent than a government, he also argues that it is typically less permanent than the state.

> The state, by contrast, is a (normally) more permanent structure of domination and coordination including a coercive apparatus and the means to administer a society and extract resources from it. . . . A state may remain in place even when regimes come and go.[29]

It is by no means obvious at first glance how state differs from regime in this formulation except in terms of its greater permanence. But an adequate conceptual distinction can be made by reference to where political power is located as opposed to how that power is exercised. States share a central common feature in that they exercise a monopoly of political power (whether this is "legitimate" or necessarily "coercive" power is another question).[30] In other words, the state is the locus of political power.[31] A regime, on the other hand, has less to do with power per se than it does with the way in which power is actually used. A regime, then, may be characterized as that part of the political system which determines how and under what conditions and limitations the power of the state is exercised. In other words, the concept of regime is concerned with the form of rule.[32] As a corollary, the regime also determines not only the manner in which governments are formed and carry out their functions, but also the basis of their legitimacy as well as the extent to which they are permitted to exercise authority. In summary, regimes embody the norms and principles of the political organization of the state, which are set out in the rules and procedures within which governments operate.

As suggested earlier, these distinctions are much easier to make at an empirical level when dealing with western democracies. But in nondemocratic nations, including much of the Third World, the distinctions are not at all clear. Although this may create problems for analysis by obscuring some of the elementary forces at work in regime change and maintenance, the very fact that there are problems in making state/regime/government

187

Comparative Politics   January 1993

distinctions in nondemocracies highlights another important distinction, namely, the distinction between democratic and nondemocratic regimes, which is the concern of the next section.

Regime Types: Democratic and Nondemocratic

It follows from the above discussion that it is at the level of how, and under what conditions and limitations, the power of the state is exercised that regime type can be distinguished. It also follows that in addressing this issue a distinction must be made between democratic and nondemocratic regimes. One objection that may be registered here is that such broad conceptual distinctions are not especially helpful when dealing with the intricate details of real world regime changes. It is perhaps for this reason that some authors have been moved to construct, largely by inductive methods, very elaborate regime typologies which more closely reflect empirical reality. One recent example is that provided by Chazan et al.[33] Such typologies may well contribute to a better understanding of the extent to which regime diversity exists in places like Africa, where once the tendency of analysts was to "overhomogenize" politics there by concentrating too hard on developmental similarities in regimes rather than divergences.[34] Nonetheless, the inductive strategies employed in complex typologizing, while capable of producing low order empirical generalizations, can not logically generate comprehensive theories with which comparativists can work.[35] Further, most typological exercises are fraught with difficulty because, as Georges Balandier points out, the noncontinuous categories they set up are not well-equipped to deal with transitions.[36] My purpose here, then, is a very different one and is prompted as much by a concern that the word "democracy" has suffered some loss of meaning since being applied to (or claimed by) a wide variety of regimes as by the more practical need to establish conceptual clarity in regime change theory.

As noted at the beginning, the literature on regime change is not only fairly vague on the state/regime/government distinction, but also tends to sidestep the problem of dealing with basic concepts like "democracy." This is not a problem confined to more recent literature. Twenty years ago Rodney Barker noted that many studies had concentrated largely on the practical conditions under which democracy could best be achieved or sustained or on those devices most appropriate to its operation. Democracy had become such a widely accepted "good" that little attention was devoted to its grounds and its character.[37] Little has changed. In a section devoted to "defining some concepts" in the O'Donnell et al. analysis, for example, scarcely a page is devoted to a discussion of democracy, and even so it is raised only in the context of "democratization."[38] In reviewing O'Donnell et al., Levine points out that, although the editors "affirm a normative bias for democracy," the level of actual discussion on democracy throughout the volumes "turns up a curiously empty set of concepts" and that "democratic political arrangements are painted in neutral colors, characterized at best by the absence of negatives, with few positive virtues of their own."[39] This is clearly illustrated in Adam Przeworski's treatment of the "characteristics of democracy," which are elaborated almost exclusively in terms of democracy as "a particular system of processing and terminating intergroup conflicts."[40] In reviewing the same volumes, Ian Roxborough attributes to Whitehead the observation that democracy "means

Stephanie Lawson

different things to different people."[41] And this no doubt suits many regime leaders because, as George Orwell so succinctly put it:

> In the case of a word like democracy not only is there no agreed definition but the attempt to make one is resisted from all sides. . . . The defenders of any kind of regime claim that it is a democracy, and fear that they might have to stop using the word if it were tied down to any one meaning.[42]

This raises the obvious question, which Giovanni Sartori poses as the title of the first chapter of his most recent work on democracy: "*can* democracy be just anything?"[43] My purpose here is to argue that the term "democracy" can not be employed in a relativistic manner, nor purely stipulatively. It describes a particular type of regime, not just any regime which lays claim to the title. By elaborating this argument, I hope also to show more clearly how democracy in contemporary mass polities requires certain minimal conditions to be satisfied before a regime can really be called "democratic."

The etymological meaning of the word "democracy" is clear enough: literally, "rule or power of the people." As Eva Etzioni-Halevy reminds us, however, if the word is used in its literal sense in application to the real world of contemporary regimes, then we have no democracies at all, since in those regimes which are now commonly described as democracies "the people as a whole rule no more, and minorities of power holders—or elites—rule no less than they do in other regimes."[44] Objections to elite theories have been canvassed in a considerable body of literature, and I do not propose to review the arguments here. Suffice it to say that in mass polities the institutional means by which the concept of "the power of the people" is expressed is through representative structures, which implies at the very least elite management or control. But the political control which is granted to elites in representative democratic regimes is always temporary and always conditional. This particular issue will be investigated more fully at a later point, especially as it bears on the problem of identifying those institutional features of modern democratic politics. For the moment, my concern is still with the meaning of "democracy" in a conceptual rather than merely etymological sense.

Part of the problem with a word like "democracy" is that it is not simply a description of certain kinds of political institutional arrangements. It is clearly an evaluative word as well, and is almost universally acclaimed as something "good" and desirable. This is one of the characteristics which Gallie says a concept must possess in order to count as essentially contested: "it must be appraisive in the sense that it signifies or accredits some kind of valued achievement."[45] There is little doubt that democracy satisfies this condition. Indeed, as Gallie notes, it has become established as "*the* appraisive political concept *par excellence*."[46]

But it was not always so, and it is only in the recent past that the speech act performed by the use of the word democracy has been transformed "from one of condemnation to one of commendation."[47] Also, as Sartori points out, it was not until around the end of the second world war that serious disputes arose in an international context about the proper application of the word in describing actual regimes. Before then, he says, there seems to have been little doubt "that fascist and communist regimes were not democracies (they actually did not claim to be such) and that democracies were Western located and Western inspired."[48] In

189

Comparative Politics   January 1993

the meantime, however, the word has been appropriated for use by all comers and conferred on regimes which may now be democratic in name but in substance reflect few, if any, of the features normally associated with the practice of democratic politics.

One of the reasons for this was the new international ideological environment created by the outcome of the war in which the triumphant Allied powers, especially the United States, vigorously promoted their own political ideals in all available forums. Under these conditions, it was often advantageous for powerful minorities "to adopt at least an appearance of sympathy for democracy" in order to "defend and preserve their privileges."[49] Furthermore, the result of American foreign policy in its attempts to promote democracy (as opposed to communism) around the world, while at the same time establishing and preserving influence and strategic interests, has been to stretch the meaning of the word "to embrace an extraordinary variety of friendly but repressive regimes."[50] These have included such notorious cases as the rule of the Somozas in Nicaragua, Pinochet in Chile, Marcos in the Philippines, and Diem in South Vietnam.

What we have seen in the last few decades is, as Sartori wryly observes, "hardly the ascendance of a common ideal that is warming the hearts of humankind" but rather "an unprecedented escalation of terminological and ideological distortion whose end result eminently is obfuscation."[51] Of course, we can not legislate the correct use of words, but we can plausibly claim that some usages are invalid, or that those who lay claim to the title should at least demonstrate some commitment to "the values or qualities for which 'democracy' originally became a term of praise."[52]

But Gallie's idea of the essentially contested nature of concepts like democracy appears to pose some problems in designating those minimal conditions which must be satisfied before a regime can be called democratic. Here is one conclusion of Gallie's general argument.

> Recognition of a given concept as essentially contested implies recognition of rival uses of it (such as oneself repudiates) as not only logically possible and humanly "likely," but as of permanent potential critical value to one's own use or interpretation of the concept in question; whereas to regard any rival use as anathema, perverse, bestial or lunatic means, in many cases, to submit oneself to the chronic human peril of underestimating the value of one's opponents' positions.[53]

Gallie's point seems to be a compelling one, since any reasonable person will, at the very least, acknowledge that their own favored interpretation is open to question and will welcome critical discussion. To do otherwise would seem dogmatic (and therefore not in the spirit of democratic discourse). And for western scholars or proponents of democracy, an unwillingness to consider alternative interpretations will also attract accusations of ethnocentric bias. But if we accord to the concept of democracy the status of essential contestability in Gallie's terms, then it seems that we are obliged, *ipso facto*, to "repudiate a wide range of restrictive or exclusivist, descriptivist or essentialist claims which are characteristically made for it by each of its rival users."[54] And if we repudiate such claims, it does not seem logically possible to insist that there is a better conception of democracy or that there are any essential features which can be taken as characteristic of democracy. In this case, and if disputes about the meaning of the concept are indeed incapable of rational resolution, then it seems we are condemned to a world of either eternal relativism or

Stephanie Lawson

skepticism. Andrew Mason puts this clearly. He says that, if essential contestability theses are committed to the view that conceptual disputes are rationally unresolvable, they either

> affirm the view that if a concept is essentially contested, it admits of a variety of different conceptions, and that none of these conceptions is better than the others from a shared or neutral standpoint—in which case they are relativist. Or they affirm the view that if a concept is essentially contested, it admits of a variety of conceptions, and that none of these conceptions can be justifiably regarded as better than the others from a shared or neutral perspective—in which case they seem to express a form of skepticism.[55]

The endorsement of relativist and skeptical views renders the concept of democracy practically and ethically unintelligible. It also means, for all practical purposes, that words like democracy can be left to the stipulative whim of any claimant. And, as Sartori points out, whatever the fine points of the doctrine that "words are mere conventions" may be, the implications are clear enough to grasp intuitively.

> If words mean, in principle, whatever we wish them to mean, then we can only be heading towards Babel. Meanwhile, the applause goes to a Humpty-Dumpty society of word magicians that earn not only a living but a reputation by tampering with language and meanings.[56]

Further, it seems that there is little point in persisting with discourse if there is no possibility of arguing for the superiority of any meaning or conception over another. If all conceptions are of equal value, then they have no value at all. Discourse, it seems, then, becomes a form of sophistry in which opposite meanings can be derived from the same words to suit the occasion or to suit the particular interests of the speaker. What is lost also is the capacity to form a community of understanding for concepts like democracy and the values associated with it like justice, equality, liberty, and community. And this means that mere expedience can serve in the place of reasoned speech over the most basic ideas of right and wrong.[57]

My argument, in short, is that if we deny the possibility of superior conceptions of democracy, then we deny also the force of practical reason whereby the ability to assign value is lost in a void of conceptual relativism. Such a void robs the concept of democracy of a context of meaning and a community of understanding. And this is precisely what happens if scholars and others run for cover when faced with accusations of dogmatism or ethnocentric bias rather than support the values of democracy. To accept that particular conceptions of democracy amount to little more than "epistemological imperialism" is to give in to a kind of ethical relativism. This is contrary to the "powerful assertion" of democratic political theory which "expresses a fundamental human aspiration, not confined to any particular territory or period of time."[58] Further, appeals to relativism are themselves dogmatic because they seek to evade criticism, and indeed to make criticism impossible.

However, the claim that there may be superior conceptions of democracy does not preclude an admission of fallibilism, which is itself a democratic attitude. Nor does it imply intolerance of other points of view, although admission of a plurality of viewpoints "does not imply any weird equality of all sincere opinions as the truth."[59] So toleration of different points of view does not signal acceptance of relativism. Rather, it is a position which allows

191

Comparative Politics   January 1993

for the legitimate expression of competing ideas without assigning to any of them the status of a universal truth, on the one hand, but without consigning them to meaningless relativism, on the other. This is, moreover, inherent in the concept of democracy itself. In other words, any conception of democracy worthy of the name implicitly provides for the free articulation of competing ideas, interests, and policies. Further, any regime which does not allow for this free articulation of ideas is not worthy of the name "democracy." It is on this basis that I make an essentialist claim for a certain conception of democracy, which I shall shortly elaborate. First, however, one thing should be made clear. The claim is qualified to the extent that it is applied to contemporary mass polities. By this I mean that it would not necessarily be applicable, for example, to the polity of the ancient Athenians, nor to other small-scale societies of the kind said to have existed in some parts of precolonial Africa where a communal style of discussion, participation, and consensus decision making engendered a distinct kind of democratic practice.[60] In other words, it is not a universalist claim, but an essentialist claim within certain limits.

Gallie's point about the essential contestability of the concept of democracy, especially in application to mass polities, may be objected to on the grounds outlined above, but there is little disagreement about the fact of its internally complex character.[61] There is a number of significant dimensions, or subconcepts, that are taken to be characteristic of democracy. These include the values mentioned above (equality, liberty, community, and justice), as well as representative institutions, electoral systems, a plurality of political parties, constitutionalism, participation, and free opposition.[62] Some of these may be regarded as more important than others. This is what Gallie means when he says that the concept of democracy is internally complex in that it "admits of a variety of descriptions in which its different aspects are graded in different orders of importance."[63] Connolly elaborates the idea of internal complexity further by employing the notion of a "cluster concept to which a broad range of criteria apply," and although the grouping together of a number of the criteria may, for example, qualify a regime as democratic, he says that it is not possible to "specify an invariant set of necessary and sufficient conditions for the proper application of the concept."[64] While this may be so, it is possible to specify some criteria as necessary, if by no means sufficient, conditions in order to qualify a regime as democratic.

Constitutional Opposition as a Necessary Condition for Democracy

The particular condition put forward here as necessary for the application of the concept of democracy to regimes in contemporary mass polities is the presence of constitutional political opposition. This is not to disregard the importance of other elements or dimensions (including other types of opposition), nor is it claimed that the presence of constitutional political opposition is in any way a sufficient condition. Furthermore, just as there are no grounds for believing that there is only one kind of government that can properly be called democratic,[65] there is no one particular set of institutional arrangements which alone secures the operation of constitutional political opposition in practice (although some may be better than others). Rather, my claim is based on the idea that constitutional political opposition is the *sine qua non* of contemporary democracy in mass polities and that its institutionalization in some form or another is required before a regime can be called "democratic" with any

Stephanie Lawson

real meaning. This is hardly a novel theme in the mainstream literature on democratic theory. As Dahl observed some time ago, "one is inclined to regard the existence of an opposition party as very nearly the most distinctive characteristic of democracy itself; and we take the absence of an opposition party as evidence, if not always conclusive proof, for the absence of democracy."[66]

The idea of constitutional political opposition reflects, amongst other things, a commitment to the right of political dissent within a general consensual framework as to how, and within what limits, that dissent can be legitimately expressed. It does not usually mean opposition to the regime itself, although particular opposition groups may argue against all or any of the regime's features and propose alternatives. But while ever an opposition remains constitutional, it does not seek to change or overthrow a regime by force. If it seeks to bring about changes at regime level, it does so only by means of the regime's own rules for change, which are normally expressed in a constitution.

In western democracies, one of the prime purposes of a constitutional political opposition is to become the government, and to do so within the rules and procedures embodied in the existing regime. And it is opposition in this context that is the focus here. The government, for its part, is required to tolerate opposition, and "the people" have the power to determine, periodically, which group has the right to rule.

> [B]oth government and opposition are bound by the rules of some kind of constitutional consensus. It is understood, on the one side, that opposition is directed against a certain policy or complex of policies, not against the legitimacy of the constitutional regime itself. Opposition rises above naked contestation; it forswears sedition, treason, conspiracy, *coup d'état*, riot, and assassination, and makes an open appeal for the support of a more or less free electorate. Government, in return, is constrained by certain limitations as to the methods it can use to counter the opposition; the free expression of oppositional views is permitted both inside and outside the halls of the parliamentary body.[67]

On this account, the power of the government in a democratic regime is, as suggested earlier, always conditional and always temporary. It is conditional because it is subject to the limitations on its power imposed by the doctrine of constitutionalism, and it is temporary because it is subject to the periodic judgment of the people, who may choose to replace it with an alternative government, the opposition. This is decisive for how and under what conditions and limitations power is exercised in practice.

The temporary status of a democratic government is especially important to the case I am making here and is well illustrated by the following observation.

> Here then is the acid test for democracy. Democracy may be defined by the toleration of opposition. In so far as alternative governments are allowed to come into existence and *into office*, democracy, in my sense, exists. In so far as opposition is persecuted, rendered illegal, or stamped out of existence, democracy is not present, and either never has existed or is in the process of being destroyed.[68]

Had democracy been defined merely in terms of the toleration of opposition, the crucial point would have been missed. Tolerated opposition of some kinds can be permitted in nondemocratic regimes, but a democratic regime requires that an opposition must be able to

193

Comparative Politics   January 1993

become the government. In other words, it must have the constitutional status of a legitimate alternative government which the people have the power to choose to actually govern. So where there is no possibility of alternation in power between governing elements and oppositional elements through a peaceful process of fair and free elections, there is no constitutional opposition, and therefore no genuine democracy.

It follows from this that the legitimacy of constitutional opposition and its right to become the government if so chosen by the people are endorsed by the principles and norms of a democratic regime and made possible in practice by its rules and procedures. Further, the conduct of democratic politics entailed in this formulation is contingent on a deeper commitment, by all elements, to the principles and norms of the regime than to their own particular platforms and policies.[69] But as Rodney Barker points out, these notions do not flourish in any soil. They presuppose, amongst other things, "certain qualities in the condition of political thinking."[70] This is a problem I shall consider more specifically in relation to nonwestern contexts shortly. For the moment, I want to address the third point raised in the introduction, the role of political parties and party systems.

In contemporary mass polities, or more specifically in representative democracies, political parties are central to the functioning of constitutional political opposition. Despite the criticisms which have been leveled at "party government," it is hard to imagine a viable alternative to their capacity for "bringing order out of the chaos of a multitude of voters."[71] The utility of party organization is not restricted to representative systems either, and the ubiquity of the political party certainly testifies to this. For, although it had its origins in the rise of representative institutions and extension of the suffrage, the political party is now a feature of virtually every type of political regime. The viability on constitutional opposition in democratic regimes, however, depends very much on the existence of a competitive, adversarial party system, and such systems are by no means found everywhere. But let us first consider briefly the role of political parties and party systems in democratic regimes in terms of their importance for constitutional opposition.

Party systems produce both governments and oppositions—any political party can compete for office by presenting itself as an alternative government, and it is through the competitive interaction between parties that governments are able actually to alternate in office. Accordingly, an important indicator of democratic maturity is when competitive elections between contending parties lead to a peaceful transition of power from one to the other.[72] This requires contending parties, and it requires especially that those who lose office as the government accept that their power is temporary as well as conditional. These norms are implicit in the notion of a democratic party system.

There is obviously a need of more than one party for there to be a "system" of this kind, and the idea that there could be any sort of real competition for office with only one participant is logically absurd.[73] Further, a single party can not claim to represent an entire political community. In contrast, adversarial party systems operate on the fallibilistic assumption that no single party, or government, has all the answers and can "propel the polity on the course of some 'general will.' "[74] Further, party systems and constitutional opposition ensure that the majoritarianism implicit in democratic politics is a qualified one. "The people" consist of the entire body of citizens, not just a majority, and constitutional opposition makes institutional provision for the expression of minority interests and dissent. But if the majority is a permanent one, then so too is the minority. These conditions are

Stephanie Lawson

incompatible with democratic politics insofar as they tend to produce permanent governments and permanent oppositions and power does not alternate.[75] This is less of a problem in western democracies, where shifting coalitions of interests tend to produce more transient majorities and minorities, although it seems more problematic elsewhere, particularly in those societies characterized as "plural." This is just one of the difficulties posed for democracy outside the West. But the more basic problem of even establishing and maintaining competitive party systems which embody the notions associated with constitutional opposition is of prior concern.

Authoritarianism and Its Implications for Opposition

Almost thirty years ago, when the "new states" of Africa and Asia were just emerging from colonial rule, David Apter wrote that the (also new) governments of these states "rarely see the necessity for a regular opposition party nor do they always accept the idea of opposition as a normal feature of government."[76] In many cases, it seems that little has changed, and the idea of political opposition, rather than being seen as something of value in itself, is still regarded as anathema. Arguably, this view of opposition is not unique to the governments of ex-colonial states or "new nations" but features in the thinking of an array of authoritarian governments which have sought to construct regimes in their own image, and indeed to mold the state itself along lines compatible with this image. It is for this reason that the state/regime/government distinction becomes more blurred in nondemocracies. This directs our attention to antithetical regime types.

The antithesis of democracy is, of course, totalitarianism, and in this type of regime the distinctions, especially the practical distinction between government and regime, are virtually nonexistent. Further, while the government constitutes the regime, it is also the case that the party, under the direct control of the leader, constitutes the government. This lack of definition between levels is implicit in the well-known catalogue of totalitarian characteristics first proposed by C. J. Friedrich in 1954 to describe this unique form of autocratic domination[77] and later elaborated by a number of other commentators.[78] The utility of this catalogue lies, amongst other things, in the distinct contrasts it provides with the "contours" of a democratic polity, which Graham Maddox draws with precision.

> [W]here the totalitarian system pins all its faith in the messianic leader, the democratic ultimately trusts no individual or group without limitations and controls; where the totalitarian leader countenances no opposition, democracy insists upon it; where totalitarianism spurns or even destroys the rule of law, democracy steadfastly upholds it through the spirit of constitutionalism; where totalitarianism breaks down institutions of state and eschews democratic values, democracy endeavors to see them preserved in concrete form; where totalitarianism destroys all sub-state associations, demanding that all loyalty be given to the leader, and all effort expended in his cause, democracy values the private and social lives of the individual citizens within it.[79]

Totalitarianism, in the communist or fascist forms embodied in Stalin's Russia, Hitler's Germany, and Mussolini's Italy, can not be applied accurately in describing more recent

Comparative Politics   January 1993

regime types. As Kitchen points out, although the dictatorships of the underdeveloped world may have learned a great deal from fascist practice, they are not themselves fascist, and regimes such as those of Pinochet in Chile and Amin in Uganda differed in some essential respects from the fascist model.[80] Similarly, Schapiro notes that it is easy to find elements of totalitarianism in other types of regimes—he lists historical examples such as Tudor England and Muscovite Russia. But these, and other regimes which we might justifiably regard as wicked and repressive, lack certain of totalitarianism's defining characteristics such as mass mobilization and mass legitimacy. However, just as democracy has become a universal word of commendation, so too has totalitarianism (and especially the variety "fascism") become a word of almost universal condemnation and is often used as such. But, as Schapiro concludes, "to apply the term 'totalitarian' to every form of morally reprehensible government is to render the term useless."[81] As with the application of the word democracy, then, it is important to ensure that the words totalitarian and fascist retain their analytic value and are not used merely for polemical purposes. Accordingly, although I intend to describe next some features of party politics which are antithetical to the contours of democracy and reflect some aspects of totalitarianism, it does not follow that the regimes in which they operate are totalitarian. Rather, they are best described simply as authoritarian, a label which covers generally those regimes which are, to greater or lesser degrees, "characterized by repression, intolerance, encroachment on the private rights and freedom of citizens, and limited autonomy for nonstatist interest groups."[82]

The particular focus of the next part of the discussion is on one party (as distinct from one party dominant) regimes. These clearly do not exhaust the category of nondemocratic types, but they provide the most convenient contrast to the multiparty systems of western democracies. Of particular importance is the notion, incorporated as a basic norm or principle of regimes in many one party states, that society is (or ought to be) a harmonious unified whole. As with the classic conservatism of the West, and with the ideology of fascism, this implies an organic view of the state. The party is portrayed as the organizational expression of organic political society and is seen to embody the "natural" unity of society.

In many cases, of course, the party is simply a "method by which a regime which was basically personal and dictatorial sought to give itself legitimacy."[83] This is illustrated, for example, by the role of the Communist Party in Cuba, which Castro has used as a vehicle to centralize power around himself.[84] Similarly, Saddam Hussein has used the machinery of the Iraqi Ba'ath Party—the guiding principal of which also emphasizes the fundamental unity of the people—as an effective instrument of control and manipulation in establishing personal rule.[85] The model of authoritarian presidential regimes in Latin America (which revolve around the rule of a "strongman" leader) also draws from an organic view of society and the state.[86] In parts of Asia and Africa, too, single party and personalized rule frequently reflects a unitary view of state and society.[87] J. A. C. Mackie notes that the period of Sukarno's autocratic rule in Indonesia was marked, amongst other things, by a "tremendous stress on ideology, indoctrination and the symbols of national unity and strength."[88] It is through a unitary view and the rhetoric that supports it that mass mobilization can often be achieved, and with it a semblance of legitimacy for the regime. Elections in these circumstances are a demonstration of support for the ruling party's mandate for continuance in office as well as

Stephanie Lawson

for its policies, and there is no sense in which elections act as a mechanism for the transfer of power as they do in democratic regimes.[89]

The arguments employed by ruling elements for the suppression of political opposition in one party regimes are usually linked to the idea of unity—"there is no need for an opposition because the ruling party and the people are one."[90] This is obviously more an aspiration than a reflection of reality. Most important, the aspiration seeks to deny a basic, ineluctable characteristic of the mass polity, which is as applicable to most of the Third World (or more so) as it is to the West, and that is social diversity or pluralism. Some of the clearest cases in which one party rule attempts to subsume a high degree of social pluralism through a unitary ideology are found in Africa. Here the processes of colonization and decolonization have produced weak states characterized by sharp, and sometimes apparently intransigent, divisions along linguistic, ethnic, religious, and other lines.[91] Although there is a diversity of regime types (as reflected in the Chazan et al. typology mentioned earlier), it is nonetheless possible to identify unitary ideology as a fairly pervasive feature of postcolonial African politics, at least amongst incumbent political leaders. This has obviously proved, *inter alia*, to be a significant obstacle to the functioning of political opposition—both constitutional and otherwise—and therefore of democratic politics. Some have argued that the institutionalization of political opposition is essentially incompatible with the African style of politics and, especially, that expectations to the contrary reflect an ethnocentric bias towards western norms of democratic political conduct. Further, it has been suggested that democratic practices are a feature as much of some African political traditions as of western traditions and, in terms of egalitarian values, perhaps even more so.[92] These, and some of the other points raised above, are worth some detailed consideration.

In the terms of modernization theory, internal integration of many of the new states of Africa was to be achieved through nationalist political parties which had won popular support through anticolonial struggles and which were therefore well placed to promote unity and development through mobilization of the populace. But on achieving independence, these parties lost the "external enemy" which had previously been instrumental in securing a degree of national solidarity, and the solution to the ethnic and regional divisions which subsequently emerged as bases for party support, and therefore disunity in the state, was the one party state.[93] The nationalist party, then, is the antecedent to the African "party-state," the role of which was to create the new nation.[94] The clearest expression of the extent to which the party was seen to embody the aspirations of state was in the slogan of Nkrumah's government: "The Convention People's Party (CPP) is Ghana," and "Ghana is the CPP."[95] This is, moreover, an explicit statement of the fusion of state, regime, and government through the party.

In the development of the African party-state and the consolidation of state power, political opposition was curtailed or eliminated as ruling elites sought to entrench their positions. The justifications employed by leaders most often revolved around the need for unity in the new state's quest for integration and economic development. This unity was equated with political uniformity, while political opposition was frequently viewed as tantamount to treason.[96] Some party-states, such as Tanzania under Nyerere, were established through popular elections and have continued to allow some avenues for the expression of criticism. Many, however, have used ruthless methods of repressing opposition, and rather than promoting the stability and unity which was the ostensible aim of

197

Comparative Politics   January 1993

these parties, the elimination of opposition has led to subversion and a number of upheavals "as those denied a fair say in running the affairs of their state have sought to change incumbent regimes by force."[97]

A common legitimating theme running through much of the rhetoric supporting all kinds of one party or party-state rule in Africa is the idea that this kind of regime is intrinsically African. Its proponents claim that it is "rooted in the African culture" while the legitimacy of opposition parties is rejected as "alien, capitalistic, and a relic of imperialism."[98] Nursey-Bray sees this as emanating, in part, from the Negritude movement, which inspired a "broad effort to enunciate genuine African values, as against the oppressive and racist views of the colonizers."[99] Following this general line of thinking, many African leaders have claimed to be continuing a process of Africanization by dispensing with alien institutions.[100] This is comparable to the goals of some millenarian and nationalist movements in the Pacific, where indigenous culture was and is promoted as a preferable alternative to that of the "alien power elite."[101] It is resonant also with the idea of the "Pacific Way" articulated by contemporary island leaders as a generalized expression and assertion of Pacific, as opposed to western, political values. But sympathy with aspirations of this kind, although they have served to counter the negative, racist images of "indigenous people" and their cultural heritage engendered by the old colonialists, should not obscure the other purposes which idealizations of a precolonial past can serve. In parts of both Africa and the Pacific, the rejection of western democratic norms in favor of political systems allegedly based on "tradition" is sometimes nothing more than a legitimating device for a variety of repressive regimes seeking to oppress or eliminate political opposition.[102]

A further aspect of this issue is that appeals to tradition frequently involve the retrospective homogenization of a variety of relatively small societies (which between them displayed quite diverse patterns of political organization). The homogeneous image of the traditional ways is then projected back into the present, thereby providing political leaders with a convenient unitary picture suitable as a contemporary standard for political practice. Although it is obvious that many contemporary states, and particularly those of Africa, are far from being culturally homogeneous internally, the unitary ideal is a powerful tool in the rhetoric of nation building and is, as suggested earlier, especially suited to the ideological underpinnings of the one party state.[103]

The idea of the intrinsic "Africanness" of the one party state has been challenged by Ibingira. He points out, first, that there is obviously no such thing as a single African political culture and that, even if one was to accept one partyism as African, it would be hard to cite an example of where it might have operated amongst the 2,000 or so ethnic groups which had very diverse systems of political organization, some of which lacked entirely the central authority which is so essentially characteristic of the one party state. He further points out that:

> If any leader were to claim to be practicing the one-party system as an indigenous African system, he should candidly and logically answer the question, *which one*? For instance, what type of African one-party system, assuming one existed, did Obote impose on Uganda? If he were to base his concepts in the Langi traditions of his kinfolks, he would almost automatically alienate the majority of his countrymen whose systems . . . differed from his. Which one-party system did Nkrumah, a Nzima, operate in Ghana among his diverse nationals? The claim of the

Stephanie Lawson

legitimacy of one-party states as based on Africa's past, therefore, is impossible to substantiate.[104]

It is clear that African polities today are very far removed from the culturally and structurally more homogeneous societies of the precolonial period which have been effectively subsumed under colonial and postcolonial state structures. So too, of course, are western democracies far removed from the polity of the ancient Athenians (which, as Aristotle pointed out, could retain its character only if it remained relatively small). What virtually all contemporary states in all parts of the world share, for better or for worse, are the conditions of the mass polity which are characterized by a high degree of social and cultural diversity—they are pluralistic rather than unitary. And while the idea of political competition between parties may seem "unnatural" in Africa and in other parts of the Third World,[105] it seems nonetheless that it is the most appropriate avenue for the expression of the diverse interests of people in mass polities. Further, while the organization of political dissent and criticism through competing parties does not necessarily prevent violence, it is less likely to occur where political opposition is regarded as legitimate. When it is regarded as treasonous or seditious, as it is in many one party states and especially where state, regime, and government are ideologically fused, the worst excesses of political violence can be perpetrated. Adolfo Gilly illustrates this very clearly.

> State-party regimes are characterized by an intrinsic difficulty, almost an inability, to absorb political change without entering into a regime crisis. . . . By identifying the ruling party both with the state and with the nation, they conceive of all attacks on the party as an attack on the state and interpret all proposals to change the government as an attempt to overthrow or destroy the state. This is the logic that led the Mexican regime to react against massive demonstrations for democracy with the killing of hundreds of students in Tlatelolco in October 1968 and led the Chinese regime to commit a similar massacre in Tiananmen in June 1989.[106]

The depiction of some of the worst consequences of authoritarianism, and much of the foregoing discussion generally, is aimed at defending a conception of democracy which clearly derives from a western tradition of constitutional democracy and which implicitly supports the norms and procedures embodied in western democratic regimes. This should not be construed, however, as a defense of all aspects of politics and society in western democracies, nor as a denigration of all nonwestern political practices. Indeed, some of the principles of liberal-democratic government, especially those which place a strong emphasis on market freedom, are at odds with the democratic values attaching to other freedoms as well as the values of equality and community.[107] In outlining some defects of constitutional government, Rawls points out that, not only has there been a failure to ensure the fair value of political liberty, but measures to rectify this have never been seriously entertained. Further, the system has tolerated disparities in the distribution of wealth and property "that far exceed what is compatible with political equality."[108] As with Rawls' theory of justice, however, the discussion of democracy here has concentrated on ideals and values, "comparison with which defines a standard for judging actual institutions."[109]

Another point that needs to be emphasized is that the doctrine of constitutionalism requires more than a mere document, or a rhetorical commitment on the part of political

Comparative Politics   January 1993

leaders, to produce anything approximating substantive democracy. This is clearly illustrated in the case of the Philippines, where, although the 1935 and 1973 constitutions enshrined democratic principles and structures of government, actual political practice reflected a considerable departure from constitutional theory.[110] What is required, then, is a commitment to the values of democracy and the espousal of democracy as a value in itself, rather than simply "a convenient instrument to be adopted and discarded at will."[111]

Conclusion

The issues canvassed in this paper have centered largely on making some important conceptual distinctions, both in terms of the formal political structures of state, regime, and government and with respect to the analytical categories of "democracy" and "nondemocracy." This does not tell us much about the process of regime change itself, nor about particular modes of transition to democracy, but it perhaps clarifies some of the difficulties posed for analysis when the question of "democratization" arises, and most especially when identifying key indicators. This is particularly so when it comes to the institutionalization of party competition and of constitutional political opposition.

A regime can incorporate any number of the features of democratic politics, including constitutional provision for elections, but these are fairly meaningless unless an opposition is able to succeed legitimately to government in an open contest. It is only in these circumstances that the power of any government is genuinely both conditional and temporary in accordance with the norms and principles of a democratic regime. And it is only when alternation in government, or succession of government, can be achieved without a change in the regime itself that a necessary condition for democratization has been achieved. This by no means excludes revolutionary or other movements of the kind that have brought about the transformations in eastern Europe from the category of democratizing forces. Rather, these are unconstitutional oppositional forces which are part of a process of change from a nondemocratic to a more democratic regime. In this context, the process must be distinguished from the result. In other words, democratizing processes will frequently emanate from unconstitutional opposition elements (they are unconstitutional almost by definition because of the nature of authoritarian regimes), which oppose the regime itself. The end result of this, if democratization is actually achieved, is the institutionalization of constitutional opposition through the rules and procedures of the new democratic regime and in accordance with the new democratic norms and principles that logically accompany it. Opposition will then be directed at other contestants for government power, and not normally at the regime itself. I use "normally" as a qualifier here because there may be legitimate calls for changes to unsatisfactory rules and procedures in democratic regimes. If such changes are brought about, however, they reflect not another regime change as such but rather an intraregime change of the kind described earlier which leaves the norms and principles unaltered.

This underscores the notion that constitutional opposition, operating within the rules and procedures of a democratic regime, does not seek to oppose the regime itself, only the government. In other words, the activities of a constitutional opposition are not regarded as treasonous but are pursued within a legitimate arena of political activity. This also highlights

Stephanie Lawson

one of the critical differences between democratic and nondemocratic regimes: the more democratic the political structures, the more clearly the differentiation among state, regime, and government (and party) is reflected empirically. And this is precisely because the activities of a constitutional opposition are legitimate and take place in accordance with the norms, principles, rules, and procedures of the regime. Similarly, the government is constrained by the same norms, principles, rules, and procedures and is not in any sense synonymous with them. On the other hand, where political structures are less democratic (or more authoritarian), the distinctions among state, regime, and government become increasingly blurred and, in the case of totalitarianism, virtually disappear altogether. Where regime change is occurring in the direction of democratization, then, an important indicator is the extent to which state/regime/government distinctions have become clearer, and this in turn depends on the establishment of competitive parties and the institutionalization of constitutional political opposition. Further, this provides one of the simplest indicators, at least of a nondemocratic regime: if a government can not be changed without changing the regime itself, then the regime is not democratic. On the other hand, the institutionalization of constitutional opposition that makes democratic alternation between parties of government possible is only a necessary, and not a sufficient condition, of a democratic regime. It certainly does not guarantee the fulfillment of democratic values and aspirations in mass polities.

NOTES

This article was written while the author was a Visiting Fellow in the Department of Political and Social Change, Research School of Pacific Studies, Australian National University, in November and December 1990. She would like to thank members of the Regime Change and Maintenance Project, and especially Ron May, John Ravenhill, and Alistair Sands, for helpful discussions during the writing of this paper.

1. Richard Joseph, "Partnership not Patronship," *Africa Report* (September-October 1990), 28.

2. Larry Diamond, Juan J. Linz, and Seymour Martin Lipset, *Democracy in Developing Countries* (Boulder: Lynne Rienner, 1988).

3. Enrique A. Baloyra, *Comparing New Democracies: Transition and Consolidation in Mediterranean Europe and the Southern Cone* (Boulder: Westview Press, 1987).

4. Guillermo O'Donnell, Philippe Schmitter, and Laurence Whitehead, eds., *Transitions from Authoritarian Rule* (Baltimore: The Johns Hopkins University Press, 1986).

5. John Herz, *From Dictatorship to Democracy: Coping with the Legacies of Authoritarianism and Totalitarianism* (Westport: Greenwood, 1982).

6. See, for example, Dankwart A. Rustow, "Transitions to Democracy: Toward a Dynamic Model," *Comparative Politics*, 2 (April 1970).

7. Terry Lynn Karl, "Dilemmas of Democratization in Latin America," *Comparative Politics*, 23 (October 1990).

8. See W. B. Gallie, "Essentially Contested Concepts," *Proceedings of the Aristotelian Society*, 56 (1956).

9. Daniel Levine, "Paradigm Lost: Dependence to Democracy," *World Politics*, 40 (1988), 393.

10. Henry Forde, "Human Rights and the Evolution of International Norms," *Round Table*, 316 (October 1990), 351.

11. Levine, p. 379.

12. Nancy Bermeo, "Rethinking Regime Change," *Comparative Politics*, 22 (April 1990), 369.

13. Charles Guy Gillespie, "Democratic Consolidation in the Southern Cone," *Third World Quarterly*, 11 (April 1989), 111.

14. Richard Sklar, "Developmental Democracy," *Comparative Studies in Society and History*, 29 (October 1987), 708.

Comparative Politics   January 1993

15. Robert M. Fishman, "Rethinking State and Regime: Southern Europe's Transition to Democracy," *World Politics*, 42 (April 1990), 428.

16. Ibid.

17. Peter Calvert, ed., *The Process of Political Succession* (London: Macmillan, 1987), p. 18. This definition suggests what I think is a fairly common, pejorative usage of regime. For example, in western democratic states regime is rarely used to refer to a particular government (or sequence of governments formed by the same party). In the United States we would normally refer instead to the "Bush administration" and in Australia to the "Hawke government." Some might be tempted to use the term "Thatcher regime" as a negative characterization of Mrs. Thatcher's relatively authoritarian leadership style and the nature of her government's policies. But the term is more commonly used to characterize authoritarian structures of government, which are sometimes personalized as in the "Marcos regime" or are otherwise spoken of in terms of a wider structure such as a "communist regime" or a "military regime." In these cases, the term is clearly employed as a pejorative label.

18. Stephen D. Krasner, ed., *International Regimes* (Ithaca: Cornell University Press, 1983), p. 1.

19. Ibid., p. 3.

20. Quoted in Jan-Erik Lane and Svante O. Ersson, *Politics and Society in Western Europe* (London: Sage, 1987), p. 279.

21. Krasner, p. 5.

22. Allan Larson, *Comparative Political Analysis* (Chicago: Nelson Hall, 1980), p. 19.

23. Calvert, ed., p. 248.

24. Naomi Chazan, Robert Mortimer, John Ravenhill, and Donald Rothchild, *Politics and Society in Contemporary Africa* (London: Macmillan, 1988).

25. I use the term "political system" as inclusive of state, regime, and government.

26. Graham Maddox, "A Note on the Meaning of 'Constitution,' " *American Political Science Review*, 76 (1982), 806–07.

27. Ibid., p. 808.

28. Fishman, p. 428.

29. Ibid.

30. Although a state can be said to exist where there is an institutional structure of social control involving a monopoly of political power, a state does not necessarily exist wherever or whenever there is a society, for there are such things as stateless societies. This is relevant to broader questions of colonization and decolonization because in many cases the most profound effect of colonization was the imposition of a state where none had existed previously. On another point, political power can not necessarily be viewed as coercive. See Pierre Clastres, *Society against the State* (New York: Urizen Books, 1977), pp. 14ff.

31. This is consistent with Calvert's view of the state as "the community organized for political purposes." One can go further and talk of the state as a "complex of institutions that constitute the organization of political authority" (Larson, p. 19), but here I think the concept of "state" begins to incorporate "regime" as well.

32. Chazan et al., p. 37.

33. Ibid., pp. 131ff. The types set out are administrative-hegemonial, pluralist, party-mobilizing, party-centralist, personal-coercive, populist, and ambiguous.

34. Roger Charlton, "Dehomogenizing the Study of African Politics: The Case of Inter-State Influences on Regime Formation and Change," *Plural Societies*, 14 (Spring-Summer 1983), 32.

35. See A. James Gregor, "Theory, Metatheory, and Comparative Politics," *Comparative Politics*, 3 (July 1971), 577–579.

36. Georges Balandier, *Political Anthropology* (Harmondsworth: Penguin, 1972), p. 44.

37. Introduction to Rodney Barker, ed., *Studies in Opposition* (London: Macmillan, 1971), p. 24.

38. O'Donnell and Schmitter, "Tentative Conclusions about Uncertain Democracies," in O'Donnell et al., eds., pp. 7–8.

39. Levine, p. 393.

40. Adam Przeworski, "Some Problems in the Study of Transition to Democracy," in O'Donnell et al., eds., p. 56.

41. Ian Roxborough, "The Dilemmas of Redemocratization," *Government and Opposition*, 23 (1988), 362.

42. Quoted in Giovanni Sartori, *The Theory of Democracy Revisited* (Chatham: Chatham House, 1987), p. 4.

43. Ibid., p. 3 (emphasis added).

44. Eva Etzioni-Halevy, *Fragile Democracy: The Use and Abuse of Power in Western Societies* (New Brunswick: Transaction Publishers, 1989), p. x.

202

Stephanie Lawson

45. Gallie, p. 171.

46. Ibid., p. 184.

47. Iain Hampsher-Monk, "The Historical Study of Democracy," in Graeme Duncan, ed., *Democratic Theory and Practice* (Cambridge: Cambridge University Press, 1983), p. 29.

48. Sartori, p. 3.

49. Lawrence Whitehead, "International Aspects of Democratization," in O'Donnell et al., eds., p. 8.

50. Ibid., p. 39.

51. Sartori, p. 4.

52. Hampsher-Monk, p. 31.

53. Gallie, p. 193.

54. John N. Gray, "On the Contestability of Social and Political Concepts," *Political Theory*, 5 (August 1977), 336.

55. Andrew Mason, "On Explaining Political Disagreement: The Notion of an Essentially Contested Concept," *Inquiry*, 33, p. 84. Cf. Gray, p. 343.

56. Sartori, p. 4.

57. Where Thucydides presents the opposing speeches of Cleon and Diodotus in debating the fate of Mytilene, for example, it becomes all too clear how the meaning of concepts can be abandoned for the sake of expedience. Although Diodotus argues against the slaughter proposed by Cleon, he abandons any appeal to the concept of justice. James Boyd White points out that, in sympathizing with the apparent leniency of Diodotus' position, the more profound implications of the discourse he uses can be overlooked, for "in the rhetoric of Diodotus anything can be said, and it invites one to think that anything can be done. To speak that way is to lose the capacity to form a community with others or to claim a consistent character for oneself; indeed it is to lose the power of practical reason." James Boyd White, *When Words Lose Their Meanings: Constitution and Reconstitution of Language, Character and Community* (Chicago: University of Chicago Press, 1984), p. 76. Noam Chomsky conveys a similar perception of the rhetoric employed in debates over the Vietnam War in America. He detects a disturbing falseness in the emotional and moral posturing of those opposed to the war whose grounds for objection were based only on "pragmatic considerations of cost and utility." See Noam Chomsky, *American Power and the New Mandarins* (Harmondsworth: Penguin, 1969), p. 11.

58. Whitehead, p. 45.

59. Bernard Crick, *Political Theory and Practice* (London: Allen Lane/Penguin, 1963), p. 91.

60. Paul Nursey-Bray, "Consensus and Community: African One-Party Democracy," in Duncan, ed., p. 100.

61. Gallie, p. 171.

62. See Graham Maddox, "Contours of a Democratic Polity," *Politics*, 21 (November 1986), 4.

63. Gallie, p. 184.

64. William Connolly, *The Terms of Political Discourse* (Oxford: Martin Robertson, 1983), p. 14.

65. William N. Nelson, *On Justifying Democracy* (London: Routledge & Kegan Paul, 1980), p. 2.

66. Robert Dahl, ed., *Political Oppositions in Western Democracies* (New Haven: Yale University Press, 1966), p. xvi. Constitutional political opposition is, however, a theme that is relatively neglected in democratic theory, perhaps because it is so taken for granted as an essential component of contemporary democracy. In Sartori's recent book, for example, it rates no more than a single textual entry in the index, although he mentions in a footnote "the centrality of opposition for democracy." See Sartori, p. 172. n. 4.

67. Richard Hofstadter, *The Idea of a Party System: The Rise of Legitimate Opposition in the United States, 1780–1840* (Berkeley: University of California Press, 1969), p. 4.

68. E. F. M. Durban, *The Politics of Democratic Socialism* (London: 1940), as reproduced in C. Cohen, ed., *Communism, Fascism and Democracy* (New York: Random House, 1962), p. 558.

69. See Fred D'Agostino, "Ethical Pluralism and the Role of Opposition in Democratic Politics," *The Monist*, 73 (1990), 439.

70. Barker, p. 8.

71. Lord Bryce, quoted in S. Neumann, *Modern Political Parties* (Chicago: University of Chicago Press, 1956), p. 396.

72. Gillespie, p. 112.

73. H. Eckstein, "Party Systems," in David Sills, ed., *International Encyclopedia of the Social Sciences*," 11 (New York: Macmillan & Free Press, 1968), p. 439.

74. Maddox, p. 6.

75. See Sartori, pp. 32–33.

203

Comparative Politics   January 1993

76. David Apter, "Some Reflections on the Role of a Political Opposition in New Nations," *Comparative Studies in Society and History*, 4 (January 1962), 154. See also C. B. Macpherson, *The Real World of Democracy* (New York: Oxford University Press, 1972), p. 25.

77. In C. J. Friedrich, ed., *Totalitarianism* (Cambridge, Mass.: Harvard University Press, 1954).

78. See especially Leonard Schapiro, *Totalitarianism* (London: Pall Mall, 1972), and S. E. Finer, *Comparative Government* (Harmondsworth: Penguin, 1970). For criticism of the catalogue and its explicit equation of communism and fascism, see Martin Kitchen, *Fascism* (London: Macmillan, 1976), and Rick Wilford, "Fascism," in Robert Eccleshall, Vincent Geoghegan, Richard Jay, and Rick Wilford, *Political Ideologies: An Introduction* (London: Unwin Hyman, 1984).

79. Maddox, p. 4.

80. Kitchen, p. 91.

81. Schapiro, p. 94.

82. Amos Perlmutter, *Modern Authoritarianism: A Comparative Institutional Analysis* (New Haven: Yale University Press, 1981), pp. 7–8.

83. Leonard Schapiro, "Can the Party Alone Run a One-Party State?," in Leonard Shapiro, ed., *Political Opposition in One-Party States* (London: Macmillan, 1972), p. 25.

84. John Griffiths, "The Cuban Communist Party," in Vicky Randall, ed., *Political Parties in the Third World* (London: Sage, 1988), p. 162.

85. Marion Farouk-Sluglett and Peter Sluglett, "The Iraqi Ba'ath Party," in Randall, ed., pp. 59–69.

86. Paul C. Sondral, "Intellectuals, Political Culture and the Roots of the Authoritarian Presidency in Latin America," *Governance*, 3 (October 1990), 418–19.

87. See especially Robert H. Jackson and Carl G. Rosberg, *Personal Rule in Black Africa* (Berkeley: University of California Press, 1982).

88. J. A. C. Mackie, "Indonesia," in Rosemary Brissenden and James Griffin, eds., *Modern Asia: Problems and Politics* (Milton: Jacandra, 1974), p. 95.

89. Paul Cammack, David Pool, and William Tordoff, *Third World Politics* (London: Macmillan, 1988), p. 87, and Rod Hague and Martin Harrop, *Comparative Government: An Introduction* (London: Macmillan, 1982), p. 126.

90. Edward Shils, "Opposition in the New States of Asia and Africa," in Barker, ed., p. 49.

91. As Rosemary Brissenden notes, these legacies of colonialism feature in many parts of the Third World, but some of the problems of regionalism and communalism that they have generated do not differ all that much from those in European disputes over places like Alsace and Trieste. See Rosemary Brissenden, "An Approach to Modern Asia," in Brissenden and Griffen, eds., p. 1.

92. See Nursey-Bray; Macpherson, ch. 3.

93. Stephen Riley and Trevor W. Parfitt, "Party or Masquerade? The All-Peoples Congress of Sierra Leone," *Journal of Commonwealth and Comparative Politics*, 25 (July 1987), 162.

94. Helen Hill, "People, Parties, Polities: Perspective on African Party-States," in Kay Lawson, ed., *Political Parties and Linkage* (New Haven: Yale University Press, 1980), p. 229.

95. Riley and Parfitt, p. 162.

96. Chazan et al., p. 46.

97. Grace Stuart Ibingira, *African Upheavals since Independence* (Boulder: Westview, 1980), p. 249.

98. Ibid., p. 252.

99. Nursey-Bray, p. 97.

100. Chazan et al., p. 45.

101. Jocelyn Linnekin, "The Politics of Culture in the Pacific," in Jocelyn Linnekin and Lin Poyer, eds., *Cultural Identity and Ethnicity in the Pacific* (Honolulu: University of Hawaii Press, 1990), p. 165.

102. See Eric Hobsbawm and Terence Ranger, eds., *The Invention of Tradition* (Cambridge: Cambridge University Press, 1983), and Stephanie Lawson, "The Myth of Cultural Homogeneity and Its Implications for Chiefly Power and Politics in Fiji," *Comparative Studies in Society and History*, 32 (October 1990).

103. See John S. Saul, "Africa," in Ghita Ionescu and Ernest Gellner, eds., *Populism: Its Meaning and National Characteristics* (London: Weidenfeld, 1970), p. 145.

104. Ibingara, p. 253.

105. Macpherson, p. 25.

106. Adolfo Gilly, "The Mexican Regime in Its Dilemma," *Journal of International Affairs*, 43 (Winter 1990), 289.

Stephanie Lawson

107. See Frank Cunningham, "The Socialist Retrieval of Liberal Democracy," *International Political Science Review*, 11, 99–110.

108. John Rawls, *A Theory of Justice* (Oxford: Oxford University Press, 1973), p. 226.

109. Ibid., p. 227.

110. See Socorro L. Reyes, "The Philippine Constitutional System," in J. Barton Starr, ed., *The United States Constitution: Its Birth, Growth and Influence in Asia* (Hong Kong: University of Hong Kong Press, 1988), p. 268.

111. Gillespie, p. 96.

Part II
Theoretical and Comparative Interpretations of Transition and Authoritarian Collapse

[4]

Transitions to Democracy

Toward a Dynamic Model

Dankwart A. Rustow*

I

What conditions make democracy possible and what conditions make it thrive? Thinkers from Locke to Tocqueville and A. D. Lindsay have given many answers. Democracy, we are told, is rooted in man's innate capacity for self-government or in the Christian ethical or the Teutonic legal tradition. Its birthplace was the field at Putney where Cromwell's angry young privates debated their officers, or the more sedate House at Westminster, or the rock at Plymouth, or the forest cantons above Lake Lucerne, or the fevered brain of Jean Jacques Rousseau. Its natural champions are sturdy yeomen, or industrious merchants, or a prosperous middle class. It must be combined with strong local government, with a two-party system, with a vigorous tradition of civil rights, or with a multitude of private associations.

Recent writings of American sociologists and political scientists favor three types of explanation. One of these, proposed by Seymour Martin Lipset, Philips Cutright, and others, connects stable democracy with certain economic and social background conditions, such as high per capita income, widespread literacy, and prevalent urban residence. A second type of explanation dwells on the need for certain beliefs or psychological attitudes among the citizens. A long line of authors from Walter Bagehot to Ernest Barker has stressed the need for consensus as the basis of democracy—either in the form of a common belief in certain fundamentals or of procedural consensus on the rules of the game, which Barker calls "the Agreement to Differ." Among civic attitudes

* This article was presented at the annual meeting of the American Political Science Association, New York City, September 1969. The author is grateful for financial support at various stages of his researches into democracy from the John Simon Guggenheim Foundation, the Ford Foundation, and the National Science Foundation. He jealously claims the full blame for his errors, foibles, and follies as revealed in this essay.

338   *Comparative Politics   April 1970*

required for the successful working of a democratic system, Daniel
Lerner has proposed a capacity for empathy and a willingness to
participate. To Gabriel Almond and Sidney Verba, on the other
hand, the ideal "civic culture" of a democracy suggests not only
such participant but also other traditional or parochial attitudes.[1]

A third type of explanation looks at certain features of social
and political structure. In contrast to the prevailing consensus
theory, authors such as Carl J. Friedrich, E. E. Schattschneider,
Bernard Crick, Ralf Dahrendorf, and Arend Lijphart have insisted
that conflict and reconciliation are essential to democracy.[2] Starting with a similar assumption, David B. Truman has attributed the
vitality of American institutions to the citizens' "multiple membership in potential groups"—a relationship which Lipset has
called one of "crosscutting politically relevant associations."[3]
Robert A. Dahl and Herbert McClosky, among others, have argued
that democratic stability requires a commitment to democratic
values or rules, not among the electorate at large but among the
professional politicians—each of these presumably linked to the
other through effective ties of political organization.[4] Harry Eckstein, finally, has proposed a rather subtle theory of "congruence":
to make democracy stable, the structures of authority throughout
society, such as family, church, business, and trade unions, must
prove the more democratic the more directly they impinge on
processes of government.[5]

Some of these hypotheses are compatible with each other,
though they may also be held independently—for example, those

---

[1] Ernest Barker, *Reflections on Government* (Oxford, 1942), p. 63; Daniel
Lerner et al., *The Passing of Traditional Society* (Glencoe, 1958), pp. 49ff., 60ff.;
Gabriel Almond and Sidney Verba, *The Civic Culture* (Princeton, 1963).

[2] Carl J. Friedrich, *The New Belief in the Common Man* (Boston, 1942);
E. E. Schattschneider, *The Semi-Sovereign People* (New York, 1960); Bernard
Crick, *In Defence of Politics*, rev. ed. (Penguin Books, 1964); Ralf Dahrendorf,
Class and Class Conflict in Industrial Society (Stanford, 1959); Arend Lijphart,
The Politics of Accommodation (Berkeley and Los Angeles, 1968).

[3] David B. Truman, *The Governmental Process* (New York, 1951), p. 514;
S. M. Lipset, *Political Man* (New York, 1960), pp. 88ff. Already A. Lawrence
Lowell had spoken of the need for a party alignment where "the line of
division is vertical," cutting across the horizontal division of classes. *Government and Parties in Continental Europe* (Boston, 1896), vol. 2, pp. 65ff.

[4] Robert A. Dahl, *Who Governs?* (New Haven, 1961); Herbert McClosky,
"Consensus and Ideology in American Politics," *American Political Science
Review*, LVIII (June 1964); James W. Prothro and Charles M. Grigg, "Funda-
mental Principles of Democracy: Bases of Agreement and Disagreement,"
Journal of Politics, XXII (May 1960).

[5] Harry Eckstein, *The Theory of Stable Democracy* (Princeton, 1961) and
Division and Cohesion in a Democracy (Princeton, 1965).

Dankwart A. Rustow **339**

about prosperity, literacy, and consensus. Others—such as those about consensus and conflict—are contradictory unless carefully restricted or reconciled. Precisely such a synthesis has been the import of a large body of writing. Dahl, for instance, has proposed that in polyarchy (or "minorities rule," the closest real-life approximation to democracy) the policies of successive governments tend to fall within a broad range of majority consensus.[6] Indeed, after an intense preoccupation with consensus in the World War II years, it is now widely accepted that democracy is indeed a process of "accommodation" involving a combination of "division and cohesion" and of "conflict and consent"—to quote the key terms from a number of recent book titles.[7]

The scholarly debate thus continues, and answers diverge. Yet there are two notable points of agreement. Nearly all the authors ask the same sort of question and support their answers with the same sort of evidence. The question is not how a democratic system comes into existence. Rather it is how a democracy, assumed to be already in existence, can best preserve or enhance its health and stability. The evidence adduced generally consists of contemporary information, whether in the form of comparative statistics, interviews, surveys, or other types of data. This remains true even of authors who spend considerable time discussing the historical background of the phenomena that concern them— Almond and Verba of the civic culture, Eckstein of congruence among Norwegian social structures, and Dahl of the ruling minorities of New Haven and of oppositions in Western countries.[8] Their key propositions are couched in the present tense.

There may be a third feature of similarity underlying the current American literature of democracy. All scientific inquiry starts with the conscious or unconscious perception of a puzzle.[9] What has puzzled the more influential authors evidently has been the contrast between the relatively smooth functioning of democracy in the English-speaking and Scandinavian countries and the recurrent crises and final collapse of democracy in the French Third and Fourth Republics and in the Weimar Republic of Germany.

This curiosity is of course wholly legitimate. The growing litera-

[6] Robert A. Dahl, *A Preface to Democratic Theory* (Chicago, 1956).

[7] Lijphart; Eckstein; Dahl, *Pluralist Democracy in the United States: Conflict and Consent* (Chicago, 1967).

[8] Almond and Verba; Eckstein; Dahl, *Who Governs?* and ed. *Political Oppositions in Western Democracies* (New Haven, 1966).

[9] See Thomas Kuhn, *The Structure of Scientific Revolutions* (Chicago, 1962).

340   *Comparative Politics   April 1970*

ture and the increasingly subtle theorizing on the bases of democracy indicate how fruitful it has been. The initial curiosity leads logically enough to the functional, as opposed to the genetic, question. And that question, in turn, is most readily answered by an examination of contemporary data about functioning democracies—perhaps with badly functioning democracies and nondemocracies thrown in for contrast. The functional curiosity also comes naturally to scholars of a country that took its crucial steps toward democracy as far back as the days of Thomas Jefferson and Andrew Jackson. It accords, moreover, with some of the characteristic trends in American social science in the last generation or two— with the interest in systematic equilibria, in quantitative correlations, and in survey data engendered by the researcher's own questions. Above all, it accords with a deep-seated prejudice against causality. As Herbert A. Simon has strikingly put it, ". . . we are wary, in the social sciences, of asymmetrical relations. They remind us of pre-Humeian and pre-Newtonian notions of causality. By whip and sword we have been converted to the doctrine that there is no causation, only functional interrelation, and that functional relations are perfectly symmetrical. We may even have taken over, as a very persuasive analogy, the proposition 'for every action, there is an equal and opposite reaction.' "[10]

Students of developing regions, such as the Middle East, Southern Asia, tropical Africa, or Latin America, naturally enough have a somewhat different curiosity about democracy. The contrast that is likely to puzzle them is that between mature democracies, such as the United States, Britain, or Sweden today, and countries that are struggling on the verge of democracy, such as Ceylon, Lebanon, Turkey, Peru, or Venezuela. This will lead them to the genetic question of how a democracy comes into being in the first place.[11] The question is (or at least was, until the Russian invasion of Czechoslovakia in 1968) of almost equal interest in Eastern Europe. The genesis of democracy, thus, has not only considerable intrinsic interest for most of the world; it has greater pragmatic relevance than further panegyrics about the virtues of Anglo-American democracy or laments over the fatal illnesses of democracy in Weimar or in several of the French Republics.

[10] Herbert A. Simon, *Models of Man: Social and Rational* (New York, 1957), p. 65.
[11] For a general discussion of the question of democracy in the context of recent modernizing countries, see Rustow, *A World of Nations: Problems of Political Modernization* (Washington, 1967), Ch. 7, which states some of the present argument in summary form.

Dankwart A. Rustow   **341**

In the following sections of this article I should like to examine some of the methodological problems involved in the shift from functional to genetic inquiry and then proceed to outline one possible model of the transition to democracy.

II

What changes in concept or method does the shift from functional to genetic inquiry imply? The simplest answer would be, "None at all." The temptation is to make the functional theories do double duty as genetic theories, to extend the perspective of Westminster and Washington versus Weimar and Paris to Ankara, Caracas, and Bucharest as well. If conditions such as consensus or prosperity will help to preserve a functioning democracy, it may be argued, surely they will be all the more needful to bring it into existence.

Alas, the simple equation of function and genesis is a little too simple, and the argument a fortiori is, in fact, rather weak.[12] The equation certainly does not seem to hold for most other types of political regimes. Military dictatorships, for instance, typically originate in secret plotting and armed revolt but perpetuate themselves by massive publicity and by alliances with civilian supporters. Charismatic leaders, according to Max Weber, establish their claim to legitimacy by performing seeming miracles but preserve it through routinization. A hereditary monarchy rests most securely on the subjects' unquestioning acceptance of immemorial tradition; it evidently cannot be erected on such a principle. Communist regimes have been installed by revolutionary elites or through foreign conquest but consolidated through the growth of domestic mass parties and their bureaucracies. From physics and chemistry, too, the distinction between the energy required to initiate and to sustain a given reaction is familiar. These arguments from analogy of course are just as inconclusive as the supposedly a fortiori one. Still, they shift the burden of proof to those who assert that the circumstances which sustain a mature democracy also favor its birth.

The best known attempts to apply a single world-wide perspective to democracy, whether nascent or mature, are the statistical correlations compiled by Lipset and by Cutright.[13] But Lipset's

---

12 ". . . a political form may persist under conditions normally adverse to the emergence of that form" (Lipset, p. 46).
13 Seymour Martin Lipset, "Some Social Requisites of Democracy: Eco-

342   *Comparative Politics   April 1970*

article well illustrates the difficulty of applying the functional perspective to the genetic question. Strictly interpreted, his data bear only on function. His statistical findings all take the form of correlations at a given single point in time. In the 1950s his "stable democracies" generally had substantially higher per capita incomes and literacy rates than did his "unstable democracies," or his unstable and stable authoritarianisms. Now, correlation evidently is not the same as causation—it provides at best a clue to some sort of causal connection without indicating its direction. Lipset's data leave it entirely open, for example, whether affluent and literate citizens make the better democrats; whether democracies provide superior schools and a more bracing climate for economic growth; whether there is some sort of reciprocal connection so that a given increase in affluence or literacy and in democracy will produce a corresponding increment in the other; or whether there is some further set of factors, such as the industrial economy perhaps, that causes both democracy *and* affluence and literacy. A corresponding objection can be urged against the findings of Almond, Verba, and others that are based mainly on contemporary opinion or attitude surveys. Only further investigation could show whether such attitudes as "civic culture," an eagerness to participate, a consensus on fundamentals, or an agreement on procedures are cause or effect of democracy, or both, or neither.

Lipset's title is true to his functional concern. He is careful to speak of "Some Social Requisites," not prerequisites, "of Democracy," and thus to acknowledge the difference between correlation and cause. But the subtlety has escaped many readers who unthinkingly translate "requisites" into "preconditions."[14] The text of the article, moreover, encourages the same substitution, for it repeatedly slips from the language of correlation into the language of causality. Significantly, on all those occasions economic and social conditions become the independent, and democracy the dependent, variable.

---

nomic Development and Political Legitimacy," *American Political Science Review,* LIII (March 1959); idem, *Political Man;* Philips Cutright, "National Political Development: Measurement and Analysis," *American Sociological Review,* XXVIII (April 1963).

[14] Rupert Emerson, *From Empire to Nation* (Cambridge, 1960), p. 278, paraphrases Lipset to this effect. M. Rejai, in his useful anthology and commentary, *Democracy: The Contemporary Theories* (New York, 1967), includes an excerpt from the article under the heading, "Socioeconomic Preconditions" (pp. 242-247).

Dankwart A. Rustow **343**

A genetic theory will have to be explicit about distinguishing correlate from cause. This does not commit us to any old-fashioned or simple-minded view of causality, whereby every effect has but one cause and every cause but one effect. It does not preclude the "probabilistic" view recently argued by Almond and, indeed, espoused by every social statistician since Emile Durkheim and before.[15] It does not rule out somewhat more sophisticated causal concepts such as Gunnar Myrdal's spiral, Karl W. Deutsch's quorum of prerequisites, Hayward R. Alker's nonlinear correlations, or the notion of a threshold which Deane Neubauer recently applied to Lipset's and Cutright's propositions.[16] Above all, a concern for causality is compatible with—indeed is indispensable to—a sceptical view that attributes human events to a mixture of law and chance. Such semideterminism is tantamount to an admission that the social scientist will never know enough to furnish a complete explanation, that he is at least as unlikely as the natural scientist to rival Laplace's Demon. Nor do scholars who would theorize about the genesis of democracy need to concur in all their epistemology and metaphysics. But to be geneticists at all they do have to inquire into causes. Only by such inquiry, I would add, can the social scientist accomplish his proper task of exploring the margins of human choice and of clarifying the consequences of the choices in that margin.[17]

It probably is no simple confusion between correlate and cause that leads Lipset's readers astray, and, on occasion, the author as well. Rather it seems to be a tacit assumption that social and economic conditions are somehow more basic, and that we must look for the significant relations in this deeper layer rather than in the "superstructure" of political epiphenomena. Our current emphasis in political science on economic and social factors is a most necessary corrective to the sterile legalism of an earlier generation. But, as Lipset (together with Bendix) has himself warned in another

[15] Gabriel A. Almond and James S. Coleman, eds. *The Politics of the Developing Areas* (Princeton, 1960), Introduction.

[16] Gunnar Myrdal, *An American Dilemma* (New York, 1944), Appendix; Hayward R. Alker, Jr., "The Long Road to International Relations Theory: Problems of Statistical Non-Additivity," *World Politics*, XVIII (July 1966); Deane Neubauer, "Some Conditions of Democracy," *American Political Science Review*, LXI (December 1967).

[17] This statement of the function of the social scientist is taken from Rustow, *A World of Nations*, p. 17; the next two paragraphs paraphrase ibid., pp. 142ff.

344   *Comparative Politics   April 1970*

context, it can easily "explain away the very facts of political life."[18] We have been in danger of throwing away the political baby with the institutional bathwater.

Note that this widespread American economicism goes considerably beyond Marx and Engels, who saw the state as created by military conquest, economic regimes defined by their legal relations of property, and changes from one to the next brought about through political revolution. If they proclaimed themselves materialists or talked like economic determinists, it was mainly in protest against the wilder flights of Hegelian "idealism."

Any genetic theory of democracy would do well to assume a two-way flow of causality, or some form of circular interaction, between politics on the one hand and economic and social conditions on the other. Wherever social or economic background conditions enter the theory, it must seek to specify the mechanisms, presumably in part political, by which these penetrate to the democratic foreground. The political scientist, moreover, is entitled to his rights within the general division of labor and may wish to concentrate on some of the political factors without denying the significance of the social or economic ones. With Truman, Dahl, and others, I would tend to see the patterns of conflict and of recurrent or changing alignments as one of the central features of any political system. With Apter, I would consider choice as one of the central concerns of the political process.[19]

What goes for economics and sociology goes for psychology as well. Here, too, the relationship with politics is one of interaction and interdependence, so that political phenomena may have psychological consequences as well as vice versa. In explaining the origins of democracy we need not assume—as does much of the current survey research literature—that beliefs unilaterally influence actions. Rather, we may recognize with Leon Festinger and other social psychologists of the "cognitive dissonance" school that there are reciprocal influences between beliefs and actions.[20] Many of the current theories about democracy seem to imply that to promote democracy you must first foster democrats—perhaps by preachment, propaganda, education, or perhaps as an automatic byproduct of growing prosperity. Instead, we should allow for the possibility that circumstances may force, trick, lure, or cajole non-

[18] Reinhard Bendix and Seymour Martin Lipset, "Political Sociology," *Current Sociology*, VI, No. 2 (1957), 85.

[19] David E. Apter, *The Politics of Modernization* (Chicago, 1965).

[20] Leon Festinger, *A Theory of Cognitive Dissonance* (Stanford, 1957).

Dankwart A. Rustow **345**

democrats into democratic behavior and that their beliefs may adjust in due course by some process of rationalization or adaptation.

To seek causal explanations, as I insisted earlier, does not imply simple-mindedness. Specifically, we need not assume that the transition to democracy is a world-wide uniform process, that it always involves the same social classes, the same types of political issues, or even the same methods of solution. On the contrary, it may be well to assume with Harry Eckstein that a wide variety of social conflicts and of political contents can be combined with democracy.[21] This is, of course, in line with the general recognition that democracy is a matter primarily of procedure rather than of substance. It also implies that, as among various countries that have made the transition, there may be many roads to democracy.

Nor does a model of transition need to maintain that democratic evolution is a steady process that is homogeneous over time. Such a notion of temporal continuity and presumably of linear correlation seems to lurk behind much of the literature of the Lipset-Cutright genre. Temporal discontinuity, on the contrary, is implicit in the basic distinction drawn earlier in this article between the functional and genetic questions. The same discontinuity may be carried into the genetic scheme itself. For instance, it may be useful to single out certain circumstances as background factors and to proceed step-by-step to other factors that may become crucial in the preparation, decision, and consolidation phases of the process.

Even in the same country and during the same phase of the process, political attitudes are not likely to be spread evenly through the population. Dahl, McClosky, and others have found that in mature democracies there are marked differences in the attitudes of professional politicians and of common citizens.[22] Nor can we take it for granted that the politicians will all share the same attitudes. In so far as democracy is based on conflict, it may take two attitudes to make a quarrel. All these differences are likely, moreover, to be compounded during the formative period when part of the quarrel must *ex hypothesi* be between democrats and nondemocrats. Finally, a dynamic model of the transition must allow for the possibility that different groups—e.g., now the citizens and now the rulers, now the forces in favor of change and now those eager to preserve the past—may furnish the crucial impulse toward democracy.

[21] Eckstein, *Division and Cohesion*, pp. 183-85.
[22] Dahl, *Who Governs?*; McClosky; Prothro and Grigg.

III

The methodological argument I have been advancing may be condensed into a number of succinct propositions.

> 1.   The factors that keep a democracy stable may not be the ones that brought it into existence: explanations of democracy must distinguish between function and genesis.
> 2.   Correlation is not the same as causation: a genetic theory must concentrate on the latter.
> 3.   Not all causal links run from social and economic to political factors.
> 4.   Not all causal links run from beliefs and attitudes to actions.
> 5.   The genesis of democracy need not be geographically uniform: there may be many roads to democracy.
> 6.   The genesis of democracy need not be temporally uniform: different factors may become crucial during successive phases.
> 7.   The genesis of democracy need not be socially uniform: even in the same place and time the attitudes that promote it may not be the same for politicians and for common citizens.

My refrain, like Sportin' Life's, has been, "It ain't necessarily so." Each proposition pleads for the lifting of some conventional restriction, for the dropping of some simplifying assumption made in the previous literature, for the introduction of complicating, diversifying factors. If the argument were to conclude on this sceptical note, it would set the researcher completely adrift and make the task of constructing a theory of democratic genesis well-nigh unmanageable.

Fortunately, the genetic perspective requires or makes possible a number of new restrictions that more than compensate for the loss of the seven others. We may continue the listing of summary propositions before elaborating this second part of the methodological argument.

> 8.   Empirical data in support of a genetic theory must cover, for any given country, a time period from just before until just after the advent of democracy.
> 9.   To examine the logic of transformation *within* political systems, we may leave aside countries where a major impetus came from abroad.

10. A model or ideal type of the transition may be derived from a close examination of two or three empirical cases and tested by application to the rest.

That diachronic data, covering more than a single point in time, are essential to any genetic theory should be obvious. Such a theory, moreover, must be based on cases where the process is substantially complete. Although control data on nondemocracies and on abortive and incipient cases may become important at a later stage of theorizing, it is more convenient to start out by studying a phenomenon where it actually has come into existence. The "advent" of democracy must not, of course, be understood as occurring in a single year. Since the emergence of new social groups and the formation of new habits are involved, one generation is probably the minimum period of transition. In countries that had no earlier models to emulate, the transition is likely to have come even more slowly. In Britain, for example, it may be argued that it began before 1640 and was not accomplished until 1918. For an initial set of hypotheses, however, it may be best to turn to countries where the process occurred relatively rapidly.

The study of democratic transitions will take the political scientist deeper into history than he has commonly been willing to go. This implies many changes in method—beginning with suitable substitutions for survey data and for interviews. Even reliable statistics are harder to come by early in any democratic experiment. The United States Constitution (Article 1, Section 2) reminds us that our decennial census was introduced at that very time so that we might begin to govern ourselves by an accurate count of noses.

Whatever the difficulties in the vastly increased use of historical data by social scientists, at least three arguments can be made in extenuation and encouragement. Man did not become a political animal in 1960 or in 1945, as much of our recent literature pretends to suppose. History, to paraphrase Georges Clemenceau, is far too important a topic to be left just to historians. And recently scholars in comparative politics have turned with increasing zest to historical themes. The list includes Almond, Leonard Binder, Dahl, Samuel P. Huntington, Lipset, Robert E. Ward, and Myron Weiner —not to speak of those like Friedrich and Deutsch to whom a political-historical perspective was natural to start with.[23]

[23] Almond, current study on nineteenth-century Britain; Leonard Binder, ed. *Politics in Lebanon* (New York, 1966); Dahl, see nn. 4, 7, and 8; Karl W. Deutsch, *Nationalism and Social Communication* (New York, 1953) and Deutsch et al., *Political Community and the North Atlantic Area* (Princeton,

348   *Comparative Politics   April 1970*

The next restriction—the omission early in the inquiry of cases where the major impulse to democratization came from the outside —is in accord with the conventional division of labor between the subfields of comparative politics and international relations. There are topics such as the theory of modernization where that division should be transcended from the start.[24] In tracing the origins of democracy, too, both perspectives may be applied at once, as witness the suggestive work of Louis Hartz, the masterly synthesis by Robert Palmer, and the current research by Robert Ward on Japanese-American interaction in the shaping of the 1947 constitution.[25] But for a first attempt at a general theory it may be preferable to stick to countries where the transition occurred mainly within a single system.

To speak of "major impulses from outside" or transitions "mainly within the system" acknowledges that foreign influences are almost always present. Throughout history, warfare has been a major democratizing force, because it has made necessary the marshalling of additional human resources.[26] Democratic ideas, moreover, have proved infectious whether in the days of Rousseau or of John F. Kennedy. And the violent overthrow of one oligarchy (e.g., France in 1830, Germany in 1918) has often frightened another into peaceful surrender (e.g., Britain in 1832, Sweden in 1918). From such ever present international influences we may distinguish situations where people arriving from abroad took an active part in the internal political process of democratization. A theory of democratic origins, that is to say, should leave aside at the beginning those countries where military occupation played a major role (postwar Germany and Japan), where democratic institutions or attitudes were brought along by immigrants (Australia and New Zealand), or where in these and other ways immigration played a major role (Canada, the United States, and Israel).

1957); Carl J. Friedrich, *Constitutional Government and Democracy* (Boston, 1950); Samuel P. Huntington, "Political Modernization: America vs. Europe," *World Politics,* XVIII (April 1966); S. M. Lipset, *The First New Nation* (New York, 1963), and Lipset and Stein Rokkan, eds. *Party Systems and Voter Alignments* (New York, 1967); Robert E. Ward and D. A. Rustow, eds. *Political Modernization in Japan and Turkey* (Princeton, 1964); Myron Weiner, current study on nineteenth-century social history of the Balkans.

[24] In this combination lies the strength of Cyril E. Black's *Dynamics of Modernization* (New York, 1966) compared to most of the other literature on the subject.

[25] Louis Hartz et al., *The Founding of New Societies* (New York, 1964); R. R. Palmer, *The Age of the Democratic Revolution,* 2 vols. (Princeton, 1959-64).

[26] See, e.g., Bertrand de Jouvenel, *On Power* (New York, 1948).

Dankwart A. Rustow **349**

The preference expressed earlier for relatively rapid instances of transition and the omission of immigrant countries amount to a very serious restriction, for they leave out of account, at this first stage of theorizing, all the English-speaking democracies. The reasons, however, seem cogent. Indeed, it may well be that American social scientists have added to their difficulties in understanding transitions to democracy by paying undue attention to Britain and the United States, which for the reasons just suggested prove to be among the hardest instances to analyze in genetic terms. The total of eight provisional exclusions still leaves (among extant democracies) about twenty-three cases on which to base a comparative analysis, thirteen of which are in Europe: Austria, Belgium, Ceylon, Chile, Colombia, Costa Rica, Denmark, Finland, France, Iceland, Ireland, India, Italy, Lebanon, Luxembourg, Netherlands, Norway, Philippines, Sweden, Switzerland, Turkey, Uruguay, Venezuela.[27]

Among these twenty-odd democracies, the last methodological proposition urges an even narrower selection at this preliminary stage of theorizing. What is here involved is a choice between three research strategies: inclusion of all relevant cases, concentration on a single country, or some intermediate course.

Completeness is of course desirable, and all the more so where the "universe" consists of no more than twenty or thirty cases. But the more nearly complete the coverage, the shallower it will have to be. The number of possible variables is so enormous (economic conditions, social cleavages, political alignments, psychological attitudes) that they could be handled only by means of the kind of simplifying assumptions that we rejected earlier on logical grounds. A test, no matter how complete, of a fallacious set of propositions would hardly yield convincing results.

The country monograph would avoid this danger. Nor does it deliberately have to be antitheoretical or "merely descriptive." Any country study nevertheless sacrifices the advantages of comparison, the social scientist's nearest substitute for a laboratory.

---

[27] This list, together with the eight omissions noted (Australia, Canada, Germany, Israel, Japan, New Zealand, United Kingdom, United States), corresponds to the one I gave in *A World of Nations*, pp. 290ff., with the following exceptions: Greece has been omitted because democracy was superseded by a military coup in 1967; Mexico was omitted because, on second thought, I do not believe that it meets the criterion of a government based on "three or more consecutive, popular, and competitive elections"—the problems of course being the severe de facto restrictions on competition; Turkey and Venezuela have been added because they now have begun to meet the criterion.

No such study can tell us which strands in a tangle of empirical factors represent the development of democracy and which the national idiosyncrasies of Monographistan.

The middle course avoids the twin dangers of inconclusive scholasticism and of fact-grubbing. Instead, it can offer a more balanced and hence more fruitful blend of theory and empiricism. The many possible variables that can affect the origins of democracy and the even more complex relations among them can best be sorted out by looking at their total configuration in a limited number of cases—perhaps no more than two or three at the start. What will emerge from this exercise is a model, or as Weber used to call it, an "ideal type," of the transition from oligarchy to democracy. Being an ideal type, it deliberately highlights certain features of empirical reality and deliberately distorts, simplifies, or omits others. Like any such construct, it must be judged initially by its internal coherence and plausibility but ultimately by its fruitfulness in suggesting hypotheses applicable to a wide variety of other empirical cases.[28] It is at this further stage of testing that the demand for completeness comes once again into its own.

The model I should like to sketch in the next few pages is based in large part on my studies of Sweden, a Western country that made the transition to democracy in the period from 1890 to 1920, and of Turkey, a Westernizing country where that process began about 1945 and is still underway. The choice of these two is accidental—except in terms of an autobiographical account for which this is not the occasion. I am now in the early stages of a study that will seek to refine the same set of hypotheses in the light of materials from a slightly larger and less arbitrary selection of countries.

IV

A.   Background Condition   The model starts with a single background condition—national unity. This implies nothing mysterious about *Blut und Boden* or daily pledges of allegiance, about personal identity in the psychoanalyst's sense, or about a grand political purpose pursued by the citizenry as a whole. It simply means that the vast majority of citizens in a democracy-to-be must have no doubt or mental reservations as to which political community they belong to. This excludes situations of latent secession, as in the

[28] For a recent, lucid restatement of the rationale for such models or ideal types, see T. B. Bottomore, *Elites and Societies* (New York, 1965), p. 32.

late Habsburg and Ottoman Empires or in many African states today, and, conversely, situations of serious aspirations for merger as in many Arab states. Democracy is a system of rule by temporary majorities. In order that rulers and policies may freely change, the boundaries must endure, the composition of the citizenry be continuous. As Ivor Jennings phrased it tersely, "the people cannot decide until somebody decides who are the people."[29]

National unity is listed as a background condition in the sense that it must precede all the other phases of democratization but that otherwise its timing is irrelevant. It may have been achieved in prehistoric times, as in Japan or Sweden; or it may have preceded the other phases by centuries, as in France, or by decades, as in Turkey.

Nor does it matter by what means national unity has been established. The geographic situation may be such that no serious alternative has ever arisen—Japan once again being the best example. Or a sense of nationality may be the product of a sudden intensification of social communication in a new idiom developed for the purpose. On the other hand, it may be the legacy of some dynastic or administrative process of unification. The various hypotheses proposed by Deutsch clearly become relevant here.[30]

I have argued elsewhere that in an age of modernization men are unlikely to feel a preponderant sense of loyalty except to a political community large enough to achieve some considerable degree of modernity in its social and economic life.[31] This sort of hypothesis must be examined as part of a theory of nationhood, not of one of democratic development. What matters in the present context is only the result.

I hesitate to call this result a consensus, for at least two reasons. First, national unity, as Deutsch argues, is the product less of shared attitudes and opinions than of responsiveness and complementarity. Second, "consensus" connotes consciously held opinion and deliberate agreement. The background condition, however, is best fulfilled when national unity is accepted unthinkingly, is silently taken for granted. Any vocal consensus about national unity, in fact, should make us wary. Most of the rhetoric of na-

---

[29] W. Ivor Jennings, *The Approach to Self-Government* (Cambridge, 1956), p. 56.

[30] Deutsch, *Nationalism and Social Communication*; Deutsch et al., *Political Community and the North Atlantic Area.*

[31] Rustow, *A World of Nations*, pp. 30ff. and *International Encyclopedia of the Social Sciences*, s.v. "Nation."

tionalism has poured from the lips of people who felt least secure
in their sense of national identity—Germans and Italians in the
past century and Arabs and Africans in the present, never English-
men, Swedes, or Japanese.

To single out national unity as the sole background condition
implies that no minimal level of economic development or social
differentiation is necessary as a prerequisite to democracy. These
social and economic factors enter the model only indirectly as one
of several alternative bases for national unity or for entrenched
conflict (see B below). Those social and economic indicators that
authors are fond of citing as "background conditions" seem somewhat implausible at any rate. There are always nondemocracies
that rank suspiciously high, such as Kuwait, Nazi Germany, Cuba,
or Congo-Kinshasa. Conversely, the United States in 1820, France
in 1870, and Sweden in 1890 would have been sure to fail one or
another of the proposed tests of urbanization or per capita income
—not to speak of newspaper copies in circulation, or doctors,
movies, and telephones available to each one thousand inhabitants.

The model thus deliberately leaves open the possibility of democracies (properly so called) in premodern, prenationalist times
and at low levels of economic development. To find a meaningful
definition of democracy that would cover modern parliamentary
systems along with medieval forest cantons, ancient city states
(the ones where slavery and metics were absent), and some of the
pre-Colombian Indians may prove difficult. It is not a task that
forms part of the present project; still, I should not like to foreclose
the attempt.

B. Preparatory Phase I hypothesize that, against this single
background condition, the dynamic process of democratization itself is set off by a prolonged and inconclusive political struggle.
To give it those qualities, the protagonists must represent well-
entrenched forces (typically social classes), and the issues must
have profound meaning to them. Such a struggle is likely to begin
as the result of the emergence of a new elite that arouses a
depressed and previously leaderless social group into concerted
action. Yet the particular social composition of the contending
forces, both leaders and followers, and the specific nature of the
issues will vary widely from one country to the next and in the
same country from period to period.

In Sweden at the turn of the century, it was a struggle first of farmers and then of an urban lower-middle and working class against a conservative alliance of bureaucrats, large landowners, and industrialists; and the issues were tariffs, taxation, military service, and suffrage. In Turkey in the last twenty years it has mainly been a contest of countryside versus city, more precisely of large and middling-size farmers (supported by most of the peasant electorate) against the heirs of the Kemalist bureaucratic-military establishment; the central issue has been industrialization versus agricultural development. In both these examples, economic factors have been of prime importance, yet the direction of causality has varied. In Sweden, it was a period of intense economic development that created new political tensions; at one crucial point, rising wages enabled the Stockholm workers to overcome the existing tax barrier for the franchise. In Turkey, conversely, the demand for rural development was the consequence, not the cause, of beginning democratization.[32]

There may be situations where economic factors have played a much lesser role. In India and in the Philippines the prolonged contest between nationalist forces and an imperial bureaucracy over the issue of self-government may have served the same preparatory function as did class conflict elsewhere. In Lebanon the continuing struggle is mainly between denominational groups and the stakes are mainly government offices. Although political struggles of this sort naturally have their economic dimensions, only a doctrinaire economic determinist would derive colonialism or religious divisions from solely economic causes.

James Bryce found in his classic comparative study that, "One road only has in the past led into democracy, viz., the wish to be rid of tangible evils.[33] Democracy was not the original or primary aim; it was sought as a means to some other end or it came as a fortuitous byproduct of the struggle. But, since the tangible evils

---

[32] For developments in Sweden see Rustow, *The Politics of Compromise: A Study of Parties and Cabinet Government in Sweden* (Princeton, 1955), Chs. 1-3, and Douglas A. Verney, *Parliamentary Reform in Sweden, 1866-1921* (Oxford, 1957). On Turkey see Ward and Rustow and the following essays by Rustow: "Politics and Islam in Turkey," in R. N. Frye, ed. *Islam and the West* (The Hague, 1957), pp. 69-107; "Turkey: The Tradition of Modernity," in Lucian W. Pye and Verba, eds. *Political Culture and Political Development* (Princeton, 1965), pp. 171-198; "The Development of Parties in Turkey," in Joseph LaPalombara and Myron Weiner, eds. *Political Parties and Political Development* (Princeton, 1966), pp. 107-133; and "Politics and Development Policy," in F. C. Shorter, ed. *Four Studies in the Economic Development of Turkey* (London, 1967), pp. 5-31.

[33] James Bryce, *Modern Democracies* (London, 1921), vol. 2, p. 602.

354   *Comparative Politics   April 1970*

that befall human societies are legion, Bryce's single road dissolves
into many separate paths. No two existing democracies have gone
through a struggle between the very same forces over the same
issues and with the same institutional outcome. Hence, it seems
unlikely that any future democracy will follow in the precise foot-
steps of any of its predecessors. As Albert Hirschman has warned
in his discussion of economic development, the search for ever
more numerous preconditions or prerequisites may end up by
proving conclusively that development always will be impossible—
and always has been.[34]

More positively, Hirschman and other economists have argued
that a country can best launch into a phase of growth not by slav-
ishly imitating the example of nations already industrialized, but
rather by making the most of its particular natural and human
resources and by fitting these accurately into the international
division of labor.[35] Similarly, a country is likely to attain democracy not by copying the constitutional laws or parliamentary practices of some previous democracy, but rather by honestly facing
up to its particular conflicts and by devising or adapting effective
procedures for their accommodation.

The serious and prolonged nature of the struggle is likely to force
the protagonists to rally around two banners. Hence polarization,
rather than pluralism, is the hallmark of this preparatory phase.
Yet there are limitations implicit in the requirement of national
unity—which, of course, must not only preexist but also continue.
If the division is on sharply regional lines, secession rather than
democracy is likely to result. Even among contestants geographically interspersed there must be some sense of community or some
even balance of forces that makes wholesale expulsion or genocide
impossible. The Turks are beginning to develop a set of democratic
practices among themselves, but fifty years ago they did not deal
democratically with Armenians or Greeks. Crosscutting cleavages
have their place in this preparatory phase as a possible means of
strengthening or preserving that sense of community.

Dahl notes wistfully that "one perennial problem of opposition
is that there is either too much or too little."[36] The first two ele-

---

[34] Albert O. Hirschman, *Journeys Toward Progress* (New York, 1963), pp. 6ff.
[35] Ibid., and Hirschman, *The Strategy of Economic Development* (New
Haven, 1958), and Hirschman, "Obstacles to Development: A Classification
and a Quasi-Vanishing Act," *Economic Development and Cultural Change*,
XIII (July 1965), 385-393.
[36] Dahl et al., *Political Oppositions in Western Democracies*, p. 397.

ments of the model between them will ensure that there is the right amount. But struggle and national unity cannot simply be averaged out, since they cannot be measured along the same scale. Strong doses of both must be combined, just as it may be possible to combine sharp polarization with crosscutting cleavages. Furthermore, as Mary Parker Follett, Lewis A. Coser, and others have insisted, certain types of conflict in themselves constitute creative processes of integration.[37] What infant democracy requires is not a lukewarm struggle but a hot family feud.

This delicate combination implies, of course, that many things can go wrong during the preparatory phase. The fight may go on and on till the protagonists weary and the issues fade away without the emergence of any democratic solution along the way. Or one group may find a way of crushing the opponents after all. In these and other ways an apparent evolution toward democracy may be deflected, and at no time more easily than during the preparatory phase.

C. Decision Phase Robert Dahl has written that, "Legal party opposition . . . is a recent and unplanned invention."[38] This accords with Bryce's emphasis on the redress of specific grievances as democracy's vehicle and with the assumption here that the transition to democracy is a complex process stretching over many decades. But it does not rule out suffrage or freedom of opposition as conscious goals in the preparatory struggle. Nor does it suggest that a country ever becomes a democracy in a fit of absentmindedness. On the contrary, what concludes the preparatory phase is a deliberate decision on the part of political leaders to accept the existence of diversity in unity and, to that end, to institutionalize some crucial aspect of democratic procedure. Such was the decision in 1907, which I have called the "Great Compromise" of Swedish politics, to adopt universal suffrage combined with pro-

[37] Mary Parker Follett, *The New State* (New York, 1918), and *Creative Experience* (New York, 1924); Lewis A. Coser, *The Function of Social Conflict* (Glencoe, 1956), p. 121 and passim. A widespread contrary position has recently been restated by Edward Shils, who writes in reference to Lebanon: "Civility will not be strengthened by crisis. It can only grow slowly and in a calm atmosphere. The growth of civility is a necessary condition for Lebanon's development . . . into a genuinely democratic system" (in Binder et al., *Politics in Lebanon*, p. 10). I find it hard to think of situations where there have been any notable advances in either civility or democracy *except* as the result of crisis.

[38] Dahl et al., *Political Oppositions in Western Democracies*, p. xi.

portional representation.[39] Instead of a single decision there may be several. In Britain, as is well-known, the principle of limited government was laid down in the compromise of 1688, cabinet government evolved in the eighteenth century, and suffrage reform was launched as late as 1832. Even in Sweden, the dramatic change of 1907 was followed by the further suffrage reform of 1918 which also confirmed the principle of cabinet government.

Whether democracy is purchased wholesale as in Sweden in 1907 or on the installment plan as in Britain, it is acquired by a process of conscious decision at least on the part of the top political leadership. Politicians are specialists in power, and a fundamental power shift such as that from oligarchy to democracy will not escape their notice.

Decision means choice, and while the choice of democracy does not arise until the background and preparatory conditions are in hand, it is a genuine choice and does not flow automatically from those two conditions. The history of Lebanon illustrates the possibilities of benevolent autocracy or of foreign rule as alternative solutions to entrenched struggles within a political community.[40] And of course a decision in favor of democracy, or some crucial ingredient of it, may be proposed and rejected—thus leading to a continuation of the preparatory phase or to some sort of abortive outcome.

The decision in favor of democracy results from the interplay of a number of forces. Since precise terms must be negotiated and heavy risks with regard to the future taken, a small circle of leaders is likely to play a disproportionate role. Among the negotiating groups and their leaders may be the protagonists of the preparatory struggle. Other participants may include groups that split off from one or the other side or new arrivals on the political stage. In Sweden these new and intermediate groups played a crucial role. Conservatives and Radicals (led by industrialists on one side and intellectuals on the other) had sharpened and crystallized the issues throughout the 1890s. Then came a period of stalemate when discipline in all the recently formed parliamentary parties broke down—a sort of randomization process in which many compromises, combinations, and permutations were devised and explored. The formula that carried the day in 1907 included crucial contributions from a moderately conservative bishop and a moderately

[39] Rustow, *The Politics of Compromise*, p. 69.
[40] Binder, ed. *Politics in Lebanon*.

liberal farmer, neither of whom played a very prominent role in politics before or after this decision phase.

Just as there can be different types of sponsors and different contents of the decision, so the motives from which it is proposed and accepted will vary from case to case. The forces of conservatism may yield from fear that continued resistance may lose them even more ground in the end. (Such thoughts were on the minds of British Whigs in 1832 and of Swedish conservatives in 1907.) Or they may belatedly wish to live up to principles long proclaimed; such was the Turkish transition to a multiparty system announced by President Inönü in 1945. The radicals may accept the compromise as a first installment, confident that time is on their side and that future installments are bound to follow. Both conservatives and radicals may feel exhausted from a long struggle or fearful of a civil war. This consideration is likely to loom large if they have been through such a war in recent memory. As Barrington Moore has aptly proposed, the English civil war was a crucial "contribution of early violence to later gradualism."[41] In short, democracy, like any collective human action, is likely to stem from a large variety of mixed motives.

The decision phase may well be considered an act of deliberate, explicit consensus. But, once again, this somewhat nebulous term should be carefully considered and perhaps replaced with less ambiguous synonyms. First of all, as Bryce suggests, the democratic content of the decision may be incidental to other substantive issues. Second, in so far as it is a genuine compromise it will seem second-best to all major parties involved—it certainly will not represent any agreement on fundamentals. Third, even on procedures there are likely to be continuing differences of preference. Universal suffrage with proportional representation, the content of the Swedish compromise of 1907, was about equally distasteful to the conservatives (who would rather have continued the old plutocratic voting system) and to the liberals and socialists (who wanted majority rule undiluted by proportional representation). What matters at the decision stage is not what values the leaders hold dear in the abstract, but what concrete steps they are willing to take. Fourth, the agreement worked out by the leaders is far from universal. It must be transmitted to the professional politicians and to the citizenry at large. These are two aspects of the final, or habituation, phase of the model.

[41] Barrington Moore, Jr., *Social Origins of Dictatorship and Democracy* (Boston, 1966), p. 3.

D. Habituation Phase A distasteful decision, once made, is likely to seem more palatable as one is forced to live with it. Everyday experience can supply concrete illustrations of this probability for each of us. Festinger's theory of "cognitive dissonance" supplies a technical explanation and experimental support.[42] Democracy, moreover, is by definition a competitive process, and this competition gives an edge to those who can rationalize their commitment to it, and an even greater edge to those who sincerely believe in it. The transformation of the Swedish Conservative Party from 1918 to 1936 vividly illustrates the point. After two decades those leaders who had grudgingly put up with democracy or pragmatically accepted it retired or died and were replaced by others who sincerely believed in it. Similarly, in Turkey there is a remarkable change from the leadership of Ismet Inönü, who promoted democracy out of a sense of duty, and Adnan Menderes, who saw in it an unprecedented vehicle for his ambition, to younger leaders in each of their parties who understand democracy more fully and embrace it more wholeheartedly. In short, the very process of democracy institutes a double process of Darwinian selectivity in favor of convinced democrats: one among parties in general elections and the other among politicians vying for leadership within these parties.

But politics consists not only of competition for office. It is, above all, a process for resolving conflicts within human groups— whether these arise from the clash of interests or from uncertainty about the future. A new political regime is a novel prescription for taking joint chances on the unknown. With its basic practice of multilateral debate, democracy in particular involves a process of trial and error, a joint learning experience. The first grand compromise that establishes democracy, if it proves at all viable, is in itself a proof of the efficacy of the principle of conciliation and accommodation. The first success, therefore, may encourage contending political forces and their leaders to submit other major questions to resolution by democratic procedures.

In Sweden, for instance, there had been a general political stalemate in the last third of the nineteenth century over the prime issues of the day—the taxation and conscription systems inherited from the sixteenth century. But in the two decades after 1918, when democracy was fully adopted by the Swedes, a whole host of thorny

[42] Festinger, *A Theory of Cognitive Dissonance*.

questions was wittingly or unwittingly resolved. The Social Democrats surrendered their earlier pacifism, anticlericalism, and republicanism, as well as the demand for nationalization of industry
(although they found it hard to admit this last point). The conservatives, once staunchly nationalist, endorsed Swedish participation in
international organizations. Above all, conservatives and liberals
fully accepted government intervention in the economy and the
social welfare state.

Of course, the spiral that in Sweden went upward to greater and
greater successes for the democratic process may also go down-
ward. A conspicuous failure to resolve some urgent political question will damage the prospects of democracy; if such a failure comes
early in the habituation phase, it may prove fatal.

Surveying the evolution of political debate and conflict in the
Western democracies over the last century, it is striking to observe
the difference between social and economic issues, which democracies handled with comparative ease, and issues of community,
which have proved far more troublesome.[43] With the advantage
of a century's hindsight, it is easy to see that Marx's estimate was
wrong at crucial points. In nationality he saw a cloak for bourgeois
class interests. He denounced religion as the opiate of the masses.
In economics, by contrast, he foresaw very real and increasingly
bitter struggles that would end by bringing bourgeois democracy
crashing down. But in fact democracy has proved most effective in
resolving political questions where the major divisions have been
social and economic, as in Britain, Australia, New Zealand, and the
Scandinavian countries. It has been the fight among religious,
national, and racial groups, instead, that has proved most tenacious
and has caused recurrent bitterness, as in Belgium, Holland, Canada, and the United States.

The reasons are not hard to find. On the socioeconomic front
Marxism itself became a sufficient force in Europe to serve to some
extent as a self-disconfirming prophecy. But beyond this there is a
fundamental difference in the nature of the issues. On matters of
economic policy and social expenditures you can always split the
difference. In an expanding economy, you can even have it both
ways: the contest for higher wages, profits, consumer savings, and
social welfare payments can be turned into a positive-sum game.
But there is no middle position between Flemish and French as

---

[43] The contrast emerges implicitly from the country studies in Dahl, ed.
Political Oppositions in Western Democracies.

360   *Comparative Politics   April 1970*

official languages, or between Calvinism, Catholicism, and secularism as principles of education. The best you can get here is an "inclusive compromise"[44]—a log-rolling deal whereby some government offices speak French and some Flemish, or some children are taught according to Aquinas, some, Calvin, and some, Voltaire. Such a solution may partly depoliticize the question. Yet it also entrenches the differences instead of removing them, and accordingly it may convert political conflict into a form of trench warfare.

The difficulty that democracy finds in resolving issues of community emphasizes the importance of national unity as the background condition of the democratization process. The hardest struggles in a democracy are those against the birth defects of the political community.

The transition to democracy, it was suggested earlier, may require some common attitudes and some distinct attitudes on the part of the politician and of the common citizen. The distinction is already apparent during the decision phase when the leaders search for compromise while their followers wearily uphold the banners of the old struggle. It becomes even more readily apparent during the habituation phase, when three sorts of process are at work. First, both politicians and citizens learn from the successful resolution of some issues to place their faith in the new rules and to apply them to new issues. Their trust will grow more quickly if, in the early decades of the new regime, a wide variety of political tendencies can participate in the conduct of affairs, either by joining various coalitions or by taking turns as government and opposition. Second, as we just saw, experience with democratic techniques and competitive recruitment will confirm the politicians in their democratic practices and beliefs. Third, the population at large will become firmly fitted into the new structure by the forging of effective links of party organization that connect the politicians in the capital with the mass electorate throughout the country.

These party organizations may be a direct continuation of those that were active during the preparatory, or conflict, phase of democratization, and a suffrage extension at the time of the democratic "decision" may now have given them a free field. It is possible, on the other hand, that no parties with a broad popular base emerged during the conflict phase and that the suffrage extension

[44] Rustow, *Politics of Compromise*, p. 231.

was very limited. Even under such conditions of partial democratization of the political structure, a competitive dynamic that completes the process may have been set off. The parliamentary parties will seek support from constituency organizations to insure a steady supply of members for their group in future parliaments. Now this and now that political group may see a chance to steal a march on its opponents by enlarging the electorate or by removing other obstacles to majority control. This, roughly, would seem to have been the nature of British developments between 1832 and 1918. Complete democratization, of course, is the only logical stopping point for such a dynamic.

V

The model here presented makes three broad assertions. First, it says that certain ingredients are indispensable to the genesis of democracy. For one thing, there must be a sense of national unity. For another, there must be entrenched and serious conflict. For a third, there must be a conscious adoption of democratic rules. And, finally, both politicians and electorate must be habituated to these rules.

Secondly, the model asserts that these ingredients must be assembled one at a time. Each task has its own logic and each has its natural protagonists—a network of administrators or a group of nationalist literati for the task of unification, a mass movement of the lower class, perhaps led by upper class dissidents, for the task of preparatory struggle, a small circle of political leaders skilled at negotiation and compromise for the formulation of democratic rules, and a variety of organization men and their organizations for the task of habituation. The model thus abandons the quest for "functional requisites" of democracy; for such a quest heaps all these tasks together and thus makes the total job of democratization quite unmanageable. The argument here is analogous to that which has been made by Hirschman and others against the theory of balanced economic growth. These economists do not deny that the transition from a primitive subsistence economy to a mature industrial society involves changes on all fronts —in working skills, in capital formation, in the distribution system, in consumption habits, in the monetary system, and so forth. But they insist that any country that attempted all these tasks at once would in practice find itself totally paralysed—that the stablest balance is that of stagnation. Hence the economic developer's

362   *Comparative Politics   April 1970*

problem, in their view, becomes one of finding backward and forward "linkages," that is, of devising a manageable sequence of tasks.

Thirdly, the model does suggest one such sequence from national unity as background, through struggle, compromise, and habituation, to democracy. The cogency of this sequence is brought home by a deviant development in Turkey in the years after 1945. The Turkish commitment to democracy was made in the absence of prior overt conflict between major social groups or their leading elites. In 1950 there was the first change of government as the result of a new electoral majority, but in the next decade there was a drift back into authoritarian practices on the part of this newly elected party, and in 1960–1961 the democratic experiment was interrupted by a military coup. These developments are not unconnected: Turkey paid the price in 1960 for having received its first democratic regime as a free gift from the hands of a dictator. But after 1961 there was a further evolution in the more appropriate sequence. The crisis of 1960–1961 had made social and political conflict far more acceptable, and a full range of social and economic issues was debated for the first time. The conflict that shaped up was between the military on one side and the spokesmen of the agrarian majority on the other—and the compromise between these two allowed the resumption of the democratic experiment on a more secure basis by 1965.

In the interests of parsimony, the basic ingredients of the model have been kept to four, and the social circumstances or psychological motivations that may furnish each of them have been left wide open. Specifically, the model rejects what are sometimes proposed as preconditions of democracy, e.g., high levels of economic and social development or a prior consensus either on fundamentals or on the rules. Economic growth may be one of the circumstances that produces the tensions essential to the preparatory or conflict phase—but there are other circumstances that might also serve. Mass education and social welfare services are more likely to be the result of democratization.

Consensus on fundamentals is an implausible precondition. A people who were not in conflict about some rather fundamental matters would have little need to devise democracy's elaborate rules for conflict resolution. And the acceptance of those rules is logically a part of the transition process rather than its prerequisite. The present model transfers various aspects of consensus from the quiescent state of preconditions to that of active elements in the

Dankwart A. Rustow   **363**

process. I here follow the lead of Bernard Crick, who has strikingly written:

> . . . It is often thought that for this "master science" [i.e., democratic politics] to function, there must already be in existence some shared idea of a "common good," some "consensus" or *consensus juris*. But this common good is itself the process of practical reconciliation of the interests of the various . . . aggregates, or groups which compose a state; it is not some external and intangible spiritual adhesive. . . . Diverse groups hold together, firstly, because they have a common interest in sheer survival, and, secondly, because they practise politics—not because they agree about 'fundamentals,' or some such concept too vague, too personal, or too divine ever to do the job of politics for it. The moral consensus of a free state is not something mysteriously prior to or above politics: it is the activity (the civilizing activity) of politics itself.[45]

The basis of democracy is not maximum consensus. It is the tenuous middle ground between imposed uniformity (such as would lead to some sort of tyranny) and implacable hostility (of a kind that would disrupt the community in civil war or secession). In the process of genesis of democracy, an element of what might be termed consensus enters at three points at least. There must be a prior sense of community, preferably a sense of community quietly taken for granted that is above mere opinion and mere agreement. There must be a conscious adoption of democratic rules, but they must not be so much believed in as applied, first perhaps from necessity and gradually from habit. The very operation of these rules will enlarge the area of consensus step-by-step as democracy moves down its crowded agenda.

But new issues will always emerge and new conflicts threaten the newly won agreements. The characteristic procedures of democracy include campaign oratory, the election of candidates, parliamentary divisions, votes of confidence and of censure—a host of devices, in short, for expressing conflict and thereby resolving it. The essence of democracy is the habit of dissension and conciliation over ever-changing issues and amidst ever-changing alignments. Totalitarian rulers must enforce unanimity on fundamentals and on procedures before they can get down to other business. By contrast, democracy is that form of government that derives its just powers from the dissent of up to one half of the governed.

---

[45] Crick, *In Defence of Politics*, p. 24.

[5]

REVISTA DE CIÊNCIA POLITICA • LISBOA • 1.º SEMESTRE DE 1985 • N.º 1

Speculations about the prospective demise of authoritarian regimes and its possible consequences (I) *

PHILIPPE C. SCHMITTER

How and why do authoritarian regimes break down? Who are the agents, and what are the motives involved in the deterioration and eventual transformation of this mode of political domination? How do past experience with authoritarian rule and the circumstances of its demise affect future democratic performance? What are the processes of democratization which ensue from such a liberation of political forces? Which possible combination of actors and actions will best ensure a viable democratic outcome? What configuration of institutions and pattern of benefits are likely to emerge from such a transformation in regime type?

Not very long ago, the posing of such questions in the context of contemporary Latin American and Southern Europe would have been considered *pura fantasia* — an imaginative exercise in political science fiction or a naive expression of wishful thinking. To the extent that scholars were explicity concerned with regime-level questions at all, their attention was directed elsewhere. Most were preoccupied with delineating the interrelated (and presumably viable) properties of «bureaucratic-authoritarian rule» and or with demonstrating the ine-

* This is a revised version of a paper first presented as «Authoritarian experiences and the prospects for democracy», at the workshop on «Prospects for democracy: transitions from authoritarian rule», sponsored by the Latin American program of the Woodrow Wilson International Center for Scholars, September 1980. A subsequent draft with the same title as the present one was initially circulated as working paper no. 60 (1980) of the Wilson Center, Washington, D. C., but has been out of print now for several years.

In any case, this version has been substantially revised. Some of its themes and concepts will appear in essays contained in Guillermo O'Donnell, Philippe C. Schmitter and Laurence Whitehead (eds.), *Transitions from Authoritarian Rule*, 4 vols. (Baltimore and London, Johns Hopkins University Press, forthcoming in 1985), especially in the fourth volume, written by Guillermo O'Donnell and myself entitled *Political Life after Authoritarian Rule: Tentative Conclusions about Uncertain Transitions*.

Despite repeated urgings by critics to divorce my speculations from those of Machiavelli, I have refused to do so in this revised edition. I apologize to the reader for what may seem an excessive preoccupation with this illustrious Florentine. Incidentally, this intellectual fascination antedates my coming to the European University Institute in Florence and, therefore, should not be interpreted as a case of «ecological determinism» or «adoptive nativism». My rediscovery of Machiavelli I owe in large part to Elissa B. Weaver, of the Department of Romance Languages of the University of Chicago. She has gently, but firmly, sought to keep me faithful to the original works and is, therefore, in no way responsible for the distortion and extensions I have no doubt forced upon them.

luctable imperatives for its emergence (and, putatively, its persistence) in the context of the regions' delayed dependent, peripheral or semi-peripheral, capitalist development. A few were keeping busy explaining away the survival of rare democratic exceptions due to mitigating circumstances and or extraordinary conditions.

Rather suddenly and quite unexpectedly, the above questions about regime transformation moved up on the agenda of public and elite attention from *pura fantasia* to, at least, *possible relevancia* and even, in a few places, to *gran actualidad*. Scholars, as usual responding belatedly and opportunistically to the demand for their services, found their recently acquired conceptual-*cum*-theoretical garments ill-fitting, if not illsuited, to the task of explaining such an unanticipated outcome. Of course, there hints scattered in the explanations of authoritarian rule about possible inconsistencies, unresolved dilemmas and eventual contradictions, and a case could be made that enough significant, if unexplained and unexpected, changes had occurred — especially in the structure of the world economy — to account for the possibility of «necessary» regime transformation. Nevertheless, the mere prospect of a resurgence of democracy in Latin America and Southern Europe was enough to provoke an «agonizing reappraisal» of assumptions about the nature of the fit between regime type, class structure, economic development and international context in those parts of the world [1].

This intriguing combination of practical urgency and theoretical embarassment no doubt motivated the decision of a group of scholars associated with the Latin American program of the Woodrow Wilson International Center for Scholars to convoke a working group on the topic of «Prospects for democracy: transitions from authoritarian rule». Several of its members had contributed significantly to the previous discussion on «bureaucratic authoritarian regimes» — and, it is only fair to point out, to the criticism of that paradigm [2]. As a member of that group, I think it accurate to say that all of us felt that a re-examination of these themes required detailed analyses of the forces and factors involved in specific — hopefully analogous — cases (past and present) of regime transformation toward democracy, as well as speculative exploration of the general processes and generic issues raised by such transformations. On the one hand, we recognized that we needed much more information and insight about what had happened and was actually happening; on the other hand, we considered it necessary to attempt, even before the necessary empirical material was available, to identify what such instances and examples might have in common, and why their outcomes might be expected to differ.

Guillermo O'Donnell and I first drafted a loose *problématique* outlining relevant issues and themes [3]. It was intended to attract attention to our joint venture and to elicit comments about its scope, content and approach. The statement also served to establish a tentative division of labor under which I was assigned the less savory, but more tractable, job of dealing with the «Demise of authoritarian rule», while Guillermo O'Donnell and Adam Przeworski would engage in the more appetizing task of speculating about the generic causes and consequences of the «Rise of democracy» [4].

When the above mentioned *problématique* was circulated among potential participants and other interested scholars, two responses particularly intrigued me: one perceptive critic accused it of being *insufficiently Machiavellian* — perhaps for not having put theoretical squerely and aggressively at the service of improving the prospect for a republican-*cum*-democratic outcome; a second, equally perceptive, critic charged that it was *excessively Machiavellian* — perhaps for its assumption that political regimes are not merely given by culture or imposed by circumstance, but are willed and chosen into being. Whatever the merit of either or both of these accusations, their paradoxical message sent me scurring back to the Florentine master, first out of curiosity and, then, for edification.

For there I not only found considerable inspiration in substantive matters, but also a sober injunction «to consider carefully how human affairs proceed» (*Discourses,* II, 29, p. 342)[5] and, therefore, not to flinch from unpleasant conclusions. He also gave me the methodological tip that «one cannot give a definite rule concerning these matters without knowing the particular details of those states wherein one had to take a similar decision» and, therefore, if one did not know those details, the way to proceed was by abstraction and deduction «in as general a manner as the subject matter will allow» (*Prince,* XX, p. 146). Finally, I received optimistic support for my implicitly comparative approach in his argument that «in all cities and all peoples there still exist and have always existed the same desires and passions. Thus it is an easy matter for him who carefully examines past events to foresee future events in a republic, or, if old remedies cannot be found, to devise new ones based upon the similarity of the events.» (*Discourses,* I, 39, p. 252.)

Within the limits imposed by my lesser talents and by the subject matter itself (alas, new desires and passions, or better new ways of satisfying and frustrating ancient desires and passions, seem to have further complicated political life since he wrote in the early 1500s), I will attempt in this essay to be *properly Machiavellian.* I doubt this would satisfy either of my initial critics. I know my reliance on Machiavelli has become obsessive. In only hope it will provide a fruitful point of departure, although I fear it exposes me to an awesome standard of comparison[6].

85

I — **«There is nothing more difficult to execute, nor more dubious of success, nor more dangerous to administer than to introduce a new system of things: for he who introduces it has all those who profit from the old system as his enemies and he has only lukewarm allies in all those who might profit from the new system.»** (*Prince,* VI, p. 94.)

Regime transformation — in whatever direction — involves a considerable risk to those promoting it and a substantial, if lesser, risk to those defending against it. Not only are «many conspiracies [...] attempted but very few reach their desired goal» (*Prince,* VI, p. 94), but even once successful in seizing power, very few conspirators, Machiavelli suggests, will manage to institute «a new system of things». Of all the acts of political courage and knavery, therefore, efforts aimed at altering the basic structure of authority and not just the occupants of office, at changing the very calculus of public choice and not just the content of policy, at affecting the established distribution of power resources and not just the pattern of political benefits — in other words, attacks on the persistences of a given regime — are likely to be among the most rationally calculated and deliberately willful. However passionate and spontaneous the behavior of rebels may appear and even become in the course of a mobilized, violent seizure of power or other form of regime change, under that behavior lies a *calculus of dissent* — a weighing of costs and benefits to be probabilistically gained from different investments in political action and different resultant configurations of authority[7]. Political action of this nature and import cannot be explained exclusively in terms of either unconscious responses to functional imperatives or instinctual reactions to cultural norms — no matter how much «necessity», as Machiavelli liked to call it, establishes the conditions of choice or «love» determines what actors would prefer to see happen. It is the calculus of dissent with respect to regime type that we will attempt to expose below.

So uncertain, however, is the calculus and so momentous may be the consequences for any given individual that most will prefer not to make it. This rational indifference to regime questions, coupled with the quasi-instinctual nature of political behavior when the stakes are low and the actions are repetitive, constitutes the strongest barrier to posible regime transformation. If, indeed, «a man who is used to acting in one way never changes» (*Discourses,* III, p. 382), and if, by changing, he would incur a high risk of political failure (not to mention personal injury), why would regime forms change at all? Why would they not merely perpetuate themselves indefinitely through marginal adjustments in policy and occasional circulations in elites?

This question of why regime transformation occurs I will address later. What is of concern here is the implication that the demise of one form and the possible rise of another form of political domination is a relatively rare event, especially when compared to most instances of political behavior which have been «scientifically» observed and analyzed. There can be no question of using effectively the powers of statistical inference or even empirical induction based on a large number of observations. Each case will be too uniquely specified in time, space and content, not to mention the fact that, through diffusion and exemplification, past cases will contaminate those occurring in the present — and the future. Purely inductive theory risks becoming a «one to one» mapping of reality with as many explanations as cases, as many variables as events[8].

We must, therefore, proceed «in as general a manner as the subject matter will allow», identify a set of generic outcomes, processes, motives and actors and seek to expose the politicologic of their interrelation, knowing full well that the types, specifications, an *Gestalten* may not fit well with any specific case whose past behavior one is attempting to explain or whose future outcome one is attempting to predict. In this vein, I propose to work backward — from a typology of *how* authoritarian regimes are overthrown, to *why* this might happen, to *who* might be involved and, finally, to *what* might be the consequences of such a demise for the possible rise of democratic replacement.

II — Authoritarian regimes commonly transform themselves or are transformed in one of four ways depending on who leads the struggle and whether actual violence is used. (P. C. S.)

No regime — authoritarian or other — collapses or is overthrown unless it and its supporters are threatened by violence. No matter how poor performance, how narrow the circle of beneficiaries or how weak the moral justification for ruling, those in power will persist in their practices and procedures (but not necessarily in their policies) until sufficiently and plausibly threatened by physical harm or forceful loss of resources[9]. When compelled to act, they may do so out of imperative necessity or anticipated reaction.

For rulers do not always wait to act until forced to do so on the terrain and at the moment of their opponents' choosing. Political actors are capable of projecting the consequences of their actions and predicting those of others. With the aid of «theory» (usually based on examples from cases elsewhere judged to have been analogous in nature), they may anticipate future outcomes and act so as to forestall unwanted outcomes. As Machiavelli put it, «in order not to lose everything, [actors were] forced to concede to [others] their own share» (*Prince,* II, p. 181). Therefore, regimes may change in nature (and not just in material benefits or symbolic trappings) without an actual mobilization of their opponents and or without the actual use of physical force — although its presence is always lurking in the background. In other words, power may be given over *(Machtuebergabe)* and not just seized *(Machtergreifung).*

Where actors in power calculate that the benefits to remaining in power clearly exceed the costs (direct and indirect) of repressing their opponents, they will resist to threat of violence with actual violence. In fact in such circumstances they have an incentive to act pre-emptively and even to provoke violence by their opponents — thereby, achieving what Machiavelli constantly strives for, i. e. «an economy of violence».

Where actors in power miscalculate their own resources and or those of their threatening opponents, or where they perceive no option of exiting from the situation with crucial resources intact, they will also act violently, but without efficiency. Quite the contrary, such miscalculated and desperate violence becomes counterproductive: «the more cruelty [they] employ, the weaker [their regime] becomes» when rulers have the general population as their enemy (*Discourses*, I, 16, p. 220). Also Machiavelli sagely warns that once regime proponents and opponents are forced to mobilize themselves and actually to confront each other with insults, insolence and violence both the stakes in the conflict and the expectations lodged in its outcome rise dangerously:

> When [false] hope enters man's breasts, it causes them to go beyond their work and, in most cases, to lose the opportunity of possessing a certain good by hoping to obtain a better one that is less certain. [*Discourses*, II, 27, p. 339.]

Regimes may also change from a sequential combination of reactions to violent mobilization and peaceful transformation. Actors who have been successful in the past at meeting the threat of violence with the use of violence against their opponents may choose to react to the prospect of renewed violence by handing over power (or a portion of it) because their former actions have temporarily eliminated their most dangerous opponents or because they are beginning to suffer the weakness brought on by their past cruelties. In this case, regime transformations coincide not with the high point of violent mobilization, but with its aftermath — even with periods of considerable quiescence.

The presence of a threat of violence against a given authoritarian regime (and not just against one or more of its policies) differentially affects the political necessity and calculation of two (not always initially clearly distinguishable) groups:

1) Those who have benefitted from and or been included in the regime; and
2) Those who have suffered or been excluded from it.

As we shall see infra, a great deal hinges on whether this differential impact produces two exclusive and polarized reactions, or whether it has a centripetal influence through its differential effect within the two «camps» of supporters and opponents.

Among regime opponents, those who have suffered direct deprivations (*antagonists*, let us call them) will be most likely to choose increased mobilization and advocate violent overthrow, but they will probably lack the necessary resources for effective collective action unless they are assisted by some external «prince», e. g. exiles or members of transnational political movements. Those who have politically excluded by authoritarian rulers, but have not suffered specific deprivations (*subjects* in my terminology) may possess the aggregate resources necessary; however, their sheer numbers, dispersion and less intense motivation normally mitigate against collective action on their part.

Among regime supporters those included with it, benefitting from it and responsible for it *(protagonists)* are most likely to respond violently in its defense, so much so that they may resort to violence even against fellow benefactors who show a willingness to compromise with real or emergent threats.

Finally, actors who benefit from the authoritarian regime, but are not directly dependent on it or responsible for its policies *(supporters)* present a real but ambiguous threat to its persistence. They are likely to possess significant (positive and negative) resources, to be small enough in number, concentrated in location, and astute enough in calculation to act collectively out of choise and not necessity — if sufficiently assured about retaining already acquired resources and future benefits under some different form of governance.

FIGURE I

Modal types/strategies for the demise of authoritarian regimes

		1) Actors leading the transformation in regime:			
		A) *Protagonists:*	B) *Supporters:*	C) *Subjects:*	D) *Antagonists:*
		Participants and beneficiaries of authoritarian rule.	Beneficiaries not participants of authoritarian rule.	Excluded but persecuted opponents.	Excluded and persecuted opponents.
2) Extent of mobilization for violence:	A) High.	Seizure of power *(Machtfestnahme)*	—	—	Overthrow of power *(Machtergreifung)*
	B) Low.	—	Transfer of power *(Machtubernahme)*	Surrender of power *(Machtubergabe)*	—

Those politico-logical distinctions can be juxtaposed to each other to produce a matrix with four modal types or strategies for the demise of authoritarian rule:

II.2 — In a *seizure of power,* some segment or faction of those who have participated and benefitted from authoritarian rule react with concerted violence, normally by *coup d'État,* to eject, even eliminate physically, the present occupants from executive office. They are most likely to attempt to institute a purified, more repressive and exclusive, type of regime, although their sheer vulnerability may lead them to broaden their basis of support by appealing to some subjects of the previous regime.

II.2 — In a *transfer of power,* the principal actors guiding regime transformation consist of ex-beneficiaries who were not directly compromised by or deeply involved with regime policies and who acquire their reins of power and office without a substantial mobilization for violence on their part.

II.3 — In a *surrender of power,* previous authoritarian rulers, faced with a greater credible threat from antagonists and or more aggressive protagonists, prudentially agree to withdraw from formal positions of authority in favor of a set of actors not compromised with the now defunct regime but not themselves capable of mobilized violence. A special case of this type consists of situations in which the transformation occurs in the context of impeding or actual defeat in war and may be presided over by an occupying foreign power.

II.4 — In an *overthrow of power,* the previous authoritarian rulers resist violently, but unsuccessfully, and are foreceably ousted by the mobilized efforts of their formely conformist subjects and victimized antagonists. Here, they lose not only formal control over the offices of public authority and the transition process, but also their informal political resources — up to and including both property and life.

*

Needless to say, any concrete historical instance of the calculus of dissent which results in the downfall of a given authoritarian regime may involve some combination of several or even all of these modal types. One could argue that «pure instances» are not only rare, but likely to fail. For example, successful seizures of power usually depend on at least the spectre of an impeding overthrow by radical antagonists. The personal sacrifice and mass mobilization involved in an overthrow are unlikely to prevail where either·a preemptive transfer or a prudential surrender of power offers a much easier and more attractive resolution to the regime crisis — unless such temptations are ruled out by hard-time protagonists.

A recent volume on the breakdown of democracies argues (implicitly) that such strategies should be regarded not as simultaneously, but as sequentially available modes for solving the problem of regime transformation [10]. Juan Linz in his introductory essay argues that the rise of authoritarian regimes from previously democratic ones involved either an inadvertent *overthrow* through civil war or, more often, a *surrender* of power, but this eventual outcome followed upon a prior *seizure* of power by a narrowly-based group within the previous democratic regime. Such prior transformations within the factional structure of power also seem characteristic of the demise of authoritarian rule.

For Machiavelli, mobilized violence was a virtual necessity (he cites with approval Juvenal's maxim that «few tyrants die a bloodless death» — *Discourses*, III, 6, p. 360). He repreatedly poured scorn on those who sought a negotiated, middle-of-the-road compromise to such a vital issue. Certainly the literature on regime transformation, scanty as it is, emphasizes the role of conspiratorial seizure and or mass overthrow. Perhaps it is my normative bias against violence or my empirical conviction that viable democracies have emerged more often historically as «second-best» compromises between stalemated political forces incapable of imposing their preferred mode of governance by regime seizure or overthrow [11], but I intent to pay special attention to strategies of transfer and surrender in which previous regime beneficiaries and passive opponents — unable and unwilling to eject forceably authoritarian rulers from power — are incapable of ruling without each other's resources of power and legitimacy. Hence, they reach a compromise and agree to establish some form of democracy which excludes only the extremes of die-hard protagonists and *revanchiste* antagonists of the defunct regime. The central property ussually stressed in the context of a declining regime is *vulnerability* to overthrow or seizure by centrifugal extremists. I will be looking for *dispensability* leading to the transfer or surrender of power to centripetal moderates. We are by no means assured of finding the latter, but we have reason to suspect that such an outcome may provide a better and more viable basis for political democracy.

III — «[Because men's] [12] desire is always greater than their power of acquisition, discontent with what they possess and lack of satisfaction [with how they obtained it] are the result [13]. From this arise the variations in their fortunes, for since some desire to possess more and others fear to lose what they have acquired. [Political enmities will constantly arise and lead to the ruin of on regime and the exhaltation of another. — P. C. S.]» (*Discourses*, I, 37, p. 247.)

Given that «human affairs are always in motion, either rising or declining» (*Discourses*, II, intro., p. 288) and, hence, that «all things of this world have a limit to their existence» (*Discourses*, III, 1, p. 351), perhaps one should wonder,

89

not why authoritarian regimes collapse or are transformed, but why any form of patterned, consensual domination can long endure. Presumably, prudence in the face of the high risks involved in changing the existing order, combined with a general inability to learn new ways of doing things [14], prevent political life from becoming completely chaotic in form and random in behavior.

Moreover, whatever the type of regime, its internal order requires some degree of self-limitation and self abnegation if it is to survive:

> Just as the states of princes have endured for a long time so too have the states of republics; both have needed to be regulated by laws, for a prince who is able to do what he wishes is mad, and a people that can do what it wishes is unwise. [*Discourses*, I, 58, p. 285.]

This «legality» is far from the element of «legitimacy» stressed by so many Neo-Weberian students of regime persistence in that it refers to self-regulated, prudential behavior by those in power, not to the belief by those out of power that their rulers are rightfully entitled to their positions of domination.

Purely arbitrary, unself-restrained, i. e. «tyrannical», forms of authoritarian rule are intrinsically unstable because they encourage «madness» among their leaders and cannot inculcate predictable and prudential ways of acting in their subjects — not because their «princes» are disliked by the people or their forms illegitimate in the eyes of the citizenry. Hence, «sultanistic», or highly personalistic, authoritarian regimes [15] face rather different problems and must rely on rather different resources (especially physical coercion and fear) to survive. The mode of their demise, the motivation and identity of their opponents and the longer-term consequences of their replacement are correspondingly likely to be different from those of their more established, impersonal, predictable, «bureaucratic-authoritarian» relatives.

III.1 — «Since human affairs are constantly changing and never remain fixed, it is necessary that they rise or fall and many things you are not compelled to do by reason, you are impelled to do by necessity.» (*Prince*, VI, p. 192.) Authoritarian regimes fall (or, better, diminish in their viability) from two intersecting and overlapping sets of motives. *By necessity,* people may have to act (be compelled to act) out of fear of losing what they have already acquired or out of need for acquiring what they feel they must have. *By reason,* people may choose to act (be impelled to act) out of calculation of what may happen in the future, unless changes intervene, or out of admiration for what they regard as a better, more just, socio-political order. Machiavelli, while acknowledging the force of reasonable anticipation and admiration, was skeptical about the constancy of its effect and the predictability of its outcome:

> Men always turn out badly for you unless some necessity makes them good. [*Prince*, XXIII, p. 137.]
> Men never do good except out of necessity, but when they have the freedom to choose and can do as they pelase, everything immediately becomes confused and disorderly. [*Discourses*, I, 3, p. 182.]

Love for a particularly just leader or admiration for good moral principles, «since men are a sorry lot is broken on every occasion in which their own self-interest is concerned; but fear is held together by a dread of punishment which will never abandon you» (*Prince*, XVII, p. 131). If one includes in the notion of necessary fear, not just the possibility of *punishing acts* by those in power, but also the more «capitalistic» response of *depriving actions* by those in control of the economy, then one might agree with Machiavelli that satisfaction of immediate self-interest provides a more prominent and predictable motive for opposing or supporting a given regime than reasonable (but more remote) calculation and or reasonable (but possibly fickle) admiration [16].

Nevertheless, the subsequent development of instruments of rational calculation in political life (e. g. professional staffs, statistical data analysis and inference, planning techniques, social science theory, etc.) and the growing role of international standards of admirable behavior in political life (e. g. Universal Declaration of Human Rights, U. N. Charter, innumerable constitutional prologues, international pressure groups, etc.) have enhanced the importance of choice with respect to regime type. Levels of living above mere subsistence and more humane punishments for violations of authority have perhaps diminished the centrality of sheer necessity and survival in the calculus of political action. Opponents and renegade supporter of authoritarian rule may feel sufficiently freed from those narrow and predictable constraints to indulge in their preference for a more legitimate and just type of regime, or to take a calculated risk on the longer-term benefits to be gleaned from a more rational and better structured form of governance — even when not enticed to do so by the opportunity for immediate benefits or forced to do so by the prospect of unbearable costs.

For these motivational categories of necessity and choice, we can deduce four modal answers to the question of *why* a given authoritarian regime may be seized or overthrown, forced to transfer or surrender power:

III.1.1 — *Success.* — If modern authoritarian regimes are the contemporary functional equivalents of classic dictatorship, their demise would be easy to understand, if still difficult to predict. Machiavelli defined the dictator as «[one] created for a cricumscribed period of time, and only in order to deal with the problem for which he was chosen. His authority encompassed the power to decide for himself the way in which to deal with this urgent danger, to do everything without consultation, and to punish anyone without appeal, but he could do nothing which would alter the form of government [...]» (*Prince,* XXXIV, p. 244.) Once the authoritarian rulers had satisfied the necessities of those who placed them in power (including their own), the «unfortunate historial parenthesis» would come to an end and the polity would return to the form of government it had known previously. The rulers, finding that «those who were at first trusted» had become increasingly hostile to the ruler's perpetration in power and being unable to obtain «more loyalty and more utility in those men who, at the beginning of their rule, were considered suspect» (*Prince,* XX, p. 148) would (or better, should) prudentially step aside. Most contemporary «liberal» justifications for authoritarian rule seem to be based on such a functionalist, problem-solving «logic» of the relation between regime type and system imperatives. These apologists tend to discount or ignore the possibility that dictators will succeed in creating or inventing new «necessities» in order to retain the support of their initial promoters, or that they will resolve the problems that brought them to power so slowly or in a manner that would irreversibly alter the pre-existing form of government, making return to it virtually impossible. In Machiavelli's terms, there is an ever-present danger that they will «corrupt the society».

III.1.2 — *Failure.* — If the authoritarian regime persistently and manifestly fails to resolve the problems which occasioned its rise (or which were occasioned by its rise), its benefactors and expectant beneficiaries will come to fear it and regard its transformation as necessary. Its initial enemies and subsequent victims will, consequently, be reinforced in their opposition. An extreme instance of regime failure — indeed, *the* most common and probable cause of the demise of such regimes — has been defeat in war. Machiavelli notes that unsuccessful republics/democracies are more threatened by «internal emergencies» because

91

they tolerate the expression of dissent in reaction to failures not even of their own making (*Prince*, XXXIII, p. 241). By inverted reasoning, unsuccessful principalities/authoritarian regimes may be more vulnerable to «external emergencies», if only because they themselves provoke failure by engaging in more adventurous and aggressive foreign policies.

In the simplest, but least likely, of circumstances the failure of authoritarian rule is so complete and convincing that it provokes what Machiavelli called «universal hatred» uniting both the common people and the notables against it. Only defeat in war seems capable of bringing about such a «catastrophic» consensus. More likely is the situation in which a broad, but diffuse, assessment of failure pervades «the general populace» while a small, privileged set of supporters continues to judge the regime successful (and yet still indispensible). Such relative failures in authoritarian governance may persist for some time — either because the extent of malperformance has not yet reached «the realm of necessity» where vital interests are threatened, or because the sheer diffuseness of its impact encourages opponents to «free ride», hoping that someone else will take the risks and pay the costs of seizing or overthrowing the regime.

In discussing «the causes of conspiracy against princes» (*Discourses*, III, 6, p. 358), Machiavelli downplays the importance of general unpopularity-*cum*-hatred. It becomes crucial, he suggests elsewhere only «in times of adversity», when the prince will be unable to call upon «the friendship of the common people» to overcome a more focused challenge to his authority and office (*Prince*, IX, p. 109). The specific type of failure which is most likely to provoke these challenges lies in «offenses against individuals» — acts of deprivation, interpreted as unjust or arbitrary, against specifically designated persons (or, by extension, small groups) who, as a consequence, come to fear for their survival. Since the certain fact of losing what one has already acquired (or the eminent prospect of such a loss) is a stronger and more predictable basis for action than the uncertain opportunity for obtaining what one does not yet have (or has lost some time ago), and since those who lose some property, privilege or honor are likely still to have more disposable political resources at hand than those who have never had them (or long since been deprived of them), it is the failures of authoritarian rulers which affect discrete groups or individuals among their own supporters and past beneficiaries that are most conducive to «causing a conspiracy» against perpetuation in power. The implication is that if a failed regime can manage to distribute its deprivations in a diffuse and proportional manner — not only across the population, but among its own supporters — it can survive periods of very poor performance, even if it is not admired or loved on other grounds.

Most authoritarian regimes are neither marked successes nor manifest failures[17]. Their mixed performance, confounded by the emergence of new problems in addition to those which brought them into existence (some of their own creation, some thrust upon them), sustains them in power much longer than would be expected if regime change were a mere instrumental-functionalist response to what liberals call «the problems of modernization» and Marxists call «the imperative contradictions of delayed-dependent capitalist development». No doubt, instances can be found of «salvationist» dictatorships which withdraw after successfully managing a particular crisis, and of «catastrophic» autocracies which collapse from threats to the survival of the geral populace and strategic supporters, but most contemporary transformations of authoritarian regimes are not motivated strictly by necessity. They involve complex elements of choice — of willful political action based on reasonable anticipation and admiration.

III.1.3 — *Decay*[18]. — Authoritarian rulers «used to acting in one way never change; [they] must come to ruin when the times, in changing, no longer are in harmony with [their] ways» (*Discourses*, III, 9, p. 382). Whatever the causes-*cum*-motives of their accession to power, whatever their success or failure in meeting these causes, those who rule for any length of time will have to adjust to a shifting panoply of new circumstances; some of which (Machiavelli reckoned about one half) are occasioned by unforesseable and unavoidable events of fortune; others of which are the unintentional product of past actions:

> One can never remove one inconvenience without causing another to arise. [*Discourses*, I, 6, p. 190.]

or the unavoidable consequence of faulty calculation:

> Shortsightedness in human nature will begin a policy that seems good but does not notice the poison that is underneath. [*Prince*, XXX, p. 123.]

All regimes, therefore, must be periodically revived and restructured. Machiavelli thought that ten years was a maximum interval «because after that amount of time has elapsed men begin to change their habits and to break the laws [...] if nothing arises that recalls the penalty to their minds and renews the fear in their hearts» (*Discourses*, III, 1, p. 353). Princes or authoritarian rulers are less capable of such acts of re-establishment of authority and revision of policies because by their nature they must draw on a narrower variety of experience than democracies (*Discourses*, III, 9, p. 382), and because their internal procedures will restrict (through strict rules of cooptation) or prohibit (through lifetime perpetuation) the succession to higher office of those capable of understanding and responding to new challenges and issues in novel ways. Whether by rotation of parties in-and-out of power or by realignment of parliamentary alliances in response to shifts in electoral fortune, democratic regimes possess a functional substitute for overcoming the fixity of individual human natures and the sclerosis induced in institutions by previously successful policies[19]. The inability of a given authoritarian regime to use predicatably the *dilemma of succession* as an opportunity to re-establish the foundations of public policy and order — more than any other factor — contributes to strategically disruptive behavior on the part of its supporters as well as its opponents. Moreover, it orients this behavior toward changes in the nature of the regime itself and not just modifications in its policies. Even actors freed from the compulsion of sheer necessity, benefitting from the regime itself and not fearful of losing what they have, may begin to calculate that their best, longer-term, interest lies with another prince or, alternatively, in a republic «ready to turn itself according to the way the winds of fortune and the changeability of affairs require» (*Prince*, XVIII, p. 135).

This strategic «indifference» to the form of political domination on the part of those near to power, coupled with the growing expectation that those in office will prove incapable of coping with the «crooked and unknown roads» of fortune or with the perverse and unexpected outcomes of previous policies, is particularly subversive of the viability of authoritarian regimes. Not only is this shift in support difficult to spot beforehand, it is difficult to attribute to any specific, immediately present, material factor and, hence, virtually impossible to buy off in any reliable fashion. Efforts to react by «recalling penalties and renewing fears» are only likely to precipitate action out of necessity. What is worse, those most inclined to react to decay have important resouces to deny the regime and or to supply its opponents. Authoritarian regimes in such a dilemma are neither clear functional successes nor failures according to their stated objectives or objective states. They have sown the «seeds of their own destruction», all right, but these have come up, not in the cultivated plots of fearful necessity, but in the fallow soil of anticipated reaction.

III.1.4 — *Delegitimation*. — Of all the motives Machiavelli considered might lead citizens to change rulers, the least likely and reliable he thought was «love» — either the loss of it on the part of those in power of the «desire to free one's city» on the part of those excluded by princely power. Doses of fear, judiciously and economically applied, would suffice — he thought — to overcome such momentary losses of popularity and to disperse such higher moral purpose. Contemporary students of politics attribute a good deal more significance to the normative basis for political action, i. e., to the need for legitimate grounds of political obligation and consent in order for regimes to persist. Presumably, this is a joint product of the diffusion and inculcation of standards of proper behavior within cultural areas and of changes in the content of state actions which demand greater voluntary compliance on the part of citizens if they are to be efficiently and effectively implemented. Fear of sanctions alone is no longer sufficient to induce people to serve (or to prevent them from disserving) the interests of the state. New and more complex linkages between a mobilized, literate, popular community and an expanded providential state make it more imperative that rulers be loved and respected — even when they are not being held accountable through the mechanisms of electoral competition and representative government to the wishes and whims of the public.

Demonstrating that delegitimation (or illegitimacy) is a plausible motive for the demise of any given authoritarian regime (or of such regimes in general) may be logically, as well as empirically, more difficult than attributing its downfall to dissatisfaction of immediate needs, threat to acquired goods or frustration of eventual opportunities.

First, actors must be shown not only to possess values antithetic to authoritarian rule with sufficient conviction and intensity [20], but these preferences about the *form* of political domination must be proven independent of the *content* of policies expected from a regime change. Citizens should demonstrably value *how* politics is conducted separately from *who benefits* from political action. If they feel it is illegitimate, regardless of whether it is perceived as a success or a failure, regardless of whether it seems capable of coping or not with emergent issues, the regime will be opposed — even when its demise may leave the opponent in a less favorable, objective circumstance. If not, if their ethical objections are hedged, such «normatively» phrased motives for opposition can safely be reduced to the more mundane (and predictable) category of self-regarding necessity or to the more ethereal (but reliable) category of calculated antecipation. They become merely a language in which political struggle takes place and through which actors with divergent needs and calculations can ally for a convergent, if fleeting, purpose.

Second, the existing regime must be shown to «need» legitimation for its survival. The values must not only clearly identify existing authorities as unworthy of respect and voluntary compliance — something these actors may make difficult by disguising themselves behind democratic façades or by themselves promising eventual conformity to democratic practices — but they must also be linked to depriving authorities of key strategic resources acquired for the perpetuation of governance. If the regime can get the compliance it needs by merely «recalling the penalty» to the mind of its subjects and «renewing the fear» in the hearts of its citizenry without seriously diverting scarce resources or upsetting future calculations, then no matter how deeply enculcated and sharply focused they are, dissenting values about the form of domination may be of little consequence.

One serious problem affecting the legitimacy of regimes which persist for some time in power is the inherent decay involved in the transmission of political values across generations. Just as respect for authority and identity with party may increase at compounding rates once a new regime is founded, so has a secular process of decline and disillusionment set in «once the generation that organized it [passes] away» (*Discourses*, I, 2, p. 179).

Inversely, the protractedness with which some authoritarian regimes persist — despite intergenerational decay in normative support — suggests another problem. Machiavelli observes that, because some polities had long suffered princely rule, their societies had become so corrupted that no manner of republican self-government could be expected to take hold. If such a regime could isolate its citizenry from the contrary influences of a democratic *Zeitgeist* either by censoring its sources of information or by convincing it of its peculiar «political culture», and if it could inculcate such a respect for hierarchy of office and privilege and inequality of access and acquisition [21], it could confine questions of legitimacy to the holders of specific positions without jeopardizing the survival of the regime itself.

*

95

Our discussion of why the demise of a given authoritarian regime might occur has been expressed in quite generic abstract terms. *Success, failure, decay* and *delegitimation* are categories obviously capable of encompassing a vast variety of much more specific interests, fears, projections and aspirations. It is precisely because contemporary instances of efforts to remove and to defend entrenched authoritarian rulers are linkely to involve a varied menu of specific motives that I have sought to structure my speculations at a general level. Once analysts have obtained enough descriptive material and identified groups of analogous experiences, then they can pass to more discriminating statements about the kinds of interests affected by regime success, the types of fear generated by failure, the ranger of anticipated reactions inspired by decay and the sorts of normative aspirations which trigger delegitimation. At present, there are only fragmentary, anecdotal illustrations of why classes, sectors, statuses, *éthnies*, regions, generations, institutions or even individuals came to oppose, became indifferent to, or stayed to support given authoritarian regimes under specific (often quite unique) circumstances.

There is also more than a hint, perhaps a persistent suspicion, that few instances of the demise of authoritarian regimes correspond exclusively and exhaustively to a single category of the already quite simplified motivational set I have sketched out above. Such regimes are often simultaneously perceived as *successful* and, therefore, dispensible in the eyes of their initial proponents; *failed* and, therefore, obstructive to the realization of the interests of some of their frustrated supporters and almost all of their opponents; *decadent* and, therefore, probably unfavorable to the future opportunities of many of their present supporters; and *illegitimate* and, therefore, offensive to the values of various publics. If consensus is even rarer at the demise of a regime at its founding, what may be most important is some optimal mix of motives for support, indifference and opposition. That mix of «whys» may be crucial both for identifying the «whos» responsible for regime seizure, overthrow, transfer or surrender, and for specifying «what consequences» such as transformation might eventually have for the viability of any ensuing democratic regime.

IV — **Because men are capable of colliding and coaligning with each other for a wide range of purposes and issues and because they exhibit differing propensities for taking risks and for discounting time, no single group of them or alliance of groups will predictably and reliably cause the demise of authoritarian rule. At some point in time, in some context of action, any group or individual may support, tolerate or oppose the persistence of an authoritarian regime. (P. C. S.)**

Here I part company rather dramatically with my illustrious Florentine predecessor. As he saw it, the polities of his time were divided into two mutually exclusive social groups: the «nobles» and the «people», each composed of different persons and interests, each with clear and incompatible regime preferences. Since the former wished only «to be free to command» and the latter «to be free from command», the identity of those supporting princely rule and those supporting republican rule was easy to establish within the social structure and relatively fixed across time. This tradition of associating dichotomously defined groups with distinctive regime preferences has, of course, prevailed (lord-peasant, bourgeois-proletarian, master-slave, creditor-debtor, producer-consumer, center-periphery, and so forth), without, however, producing a convincing explanation or description of who provokes either the rise or the demise of authoritarian rule. Some of those who «should» have resisted oppression, exploitation, enslavement, dependency, etc., by struggling for «freedom from command» have turned up on the wrong side of the barricades (or, more often, chosen to remain indifferent until others had taken the risk and paid the cost of a «beneficial» regime change). Inversely, the ranks of those assaulting authoritarian regimes have often been swelled (if not lead) by those who had formerly been «free to command». *More often than not, regime preference and tolerance have divided categories of actors and rarely brought together groups of economic or social homogeneity.* One could go so far as to claim that part of the process undermining regime viability involves the fragmentation of previously coherent economic and social interests and their recombination into unprecedented alliances oriented around alternative strategies for regime defense and demise. Hence, even if one could analytically identify and empirically isolate two warring coalitions [22]: one of privileged, defensive, commanding «nobles» and another of aspiring, aggressive, freedom-loving «plebes», it is by no means clear that the two camps would be composed of distinctive and mutually exclusive economic classes, social statuses, geographic locuses, productive sectors or institucional situses — not even to mention the thorny issue of ethnic identities and national loyalties.

Given this social heterogeneity in the contemporary basis of both support for and opposition to authoritarian rule, the best one can expect is to specify the generically relevant features of actors with respect to such regimes — and then, in efforts aimed at explaining distinctive historical instances of their transformation, to fill in these categories with the class, sectoral, locational and generational units specifically appropriate to the case and time period at hand.

The most obvious and elementary categorization of *positional* actors with respect to existing regimes involves whether they are in or out of power. Those «in power» can be further subdivided, as we have argued above, into those directly involved in and responsible for the acts of the regime *(protagonists),* i. e., those whose office or status is primarily dependent upon the regime, and those whose support is courted, whose opinions are solicited and whose actions are encouraged and subsidized by the regime, but whose position and property are independent of it *(supporters).* Actors «out of power» can also be usefully dichotomised into those who are ignored, acted upon or controlled by the regime but whose existence is tolerated proved they do not act collectively to thwart its pur-

96

poses or challenge its existence *(subjects)*, and those who are deliberately deprived or persecuted by it *(antagonists)*. The latter two categories constitute the great bulk of the population under authoritarian rule, except for «populist» varieties which seek to fuse the passive categories of supporter and subject. Nevertheless, policies of paternalistic concession and benign neglect may be sufficient to contain most persons within the realm of passive obedience and to isolate successfully most potential antagonists. These most intransigeant opponents, in turn, are likely to be subdivided into those driven into exile by persecution [23] and those who continue to reside precariously without the country.

The second generic factor of differentiation is *strategic* in nature and is furnished by Machiavelli. He suggested that actors responded to political choice with one of two dispositions:

1) They could seek to minimize losses and protect what they had already acquired; or

2) They could be driven by the desire to expand their resources and benefits further, thereby, exhibiting a much greater propensity for taking risks in the prospect of maximizing gains.

FIGURE II

Generic types of political actors

97

I) Position with respect to incumbent regime: II) Basic disposition for acting in politics:	1) Those in power	
	A) Those directly involved in and responsible for regime policies.	B) Those consulted by regime policy makers and associated indirectly with regime policies.
Loss minimizers: Those who primarily desire to protect what they have already acquired by political action (or inaction).	*Conservative protagonists.* [*Examples:* upper-level executive personnel; technocrats, military & police officers; foreign advisors (?); dependents and family members.]	*Conservative supporters.* [*Examples:* subsidized & protected bourgeois; some large landowners; privileged «leaders» of middle & working class associations; technocrats; civil servants; foreign capitalists (?).]
Gain maximizers: Those who primarily desire to acquire more than they presently have through political action.	*Agressive protagonists.* (*Examples:* leaders of dissident faction; displaced rivals; interservice competitors; lower-ranking officers & technocrats; «state capitalists».)	*Acquisitive supporters.* (*Examples:* emergent, competitive bourgeois; middle-level civilian bureaucrats; new agrarian capitalists; new middle class.)

I) Position with respect to incumbent regime: II) Basic disposition for acting in politics:	2) Those out of power:	
	A) Those ignored by regime policy-makers but tolerated by regime policies.	B) Those persecuted by regime policy makers & deprived by regime policies.
Loss minimizers: Those who primarily desire to protect what they have already acquired by political action (or inaction).	*Defensive subjects.* (*Examples:* peripheral landed notables & provincial elites; old middle class; petty bourgeoisie; small landholders & peasants; some skilled workers.)	*Defensive antagonists.* (*Examples:* leaders & militants of traditional parties; rival technocrats; domesticated CP; leaders-followers of liberal professions; assimilated exiles; emigrants.)
Gain maximizers: Those who primarily desire to acquire more than they presently have through political action.	*Acquisitive subjects.* (*Examples:* bulk of urban working class; landless rural workers and share-croppers; urban «marginals».)	*Agressive antagonists.* (*Examples:* students; underground leaders and militants; union leaders; peasant militants; some intellectuals; exiled leaders;· foreign-sponsored militants.)

Figure II displays these two dimensions of political position/disposition in a matrix which generates six generic types of actors — each with a presumed different propensity for acting with respect to the authoritarian regime in power. The examples of social, political and economic groups at the bottom of each cell are merely illustrative since, as I noted above, the mix of those supporting or opposing authoritarian rule varies considerably from one case to another and over time with a single case.

IV.1 — In one of his most apposite passages, Machiavelli argues rather counter-intuitively that *defensive* or *conservative* actors may be more dangerous to regime persistence than *acquisitive* or *aggressive* ones for «in most cases [...] disturbances are caused by those who possess for the fear of losing generates in them the same desires that those who desire to acquire possess [...] Furthermore, those who possess more can with greater force and speed effect changes. And what is more serious, their unchecked and ambitious behavior kindles the desire for possession in the minds of those who do not possess.» (*Discourses*, I, 5, pp. 187-188.)

Actors oriented toward acquiring resources, positions and benefices they do not presently have are easier do deal with. Their chosen goals are less certain and, perhaps, less tangible (honor, freedom and future property instead of security, command and present property). Their available resources are less substantial and, perhaps, less concentrated. Their disturbances are less likely to become contagious. Most important, defensively motivated actions against regime persistence can be more difficult to predict and recognize than acquisitive ones since they may represent rapid reversals of position and or since they may come disguised as supportive in intent.

98

IV.2 — Machiavelli also warns authoritarian rulers-*cum*-princes that they can rarely rule by themselves, but must rule through or with others. They should, therefore, be more wary of those in or near power than those subjected to it or far removed from it. As with the *defensive* actors, *protagonists* and *supporters* typically have more opportunity and resources to act. The distribution of offices and favors to those in power or supportive of it tends to create new and further obligations; gratitude for benefits received is quickly forgotten or discounted in favor of expanded expectations (*Prince*, X, p. 112)[24]. «All conspiracies have been formed by those closest to the prince» — because those farther removed are too weak indidually and too numerous collectively to organize a successful challenge. *Subjects* and *antagonists*, he suggested: «When they are tired of a prince, they turn to cursing him and wait for others who have greater power than they possess to avenge them.» Although Machiavelli might marvel at the disruptive power and dedicated effort of small groups of intense antagonists in modern, interdependent, ideologically mobilized and media conscious polities, he probably would conclude, as he did in the early 1500s, that such quixotic attempts deserved to be praised for their intentions, but not for their prudence or intelligence.

IV.3 — Just as modern princes can rarely rule alone, modern conspirators can rarely activate their calculus of dissent without allies. Heroic, individualistic action, say tyrannicide by lone assassin or small band, may still suffice against highly personalistic dictators (although replacement by family or friend without regime change is the usual outcome), but the removal of established, bureaucratized and impersonal, authoritarian rulers invariably involves coalitional behavior, frequently over a protracted period of time. It may ber possible to locate after the event, even to predict before its occurrence, which category of actor will attempt to build a dissenting coalition. However, the success of the effort will depend on its choice of allies which will, in turn, vary according to whether the strategy chosen aims at seizure, overthrow, transfer to surrender of power and whether the motivational incentives of success, failure, decay or delegitimation are sufficiently and appropriately diustributed across the conspiratorial alliance. The fact that different types of actors are likely to prefer different strategies and possess different motives for regime transformation may prevent the demise of even the most unsuccessful, decadent and delegitimated of authoritarian regimes for some time. This may especially be the case if, to the inevitable difficulties of putting together a heterogeneous coalition of dissent, one adds the deliberate tactics of the regime itself at differential repressions and selective concession intended to *divide et impera* its opponents in general and the possible efforts of its *agents provocateurs* aimed at discrediting specific groups and actions.

IV.4. — One specific institutional actor occupies a unique position within the generic categories I have identified, simply because under normal circumstances, it alone possesses sufficient resources which, if applied concertedly, could countermand, if not suppress outright, all threats to regime persistence. Machiavelli observes that because of the existence of a sizable standing army, in the Roman Empire [25], «it was then necessary to satisfy the soldiers more than the common people [since] the soldiers could do more than the common people» and no regime change was likely to occur without their connivance or tolerance. Since then the situation had altered, he thought, and it had become more imperative to satisfy the common people, «since [they] can do more than the soldiers» (*Prince*, XIX, p. 145). No doubt, the perpetuation of this imbalance of forces and the implications of this for republican governance lay behind Machiavelli's firm advocacy of a popular militia. In the more recent period, however, modern armies with rare exceptions are permanently standing, more-or-less professionally organized, hierarchically directed and usually superior in their capacity for exercising violence than the common people or aroused elites. Soldiers (or, more explicitly, their officers) have to be satisfied or be rendered prudentially fearful not only before potential opponents, but also before other actual supporters — if any given authoritarian regime is to survive.

99

If this is the case, if the armed forces have not become so decadent, venal, fragmented and or infiltrated that they can plausibly be defeated in a violent confrontation, then any strategy for peacefully exiting from authoritarian rule must include a military component if it is to be successful. Put in other terms, the armed forces, or some significant part of them, must become «members» of the dissenting alliance, if not by commission then by omission.

The safest strategy is to appeal to the military and attempt to convince them that, as the *conservative protagonists* they usually are, they can best defend their corporate interests by supporting or, at the best, remaining neutral during a transfer or surrender of power. To act otherwise in the fact of impending regime demise would be to risk becoming so internally politicized, so ethically compromised or so functionally denatured as to risk losing their effective monopoly over organized violence and, ultimately, to be displaced or disbanded in the aftermath of a violent overthrow of the regime.

Much more risky — in the likelihood either that it will lead to a change in regime or to eventual democratic rule — is the strategy of appealing to dissident factions, interservice rivals or frustrated cliques of officers with blocked promotions to act as *aggressive protagonists* and to seize power in anticipation:

> For when the nobles see that they cannot resist the populace, they begin to support one among them and make him prince in order to be able, under his shadow, to satisfy their appetites. [*Prince*, IX, p. 108.]

Such an alliance of *conservative supporters* and *aggressive protagonists* is most likely simply to perpetuate authoritarian rule, although with a different basis of support. Particularly interesting are those situations where preemptive coups of this sort induce those who have seized power to consolidate their position by forging a populist alliance with previous subjects and even antagonists within their ranks.

More promising but much less frequent are seizures of power from within an authoritarian regime by an isolated group of its own protagonists (usually a military clique). If they are momentarily successful, their vulnerability may induce a spontaneous overthrow of power through the massive mobilization of previous subjects and repressed antagonists — a spoiling of power into the streets, so-to-speak — in which not merely the regime is transformed but the state structure itself may be threatened.

---

[1] One is tempted to regard all this as a confirmation of the malicious accusation (of unknown authorship) that social scientists only manage to explain something to their collective satisfaction once it has already disappeared or changed into something else. Marx asserted that societies only pose those problems to themselves which they stand some chance of resolving. Social scientists, *par contre*, only seem to answer satisfactorily those questions which no longer exist.

[2] See the essays in David Collier (ed.), *The New Authoritarianism in Latin America*, Princeton, Princeton University Press, 1979, by Fernando Henrique Cardoso, Albert Hirschman and Guillermo O'Donnell, all members of the Academic Advisory Committee of the Woodrow Wilson Center.

[3] Guillermo O'Donnell and Philippe C. Schmitter, with the assistance of Abraham F. Lowenthal and Fernando Henrique Cardoso, «Prospects for democracy: transition from authoritarian rule — A proposal for a series of discussions at the Wilson Center», Washington, D. C., April 1979.

[4] While in part the product of convenience and personal inclination, this division of labor is based on an important theoretical assumption — that the demise of established authoritarian rule and the emergence of viable democracy are two different occurrences. Fritz Stern may have been the first to defend this premise openly:

> The implicit thesis of the book [is that] the disintegration of the Weimar Republic and the rise of Nazism were two distinct if obviously overlapping historical processes. By 1932, the collapse of Weimar had become inevitable; Hitler's triumph had not. [T. Eschenburg *et al.*, *The Path to Dictatorship 1918-1933*, Garden City, N. Y., Anchor Books, 1966, p. xvii.]

Inverting the direction of regime transformation, we would assert that, beyond some point, the collapse or displacement of a given authoritarian regime becomes unavoidable, but the prospect of a democratic outcome has not therefore become inevitable.

[5] All the direct citations from Machiavelli are taken from a new translation and the page references are to Peter Bondanella and Mark Musa (eds. and transl.), *The Portable Machiavelli*, New York, Penguin Books, 1979.

[6] Machiavelli, however, provides me with an excuse for so proceeding:

> A prudent man should always enter those paths taken by great men and imitate those who have been most excellent, so that if one's own skill does not match theirs, at least it will have the smell of it. [*Prince*, VI, p. 92.]

[7] This should not be read so as to exclude the possibility of an unintended, «accidental», regime change in which actors thinking they are mere «purifying» or «recasting» a given regime make demands and pursue policies which irrevocably undermine the regime's viability. While this would seem to be a rare occurrence, any realistic theory of regime transformation should incorporate the possibility that crucial actors may be unaware of what is at stake.

[8] Machiavelli, although he relied heavily on illustrations from the past (and a few from his pre-

sent) to support his assertions, did not use them as the basis for deriving them. He was also skeptical about the quality of this «data base»:

> I believe we do not know the complete truth about antiquity; most often the facts that would discredit those times are hidden and other matters which bestow glory upon them are reported magnificently and most thoroughly. [*Discourses*, II, intro., p. 28F.]

Modern authoritarian regimes possess greater means to hide «discrediting» events and amplify «magnificent» ones, but their efforts are at least partially cancelled out by a much greater variety of sources for data. Nevertheless, the sullen persistence of most authoritarian regimes contrasts with the noisy travails of almost any democracy.

[9] The threat of violence must be sufficiently credible and salient, not only to those in power to command their concern, but also to those out of power so that the rulers cannot «keep the populace occupied with festivals and spectacles» (*Prince*, XXI, p. 153).

[10] Juan Linz and Alfred Stepan (eds.), *The Breakdown of Democratic Regimes*, Baltimore and London, Johns Hopkins University Press, 1978, pp. 3-124.

[11] Dankwart Rustow, «Transitions to democracy: toward a dynamic model», in *Comparative Politics*, II, 3 (April 1970), pp. 337-364.

[12] Please excuse the sexism, but it stems from my feeble attempt to imitate Machiavelli's style.

[13] Machiavelli puts it more poetically later in the *Discourses:*

> We are endowed by Nature with the power and wish to desire everything and by Fortune with the ability to obtain little of what we desire. The result is an unending discontent in the minds of men and a weariness with what they possess: this makes men curse the present, praise the past and hope in the future, event though they do this with no reasonable motive. [*Discourses*, II, intro., p. 290.]

101

[14] But *not bene*, elsewhere, Machiavelli states that «men desire novelty to such an extent that those who are doing well wish for change as much as tose who are doing badly» (*Discourses*, III, 11, p. 392). Presumably these fickle-minded actors have never tried, or been denied, the opportunity to learn established ways of acting.

[15] For a discussion of sultanistic and caudillistic rule, see J. Linz, «Totalitarian and authoritarian regimes», in *Handbook of Political Science*, vol. III (Reading, Mass.: Addison-Wesley, 1975), pp. 259-264.

[16] Machiavelli lived «in a universe hushed in moral stillness», to use Sheldon Wolin's expressive phrase. Machiavelli, himself, said of his times: «It looks as if the world were become effeminate [i. e., fickle — P. C. S.] and as if Heaven were powerless.»

[17] For an analysis of Latin American military and civilian, competitive and non-competitive regimes which demonstrates empirically their «unexceptional» performance in meeting key economic and social goals, see my «Military intervention, political competitiveness and public policy in Latin America: 1950-1967» as excerpted in A. F. Lowenthal (ed.), *Armies and Politics in Latin America*, New York & London, Holmes and Meier, 1976, pp. 113-164.

[18] Actually the label «decay» is not very appropriate. What I had in mind is a situation in which a regime (or its leaders) come to be regarded by key supporters and opponents as lacking *Virtù:* the capacity to assess changing situations, to recognize the unintended consequences of one's acts and to modify one's potential response accordingly. A growing rigity in behavior, a sclerotic incapacity to learn, a tendency to maximize short-run returns without regard for their eventual impact — all these are the properties of a decadent or decayed regime in the sense I wish to use it here.

[19] «There are two reasons why we cannot change ourselves: first, because we cannot oppose the ways in which nature inclines us; second, because once a man [and especially an agency — P. C. S.] has truly prospered by means of one method of procedure it is impossible to convince him that he can benefit by acting otherwise.» (*Discourses*, III, 9, p. 383.)

[20] While it seems to be the presupposition of numerous analysts that the present period has none of the «moral stillness» that so plagued Machiavelli's time, and that «non-democratic» forms of governance are *eo ipso* incapable of legitimating themselves in such a democratic age — in contrast

to the interwar period —, this has never to my knowledge been empirically demonstrated. The fact, however, that so many authoritarian rulers (in Latin America, if not in Southern Europe) promise an eventual return to democratic practices could be taken as indirect evidence for the existence and strength of such values.

21 In his discussion of the «goodness» of German society and, hence, its appropriateness for republican rule, Machiavelli stressed that «[the Germans] do not have many dealings with their neighbors [...] [hence] have had no opportunity to acquire the custom of France, Spain or Italy — nations which taken together represent the corruption of the world»; and that they «do not allow any of their citizens to be or to live in the style of a gentleman; indeed, they maintain among themselves a complete equality». (*Discourses,* III, 6, p. 326).

22 Setting aside for the moment the probable existence of a large, intermediary coalition of indifferents and *attentistes* who merely wish to be free from politics and will conform to whatever regime emerges provided it leaves them more-or-less alone.

23 Machiavelli, himself an exile, called attention to «how dangerous it is to believe those who have been driven from their native city...» (*Discourses,* III, 30, p. 348). Perhaps fortunately, exiles rarely have played a significant role in authoritarian regime transformation, but they have occasionally been a factor complicating the politics of successor regimes.

24 «Many are led to conspire as a result of too many favors rather than too many injuries.» (*Discourses,* III, 6, p. 361.)

25 «Where in other principalities one has only to contend with the ambition of the nobles and the arrogance of the people, the Roman emperors had a third problem: they had to endure the cruelty and the avarice of soldiers.» (*Prince,* XIX, p. 140.)

[6]

Transitions to Democracy

Juan J. Linz

RECENT SUCCESSFUL TRANSI-
TIONS to democracy in Europe,
Latin America, and Asia have led
scholars to expand their inquiry into
political regime transitions, the ingredients of successful transitions, and
the prospects for democratization in
still undemocratic countries. The
hope and desire for further democratization have inspired some to use the
knowledge acquired for the purpose of
political engineering, so as to carry forward the democratic banner. Until recently, what was known about regime
change was based largely on the research of historians on the transformations leading to the emergence of
the modern democracies as well as the
crises and breakdown of democracies
in Europe between the two wars.[1]
Now there is a growing body of scholarship on the crises of nondemocratic
regimes and the transitions to democracy, or to use the title of the important work of Guillermo O'Donnell and
Philippe C. Schmitter, to "uncertain
democracies."[2]

Defining the Focus

There are many types of regime
change, but this article will address
just those leading to political democracy. Even with this specific focus,

there are a variety of categories to be
explored. There are as many types of
democratic regimes as there are democratic governments in societies of
varying levels of economic and social
development, to say nothing of quite
different degrees of realization of the
ideals of political democracy. There is,
however, or can be, considerable
agreement on the characteristics defining a democratic political system.[3]
Moreover, this essay will focus strictly
on the establishment and consolidation of democratic regimes emerging
in a transition *from authoritarian regimes.* This excludes from the analysis
the slow emergence of democratic political institutions in Western Europe
and some of the fragments of European societies overseas, beginning in
the 18th century, that constitute the
small group of continuous and stable
democracies that have not experienced any breakdown of their political
institutions once installed.

Much can be learned from the complex and long process of development
of democratic institutions from absolute states to constitutional monarchies and the more or less continuous
process of increasing democratization.
It would be a mistake, however, to
think that any society today could follow the path that led to democracy in
the United Kingdom, Sweden, the
United States, or Switzerland. Contemporary societies must telescope
such a long historical process into a
few critical years, and the social, economic, cultural, ideological, and inter-

Juan J. Linz is Sterling Professor of Political
and Social Science at Yale University. He is
coeditor with Larry Diamond and Seymour
Martin Lipset of *Democracy in Developing
Countries,* (Boulder, Colo.: Lynne Rienner
Publishers, 1988 and 1989).

Juan J. Linz

national context is too different to extrapolate from their experience to contemporary societies.

This study also does not concern itself with those few societies that still or until recently were subject to the traditional rule of kings, sultans, or shaykhs, that in the Weberian terms would be feudal or patrimonial systems. For purposes of clarity, it is prudent also to disregard the transfer of democratic institutions to former colonies and attempts to consolidate them, particularly in the case of the African states.

The focus of this article is nondemocratic and nontraditional regimes and the political, institutional characteristics related to their demise, the probability of transitions to democracy, and the consolidation of competitive regimes. It is important to distinguish at the outset between those societies that already have enjoyed some significant period of democratic rule that was displaced by a nondemocratic one, such as Germany, Austria, Italy, Spain, Czechoslovakia, and a number of Latin American countries, and those societies in which the nondemocratic regime succeeded traditional or colonial rule without having been preceded by democracy. The first case involves a process of redemocratization, of which restoration of the previous democratic regime would be a particular case.[4] In the second case, where democracy is being created for the first time, there will be no experience of the functioning of democratic institutions or a collective memory of the past difficulties of those institutions leading to their crisis and breakdown. To a large extent, this analysis focuses on the first case, redemocratization, because the number of successful transitions from authoritarian rule to democracy in the last half century, leaving aside the former col-

onies, have been cases of redemocratization.

It is essential to emphasize that the crisis and breakdown of nondemocratic regimes is a process that should be kept analytically separate from that of transitions to political democracy. The collapse of an authoritarian regime may or may not create the conditions for the successful establishment of political democracy. Not infrequently, the crises of a particular authoritarian government or regime lead to its substitution by another such regime, and many countries have seen successive military coups d'état, sometimes of different ideological orientation, and, in other cases, the collapse of such a regime has led to revolutionary authoritarian alternatives. The instability of the nondemocratic regime, therefore, should not lead necessarily to the establishment of democracy, unless some other factors intervene.

Totalitarianism vs. Authoritarianism

Social scientists have formulated important distinctions between totalitarian, and authoritarian regimes, to which one could add "sultanistic" regimes.[5] Space limitations do not allow an attempt to define those ideal types that seem to be relevant to the processes of regime change, the likelihood of crisis and breakdowns, the form the transition takes, and the outcome of those processes. If a strict definition of totalitarianism is used, it would apply to the rule of Hitler, Stalin, and other Communist regimes, but not all of them, probably not even to Mussolini's Italy. Such regimes were not overthrown internally and did not lead directly to a transition to democracy. As the history of the Soviet Union shows, however, those re-

Transitions to Democracy

gimes have changed over time to a type of rule that might be called post-totalitarian authoritarianism.

There is no agreement about when and how that process took place in the Soviet Union and in different Communist countries, but it seems an important antecedent to the present processes of transition. In some Communist states, such as Poland, the pre-Communist social pluralism asserted itself early, and the Communist authoritarian regime correspondingly granted rather early an independent political role to the Church and facilitated the emergence of Solidarity. Until the advent of the important changes that took place in the Soviet Union with Mikhail Gorbachev, the weak legitimacy of Communist rule in Eastern Europe was reflected in ideological crisis, in tentative efforts of liberalization, including the Prague Spring, in economic reforms in Hungary, but not in the process of regime crisis and transition that would lead possibly to democracy. The increasing cost of repression without Soviet assistance and the growing feeling by the opposition and average citizens that change was possible forced the rulers to initiate or accept political change. In the case of Hungary, this has taken a form not too dissimilar from the *reforma pactada–ruptura pactada* in Spain, while in East Germany and Czechoslovakia the pressures from the opposition and popular protest have led to some form of power sharing, even before free elections. Only in Romania, where the totalitarian features of the regime were combined with the sultanistic characteristics of the rule of Nicolae Ceauşescu (which some likened to the rule of the Somozas in Nicaragua), was any reform or negotiated transition impossible. This led to a popular revolutionary explosion, and ultimately to Ceauşescu's death. Any

comparative study of those transitions, however, should not forget the legacy of totalitarianism, which is particularly important in the two Greek Orthodox Communist countries, Bulgaria and Romania, and their inefficient socialist economies.

Sultanistic Regimes

Among the nondemocratic regimes, a few are based on personal rule with loyalty to the ruler derived not from tradition, ideology, personal mission, or charismatic qualities, but from a mixture of fear and rewards to collaborators.[6] The ruler exercises power without restraint, at his own discretion, and above all, is unencumbered by rules or by any commitment to an ideology or value system. The binding norms and relations of bureaucratic administration are being subverted constantly by the personal and arbitrary decisions of the ruler, which the ruler does not feel constrained to justify in ideological terms.

The staff of such rulers is constituted not by an establishment with distinct career lines, recruited by more or less universal criteria, but largely by individuals chosen directly by the ruler. They often are people who would not enjoy any prestige or esteem in a society on their own account and whose power is derived exclusively from the ruler. Among them often are members of the ruler's family, friends, cronies, business associates, and individuals directly involved in the use of violence to sustain the regime.

In the extreme, the personalistic and particularistic use of power for essentially the private ends of the ruler and collaborators makes the country essentially a huge domain. Support is based not on a coincidence of interest between the preexisting private social

Juan J. Linz

groups and the ruler, but on the interests created, the rewards offered for loyalty, and the fear of vengeance. Although such rulers make few demands of active support from the population, everybody is threatened by their arbitrary exercise of power, diffuse fear prevails, and opponents or suspected opponents are punished arbitrarily and harshly, creating an atmosphere of terror.

The mode of demise of such rulers, the motivation and identity of their opponents, and the longer-term consequences of their replacement likely will differ from the more established and impersonal, predictable, bureaucratic authoritarian regimes. In these regimes, the ruler cannot rely on a broad basis of support from organizations, such as a single party, a disciplined professional army, organized interests, or a religious community, because this type of rule has destroyed and corrupted such social institutions.

The vacuum created by sultanistic rule makes organized opposition based on preexisting social structures difficult, and assures continuation of such regime systems until a popular rebellion or a conspiracy eliminates physically the ruler and supporters. Sultanistic rule leaves a vacuum in a society that makes the establishment and consolidation of democratic politics extremely difficult. Its overthrow is more likely to lead to another nondemocratic regime, sometimes with characteristics similar to the one overthrown, or to a revolutionary regime that attempts to create *ex novo* organized social forces, assuming power without allowing the development of competitive social and political forces and the relatively free competition of democratic politics. The breakdown and aftermath of the rule of Fulgencio Batista in Cuba, Anastasio Somoza in Nicaragua, Jean-Claude Duvalier in

Haiti, Mohamed Reza Pahlavi in Iran, and Nicolae Ceauşescu in Romania are examples.[7]

Stability and Instability of Authoritarian Regimes

In attempting to understand the sources of crisis and ultimate collapse of authoritarian regimes, it is useful to explore the ways in which those sources are unique or common to the collapse of other types of regimes, including democracies. Some sources will be common to quite different types of regimes, while others would be specific to authoritarian rule or to particular types of authoritarian regimes. Inadequate legitimacy and effectiveness are factors in the crisis and breakdown of many different types of political systems.[8]

The relative efficacy of authoritarian regimes is particularly important. Defined as the incapacity to satisfy the expectations of society, to solve pressing problems, whether internal or external, it is a basic source of crisis. Authoritarian regimes have a mixed efficacy, in that their performance on such matters is sometimes creditable. Such regimes cannot, however, translate that efficacy into political legitimacy in the way that democracies can.

A particularly difficult challenge confronting authoritarian regimes is the renewal of leadership and particularly succession. This is an acute problem in highly personalized regimes in which founders consider themselves indispensible, are unwilling to relinquish power while still living, and are fearful of naming any heir apparent. However, this instability should not be overemphasized, as some authoritarian regimes have found institutional mechanisms to avoid the personalization of power, as evident in the recent military regimes, including

Transitions to Democracy

those of Uruguay, Peru, and Brazil. It would be a mistake to think that all authoritarian regimes are vulnerable to succession crises.

The importance of what Max Weber deemed legitimacy in the stability of regimes has been the object of considerable dispute.[9] Clearly, it is impossible to ignore the role played by the popular and elitist belief in the right of those in power to rule by virtue of some undefined principle, and the concomitant belief of those exercising power in their right to do so. At a minimum, those beliefs imply that a particular form of political organization is the best possible in a given society and time. In many authoritarian regimes, this idea is generated by the conviction of significant segments of society that a democratic regime did not satisfy that minimum requirement. History demonstrates, however, that this conviction is likely to erode as time goes by. There can be little question that the democratic formula for legitimation of authority today is regarded as more desirable and valuable in most countries. The democratic alternative appears more legitimate than power not accountable to the society.

The absence or severe weakness of legitimation principles of contemporary authoritarian regimes has many sources. There is today no major Western capitalist country with an authoritarian political organization and ideology that stands as a legitimate example for authoritarian regimes elsewhere to follow. The defeat of fascism as a worldwide ideological movement in World War II and the abandonment by the Catholic Church of the conservative interpretation of corporatism has left authoritarian regimes the world over without an articulated ideological system of legitimation that could be appealing to those sectors of society

whose politics are based not on interests but on ideological conceptions of the best political order. Whereas in the 1930s a number of respectable and even outstanding intellectuals and literary figures were passingly attracted to fascism, none of the contemporary authoritarian regimes has held a comparable attractiveness.[10] Perhaps the only exception has been the Yugoslav experiment with self-management as an alternative to political democracy. Faced with a crisis and with viable democratic alternatives on the horizon, authoritarian regimes have found themselves severely constrained by their absence of legitimacy, in terms of their ability to activate commitments in support of the regime.

Any understanding of the stability or instability of authoritarian regimes requires attention to the circumstances of their birth, to the social and economic changes taking place under them, to the changes in the political and ideological climate between the moment of their installation and later stages, and to the changes in leadership composition in the course of their existence, rather than perceiving them as unchanging societies and regimes. In this context, the duration of the regime becomes an important factor and, perhaps in contrast with democracies, a factor accounting for their dispensibility and vulnerability. Such regimes find it much more difficult to incorporate and assimilate changes in their social, political, and ideological environments than do democracies, where the responsiveness of ruling parties or their replacement by alternate parties makes it far easier to respond to such changes.

Authoritarian rulers often are compelled to undertake a certain amount of liberalization in the hope of reducing opposition or even co-opting it. However, it is unlikely that such lib-

Juan J. Linz

eralization will satisfy expectations. The process of liberalization reduces in turn the incentives for participation in the institutions of the regime and gives increased room to test the limits of freedom and power, leading often to reversals of the process, in terms of repression that disappoints expectations and increases frustrations. In this way, liberalization may contribute to, rather than prevent or neutralize, the growth of opposition. On the other hand, the return to oppression is made without the limited popular support it may once have had, and without legitimacy it becomes increasingly costly.

The record of recent decades suggests that growing liberalization in no way assures the transition to political democracy. Under certain circumstances, it may contribute to that process. It also can lead to a crisis involving growing repression and perhaps ultimately a violent overthrow that will make democratization more difficult. Liberalization does not involve a process essential to the transition to democracy: a transfer of power *(Machtübergabe)*, the abdication of power, or the takeover of power *(Machtergreifung)* by some group willing to open the doors to democratic political processes, or ready to turn over power to those who would do so.[11]

Ten Paths to Democracy

Alfred Stepan has listed at least 10 alternative paths from nondemocratic regimes to political democracy.[12] Like all social science typologies, his list is merely an analytical simplification of a more complex reality, often involving a mixture of paths, some tried simultaneously and others tried sequentially.

The first three paths are of limited relevance in the present historical con-

text, but they were decisive for the redemocratization of a number of democracies that today are considered among the most stable, including the Federal Republic of Germany and Japan. The first of the types, internal restoration after external occupation, is the least problematic, because the democracies restored had not themselves experienced internal crisis and in one case, Denmark, even had continued operating under Nazi occupation. The continuous legitimacy of an exile government remained unquestioned internally except by small marginal minorities and by the foreign military occupying authority.

The second path is that of internal democratic reformulation after external liberation. Under quite different circumstances and, therefore, with quite different outcomes, this was the path pursued in France and Greece. In some respects, Italy after 1943 fits into this type.

The third and most interesting path is the one characterized as externally monitored installation. The purest case is that of Germany where the total debellicization of the German state gave to the Allied powers full control of political development. Thus, the Western allies created a working political democracy, and the Soviet Union created a sham multiparty system parallel to the Western one but in which the undisputed hegemony of the Communist Party was assured. It is useful to note that an externally controlled process of democratization was not incompatible with the creation of stable democratic institutions, did not contribute to their delegitimation, and might have influenced social and political development in ways that contributed to the future stability of the Federal Republic of Germany.

These first three paths in Stepan's list of alternatives are grouped to-

Transitions to Democracy

gether by virtue of their connection to international war and external intervention. A second group derives from the experience of those states where authoritarians initiate and control the process of democratization. The third group relates to those where forces of the opposition play the major role.

Stepan describes three types of transition in which authoritarian powers make the move toward democracy. He distinguishes between transformation led from within the authoritarian regime, transition initiated by the military as government, and extrication led by the military as an institution. The examples he discusses are those of recent transitions to democracy in southern Europe and in Latin America. Certainly, these three paths are the ones most relevant today for the transition to democracy in a large number of authoritarian regimes.

The four additional types of transition are determined by the different roles of the opposition. In two such types, the opposition forces play the major role, whether society as a whole expels the authoritarian regime or through a pact of political parties in the opposition with or without consociational elements.[13] In the remaining two types, violent revolt or revolutionary war are involved.

Stepan rightly emphasizes that the paths pursued are a result of the constellation of social and political forces in the different societies, the nature of the authoritarian regime, and to some extent the international context in which the transition takes place. He points out that to follow one or the other path leads to different types of democracies, processes of socioeconomic change, and probabilities of stability of the resulting regimes.

Robert Fishman, in his essay on south European transitions, has refined Stepan's analysis by distinguish-

ing regime-led transitions with the passivity or even hostility of state institutions, such as the armed forces, from those led by the structures of the state, such as the armed forces against the regime, and finally those where the state disintegrates and a segment of the armed forces overthrows the regime. An example of the first case would be Spain, where part of the political class of the regime of Francisco Franco took the initiative of the transition. The second case would be that of Greece, where the armed forces supporting the return of Konstantinos Karamanlis against the colonels ended their rule. The third would be the movement of the captains that overthrew Marcelo Caetano in Portugal, leading to a profound restructuring of the state and revolutionary changes.

The emphasis here is on understanding the types of regime transition embodied in the middle set of three paths in Stepan's framework—namely, regime-led transitions. As he describes it, this path highlights the role of the authoritarian leadership in initiating the process. It also requires the cooperation of the democratic opposition to be successful, as demonstrated by the transition in Spain.

One of the most interesting questions about the process of transition relates to deciding who shall govern in the interim between the decision to liquidate an authoritarian regime and the moment in which a government can be formed that would be based on a free democratic election. This question is far from academic and involves basic options of considerable importance for the transition process itself, the nature of the emerging democratic system, and its future stability.[14]

There are two alternatives. The democratic opposition naturally will argue that the authoritarian regime lacks the legitimacy to continue gov-

Juan J. Linz

erning, calling for the installation of a wholly "democratic" provisional government. The counterargument is that newly self-defined parties also lack democratic legitimacy until their support by the electorate has been established. The question being debated is not one of democratic legitimacy; rather, it is one of who shall control many political resources in the period of transition and if the democratic opposition shall have the opportunity to attempt important transformations in the society before elections.

Neither option guarantees in all cases a successful transition to democracy, and overt conflict on this question might well set back the process of transition. As much depends on the level of trust in the fairness of those participating in the institutionalization of democracy as on the relative balance of power among the parties. The continuity of power in the legal successors of the authoritarian regime is likely to neutralize the fears of the defenders of the status quo, and particularly of the military institution. Such continuity also can contribute to moderate the demands and activities of those desiring radical social change and thereby reduce the fears in the crucial transition period. This solution, however, is available only when the state apparatus of the previous regime has not disintegrated, when those assuming power are not made directly responsible for the worst features of the old regime, and, therefore, when the latter has a capacity to negotiate with the opposition some ground rules for the transition and to give some evidence of their good faith.

The alternative of the transfer of power to the opposition before elections results from the opposite situation: the disintegration of the state apparatus, particularly the division within the armed forces, the creation

of the power vacuum that allows rapid mobilization of the masses and successful spontaneous actions by them, and the weakness or absence of a leadership emerging out of the old regime as ready to hold onto power as to open the door to decision making by a free election. Although a government of committed democrats, the power of a provisional government is closer to that of a dictatorship in the classical meaning of the term than to a caretaker government preparing elections. In fact, some elements in such a provisional government might be tempted to expand their power beyond a certain base, to establish conditions for participation in the electoral process of political parties, and set up guidelines for future development of the constitution.

One of the great challenges of the period between authoritarian rule and the first government based on free elections is the setting up of basic rules of the future political process, meaning both the characteristics of the representative institutions to be elected and the electoral law.

Reforma or *Ruptura:* A False Dilemma

The two Spanish words that became part of the political language during the transition to democracy in Spain have been and are presented as two alternative paths to democracy. Both have their apologists and critics and much of the political debate turns around them in countries where the stabilization of an authoritarian regime has failed or such a regime nears a state of crisis.

Transitions from authoritarianism to democracy tend to be initiated when leaders in the authoritarian regime start considering the possibility of a reform leading to some form of polit-

Transitions to Democracy

ical democracy. The opposition to an authoritarian regime favors in principle a *ruptura*, a break with the existing institutional arrangements, a change not controlled and even without any participation by those who, to one or another extent, had a share in the previous regime. Carried by moral indignation, they would like to see those who have had a share of power deprived of all opportunity to participate in the process, if not formally of political rights and access to public office. These positions in principle are irreconcilable and unless the partisans of the *ruptura* gain the support of a significant segment of the armed forces, or are able to mobilize the people for a violent overthrow of the regime, it seems unlikely that those in power would acquiesce freely to abdicate and make room for the partisans of ·he *ruptura*. The strategy of a clean break is viable only in a revolutionary or potentially revolutionary situation.

Under certain circumstances, a transformation led by those in power without the participation of the opposition might be possible, as in the case of the transition to democracy in Turkey in 1947. There also are cases of successful *ruptura*, as demonstrated by the example of Portugal in 1974. These should not obscure the fact, however, that in most authoritarian regimes, neither of those strategies really is available to those in power or those in the opposition.

Paradoxically, the transition is sometimes made possible by the simultaneous formulation of both positions as postures, for bargaining purposes rather than as final stands. In fact, if both positions have comparable power resources, although of different natures, or both are relatively weak because of the apathy of large segments of the population, transition will be possible only through a complex process that involves both reform and *ruptura*.[15]

There is not room to describe the multiple moves of the various players in the complex political game embodied in transitions, the doubts of the opposition leaders about accepting the offers of the reformers, the ensuing tensions between the persistent advocates of *ruptura* and those ready to test the will of the reformers, the show of force of the different actors to convince the negotiators to find solutions to the many specific complex issues, the working out of agreements on an electoral law, conditions for the campaign, and the counting of ballots, etc.[16] The point is that each of those decisions can create crises that would seem to threaten the whole process. In some cases, it is the leadership of the reformers within the regime that takes the initiative rather than being pressured by events and the dynamics of a volatile situation.[17] In others, it takes the right steps too late and in a half-hearted way, thereby frustrating the possibility of agreement.

Many of the proposals of the reformers will fall short of real democratization, and should the attempt fail, the whole process might be delayed or even aborted by the radicalization of the frustrated opposition, and the angry response of some would-be reformers. This was, in part, the fate of Caetano in Portugal and a possibility had Arias Navarro continued as head of government in Spain.

It is useful to note that the commitment to free and fair elections accelerates the process of transition and legitimizes temporarily the existing government for the moderate opposition, deflates the mobilization for the overthrow of the government, and forces the leaders of the opposition to assume responsible positions and to postpone demands for substantive pol-

Juan J. Linz

icy changes that it now can hope to achieve after the elections.

To successfully navigate these dangerous waters requires political actors with a considerable degree of rationality, a capacity to see through the bluff and threats of others, the maintenance of public order and of the monopoly of organized violence by the government, and probably increasing contacts and trust between the most important and responsible leaders. Undoubtedly, the international situation, by giving support to the process and discouraging on the one side revolutionary hopes and on the other the maintenance of the status quo, can contribute positively or negatively to this complex process.[18]

There can be little doubt that the model of negotiation and compromise among the forces of *reforma* and *ruptura* described above will not succeed equally well in all societies, even if supported by the leadership of the reformist wing of the government and the moderates of the opposition. Although the process of democratization is fundamentally a political process, it would be foolish to ignore the constraints and confining conditions imposed by the socioeconomic structure of different societies. What was possible in Spain and more slowly might be in Brazil, certainly will be infinitely more difficult in Bolivia or Guatemala.

One aspect that cannot be discussed here at length is the role of organized interests, such as trade unions, financial groups, employer's associations, and peasant leagues, in this period. It should not be forgotten that the climate of increased freedom is likely to encourage the mushrooming of such organizations, the expressions of pent-up demands, the corresponding disruption of the productive process and of the normal functioning of public

services, the fears of the owning classes, and even acts of personal revenge. One of the consequences can be the lowering of production and an increase of wages and prices, provoking an inflationary spiral.

The analysis of the different paths leading from authoritarianism to democracy, most particularly the transition by transaction (the *reforma pactada–ruptura pactada* model), tends to focus attention on elite settlements, the roles of the leaders of the regime and the opposition, the "bunker," the democrats, and the revolutionaries, and inevitably reduces the role of the people.

It should never be forgotten that in transitions, average men and women, students, and workers are demonstrating in the streets, taking risks in organizing illegal groups, distributing propaganda, and in a few cases, such as in Romania and Nicaragua, assaulting the seats of power. These people and their actions play an important and even decisive role. This is true even in those transitions initiated by the regime or the state that without the pressure from below would not be justified or supported. However, a leaderless and disorganized people filling the squares and demanding a change of regime may be unable to negotiate a transfer or sharing of power, or processes to achieve such a goal, and may be pushed to intransigent positions, and, thus, their efforts will end if not in revolutions, then in repression. Therefore, the limited social pluralism, the semi- or pseudo-freedom of many authoritarian regimes, or a prolonged period of crisis of the regime sometimes has made possible the emergence of structured opposition of the type necessary to play a role in the transition, and, if committed to democracy, bring it about.

Transitions to Democracy

Redemocratization and Regime Type

At first sight, it would seem as if the choice between authoritarianism and political democracy were a simple matter of agreeing that in the future power should go to those enjoying popular support as measured in free and fair elections. However, matters are not that simple, because democracies differ considerably in the way in which power is allocated through the process of elections. It should not be forgotten that democratic government is also constitutional government, that is, rule within certain institutional arrangements agreed upon by the participants for more than one situation, not to be changed easily and every day. Constitution-making and debates about alternative constitutional provisions were the center of political science and the political debate in the nineteenth century and even in the first decades of the twentieth, but with the behavioral revolution and the increased emphasis on socioeconomic factors and policy alternatives, that interest largely has been lost. The current typologies of democracy pay little attention to institutional factors and constitutional provisions are left to the debates of professors in the law schools and to the lawyers. Politicians in practice cannot ignore those issues either.

Does it make any difference for the success of the transition to democracy that the new regime be presidential or parliamentary, unitary or federal, unicameral or bicameral? The literature offers few answers to these questions, although they should be at the core of interest of students of transitions. The choice between parliamentarism, presidentialism, and a semipresidential regime has important implications for

the transition to democracy and its consolidation.[19] Although a thorough study of the empirical evidence has not been undertaken, the historical record suggests that a presidential democracy, such as that of the United States and many Latin American constitutions, creates particular difficulties in the process of redemocratization. A presidential system increases the threat that the transition to democracy, with its uncertainties about who and in what way someone should rule, represents for those who might be defeated. Presidentialism is more likely than parliamentarism to create a zero-sum situation, by giving to an individual leader considerable power for a fixed period of time. A presidential system limits the expectations to influence the political process of those who might be in the minority. Presidentialism even limits the influence after the election of the different parties in a coalition formed to elect a particular candidate, unless they turn to oppositional tactics that can contribute to the creation of a crisis situation. Presidentialism is likely to foster a process of polarization in a divided society and often requires a coalition of the moderates with those taking more extreme positions.

Parliamentarism can avoid some of these rigidities of presidentialism. The first free election does not necessarily give a single leader a dominant position for a four-year (or more) period, although in practice, the desire for governmental stability will lead to provisions like the German constructive no-confidence vote and the chancellor-type of government. Combined with proportional representation, the different parties can maintain their identity, agree on some issues, and disagree on others. The more extreme positions can be isolated or incorpo-

Juan J. Linz

rated into the process in an ad hoc manner. The moderates closer to the opposition and to the past authoritarian regime can cooperate in the institution-building phase of the installation process, but also diverge on policy matters.

To be sure, parliamentarism can contribute to the instability of democratic government, making governing more difficult and inefficient. The point is that in the installation phase, a parliamentary form of democracy allows for a greater distribution of the costs and benefits of change and the threatening implications of some decision making.

It could be argued that an outstanding president in such a difficult transition phase could play a role similar to the political leaders in parliament and make decisions by complex bargaining. This assumes, however, the availability of a candidate of those characteristics to occupy the presidency.

The Military and Democratization

Social scientists speculate about whether there is a direct connection between different types of authoritarian regimes and the paths to democracy they navigate. Such speculation is short-lived, because the answer seems to be that there is not such a direct connection; politics is far too complex an undertaking. However, one feature of the process that does seem to shape outcomes significantly is the relative importance of bureaucratic-military forces in the outgoing authoritarian regimes.[20]

There is the possibility of democratization initiated by individual leaders of the military government rather than by the military as a corporate institution. This has been the case in

Brazil where the opening initiated by President Geisel and his chief ally General Golbery led to a process of liberalization, progressively greater autonomy of civil society, increasingly free elections for certain offices, and ultimately, because of growing public pressure, to the election by an electoral college of a civilian president. This slow process was not seen with favor by important sectors of the military.

This pattern contrasts with those cases in which the military as an institution wishes to extricate itself from power, such as the Greek Army after the Cyprus crisis or the Peruvian Army, in order to defend the autonomy of the institution and its capacity for national defense without being blamed for the role as governor.

A decision taken this way is something different from the acquiescence or toleration of the process of democratization by the armed forces as led by a civilian government. Although social scientists are prone to forget it, there is a fundamental difference between informal and formal power, between influence and formal authority.

Even in an authoritarian regime, civilians have closer ties with civil society, live in a less isolated and restricted world than officers, and engage in professional activities that bring them into contact with a more representative segment of the population. In the course of their careers, many civilians establish personal links with those who will be leaders of the opposition, something much less likely in the case of army officers. Those multiple links and associations become quite important in the process of negotiating the transition.

Apart from the position that the military occupies in the formal structures of power in an authoritarian regime,

Transitions to Democracy

its position toward democratization will be important. Unlike any other group in society, the military can enforce its will by moving tanks into the streets. Some cases of redemocratization were initiated by a sector of the armed forces, as in Portugal, or with the cooperation of the military, as in Venezuela. On the other hand, the military can veto such a process of reform by force. It is useful to remember the dictum of Machiavelli that it is not reasonable that those armed should obey those who are disarmed, and in most societies only the armed forces are armed effectively. It would be a great mistake to assume that military establishments necessarily are hostile to democratic and party politics, although their mentality makes them less sympathetic to or understanding of some of the vagaries of party politics and the lack of unity of purpose and discipline so often associated with democracy. One should not forget the other side of the story—the latent or overt antimilitary outlook of many democratic politicians, often as ill-informed and insensitive to the problems of the military world as the dislike of some officers of civilians. In a stable democracy, and to some extent in a stable authoritarian regime, these latent tensions and the differences in mentality are not politically relevant, but they become central in a period of political change.

The active involvement of the military in the democratization of certain societies poses dilemmas not unlike those posed by multinational, multiethnic societies, raising questions about whether the abstract, normative, pure model of democratic politics is realizable immediately in all societies. This dilemma suggests that more imperfect, limited, partly distorted democratic institutions might some-

times be viable when it is unviable in the short run to implement the full sovereignty of the people and their elected representatives. This raises the difficult and delicate question of how much deviation from the ideal model is possible without giving up the fundamental principle and the hope for further implementation of the ideal.

This problem is compounded by the fact that the military also is likely to have strong beliefs about the international position of the country derived from geopolitical considerations, beliefs limiting foreign policy options and indirectly some of the economic and social policy alternatives of whatever type of regime is in power. Although citizens might bemoan this fact, social scientists are forced to deal with its import regarding the democratization process and its relevance for a more limited realization of political democracy, which poses a basic question about whether democracy is worth compromise. It is prudent to recall that the process of democratization of today's stable and fully sovereign democracies in Europe was achieved by constant compromises and conflicts with royal authority and with the residual powers of aristocratic or notable second chambers.

It seems doubtful that formalized mechanisms or pacts and legal and constitutional provisions can or should be worked out in the transition phase to manage these problems of the military and democratization. Recent experience suggests that it would be more desirable informally to reach binding understandings and to develop certain acceptable limits and practices. However, this requires a certain honest commitment of the leadership to those compromises and a capacity to defend them to others.

Juan J. Linz

Here, as in so many places, the difficulty lies in the vacuum of leadership and of organizational density so often left as a heritage of the authoritarian regime.

The sudden and rapid political change in the Communist countries of Europe and in the Soviet Union has taken social scientists largely by surprise. Obviously, totalitarianism had been displaced by authoritarianism in Poland some years ago. Even the Soviet Union long could not be fitted into the ideal type of totalitarianism, although there was no consensus on precisely when this occurred or on how to conceptualize Soviet politics. Certainly many East European Communist states were posttotalitarian, having experienced periods and processes of liberalization, a decay of ideology, and crises of mass organizations. Even so, a transition to pluralist political democracy did not seem to be in the cards. It is too early to analyze the processes that have led to change, the different paths democratization has taken, and even less, the types of regimes currently emerging, particularly in the case of the Soviet Union. There are, however, similarities with the processes that have taken place elsewhere.

The changes initiated by Mikhail Gorbachev—*glasnost* and *perestroika*—are changes from above reinforced and accelerated from below, and going probably beyond their original intent. The withdrawal of the protective umbrella of the Soviet Union made visible the low legitimacy of the imposed postwar regimes in Eastern Europe. Soviet withdrawal made the cost of repression greater and greater as the opposition gained courage to manifest itself and as the cost of tolerance, in terms of the risk of Soviet intervention, became less. At the same time, the crisis of efficacy of the socialist

economies, including that of the Soviet Union, made it imperative to search for new solutions including political change.

Significantly, there seems to be no single model for transitions in Communist countries, but varying responses reflecting the different evolution of the regime in previous years. On one extreme, there is Romania, where Ceauşescu's regime, between sultanistic and totalitarian, left no way out except popular uprising and led to a provisional government whose plans are uncertain and might not lead to a democracy. On the other extreme, there is Poland, where limited pluralism had developed over the years and a well-organized opposition gained power in an election, although it still had to share it with the Communists. The latter case reminds one of the dyarchy of the democratic parties and the military in the Brazilian transition. Hungary seems to follow more the Spanish model, with the regime initiating change and retaining power until after the elections. The Czech and the German solutions, with a limited power sharing between the regime and the opposition, have not had a parallel in Western transitions in the period before elections. All of the transitions in the Communist countries, however, are fundamentally different from those in the West, because of the presence of their ineffective centrally planned socialist economies. Those countries must proceed with economic reforms and with transitions to some form of market economy, while simultaneously undertaking political reform or as a result of political change. There are indications that changes in the economic system present greater difficulties than political change, partly because as yet there is no model of transition from a command to market economy and some form of capitalism.

Transitions to Democracy

The crisis of state socialism and centralized planned economies has brought a recognition of the need to introduce market mechanisms even with private ownership of the means of production. This is something that many would call capitalism, but in practice will remain a mixed economy, with implications not limited to Communist countries. It must not be forgotten that in many democracies close to a majority of the population favored, in principle, a socialized economy, although not necessarily in practice, and that the democratic governments that did not socialize the means of production were indirectly protecting or legitimizing capitalist economic systems, sometimes more effectively than any authoritarian regime could. In doing so, in some cases they were bearing a cost for not realizing the will of the people. Now, with the greater legitimacy of the market economy, that strain is likely to be reduced. Indirectly, the crisis of full socialism, not the welfare state principle or mixed economies, contributes to the stability and legitimacy of democracies unwilling or unable to move toward socialism.

Democratic Consolidation

When has the transition finished? How does one know when consolidation is complete? The transition generally starts with a particularly dramatic event, although the power of such an event often is manifest as a culmination of a series of events. Such an event often results in the public and official commitment of the authoritarian rulers to hold free elections and to revert power to the electorate by a specified deadline. Such an event also may result in a coup or revolutionary insurrection compelling the rulers to abandon power and flee or be killed,

leaving a new group of self-described caretaker power holders who appear committed to hold elections or to transfer power to the electorate. The essential ingredient of a transition is the expectation on the part of both the people and the power holders that political authority soon will be derived only from the free decision of an electorate.

At what point does this transition period, strictly defined, end? Again, the choice is to some extent arbitrary, but there is little doubt that the successful realization of a free election, the convening of a new parliament on whose confidence the government depends, or the installation of a new president in office, would be such a moment.

This is the strictest definition of the transition period, but it seems reasonable to say that, until the elected representatives create or restore a basic constitutional framework, defining the functions of the different organs of the government, a democracy cannot be considered fully established. From this perspective, the constitution-making phase still is part of the transition, because it cannot be considered finished until there is a legal framework defining the procedures by which those who exercise executive power are to be designated as well as the respective powers of the legislature, the executive, and in some cases the judiciary to decide the constitutional conflicts.

The period of the writing of the constitution is integral to the period of transition, because the degree of consensus achieved will be an important element of stability or instability in the future politics of the society. The approval of the constitution satisfying only the majority and totally rejected by the opposition hardly can be seen to have created a framework for day-

Juan J. Linz

to-day politics and stable governance. In this sense, Spanish democracy started on a stronger basis with the 1978 constitution than the republic in 1931 with a highly contested one.

The emergence of a significant number of new democratic regimes raises the question of their degree of consolidation or stability. There are those who feel that the completion of the transfer of power to an elected president or government is insufficient proof of consolidation, particularly in view of the staggering task that some of those governments confront. There is no scholarly consensus on how to define consolidation. Opinions range from a minimalist conception to one which would include the development of all the institutions of the new democracy: all the patterns of interest mediation, the consolidation of a party system, the successful transfer of power to an opposition party, etc. In this author's view, a maximalist definition of consolidation will make it almost impossible to say that any democratic regime is ever fully consolidated and would lead to future crises being explained as a result of unsuccessful consolidation rather than the incapacity of the regime to confront them.

This author will argue for a minimalist conception of a consolidated democratic regime, that is, one in which none of the major political actors, parties, or organized interests, forces, or institutions consider that there is any alternative to democratic processes to gain power, and that no political institution or group has a claim to veto the action of democratically elected decision makers. This does not mean that there are no minorities ready to challenge and question the legitimacy of the democratic process by nondemocratic means. It means, however, that the major actors

do not turn to them and that they remain politically isolated. To put it simply, democracy must be seen as the "only game in town."

The fact that certain institutions, such as the armed forces in some Latin American countries and perhaps the Communist Party and *nomenklatura*, might attempt to exercise a veto or share power independently of the result of elections would lead one to consider those democracies as not fully consolidated. For example, Chilean democracy, until the 1980 constitution is reformed—given the powers that would be retained by the military—probably would not be considered fully consolidated. The response of all the political forces to the attempted coup in Spain of February 23, 1981, which brought together to condemn it the leaders of the trade unions and employers' federation, of the Communist Party and of the conservative *Alianza Popular*, with the capacity of the then-Spanish government to bring its leaders to trial is an example of consolidation. The fact that some democracies might be inefficient in solving major problems should not be confused with the lack of consolidation, although it might qualify them as democracies risking instability. Undoubtedly, some democracies might be both not fully consolidated and embattled by the problems they face and, therefore, at risk of breakdown.

Democratic consolidation often faces a keen challenge in dealing justly with the previous nondemocratic rulers, particularly as regards civil rights violations. Steps to mete out some form of justice are especially important when those abuses were unjustifiable even in terms of the legislation of the predecessor regime, such as disappearances and torture.[21] There is also the difficult question of purging partners of the old regime from the armed

Transitions to Democracy

forces, the bureaucracy, and even from private activities like large business enterprises. New democratic regimes have followed quite different policies in this area and it is not clear how they contribute to consolidation or whether they create more problems than they solve.

Some argue that democracy is not fully consolidated until power has alternated from one set of elected leaders to another, until the party or parties that ruled as a result of the first democratic election have been substituted without major strains or crisis by the opposition. This seems an unnecessarily strict interpretation, given that party hegemony often is durable, and that such alternation is the exception rather than the rule in democracies. Carried to the logical extreme, this argument would lead to the absurdity that Japanese democracy has not been consolidated.

It is difficult to separate the process of the establishment of democratic political institutions, the defense of those institutions, and their legitimation from the processes of social, cultural, and economic change that result from their implementation. The less such fundamental changes become associated with the regime transition, the easier it will be for certain segments of society to sustain the deprivations of such change, meaning that democratic institutions will not suffer at a later date their anger or attempt to set aside the political system. To put it somewhat epigrammatically, there are changes within a democratic regime but not changes by the democratic regime. One of the bases of legitimacy of democracy is its relative openness to changing substantive policy content. On the other hand, people might not identify with democratic institutions and processes in the abstract, and newly democratic regimes

only can gain allegiance of the people by bringing about real social changes affecting their daily lives.

It is far from easy to decide which of these alternatives can contribute more to the consolidation and ultimate stabilization of a new democratic regime. On the one hand, in societies with serious social and economic problems in which large segments of the population have felt very deprived, a democracy that does not implement relatively soon major social change will be challenged by the discontent of the masses, producing perhaps violent conflicts that lead either to revolutionary violence or, more likely, to counterrevolutionary responses. On the other hand, a process of fundamental change might not be essential in more developed societies where the socioeconomic order enjoys a certain legitimacy and moderate policies would not alienate the people from the new regime, where the gains in personal and political freedom can be valued positively in and of themselves.

Every regime, and the new democracies are no exception, is likely to face crisis and the threat of breakdown, but it is important to keep analytically distinct the problem of regime consolidation and that of its performance, problems, and crisis. There is an obvious temptation to attribute any serious difficulties after the establishment of a new democracy to the legacies of the past, the persistent attachments of some sectors of the society to the authoritarian regime, identification of certain interests with that regime, and to start a debate about the extent to which different decisions during the transition period would have prevented the emergence of those problems at a later date. The temptation to argue that the transition has not been completed, the consolidation has not been achieved, or even

Juan J. Linz

started, is great given its political convenience for new leaders facing hard
times. By providing a sort of political
alibi, they would be exonerated from
responsibility for their own failures,
for creating problems that did not
need to arise, and would allow them a
kind of scapegoating rather than compel a sober analysis of their own actions. Although it will be difficult to
decide to what extent the crisis of
posttransition   democratic   regimes
should be attributed to the legacies of
the past, to decisions made during the
transition, or to the performance of the
new regime and its leadership, the
making of this distinction is not only
intellectually important but also politically significant.

The reality and the perceptions of
transition, sometimes even the mis-
perceptions of what happened or what
could have happened, become part of
the reality of politics in that constant
process of creating stable democratic
regimes. Newly democratic societies
should not forget their authoritarian
pasts and the difficulties of the transition and consolidation. Still, their
leaders must be responsible enough to
conduct a political debate recognizing
that a stable political future is the responsibility and possibility of citizens
enjoying their rights and responsibilities under a democratic government.

It should be highlighted that a democratic government that has considerable support and political legitimacy is
able to survive considerable inefficacy
in the economic system and in social
performance. Historical evidence and
reliable data from a number of surveys
indicate that the level of legitimacy of
democracy has not been affected by
the level of dissatisfaction with the
performance of the government. The
world depression that presumably destroyed the democracy in Weimar and
Austria created more unemployment

in Norway and in the Netherlands and
in fact consolidated the Norwegian democracy. The Dutch government was
one of the most long-lasting after the
depression. The degree of institutional legitimacy was more decisive
than the economic crisis.[22]

This is not to say that in the medium or long run inefficacy of the government is not likely to hurt democracy. In the short run, however, a
democracy that does not promise that
it will solve all problems, and instead
admits to problems that cannot be
solved immediately, convinces people
of that fact, solves the problem of human rights and liberty, and maintains
a degree of honesty, has a certain leeway. In addition, an interesting mechanism of democracy is that those who
are in power can lose the first election.
Given changes in administrations,
there normally remains eight years to
survive such crises, if there are legitimate democratic institutions. Therefore, the greatest challenge in many
countries is how and under what circumstances legitimate democratic institutions can be created.

Conclusion

In the 1970s, it made sense to say that
the safest bet about a country's regime
in a succeeding generation was that it
would be somewhat different, but not
radically different from what it was
then. By 1990, one could say that the
safest bet in many countries would be
that it will be a democracy. However,
this optimistic picture is blurred by the
fact that quite a few of the emerging
democracies are far from consolidated,
that their authority is constrained in
many cases by the considerable political autonomy of the armed forces, and
that they face the impossibility of satisfying a desire of justice after years of
violation of basic human rights. In ad-

Transitions to Democracy

dition, in both Latin America and probably in Eastern Europe, the democracies face near unsolvable economic and, consequently, social problems.

Nevertheless, the experience of European countries during the depression, including some of the new democracies in Europe, and that of the recent economic crisis suggest that legitimate democratic regimes can survive considerable failures in efficacy, at least for some time. No one can exclude, however, that a continuous failure of performance, particularly after change of the ruling parties, might not lead to blame being placed on the system and serve as a basis for the appeal of an antidemocratic disloyal opposition, the temptation for military intervention, or in some cases continuous unrest and disillusionment. The absence of alternative ideologies to democracy makes their overthrow less likely, but does not exclude loss of support, violence, and recurrent crisis. Ahead, there might be some embattled or difficult democracies, of which today the Philippines is an example.

Much depends on the leadership of the new democracies. Their leaders must convince people of the value of newly gained freedoms, of security from arbitrary power, and of the possibility to change governments peacefully, and at the same time they must convey to them the impossibility of overcoming in the short-run the dismal legacy of some nondemocratic rulers and the accumulated mistakes that have led to or contributed to their present crisis. Leaders have the hard and ungrateful task of telling people that with democracy the economy will not improve immediately; that without economic change, social change and justice will not be achieved, although some improvements might be possi-

ble; and that, ultimately, the success of a society is not the result of activities of the state or even the best possible government, but of the efforts of the whole society. Democratic leaders must avoid the danger of overselling democracy. Their task is to lower expectations, while maintaining the hope that a society freed from arbitrary power might develop autonomously in freedom.

This article summarizes a longer research paper entitled "Transition to Democracy: A Comparative Perspective," prepared for the International Political Science Association Roundtable in Tokyo, March 29–April 1, 1982.

Notes

1. Juan J. Linz and Alfred Stepan, eds., *The Breakdown of Democratic Regimes* vols. 1, 2, and 3 (Baltimore: Johns Hopkins, 1978). The three volumes include references to the relevent literature.

2. The classic reference is: Guillermo O'Donnell, Philippe Schmitter, and Laurence Whitehead, eds., *Transitions from Authoritarian Rule, Prospects for Democracy* (Baltimore: Johns Hopkins, 1986).

   See also Scott Mainwaring, *Transitions to Democracy and Democratic Consolidation: Theoretical and Comparative Issues*, Kellogg Institute for International Studies, Working Paper 130 (Notre Dame, Ind.: University of Notre Dame, 1989).

   Guiseppe Di Palma and Laurence Whitehead, eds., *The Central American Impasse* (London: Croom Helm, 1986).

   James Malloy and Mitchell Seligson, eds., *Authoritarians and Democrats: Regime Transition in Latin America* (Pittsburgh: University of Pittsburgh Press, 1987).

   John H. Herz, ed., *From Dictatorship to Democracy, Coping with the Legacies of Authoritarianism and Totalitarianism* (Westport, Conn.: Greenwood, 1982). See relevant chapters on Germany, Italy, Austria, France, Japan, Spain, Portugal, and Greece.

   Guiseppe Di Palma, *To Craft Democracies. Reflections on Democratic Transitions and Beyond* (Forthcoming).

3. It is not possible to enter the debate on

Juan J. Linz

the definition of democracy, nor refer to the contributions of Kelson, Schumpeter, Lipset, Dahl, nor the classic work of Sartori and their critics. My own approach can be found in Linz and Stepan, eds., *The Breakdown of Democratic Regimes*, vol. 1, in my contribution to the *Handbook of Political Science*, vid infra., and in my introduction to Robert Michels' *La Sociologia del partito politico* (Bologna: Il Mulino), 1960.

4. Robert A. Kann, *The Problem of Restoration: A Study of Comparative Political History* (Berkeley/Los Angeles: University of California, 1968). Kann presents interesting ideas on the problem.

5. For the typology of nondemocratic political systems and my own conceptualization, refer to Juan Linz, "Totalitarian and Authoritarian Regimes," Nelson Polsby and Fred Greenstein, eds., *Handbook of Political Science*, vol. III (Reading, Mass.: Addison Wesley Press, 1975), pp. 175–482.

6. The term "sultanistic" is derived from the use by Max Weber in Guenther Roth and Claus Wittich, *Economy and Society* vol. I, (New York: Bodminster, 1968), pp. 231–232. For my analysis of contemporary sultanistic regimes, see *Ibid*, pp. 259–263.

7. Fazdeh Farhi, "State Disintegration and Urban-based Revolutionary Crisis: A Comparative Analysis of Iran and Nicaragua," *Comparative Political Studies* 21, pp. 231–256.

8. On legitimacy, efficacy, and effectiveness in the crises and breakdown of regimes, see Linz, *The Breakdown of Democratic Regimes*, vol. I, pp. 16–24, and the references therein.

See also "Legitimacy of Democracy and the Socioeconomic System," Mattei Dogan, ed., *Comparing Pluralist Democracies* (Boulder, Colo.: Westview, 1988), pp. 65–113; and "Il rapporto tra legittimazione ed efficacie di governor," *Mondo Operaio* 3, 1989, pp. 111–116.

For an argument against the use of the concept of legitimacy, see Adam Przeworski, "Some Problems in the Study of the Transition to Democracy," O'Donnell, Schmitter, and Whitehead, eds., *Transitions from Authoritarianism*, vol. III, pp. 47–84.

9. See Linz, *The Breakdown of Democratic Regimes*, vol. I, pp. 16–24.

10. Alistair Hamilton, *The Appeal of Fascism* (New York: Avon, 1971).

11. Rainer M. Lapsius, "*Machtübernahme und Machtübergabe: Zur Strategie des Regimewechsels*," Hans Albert et al, eds., *Sozialtheorie und Soziale Praxis: Homage to Eduard Baumgarten*, Mannheimer Sozialwissenschaftliche Studien, vol. 3, (Meisenheim: Anton Hain, 1971), pp. 158–173.

12. Alfred Stepan, "Paths toward Redemocratization: Theoretical and Comparative Considerations," O'Donnell, Schmitter, and Whitehead, *Transitions from Authoritarian Rule*, part III, pp. 64–84.

13. The "consociational" element is the type of conflict management described by Lijphart and many others contributing to the theory of consociational democracy. For discussion of Colombia and Venezuela, see Kenneth McRae, ed., *Consociational Democracy, Political Accommodation in Segmented Societies* (Toronto: McClelland and Steward, 1974). See Alexander Wilde, "Conversations among Gentlemen: Oligarchic Democracy in Colombia," Linz and Stepan, eds., *The Breakdown of Democratic Regimes*, vol. II, pp. 28–81. See Daniel J. Levine, "Venezuela Since 1958: The Consolidation of Democratic Politics," *Ibid*, pp. 82–109.

See also Jonathan Hartlyn, *The Politics of Coalition Rule in Colombia* (Cambridge: Cambridge University Press), 1988.

In both Colombia and Venezuela, the pacts between parties and leaders helped to erode the basis of the authoritarian regime, depriving it of its rationale that a bloody conflict would ensue in its absence. The fact that parties and leaders, institutions and interests, whose bitter conflicts had contributed to the breakdown of democracy, could agree in the opposition to authoritarianism and in a process of redemocratization and consolidation of democracies was decisive in the ousting of the authoritarian rulers. The consociational mechanisms have been central to the process of consolidation of Austrian democracy, during the period of the *consenso* in Spain after the first election in 1977 until 1979, and the process of constitution-making has much in common with conso-

Transitions to Democracy

ciational practices, as Carlos Huneeus and Richard Gunther have noted.

14. Robert M. Fishman, "Rethinking State and Regime: Southern Europe's Transition to Democracy," *World Politics,* forthcoming.

15. Juan J. Linz, "Il Fattore tempo nei mutamenti di regimi," *Teoria Politica* 1, 1986, pp. 3–48. See in particular pp. 16–23.

16. On the Spanish transition, see José Féliz Tezanos, Ramón Cotarelo, and Andrés de Blas, eds., *La transición democrática española* (Madrid: Editorial Sistema, 1989). In addition to the essays, it includes a detailed bibliography and a chronology of the transition. See José María Maravall and Julián Santamaría, "Political Change in Spain and the Prospect for Democracy," O'Donnell, Schmitter, and Whitehead, eds., *Transitions from Authoritarian Rule,* part I, pp. 71–108. See Paul Preston, *The Triumph of Democracy in Spain* (London: Methuen, 1984).

See Scott Mainwaring and Donald Share, "Transitions Through Transaction: Democratization in Brazil and Spain," Wayne Selcher, ed., *Political Liberalization in Brazil* (Boulder, Colo.: Westview, 1986), pp. 175–215.

See Donald Share, "Transitions to Democracy and Transition Through Transaction," *Comparative Political Studies* 19, January 1987, pp. 525–548.

17. Juan J. Linz, "Innovative Leadership in the Transition to Democracy and a New Democracy: The Case of Spain," a paper presented at the Conference on Innovative Leadership and International Politics, Leonard Davis Institute for International Relations, Hebrew University, Jerusalem, June 8–10, 1987.

18. This development is well stated in the First Thesis submitted to the Congress of the Partido Comunista de España (April 1978): "The radical political *ruptura* realized in one stroke, with the instoration of a provisional government as was advocated by the Communist Party and the *Junta Democrática,* was not possible due to various factors, among which one can stress the reformist orientation taken by the forces in the opposition and those that emerged out of the franquist regime itself,

as well as the international pressure, fundamentally European and American, fearful of the hegemony of the working class and the forces of the left. These factors contributed to the mass movement, in spite of its breath and importance, not having achieved the strength necessary to determine a radical break *ruptura.* That situation obliged the PCE to nuance its ruptural theses in the solution of the *ruptura pactada.* In fact, the process of change has taken place as such a *ruptura pactada,* although the pact would be purely tacit after the displacement by the mass struggle of the reactionary and inmobilist government of Arias Navarro."

19. See Juan J. Linz, "Democracy: Presidential or Parliamentary. Does it Make a Difference?," presented at a workshop at the Woodrow Wilson International Center for Scholars in 1984, from which short a short excerpt was published, Juan J. Linz, "Perils of Presidentialism," *Journal of Democracy* 1:1 (Winter 1990), pp. 51–69. The extended version is in Oscar Godoy, ed., *Hacia una democracia moderna, La opción parlamentaria* (Santiago, Chile: Ediciones Universidad Católica de Chile, 1990). At a conference at Georgetown University organized by Arturo Valenzuela and the author, papers on the problem were presented by scholars from different countries that will be published in the near future. See also Scott Mainwaring, "Presidentialism in Latin America," *Latin American Research Review,* pp. 157–179.

20. Alfred Stepan, *Rethinking Military Politics: Brazil and the Southern Cone* (Princeton, N.J.: Princeton University Press, 1988).

Felipe Agüero, "The Military in the Processes of Political Democratization in South America and Southern Europe: Outcomes and Initial Conditions," a paper presented at the Fifteenth International Congress of the Latin American Studies Association, 1989.

Alain Rouquie, "Demilitarization and the Institutionalization of Military-Dominated Politics in Latin America," in O'Donnell, Schmitter, and Whitehead, eds., *Transitions from Authoritarian Rule,* part III, pp. 108–136.

21. Juan J. Linz, "Political Regimes and Respect for Human Rights: Historical and

Juan J. Linz

Cross National Perspectives," Bernt Hagt-
vet, ed., Symposium on the Human Rights
at the Nobel Institute, 1988.

22. Juan J. Linz and Alfred Stepan, "Political
Crafting of Democratic Consolidation or Destruction: European and South American Comparisons," Robert A. Pastor, ed.,
*Democracy in the Americas: Stopping the Pen-
dulum* (New York: Holmes and Meier,
1984), pp. 41–61.

[7]

DEMOCRACY'S THIRD WAVE

Samuel P. Huntington

Samuel P. Huntington *is Eaton Professor of the Science of Government and director of the John M. Olin Institute for Strategic Studies at Harvard University. Material in his article is based upon the 1989 Julian J. Rothbaum Lectures at the Carl Albert Center of the University of Oklahoma, to be published as* The Third Wave: Democratization in the Late Twentieth Century *(University of Oklahoma Press, 1991), and is used here by permission of the Press.*

Between 1974 and 1990, at least 30 countries made transitions to democracy, just about doubling the number of democratic governments in the world. Were these democratizations part of a continuing and ever-expanding "global democratic revolution" that will reach virtually every country in the world? Or did they represent a limited expansion of democracy, involving for the most part its reintroduction into countries that had experienced it in the past?

The current era of democratic transitions constitutes the third wave of democratization in the history of the modern world. The first "long" wave of democratization began in the 1820s, with the widening of the suffrage to a large proportion of the male population in the United States, and continued for almost a century until 1926, bringing into being some 29 democracies. In 1922, however, the coming to power of Mussolini in Italy marked the beginning of a first "reverse wave" that by 1942 had reduced the number of democratic states in the world to 12. The triumph of the Allies in World War II initiated a second wave of democratization that reached its zenith in 1962 with 36 countries governed democratically, only to be followed by a second reverse wave (1960-1975) that brought the number of democracies back down to 30.

At what stage are we within the third wave? Early in a long wave, or at or near the end of a short one? And if the third wave comes to a halt, will it be followed by a significant third reverse wave eliminating many of democracy's gains in the 1970s and 1980s? Social science cannot provide reliable answers to these questions, nor can any social scientist. It may be possible, however, to identify some of the factors that will affect the future expansion or contraction of democracy in the world and to pose the questions that seem most relevant for the future of democratization.

One way to begin is to inquire whether the causes that gave rise to the third wave are likely to continue operating, to gain in strength, to weaken, or to be supplemented or replaced by new forces promoting democratization. Five major factors have contributed significantly to the occurrence and the timing of the third-wave transitions to democracy:

1) The deepening legitimacy problems of authoritarian regimes in a world where democratic values were widely accepted, the consequent dependence of these regimes on successful performance, and their inability to maintain "performance legitimacy" due to economic (and sometimes military) failure.

2) The unprecedented global economic growth of the 1960s, which raised living standards, increased education, and greatly expanded the urban middle class in many countries.

3) A striking shift in the doctrine and activities of the Catholic Church, manifested in the Second Vatican Council of 1963-65 and the transformation of national Catholic churches from defenders of the status quo to opponents of authoritarianism.

4) Changes in the policies of external actors, most notably the European Community, the United States, and the Soviet Union.

5) "Snowballing," or the demonstration effect of transitions earlier in the third wave in stimulating and providing models for subsequent efforts at democratization.

I will begin by addressing the latter three factors, returning to the first two later in this article.

Historically, there has been a strong correlation between Western Christianity and democracy. By the early 1970s, most of the Protestant countries in the world had already become democratic. The third wave of the 1970s and 1980s was overwhelmingly a Catholic wave. Beginning in Portugal and Spain, it swept through six South American and three Central American countries, moved on to the Philippines, doubled back to Mexico and Chile, and then burst through in the two Catholic countries of Eastern Europe, Poland and Hungary. Roughly three-quarters of the countries that transited to democracy between 1974 and 1989 were predominantly Catholic.

By 1990, however, the Catholic impetus to democratization had largely exhausted itself. Most Catholic countries had already democratized or, as in the case of Mexico, liberalized. The ability of Catholicism to promote further expansion of democracy (without expanding its own ranks) is limited to Paraguay, Cuba, and a few

Francophone African countries. By 1990, sub-Saharan Africa was the only region of the world where substantial numbers of Catholics and Protestants lived under authoritarian regimes in a large number of countries.

The Role of External Forces

During the third wave, the European Community (EC) played a key role in consolidating democracy in southern Europe. In Greece, Spain, and Portugal, the establishment of democracy was seen as necessary to secure the economic benefits of EC membership, while Community membership was in turn seen as a guarantee of the stability of democracy. In 1981, Greece became a full member of the Community, and five years later Spain and Portugal did as well.

In April 1987, Turkey applied for full EC membership. One incentive was the desire of Turkish leaders to reinforce modernizing and democratic tendencies in Turkey and to contain and isolate the forces in Turkey supporting Islamic fundamentalism. Within the Community, however, the prospect of Turkish membership met with little enthusiasm and even some hostility (mostly from Greece). In 1990, the liberation of Eastern Europe also raised the possibility of membership for Hungary, Czechoslovakia, and Poland. The Community thus faced two issues. First, should it give priority to broadening its membership or to "deepening" the existing Community by moving toward further economic and political union? Second, if it did decide to expand its membership, should priority go to European Free Trade Association members like Austria, Norway, and Sweden, to the East Europeans, or to Turkey? Presumably the Community can only absorb a limited number of countries in a given period of time. The answers to these questions will have significant implications for the stability of democracy in Turkey and in the East European countries.

The withdrawal of Soviet power made possible democratization in Eastern Europe. If the Soviet Union were to end or drastically curtail its support for Castro's regime, movement toward democracy might occur in Cuba. Apart from that, there seems little more the Soviet Union can do or is likely to do to promote democracy outside its borders. The key issue is what will happen within the Soviet Union itself. If Soviet control loosens, it seems likely that democracy could be reestablished in the Baltic states. Movements toward democracy also exist in other republics. Most important, of course, is Russia itself. The inauguration and consolidation of democracy in the Russian republic, if it occurs, would be the single most dramatic gain for democracy since the immediate post-World War II years. Democratic development in most of the Soviet republics, however, is greatly complicated by their ethnic heterogeneity

and the unwillingness of the dominant nationality to allow equal rights
to ethnic minorities. As Sir Ivor Jennings remarked years ago, "the
people cannot decide until somebody decides who are the people." It
may take years if not decades to resolve the latter issue in much of the
Soviet Union.

During the 1970s and 1980s the United States was a major promoter
of democratization. Whether the United States continues to play this role
depends on its will, its capability, and its attractiveness as a model to
other countries. Before the mid-1970s the promotion of democracy had
not always been a high priority of American foreign policy. It could
again subside in importance. The end of the Cold War and of the
ideological competition with the Soviet Union could remove one rationale
for propping up anti-communist dictators, but it could also reduce the
incentives for any substantial American involvement in the Third World.

American will to promote democracy may or may not be sustained.
American ability to do so, on the other hand, is limited. The trade and
budget deficits impose new limits on the resources that the United States
can use to influence events in foreign countries. More important, the
ability of the United States to promote democracy has in some measure
run its course. The countries in Latin America, the Caribbean, Europe,
and East Asia that were most susceptible to American influence have,
with a few exceptions, already become democratic. The one major
country where the United States can still exercise significant influence
on behalf of democratization is Mexico. The undemocratic countries in
Africa, the Middle East, and mainland Asia are less susceptible to
American influence.

Apart from Central America and the Caribbean, the major area of the
Third World where the United States has continued to have vitally
important interests is the Persian Gulf. The Gulf War and the dispatch
of 500,000 American troops to the region have stimulated demands for
movement toward democracy in Kuwait and Saudi Arabia and
delegitimized Saddam Hussein's regime in Iraq. A large American
military deployment in the Gulf, if sustained over time, would provide
an external impetus toward liberalization if not democratization, and a
large American military deployment probably could not be sustained over
time unless some movement toward democracy occurred.

The U.S. contribution to democratization in the 1980s involved more
than the conscious and direct exercise of American power and influence.
Democratic movements around the world have been inspired by and have
borrowed from the American example. What might happen, however, if
the American model ceases to embody strength and success, no longer
seems to be the winning model? At the end of the 1980s, many were
arguing that "American decline" was the true reality. If people around
the world come to see the United States as a fading power beset by

political stagnation, economic inefficiency, and social chaos, its perceived failures will inevitably be seen as the failures of democracy, and the worldwide appeal of democracy will diminish.

Snowballing

The impact of snowballing on democratization was clearly evident in 1990 in Bulgaria, Romania, Yugoslavia, Mongolia, Nepal, and Albania. It also affected movements toward liberalization in some Arab and African countries. In 1990, for instance, it was reported that the "upheaval in Eastern Europe" had "fueled demands for change in the Arab world" and prompted leaders in Egypt, Jordan, Tunisia, and Algeria to open up more political space for the expression of discontent.[1]

The East European example had its principal effect on the leaders of authoritarian regimes, not on the people they ruled. President Mobutu Sese Seko of Zaire, for instance reacted with shocked horror to televised pictures of the execution by firing squad of his friend, Romanian dictator Nicolae Ceauşescu. A few months later, commenting that "You know what's happening across the world," he announced that he would allow two parties besides his own to compete in elections in 1993. In Tanzania, Julius Nyerere observed that "If changes take place in Eastern Europe then other countries with one-party systems and which profess socialism will also be affected." His country, he added, could learn a "lesson or two" from Eastern Europe. In Nepal in April 1990, the government announced that King Birendra was lifting the ban on political parties as a result of "the international situation" and "the rising expectations of the people."[2]

If a country lacks favorable internal conditions, however, snowballing alone is unlikely to bring about democratization. The democratization of countries A and B is not a reason for democratization in country C, unless the conditions that favored it in the former also exist in the latter. Although the legitimacy of democratic government came to be accepted throughout the world in the 1980s, economic and social conditions favorable to democracy were not everywhere present. The "worldwide democratic revolution" may create an external environment conducive to democratization, but it cannot produce the conditions necessary for democratization within a particular country.

In Eastern Europe the major obstacle to democratization was Soviet control; once it was removed, the movement to democracy spread rapidly. There is no comparable external obstacle to democratization in the Middle East, Africa, and Asia. If rulers in these areas chose authoritarianism before December 1989, why can they not continue to choose it thereafter? The snowballing effect would be real only to the extent that it led them to believe in the desirability or necessity of democratization. The events of 1989 in Eastern Europe undoubtedly encouraged democratic opposition groups and frightened authoritarian leaders elsewhere. Yet given the previous weakness of the former and the long-term repression imposed by the latter, it seems doubtful that the East European example will actually produce significant progress toward democracy in most other authoritarian countries.

By 1990, many of the original causes of the third wave had become significantly weaker, even exhausted. Neither the White House, the Kremlin, the European Community, nor the Vatican was in a strong position to promote democracy in places where it did not already exist (primarily in Asia, Africa, and the Middle East). It remains possible, however, for new forces favoring democratization to emerge. After all, who in 1985 could have foreseen that Mikhail Gorbachev would facilitate democratization in Eastern Europe?

In the 1990s the International Monetary Fund (IMF) and the World Bank could conceivably become much more forceful than they have heretofore been in making political democratization as well as economic liberalization a precondition for economic assistance. France might become more active in promoting democracy among its former African colonies, where its influence remains substantial. The Orthodox churches could emerge as a powerful influence for democracy in southeastern Europe and the Soviet Union. A Chinese proponent of *glasnost* could come to power in Beijing, or a new Jeffersonian-style Nasser could spread a democratic version of Pan-Arabism in the Middle East. Japan could use its growing economic clout to encourage human rights and democracy in the poor countries to which it makes loans and grants. In 1990, none of these possibilities seemed very likely, but after the surprises of 1989 it would be rash to rule anything out.

A Third Reverse Wave?

By 1990 at least two third-wave democracies, Sudan and Nigeria, had reverted to authoritarian rule; the difficulties of consolidation could lead to further reversions in countries with unfavorable conditions for sustaining democracy. The first and second democratic waves, however, were followed not merely by some backsliding but by major reverse waves during which most regime changes throughout the world were from democracy to authoritarianism. If the third wave of democratization slows down or comes to a halt, what factors might produce a third reverse wave?

Among the factors contributing to transitions away from democracy during the first and second reverse waves were:

1) the weakness of democratic values among key elite groups and the general public;

2) severe economic setbacks, which intensified social conflict and enhanced the popularity of remedies that could be imposed only by authoritarian governments;

3) social and political polarization, often produced by leftist governments seeking the rapid introduction of major social and economic reforms;

4) the determination of conservative middle-class and upper-class groups to exclude populist and leftist movements and lower-class groups from political power;

5) the breakdown of law and order resulting from terrorism or insurgency;

6) intervention or conquest by a nondemocratic foreign power;

7) "reverse snowballing" triggered by the collapse or overthrow of democratic systems in other countries.

Transitions from democracy to authoritarianism, apart from those produced by foreign actors, have almost always been produced by those in power or close to power in the democratic system. With only one or two possible exceptions, democratic systems have not been ended by popular vote or popular revolt. In Germany and Italy in the first reverse wave, antidemocratic movements with considerable popular backing came to power and established fascist dictatorships. In Spain in the first reverse wave and in Lebanon in the second, democracy ended in civil war.

The overwhelming majority of transitions from democracy, however, took the form either of military coups that ousted democratically elected leaders, or executive coups in which democratically chosen chief executives effectively ended democracy by concentrating power in their own hands, usually by declaring a state of emergency or martial law. In the first reverse wave, military coups ended democratic systems in the new countries of Eastern Europe and in Greece, Portugal, Argentina, and Japan. In the second reverse wave, military coups occurred in Indonesia, Pakistan, Greece, Nigeria, Turkey, and many Latin American countries. Executive coups occurred in the second reverse wave in Korea, India, and the Philippines. In Uruguay, the civilian and military leadership cooperated to end democracy through a mixed executive-military coup.

In both the first and second reverse waves, democratic systems were replaced in many cases by historically new forms of authoritarian rule. Fascism was distinguished from earlier forms of authoritarianism by its mass base, ideology, party organization, and efforts to penetrate and control most of society. Bureaucratic authoritarianism differed from earlier forms of military rule in Latin America with respect to its institutional character, its presumption of indefinite duration, and its economic policies. Italy and Germany in the 1920s and 1930s and Brazil and Argentina in the 1960s and 1970s were the lead countries in introducing these new forms of nondemocratic rule and furnished the examples that antidemocratic groups in other countries sought to emulate. Both these new forms of authoritarianism were, in effect, responses to social and economic development: the expansion of social mobilization and political participation in Europe, and the exhaustion of the import-substitution phase of economic development in Latin America.

Although the causes and forms of the first two reverse waves cannot generate reliable predictions concerning the causes and forms of a possible third reverse wave, prior experiences do suggest some potential causes of a new reverse wave.

First, systemic failures of democratic regimes to operate effectively could undermine their legitimacy. In the late twentieth century, the major nondemocratic ideological sources of legitimacy, most notably Marxism-Leninism, were discredited. The general acceptance of democratic norms meant that democratic governments were even less dependent on performance legitimacy than they had been in the past. Yet sustained inability to provide welfare, prosperity equity, justice, domestic order, or external security could over time undermine the legitimacy even of democratic governments. As the memories of authoritarian failures fade, irritation with democratic failures is likely to increase. More specifically, a general international economic collapse on the 1929-30 model could undermine the legitimacy of democracy in many countries. Most democracies did survive the Great Depression of the 1930s; yet some succumbed, and presumably some would be likely to succumb in response to a comparable economic disaster in the future.

Second, a shift to authoritarianism by any democratic or democratizing great power could trigger reverse snowballing. The reinvigoration of authoritarianism in Russia or the Soviet Union would have unsettling effects on democratization in other Soviet republics, Bulgaria, Romania, Yugoslavia, and Mongolia; and possibly in Poland, Hungary, and Czechoslovakia as well. It could send the message to would-be despots elsewhere: "You too can go back into business." Similarly, the establishment of an authoritarian regime in India could have a significant demonstration effect on other Third World countries. Moreover, even if a major country does not revert to authoritarianism, a shift to dictatorship by several smaller newly democratic countries that lack many of the usual preconditions for democracy could have ramifying effects even on other countries where those preconditions are strong.

If a nondemocratic state greatly increased its power and began to expand beyond its borders, this too could stimulate authoritarian movements in other countries. This stimulus would be particularly strong if the expanding authoritarian state militarily defeated one or more democratic countries. In the past, all major powers that have developed economically have also tended to expand territorially. If China develops economically under authoritarian rule in the coming decades and expands its influence and control in East Asia, democratic regimes in the region will be significantly weakened.

Finally, as in the 1920s and the 1960s, various old and new forms of authoritarianism that seem appropriate to the needs of the times could emerge. Authoritarian nationalism could take hold in some Third World countries and also in Eastern Europe. Religious fundamentalism, which has been most dramatically prevalent in Iran, could come to power in other countries, especially in the Islamic world. Oligarchic authoritarianism could develop in both wealthy and poorer countries as a reaction to the leveling tendencies of democracy. Populist dictatorships could emerge in the future, as they have in the past, in response to democracy's protection of various forms of economic privilege, particularly in those countries where land tenancy is still an issue. Finally, communal dictatorships could be imposed in democracies with two or more distinct ethnic, racial, or religious groups, with one group trying to establish control over the entire society.

All of these forms of authoritarianism have existed in the past. It is not beyond the wit of humans to devise new ones in the future. One possibility might be a technocratic "electronic dictatorship," in which authoritarian rule is made possible and legitimated by the regime's ability to manipulate information, the media, and sophisticated means of communication. None of these old or new forms of authoritarianism is highly probable, but it is also hard to say that any one of them is totally impossible.

Obstacles to Democratization

Another approach to assessing democracy's prospects is to examine the obstacles to and opportunities for democratization where it has not yet taken hold. As of 1990, more than one hundred countries lacked democratic regimes. Most of these countries fell into four sometimes overlapping geocultural categories:

1) Home-grown Marxist-Leninist regimes, including the Soviet Union, where major liberalization occurred in the 1980s and democratic movements existed in many republics;

2) Sub-Saharan African countries, which, with a few exceptions, remained personal dictatorships, military regimes, one-party systems, or some combination of these three;

3) Islamic countries stretching from Morocco to Indonesia, which except for Turkey and perhaps Pakistan had nondemocratic regimes;

4) East Asian countries, from Burma through Southeast Asia to China and North Korea, which included communist systems, military regimes, personal dictatorships, and two semidemocracies (Thailand and Malaysia).

The obstacles to democratization in these groups of countries are political, cultural, and economic. One potentially significant political obstacle to future democratization is the virtual absence of experience with democracy in most countries that remained authoritarian in 1990. Twenty-three of 30 countries that democratized between 1974 and 1990 had had some history of democracy, while only a few countries that were nondemocratic in 1990 could claim such experience. These included a few third-wave backsliders (Sudan, Nigeria, Suriname, and possibly Pakistan), four second-wave backsliders that had not redemocratized in the third wave (Lebanon, Sri Lanka, Burma, Fiji), and three first-wave democratizers that had been prevented by Soviet occupation from redemocratizing at the end of World War II (Estonia, Latvia, and Lithuania). Virtually all the 90 or more other nondemocratic countries in 1990 lacked significant past experience with democratic rule. This obviously is not a decisive impediment to democratization—if it were, no countries would now be democratic—but it does make it more difficult.

Another obstacle to democratization is likely to disappear in a number of countries in the 1990s. Leaders who found authoritarian regimes or rule them for a long period tend to become particularly staunch opponents of democratization. Hence some form of leadership change within the authoritarian system usually precedes movement toward democracy. Human mortality is likely to ensure such changes in the 1990s in some authoritarian regimes. In 1990, the long-term rulers in China, Côte d'Ivoire, and Malawi were in their eighties; those in Burma, Indonesia, North Korea, Lesotho, and Vietnam were in their seventies; and the leaders of Cuba, Morocco, Singapore, Somalia, Syria, Tanzania, Zaire, and Zambia were sixty or older. The death or departure from office of these leaders would remove one obstacle to democratization in their countries, but would not make it inevitable.

Between 1974 and 1990, democratization occurred in personal dictatorships, military regimes, and one-party systems. Full-scale democratization has not yet occurred, however, in communist one-party states that were the products of domestic revolution. Liberalization has taken place in the Soviet Union, which may or may not lead to full-scale democratization in Russia. In Yugoslavia, movements toward democracy are underway in Slovenia and Croatia. The Yugoslav communist revolution, however, was largely a Serbian revolution, and the prospects for democracy in Serbia appear dubious. In Cambodia, an extraordinarily brutal revolutionary communist regime was replaced by a less brutal communist regime imposed by outside force. In 1990, Albania appeared to be opening up, but in China, Vietnam, Laos, Cuba, and Ethiopia, Marxist-Leninist regimes produced by home-grown revolutions seemed determined to remain in power. The revolutions in these countries had been nationalist as well as communist, and hence nationalism reinforced communism in a way that obviously was not true of Soviet-occupied Eastern Europe.

One serious impediment to democratization is the absence or weakness of real commitment to democratic values among political leaders in Asia, Africa, and the Middle East. When they are out of power, political leaders have good reason to advocate democracy. The test of their democratic commitment comes once they are in office. In Latin America, democratic regimes have generally been overthrown by military coups d'état. This has happened in Asia and the Middle East as well, but in these regions elected leaders themselves have also been responsible for ending democracy: Syngman Rhee and Park Chung Hee in Korea, Adnan Menderes in Turkey, Ferdinand Marcos in the Philippines, Lee Kwan Yew in Singapore, Indira Gandhi in India, and Sukarno in Indonesia. Having won power through the electoral system, these leaders then proceeded to undermine that system. They had little commitment to democratic values and practices.

Even when Asian, African, and Middle Eastern leaders have more or less abided by the rules of democracy, they often seemed to do so grudgingly. Many European, North American, and Latin American political leaders in the last half of the twentieth century were ardent and articulate advocates of democracy. Asian and African countries, in contrast, did not produce many heads of government who were also apostles of democracy. Who were the Asian, Arab, or African equivalents of Rómulo Betancourt, Alberto Llera Camargo, José Figueres, Eduardo Frei, Fernando Belaúnde Terry, Juan Bosch, José Napoleón Duarte, and Raúl Alfonsín? Jawaharlal Nehru and Corazon Aquino were, and there may have been others, but they were few in number. No Arab leader comes to mind, and it is hard to identify any Islamic leader who made a reputation as an advocate and supporter of democracy while in office. Why is this? This question inevitably leads to the issue of culture.

Culture

It has been argued that the world's great historic cultural traditions vary significantly in the extent to which their attitudes, values, beliefs, and related behavior patterns are conducive to the development of democracy. A profoundly antidemocratic culture would impede the spread of democratic norms in the society, deny legitimacy to democratic institutions, and thus greatly complicate if not prevent the emergence and effective functioning of those institutions. The cultural thesis comes in two forms. The more restrictive version states that only Western culture provides a suitable base for the development of democratic institutions and, consequently, that democracy is largely inappropriate for non-

Western societies. In the early years of the third wave, this argument was explicitly set forth by George Kennan. Democracy, he said, was a form of government "which evolved in the eighteenth and nineteenth centuries in northwestern Europe, primarily among those countries that border on the English Channel and the North Sea (but with a certain extension into Central Europe), and which was then carried into other parts of the world, including North America, where peoples from that northwestern European area appeared as original settlers, or as colonialists, and laid down the prevailing patterns of civil government." Hence democracy has "a relatively narrow base both in time and in space; and the evidence has yet to be produced that it is the natural form of rule for peoples outside those narrow perimeters." The achievements of Mao, Salazar, and Castro demonstrated, according to Kennan, that authoritarian regimes "have been able to introduce reforms and to improve the lot of masses of people, where more diffuse forms of political authority had failed."[3] Democracy, in short, is appropriate only for northwestern and perhaps central European countries and their settler-colony offshoots.

The Western-culture thesis has immediate implications for democratization in the Balkans and the Soviet Union. Historically these areas were part of the Czarist and Ottoman empires; their prevailing religions were Orthodoxy and Islam, not Western Christianity. These areas did not have the same experiences as Western Europe with feudalism, the Renaissance, the Reformation, the Enlightenment, the French Revolution, and liberalism. As William Wallace has suggested, the end of the Cold War and the disappearance of the Iron Curtain may have shifted the critical political dividing line eastward to the centuries-old boundary between Eastern and Western Christendom. Beginning in the north, this line runs south roughly along the borders dividing Finland and the Baltic republics from Russia; through Byelorussia and the Ukraine, separating western Catholic Ukraine from eastern Orthodox Ukraine; south and then west in Romania, cutting off Transylvania from the rest of the country; and then through Yugoslavia roughly along the line separating Slovenia and Croatia from the other republics.[4] This line may now separate those areas where democracy will take root from those where it will not.

A less restrictive version of the cultural obstacle argument holds that certain non-Western cultures are peculiarly hostile to democracy. The two cultures most often cited in this regard are Confucianism and Islam. Three questions are relevant to determining whether these cultures now pose serious obstacles to democratization. First, to what extent are traditional Confucian and Islamic values and beliefs hostile to democracy? Second, if they are, to what extent have these cultures in fact hampered progress toward democracy? Third, if they have significantly retarded democratic progress in the past, to what extent are they likely to continue to do so in the future?

Confucianism

Almost no scholarly disagreement exists regarding the proposition that traditional Confucianism was either undemocratic or antidemocratic. The only mitigating factor was the extent to which the examination system in the classic Chinese polity opened careers to the talented without regard to social background. Even if this were the case, however, a merit system of promotion does not make a democracy. No one would describe a modern army as democratic because officers are promoted on the basis of their abilities. Classic Chinese Confucianism and its derivatives in Korea, Vietnam, Singapore, Taiwan, and (in diluted fashion) Japan emphasized the group over the individual, authority over liberty, and responsibilities over rights. Confucian societies lacked a tradition of rights against the state; to the extent that individual rights did exist, they were created by the state. Harmony and cooperation were preferred over disagreement and competition. The maintenance of order and respect for hierarchy were central values. The conflict of ideas, groups, and parties was viewed as dangerous and illegitimate. Most important, Confucianism merged society and the state and provided no legitimacy for autonomous social institutions at the national level.

In practice Confucian or Confucian-influenced societies have been inhospitable to democracy. In East Asia only two countries, Japan and the Philippines, had sustained experience with democratic government prior to 1990. In both cases, democracy was the product of an American presence. The Philippines, moreover, is overwhelmingly a Catholic country. In Japan, Confucian values were reinterpreted and merged with autochthonous cultural traditions.

Mainland China has had no experience with democratic government, and democracy of the Western variety has been supported over the years only by relatively small groups of radical dissidents. "Mainstream" democratic critics have not broken with the key elements of the Confucian tradition.[5] The modernizers of China have been (in Lucian Pye's phrase) the "Confucian Leninists" of the Nationalist and Communist parties. In the late 1980s, when rapid economic growth in China produced a new series of demands for political reform and democracy on the part of students, intellectuals, and urban middle-class groups, the Communist leadership responded in two ways. First, it articulated a theory of "new authoritarianism," based on the experience of Taiwan, Singapore, and Korea, which claimed that a country at China's stage of economic development needed authoritarian rule to achieve balanced economic growth and contain the unsettling consequences of development. Second, the leadership violently suppressed the democratic movement in Beijing and elsewhere in June of 1989.

In China, economics reinforced culture in holding back democracy. In Singapore, Taiwan, and Korea, on the other hand, spectacular growth created the economic basis for democracy by the late 1980s. In these countries, economics clashed with culture in shaping political development. In 1990, Singapore was the only non-oil-exporting "high-income" country (as defined by the World Bank) that did not have a democratic political system, and Singapore's leader was an articulate exponent of Confucian values as opposed to those of Western democracy. In the 1980s, Premier Lee Kwan Yew made the teaching and promulgation of Confucian values a high priority for his city-state and took vigorous measures to limit and suppress dissent and to prevent media criticism of the government and its policies. Singapore was thus an authoritarian Confucian anomaly among the wealthy countries of the world. The interesting question is whether it will remain so now that Lee, who created the state, appears to be partially withdrawing from the political scene.

In the late 1980s, both Taiwan and Korea moved in a democratic direction. Historically, Taiwan had always been a peripheral part of China. It was occupied by the Japanese for 50 years, and its inhabitants rebelled in 1947 against the imposition of Chinese control. The Nationalist government arrived in 1949 humiliated by its defeat by the Communists, a defeat that made it impossible "for most Nationalist leaders to uphold the posture of arrogance associated with traditional Confucian notions of authority." Rapid economic and social development further weakened the influence of traditional Confucianism. The emergence of a substantial entrepreneurial class, composed largely of native Taiwanese, created (in very un-Confucian fashion) a source of power and wealth independent of the mainlander-dominated state. This produced in Taiwan a "fundamental change in Chinese political culture, which has not occurred in China itself or in Korea or Vietnam—and never really existed in Japan."[6] Taiwan's spectacular economic development thus overwhelmed a relatively weak Confucian legacy, and in the late 1980s Chiang Ching-kuo and Lee Teng-hui responded to the pressures produced by economic and social change and gradually moved to open up politics in their society.

In Korea, the classical culture included elements of mobility and egalitarianism along with Confucian components uncongenial to democracy, including a tradition of authoritarianism and strongman rule. As one Korean scholar put it, "people did not think of themselves as citizens with rights to exercise and responsibilities to perform, but they tended to look up to the top for direction and for favors in order to survive."[7] In the late 1980s, urbanization, education, the development of a substantial middle class, and the impressive spread of Christianity all weakened Confucianism as an obstacle to democracy in Korea. Yet it remained unclear whether the struggle between the old culture and the new prosperity had been definitively resolved in favor of the latter.

The East Asian Model

The interaction of economic progress and Asian culture appears to have generated a distinctly East Asian variety of democratic institutions. As of 1990, no East Asian country except the Philippines (which is, in many respects, more Latin American than East Asian in culture) had experienced a turnover from a popularly elected government of one party to a popularly elected government of a different party. The prototype was Japan, unquestionably a democracy, but one in which the ruling party has never been voted out of power. The Japanese model of dominant-party democracy, as Pye has pointed out, has spread elsewhere in East Asia. In 1990, two of the three opposition parties in Korea merged with the government party to form a political bloc that would effectively exclude the remaining opposition party, led by Kim Dae Jung and based on the Cholla region, from ever gaining power. In the late 1980s, democratic development in Taiwan seemed to be moving toward an electoral system in which the Kuomintang (KMT) was likely to remain the dominant party, with the Democratic Progressive Party confined to a permanent opposition role. In Malaysia, the coalition of the three leading parties from the Malay, Chinese, and Indian communities (first in the Alliance Party and then in the National Front) has controlled power in unbroken fashion against all competitors from the 1950s through the 1980s. In the mid-1980s, Lee Kwan Yew's deputy and successor Goh Chok Tong endorsed a similar type of party system for Singapore:

> I think a stable system is one where there is a mainstream political party representing a broad range of the population. Then you can have a few other parties on the periphery, very serious-minded parties. They are unable to have wider views but they nevertheless represent sectional interests. And the mainstream is returned all the time. I think that's good. And I would not apologize if we ended up in that situation in Singapore.[8]

A primary criterion for democracy is equitable and open competition for votes between political parties without government harassment or restriction of opposition groups. Japan has clearly met this test for decades with its freedoms of speech, press, and assembly, and reasonably equitable conditions of electoral competition. In the other Asian dominant-party systems, the playing field has been tilted in favor of the government for many years. By the late 1980s, however, conditions were becoming more equal in some countries. In Korea, the government party was unable to win control of the legislature in 1989, and this failure presumably was a major factor in its subsequent merger with two of its opponents. In Taiwan, restrictions on the opposition were gradually lifted. It is thus conceivable that other East Asian countries could join Japan in providing a level playing field for a game that the government party always wins. In 1990 the East Asian dominant-party systems thus spanned a continuum between democracy and authoritarianism, with Japan at one extreme, Indonesia at the other, and Korea, Taiwan, Malaysia, and Singapore (more or less in that order) in between.

Such a system may meet the formal requisites of democracy, but it differs significantly from the democratic systems prevalent in the West, where it is assumed not only that political parties and coalitions will freely and equally compete for power but also that they are likely to *alternate* in power. By contrast, the East Asian dominant-party systems seem to involve competition for power but not alternation in power, and participation in elections for all, but participation in office only for those in the "mainstream" party. This type of political system offers democracy without turnover. It represents an adaptation of Western democratic practices to serve not Western values of competition and change, but Asian values of consensus and stability.

Western democratic systems are less dependent on performance legitimacy than authoritarian systems because failure is blamed on the incumbents instead of the system, and the ouster and replacement of the incumbents help to renew the system. The East Asian societies that have adopted or appear to be adopting the dominant-party model had unequalled records of economic success from the 1960s to the 1980s. What happens, however, if and when their 8-percent growth rates plummet; unemployment, inflation, and other forms of economic distress escalate; or social and economic conflicts intensify? In a Western democracy the response would be to turn the incumbents out. In a dominant-party democracy, however, that would represent a revolutionary change. If the structure of political competition does not allow that to happen, unhappiness with the government could well lead to demonstrations, protests, riots, and efforts to mobilize popular support to overthrow the government. The government then would be tempted to respond by suppressing dissent and imposing authoritarian controls. The key question, then, is to what extent the East Asian dominant-party system presupposes uninterrupted and substantial economic growth. Can this system survive prolonged economic downturn or stagnation?

Islam

"Confucian democracy" is clearly a contradiction in terms. It is unclear whether "Islamic democracy" also is. Egalitarianism and voluntarism are central themes in Islam. The "high culture form of Islam," Ernest Gellner has argued, is "endowed with a number of features—unitarianism, a rule-ethic, individualism, scripturalism, puritanism, an egalitarian aversion to mediation and hierarchy, a fairly small load of magic—that are congruent, presumably, with requirements of modernity or modernization." They are also generally congruent with the requirements of democracy. Islam, however, also rejects any distinction between the religious community and the political community. Hence there is no equipoise between Caesar and God, and political participation is linked to religious affiliation. Fundamentalist Islam demands that in a Muslim country the political rulers should be practicing Muslims, *shari'a* should be the basic law, and *ulema* should have a "decisive vote in articulating, or at least reviewing and ratifying, all governmental policy."[9] To the extent that governmental legitimacy and policy flow from religious doctrine and religious expertise, Islamic concepts of politics differ from and contradict the premises of democratic politics.

Islamic doctrine thus contains elements that may be both congenial and uncongenial to democracy. In practice, however, the only Islamic country that has sustained a fully democratic political system for any length of time is Turkey, where Mustafa Kemal Ataturk explicitly rejected Islamic concepts of society and politics and vigorously attempted to create a secular, modern, Western nation-state. And Turkey's experience with democracy has not been an unmitigated success. Elsewhere in the Islamic world, Pakistan has made three attempts at democracy, none of which lasted long. While Turkey has had democracy interrupted by occasional military interventions, Pakistan has had bureaucratic and military rule interrupted by occasional elections.

The only Arab country to sustain a form of democracy (albeit of the consociational variety) for a significant period of time was Lebanon. Its democracy, however, really amounted to consociational oligarchy, and 40 to 50 percent of its population was Christian. Once Muslims became a majority in Lebanon and began to assert themselves, Lebanese democracy collapsed. Between 1981 and 1990, only two of 37 countries in the world with Muslim majorities were ever rated "Free" by Freedom House in its annual surveys: the Gambia for two years and the Turkish Republic of Northern Cyprus for four. Whatever the compatibility of Islam and democracy in theory, in practice they have rarely gone together.

Opposition movements to authoritarian regimes in southern and eastern Europe, in Latin America, and in East Asia almost universally have espoused Western democratic values and proclaimed their desire to establish democracy. This does not mean that they invariably would introduce democratic institutions if they had the opportunity to do so, but at least they articulated the rhetoric of democracy. In authoritarian Islamic societies, by contrast, movements explicitly campaigning for democratic politics have been relatively weak, and the most powerful opposition has come from Islamic fundamentalists.

In the late 1980s, domestic economic problems combined with the snowballing effects of democratization elsewhere led the governments of several Islamic countries to relax their controls on the opposition and to attempt to renew their legitimacy through elections. The principal initial beneficiaries of these openings were Islamic fundamentalist groups. In Algeria, the Islamic Salvation Front swept the June 1990 local elections, the first free elections since the country became independent in 1962. In the 1989 Jordanian elections, Islamic fundamentalists won 36 of 80 seats in parliament. In Egypt, many candidates associated with the Muslim Brotherhood were elected to parliament in 1987. In several countries, Islamic fundamentalist groups were reportedly plotting insurrections. The strong electoral showings of the Islamic groups partly reflected the absence of other opposition parties, some because they were under government proscription, others because they were boycotting the elections. Nonetheless, fundamentalism seemed to be gaining strength in Middle Eastern countries, particularly among younger people. The strength of this tendency induced secular heads of government in Tunisia, Turkey, and elsewhere to adopt policies advocated by the fundamentalists and to make political gestures demonstrating their own commitment to Islam.

Liberalization in Islamic countries thus enhanced the power of important social and political movements whose commitment to democracy was uncertain. In some respects, the position of fundamentalist parties in Islamic societies in the early 1990s raised questions analogous to those posed by communist parties in Western Europe in the 1940s and again in the 1970s. Would the existing governments continue to open up their politics and hold elections in which Islamic groups could compete freely and equally? Would the Islamic groups gain majority support in those elections? If they did win the elections, would the military, which in many Islamic societies (e.g., Algeria, Turkey, Pakistan, and Indonesia) is strongly secular, allow them to form a government? If they did form a government, would it pursue radical Islamic policies that would undermine democracy and alienate the modern and Western-oriented elements in society?

The Limits of Cultural Obstacles

Strong cultural obstacles to democratization thus appear to exist in Confucian and Islamic societies. There are, nonetheless, reasons to doubt whether these must necessarily prevent democratic development. First, similar cultural arguments have not held up in the past. At one point many scholars argued that Catholicism was an obstacle to democracy. Others, in the Weberian tradition, contended that Catholic countries were unlikely to develop economically in the same manner as Protestant countries. Yet in the 1960s, 1970s, and 1980s Catholic countries became democratic and, on average, had higher rates of economic growth than Protestant countries. Similarly, at one point Weber and others argued that countries with Confucian cultures would not achieve successful capitalist development. By the 1980s, however, a new generation of scholars saw Confucianism as a major cause of the spectacular economic growth of East Asian societies. In the longer run, will the thesis that Confucianism prevents democratic development be any more viable than the thesis that Confucianism prevents economic development? Arguments that particular cultures are permanent obstacles to change should be viewed with a certain skepticism.

Second, great cultural traditions like Islam and Confucianism are highly complex bodies of ideas, beliefs, doctrines, assumptions, and behavior patterns. Any major culture, including Confucianism, has some elements that are compatible with democracy, just as both Protestantism and Catholicism have elements that are clearly undemocratic. Confucian democracy may be a contradiction in terms, but democracy in a Confucian society need not be. The real question is which elements in Islam and Confucianism are favorable to democracy, and how and under what circumstances these can supersede the undemocratic aspects of those cultural traditions.

Third, cultures historically are dynamic, not stagnant. The dominant beliefs and attitudes in a society change. While maintaining elements of continuity, the prevailing culture of a society in one generation may differ significantly from what it was one or two generations earlier. In the 1950s, Spanish culture was typically described as traditional, authoritarian, hierarchical, deeply religious, and honor-and-status oriented. By the 1970s and 1980s, these words had little place in a description of Spanish attitudes and values. Cultures evolve and, as in Spain, the most important force bringing about cultural changes is often economic development itself.

Economics

Few relationships between social, economic, and political phenomena are stronger than that between the level of economic development and the existence of democratic politics. Most wealthy countries are democratic, and most democratic countries—India is the most dramatic exception—are wealthy. The correlation between wealth and democracy implies that transitions to democracy should occur primarily in countries at the mid-level of economic development. In poor countries democratization is unlikely; in rich countries it usually has already occurred. In between there is a "political transition zone": countries in this middle economic stratum are those most likely to transit to democracy, and most countries that transit to democracy will be in this stratum. As countries develop economically and move into the transition zone, they become good prospects for democratization.

In fact, shifts from authoritarianism to democracy during the third wave were heavily concentrated in this transition zone, especially at its upper reaches. The conclusion seems clear. Poverty is a principal—probably *the* principal—obstacle to democratic development. The future of democracy depends on the future of economic development. Obstacles to economic development are obstacles to the expansion of democracy.

The third wave of democratization was propelled forward by the extraordinary global economic growth of the 1950s and 1960s. That era of growth came to an end with the oil price increases of 1973-74. Between 1974 and 1990, democratization accelerated around the world, but global economic growth slowed down. There were, however, substantial differences in growth rates among regions. East Asian rates remained high throughout the 1970s and 1980s, and overall rates of growth in South Asia increased. On the other hand, growth rates in the Middle East, North Africa, Latin America, and the Caribbean declined sharply from the 1970s to the 1980s. Those in sub-Saharan Africa plummeted. Per capita GNP in Africa was stagnant during the late 1970s and declined at an annual rate of 2.2 percent during the 1980s. The economic obstacles to democratization in Africa thus clearly grew during the 1980s. The prospects for the 1990s are not encouraging. Even if economic reforms, debt relief, and economic assistance materialize, the World Bank has predicted an average annual rate of growth in per capita GDP for Africa of only 0.5 percent for the remainder of the century.[10] If this prediction is accurate, the economic obstacles to democratization in sub-Saharan Africa will remain overwhelming well into the twenty-first century.

The World Bank was more optimistic in its predictions of economic growth for China and the nondemocratic countries of South Asia. The current low levels of wealth in those countries, however, generally mean that even with annual per capita growth rates of 3 to 5 percent, the economic conditions favorable to democratization would still be long in coming.

In the 1990s, the majority of countries where the economic conditions for democratization are already present or rapidly emerging are in the Middle East and North Africa (see Table 1). The economies of many of these countries (United Arab Emirates, Kuwait, Saudi Arabia, Iraq, Iran,

Table 1 — Upper and Middle Income Nondemocratic Countries - GNP Per Capita (1988)

INCOME LEVEL	ARAB- MIDDLE EAST	SOUTHEAST ASIA	AFRICA	OTHER
Upper Income (>$6,000)	(UAE) (Kuwait) (Saudi Arabia)	Singapore		
Upper Middle Income ($2,000- 5,500)	(Iraq) (Iran) (Libya) (Oman)* Algeria*		(Gabon)	Yugoslavia
Lower Middle Income ($500-2,200) $1,000	Syria Jordan* Tunisia*	Malaysia* Thailand*	Cameroon*	Paraguay
	Morocco* Egypt* Yemen* Lebanon*		Congo* Côte d'Ivoire Zimbabwe Senegal* Angola	

Note: ( ) = major oil exporter
  * = average annual GDP growth rate 1980-1988 > 3.0%

Source: World Bank, *World Bank Development Report 1990* (New York: Oxford University Press, 1990), 178-181.

Libya, Oman) depend heavily on oil exports, which enhances the control of the state bureaucracy. This does not, however, make democratization impossible. The state bureaucracies of Eastern Europe had far more power than do those of the oil exporters. Thus at some point that power could collapse among the latter as dramatically as it did among the former.

In 1988 among the other states of the Middle East and North Africa, Algeria had already reached a level conducive to democratization; Syria was approaching it; and Jordan, Tunisia, Morocco, Egypt, and North Yemen were well below the transition zone, but had grown rapidly during the 1980s. Middle Eastern economies and societies are approaching the point where they will become too wealthy and too complex for their various traditional, military, and one-party systems of authoritarian rule to sustain themselves. The wave of democratization that swept the world in the 1970s and 1980s could become a dominant feature of Middle Eastern and North African politics in the 1990s. The issue of economics versus culture would then be joined: What forms of

politics might emerge in these countries when economic prosperity begins
to interact with Islamic values and traditions?

In China, the obstacles to democratization are political, economic, and
cultural; in Africa they are overwhelmingly economic; and in the rapidly
developing countries of East Asia and in many Islamic countries, they
are primarily cultural.

Economic Development and Political Leadership

History has proved both optimists and pessimists wrong about
democracy. Future events will probably do the same. Formidable
obstacles to the expansion of democracy exist in many societies. The
third wave, the "global democratic revolution" of the late twentieth
century, will not last forever. It may be followed by a new surge of
authoritarianism sustained enough to constitute a third reverse wave.
That, however, would not preclude a fourth wave of democratization
developing some time in the twenty-first century. Judging by the record
of the past, the two most decisive factors affecting the future
consolidation and expansion of democracy will be economic development
and political leadership.

Most poor societies will remain undemocratic so long as they remain
poor. Poverty, however, is not inevitable. In the past, nations such as
South Korea, which were assumed to be mired in economic
backwardness, have astonished the world by rapidly attaining prosperity.
In the 1980s, a new consensus emerged among developmental economists
on the ways to promote economic growth. The consensus of the 1980s
may or may not prove more lasting and productive than the very
different consensus among economists that prevailed in the 1950s and
1960s. The new orthodoxy of neo-orthodoxy, however, already seems to
have produced significant results in many countries.

Yet there are two reasons to temper our hopes with caution. First,
economic development for the late, late, late developing
countries—meaning largely Africa—may well be more difficult than it
was for earlier developers because the advantages of backwardness come
to be outweighed by the widening and historically unprecedented gap
between rich and poor countries. Second, new forms of authoritarianism
could emerge in wealthy, information-dominated, technology-based
societies. If unhappy possibilities such as these do not materialize,
economic development should create the conditions for the progressive
replacement of authoritarian political systems by democratic ones. Time
is on the side of democracy.

Economic development makes democracy possible; political leadership
makes it real. For democracies to come into being, future political elites
will have to believe, at a minimum, that democracy is the least bad form

of government for their societies and for themselves. They will also need the skills to bring about the transition to democracy while facing both radical oppositionists and authoritarian hard-liners who inevitably will attempt to undermine their efforts. Democracy will spread to the extent that those who exercise power in the world and in individual countries want it to spread. For a century and a half after Tocqueville observed the emergence of modern democracy in America, successive waves of democratization have washed over the shore of dictatorship. Buoyed by a rising tide of economic progress, each wave advanced further—and receded less—than its predecessor. History, to shift the metaphor, does not sail ahead in a straight line, but when skilled and determined leaders are at the helm, it does move forward.

NOTES

1. *New York Times*, 28 December 1989, A13; *International Herald Tribune*, 12-13 May 1990, 6.

2. *The Times* (London), 27 May 1990; *Time*, 21 May 1990, 34-35; *Daily Telegraph*, 29 March 1990, 13; *New York Times*, 27 February 1990, A10, and 9 April 1990, A6.

3. George F. Kennan, *The Cloud of Danger* (Boston: Little, Brown, 1977), 41-43.

4. See William Wallace, *The Transformation of Western Europe* (London: Royal Institute of International Affairs-Pinter, 1990), 16-19.

5. See Daniel Kelliher, "The Political Consequences of China's Reform," *Comparative Politics* 18 (July 1986): 488-490; and Andrew J. Nathan, *Chinese Democracy* (New York: Alfred A. Knopf, 1985).

6. Lucian W. Pye with Mary W. Pye, *Asian Power and Politics: The Cultural Dimensions of Authority* (Cambridge: Harvard University Press, 1985), 232-236.

7. *New York Times*, 15 December 1987, A14.

8. Goh Chok Tong, quoted in *New York Times*, 14 August 1985, A13.

9. Ernest Gellner, "Up from Imperialism," *The New Republic*, 22 May 1989, 35-36; R. Stephen Humphreys, "Islam and Political Values in Saudi Arabia, Egypt, and Syria," *Middle East Journal* 33 (Winter 1979): 6-7.

10. World Bank, *World Development Report 1990* (New York: Oxford University Press, 1990), 8-11, 16, 160; and *Sub-Saharan Africa: From Crisis to Sustainable Growth* (Washington: World Bank, 1990).

[8]

Modes of transition in Latin America, Southern and Eastern Europe*

Terry Lynn Karl and Philippe C. Schmitter

The recent demise of authoritarian rule and the advent of democracy in so many places under such different circumstances presents a challenge – and an opportunity – to students of comparative politics. These almost simultaneous transformations in regime·type are a sobering reminder of what John Stuart Mill long ago warned was the most serious impediment to the accumulation of scientific knowledge about social reality. namely, the prospect that different causes could produce the same effect. How could such (generically) similar outcomes emerge from such a diversity of national and regional situations? What possible communalities could have propelled the autocratic regimes of Southern Europe (Portugal, Spain, Greece and Turkey). South America (Argentina. Bolivia, Brazil. Chile, Ecuador, Paraguay, Peru and Uruguay), Central America (El Salvador, Guatemala, Honduras, and Nicaragua) and Eastern Europe (Bulgaria, East Germany, Czechoslovakia, Hungary, Poland, Romania and Yugoslavia) towards the convocation of free competitive elections of uncertain outcome within the last two and a half decades?[1]

This puzzling equifinality with regard to the causes of regime change only raises further questions about its consequences: will these newly emergent and fragile democracies survive? Will they succeed in significantly improving the life chances and welfare of their recently enfranchised citizens – especially in the face of intense international competition and some of the worst economic conditions since the 1930s? Even if they do persist, will they merely be 'condemned' to remain democratic for some period by the lack of any viable alternative, but fail to consolidate into legitimate and valued institutions?[2]

Terry Lynn Karl is associate professor of political science and director of the Center for Latin American Studies at Stanford University. Stanford CA 94305-2044. USA and is the author of *The Paradox of Plenty: Oil Booms and Petro-States* (forthcoming).
Philippe C. Schmitter is professor of political science and director of the Center for European Studies at Stanford University. He is the co-author (with Guillermo O'Donnell) of *Transitions from Authoritarian Rule: Tentative Conclusions about Uncertain Democracies* (1986).

Some orienting hypotheses

Let us start with the following (disputable) assumptions about contemporary politics: (1) polities undergoing regime change from autocracy do so by a variety of means; (2) these can be specified and clustered into a limited number of 'modes of transition'; (3) these modes, to a significant extent, determine which 'types of democracy' will emerge; (4) whether or not they will be consolidated; and (5) what the long-range consequences will be for different social groups. This article will take (1) for granted and explore the plausibility of (2). Assumptions (3), (4) and (5) have been left for future speculation.

On the surface, these assumptions – especially (3), (4) and (5) – might seem dubious.

if not counter-intuitive. As we shall see, the transition is a period of great political uncertainty. It is subject to unforeseen contingencies, unfolding processes and unintended outcomes. The 'normal' constraints of social structures and political institutions seem temporarily suspended; actors are often forced into making hurried and confused choices; and the alliances they enter are usually fleeting and opportunistic. The result of these interactions is often not what any one group preferred initially. Why, then, should such an improbable and *under*determined 'founding moment' have a lasting effect? Would it not be more plausible to assume that these 'events' would prove epiphenomenal and that, ultimately, the polity will acquire the regime configuration that it deserves, given its entrenched social structures, its standing citizen preferences, or its established constitutional history?

Our argument is not based on deductive principles of rational choice or historical inertia, but on inductive observation from a limited range of recent experiences in Europe and Latin America and their tentative extension to the even more recent experiences of Eastern Europe. In a sense, it bears a generic resemblance to the currently fashionable attention being paid to 'chaos theory' and to 'path dependency'. Small differences and minor choices, whose relevance is often unknown to those experiencing them, may be capable of producing major effects and channelling a system in quite different and lasting directions.

Revised thoughts about requisites

If true, there may be a pressing need for important revisions, even reversals, in the way democratization has heretofore been conceptualized. For example, there may be no single precondition (or even set of preconditions) necessary for the emergence of a democratic polity, and there surely is no single precondition that is sufficient to produce such an outcome. Searching for the causes of democracy from probabilistic associations with economic, social, cultural, psychological or international factors has not so far yielded any general law of democratization, nor is it likely to do so in the near future, despite the recent proliferation of cases.[3] This quest for a set of unique and identical

conditions that can explain the presence or absence of democratic regimes should be abandoned and replaced by a more modest effort to develop a contingently sensitive understanding of the variety of circumstance under which they may emerge.

Moreover, what the literature has considered in the past to be the preconditions for democracy may be better conceived in the future as the outcomes of different types of democracy. Patterns of greater economic growth and more equitable income distribution, higher levels of literacy and education, increases in social communication and media exposure may be better treated as the products of stable democratic processes, rather than as the prerequisites for their existence. A 'civic' political culture characterized by high levels of mutual trust, a willingness to tolerate diversity of opinion and a propensity to accommodation and compromise could be the result of the protracted functioning of democratic institutions that generate appropriate values and beliefs rather than a set of cultural obstacles that must initially be overcome. There is evidence for this contention in the fact that most democracies in Europe and Latin America's oldest democracy in Costa Rica have emerged from quite 'uncivic' warfare. In other words, what have been emphasized as independent variables in the past might be more fruitfully conceived as dependent variables in the future.

From contingent choice to structured contingency

This rejection of the search for prerequisites, plus the hunch that much of what had been thought to produce democracy should be considered as its product, has caused some recent theorists to divert their attention from structures to the strategic choices, shifting alliances, emergent processes and sequential patterns involved in moving from one type of political regime to another. As we shall see below, these elements of intention and uncertainty are important even when the transition takes place under 'controlled conditions', i.e. when authoritarian incumbents dictate the pace and content of changes, when violence is ruled out and when continuity in property rights and social relations is imposed. In this approach, democratization is conceived as a complex historical process with analytically distinct, if empirically overlapping, stages of transition, consolidation, persistence and, eventually, deconsolidation.[4]

Different sets of actors with different followings, preferences, calculations, resources and time horizons come to the forefront during these successive stages. Each is 'punctuated' by specific events or accomplishments, even if their significance is not immediately apparent to the actors themselves. For example, elite factions and social movements seem to play the key roles in bringing about the demise of authoritarian rule; political parties move to centre stage during the transition itself when the convocation and holding of 'founding elections' privileges their capacity for aggregating actor preferences across territorial constituencies; while the more discrete and specialized activity of interest associations and state agencies may become major determinants of the type of democracy that is ultimately consolidated.

The notion of contingency, i.e. that outcomes depend less on objective conditions circumscribing routinized actions than on subjective evaluations surrounding unique strategic choices, has the advantage of stressing collective decisions and political interactions that have largely been underemphasized in the search for preconditions. Instead of the familiar sociopolitical world where most outcomes are *overdetermined* by complex sets of mutually reinforcing conditions, the realm of the transition appears *under*specified by episodically convergent purposes. But this understanding of democracy risks descending into excessive voluntarism, if it is not explicitly confined to specific transitory periods and eventually placed within a framework of structural-historical constraints. Even in the midst of the tremendous uncertainty provoked by a regime change, the decisions made by various actors respond to, and are conditioned by, socio-economic structures and political institutions already present, or existing in people's memories. These can be decisive in that they may either restrict or enhance the options available to different political actors attempting to construct one or another type of democracy.

Certain social structures do seem to make the consolidation of any form of political democracy highly improbable; inversely, it is reason-

able to presume that their absence may make accommodative strategies more viable and reinforce the position of democratic actors. For example, political democracies have lasted only in countries where the landed class, generally the most recalcitrant of interests, played a secondary role in the export economy (e.g. Venezuela or Chile), or where non-labour repressive agriculture predominated (e.g. Greece, Northern Italy, Costa Rica, Argentina and Uruguay). Thus, the survival capacity of political democracy does seem to depend on a structural space defined either by the absence of a strong landowner elite engaged in labour-repressive agriculture or its subordination to interests tied to other economic activities. Barrington Moore, Jr. carried this argument one step further when he proclaimed: 'No bourgeoisie, no democracy'! It was not enough just to undermine the power of landed aristocracy and commercialize agriculture, but a new dominant class of urban merchants and industrialists had to be consolidated *before* democracy could emerge.[5]

The implications of this contrast could be quite significant for many of the countries now undergoing regime changes. In Southern Europe and South America, all countries have thoroughly capitalist agricultural sectors. Most are no longer dependent upon traditional agricultural exports, but few (except Spain) can be said to have well-established national bourgeoisies. In Eastern Europe, the 'structural space' is even more ambiguous. Poland has left agriculture in private hands, although the capitalist status of its farmers is somewhat doubtful; Hungary has a mixed public–private system; the rest are characterized by state farms, all of which produce for a commercial, if controlled, market. As for the allegedly necessary bourgeoisie, it must be created almost *de toutes pièces* from foreigners, exiles and former *apparatchniks*, except where existing elements from the 'second economy' can be pressed into service as in Poland and Hungary.[6] For different reasons, ambiguity characterizes the Central American cases as well. In Guatemala, El Salvador, and to a lesser extent Honduras, labour repressive agriculture still predominates while partnerships between militaries and commercialized, but still traditional, agrarian interests control local economies. In Nicaragua, there is a mixed public–private agricultural system, but nothing that can faintly be construed as a national bourgeoisie.[7]

The inheritance from the past

But what about the 'political institutional space' inherited from the *ancien régime*? Are there certain configurations which preclude a democratic outcome, regardless of social structure? Here, Latin America offers an interesting contrast with Eastern Europe. In the former, the overriding constraint during the transition comes from the nature of civil–military relations: will the armed forces tolerate a return to competitive civilian rule, especially forms of it which seek to reduce their privileges and direct political role in the future? In the latter, it comes from the nature of state–civil society relations: will the party/state apparatus permit elected governments to undermine their monopoly on certain administrative roles and transfer substantial productive assets to private persons?

Stated another way, Latin Americans tend to be preoccupied with 'the *Gorilla* question' and may go to unusual lengths in their alliances and policies to avoid the possibility of a *golpe*. However, they are usually quite sanguine about whether high-level civil servants and *técnicos* can be expected to co-operate with the fledgling democracy. Eastern Europeans tend to worry about 'the *Nomenklatura* question' and may wonder how they can avoid the sabotage of their programmes by well-entrenched networks of party officials and state managers. However, they at least profess to be unconcerned (except in Romania) about a possible violent reaction by their national armed forces. They may, however, continue to worry about the possibility of invasion by foreign armed forces, i.e. those of the Soviet Union.

The cases in Southern Europe lie somewhere in between. In Spain, the Franco regime had already asserted civilian control over the military and scaled down its privileges, but there was a diffuse fear that a *bunker* had formed within the state and para-state apparatus which could impede reforms and even bring down governments. In Portugal, the problem was virtually inverted: how to get a progressive Armed Forces Movement out of power after it had brought about the fall of the Caetano regime and threatened to dictate the terms of a new

institutional arrangement. Only in Greece and Turkey was there a Latin American-like fear of military intervention, conditioned in the latter case by the fact that the armed forces had both installed and restored democracy in the past. In Latin America, the prospect of a *Nomenklatura* emerging as a crucial element in the transition has been mitigated by the absence of an effective dominant political party and the penetrated, clientelistic nature of the public administration.

These cases illustrate the different limits, as well as opportunities, that entrenched social and political structures can place upon contingent choice. If the focus in explaining the transition to democracy had been solely upon voluntary choices and strategic interaction, the pact-making that characterized the Venezuelan, Spanish or Uruguayan transitions, the pattern of gradual expansion of the suffrage that emerged earlier in Chile, the suppression of the MFA in Portugal, the unwillingness of Egon Krenz to put down popular demonstrations in Leipzig by force, or even King Juan Carlos' refusal to accede to *golpista* demands in Spain would all appear to be simply the result of skilful leadership by astute politicians.[8] Instead, by focusing either on the social dynamics produced by a particular form of insertion into the international economy or on the political interactions between military and civilian institutions, one becomes aware of how different contexts make such 'statecraft' more or less possible. This is *not* to argue that individual decisions made at particular points in time are merely epiphenomenal, or that all observable outcomes can be linked predictably to pre-existing social, economic or political relations. It is merely to claim that historically-created structures may constitute 'confining conditions' that restrict (or in some cases enhance) the choices available. In other words, they may determine the range of options available to decision-makers and even predispose them to choose a specific option.[9]

Modes of transition to democracy

Once these links between pre-existing structures and contingent choice have been made explicit, it becomes apparent that the arrangements 'crafted' by key political actors during a regime

The Polytechnic of Athens, Greece, in 1973, under the military dictatorship. The text on the pavement reads: 'The people will bring down the junta – peace, education, liberty'. Edimedia

transition establish new rules, roles and behavioural patterns which may (or may not) represent an important rupture with the past. These, in turn, become the institutions shaping the prospects for regime consolidation in the future. Electoral laws, once adopted, encourage some interests to enter the partisan political arena and discourage others. The specific manner in which freedom of association is defined and different means of collective action are regulated (or tolerated) can have a major impact on which interests get recognized and who joins what organizations. Certain models of economic development, once initiated through compromises between capital and labour, systematically favour some groups over others in patterns that become difficult to change. Informal accords between political parties and the armed forces can establish the initial parameters of civilian and military spheres in ways that deviate from

formal constitutional norms. Thus, what at the time may appear to be temporary alliances during the uncertain transition may become persistent barriers to change. Nascent democracies can be scarred with accidental, but lasting, 'birth defects'.

The issue of comparability

Before distinguishing between possible modes of transition to democracy, let us first consider briefly whether these recent cases can all be considered sub-species of the same *genus*. In their comparative exploration of Southern Europe and South America, the authors, in the four-volume compilation on *Transitions from Authoritarian Rule*, took it for granted that they were examining analogous experiences and, to a certain extent, were able to use a common set of concepts and assumptions in their respective analyses.[10] This, however, depended upon two very important 'parametric' conditions:

(1) each case was regarded as an independent occurrence. While there were some significant diffusion effects as late-comers learned from their predecessors and certain successful cases, e.g. Spain, served as models for others, none of the countries was so controlled in its options that the outcome could be attributed to a foreign, 'hegemonic' power. Indeed, one major conclusion was that external factors tended to play a relatively minor role and 'the reasons for launching a transition can be found predominantly in domestic, internal factors'.[11] This assumption cannot be sustained in the cases of Eastern Europe and Central America. In the former, it is at least arguable that none of the transitions would have occurred had it not been for the prior (and independent) change in the threat to intervene by the Soviet Union. Only after the 'Sinatra Doctrine' – 'you can do it your own way' – was pronounced (and believed) could the transition to some type of democracy begin. In the latter, while the initiation of transitions has generally been located in domestic rather than external factors, the form taken by these transitions has been very much the product of decisions taken by the US government. Its insistence on imposing 'electoralism', for example, has shaped the type of hybrid, civilian-led repressive regimes that have emerged throughout the region.[12]

(2) In each case the transitions in Southern Europe and South America were 'self-limited'. Actors decided, sometimes against considerable resistance, to restrict the change in regime to the sphere of the organization of public authority and citizen representation. They abstained from making major modifications in the definition of property rights or the distribution of social product – except in the case of Portugal, where extensive nationalizations of industry and expropriations of land took place and rendered the subsequent consolidation of political democracy much more difficult. The basic systems of capitalist production and distribution were left largely untouched, even if the role of the state as regulator and employer tended to expand somewhat. This has not been the case in Eastern Europe or Central America. In the former, the state socialist system of production and distribution is in the process of being dismantled

– admittedly to differing degrees and at differing paces – *pari passu* with the structures of autocratic political domination. In the latter, what is at stake is the demise of traditional agro-export models supported by reactionary and despotic political regimes. A more dramatic way of putting it would be that the countries of Southern Europe and South America underwent a common process of political reform in the 1970s and 1980s, whereas those of Eastern Europe and Central America have been experiencing a compound and simultaneous process of social, economic and political revolution.[13]

Given these two sizeable parametric differences, it is certainly legitimate to question, as we now turn to an effort at defining the modes of transition in these four areas of the world, whether we are not dealing with differences in *genus* and not just distinctions between subspecies. Our practical inclination is to proceed for the moment as if the cases were comparable, but to be prepared to abandon that assumption if and when otherwise inexplicable patterns emerge.

Transitions are 'produced' by actors who choose strategies that lead to change from one kind of regime to another. As we have argued above, they may be constrained in the choices available to them by prevailing social, economic and political structures and the interaction of strategies may often result in outcomes that no one initially preferred, but nevertheless we believe that actors and strategies define the basic property space within which transitions can occur and that the specific combination of the two defines which type of transition has occurred.

In Figure 1, we have depicted the relevant space by cross-tabulating variation in strategy by variation in actors. Simplifying considerably on the y-axis, strategies of transition can vary along a continuum that runs from unilateral recourse to force to multilateral willingness to compromise. In between lies a muddled and ambiguous zone of action in which mutual threats are exchanged, acts of physical intimidation and coercion may be committed and substantial mobilizations of support may occur. On the x-axis, we distinguish between cases in which most, if not all of the impetus for change comes 'from below', from actors in subordinate or excluded positions in the social, economic and

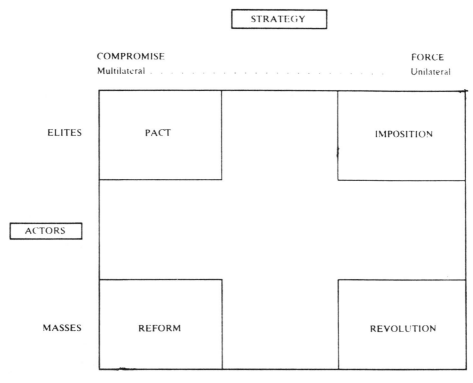

FIGURE 1. Modes of transition: the property space

political order of the *ancien régime*, and those in which elite actors 'from above', i.e. from within the dominant institutions of authoritarian rule, social prestige and/or economic exploitation, play the leading role in moving the system towards some form of democracy. Again, we concede that the range of variation cannot be collapsed into a net dichotomy and have left room for a 'messy' intermediate category in which elites and non-elites mingle and compete for the direction of the transition. This is also an area where actors coming 'from outside' may intervene directly and significantly – often because they have defeated the previous authoritarian regime in international warfare!

From the four 'extreme' corners of the plot in Figure 1 emerge four ideal-types of regime transition: by *Pact* when elites agree upon a multilateral compromise among themselves; by *Imposition* when elites use force unilaterally and effectively to bring about a regime change against the resistance of incumbents; by *Reform* when masses mobilize from below and impose a compromised outcome without resorting to violence, and by *Revolution* when masses rise up in arms and defeat the previous authoritarian rulers militarily. In the capacious space in between the four extremes presumably lie a large number of situations in which both the identity of the relevant actors and the selection of strategies are 'mixed'. Violence is tempered by compromise before it becomes dominant; masses are aroused and active, but still under the control of previous elites; domestic actors

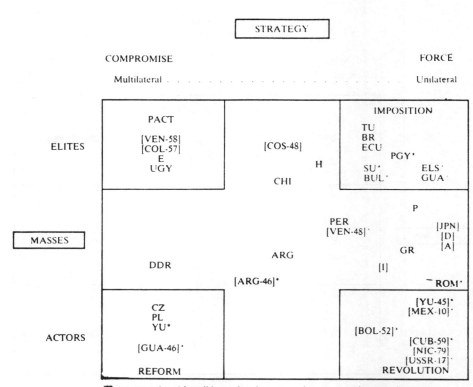

FIGURE 2. Modes of transition: the distribution of recent cases

and strategies are significant. but the outcome hinges critically on what foreign occupiers or intervenors do.

In Figure 2 we have attempted to 'score' recent cases in Latin America. Southern and Eastern Europe according to type of transition. In brackets [ ]. we have included a few 'representative' historical cases. These placements are, of course, tentative and subject to revision by specialists in the politics of the countries concerned. Moreover. they seek to resume in a single evaluation what is. in many cases. a very complex historical pattern. Take, for example. Poland's (PL) transition. It began in 1981 in the Reform box with the rise of *Solidarnosc* – a mass-based movement advocating regime

change by non-violent means. This 'phase' ended with a Pact in 1981, which was subsequently broken by the Imposition of a military regime, whose temporary effect was to abort the transition process altogether. In 1989. these autocratic rulers chose. under pressure from two successive strike waves but without being compelled to do so by the organized violence of their adversaries. to enter into 'round table' negotiations that subsequently produced another Pact. which in turn led to restricted elections in June that brought to power a mass-based, alliance-prone Reform government. Since its transition began and ended in the Reform box. and since it was conditioned all along by the presence of a mass movement. we have placed Poland there, in effect ignoring the tortuous path by which it left and returned.

Among the recent cases, some are relatively easy to classify. Spain (E) and Uruguay (UGY) are leading contemporary instances (and frequently taken as examplary models) of pacted transitions. Czechoslovakia (CZ) and Yugoslavia (YU) fit the reform model quite well in that change came about as a result of mass mobilization, non-violence and multilateral negotiations. In Turkey (TU), Brazil (BR), Ecuador (ECU) and the Soviet Union (SU), the change in regime was largely initiated from above and the coercive power of the state was consistently brought to bear to determine the timing, pace and content of change. Paraguay (PGY) and Bulgaria (BUL) were more ambiguous cases in that actual violence was used and popular mobilization occurred in the process of ousting Stroessner and Zhivkov, but incumbent elites retained subsequent control. In El Salvador (ELS) since 1982, there has been an attempt to impose a transition via restricted elections, but protracted resistance by those excluded has prevented such an outcome. The revolutionary cases are well-known: Mexico (MEX) in 1910, Cuba (CUB) in 1959, Nicaragua (NIC) in 1979, Russia (USSR) in 1917, with Bolivia (BOL) in 1952 meriting a more ambiguous score.

Many cases are, however, even more difficult to classify. Take Portugal (P). It began its transition suddenly and unexpectedly by imposition – a *coup d'état* launched by junior military officers in the context of impending military defeat in Guinea-Bissau. Virtually overnight, the successful seizure of power triggered a mass response that first pushed the process in a reformist direction and, then, in the spring and summer of 1975 seemed to be leading toward a revolutionary outcome. The defeat of radical military elements in November prevented that and for some time the Portuguese polity remained suspended between reform and imposition (efforts to negotiate pacts failed), until the elections of 1987 and consequent changes in the constitution seemed at last to place the country on the road to consolidation.[14]

Chile (CHI) is another hard case to classify. It was firmly (and protractedly) entrenched in the imposition mode until General Pinochet misjudged his capacity to win a key plebiscite in 1988. Since then, Chile's revived civilian politicians have opted for a pacted transition based on a 'grand alliance' of all opposition parties. Hungary (H) is a somewhat similar case in which the initial impetus came from within the dominant party, but these elites lost control and were forced to 'round table' with opposition groups who, themselves, aroused little popular support. The German Democratic Republic (DDR) would have been a standard case of reform from below were it not for the substantial interference of elites from the neighbouring Federal Republic at key moments in its transition. Similarly, Romania (ROM) may have first undergone an accelerated regime change under revolutionary conditions of violence and mass involvement, but the (unclear) role of the Soviet Union and the subsequent recuperation of the *Nomenklatura* and military apparatus resemble the imposition mode.[15]

At the very centre of our property space are three cases that literally defy classification: Argentina (ARG), Greece (GR) and Peru (PER). Here, we find elements of imposition since important fragments from the previous autocratic regime – military in all three cases – played a key role in the transition, but in the context of considerable mobilization of urban masses and some resort to violence. In the former two cases, the scenario also included defeat in international war as the result of adventurous foreign policies, but without the subsequent occupation by foreign conquerors as in the cases of Germany (D), Japan (JPN) and Austria (A).

Some tentative conclusions

The first general observation is that all modes of transition have been tried, at one time or another. Revolutions have become less frequent, although the Romanian case of 1989 came close to repeating the broad conditions of the Nicaraguan one of 1979. Latin America is particularly rich in the diversity of ways in which regime change has occurred, although that should be tempered by noting that few of these have given rise to any stable type of democracy. The Southern European cases are virtually all in the upper half of Figure 2, an indication of

Spain is a case of successful transition to democracy. *Left:* The failed military *coup d'état* of 22 February 1987. Thomas imapress

Above: Socialist Party electoral poster in Valencia, 1982, with Felipe Gonzáles, who won the election. Reininger Contact Press

the dominant role played by elites there. The Eastern European transitions are strung out along the diagonal running from imposition to reform. Despite the frequency with which 'round tables' have been convoked, none of these cases could be unambiguously labelled as 'pacted', although Hungary comes the closest. Romania, as we have said, is an outlier with its near-revolutionary conditions.

The second generalization stems from the distribution of asterisks (*) indicating that the transition in question did **not or** has not yet resulted in some form of stable democracy. Imposed and reformist transitions may or may not lead to democracies. Revolutions are less ambiguous; they may produce relatively enduring patterns of domination – witness Russia since 1917, Mexico since 1929, China since 1949, and Cuba since 1959 – but they have rarely evolved into patterns of fair competition, unrestricted contestation, tolerance for rotation in power and free associability. This clashes frontally with the oft-cited generalization of Barrington Moore, Jr. that 'revolutions are necessary for democracy'.[16] Admittedly, his assertion is based on different cases (Britain, the United States and France), a longer time frame (almost a hundred years in the case of France and longer for the UK), and a counterfactual assumption (that previous autocratic regimes would not have evolved toward democracy without such a violent, mass-based rupture with the past). Nevertheless, our 'sample' strongly suggests the contrary, i.e. that where authoritarian incumbents have been removed by force and replaced by a new elite representing mass constituencies, the subsequent emergence of political democracy is unlikely. We would note, however, that developments currently under way in the Soviet Union, Nicaragua and Mexico may (belatedly) be challenging this assertion.[17]

The experience of the Latin American cases tentatively suggests a counter-intuitive conclusion: the reform mode of transition has rarely led to the consolidation of democracy. The prevailing wisdom has long been that peaceful pressure from below through the mobilization of excluded groups which compels ruling elites to expand rights of contestation and to extend the franchise is *the* most successful formula for democratization, especially where it occurs sequentially and gradually.[18] This may have

worked well in Chile prior to 1971–3, but not in response to the socialist reforms of Allende. Analogous experiences in Argentina (1946–55) and Guatemala (1946–54) resulted in regressions to authoritarian rule. It is important to note, however, that these failures of democratization took place in the context of the Cold War and were greatly influenced by it. With Czechoslovakia, Poland, Yugoslavia and Nicaragua currently well-ensconced in this mode of transition, we shall see whether in a different time-period and international context, this pessimism remains justified.

The modes that have most often resulted in the implantation of some type of political democracy are 'transitions from above'. In these cases, traditional rulers remain in control, even if pressured from below, and successfully use strategies of either compromise or force, or some mix of the two, to retain at least part of their power.

–Of these two modes of transition, democratization by pure imposition is the most common, especially if we include cases in which force or the threat of force is applied by foreign as well as domestic actors. Indeed, some of the most notoriously successful stable democracies were imposed upon defeated countries in the wake of the Second World War, although the Republic of Korea and the Philippines are witnesses to the possibility that the 'formula' can fail. In Figure 2, the box labelled Imposition includes Brazil, Ecuador, Paraguay and Turkey, where the military used its dominant position to establish unilaterally the rules for eventual civilian governance, and Bulgaria and the Soviet Union where an incumbent civilian elite has (so far) controlled the timing and pace of regime change. In the former four cases, the transition has been drawn out, real limits have been placed upon the extent of democratization, and consolidation seems very difficult to reach, although no regression to autocracy has yet occurred. In the case of the Soviet Union and Bulgaria, it is still too early to judge what the outcome will be, although the continued precariousness of citizen rights and the absence of institutionalized structures of partisan competition are hardly encouraging signs.

Where democracies that have endured for a respectable length of time appear to cluster is in the cell defined by relatively strong elite actors who engage in strategies of compromise. This category includes the historical cases of Venezuela (1958–) and Colombia (1957–), and the recent redemocratizations in Spain(1975–) and Uruguay (1984–).[19] What unites these otherwise diverse cases is the presence of foundational pacts, that is, explicit (though not always public) agreements between contending elites, which define the rules of governance on the basis of mutual guarantees for the 'vital interests' of those involved. Indeed, an argument could be made that under the conditions of modern politics, i.e. where mass enfranchisement and extensive individual freedoms are presumed, where class, sectoral and professional interests are likely to be well defended by specialized organizations, where the armed forces possess an overwhelming superiority in the use of violence, where the state probably has extensive responsibilities for the regulation of the market and redistribution of income, and where the economic system is tightly integrated with, and hence vulnerable to, the international market, some such explicit 'social contract' is a virtual necessity. The previous liberal contract based on implicit individual consent to legitimate authority will no longer be sufficient. It simply does not cover the range of probable rights and obligations, nor is it capable of delivering the requisite conformity of key social groups.[20]

These explicit, 'foundational' pacts have several essential components. First, they are necessarily comprehensive and inclusive of virtually all politically significant actors. Because pacts are negotiated compromises in which contending forces agree to forego their capacity to harm each other by extending guarantees not to threaten each other's vital interests, they are only successful when they include *all* potentially threatening interests. Second, they are actually a series of accords that are interlocking and dependent upon each other. They necessarily include an agreement between the military and civilians over the conditions for establishing civilian rule, an agreement between political parties to compete under the new rules of governance, and a 'social contract' between state agencies, business associations and trade unions regarding property rights, market arrangements and the distribution of benefits. Third, while they are ultimately both substantive (about the main tenets of policy) and procedural (about the

rules of policy-making), they initially emphasize rule-making because 'bargaining about bargaining' is the first and most important stage in the process of compromise.

Finally, foundational pacts serve to ensure survivability because, despite their inclusionary nature, they are also and simultaneously aimed at restricting the scope of representation in order to reassure traditional dominant classes that their vital interests will be respected. In essence, they are anti-democratic mechanisms, bargained by elites, which seek to create a deliberate socioeconomic and political contract that demobilizes emerging mass actors while delineating the extent to which all actors can participate or wield power in the future. They may accomplish this task by restricting contestation (as Colombian parties did in 1958 by agreeing to alternate in power regardless of the outcome of elections), by restricting the policy agenda itself (as Venezuelan parties did in 1958 by agreeing to implement the same economic programme), or by restricting the franchise (as Chilean elites did, beginning with the electoral law of 1874).

There are a number of cases that do not fit neatly into any of the ideal-typic categories which we have presented. Instead, they combine some of the features of these various types. For example, in Costa Rica in 1948 an opposition party militarily defeated the governing party in a short civil war, but then immediately resorted to pact-making to lay the foundation for an enduring democracy.[21] In Chile, Pinochet's strategy of unilateralism was curbed by his defeat in the 1988 plebiscite and subsequently replaced by *pactismo* among civilian politicians.[22] Hungary is another case that shares this intermediate ground between the two elitist modes – a location that seems to bode well for a democratic outcome.

The same cannot be said for those cases which occupy positions *below* the elitist line. In Peru after 1978, the military's control over the timing and shape of the transition was strongly influenced by a mass popular movement; in Guatemala (1984–) and El Salvador (1982–), an imposed transition led by civilian elites tied to the United States (and grudgingly tolerated by the armed forces) has been stalemated by the refusal of traditional elites to incorporate armed rebels and organized workers and peasants into the polity. In Argentina, placed right in the centre of Figure 2, one is hard pressed to imagine what dominant strategy could possibly dislodge it from permanent regime instability – whether of a democratic or an autocratic cast![23] Common to these cases is a loss of elite control and an inability of mass organizations successfully to impose a new coherent strategy for either domestic or external reasons.

Since the Portuguese 'Revolution of the Carnations' in 1974, one autocratic regime after another has given way to some type of democracy – first in Southern Europe, then in South and to a lesser extent Central America and, most recently, in Eastern Europe. These transitions can all be considered part of the same process in that each successive one has contributed to the likelihood of the next. Despite these diffusion effects, in most cases the changes were deliberately confined to the realm of political authority alone; in others, they involved a simultaneous and compound transformation of political, social and economic relations. The actual means whereby these regime changes were accomplished has varied a great deal.

In this article, we have explored the hypothesis that the mode of transition from autocratic rule is a principal determinant of whether democracy will emerge. Distinguishing between situations in which previous elites continued to dominate political life and those in which they were displaced by mass movements and between those in which actors chose strategies of multilateral compromise or unilateral imposition, we have concluded that 'transitions by pact' are the most likely to lead to political democracy, followed by 'transitions by imposition'. Because of the nature of these two modes of transition, however, they are likely to produce restricted types of democracy. Where incumbents lost control over the process of regime change and the new structures of power and authority emerged from below, either by reform or revolution, the probability of a successful outcome diminished – at least in the past. Most problematic were those situations which mixed elements of several modes of transition and from which no dominant winning strategy or coalition could emerge. Not only is the mode of transition a principal determinant of whether democracy will emerge, but it may also be a major factor influencing the specific type of democracy that will eventually be consolidated. That, however, is an argument that we must pursue elsewhere.

Notes

* An earlier version of this article covering only the Latin American cases and written by Terry Karl only, was published as 'Dilemmas of Democratization in Latin America', *Comparative Politics*, Vol. 23, No. 1, October 1990, pp. 1–21. It was originally presented at the Conference on 'Latin America at the Threshold of the 1990s', sponsored by The Institute of Latin America of the Chinese Academy of Social Sciences and the Ford Foundation, Beijing, 8–16 June, 1988.

1. This article focuses on cases within these four 'regions' and, therefore, ignores analogous developments in Asia (e.g. Pakistan, the Philippines, the Republic of Korea and Taiwan) and Africa (e.g. Gambia, Nigeria, Namibia and, most recently, South Africa). There have even been 'rumblings' about democratization and attempts at liberalization in the Arab world (e.g. Tunisia, Jordan and Egypt). This (quite unanticipated) series of regime changes threatens to eliminate one of the methodological reasons why the techniques of 'normal' social science have not been brought to bear on the subject, namely, the absence of a sufficient number of cases to support probabilistic statistical estimation. There remains, however, the more important theoretical issue of the 'abnormal' role of uncertainty and contingency in such processes. This is explored in Guillermo O'Donnell and Philippe C. Schmitter, *Tentative Conclusions about Uncertain Transitions*, Vol. 4 of *Transitions from Authoritarian Rule*. Baltimore: Johns Hopkins University Press, 1986.

2. These questions underlie the flood of recent comparative volumes on democratization, in Latin America and Southern Europe. See, for example, Julian Santamaria (ed.), *La Transición a la Democracia en el Sur de Europa y América Latina*. Madrid: Centro de Investigaciones Sociológicas, 1982; Guy Hermet, *Aux frontières de la démocratie*. Paris: PUF, 1983; Geoffrey Pridham (ed.), *The New Mediterranean Democracies*. London: Frank Cass, 1984;

Fundacion Pablo Iglesias, *Caminos de la Democracia en America Latina*. Madrid: Editorial Pablo Iglesias, 1984; Isidoro Cheresky and Jacques Choncol (eds.), *Crisis y Transformacion de los Regimenes Autoritarios*. Buenos Aires: EUDEBA, 1985; Augusto Valas (ed.), *Transicion a la Democracia*. Santiago: FLACSO, 1985; *Los Limites de la Democracia, (two volumes)*. Buenos Aires: CLACSO, 1985; Alain Rouquie, Bolivar Lamounier and Jorge Schvarzer (eds.), *Como Renascem as Democracias*. São Paulo: Editora Brasilense, 1985; Alain Rouquie, *La démocratie ou l'apprentissage de la vertu*. Paris: Metailie, 1985; Guillermo O'Donnell, Philippe Schmitter and Laurence Whitehead (eds.), *Transitions from Authoritarian Rule* (four volumes). Baltimore: Johns Hopkins University Press, 1986; Paul W. Drake and Eduardo Silva (eds.), *Elections and Democratization in Latin America, 1980–1985*. San Diego: Center for Iberian and Latin American Studies, University of California, 1986; Enrique A. Baloyra (ed.), *Comparing New Democracies: Transition and Consolidation in Mediterranean Europe and the Southern Cone*. Boulder: West View Press, 1987; Carlos Huneeus (ed.), *Para Vivir La Democracia*. Santiago: Editorial Andante, 1987. James L. Malloy and Mitchell A. Seligson (eds.), *Authoritarians and Democrats: The Politics of Regime Transition in Latin America*. Pittsburgh: University of Pittsburgh Press, 1987; George A. Lopez and Michael Stohl (eds.), *Liberalization and Redemocratization in Latin America*. New York: Greenwood Press, 1987; Dieter Nohlen and Aldo Solari (eds.), *Reforma Politica y Consolidacion Democrática*. Caracas: Editorial Nueva Sociedad, 1988; Larry Diamond, Juan J. Linz and Seymour Martin Lipset (eds.), *Democracy in Developing Countries* (four volumes). Boulder: Lynne Rienner Publishers, 1988; Benno Galjart

and Patricio Silva (eds.), *Democratization and the State in the Southern Cone*. Leiden: CEDLA, 1989

The literature on democratization in Eastern Europe is just beginning to appear and almost all of it deals with single cases: Jadwiga Staniszkis, *Poland's Self-Limiting Revolution*. Princeton: Princeton University Press, 1984; 'Central and Eastern European Social Research'. Special Issue. *Social Research*. Vol. 55, Nos. 1–2, Spring Summer, 1988; John Keane (ed.), *Civil Society and the State*. London: Verso, 1988; 'Perestroika in Eastern Europe'. Special Issue. *Telos*, No. 79, Spring 1989.

3. Albert Hirschman has even claimed that this search can be pernicious. In his view, to lay down strict preconditions for democracy, such as 'dynamic growth *must* be resumed, income distribution *must* be improved, . . . political parties *must* show a co-operative spirit . . .' may actually encourage the de-consolidation of existing democracies. Hirschman argues that this will almost certainly obstruct constructive thinking about the ways in which democracies may be formed, survive and even become stronger *in the face of and in spite of* continuing adversity. See his 'Dilemmas of Democratic Consolidation in Latin America', unpublished notes for the São Paulo Meeting on Democratic Consolidation in Latin America and Southern Europe. 1986.

4. See, especially, Guillermo O'Donnell and Philippe C. Schmitter. *Tentative Conclusions about Uncertain Transitions*. Vol. 4 of the study cited in note 1; Adam Przeworski, 'Some Problems in the Study of the Transition to Democracy', in Vol. 3 of the same study, and ibid., 'Democracy as a Contingent Outcome of Conflicts', in Rune Slagsted and Jon Elster (eds.), *Constitutionalism and Democracy*. New York: Cambridge University Press, 1989.

5. *Social Origins of Dictatorship and Democracy*. Boston: Beacon Press, 1966, pp. 418–19, 423–5.

6. See Jadwiga Staniszkis, 'The Obsolescence of Solidarity', *Telos*, No. 80, Summer 1989, pp. 37–50.

7. See John Weeks, 'An Interpretation of the Central American Crisis'. *Latin America Research Review*, Vol. XXI, No. 3, 1986.

8. This is the thrust of Daniel Levine's analysis of Venezuela, which attributes the emergence of a democratic regime primarily to statecraft and the ability of political actors to compromise. See his 'Venezuela since 1958, the Consolidation of Democratic Politics', in Juan Linz and Alfred Stepan (eds.), *The Breakdown of Democratic Regimes: Latin America*. Baltimore: Johns Hopkins University Press, 1978.

9. Cf. Terry Lynn Karl, 'Petroleum and Political Pacts: the Transition to Democracy in Venezuela', *Latin America Research Review*, January 1987, pp. 63–94, and Otto Kirchheimer, 'Confining Conditions and Revolutionary Breakthroughs', *American Political Science Review*, No. 59, 1965, pp. 964–74.

10. See the respective 'Introductions' to Vols. 1 and 2 of G. O'Donnell, P. Schmitter and Laurence Whitehead (eds.), *Transitions from Authoritarian Rule*, op. cit.

11. G. O'Donnell and P. Schmitter (eds.), *Tentative Conclusions*, op. cit., p. 18.

12. See Terry Lynn Karl, 'Imposing Consent? Electoralism versus democratization in El Salvador', in Paul W. Drake and Eduardo Silva (eds.), *Elections and Democratization in Latin America, 1980–1985*. San Diego: Center for Iberian and Latin American Studies, University of California, 1986, pp. 9.–36.

13. Although consider the following quotation from a thoughtful essay by Víctor-Pérez Díaz: 'In the life span of one generation Spain has become a modern capitalist economy. a liberal democratic polity and a tolerant and plural society. largely secular with regard to most economic and political concerns and based on values common to all Western European countries. with those of individual freedom and human rights in the forefront. This has been the result of a profound institutional and cultural transformation of which the democratic transition is only one, although a decisive. aspect.' 'The Emergence of Democratic Spain and the "Invention" of a Democratic Tradition'. Unpublished MS. March 1990. p. 6. Elsewhere in this work. Pérez-Díaz argues convincingly that most of the economic and social changes began under the Franco regime. so that they were never as simultaneous and sudden as in contemporary Eastern Europe.

14. See Philippe C. Schmitter. 'Liberation by *Golpe*: Retrospective Thoughts about the Demise of Authoritarian Rule in Portugal'. *Armed Forces and Society*. Vol. 2, No. 1. Fall 1975.

15. Cf. Michel Castex. *Un mensonge gros comme le siècle: Roumanie. histoire d'une manipulation*. Paris: Albin Michel. 1990: also 'Enigmas of a Revolution'. *The Economist*. 6 January. 1990.

16. Barrington Moore. Jr.. op. cit.. pp. 426–32.

17. There are interesting changes taking place in both post-revolutionary Nicaragua and Mexico. Nicaragua was the first revolutionary regime in Latin America to hold national elections in which a number of political parties were allowed to run. In 1984. the traditional Liberal and Conservative parties and several small leftist parties competed with the FSLN and won almost 35 per cent of the vote. In 1990, the UNO, a coalition of 14 anti-Sandinista parties, defeated the Sandinistas. who have so far respected the mandate of the electorate. In Mexico. the PRI has begun to permit greater contestation at the municipal and regional levels. but these elections are still characterized by numerous restrictions. fraud and localized violence.

18. Robert Dahl. *Polyarchy*. New Haven: Yale University Press. 1971. pp. 1–9.

19. On these cases. see Charles G. Gillespie. 'Uruguay's Transition from Collegial Military-Technocratic Rule'. in O'Donnell et al.. op. cit.. Vol. 2: Jonathan Hartlyn. 'Democracy in Colombia: the Politics of Violence and Accommodation'. in Larry Diamond. Juan J. Linz and Seymour Martin Lipset (eds.). *Democracy in Developing Countries: Latin America*. Vol. 4. Boulder: Lynne Rienner Publishers. 1989: Alexander W. Wilde. 'Conversations Among Gentlemen: Oligarchical Democracy in Colombia'. in Juan Linz and Alfred Stepan (eds.). *The Breakdown of Democratic Regimes: Latin America*. Baltimore: Johns Hopkins Press. 1978 and Terry Karl. 'Petroleum

and Political Pacts: the Transition to Democracy in Venezuela'. op. cit.. Vol. 2.

20. We are grateful to Samuel Valenzuela for this point. See his *Democratización Via Reforma: La Expansion del Sufragio en Chile*. Buenos Aires: Ediciones IDES. 1985.

21. There is little information on the dynamics of regime transition in Costa Rica. See Jacobo Schifter. *La fase oculta de la guerra civil en Costa Rica*. San Jose: EDUCA. 1979.

22. Even where the military retained control over the transition in Latin America. it systematically engaged in a process of consultation with civilian parties. See Francis Hagopian and Scott Mainwaring. 'Democracy in Brazil: Origins. Problems and Prospects'. *World Policy Journal*. Summer 1987. pp. 485–514. and Manuel Antonio Garretón. 'El Plebiscito de 1988 y la transición a la democracia'. Santiago: FLACSO. 1988.

23. For an analysis of this most difficult case which. however. does not stress the particular conditions surrounding its successive efforts at regime change. but rather long-term structural factors. see Carlos Waisman. *Reversal of Development in Argentina*. Princeton: Princeton University Press. 1987. For a detailed analysis of one specific 'cycle' of this agonizing pattern. see Guillermo O'Donnell. *Bureaucratic Authoritarianism: Argentina in Comparative Perspective*. Berkeley: University of California Press. 1988.

Part III
National Case-Studies of Transition:
Three Area Studies

Southern Europe

[9]

Arend Lijphart

The Southern European Examples of Democratization: Six Lessons for Latin America*

THE RETURN TO DEMOCRACY OF SPAIN, PORTUGAL, AND Greece in the 1970s is an encouraging and inspiring example to democrats everywhere — but especially to Latin American democrats because of their region's close historical and cultural ties with two of the Southern European countries. However, apart from the general feeling of optimism that the Southern European experience legitimately engenders, are there any specific lessons and lessons specifically relevant to Latin America that can be learned from it? In this article, I shall suggest six such lessons. Some of these are positive lessons — examples to be followed, such as choosing a form of democracy that is suitable to a country's size and to its political and social divisions; others are negative — examples to be avoided, such as Portugal's and Greece's experimentation with a presidential form of government. Some lessons are based on common characteristics of the new Southern European democracies; others concern traits on which they differ.

In a recent co-authored study of these three newly democratic countries, plus Italy, the fourth Southern European democracy, I have shown that the differences among them are more important than the similarities: differences in their forms of democracy and in the process of moving from authoritarian to democratic regimes.[1] The differences in their forms of democracy are particularly striking. As I have argued in my book *Democracies*,

*This article is a revised version of a paper presented at the International Seminar on 'Las Perspectivas de la Estabilidad Democrática en los Países Andinos', organized by the Department of Political Science of the Universidad de los Andes, in Villa de Leyva, Colombia, August 8–12, 1988.

[1] Arend Lijphart, Thomas C. Bruneau, P. Nikiforos Diamandouros, and Richard Gunther, 'A Mediterranean Model of Democracy? The Southern European Democracies in Comparative Perspective', *West European Politics*, 11, 1, January 1988, pp. 7–25.

SIX LESSONS FOR LATIN AMERICA   69

two basic forms of democracy, majoritarian and consensus, differ along two dimensions.[2] Each of these dimensions is divided in four categories in Figure 1, creating a matrix with sixteen cells. The democracies classified in these cells are the three newly democratic Southern European countries plus the twenty-one democracies that have been continually democratic since the end of the Second World War; since France underwent a major change in democratic regime in 1958, the French Fourth and Fifth Republics are treated as two separate cases.

The executives-parties dimension is based on a cluster of five characteristics of the party and electoral systems and of the arrangement of executive power. The majoritarian and the contrasting consensual elements are 1) single-party governments versus broad coalition governments, 2) executive dominance versus executive-legislative balance, 3) two-party versus multiparty systems, 4) parties that differ mainly with regard to socio-economic issues versus parties divided by religious, cultural, foreign policy, and regime support issues as well, and 5) plurality or first-past-the-post electoral systems versus proportional representation. Each of these contrasting characteristics represents a continuum from pure majoritarianism to pure consensus democracy; they were operationalized and scores on them were assigned to the 25 democratic systems. Since these scores use different scales, they were all standardized (so as to have a mean of 0 and a standard deviation of 1). The total scores on the executives-parties dimension as a whole are the averages (again standardized) of the five individual scores. Democracies that are majoritarian on the executives-parties dimension are shown in the top half of Figure 1, the consensus democracies at the bottom.

The second dimension has to do with the three related variables of 1) government centralization, measured in terms of the central government's taxing powers, 2) constitutional flexibility, ranging from an unwritten constitution to a written constitution that is difficult to amend and protected by judicial review, and 3) unicameralism versus strong bicameralism. Since these differences are commonly associated with the contrast between federalism and unitary government, this dimension is called the federal-unitary dimension. The country scores on this dimension are again the standardized averages of the three standardized

[2] Arend Lijphart, *Democracies: Patterns of Majoritarian and Consensus Government in Twenty-One Countries*, New Haven, Yale University Press, 1984.

70   GOVERNMENT AND OPPOSITION

FIGURE 1
Twenty-Five Democracies Classified According to the Two Majoritarian-Consensus Dimensions
II Federal-unitary dimension

		Strongly majoritarian	Majoritarian	Consensual	Strongly consensual
I Executives-Parties Dimension	Strongly majoritarian	New Zealand United Kingdom	*Greece* Ireland	Austria	Australia Canada United States
	Majoritarian		France v Luxembourg Sweden	*Spain*	Germany Japan
	Consensual	Iceland	Belgium Denmark Norway *Portugal*		
	Strongly consensual	Israel	Finland France IV Netherlands	*Italy*	Switzerland

Notes: 1. The dividing points between the four categories of each dimension
          are the standardized means of .75, 0. and − .75.
       2. The period covered is approximately 1945 − 80 for most of the
          countries and approximately 1975 − 86 for Spain, Portugal and
          Greece.

Source: Adapted from Arend Lijphart, Thomas C. Bruneau, P. Nikiforos
        Diamandouros, and Richard Gunther, 'A Mediterranean Model of
        Democracy? The Southern European Democracies in Comparative
        Perspective', *West European Politics*, 11, 1 January 1988, p. 12.

scores. The 'unitary' (majoritarian) democracies are shown on
the left-hand side of Figure 1, the 'federal' (consensual)
democracies on the right.

As Figure 1 shows, there are relatively few democracies that
occupy an extreme position on both dimensions. New Zealand
and the United Kingdom are unambiguous examples of the
majoritarian model and Switzerland of the consensus model.
Israel is a virtually perfect example of majoritarianism on the first
dimension and unitary government on the second; Australia,
Canada, and the United States exhibit the exactly opposite
characteristics to a high degree. Most of the other countries —

SIX LESSONS FOR LATIN AMERICA   71

including the four Southern European democracies, italicized in
the figure — are more in the middle. Spain, Portugal, Italy,
Greece clearly do not form a distinctive cluster: they are located
in different and non-contiguous cells, and they differ from each
other particularly as far as the executives-parties dimension is
concerned.

Spain's, Portugal's, and Greece's contemporaneous democratization in the 1970s should not divert our attention from the
different circumstances of their return to democracy. For one
thing, their previous authoritarian periods were of widely
different durations: a mere seven-year interlude in Greece,
compared with more than a third of a century of authoritarianism
in Spain, and almost half a century in Portugal. Moreover, their
authoritarian regimes came to an end as a result of very different
events: the dictator's death in the case of Spain, war and
institutional exhaustion in Portugal, and a combination of
internal crisis and foreign-policy adventurism in Greece. Finally,
the transition to democracy occurred under quite dissimilar
ideological leaderships: the conservatives in Greece, the left-
leaning military in Portugal, and a broad coalition in Spain that
practised what was referred to as 'the politics of consensus'.

There are also important differences within Latin America to
be noted, as well as differences between Southern Europe and
Latin America. In the concluding part of this article I shall
consider to what extent the inter-regional differences affect the
relevance of the Southern European lessons to the Latin
American situation. But let me first turn to the substance of these
lessons.

LESSON ONE: OPPORTUNITIES FOR DEMOCRATIC ENGINEERING

In contrast with the striking differences among the Southern
European democracies with regard to their forms of and
transitions to democracy, there are many background
characteristics that they have in common — cultural, social,
economic, historical-developmental, and geographical. For
instance, in addition to their shared Southern European
geographical location, they are economically less developed than
most other European countries. Spain, Portugal, and Italy have
agricultural sectors characterized by latifundia in the south and
small farms in the north — a division that has strongly affected
politics in the past and present. These same three countries share

a Latin culture and also a common religious condition; unlike in many other European countries, there was never a Catholic-Protestant split but a deep and politically very salient clerical-anticlerical cleavage.

The contrast between these similarities in background conditions and the differences with regard to type of democratic regime and the process of democratization is theoretically very significant. It reveals the limitations of socio-economic and cultural reductionist arguments: political institutions and the basic rules of the game of democratic politics are not merely a 'superstructure' that grows out of a socio-economic-cultural base. Politics, including democratic politics, has an independent life of its own.

This theoretical conclusion has a significant practical relevance. It means that there is ample room for political and constitutional engineering. While politics remains the art of the possible, democratic engineers need not feel too constrained in making the necessary choices of rules and institutions that will serve their democratic systems best.

LESSON TWO: DEMOCRACY IN DIVIDED SOCIETIES

Several conclusions as well as practical lessons emerge when we try to explain why particular countries occupy particular positions in Figure 1. There are three explanations: the degree of pluralism, population size, and the influence of the majoritarian Westminster model on countries with a British heritage. The first and second contain positive practical lessons, the third a negative lesson.

Let us turn to the question of pluralism first. Figure 1 shows a connection between both dimensions of the majoritarian-consensus contrast on the one hand and the degree to which the countries are plural societies on the other. Plural societies are societies that are sharply divided along religious, ideological, linguistic, cultural, ethnic, or racial lines into virtually separate sub-societies with their own political parties, interest groups, and media of communication. No country is either 'completely' plural or 'completely' nonplural, of course, but we can make a rough threefold classification into plural, semiplural, and nonplural societies. As we move from the upper left-hand corner to the lower right-hand corner of Figure 1, we encounter plural and semiplural societies with increasing frequency. The four cells on the diagonal from Israel to Australia contain nonplural societies (Denmark, Norway, Portugal, and Australia) and plural and semiplural ones in approximately equal numbers. Above and to the left of this diagonal, all countries except Austria, the French Fifth Republic, and Luxembourg are plural or semiplural; below and to the left of the diagonal, only one country — Japan — is nonplural. Of these four exceptions, Austria is probably not really deviant; my coding system probably resulted in a too high majoritarian score for this country on the first dimension.[3] The other three are true exceptions, but the important point is that there are only three such deviant cases out of a total of 25. The relationship would be even stronger if it were not for the other two factors — British political traditions and population size — that also have strong influence. I shall discuss these subjects shortly.

The general pattern is that countries with significant societal divisions tend to adopt forms of democratic government that can accommodate these divisions, namely, rules and institutions of consensus democracy. And the practical lesson for political engineers is explicitly to take such deep divisions and differences into account wherever they exist and to be creative and constructive in establishing the appropriate consensus-oriented and consensus-inducing democratic arrangements. Moreover, it is important not to think of plural societies too narrowly as countries divided by ethnic or other primordial cleavages. Consensus democracy is clearly needed by all countries that have deep divisions of any kind or that face immense problems, including countries with a recent history of military dictatorship and civil war, countries with huge socio-economic inequalities, and so on. Many Latin American countries can be described in these terms.

If we look at the placement of the four Southern European democracies in Figure 1, we see that, as expected, religiously and ideologically divided Italy and linguistically plural Spain are located to the right of nonplural Greece and Portugal. On the

[3] One of the reasons for Austria's high majoritarian score is that the country was governed from 1949 to 1966 by a 'grand coalition' of the large Socialist and People's Parties, neither of which had a majority in parliament. Technically, therefore, this coalition had to be classified as a highly majoritarian 'minimum winning coalition' (or bare-majority coalition) in spite of the fact that together these parties enjoyed overwhelming parliamentary support. If the minimum-winning criterion could be relaxed so as to allow the Austrian grand coalition to be classified as an inclusive 'oversized' coalition government, Austria would move down one cell in Figure 1.

other hand, it is surprising that on the executives-parties dimension Greece is among the most majoritarian regimes and that Spain is on the majoritarian side, too, given the severe political and ideological divisions in these countries in the recent past and the continuing cultural-linguistic cleavages in Spain. Greece had single-party majority cabinets between its return to democracy in 1974 and the middle of 1989, and Spain has abandoned its earlier reliance on 'the politics of consensus' and has had one-party majority governments since 1982. This emphasis on straight majority rule has not led to a serious crisis, mainly because the ruling parties have behaved with moderation, but it has entailed a serious risk for these newly democratic countries — a risk that I would not want to recommend as an example to be followed.

LESSON THREE: PR AND PROPORTIONALITY

The next lesson follows immediately from the above point. What has made single-party majority cabinets possible in Spain and Greece is that their parliamentary elections have resulted in many victories for one party; this is true for four of the six elections in Greece held so far (the 1989 elections are the exception) and in the last three of the five Spanish elections. It is important to note that six of these seven one-party majorities won at the polls were what Douglas W. Rae calls 'manufactured majorities': a party winning a majority of the legislative seats with only a minority of the popular vote.[4] Such manufactured majorities are quite common in plurality systems but rare under proportional representation (PR). Spain uses PR but applies it in small districts, which discriminates against minor parties and in favour of the large parties. Until the 1989 elections, Greece used a PR system that was usually referred to as 'reinforced PR', but what was being reinforced was the large parties rather than proportionality.

The lesson to democratic engineers is: if you want to encourage power-sharing coalition government instead of one-party rule, and if you want to avoid the artificial manufacturing of majorities, you should choose a PR system that is proportional in reality as well as in name — unlike the Spanish and Greek examples. This lesson is of special importance to Latin America

[4] Douglas W. Rae, *The Political Consequences of Electoral Laws*, New Haven, Yale University Press, 1967, p. 74.

since many countries in this region have strong traditions of conducting their legislative elections by PR. It is worth noting that these traditions constitute an unexpected deviation from the United States model of mainly plurality and majority electoral systems; as I shall show later, the American model of democracy is very strong in Latin America in other respects, especially as far as the reliance on presidential forms of government is concerned.

It should also be pointed out, however, that presidentialism and PR elections of the legislature are related to each other: presidentialism tends to limit the operation of PR. The reason is that the presidency is the biggest political prize to be won and that only the largest parties have a chance to win it. This creates a major advantage for the large parties and a disadvantage for the smaller ones not only in the presidential elections themselves but also indirectly in the legislative elections even when the latter are conducted by PR. As Matthew Shugart has pointed out, this is especially the case when the legislative election is held at the same time or shortly after the presidential election.[5] In addition to this indirect effect of presidentialism on limiting proportionality and minority representation, presidentialism also has a direct negative effect on proportionality, of course: the fact that a presidential election entails the election of one person necessarily means that plurality or majority methods have to be used and that PR is logically excluded.

LESSON FOUR: THE TRADITION OF PRESIDENTIALISM

The second explanation of the configuration of democracies in Figure 1 has an indirect but quite important relevance to our concerns: the countries with a British political heritage (Britain itself, New Zealand, Ireland, Australia, Canada, and the United States) are all highly majoritarian on the executives-parties dimension and are all located in the top row of the figure. The influence of the Westminster model as a normative example has tended to interfere with the need for more consensual arrangements in some of the countries. In particular, had it not been for the strong British influence, it is quite unlikely that

[5] Matthew S. Shugart, 'Duverger's Rule and Presidentialism: The Effects of the Timing of Elections', paper presented at the Annual Meeting of the American Political Science Association, Washington, D.C., 1988.

linguistically plural Canada would have developed along such strongly majoritarian lines (on the first dimension).

There are other examples of dominant and potentially dangerous foreign models that have been obstacles to an optimal choice of democratic type based on a country's needs. The presidential form of government of the French Fifth Republic was such a model for Portugal and Greece; because of the fortunate circumstance of having a monarchy, Spain escaped this influence. And the US presidential model has had a powerful impact in Latin America. Without going into a full evaluation of the advantages and disadvantages of presidentialism, let me emphasize two serious problems.[6] One is that it entails a strong predisposition toward majoritarian democracy: it means the concentration of all executive power in the hands of one person, which is incompatible with broad coalition government and power-sharing. Guillermo O'Donnell notes 'the infrequent recourse to formal and explicit political and economic pacts as transitional devices in Latin America', in contrast with *pactismo* in Southern Europe. He tries to explain this phenomenon in terms of popular pressures that make compromises difficult and in terms of the absence of strongly institutionalized party systems.[7] In addition, it seems to me, presidentialism is to blame: by its very nature it is inimical to collective and collegial decision-making and hence to compromises either on an ad hoc or regularized basis. Moreover, where pacts have been successfully established in presidential regimes, as in Colombia and Venezuela, they have entailed more drastic limitations on democratic participation and the rights of oppositions than similar pacts in more flexible parliamentary systems.

The second major problem of presidentialism is that it is based on the principle of separation and balance of executive and legislative powers but that, in practice, most presidential systems have found it impossible to achieve this balance. The United States itself is an exception, although historically it has also experienced swings between, in Woodrow Wilson's words,

[6] For an excellent and much more extensive analysis, see Juan J. Linz, 'Democracy, Presidential or Parliamentary: Does It Make a Difference?', paper presented at the Annual Meeting of the American Political Science Association, Chicago, 1987.

[7] Guillermo O'Donnell, 'Introduction to the Latin American Cases', in Guillermo O'Donnell, Philippe C. Schmitter, and Laurence Whitehead (eds), *Transitions from Authoritarian Rule: Prospects for Democracy*, Baltimore, Johns Hopkins University Press, vol. 2, pp. 11 – 12.

'Congressional government' and the so-called 'imperial presidency'.[8] The usual interpretation of presidential power in Latin America is that is has overwhelmed the power of the legislature and that it has tended to turn into dictatorial power. One typical response to this danger has been to limit the president's right to be re-elected. As Harry Kantor points out, however, such rules 'are infractions upon true democracy, which demands that voters be allowed to vote for whomever they choose'.[9] I would add that they also conflict with the democratic assumption that the opportunity to be re-elected is a strong incentive for elected officials to remain responsive to the voters' wishes. The fact that parliamentary executives do not need to be limited by such basically undemocratic rules shows that they are much safer for democracy. In addition to restrictions on presidential succession, many other limitations on presidential prerogatives have often been adopted, based on the same fear of too strong presidential power. Ironically, this has often meant that presidents have become virtually powerless and frustrated. In fact, the increasingly prevalent interpretation of the problem of presidentialism in Latin America is that presidents suffer from too little instead of too much power.[10]

Portugal had a French-style presidential government — a strong president combined with a cabinet dependent on the legislature's confidence — from 1976 to 1982. The constitution gave the president extensive powers, and his popular election added to his political stature. However, the president's powers were severely reduced in the 1982 constitutional revision and, although popular election was not changed, Portugal reverted to a parliamentary system — similar to the Austrian, Irish, and Icelandic parliamentary systems which have weak, albeit popularly elected, presidents, too. Greece also adopted a strong presidency, inspired by the French model, although the president was not popularly elected; President Constantine Karamanlis's great personal prestige partly compensated for this lack of popular legitimation. The 1986 constitutional amendments eliminated

---

[8] See Fred W. Riggs, 'The Survival of Presidentialism in America: Para-Constitutional Practices', *International Political Science Review*, 9, 4, October 1988, pp. 247 – 78.

[9] Harry Kantor, 'Efforts Made by Various Latin American Countries to Limit the Power of the President', in Thomas V. DiBacco (ed.), *Presidential Power in Latin American Politics*, New York, Praeger, 1977, pp. 23 – 24.

[10] See Scott Mainwaring, 'Presidentialism in Latin America: A Review Essay', *Latin American Research Review*, forthcoming, 1990.

almost all of the special powers of the president, making the regime unambiguously parliamentary.

These Portuguese and Greek examples of constitutional adaptation should be regarded as positive and highly instructive models to democrats, especially in the Western hemisphere, who are predisposed to think in presidential terms. Shifting from presidential to parliamentary government entails a drastic and difficult, but clearly not impossible, regime change. On the other hand, there are two reasons why such a change was easier for Portugal and Greece than it would be for the Latin American democracies. One is that the French presidential model already contains some parliamentary features — the model is, in fact, often called merely *semi*-presidential — and hence that it can be turned into parliamentarism more easily than the US presidential model. Secondly, presidential government in Greece and Portugal did not last long enough to become a firm tradition, while the problem in Latin America is not just the influence of the US presidential model but also the fact that presidentialism has become a strong Latin American tradition, too.

LESSON FIVE: POPULATION SIZE, DECENTRALIZATION, AND FEDERALISM

Let us now turn to the third and last explanation of the distribution of the 25 democratic systems in Figure 1: the respective sizes of the countries' populations. Figure 1 shows that this variable is correlated with the federal-unitary contrast, although the relationship is obviously not a perfectly monotonic one. As we move from strong majoritarianism ('unitary government') on the left to strong consensus ('federalism') on the right, we find that population size tends to go up. The most striking exceptions are the United Kingdom which, in terms of this explanation, is placed too far to the left in the figure, and Switzerland which is similarly much too far on the right-hand side. The four Southern European democracies display roughly the differences that we would expect on the basis of their different population sizes: the two smaller countries, Greece and Portugal, with populations of about ten million each, are located higher than Spain and Italy, which have respectively about four and six times larger populations.

It is not surprising that we find this link between population size and type of democracy: larger countries need more provisions for regional autonomy and more of the supporting 'federal' institutions than small countries. The practical lesson for democratic engineers is that the form of democracy chosen should be appropriate to their particular country in this respect. Democracies do not have to be formally federal in order to be rated as 'federal' (consensual) in Figure 1. The criteria for classification on the federal-unitary dimension are the degree of government centralization, the organization of the national legislature (unicameralism versus strong bicameralism), and constitutional flexibility; in other words, whether or not a country is formally federal is *not* a criterion. And, in fact, of the nine countries classified in the consensual and strongly consensual cells on the federal-unitary dimension in Figure 1, three are formally unitary states: Japan and our two more 'federal' Southern European countries, Spain and Italy. On the other hand, formal federalism does appear to be a factor of considerable importance: the six countries that have explicit federal constitutions are all on the right-hand side of the figure, and five of the six are on the far right-hand side. In Latin America, there is a similar relationship between population size and formal federalism. Most of the larger countries have federal constitutions — Brazil, Mexico, Argentina, and Venezuela — but there is no strong tradition of actual government decentralization. For instance, Daniel J. Elazar states that in Mexico the states 'exercise limited autonomy [under] a very strong federal government', and he describes Argentina as 'a federation in which most power is lodged in the federal capital'. On the other hand, Colombia is a 'decentralized unitary state' in which decentralization is maintained by 'the strong demands for autonomy that exist in some of the major provinces'.[11]

In the previous section, I emphasized the negative influence of the United States model of presidential government. I should now state with equal emphasis that in two other respects the US model should be regarded as beneficial for the Latin American countries, since the model also includes federalism and a strong written constitution; I shall discuss the latter in the next section. As far as the federal model is concerned, Sir Arthur Lewis's analysis of the failure of democracy in West Africa is highly pertinent. He attributes a large part of the blame to the pernicious

---

[11] Daniel J. Elazar, 'Arrangements for Self-Rule and Autonomy in Various Countries of the World: A Preliminary Inventory', in Daniel J. Elazar (ed.), *Federalism and Political Integration*, Lanham, Maryland, University Press of America, 1984, pp. 230–31.

influence of the majoritarian model, including its unitary and centralist bias. These states 'would have fared better if they had not had to assume that British and French constitutional ideas were superior to all others. With an American heritage, they would have taken the federal idea for granted, and it would have been the centralizers who were arguing an unpopular case'. He concludes that the West African countries 'will need much un-brainwashing before they grasp their problems in true perspective'.[12] Lewis would undoubtedly regard the Latin American countries as very fortunate for not having to undergo the same 'un-brainwashing' due to the strong influence of the US model.

Because the federal component of the US model must be judged positively but the presidential component negatively, it is important to stress that the two are not logically linked with each other. Klaus von Beyme points out that 'right into the twentieth century the prejudice persisted vigorously that federalism and parliamentary majority government could not be combined'. Citing the Argentinian, Brazilian, Mexican, and Venezuelan examples, he adds that 'this message was taken especially to heart in Latin America'. Among Europeans, the examples of federal-cum-parliamentary government in Australia and Canada were long ignored, and it is only after the adoption of the similar constitutional mixes in Austria and West Germany that 'this prejudice has died out — at least in Europe.[13] To the extent that the myth persists in Latin America, it also deserves to die out there.

LESSON SIX: CONSTITUTIONAL PROTECTION

While the new Southern European democracies have different positions on the federal-unitary dimension, they are strikingly alike with regard to one of the variables that goes into this dimension: the rigidity of their constitutions. All three have written constitutions that can be amended only by extraordinary majorities and are protected by judicial review. Their emergence from dictatorial rule accounts for much of this similarity. Of the other democracies in Figure 1 only seven have equally firm and

[12] W. Arthur Lewis, *Politics in West Africa*, London, Allen & Unwin, 1965, p. 55.

[13] Klaus von Beyme, *America as a Model: The Impact of American Democracy in the World*, New York, St Martin's Press, 1987, p. 76 (italics omitted).

protected constitutions, and three — Austria, Germany, and Japan — have similar backgrounds of authoritarianism.

Since this background is unfortunately also common in Latin America, the Southern European model of strong constitutional protection is a positive example. Flexible constitutions, such as the unwritten constitutions of Great Britain and New Zealand and the surprisingly many written constitutions that can be amended by majority rule and/or are not protected by the courts' ability to test the constitutionality of laws, are a luxury that some older and completely self-confident democracies may be able to afford. It is a luxury that cannot be recommended for new and less firmly established democratic systems.

As indicated earlier, constitutional rigidity and judicial review are important parts of the US model of democracy; Karl Loewenstein even called them 'America's most important export'.[14] In fact, it can be argued that judicial review is a logical corollary of both separation of powers (presidential government) and division of powers (federalism) since an impartial authority is needed to decide where exactly these powers should be separated and divided.[15] On the other hand, there is no logical reason why judicial review and rigid constitutions cannot be combined with parliamentary government or, for that matter, with unitary and centralized systems. In practice, as von Beyme points out, 'today more parliamentary systems than presidential ones have established a variation on the theme of constitutional jurisdiction'.[16] Very clearly, the combination of parliamentary government, strong constitutional protection, and, for the larger countries, federalism and decentralization is both possible and advisable.

CONCLUSION

I believe that these six lessons are both valid and valuable in spite of the obviously many and considerable differences among the Southern European countries, among the Latin American countries, and also between Southern Europe and Latin America. I have already repeatedly referred to the first two sets of

---

[14] Cited in von Beyme, *America as a Model*, op. cit., p. 85.

[15] See K. C. Wheare, *Federal Government*, 4th ed., New York, Oxford University Press, 1984, pp. 53 – 74.

[16] Von Beyme, *America as a Model*, op. cit., p. 85.

differences, those within Southern Europe and within Latin America. However, the most important reason for doubting the relevance of the Southern European examples for Latin America would be the difference between the two regions. It is precisely this difference that several scholars have recently emphasized. For instance, Guillermo O'Donnell writes that 'the prospects for political democracy in Latin America are not very favorable, certainly less so than in Southern Europe'.[17] O'Donnell's co-author of the authoritative four-volume work *Transitions from Authoritarian Rule*, Philippe C. Schmitter, is equally pessimistic. In my opinion, both this forecast and the grounds for it are exaggerated.

One of the reasons for their pessimism, with which I find myself largely in agreement, concerns the considerable socio-economic differences between the two regions. What is important here is not the overall level of economic development. Italy and Spain may be economically more developed than any of the Latin American countries, but Portugal and Greece are clearly not. The crucial difference is that socio-economic inequality is substantially greater in Latin America than in Southern Europe. O'Donnell speaks of 'acute, pervasive, and blatant inequalities' in the latter region.[18] But O'Donnell's diagnosis should yield two conclusions, instead of one: this major cleavage makes viable democracy less likely, but the likelihood can be improved by using the appropriate consensual instruments.

Another reason why O'Donnell and Schmitter are pessimistic is that the Latin American countries do not share the Southern European advantage of 'the relatively modest, not to say minor, role played by the armed forces in the defunct regime'. But Greece is at least a partial exception to this pattern and, as Schmitter himself points out, there is the countervailing disadvantage that the Southern European countries have...experienced bureaucratic-authoritarian rule more continuously and for a longer period of time'. Another difference is that the international context has been more favourable to Southern Europe than to Latin America. For one thing, 'the United States, whose policies toward democratization in Latin America have been ambiguous and variant from one case to another, has consistently supported it in Southern Europe'. But Schmitter himself concludes that such external forces have been of

[17] Guillermo O'Donnell, 'Introduction to the Latin American Cases', op. cit., p. 14.
[18] ibid., p. 11.

minor importance and that the transitions from authoritarian rule and the prospects for democracy must be largely explained 'in terms of national forces and calculations'.[19]

Schmitter also emphasizes the differential role of dominant models: 'The Southern European countries may have also benefited from their distance from the American system of government. Western Europe may seem to be monolithically democratic in the contemporary period, but beneath that overall similarity lie many differences in institutional configuration [such as] pure parliamentarism, semipresidentialism, and consociation-alism, coupled with a wide range of party systems, electoral arrangements, and territorial distributions of authority'. The Latin American political engineers, by contrast, 'may be compelled to choose from a more restricted menu. The hegemony of the United States as a model of political democracy, not to mention the legacy of their own nineteenth-century constitutions, makes it less likely that they will deviate from the presidentialist, bicameral, formal checks-and-balances, first-past-the-post "ideal" with its implied two-party system'.[20] After all that I have said myself about the importance of normative models of democracy, I have to endorse much of what Schmitter is arguing, but I would add three qualifications. First, as I have emphasized several times, parts of the US model are positive and valuable for Latin America. Secondly, Schmitter's statement that the Latin Americans may be 'compelled' to choose from the US model and their own political traditions is too strong and too deterministic; in fact, there has been considerable interest in studying the European, and especially Southern European, examples. My third, relatively minor, point concerns the choice of electoral systems. Here the variation in Europe is much more limited — PR is the nearly universal norm — and the Latin American experience is much more varied — including a strong PR tradition — than Schmitter claims.

Finally, in spite of all his pessimism, O'Donnell argues that the chances for democracy in Latin America may not be so small after all because of the widespread revulsion against the excesses of recent authoritarian regimes. As a result, 'never has the

---

[19] Philippe C. Schmitter,'An Introduction to Southern European Transitions from Authoritarian Rule: Italy, Greece, Portugal, Spain, and Turkey', in O'Donnell, Schmitter, and Whitehead (eds), *Transitions from Authoritarian Rule*, op. cit., vol. 1, pp. 4 – 5.
[20] ibid., p. 9.

ideological "prestige" of political democracy been higher in Latin America than now' — offering an unprecedented opportunity for the establishment and consolidation of democracy. 'This is the terrain', he continues, 'where that unpredictable combination of *virtù* on the part of leaders, and *fortuna* in the combination of circumstances, may make the crucial difference'.[21] The message of this article has been that the political engineers' *virtù* should include not only a strong commitment to democracy but also the willingness and ability to be creative, to be not over constrained by existing political traditions, to examine all of the available options, and to learn from the positive and negative examples of other democracies.

[21] O'Donnell, 'Introduction to the Latin American Cases', op. cit., p. 11.

[10]

Government Performance:
An Issue and Three Cases in Search of Theory

Giuseppe Di Palma

> A people who were not in conflict about some rather fundamental matters would have little need to devise democracy's elaborate rules for conflict resolution.
>
> Dankwart Rustow[1]

This essay is not a full account of the relative performance of the new democratic governments of southern Europe. Since the proper evaluation of performance and its correlates – especially when it comes to new democracies – seems to me to be still very much at issue, this essay is rather a critical exploration of this question with examples drawn from the region.

Is there something especially difficult about government performance in new democracies, something debilitating in their newness? To support this view there is as a minimum the double notion that new democracies are born with a legitimacy problem and that effective performance is closely connected with legitimacy. Democracy – so goes the argument – is an inherently incohesive system of government; it is a system of compromise, a set of rules for mediating plural and competing interests, to which a country takes poorly after the inevitable trauma of authoritarian or totalitarian demise. For one thing, resentment against democracy builds among those leaders and supporters of the old regime who have lost benefits, power or more, as a consequence of its demise. For another, there are many who do not subscribe to democracy as a system of government, irrespective of personal costs or benefits. These principled opponents are to be found not only among the loyalists of the past regime but also among those who fought it hoping to replace it with their own brand of totalitarianism/authoritarianism. But democracy cannot rely on force and repression alone to resist its opponents without imperilling its authenticity. In fact the use of force, even when needed to save democracy, may end up by alienating whatever democratic support there exists. How then can a new democracy consolidate itself if it can only rely on competitive means – means that its opponents shun and its practitioners plainly cannot practise? Immobilism and indecisiveness in a vast area of crucial policy issues seem natural outcomes of this predicament, feeding in turn on to illegitimacy.

Given the predicament, the successful redemocratisation of West Germany (or for that matter postwar Japan) and the widely acclaimed effectiveness of their governments have been seen as fully exceptional cases, in which the decisive but exogenous factors that tilted the scale in favour of democracy are taken to be prolonged Allied occupation and carefully staged political reconstruction under close supervision by the occupying powers. At the same time, the clearest examples, and somehow the rule, when it comes to the plight

GOVERNMENT PERFORMANCE   173

of new democracies have been taken to be Italy and France; two countries that rebuilt democracy with little if any foreign supervision and little if any restraint upon domestic centrifugal forces. Thus, not for anything, Italy is still regarded as Europe's permanently sick democracy, and in France the Fourth Republic lasted only thirteen years.

Without fully discounting this line of analysis and its bearing on the particular cases, I propose a second look. Exactly because, I will argue, transferring allegiance, support and loyalty to a new regime is largely a matter of calculus and interest, it is not inescapably true that new democracies suffer from a problem of legitimacy – on the contrary. And though in a new and untried democracy, born naturally through and into conflict, problems of government performance *seem* aplenty, neither is it necessarily true that any such problem hides one of legitimacy and/or will feed negatively on to legitimacy – even if we understand the latter as a fact of calculus and interest. In a competitive democracy, new or old, government performance is always at issue. But whether the issue is or becomes unmanageable, leaving governments without space for choice and manoeuvre, depends on how the problem of legitimacy has been resolved to begin with. All of which, I will also argue, points to a sturdier view of new democracies overall; though, within this view, significant differences exist between the three southern European cases at hand – Spain, Portugal and Greece.

Dankwart Rustow wrote in 1970 that, for the historical record, democracies have been born nearly always as nothing more than a compromise. The compromise brought together forces who were or could be engaged in an otherwise inconclusive struggle for regime supremacy, and served therefore to terminate or forestall political confrontation. Rustow's remarks have two interesting and promising implications for new democracies – especially those which, like ours, return for the second time to democracy after a dictatorial interlude. First, 'genuine' democrats need not pre-exist democracy, and in point of fact they rarely do so in any substantial numbers. Second, being a means for reconciliation, the democratic compromise need not be more than a second best for the parties that negotiate it.[2] In other words, the rules of the democratic game are more a matter of instrumental agreement worked out among competing leaderships and institutions, *which accept to remain competitive within the new agreement*, than one of pre-existing popular or elite consensus on fundamentals. This much is forcefully implied in the quote from Rustow with which I open this paper. Therefore the transfer of allegiance from dictatorship to democracy, though always difficult, does not require exceptionally favourable circumstances, and the viability of a new democracy rests ultimately in making the transfer, if at all possible, attractive, convenient or compelling. It is to what make the transfer finally attractive, convenient or compelling though initially difficult that I now turn my attention.

TRANSFERRING ALLEGIANCE TO DEMOCRACY

I will leave out of my analysis those rare and intellectually less absorbing cases in which the transfer of allegiance is made almost inescapable by objective circumstances;[3] I will instead concentrate on those cases in which calculus, choice and leadership prove more decisive, as well as challenging and difficult. I suggest two sources of challenge.

In the first place, short of a holocaust brought upon the dictatorship by its own wars, it is unlikely that its crisis is so total as to leave a perfect vacuum of interests, organisations and allegiances in which a new democracy can safely step. Even if a dictatorship were to be overthrown by a revolt of its domestic enemies and nothing else – an unlikely occurrence, since either the dictatorship has a monopoly of force or it is already coming apart internally – it is most improbable that armed victory can cancel and reverse in one stroke the legacy that the dictatorship has left in the institutions and in the minds of people. The job begins, rather than ending, with armed victory. This is the more true if – as in our countries – to be overthrown is in fact an authoritarian rather than a totalitarian dictatorship; that is, a dictatorship that does not exercise command through newfangled and ruthless institutions of its own but makes do by penetrating and co-opting the existing structures and institutions (armies, bureaucracies, regular courts, conservative economic interests . . .). And it is even truer if the authoritarian regime, instead of falling in one piece at the hand of its enemies, falls apart because of internal exhaustion. Indeed, this seems to me the way in which authoritarian regimes go down most of the time: without having done anything so irreparably wrong to doom themselves unequivocally, they become, by the nature of their closed system, sluggish, inefficient, unable to adjust to changing times, irrelevant; or by liberalising they trigger higher expectations; or they substantially alter the place that some of their organised constituencies (most dangerously, the army) occupy in the regime; or worst of all, they show inability to accommodate the crisis of confidence that typically accompanies the death or incapacitation of the first dictator. It is in response to any combination of these circumstances that forces that are part of the coalitions supporting or running a dictatorship may come to consider it as finally expendable and disposable and may be tempted to secede.[4] Whether it is a matter of values and beliefs or one of self-interest, allegiance to dictatorship is not eternal and locked in. In all these cases of dictatorial crises, from revolution to secession, the challenge for the democratic forces is largely similar: since old interests have not disappeared into thin air, but may also be tempted to transfer allegiance, how can a new democracy accommodate them in the new compromise while removing those structures, through which the interests operated, that are incompatible with political democracy?

The challenge just described accurately depicts the predicament of our three southern European countries. Though there are interesting differences between them as to the precise status of the challenge – differences which will be of relevance later – what is important to stress at this point is the underlying commonality. In none of the countries did the transition make a clean slate of the past, except in its specific institutional forms. In all cases therefore the question of democratic legitimacy hinged on the treatment of the authoritarian past.

But this is only the first challenge. The second challenge does not come from inside the authoritarian regime. In countries like ours, which experienced a

GOVERNMENT PERFORMANCE   175

liberal or outright democratic period before the dictatorship, it comes from
the fact that the various social and political forces called to set up the
institutions of the reborn democracy tend to draw different lessons from the
failure of the first competitive experiment. Of major importance is the fact
that the left, even when recognising its own mistakes at the time (sectarianism,
internal dissension, excessive self-confidence) puts less emphasis than the
moderate and conservative forces on the past excesses of unbridled
parliamentarism. Rather, it tends to blame the old parliamentary system for
having been socially backward, elitist, insufficiently democratic, wavering in
the face of the authoritarian threat, or even hiding and abetting already
existing authoritarian practices. Therefore a new democracy that wants to aid
the conversion of the authoritarian right is compelled, because of this, to be
especially sensitive to the left's concerns as well – lest it appear to be a
democracy as narrow as the old. For example, measures that could be taken to
rationalise political democracy by rationalising the party system, parliamentarism, the electoral process, executive powers and management of class
conflict may be regarded by the left as tampering with its freedom of action in
particular. The challenge to democratic leadership stemming from the
concerns of the left is the more significant as, short of the catastrophic
obliteration of totalitarianism that brings disgrace upon *any* extremism and
advises moderation instead, any other resumption of democracy is likely to
witness the emergence in full of a potentially extremist or 'maximalist' left.

   The double challenge which I just described indicates that all sorts of
coalitions of dissent from dictatorship take shape during the transition. They
involve the traditional enemies of the dictatorship, themselves minimally
divided on whether their aspirations are democratic, uncertain or clearly nondemocratic. They also involve forces seceding from the dictatorship yet (since
secession is not necessarily toward democracy) similarly divided on their
aspirations. The point is to transform these essentially negative, uncertain,
shifting and even conflicting coalitions into one coalition of consent for
democracy. Though the transformation is by no means a sure thing,
democracy has some trump cards to play.

   The best trump card is actually what we often consider to be democracy's
weakness. It is exactly because democracy is a system of compromise, it is
exactly because of its openness and open-endedness, because its game is never
final, because nobody loses once and for all and on all arenas, that under
certain circumstances the democratic game may finally appear attractive,
convenient or compelling even to its detractors – be they loyalists or enemies
of the old dictatorship. In other words, a coalition of consent for democracy
can rely upon and draw strength from a moderate compromise: a compromise
that attracts as wide a spectrum of opponents as well as former loyalists of the
dictatorship, leaving out if necessary only a few weakened dissenters.

MATERIAL AND REGULATORY-INSTITUTIONAL BASES OF THE TRANSFER

Naturally, however, this type of compromise must rest in turn – and can in fact
rest by the nature of democracy – on material bases. There are basically three
such bases, three also being the key constituencies whose consent to
democracy must be secured:

1. Since we are talking of capitalist democracies, there must be collective consent to the reproduction of capital. Though the matter seems obvious, this requires less obviously avoiding policies of democratic reconstruction designed to hamper significantly capital's capacity to accumulate and invest or, worse, designed to punish capitalists collectively for their real or alleged class role in the advent and running of the dictatorship.[5]

2. Similarly, most of the state institutions that served the authoritarian regime (army, bureaucracy) are meant to serve democracy as well. Therefore, in order to secure such service, their internal self-rule may have to be preserved. Otherwise said, in the transition to democracy policies should be avoided that can be construed as retroactive punishment of the state institutions' personnel *as a class*, rather than as necessary removal of legal features added by the dictatorship or as well-meant reforms. And reforms should come to terms with the preservation of internal self-rule and the institutions' involvement in those reforms.

3. Crucial to this first part of the compromise is the consent of the left. But how to secure its consent, and possibly even its participation in promoting the compromise? The answer is that the left in turn must be secured ample space for democratic action in the party, electoral, parliamentary and labour arenas. Sooner or later, in other words, it must feel in the legitimate position to weigh publicly and contractually in the stimulation, allocation and social uses of privately produced wealth. I should add that this strategy of co-optation of the left, if successfully executed, may even attract to the democratic game a left that is potentially extremist by label or advocacy if not by deeds.

Though I have referred to the three parameters of the compromise as material, to convey readily the idea that there must be tangible incentives, it should be clear that the compromise is not about a fixed distribution of corporate spoils: it does not and cannot guarantee ahead of time exactly how often, how much and when each actor will win or lose. The point is of importance to understand what constitutes democratic legitimacy and how it relates to democracy's authoritative performance. To be sure, each of the three social and state formations aspires to a corporate voice, resources and rewards of its own. And these aspirations the democratic compromise recognises. Still, within the parameters just described the compromise is really about a competitive political market. More precisely, it is about what Adam Przeworski calls uncertainty[6]– the shared uncertainty of political outcomes that naturally results from a competitive market with multiple arenas, in which politico/institutional and societal positions of relevance for outcomes are deployed in dispersed and countervailing fashion. In other words, the compromise is not about results but about a set of rules of the game: norms, procedures and institutions whose operation will probabilistically and therefore only uncertainly effect a fair balance of winning and losing. This is all that democracy can at best offer those who enter the compromise. Conflict, as Rustow's opening quote implies, will remain – except on the rules themselves. But this is an important point. If rule agreement is reached, its institutional nature and the very knowledge that each institution will impinge

GOVERNMENT PERFORMANCE   177

on outcomes only partially and probabilistically mean that the agreement, by allowing substantial leeway on actual performance to come, has a span of endurance. It means that democratic legitimacy does not rest on a specific set of policies, on delivery, on performance, but rests precisely (and more safely) on rule agreement.[7]

To be sure, the agreement is instrumental, a means to an end; and political actors, even when they consent to sharing losses and victories and are reassured that the sum-total of the game is positive, will try to bend both means and ends in their favour. Therefore, agreement on rules will be implicitly tested against performance and may at times require renegotiation if, for reasons having to do with the rules' actual performance or their changing environment, performance falls eventually outside a tolerable range of expected outcomes. In sum, it would be wrong to think that political actors who manage to reach and maintain rule agreement do it in a peaceful, orderly and undramatic manner. On the contrary, hammering out the agreement and keeping it in place will naturally be accompanied by confrontation, tension and animosity – a target of which is performance itself.

Yet a crisis of legitimacy stemming from the latter remains an unlikely occurrence, given the range of performance which rule agreement tolerates. Thinking of the corporate interests and aspirations of the main social and state formations discussed above, it can be said that as long as the rules of the democratic game seem designed to protect mutually those interests and aspirations, each formation will still be capable of adapting to variance in performance that – either by policy choice or exogenous circumstances – affects the formation negatively. Also, a democratic government that can rely on rule agreement will feel more comfortable about pursuing partisan majority policies over the possible objections of the opposition and about exercising in effect its 'market supremacy', without fearing that it violates mutually expected outcomes. In simple terms, government performance will gain from rule agreement.

TRANSFERRING ALLEGIANCE IN THE EUROPEAN HISTORICAL AND INSTITUTIONAL CONTEXT

If we bear in mind all the above, we should be able to keep the drama that marks every democratic transition and consolidation – irrespective, in my view, of final accomplishments – separate from those accomplishments. But have we always been so capable? In assessing the events of Greece, Portugal and Spain we seem to have been victims, especially in the first and more uncertain phase of their transitions, of dire historical memories and cultural-geographical preconceptions. In at least two of the cases, and in some way all of them, I will argue that we have given excessive substance to drama, for those dire historical memories seem actually to have worked to deny their own prophecy. We have hence attributed problems of performance that have other causes to a crisis of legitimacy, exaggerated such problems or made them too close a harbinger of such crisis.

Certainly, a scenario in which drama and substance do coincide is not at all unthinkable. It is a scenario that speaks against the three-pronged democratic

12

compromise I outlined above. It has been presented in paradigmatic form by Guillermo O'Donnell with Latin America and the crisis of bureaucratic authoritarianism as referents, but I can cast it as well in terms of the southern European *problématique* of the seventies.[8] The point however is that – as I will show in a moment – the scenario is not necessary. The scenario starts, as O'Donnell sets it up, with the full revival of civil society in its old as well as new economic, social and cultural components. The new components – which find expression through *movimientos de base, groupuscules, asociaciones vecinales* and similar – are themselves the product of the new culture of demands and autonomous participation of the seventies and are therefore not limited to aspiring democracies. However, by combining with the inevitable post-dictatorial escalation of long-suppressed labour and economic demands by workers and various sectors of the middle classes, they can mobilise strata of society ranging from the latter to previously unorganised and marginal urban poor. A climate of apparent disorder, unruliness and anarchy will ensue, triggering actual fears among sectors of the bourgeoisie and the state. If we combine the new mobilisation, the fears and the general economic weakness of the region (whether southern Europe or Latin America) especially visible in the seventies, it is not difficult to forecast inflation, unemployment, state deficits, disinvestments, flights of capital and balance of payment problems.

This, however, is as far as the scenario will inescapably travel. Whether it will escalate into an economic crisis of major proportions, continues O'Donnell, and into a crisis of legitimacy, I would add, depends on something else. It depends above all on the role of the politically organised left and its relation with civil society. A left that is maximalist in its economic and political demands, bent perhaps on purging the elements of the old regime, and perhaps even in control of the transition, will end up by threatening capital's capacity for reproduction as well as the state's need for order and self-rule. Being as uncertain as they are historically about their strength and hegemony, and being therefore not alien from repression, sectors of the regional bourgeoisie or more so of the state will likely react with *contragolpismo,* thus bringing the initial steps of the scenario to their 'logical' conclusions.

But another type of left can also be envisioned. A left that understands the threat of *contragolpismo,* and can also afford to act with greater caution without imperilling, or thinking of imperilling its future role; a left that can subscribe to the following words by a member of the executive committee of the Spanish Socialist Party: 'Democracy and its consolidation come first, before our political programs ... because the Spanish right has shown that it can live very well under both authoritarian and democratic regimes, while the left can only survive within a democratic framework.'[9] A left, in sum, that understands how the right is perfectly capable of living in a democracy, but will not do so without institutional guarantees and cannot otherwise be easily routed. This does not require that the initiative for a democratic compromise should come from the left (it can as well come from the right), but it does require that the compromise rest largely on the participation – because of attraction, convenience or compulsion – of the left.

GOVERNMENT PERFORMANCE   179

In view of the quote above, my claim that such a left (and a similarly accommodating right) have evolved in southern Europe will not come as a surprise to the reader. Indeed, the generalisations I have been presenting originate in a reflection on the southern European redemocratisations of the seventies. They best fit the Spanish case. They are not far removed from the Greek one. And they will only need some firm amendments when we come to Portugal.[10]

The question I am now ready to address is why the social and state formations of these three countries came to accept the democratic compromise. With individual amendments to be introduced when necessary, the answer applies as well to all European cases of redemocratisation following the Second World War. It begins by recognising something special in the European experience of redemocratisation. What is special is that, in replacing fascist or pseudo-fascist dictatorships, European countries could count on reviving or recycling for democracy a series of political and state institutions with a long historical tradition of their own – longer in fact than the life-span of any particular regime and predating dictatorship. Some of these institutions (political parties, unions and lay organisations of the Church) may have gone underground under the dictatorship; yet they never disappeared. Others may have served the dictatorship (bureaucracies, armies, judiciaries, business associations); yet they never became coterminous with it, never defined or were defined by it, and were possibly shunted aside by new and specifically totalitarian institutions (single parties, corporatist syndicates, special tribunals, party militias, secret police). It is true that in some cases (the army in Spain) the state apparatus or parts of it installed and ran the dictatorship. But what is important to remember is that in such cases the dictatorship emphasised depoliticisation and demobilisation, while the state apparatus still presented itself as the historical and impartial guarantor of domestic law and order. All of which confirms the fact that in Europe the state apparatus has always been concerned (not always successfully) with protecting its impersonal, non-political, legal-professional status. Exactly the type of status which democracy can also guarantee.

This institutional weight of the past (and a past that had been liberal and even democratic) has been in my opinion at least necessary in making European returns to competitive politics successful. In the first place, it helped state institutions placed at the service of dictatorship to secede, as a first step toward reaffirming their legal-professional autonomy within the state. In the second place, of all possible outcomes of the crisis the institutional weight of the past favoured democracy *tout court*, over another dictatorship or some 'guided' democracy. One consistent aspect of the various crises of dictatorship in Europe has been the prompt re-emergence of political parties and party allegiances, even after decades of interruption of competitive politics. But this re-emergence has been possible exactly and only because each of the two key European social formations – the bourgeoisie and the working class – had party traditions to return to and with which to vie within the crisis. In turn, once and because these traditions were revived, it made much less difference what the 'natural and instinctive' regime affinities of those social formations might have been. What became instead of paramount importance was the preservation and consolidation of the party-political space of each social formation, in a political arena that proved immediately to be highly competitive.

Thus, once the crisis of a European dictatorship was under way, the country's institutions and social formations, each with their own coveted spheres of autonomy and social presence, were sooner or later compelled toward coexistence. They were compelled by the very weight of their diversity and co-presence, and so as to avoid the prospect of a dragged-out and inconclusive fight. That is why they ended up by accepting exactly the three-pronged moderate institutional compromise which is at the heart of democracy. In addition, the international economic context of stagflation, industrial adjustment and global re-equilibration within which the transition of the seventies occurred also spurred those compromises by giving them a specific content, compelling in its own terms. It decisively tilted the compromises toward a self-imposed deferral of labour's economic demands – without however ruling out (quite on the contrary) governments of the left in the near future.

THE CASE OF SOUTHERN EUROPE

I have presented democracy as a method, an institutional set-up for conducting a competitive game which, exactly because it is competitive, is not called to secure any specific set of policies. Thinking of democracy otherwise, and trying in fact to define and achieve democracy exclusively by radical policies that are 'socially advanced and popularly orientated' either backfires or leads to forms of guided or organic democracy that differ little in methods from the authoritarian regime they replace. Conflict involving these two antagonistic conceptions of democracy, between and within the army and the political parties is what made the first steps of Portuguese democracy so perilous, at least when compared with the other two countries. In view of the model of European transitions presented above, there are no simple explanations for the conflict, but the role of the army is of special importance. To begin with, the fall of the dictatorship came through an easy and bloodless army coup inside a wavering and backward regime, militarily in serious trouble. Mistaken for a popular revolution, the coup created a feeling of dangerous elation among the victors as to the radical transformations that the revolution, guided by an organised army, should and could legitimately bring about in the apparent vacuum of power and interests suddenly left by the dictatorship. Further, opposition to what appeared to be taking quickly the features of a guided democracy came not only from the civilian parties but from within the rebellious army itself; something which made the initial resolution of the conflict less a matter of negotiations and more one of showdowns. It could be said that all three minimum ingredients for a democratic compromise were violated at the time – including the third one, given the constraints imposed by the military-civilian extreme left on the democratically orientated and dominant Socialist Party. Nevertheless even in Portugal a gradual rerouting of the transition toward a workable democratic compromise has been possible. It took the victory of the electoral over the

GOVERNMENT PERFORMANCE   181

guidance principle in 1975–6, the eventual emergence (of all things) of a dominant centre-right government coalition in 1979, and the recent repeal of the guidance features contained in the 1976 constitution, with the preservation at the same time of some of the social reforms that give space to a democratic left.

By comparison with Portugal, the return to democracy in Spain was instead characterised by a much greater attention to the problem of easing the transfer of allegiance and accommodating vastly different constituencies. The example of Spain in this regard is almost paradigmatic, in view of the fact that the death of Franco left a regime otherwise entrenched, mildly liberalised in politics and with an expanded economy purposely integrated into that of western Europe. Since that death was not the kind of event that necessitates dictatorial collapse, any pressure for significant change could have lead, as anticipated at the time, to a showdown and a bitter outcome no matter what. But perhaps the secret of Spain's success, and what puts into question the conventional view that allegiances cannot be transferred, is the very fact that the transition to democracy was initiated and lead throughout by legitimate heirs of the dictator. This, plus the fact that this leadership made it a point of skilfully using the constititional means offered by the dictatorship itself to achieve the explicit aim of full electoral competition, forestalled, co-opted and even transformed two likely sources of dissent: dissent from the unrepented nostalgics of the dictator, and dissent from those opponents of the same who were entitled to suspect a transition guided of all by *los de siempre*. The success of this strategy has allowed what I have elsewhere called a mutual 'backward and forward' legitimation easing the convergence of allegiances on the new democracy.[11] But, to repeat, the very fact that past and present co-existed in the transition demanded the respect of the three minimum components of the democratic compromise: a capitalist economy and economic culture, the rehabilitation of the old state institutions, and a social democratic political culture likely to govern in the foreseeable future.

The Greek transition to democracy presented some features in its early stages that, without in any way approaching in seriousness those of Portugal, raised some questions about the evolution of the democratic compromise in that country. However, those questions have not withstood the test of time. The original picture was mixed. For a variety of reasons which I examined elsewhere, [12] and which placed the nostalgic right (and the left) in a weaker position at the transition, prime minister Karamanlis was able to implement on his own a plan to authenticate and extend the new democratic order that is without precedent in modern Greek history (rejection of the monarchy by overwhelming popular vote, trial of junta leaders but not of the army, freedom of action for the communist parties ...). At the same time, however, though the Greek transition did not show the conflict between opposite transitional strategies so typical of Portugal in 1974–5, it did not adopt Spain's explicit *politica de consenso* either. Instead, the same conditions that allowed a swift authentication of the democratic order also allowed Karamanlis to leave the left opposition, in particular PASOK, out of the constitutional process and to implement a 'gaullist' constitution whose aim appeared to be the perpetuation of his party's rule. In effect, not only has that monopoly over time proven

182   THE NEW MEDITERRANEAN DEMOCRACIES

quite ephemeral; more important, PASOK'S successful response to the
constrictions of the gaullist model has not been one of progressive
polarisation and centrifugation but one of convergence toward the centre in
images and appeals. In pursuing convergence, PASOK never raised any
question about the enduring appropriateness of Karamanlis' constitutional
set-up,[13] never repudiated as lenient the already firm conditions under which
the nostalgic right and compromised state institutions had been allowed to
partake of the democratic compromise, and considerably diluted its much
touted and strident Third World socialism.[14]

ON THE FINAL QUESTION OF PERFORMANCE

There is now the problem, to return to the theme of this paper, of fitting this
sturdier picture of southern European democracies with the palpable evidence
of poor performance, especially in the economic sphere, not just of Portugal –
as one might expect from the above – but of all three countries. But is it really a
problem? So far I have mainly argued forward, from legitimacy to
performance. I will now argue in reverse, starting from performance.

In the first place, it is incorrect to equate economic performance specifically
with government performance. Economic performance refers generically to
how well the economy of a country is doing, its actual health. Indeed, its
typical indicators (especially in analyses of southern Europe) are in the form
of aggregate statistics – rate of inflation and unemployment, balance of
payments, budgetary outlays and deficits, GNP, money supplies, investments,
prime rates .... In sum, the evidence really points to what in policy analysis are
called outcomes. And policy analysis reveals that outcomes have no clear
connection with what analysts mean by government performance, i.e. policies
instituted by governments with a given intent in mind. A recent assessment of
comparative policy studies sums up the case as follows:

> Often budgetary outlays and assumed performance variables, such as
> income, education or health levels were used as the dependent variables.
> Not only were such variables relatively crude indicators of the concepts
> of policy process and outcomes, but their use involved a chain of casual
> inferences of questionable merit. As the growing literature on policy
> implementation suggests, it is often difficult to assume that budgetary
> expenditures reflect changes in policy, that such expenditures then are
> actually turned into effectively implemented programs, and that these
> programs in turn achieve the expected results. Each link in this chain
> ought to be examined before we conclude that a regime has failed or
> succeeded in reallocating resources and in affecting income, health or
> education levels.[15]

In sum, while policies have consequences that deserve study, starting from
outcomes leaves the matter unanswered. Yet most of the studies of policy
performance abroad, in particular the studies of our three new democracies,
are narrowly focused on the outcomes of a yet unchartered implementation
process.[16]

In the second place, if we cannot equate economic performance with

GOVERNMENT PERFORMANCE   183

government performance specifically, much less can we infer that problems of performance stem from the fact that the governments we are dealing with are democratic and new. Indeed, even if we were to take for proven that poor performance reflects a problem of governance, it does not follow that the problem is connected with democraticity and newness. For one thing, problems of governance in the economic sphere (assuming that they are such) are nowadays shared by almost all western societies, some of them (Latin America) not at all democratic. For another, though it is true that the question of economic performance is particularly acute in our countries, we cannot overlook the fact that what is specific to these countries is not only the novelty of their democratic governments but also the fact that these governments have inherited particularly weak economies, further weakened by readjustments in the international economic order. Could the old authoritarian governments or more consolidated democracies have done better? Alternatively, though the problems of governance may be general, could the reasons be specific to each type of regime? I am not ruling out any of these possibilities, but at the level at which performance has been studied in our countries we are not equipped to test them.

It may be true that democratic government performance cannot be assessed by objective means-end criteria of the type implicit above, but rather by criteria of public expectations – performance thus being in the eyes of the beholder. But this still would not make our countries a clear case of poor performance, closely connected with regime legitimacy. We can readily recognise that when it comes to public reactions to governance it does not always matter whether or not specific governments are actually responsible for economic outcomes. I have already implied that, as part of the natural drama of new democracies all sorts of accusations can be laid down against their governments and their policies. They come not only from residual nostalgics but also from disappointed democrats of all shades, as well as from oppositions drumming up electoral support and not at all alien in the process from charging the government with mismanagement of the transition. Greece, Portugal, and Spain are certainly no exception to the pattern. Given the particular temper of the seventies, what has been consistently at issue in the accusations of the opposition has been economic performance – whether the betrayal by the Spanish *Centro Democratico* of its early social democratic promises, or the economic chaos brought about in Portugal by the policies of nationalisation and agrarian reform adopted by the military/left coalitions, or the unwillingness of the Greek *Nea Democratia* to free the economy of the country from the spiral of dependency.

However, if we choose the criterion of public expectations we obviously cannot equate each and all policy dissatisfaction with poor performance. Since it is in the nature of a competitive democracy that some interests lose some of the time, every democratic government by that criterion would perform 'poorly'.[17] Hence we must recognise that, despite overt political language often to the contrary, what is at issue is broader and more difficult to assess than concrete demand satisfaction. Government decisions emerge out of a process of aggregation, elimination, reformulation, deferment, give-and-take and the conflict that often surrounds the process is not only about which

184   THE NEW MEDITERRANEAN DEMOCRACIES

demands should be entertained, which decisions should be made, which deferred, but also about how the process should be conducted, what role the contestants in and out of government should have, what symbolic or tangible side rewards the losers should reap.[18] In other words, the outcome of the process – decisions – will not be evaluated by the affected parties in the light of immediate demand satisfaction alone but in the light of a more distant and aleatory, as well as more encompassing calculus of reciprocal and prospective gains and losses. Within this calculus the criterion of individual demand satisfaction becomes a criterion of mutual decisional equity. And since equity can only be safeguarded (and only probabilistically) by a set of agreed-upon decisional rules, this discussion takes us back to my earlier discussion of the democratic compromise and the rules of the game.

There, I wrote that the presence of rule agreement allows governments a degree of decisional leeway and choice, without fearing violation of the democratic compromise. I now propose more precisely that if we assess democratic government performance in the light of public opinion and societal interests – a sensible criterion in view of the fact that democratic performance seems to be very much in the eyes of the beholder – then the least elusive and most generalisable if indirect way of assessing whether performance is satisfactory/equitable and therefore generally free of conflict-generated political constraints is to see whether or not there exists agreement on the rule for democratic decision among those actors who could otherwise stalemate governance.

I have already argued that, with the partial exception of Portugal, our three countries have developed rule agreement in the transition. We can now point to evidence that the agreement endures past the transition. One democratic decisional rule, in fact the classical one as well as the simplest, but also the one that a difficult democracy can least afford, is the rule of alternating majorities. Clear-cut changes in government have recently occurred in all three countries – in 1981 in Greece, in 1982 in Spain, and in 1979 and 1983 in Portugal. The historical importance of these changes is double. Other contributors to this issue rightly stress the historical novelty of socialist governments, and in all three countries contemporaneously. I would like to stress another aspect: major government changes of the type that have taken place in our countries are a good test of whether rule agreement and the democratic compromise that the rules are supposed to sustain are really holding up. Despite the electoral rhetoric and the fact that the oppositions have not been averse to accusing previous governments of mismanaging the transition, the victory of the oppositions has not set in motion a process of reciprocal delegitimation, a coming apart of original agreements and therefore a crisis of regime legitimacy. Nor has the coming into power of socialist governments led to a flurry of radical policies. On the contrary, early rhetoric notwithstanding (the case of Papandreou's PASOK being by far the most glaring), the basic policies of the socialist governments, especially in the economic sphere, are above all remarkable for the fact of differing only incrementally and sectorally from those of their predecessors.

One way of looking at this convergence is to say that the reality of the domestic and international economies of the seventies has undercut the

GOVERNMENT PERFORMANCE   185

socialists' room for manoeuvre, and since the socialists do not seem to be
appreciably better at curing the economy, this speaks poorly for the viability
of our young democracies. I prefer to remind the reader that the fact that
alternating governments are not bent on undoing each other's work is exactly
what makes the rule of alternance acceptable – and the advantage is the
greater in view of the poor or poorly understood fit between government
policies and economic outcomes anyway. Otherwise, alternance could
threaten the expectations that are built in the democratic compromise. It may
be true that the capitalist reality of the seventies has locked our countries in a
conservative version of the compromise, and one may wish a more innovative
democratic model for the future of these countries. But though such
conservative compromise and the limited room for manoeuvre it leaves may
feed *desencanto* with democracy, the political risks of forcing a substantial
alteration in the terms of the compromise may be considerable, while the
policy results may be ironically meagre or downright perverse.

Awareness of these risks may be another reason why the socialist
governments of southern Europe have chosen to distinguish themselves less
for their economic policies and more for their stand on moral, civic and
symbolic issues, as well as on foreign and international affairs. But here as well
much is a matter of image more than policies. Moral and civic issues have been
historically employed by the southern European left as an avenue for social
regeneration and for striking at collective class, religious and institutional
enemies. The reforms of the leftist governments during the Second Spanish
Republic are just one example. But the socialist governments of the eighties
seem decidedly more guarded on these matters. Much of the moralisation has
not taken the form of policies, but remains at the level of expressive gestures.
As well, governments have avoided using civic reforms for the purpose of
frontally attacking specific groups and institutions – usually connected with
the old regime.

Similarly, it is at least an overstatement to say that foreign and international
affairs have been used as an area for socialist distinctiveness. In Greece the
greater international assertiveness of Papandreou's government – again more
often a matter of gestures and declarations than one of actual policies – has
actually found sympathetic ears among more conservative groups and state
institutions, and can also be seen as a strategy of consensus and party
legitimation within the democratic framework. In Portugal foreign and
international affairs do not seem, in fact, to be among the most salient
government concerns. Only in Spain do they seem to be more divisive, but
only by comparison with the other two countries – and at any rate, always in a
context within which the socialist government does not distinguish itself for
programmatic determination. Again, here too the limited margins for
manoeuvre by domestic governments may well reflect the international
constraints of the day. But the unwillingness of socialist governments to
challenge those constraints in ways that can be resented domestically
represents also a choice, and one of significance in the maintenance of a
smooth rule of alternance.

186 THE NEW MEDITERRANEAN DEMOCRACIES

CONCLUSIONS

There is no denying that the young democracies of southern Europe were born and will continue to function in an era in which problem solving is very much in demand. There is also no reason to believe that they are behaving any differently at problem solving than other western societies i.e. poorly. Nor is it surprising that their governments, being new and untried, as well as saddled with particularly weak economies and the re-emergence of demanding civil societies, are being held responsible, correctly or incorrectly, for failures at problem solving. The thrust of my paper has been a cautionary one. Before drawing dire inferences we should reflect on a point made by Dankwart Rustow: the democratic game, once the initial momentum is set, rewards those who play it; and even those who come to play it out of *force majeure* rather than conviction may find their decision more palatable once they begin to live with it.[19] The fact that the game is competitive, rough, conflictive and even a source of *desencanto* does not subtract from the fact that it is shared. It takes more to dislodge agreement once it is set. Even in Portugal, where the search for agreement has been protracted and difficult, it appears that the threshold has finally been past.

Besides, when it comes to transitions, crises and the like the very fact that loyalties are a relative matter also means that they are not likely to be transferred or simply withheld unless some other game is available. But a return to an authoritarian game, only years after it has shown itself unable to satisfy its own supporters, seems a remote possibility.

Of course, we may be wrong and events may overtake us. Crises and transitions are set in motion and evolve by a concatenation of events; the probable effect of each one on the next escapes social scientists at this stage of their arts. But this is not the point. The point is more simply to recognise the type of events and circumstances that are more likely to set the stage for a crisis (without determining its evolution). Since they must have something to do with the dislodging of rule agreement, I venture to say that the type of policy problems our new democracies suffer from do not, even in the context of newness, quite fit the bill.

NOTES

1. Dankwart Rustow, 'Transitions to Democracy,' *Comparative Politics*, Vol. 2, No. 3 (April 1970), p.362.
2. Ibid., p.357.
3. I am thinking of cases such as the fall of Nazism, and possibly Imperial Japan. Nazism's total defeat in a war designed to secure the thousand-year Reich could not but leave an utter organisational and power vacuum, a final sense of apocalyptic and self-induced failure, and an ingrained fear of any new totalitarian experiment. Without overlooking the very important role played by Allied and German leadership in guiding and rationalising democratic reconstruction, it could thus be said that – once West Germany had been made geopolitically safe from the Soviet Union – choice and leadership in the transition overdetermined the final result. In West Germany there was no question of allegiance to anything other than democracy.

GOVERNMENT PERFORMANCE   187

4. See the ample observations on these points in Philippe Schmitter, 'Speculations about the Prospective Demise of Authoritarian Regimes and its Possible Consequences,' paper presented at the Conference on the Prospects for Democracy: Transitions from Authoritarian Rule. Woodrow Wilson Center, Washington, DC, 1980.

5. For the record, I do not believe that the bourgeoisie as a *class* can play a significant role in the advent and survival of dictatorship – at least not in the highly institutionalised party and state context of Europe.

6. Adam Przeworski, 'Some Problems in the Study of the Transition to Democracy,' paper presented at the Conference on the Prospects of Democracy, op. cit.

7. A more exhaustive discussion of the points made in this paragraph is contained in Giuseppe Di Palma, 'Party Government and Democratic Reproducibility: The Dilemma of New Democracies,' in Francis Castles (ed.), *The Future of Party Government: Problems and Concepts* (The Hague: De Greuter, 1984).

8. Guillermo O'Donnell, 'Nota Para el Estudio de Procesos de Democratization Politica a Partir del Estado Burocratico-Autoritario,' paper presented at the Conference on the Prospects of Democracy, op.cit.

9. Interview by author reported in Donald Share, 'Two Transitions: Democratization and the Evolution of the Spanish Socialist Left,' paper presented at the Annual Meeting of the American Political Science Association, Chicago, September 1983, p.12.

10. The view I will present is a somewhat sturdier view of those transitions – the Portuguese in particular – than the one I presented in 'Founding Coalitions in Southern Europe: Legitimacy and Hegemony,' *Government and Opposition*, Vol.15, No.2 (Spring 1980), pp.162–89.

11. Ibid., p.170.

12. Ibid., pp.175–8, 187.

13. At the same time, not unlike in Portugal, the president of the republic, despite the gaullist potentials of the office, has come to play a role as guarantor of constitutional equilibria and collective interests. With Karamanlis as president and Papandreou as prime minister, this has made possible what George Mavrogordatos calls a 'charismatic tandem'. George Mavrogordatos, 'Rise of the Green Sun', Centre of Contemporary Greek Studies, King's College, London, Occasional Paper 1, 1983, p.20.

14. An exhaustive and revealing analysis of PASOK's electoral convergence and why the party should be considered a centrist rather than a socialist party is contained in ibid. Of special interest are opinion data showing that the distribution of PASOK's supporters on the left-right scale is typical of a centrist party. A comparison with Giacomo Sani's identical data for Italy and Spain reveals a curve strikingly similar to that of Italy's Christian Democracy and smaller secular parties. See Giacomo Sani, 'Partiti e atteggiamenti di massa in Spagna e Italia,' *Rivista Italiana di Scienza Politica*, Vol.11, No.2, (August 1981), pp.235–79.

15. Thomas John Bossert, 'Can We Return to the Regime for Comparative Policy Analysis? or, the State and Health Policies in Central America,' *Comparative Politics*, Vol. 15, No.4 (July 1983), p.420.

16. This focus on outcomes has a reason. An extensive survey of available policy analyses reveals that almost all of them, even when authored by accredited scholars, are journalistic in style – appearing in such publications as *The Economist* and *Current History*.

17. In a formal analysis of decisional rules in democratic institutions Douglas Rae shows that more democratic institutions do not necessarily produce greater satisfaction with decisions. Douglas Rae, 'Political Democracy as a Property of Political Institutions,' *American Political Science Review*, Vol. 65, No.1 (March 1971) pp.111–29.

18. The sentence is paraphrased from my *Surviving without Governing: The Italian Parties in Parliament*, Berkeley: University of California Press, 1977, p.19. For a more extended treatment of the criterion of expectations and how it affects the evaluation of performance see ibid., pp.15–24.

19. Rustow, op.cit., p.358.

[11]

Review Article

RETHINKING STATE AND REGIME:
Southern Europe's Transition to
Democracy

By ROBERT M. FISHMAN*

Guillermo O'Donnell, Philippe C. Schmitter, and Laurence Whitehead, eds., *Transitions from Authoritarian Rule: Southern Europe*. Baltimore: The Johns Hopkins University Press, 1986, 212 pp.

Richard Gunther, Giacomo Sani, and Goldie Shabad, *Spain after Franco: The Making of a Competitive Party System*. Berkeley: University of California Press, 1986, 516 pp.

Walter C. Opello, *Portugal's Political Development: A Comparative Approach*. Boulder, CO: Westview Press, 1985, 235 pp.

M ORE than ten years have passed since democracy returned to the last of the Western European countries that had been ruled by one form or another of authoritarian political system during much of the twentieth century. The historical clustering of distinct national processes of redemocratization in Portugal, Greece, and Spain—all occurring in the mid-1970s—rapidly transformed the political map of non-Communist Europe and eliminated the last nondemocratic model of political rule (except in Turkey, which experienced a period of authoritarian rule after the transitions discussed in this essay). This historical clustering of three instances of regime change encourages one to search for common causes and trajectories. In comparative discussions of the transitions, much emphasis has been directed to the effort to uncover common patterns of and explanations for the developments in Southern Europe.[1] The literature

* For helpful comments on an earlier draft of this essay I thank José Alvarez Junco, H. E. Chehabi, Jeff Goodwin, Peter Hall, Juan Linz, Ted Perlmutter, Edward Robbins, Theda Skocpol, Basilios Tsingos, and members of the CROPSO seminar, Harvard University.
[1] See, for example, the discussion by Geoffrey Pridham, "Comparative Perspectives on the New Mediterranean Democracies: A Model of Regime Transition?" in *West European Politics* 7 (April 1984).

RETHINKING STATE AND REGIME   423

has not been very helpful, however, in conceptualizing differences among the three countries. I will argue that a comparative understanding of the transitions requires the use of analytical distinctions—such as the difference between state and regime—which will allow us to perceive the widely divergent paths of the Southern European cases along several dimensions.

A number of important scholarly works on the return of democracy to Portugal, Greece, and Spain have been published in addition to those devoted to the many countries in other parts of the world that have recently returned to democratic rule. Most analysts have shied away from broad comparative generalizations, however; with few exceptions, the most important contributions have come from country-specific studies, many of them emphasizing the distinctiveness of their national cases.[2] The great exception to the general absence of significant comparative and theoretical work on the redemocratizations is *Transitions from Authoritarian Rule* (one volume in hardback and four separate volumes in paper), edited by O'Donnell, Schmitter, and Whitehead. In his introductory essay to the volume on Southern Europe, Schmitter notes that the contributors to the project concluded that "transitions from authoritarian rule and immediate prospects for democracy were largely to be explained in terms of national forces and calculations" (p. 3) rather than of international dynamics, although the international context of the Southern European cases rendered successful redemocratization more likely there than in Latin America. The excellent country chapters, which cover Italy[3] and Turkey in addition to the three cases under discussion, tend to emphasize specifically political actions and paths—including significant contributions to regime change by some of the very forces that held, or helped to exercise, authoritarian political power. Earlier narrowly class-based and internationally oriented theories of the

[2] Unfortunately, the insightful work of Juan Linz on transitions to democracy is not yet available in one volume. His essays on the topic include "Il fattore tempo nei mutamenti di regime" [The time factor in regime change], in *Teoría Política* 2, No. 1 (1986); "Lideranca inovadora na transicao para a democracia a uma nova democracia: o caso da Espanha" [Innovative leadership in the transition to democracy and in a new democracy: The case of Spain], in Gilberto Dupas, ed., *A transicao que deu certo: O exemplo da democracia espanhola* [The transition that worked out: The Spanish case] (Sao Paulo: Trajetoria Cultural, 1989), and "The Transitions from Authoritarian Regimes to Democratic Political Systems and the Problems of Consolidation of Political Democracy" (paper presented at the IPSA Roundtable, Tokyo, March 29-April 1, 1982).

[3] Excellent complementary essays on Italy's return to democracy after Fascism include Gianfranco Pasquino's chapter in the *Transitions* volume and an earlier chapter by Giuseppe Di Palma, "Italy: Is There a Legacy and Is It Fascist?" in John H. Herz, ed., *From Dictatorship to Democracy* (Westport, CT: Greenwood Press, 1982).

Southern European transitions,[4] already significantly contradicted by empirical work,[5] find little resonance in the interpretive essays of this volume.

The major attempt in the *Transitions* volume on Southern Europe to account for the rough political parallelism—that is, the historical simultaneity of roughly similar political developments across national boundaries—long noted by many analysts of this region is the broadly posed and subtle analysis of sociologist Salvador Giner. In a contribution that encompasses nineteenth- and twentieth-century political development, Giner emphasizes the "unevenness" of Southern European societies and political forces—their heterogeneity and contradictions—rather than focusing on any specific and immutable configuration of sociopolitical forces. He maintains that

> the inner contradictions of each one of these basic components—limited parliamentarianism, restricted and divided liberalism, stunted reformism, and utopian imperialism—irrevocably led these societies toward a specific form of class despotism, namely Fascist or fascistisant dictatorship . . . (p. 23).

What remains somewhat unclear is how such a complex and subtly described syndrome of unevenness and contradiction can "irrevocably" lead to a "specific form of class despotism." Enormous differences among the four cases (Giner includes Italy in his analysis) in the timing of political changes, the longevity of nondemocratic regimes, and the political forms taken by nondemocratic rule make it difficult to sustain the strong assertion of an irrevocable tendency toward equivalence in the political development of these countries.

Although Giner's essay is enormously suggestive, it fails to resolve adequately the large question of (imperfect) political parallelism and historical clustering. Strong causal claims prove difficult to advance unless the differences as well as the similarities among the cases are systematically incorporated into the analysis; in order to do that, we need conceptual distinctions that allow us to delineate crucial differences. Unless one acknowledges and makes sense out of the variations among the coun-

[4] The most influential example is Nicos Poulantzas, *The Crisis of the Dictatorships* (London: New Left Books, 1976). Although few empirical data are supplied by Poulantzas or others in support of his interpretation, some important insights may be found in this work. For more recent essays stressing international political economic arguments and class arguments, see Giovanni Arrighi, ed., *Semiperipheral Development: The Politics of Southern Europe in the Twentieth Century* (Beverly Hills, CA: Sage, 1985).

[5] See, for example, the important study of Spanish business and political change by Robert Martinez, "Business Elites in Democratic Spain" (Ph.D. diss., Yale University, 1984).

RETHINKING STATE AND REGIME   425

tries, one is left with too many exceptions to any comparative assertion, whether it concerns the political role of the military, the place of a single party in nondemocratic rule, or the character of the crisis leading to the demise of authoritarian rule.

In accounting for the recent return to democracy, Giner emphasizes the erosion of legitimacy for the authoritarian systems, the consequences of economic development, and the contribution to democratization by some of the political forces inside the structure of authoritarian political power. In his emphasis on the delegitimation of authoritarian regimes as well as in his discussion of the role of forces to be found *within* the circle of power, Giner touches upon themes widely emphasized by analysts of the transitions. It is precisely on these two questions—the sources of the delegitimation of authoritarian rule and the location of the impetus toward democratic change within the circles of political power—that an analysis of the differences among the Southern European cases yields significant insights.

Despite the differences among the cases and the absence of any strong evidence for a parsimonious, largely class-based or internationally focused macro-level explanation,[6] the historical clustering of the experiences of Spain, Portugal, and Greece remains an intriguing fact. There is a sense in which authoritarian rule was 'exhausted' in all three societies at about the same time—unable to resolve the basic political challenges of legitimation and institutionalization at a time when crisis, to one degree or another, prevented the regimes from continuing on effortlessly through the sheer force of inertia. But the fact that the exhaustion of authoritarian rule set in at about the same time in the three societies in no sense guarantees that the causes of this exhaustion were the same, or that the path of redemocratization would be similar.

The contributors to the *Transitions* volume have largely chosen to focus on political forces, choices, and dynamics, following the earlier emphasis of Juan Linz and others in their work on the breakdown of democratic regimes.[7] Indeed, the emphasis on strictly political factors is so strongly drawn in many of the contributions—above all in Schmitter and O'Donnell's concluding theoretical volume, *Tentative Conclusions about Uncertain Democracies*—that (with the exception of a few of the country

---

[6] This is not to argue that class forces or the international context are irrelevant; rather, the point is that these forces are not the *sole* determinants of political developments and actions.

[7] See Juan Linz, *The Breakdown of Democratic Regimes: Crisis, Breakdown & Reequilibration*, and the other three volumes included in Juan Linz and Alfred Stepan, eds., *The Breakdown of Democratic Regimes* (Baltimore: The Johns Hopkins University Press, 1978).

chapters) the importance of social forces in undermining authoritarian rule is almost certainly somewhat understated.[8] Nevertheless, the political focus of the *Transitions* volume, including the attention directed to the issue of legitimation—or delegitimation—and the emphasis on the political orientation of forces located within the circle of political power, appears consistently useful in analyzing the Southern European cases.

THE LOCATION WITHIN THE CIRCLES OF POWER OF THE IMPETUS TOWARD POLITICAL CHANGE: STATE OR REGIME?

The earliest major theoretical statement, in the context of the recent transitions, on the tendency of the impetus for change to emerge from within the structure of political power is "Liberation by Golpe," Philippe Schmitter's strongly argued analysis of the events in Portugal.[9] In this article, written in the aftermath of the revolutionary coup of April 25, 1974, Schmitter asserts that the principal weak point in authoritarian rule—and thus the best hope for the restoration of democracy—is to be found not so much in the relations between state and civil society as within the structure of authoritarian rule itself. Specifically, he asserts that "the sources of contradiction, necessary if not sufficient for the overthrow of authoritarian rule, lie within the regime itself, within the apparatus of the state, not outside it in its relations with civil society."[10] Thus, Schmitter explicitly focuses on both the authoritarian *regime* and

[8] A significant literature does exist on social forces and the transitions. For insightful essays with abundant data on civil society and political change in Spain, see Víctor Pérez Díaz, *El retorno de la sociedad civil* [The return of civil society] (Madrid: Instituto de Estudios Económicos, 1987). An important recent comparative analysis of labor and the transitions is J. Samuel Valenzuela, "Labor Movements in Transitions to Democracy: A Framework for Analysis," *Comparative Politics* 21 (July 1989).

Strong arguments for the central role of social forces in undermining authoritarian rule may be found in two recent articles by Joseph Foweraker: "The Role of Labor Organizations in the Transition to Democracy in Spain," in Robert Clark and Michael Haltzel, eds., *Spain in the 1980s* (Cambridge, MA: Ballinger, 1987), and "Corporatist Strategies and the Transition to Democracy in Spain," *Comparative Politics* 20 (October 1987). This view contrasts sharply with the position of Donald Share, *The Making of Spanish Democracy* (New York: Praeger, 1986), and Raymond Carr and Juan Pablo Fusi, *Spain: Dictatorship to Democracy* (London: George Allen & Unwin, 1979), both of whom stress the internal evolution of the Franco regime itself. Other analysts, such as José María Maravall, in *La política de la transición* [The politics of the transition] (Madrid: Taurus, 1981), adopt an intermediate position stressing both the pressure "from below" and the reform "from above." In *Working Class Organization and the Return to Democracy in Spain* (Ithaca, NY: Cornell, 1990), I analyze the role of labor in the larger political transformation. However, this is not the place to focus on the role of social forces such as labor, despite their importance, or to attempt to draw a compelling balance between social and political determinants.

[9] Philippe C. Schmitter, "Liberation by Golpe," *Armed Forces and Society* 2 (November 1975).

[10] *Ibid.*, 20.

the *state apparatus* without drawing a distinction between the two. This emphasis on forces within the structure of authoritarian power appears to fit the Portuguese case, and it has proved highly stimulating to analysts of the other Southern European transitions. Given the fact that the remnants (or successors) of the Franco regime helped orchestrate the reform-oriented process of change in Spain, and that the Greek military extricated itself from political power, Schmitter's perspective appears to be useful for all three cases; indeed, it has helped to orient the work of many country-specific analysts.

I shall attempt to show, however, that this broad focus on sources of change located within the structure of political power masks important differences relating to where the impetus for change is to be found. The crucial move toward democracy—to the extent that it does emerge from within the authoritarian power system itself—may be located within the *regime* or within the *state*; the results differ decidedly. In the case of Spain, it is clear that the reformist sectors were located within the remnants of the Franco regime; from this position, they helped to launch and channel the return to democracy (under pressure from the opposition). In the case of Portugal, by contrast, the regime proved incapable or unwilling to reform itself fundamentally even after 1968, when Caetano replaced Salazar;[11] the impetus for change emerged instead from within the armed forces. The Greek case is somewhat more difficult to place in this scheme, given the problem of distinguishing between regime and state when the military itself rules; in some respects, it falls analytically between the Spanish and Portuguese cases. These differences suggest the existence of divergent causal processes—processes that have, in fact, led to rather different outcomes.[12]

The distinction I emphasize here between state and regime is not a new one; it rests on broadly shared understandings of these two much-used concepts. On occasion, this distinction has been explicitly drawn,[13]

[11] On the failure of the Portuguese regime to reform itself, and the contrast with Spain, see Juan Linz, "Spain and Portugal: Critical Choices," in David Landes, ed., *Western Europe: The Trials of Partnership* (Lexington, MA: Lexington Books, 1977). A comparison of the Spanish and Portuguese transitions that features, in part, differences in the relations between regime and opposition in the two cases, is Nancy Bermeo, "Redemocratization and Transition Elections: A Comparison of Spain and Portugal," *Comparative Politics* 19 (January 1987).

[12] For a recent analysis emphasizing the differences in the current democratic polities of Southern Europe, see Arend Lijphart, Thomas Bruneau, P. Nikiforos Diamandouros, and Richard Gunther, "A Mediterranean Model of Democracy? The Southern European Democracies in Comparative Perspective," in *West European Politics* 11 (January 1988).

[13] See, for example, the useful essay by Fernando Henrique Cardoso, "On the Characterization of Authoritarian Regimes in Latin America," in David Collier, ed., *The New Authoritarianism in Latin America* (Princeton: Princeton University Press, 1979). Despite Cardoso's insights, the essay is somewhat marred by its unresolved ambivalence between a Marxian and Weberian conception of the state, thereby limiting its ability to clarify the issue.

but it is not consistently maintained even in many works by the best analysts of these systems. Thus, it has not been adequately developed in recent analyses of the transitions[14] despite the many theoretical works on regimes[15] and on the state.[16]

A regime may be thought of as the formal and informal organization of the center of political power, and of its relations with the broader society. A regime determines who has access to political power, and how those who are in power deal with those who are not. The distinction between democracy, totalitarianism, and authoritarianism thus deals with the question of *regime type*. (However, full penetration of the state by the regime might be thought of as one of the defining characteristics of pure totalitarianism; in a different sense, in cases of personal rulership or "sultanism," state and regime may be thoroughly entangled with one another, both closely identified with the ruler.) Regimes are more permanent forms of political organization than specific governments, but they are typically less permanent than the state. The state, by contrast, is a (normally) more permanent structure of domination and coordination including a coercive apparatus and the means to administer a society and extract resources from it.

Although the two concepts are analytically distinct, the empirical realities to which they refer may be more or less tightly interwoven in some political formations. In many instances, however, the empirical realities are distinguishable from one another. A state may remain in place even when regimes come and go, as has happened at many points in the history of Spain and numerous other countries. Somewhat less frequently, and only for rather brief periods of time, a regime may remain relatively

[14] To some extent, the distinction is suggested by Alfred Stepan in "Paths to Redemocratization: Theoretical and Comparative Considerations," in O'Donnell, Schmitter, and Whitehead, eds., *Transitions from Authoritarian Rule: Comparative Perspectives* (Baltimore: The Johns Hopkins University Press, 1986). In that essay and in his recent book, *Rethinking Military Politics* (Princeton: Princeton University Press, 1988), Stepan differentiates three forms of what he calls "redemocratization from within the authoritarian regime": transition initiated by a civilian political leadership, by the military as government, and by the military as an institution. However, Stepan's insightful discussion still fails to emphasize the major analytical distinction between state and regime, and ends up placing in the same category (transition initiated by the military as institution) two quite different cases: Portugal and Greece.

[15] See especially the extremely broad and insightful essay by Juan Linz, "Totalitarian and Authoritarian Regimes," in Fred Greenstein and Nelson Polsby, *Handbook of Political Science*, Vol. III, *Macropolitical Theory* (Reading, MA: Addison-Wesley, 1975).

[16] My own understanding of the state is clearly Weberian, and follows the rich discussion in *Economy and Society* (American ed., Berkeley: University of California Press, 1978) and "Politics as a Vocation," in Hans Gerth and C. Wright Mills, eds., *From Max Weber: Essays in Sociology* (New York: Oxford University Press, 1946) as well as the strongly argued thesis on the state in Theda Skocpol, *States and Social Revolutions* (Cambridge: Cambridge University Press, 1979), and in her other writings.

cohesive and determined to remain in power even as the state on which it relies crumbles away and loses its ability or resolve to coerce, administer, and extract resources.[17] Where a state does not disintegrate in the context of a political transition, it may (or may not) serve a new democratic regime as well as it served an earlier authoritarian one. The ability of new regimes to restructure or "purge" the state, moreover, varies significantly from case to case. Indeed, the state/regime distinction may prove analytically useful even for cases in which it does not correspond to easily differentiated empirical entities.

More concretely, the individuals and collectivities that fill the central roles in states are not always the same as those who do so in regimes. The military, a central institution in any state, is quite marginal in some authoritarian regimes. Without question, official parties in authoritarian systems are part of the regime, but it is not at all clear that they should be viewed as part of the state. Intellectuals, policy advisers, and journalists, as well as former government officials—including well-known former ministers—all may be part of the political community in an authoritarian regime even if they hold no state office or duty. Such 'regime figures,' or regime actors, may play a significant part in authoritarian systems both in normal times and during moments of systemic transformation. Their role is not limited to the objective of legitimation (or delegitimation), but encompasses matters of political strategy and intrigue that may prove central to the political trajectory followed by a regime. By contrast, many centrally important state actors—for example, the judiciary and the civil service as well as the military—play little or no role in regime politics in nonmilitary authoritarian regimes such as Franco Spain. But their capacity to disrupt the regime, should they choose to ignore their traditional marginalization from politics, is clear to all and could be decisive in crucial moments, especially during a transition or attempted transition.

In the case of Spain, the objective of returning to democracy eventually came to be assumed by significant sectors within the regime. Following the death of Franco, and under pressure from the opposition, these sectors began the difficult but ultimately successful process of transition by negotiated reform. The initiative for reform, however, should not be viewed as the clear policy of a united government; some governmental figures, such as Prime Minister Carlos Arias Navarro did not cooperate

---

[17] This seems to have been the case in the waning days or months of the Shah's regime in Iran when first government bureaucrats and ultimately the army itself refused to carry out state functions. Such a configuration, if sustained for any significant period of time, is likely to lead to the type of crisis that, according to Skocpol (fn. 16), underpins social revolution.

fully and nevertheless remained in office until summer 1976. On the other hand, many 'regime figures'—including some who held no formal governmental responsibilities—did play a fundamentally important role.[18] By contrast, state actors (with the extremely important exception of King Juan Carlos[19] who, in some sense, represented both state and regime) never moved to advance the cause of redemocratization; to the extent that they have been a factor at all, they have appeared to threaten the political opening at various points. The most dramatic incident occurred on February 23, 1981, when an attempted military coup by a minority within the armed forces seriously endangered the new democratic system.[20] Indeed, reformist Prime Minister Adolfo Suarez (named to that post in July 1976) found it necessary to override significant pressure from the military in order to implement democratic reforms such as the legalization of the Communist party in April 1977; frequent rumors of pro-coup conspiracies within the military punctuated the transition.

This specific location of the impetus for change helped produce a new political system in which the authoritarian regime was never totally rejected symbolically even though it was fully superseded and transformed. Moreover, regime actors from the old Franco system have been able to play central roles in the new democratic system to the extent that they accept the political change. Adolfo Suarez, the founding prime minister of the new democracy and a political veteran of the *Movimiento*, the old regime party, is only the most obvious example of this broader pattern. By helping to initiate and guide the transition, the reformist sector of the old regime participated in the shaping of the new one. And the marginality in the transition of the state, as such, left its structures intact. The Spanish transition was the only one in Southern Europe in which no purge of the state was possible; moreover, the fear of a military intervention against democracy helped to restrain the more radical instincts of some political actors.

In Portugal, on the other hand, the regime proved incapable of reforming itself to any significant degree even after Salazar passed from the scene. Thus, political actors from the old regime lost the ability to shape the new democracy or the transition period. Instead, the impetus for change came from within the state in the form of a middle-level

[18] Good sources in English include Paul Preston, *The Triumph of Democracy in Spain* (London: Methuen, 1986); Carr and Fusi (fn. 8); and Share (fn. 8).

[19] For an analysis of the role of Juan Carlos in the transition to democracy, see Joel Podolny, *The Role of Juan Carlos, the King of Spain, in the Consolidation of the Spanish Parliamentary Monarchy* (Social Studies Honors Thesis, Harvard College, Spring 1986).

[20] For an especially good discussion in English of the coup attempt and its political antecedents, see Preston (fn. 18).

RETHINKING STATE AND REGIME   431

officers' revolt in the military. The regime was overthrown—something
that never happened in Spain—because it had failed to initiate or channel the process of political change. Moreover, the location of the revolt
within the military—specifically at the captains' level—seriously undermined the structure of hierarchy in that institution. With the ensuing
politicization and division of the military, the stage was set for revolutionary mobilizations that have left an enduring mark on Portugal.[21] Unlike in Spain, where the military remained a cohesive force and a potential threat to a moderate and reformist process of democratization, the
military in Portugal helped initiate leftist popular mobilizations and
quickly lost the cohesion and discipline necessary to serve as an effective
and predictable instrument of state coercion. The ensuing revolutionary
mobilizations—in part a result of the shifting balance of power and strategies within the state[22]—transformed the ownership of land in large areas of the country and led to numerous expropriations in urban centers
as well, including the entire banking sector. Significant numbers of those
involved in the old authoritarian structure of power, including the secret
police, were purged.[23]

At a certain level of abstraction, it may be valid to argue that the
transitions in both Spain and Portugal were initiated or led by forces
within the circle of political power or domination; but the causes and the
consequences of the two transitions, as well as the actors and the processes, differ enormously. It is in no sense sufficient to summarize the
entire difference with the common dichotomy *reforma/ruptura*.

In Greece, as in Portugal, the military helped to initiate the political
change. In the Greek case, however, it is difficult to locate this initiative
squarely in the regime or the state, given the military character of the
regime and the consequent overlapping of these two analytically distinct
entities. In a sense, one can argue that, when removing itself from power,
the military acted more as an institution of the state than of the regime.
In the summer of 1974, in the wake of the military crisis with Turkey
over Cyprus, the armed forces' highest leadership reinstituted military-
institutional control over the political hierarchy of the junta and then
quickly handed over power to civilian democratic politicians. Nikiforos

[21] For excellent discussions of the Portuguese transition, with the expected emphasis on
the role of the military, see the chapters by Kenneth Maxwell in the *Transitions* volume, and
in Herz (fn. 3). An outstanding analysis of the revolution in agrarian social relations is found
in Nancy G. Bermeo, *The Revolution within the Revolution* (Princeton: Princeton University
Press, 1986).

[22] Bermeo, *ibid.*, emphasizes this point.

[23] See Antonio Costa Pinto, "Revolution and Political Purge in Portugal's Transition to
Democracy" in Stein U. Larsen, ed., *Modern Europe after Fascism: 1945-1980's* (Bergen: Norwegian University Press, forthcoming).

Diamandouros, in his compelling analysis in the *Transitions* volume, states that "the Joint Chiefs, invoking the threat of war, reasserted the hierarchical lines of command within the armed forces and effectively neutralized ... the hard-liners" (p. 157). The change occurred rapidly and provided no opportunity for the military to shape the new democracy (as is possible in a regime-initiated transition). In view of the broad support for political intervention within the military, it would, however, be a mistake to completely counterpose the armed forces as a state institution against the junta as a military regime.[24]

In any event, the Greek military acted as an institution and preserved its discipline and hierarchy. By contrast, in the Portuguese case, the location of the coup at the captains' level and the actual exercise of power by the military initiated a period of politicization and internal division within the armed forces. Although the cases of both Greece and Portugal can be seen as state-initiated transitions, the institutional integrity and quick withdrawal from political power of the Greek military explain why no revolutionary mobilization took place in Greece. In Greece, as in Portugal, however, a symbolic break occurred between regimes, and a purge of leaders from the authoritarian period was feasible, even if limited. In Spain, such a purge never took place; the loyalty of the military remained a troublesome question for democratic political leaders for several years. In some respects, the Greek case may thus be seen as lying between the other two.

The distinction between state and regime is important not only for identifying the source of the democratizing initiative, but also for understanding the subsequent trajectory of political change: the location of the impetus for political change within the circles of power has implications for the ability of the transitional political formation to carry out functions associated with state and regime. Thus, regime-initiated transitions like the Spanish one are better able to channel links between society and the center of political power and to determine who will have access to the latter. Regime reformists are able to help steer the transition and define the boundaries of the new democratic system. They may, however, be vulnerable to pressure or threats from within the state itself. By contrast, where state actors initiate the transition, they will probably not be able to participate to the same extent in defining the new political system, but they can at least guarantee the ability of the new civilian political lead-

---

[24] For data from an empirical study of the Greek military during the junta's time in power, see George Andrew Kourvetaris, "Professional Self-Images and Political Perspectives in the Greek Military," *American Sociological Review* 36 (December 1971).

RETHINKING STATE AND REGIME   433

ership to administer and coerce effectively—so long as state institutions
maintain their unity and internal discipline. Where state cohesion and
institutional hierarchy are undermined by the transition, however, as in
Portugal, some state functions may no longer be reliably carried out, and
the stage is prepared—following Skocpol's formulation—for social revolutionary mobilization, provided that revolutionary actors are available.[25]

Each type of transition suggests specific analytical inquiries. For regime-initiated redemocratizations where the state remains in place, perhaps the most important question concerns the relationship between state
and regime in both political settings—under authoritarian rule and in
the new democratic context.[26] Was the state, under authoritarian rule,
closely associated with the specific form of the regime, or was it seen as
more or less politically neutral and bureaucratic (with the possible exception of certain highly specific and isolated state institutions that were
strongly linked to repressive authoritarian policies)? Furthermore, are
state institutions, under democracy, predictable and effective in carrying
out state functions within the structure of democratic legality? Are state
entities effectively subject to democratic political control?

Where state actors initiate the transition, the crucial question is
whether they retain their internal discipline and unity (as in Greece), or
lose those qualities (as in Portugal). If the state initiators of a transition
undermine the existing hierarchy and cohesion of state institutions, the
state is less able to fulfill its distinctive functions; the result may be more
wide-ranging mobilization and transformation.

Where state and regime are closely intertwined, as in Greece, a distinctive question is whether the institutions or actors that initiate the
transition behave, during the transition, as regime or as state. The Greek
transition tended to take the latter form, initiated by what Stepan calls
"the military as institution"; this helps to explain how so much could be
changed so quickly by the new democratic political leadership—including the purging of some military elements strongly associated with repressive policies. Other factors are undoubtedly also important in accounting for the ability of Greece's new democratic rulers to impose a
decisive political opening quickly and to purge a significant number of
military hard-liners within a year after the transition. In other parts of

[25] See Skocpol (fn. 16).
[26] A rich discussion of differing configurations of relations (under authoritarianism)
between the coercive apparatus and the governmental institutions is presented by Stepan
(fn. 14, 1988).

the world, some military-led transitions have given way to limited—or even facade—regimes of democracy that coexist with unaccountable centers of repression within the state apparatus.[27]

This line of analysis suggests that democratic transition is more likely to be successful where state and regime can be distinguished from one another. Where the distinction is not easily drawn—because of "fusion" between the two in a military dictatorship, or totalitarian penetration of the state by the regime, or confusion between the two under personal rulership—special problems are likely to emerge in the process of democratization.

The distinction between state and regime is a useful starting point for the comparative analysis of transitions, but it is only a starting point. Major differences between the Portuguese and Greek cases underscore the importance of moving beyond this distinction in order to incorporate other significant factors within any causal analysis. No matter where we choose to locate the actors analytically, their political perspective(s), their internal cohesion or division, and the political mechanisms available to them, all help to determine the role assumed by the initiators of a transition.

If the consequences and the broad outlines of different patterns of political transition are sharply divergent, their causes may be quite dissimilar as well, despite the historical clustering of the processes. It is certainly reasonable to inquire whether the types of factors that help to push a regime toward transition differ from those that induce pressure for political change from sectors of the state largely outside the regime. It is not possible here to provide a complete inventory of relevant factors, but at least one centrally important political component of transitions should be considered: the delegitimation of the old regime and the legitimation of new forms of political rule.

THE DELEGITIMATION OF AUTHORITARIAN RULE: NEW CRISES OR HISTORICAL OBSOLESCENCE?

Despite the emphasis placed on the issue of legitimacy by analysts of the transitions, the problem is rarely posed in terms of the *original* legitimation formula for authoritarian rule and the means available for its

[27] This is most clearly the case in some Central American countries; see Jennifer Schirmer, "Oficiales de la Montaña: Based on an Exclusive Interview with the Guatemalan Golpistas of May 11, 1988," *Human Rights Internet Reporter* 13 (Spring 1989), 13-16. In the case of Brazil, analysts have questioned the fully democratic character of the political formation; see Frances Hagopian, " 'Democracy by Undemocratic Means'?: Elites, Political Pacts, and Regime Transition in Brazil," *Comparative Political Studies* (forthcoming), and Stepan (fn. 14).

RETHINKING STATE AND REGIME   435

undoing. Authoritarian rule frequently legitimates itself through reference to a founding crisis, an event, or a series of occurrences that the
regime asserts it is uniquely able to overcome. It follows that the delegitimation of such a regime may occur through the appearance of a new
crisis that it manifestly fails to handle adequately; alternatively, relevant
political sectors may seek to demonstrate that the founding crisis of authoritarian rule has been historically superseded, and that therefore the
regime is obsolete. We may think of these two alternatives for delegiti-
mizing authoritarianism as *crises of failure* and *crises of historical obsolescence*.[28] The delegitimation of the Portuguese and Greek regimes took
the form of crises of failure—in both instances of a military nature. In
the Spanish context, the forces of democracy were not blessed with any
equivalent glaring failure of the regime. In this setting, the delegitimation of authoritarian rule required that the relevant political sectors (in
the opposition and within the reformist wing of the regime) demonstrate
repeatedly that the founding crisis of authoritarian rule had been historically overcome, and that the country was no longer divided into two
opposed camps. Authoritarian rule—and most specifically its claim to
legitimacy—was thus faced with a crisis of historical obsolescence. The
effort of regime reformists and the opposition to delegitimize authoritarianism pushed both political sectors toward accommodation and moderation, thus further tending to preclude any purge of the state.

The character and depth of the foundational crisis of authoritarian
regimes—and the coherence of the associated legitimation claims—help
to account for the form taken by subsequent transitions. The Greek regime of 1967-1974 emerged from a much less overwhelming crisis than
did those of the other two countries.[29] Indeed, Diamandouros maintains

[28] This distinction is to some extent suggested by the formulation of Adam Przeworski in
his essay, "Some Problems in the Study of the Transition to Democracy," in *Transitions from
Authoritarian Rule: Comparative Perspectives* (fn. 14). Synthesizing the arguments of others,
Przeworski proposes that, to the extent that legitimation is a significant factor, a regime may
lose its legitimacy when "it has realized the functional needs that led to its establishment" or
for other reasons (p. 50). This suggests that we might counterpose crises of failure and of
success. However, I prefer to think in terms of historical obsolescence rather than success
since regimes may be overtaken by historical developments that are in no sense their own
successes. Moreover, the notion of historical obsolescence suggests more forcefully the need
of central political actors to argue that the regime is obsolete, and to support this assertion
with their actions and rhetoric. Political arguments (albeit with material referents) rather
than objective conditions such as 'the realization of functional needs' are, after all, the essence
of legitimation or delegitimation.

[29] On the virtual disintegration from within of the Portuguese First Republic and the
foundations for five decades of authoritarian rule, see Douglas Wheeler, *The First Portuguese
Republic* (Madison: University of Wisconsin Press, 1978), and Stanley Payne, *A History of
Spain and Portugal* (Madison: University of Wisconsin Press, 1973). The bibliography on the
social and political conflict in Spain in the 1930s, culminating in the outbreak of civil war, is
too lengthy to be covered adequately here.

that the junta never enjoyed the same legitimacy with its potential socio-political base on the right as did its Iberian counterparts; thus, "the regime's ideological legitimation strategy assigned a preeminent role to the eventual return to democratic institutions and competitive politics" (p. 148). The weakness of the regime's initial claim to legitimacy and its associated inability to institutionalize itself in any serious fashion, as much as the ultimate crisis of failure and the state-led character of the transition, may account for the significant political room for maneuver enjoyed by Greece's new democratic regime.[30] The changes rapidly instituted under the new democracy should not be underestimated: in addition to the purge of some pro-authoritarian sectors within the state apparatus, these changes included the legalization of the Communist party (which had been banned since the civil war) and the end of the monarchy.

As the reader may have noted, there is an affinity between crises of obsolescence and regime-led transition on the one hand, and crises of failure and state-led transitions on the other. It is not likely, however, that the type of crisis alone determines whether state or regime will initiate a transition. Among the factors that shape the way in which states and regimes respond to crises are the political perspectives within them, their internal unity or division, and the mechanisms available to them to influence political life. Thus, neither all states nor all regimes would respond in equivalent ways to similar crises. The Portuguese regime did, in a sense, face a crisis of obsolescence—given the great historical distance of its founding justification—but it was unable to reform itself. One might speculate also that the Spanish state—or, more specifically, the military—even if faced with a severe crisis of failure, would have been slower than the Greek or Portuguese army to call an end to authoritarian rule.

Despite the considerable attention that analysts of transitions have given to the dynamics of legitimation or delegitimation, the explanatory value of legitimacy has been challenged by Przeworski and others.[31] In response to such criticisms, it is worth noting that the concept of legitimacy refers to phenomena that are much more specific than certain types of political behavior—such as obedience, diffuse ill-defined support, or political preference—with which it is sometimes confused. Legitimacy

---

[30] These features of the Greek case obviously raise the question whether it should be seen as an "authoritarian situation" in the terms of Juan Linz's formulation of the Brazilian case. See Linz, "The Future of an Authoritarian Situation or the Institutionalization of an Authoritarian Regime: The Case of Brazil" in Alfred Stepan, ed., *Authoritarian Brazil* (New Haven: Yale University Press, 1973).

[31] See Przeworski (fn. 28).

Transitions to Democracy

RETHINKING STATE AND REGIME

in the Weberian sense involves the issuing of a rather specific claim by those in power to justify their position of domination and affirm their right to issue *binding* commands; full legitimacy also entails that staff and subjects accept that claim as valid. It is of course possible to obey, and perhaps even accept as relatively benign, an authoritarian regime without actually supporting its claim to legitimacy. Authoritarian regimes would certainly like to be considered legitimate by all or most citizens; but to survive, they require legitimacy only within the fairly specific circles of their own political supporters and the state. Democracy, on the other hand, probably requires a more broad-based legitimacy if it is to be stable. Thus, a successful transition requires not only the delegitimation of authoritarian rule for some of its former supporters, but also the legitimation of the new democratic regime.

Researchers using both inferential and direct measures have studied the legitimacy of the new democracy more thoroughly in the Spanish case than in the other two.[32] The legitimacy of democracy—and, more importantly, of the state under democracy—has been widely accepted in Spain, which has helped to assure the success of the transition.[33] This legitimacy would probably have been far more tenuous if the state as a whole (rather than only certain limited components of it) had been tightly identified with the Franco regime. Of course, some elements of the state—most dramatically during the attempted coup of February 23, 1981—have identified with the authoritarian past. Their sentiments, and the widespread concern over the potential disloyalty of others, helped to restrain governmental and political action. But ultimately, the pockets of disloyalty within the state were isolated and deactivated. At this time, Spain's democracy rests not just on a regime of competition among more or less mutually secure parties,[34] but also on the existence of state structures of coercion and administration which are legitimate for most Spaniards and loyal to the democratically elected authorities. The behavior of state institutions may at times be a source of frustration to Spaniards; but

[32] For differing approaches to the legitimacy of democracy in Spain, see Peter McDonough, Samuel Barnes, and Antonio Lopez Pina, "The Growth of Democratic Legitimacy in Spain," *American Political Science Review* 80 (September 1986), and chaps. XIV and XV of Juan Linz, Manuel Gomez-Reino, Francisco Andres Orizo, and Dario Vila, *Informe Sociológico sobre el cambio político en España: 1975-1981* [Sociological report on the political change in Spain: 1975-1981] (Madrid: Euramerica, 1981).

[33] I attempt an operationalization of the Weberian conception of legitimacy in *Working Class Organization and the Return to Democracy in Spain* (fn. 8). My research findings show the legitimacy of the state under democracy to be a remarkably good 'predictor' of workplace union leaders' support for nationally negotiated wage restraints. See esp. chaps. 5 and 7.

[34] Robert Dahl, in *Polyarchy* (New Haven: Yale University Press, 1971), stresses the fundamental importance of mutual security for democracy to survive.

ultimately, civilian political actors have been free to design a solid new democratic regime on their own.

DISTINCT POLITICAL TRAJECTORIES: NATIONAL CASE STUDIES

The national case studies and monographic investigations of the various transitions represent an important scholarly achievement. These studies are at their best—and are most useful for comparative analysis—when they focus on the most salient, and in many cases distinctive, features of each national case. Indeed, there are important differences among the cases, which must be explored empirically, analyzed, and explained. Distinctive to the Spanish case—in addition to the absence of any purge of state institutions—was the "politics of consensus" encompassing all significant political actors (except for some sectors within the Basque Country).[35] The pervasive moderation (with notable but isolated exceptions on the far right, the far left, and among regional nationalists) and the political forces' joint consultations on major matters have made possible the establishment of a new democratic regime that is accepted by a wide spectrum of adversaries who only four decades earlier were engaged in a bitter civil war.

Spain after Franco, the outstanding book by Richard Gunther, Giacomo Sani, and Goldie Shabad, provides an extraordinarily thorough and compelling analysis of the forging and the practice of this "politics of consensus," and of its impact on the emergence of a new party system. Thanks to an exhaustive program of research, including extensive qualitative interviewing at the elite level and a large sample survey of public opinion at the mass level, the rich work presents many original findings. Moreover, in addition to providing survey data and political science concepts, the work serves as an excellent history of the period; it details little-known facts, especially in the area of elite strategies and of negotiations concerning the constitution and regional policy. At the same time, the authors present a broad and compelling interpretive overview of the foundation of a new democratic system, focusing on the emergence of the party system. They explore the historical foundations—in the memories of the civil war, the transformation of Spanish society, and the dynamics of the transition itself—of the politics of consensus that characterized the early years of democracy. The authors argue convincingly that this consensus rested on a complex interplay between mass-level predispositions and elite-level political initiatives.

[35] On the complexities and internal divisions of Basque politics, see Juan Linz, *Conflicto en Euskadi* [Conflict in the Basque Country] (Madrid: Espasa Calpe, 1986).

RETHINKING STATE AND REGIME   439

The forging of political parties and of a competitive political arena that permitted veterans of the Franco regime and opposition forces to coexist democratically is shown to have been a difficult process requiring favorable conditions as well as political skill and good will. Clearly, the shape of the new democracy and its chances for survival were powerfully influenced both by the participation in the transition of regime reformers like Adolfo Suarez and the mechanisms used by all democratic forces for 'delegitimating' or undercutting the case for authoritarianism. *In Spain after Franco*, the distinctive contours of Spanish democracy are richly analyzed; far from representing mere idiographic description, the volume provides the basis for comparative analysis and for the explanation of why this case is "so and not otherwise."[36]

The Portuguese case, by contrast, was characterized not only by a purge of state institutions, but also by dramatic political conflicts and revolutionary mobilizations (including the seizing of much property) during the years of regime transition. Most of the recent scholarship on postauthoritarian Portugal has focused on the explanations and consequences of the revolutionary surge. An exception to the general tendency in recent work on Portugal is Walter Opello's *Portugal's Political Development: A Comparative Approach*. Although the book represents much effort and conveys a good deal of interesting information, it avoids or even denies much of what is distinctive about the Portuguese case. The author is so eager to place Portugal within a Western European framework of analysis that he tends to pose only those questions that have been asked before, about rather different cases, by students of political development. Even the survey data deal largely with the most general questions that might be posed in any political system. Opello actually argues strongly against the dominant interpretation of the transition period as a revolutionary (or partially revolutionary) episode. Emphasizing that the end of authoritarianism was precipitated by military initiative rather than popular rebellion, he argues that the dominant interpretation of the period tends "to confuse the rhetoric of revolution with the reality of events that were actually taking place" (p. 65). Opello attributes little importance to the frequently bitter conflicts over control and power in the economy and the state—conflicts that involved mass mobilizations and engendered, at a minimum, highly anxious observation by international powers. The book's argument reflects a limited conception of revolution and a failure to appreciate the particular configuration of state and regime forces that shaped this decisive period of political change in

---

[36] This is, in Max Weber's phrase, a fundamental objective of the social sciences.

Portugal. It is, after all, not sufficient to observe that the crucial initiative came "from above"; the distinctive contours of that initiative in Portugal set the case apart from Southern Europe's other two instances of regime- or state-led transition and contribute powerfully to explaining the (ulti- mately arrested) social revolution of postauthoritarian Portugal. Without some attention to what is distinctive and salient, a case such as that of Portugal cannot be effectively placed in a broader comparative perspec- tive.

To sum up: despite the historical convergence in the mid-1970s of the redemocratization of Spain, Portugal, and Greece, the political processes in these three cases have been remarkably different along several dimen- sions. The causes of political transition, the identity of the central actors, the paths followed by the political changes, and the broad outlines of the political outcomes are sharply divergent. In Spain, state actors remained uninvolved in the transition process and stood as a potential impediment to change while regime reformists helped to initiate and guide the tran- sition; the result is a polity that is in many respects moderate and re- strained. In Portugal, regime actors failed to initiate the move to democ- racy; a coup of the politicized middle ranks of the military set the stage for a partially successful social revolution, ultimately halted in part by the democratically expressed preferences of the people. In Greece, the military hierarchy, acting as a state institution, took power away from the junta and transferred it to democratic civilian leaders who (after the failure of a coup attempt several months later) were able to carry out a purge of military officers implicated in the abuses of authoritarian rule.

Although international and cross-national historical contexts un- doubtedly contributed somewhat to each of the transitions, the three cases do not follow a unified logic. When comparative analysis focuses on differences as well as on similarities, one must be prepared to find that some instances of historical convergence may owe as much to acci- dents in timing as to any overarching causal configuration.

To emphasize the distinctiveness of specific cases in no sense implies that the comparative enterprise has been abandoned. It simply avoids the false assertion that there is one comprehensive causal constellation ac- counting for significantly different outcomes and processes. Comparative analysis must delineate and account for differences as well as similarities; it requires the use of concepts that discriminate in useful ways among partially similar and partially different cases. It is to that end that the distinctions drawn in this essay are advanced.

[12]

Democratization from authoritarian rule has been an important focus of scholarly interest
in the 1980s. However, no typology of democratic transitions currently exists. This article
introduces a typology of transitions from authoritarianism to democracy with four major
types: incremental democratization, transition through rupture, transition through
protracted revolutionary struggle, and transition through transaction. The remainder of
the article discusses the conditions for one type of democratic transition, transition
through transaction, in Spain (1975-1978). As the Spanish case suggests, the conditions
for this type of transition are quite different from those required for other forms of
transition. The summary discussion of the Spanish case is divided into a consideration of
the conditions for the initiation of transition through transaction, and an examination of
the conditions for the implementation of transition through transaction. Both sections
emphasize the crucial role of elite attitudes and skill in transitions through transaction.

TRANSITIONS TO DEMOCRACY
AND TRANSITION THROUGH
TRANSACTION

DONALD SHARE
University of Puget Sound

Democratization from authoritarian rule has been one of the most
intensely studied topics of the 1980s.[1] Students of comparative
politics have explored the erosion of authoritarian rule, the conditions
for democratic transition, the process of democratic regime change, the
foundation and consolidation of new democracies, and the consequences of democratic transition for the future of democratic rule.

AUTHOR'S NOTE: *This article was presented at the 1985 Annual Meeting of the
American Political Science Association in New Orleans. Earlier versions appeared as part
of my "Transition Through Transaction: The Politics of Democratization in Spain,
1975-1977" (Ph.D. dissertation, Stanford University, 1984).*

COMPARATIVE POLITICAL STUDIES, Vol. 19 No. 4, January 1987 525-548
© 1987 Sage Publications, Inc.

526   COMPARATIVE POLITICAL STUDIES / January 1987

This concern about democratization follows a decade of scholarly inquiry into the difficulties confronting democratic rule in both the developed and developing world, and ultimately, the nature of and causes for its breakdown. The shifting focus is partly explained by contemporary political developments. From the mid-1960s until the early-1970s "liberal" notions of democratic rule came under attack, with the end of democracy in such developing nations as Argentina, Greece, Brazil, Chile, and Uruguay. Not surprisingly, scholarly attention was directed to the economic, social, and international constraints obstructing democratic rule in less developed nations. The "dependency" literature, by explaining how internal and external forms of political economic domination undermined democracy in dependent countries, was especially influential.[2]

This return to democracy in Latin Europe (Greece and Portugal in 1974 and Spain after 1975) and Latin America (Peru in 1980, Bolivia and Argentina in 1982, and Brazil more recently) kindled a renewed interest in democratization. Unlike the "political development" literature of the past, with its emphasis on the maintenance of stable democracy, or with its selective focus on the "classical" models of democratic evolution (England and Sweden), the recent writings have focused more narrowly on the *genesis* of democratic rule. These writings have given rise to what may be seen as a cautious optimism about the possibilities for democratic rule, in marked contrast to the scholarly pessimism of the previous decade.

The new writings on democratization have, with some exceptions, heeded the warnings of Dankwart Rustow, issued more than 10 years ago (Rustow, 1970). Democracy's genesis has been studied separately from the functional requisites for its maintenance. Explanations of democratization have attempted to pinpoint causes rather than draw attention to correlations. Emphasis on structural variables (the international system, the class structure, economic performance, and political institutions) has not displaced concern about political strategy, skill, and beliefs. There has been a recognition that more than one road leads to democratic rule, and that such roads will vary depending on historical and contextual factors. Finally, Rustow was correct when he predicted that "The study of democratic transitions will take the political scientist deeper into history than he/she has commonly been willing to go" (Rustow, 1970: 347).

Surprisingly, despite the attention recently attributed to the question of democratization from authoritarian rule, there has been little effort to develop a typology of democratic transitions.[3] Attempts to develop theoretical explanations for the emergence of democratic rule have failed in part because the universe of transitions to democracy is so large and diverse. This article proposes a broad typology of democratic transitions from authoritarian rule. It argues that such a typology is necessary for any examination of the conditions for democratic transition, since the conditions for each subtype are likely different. In order to illustrate this point, the article will briefly discuss one subtype, referred to here as "transition through transaction," drawing on the Spanish case in particular. It will be argued that the conditions for Spain's transition through transaction differed from those associated with the most common subtype, "transition through rupture."

SOME PRELIMINARY DEFINITIONS

This article is concerned with transitions from authoritarian to democratic regimes. By regime, I mean the formal and informal structure of governmental roles and processes. Included within this concept of regime are methods of inauguration of governments, formal and informal representative mechanisms, and patterns of coercion. Authoritarian regimes will be defined as political systems with significant procedural proscriptions on political contestation or inclusiveness. The notion of democracy employed here will be Robert Dahl's definition of polyarchies, or "regimes that have been substantially popularized and liberalized, that is highly inclusive and extensively open to public contestation" (Dahl, 1971: 8). More concretely, democracies must provide for (1) free and contested elections for the selection of political representatives, (2) basic civil rights, and (3) clearly established "rules of the game" that protect these democratic liberties. Thus this article adopts a relatively narrow, easy to operationalize, and procedurally oriented definition of democracy.

It should be noted from the start that a common problem facing students of the transition to democracy is defining its chronological parameters. It is often observed that the transition to democracy may have its roots deep within the process of change during the authoritarian regime. For example, the political thaw of the 1960s in franquist Spain clearly contributed to the emergence of forces favoring democratic rule. For the purposes of this article, such easing of repression and

restoration of civil liberties will be termed "liberalization." Democratization will refer to the establishment of institutions and procedures
that allow for all three aspects of our definition of democracy.
Liberalization of an authoritarian regime may or may not occur prior to
democratization.[4]

Just as it is hard to mark the beginning of the process of democratic
transition, it is also difficult to define its end point. The transition to
democracy may be viewed as complete when democratic procedures,
rights, and rules of the game have been clearly delineated and widely
accepted by a majority of elites and citizens. In many democratic
transitions, such as post-World War II West Germany or contemporary
Brazil, the end of the transition process is more difficult to define, since
direct popular endorsement of the newly established rules of the game
may be postponed or delayed indefinitely. Even in the Spanish
transition to democracy, where the 1978 referendum demonstrated an
overwhelming popular approval of a new constitution, some considered
the transition incomplete until the regime experienced its first alternation of power in 1982.

Although it is useful to delimit beginning and end of the transition to
democracy for analytical purposes, such artificial boundaries are
necessarily imperfect. The boundaries between the breakdown of
authoritarian rule and the initiation of democratization are often
blurred. Likewise, the process of democratization often overlaps with
the consolidation, institutionalization, and early maintenance of a new
democratic regime.

A TYPOLOGY OF
TRANSITIONS TO DEMOCRACY

Two caveats are in order before proposing a typology of transitions
to democracy.[5] First, this exercise will only consider transitions from
authoritarian rule to democracy, using the strict definitions of both
terms introduced in the previous section. Thus, the universe of
postcolonial democracies that have evolved after periods of neither
authoritarianism nor complete democracy (for instance, the United
States) are not considered here. Second, the typlogy establishes ideal-
types, recognizing that most historical cases of democratic transition
may manifest characteristics of more than one form of democratization.

In developing the typology of transitions to democracy, illustrated in Figure 1, two classificatory questions were asked. First, is the democratic transition brought about with the participation or consent of leaders of the authoritarian regime, or does it transpire without such participation or consent? Transitions which enjoy the support of authoritarian rulers may be termed consensual. According to Giovanni Sartori (1976: 275), these types of transitions occur "whenever they can be imputed to the working principles or to the rules of the game, inherent in that system. In short, continuous change amounts to self-change, to transformations resulting from, and permitted by, the inner constituent mechanisms of each political structure." This support for democratization can be manifest in two ways: Authoritarian leaders may simply tolerate democratic political change, refraining from active stewardship over it; or they actively participate in the process of change, hoping thereby either to control and limit such change, or to forestall more distasteful change.

Consensual transitions entail at least some degree of political continuity between the authoritarian and democratic period. Because authoritarian elites are willing and able to allow the birth of democratic rule—and are partly or largely responsible for its genesis—the legitimacy of the authoritarian and democratic regimes are not mutually exclusive. Consensual transitions are able to foster simultaneously "backward" and "forward" legitimation; democratic rule is established upon, not at the expense of authoritarianism.[6] Thus consensual transitions usually avoid open confrontation between supporters of authoritarian and democratic rule, and may gain adherents from both camps. Logically, in such cases one would expect to detect democratic features within the preceding authoritarian regime, as well as nondemocratic vestiges in the succeeding democracy.

Transitions to democracy that are initiated without the consent or cooperation of authoritarian rulers may be termed nonconsensual. In nonconsensual transitions to democracy, the legitimacy of authoritarian and democratic rule are mutually exclusive: Support for authoritarian rule cannot be reconciled with acceptance of a democratic regime. In such cases, authoritarian leaders, out of ignorance, incompetence, sheer stubbornness, or some mixture thereof, oppose the transition to democracy. They may stifle attempts by political forces to initiate it, or they may simply neglect to place the question of democratic rule on the political agenda. Either way, when democratization results, it is at the expense of the legitimacy of authoritarian rule. The resulting

530   COMPARATIVE POLITICAL STUDIES / January 1987

Democratization by or Against Regime Leaders?

	By Regime Leaders (Consensual)	Against Regime Leaders (Non-Conensual)
Gradual:	Incremental Democratization	Transition Through Protracted Revolutionary Struggle
Rapid:	Transition Through Transaction	Transition Through Rupture a) Revolution b) Coup c) Collapse d) Extrication

(Pace of Democratization)

Figure 1: Types of Democratization from Authoritarian Rule

democracy will likely eschew the support—and may actively prohibit the participation—of political forces linked with the authoritarian past. Purges, deportation, imprisonment, and other proscriptions are the mark of nonconsensual transitions. Severe discontinuities between authoritarian and democratic periods are often manifest in political institutions, political symbols, political culture, and even socioeconomic arrangements.

A second question regarding the universe of transitions to democracy concerns the duration of the transition. Does the transition to democracy occur gradually, transcending a single generation of political leaders, or is it a relatively rapid phenomenon? This question has both theoretical implications, that will be become apparent below, and practical importance. As Dahl has noted, *incremental democratization* of the consensual type is increasingly impractical in the contemporary world, where mass communications, combined with the demonstration effect, make an incremental opening of the political process extremely difficult to affect (Dahl, 1971: 39). Likewise, the incremental growth of democratic oppositions in the face of rigidly authoritarian regimes *(protracted revolutionary struggles)* seems to be the perfect breeding ground for revolutionary movements, seldom dominated by forces adhering to the definition of democracy established here.[7]

For these reasons, it seems likely that the interest both of political leaders and scholars will emphasize rapid transitions to democracy. Despite their apparent desirability, rapid transitions to democracy present some real difficulties. The speed with which the rules of the game shift from democratic to authoritarian notions of power opens the door for political instability. The problems associated with rapid transitions differ according to whether they are consensual *(transitions through transaction)* or nonconsensual *(transitions through rupture)*. Some of these difficulties will be discussed in the following section.

While incremental transitions have been the most studied, they are not the most common. Outside of the United Kingdom and some northern European cases, there are few cases of incremental democratization. Most modern democracies have resulted from transition through rupture. Within this category, four subtypes of democratic transition can be differentiated. Most democracies in this category were produced by the collapse of the preceding authoritarian regime, usually because of defeat and occupation by a foreign power. Many of the democracies of postwar Western Europe, along with Japan, illustrate this subtype. A second subtype, extrication, occurs when authoritarian regimes experience a sudden loss of legitimacy, and abruptly hand power over to the democratic opposition. The recent events in Argentina, and possibly those in Peru in 1980, serve as examples. Transition through rupture may also take the form of a coup, in which the authoritarian regime is dislodged from power by an elite group within the military or police forces. The Portuguese transition, at least in its initial phase, is an example of this subtype, since a group of young, disaffected military officers toppled the Salazar-Caetano regime. Finally, transitions through rupture may come about via mass mobilization, or revolution, of which the French Revolution serves as a prototype.

Although transitions through rupture may take many forms, their nonconsensual nature, and their rapidity, make them similar for analytical purposes. Transitions through rupture all involve the repudiation, or at least significant delegitimation of, the extinct authoritarian regime. Often, the ability to delegitimate the previous regime is all that gives legitimacy to the emerging regime. Consequently, the regimes emerging from these transitions almost always attempt to purge those implicated with authoritarian rule from positions of importance.

532   COMPARATIVE POLITICAL STUDIES / January 1987

Punishment for past abuses, including imprisonment, exile, and occasionally public trials, are characteristically part of such transitions. Symbolic measures, such as the change of street names or banning of cultural works associated with the authoritarian period, will be undertaken both to further discredit the previous regime, and to reward psychologically the opponents of authoritarian rule.

There are two general sets of drawbacks associated with transitions through rupture. Most obviously, it is apparent that the conditions for such transitions do not often or readily emerge in contemporary cases of authoritarian rule. The total collapse of authoritarian regimes has most often come about through military defeat. While such an eventuality is not impossible, as the Argentine debacle recently demonstrated, military defeat cannot be expected to undermine authoritarian rule very often. Moreover, the dangers of such a form of collapse in the nuclear age need not be emphasized.

Even in cases of extrication, where the authoritarian regime has not completely collapsed, but in which its legitimacy has been critically eroded, serious drawbacks are evident. In this set of cases, the legitimacy of authoritarian rule is most often undermined by a set of conditions that may also obstruct the consolidation of democratic rule. Severe economic crisis, or a foreign policy catastrophe, can easily encourage the military to run for the shelter of the barracks, while bestowing on the democratic opposition a series of unsolvable problems.

Likewise, military coups may destroy authoritarian rule, but they inevitably politicize (and usually divide) the military. As the Portuguese Armed Forces Movement demonstrated, the consequences of a politicized military may be unfavorable for democratic rule, and can even directly threaten democracy. In addition, military coups always involve some possibility of political violence, and may create the conditions for the victory of hardline sectors (rightist or leftist) in the armed forces.

Democratization through protracted revolutionary struggle is conceivable, but there are reasons to suspect that its occurrence will be rare. The protracted nature of a revolutionary struggle usually indicates the presence of a particularly intransigent and powerful authoritarian regime, or a revolutionary opposition whose aspirations do not conform to the definition of democracy advanced earlier, or both. Of course, in some cases the intransigence or repressiveness of an authoritarian regime is encouraged by a persistent undemocratic revolutionary opposition. Also, an initially democratic opposition may abandon its faith in democratic procedures when faced with an intransigent authoritarian regime. These two factors have often fed on each other, producing a vicious cycle of intolerance and intransigence that hardly augurs well for the emergence of democratic rule. Although revolutionary movements may be able to dislodge authoritarian regimes and install democratic rule, the likelihood of such an outcome would appear to be minimal.[8] The recent events in Nicaragua appear to lend support to this argument.

Logically, it is to transitions through transaction that many have turned in search of a form of democratization that is peaceful and rapid.[9] Unfortunately, transition through transaction demands a particularly restrictive set of conditions that may not appear in most authoritarian regimes.[10] Perhaps the most difficult prerequisite is the authoritarian regime's *willingness to initiate* the transition to democracy. After all, as Philippe Schmitter (1979: 7) has pondered,

> If by changing [regime leaders] would incur a high risk of failure (not to mention personal injury), why would regime forms change at all? Why would they not merely perpetuate themselves indefinitely through marginal alterations in policy and occasional circulations in elites?

Adam Przeworski (1979: 4) notes that "The most difficult question is what would make [the dominant groups of the regime] decide to begin the process of transition, or perhaps more realistically, what would make them tolerate any articulation of pressures for transition."

A second question concerns the authoritarian regime's *ability to implement* transition through transaction. Sartori (1976: 276) suggests that "the pertinent question is whether [authoritarian and democratic] systems *can* be converted into one another without breakdown, i.e., continuously, via inner transformation." Leaders of transitions through transaction confront a plethora of obstacles. Authoritarian hardliners will almost certainly oppose democratization, or at least seek to limit it in ways unacceptable to the democratic opposition. The democratic opposition will not readily accept a transition to democracy led by members of a regime that only recently persecuted it. Dahl (1971) notes that such transitions can easily be undermined by forces within the regime or democratic opposition:

> . . . the search for a system of mutual guarantees is likely to be complex and time consuming. During the transition, when conflict erupts, neither side can be entirely sure that it will be safe to tolerate the other. Because

534   COMPARATIVE POLITICAL STUDIES / January 1987

the rules of the political game are ambiguous, and the legitimacy of competitive politics is weak, the costs of suppression may not be inordinately high. The danger is, then, that before a system of mutual security can be worked out among the contestants, the emerging but precarious competitive regime will be displaced by a hegemony ruled by one of the contestants [pp. 38-39].

On the societal level, the prospect of democratization will almost certainly release pent-up demands for economic, social, cultural, and political change.[11] The heightened politicization and mobilization of society may frighten and threaten authoritarian hardliners. On the elite level, the initiation of transition through transaction may unravel the authoritarian coalition, as some elites abandon ship with eyes to a future democratic system, while others maneuver against the reformist leadership or dig in for a last stand. In short, this type of democratization "poses an enigma that severely tests the ingenuity of the 'social engineers' who offer their expertise to accomplish a task which amounts to squaring a circle" (O'Donnell, 1979a: 315).

THE CONDITIONS FOR TRANSITION THROUGH TRANSACTION IN SPAIN

By providing a brief overview of how the circle was squared in Spain after Franco, it is possible to highlight the difficult conditions for transition through transaction, and to illustrate this most interesting subtype. The following discussion is a highly abridged version of arguments appearing elsewhere (Share, 1984; Share and Mainwaring, 1986).

For analytical purposes, it is useful to divide the discussion according to conditions facilitating the initiation of transition through transaction and conditions facilitating its implementation. A third area of importance, the conditions for the consolidation of transition through transaction, will not be dealt with here, although it has received important treatment elsewhere.[12]

THE INITIATION OF TRANSITION THROUGH TRANSACTION

Unlike some Latin American authoritarian regimes, where military rule may perform a "caretaker" function, the franquist regime declared no original intentions to democratize. Franquism was the antithesis of parliamentary democracy: It eliminated all parties and democratic institutions, ended the regional autonomy established under the Republic, and abolished all of the political symbols associated with the democratic period. While in the 1960s there were attempts to introduce a modicum of democratic discourse and behavior, such measures never went beyond what the Portuguese refer to as *para ingles ver* (show for the English). The facade democracy of the late franquist period may have reflected the increasing legitimacy of democratic symbols and procedures, but it did not symbolize a commitment on the part of the franquist elite to democratize.

Nor can the decision to democratize be understood solely in terms of "imperatives" brought about by any combination of economic crisis, mass pressure, or the international environment.[13] In its twilight, the franquist regime was faced with numerous challenges: the increasingly politicized and militant working class, a democratic student movement, a rejuvenated and increasingly unified political opposition, a hostile and partially radicalized Church, an inhospitable international environment, and most visibly, the persistent terrorist violence.[14] These challenges were a sign of the eroding legitimacy of authoritarian rule, but they were never successful in toppling the franquist regime. Ironically, the regime's unusual sense of security appears to have facilitated its willingness to tolerate a transition through transaction. Franquism consistently demonstrated an ability to contain direct threats to its existence. While the regime's reservoir of active support dwindled as the dictator's death became imminent, the multifarious challenges were more than offset by a combination of passive tolerance of authoritarian rule and selective repression.

Nevertheless, the changing socioeconomic environment of Spanish authoritarianism did form the context within which democratic change took place. While the regime's ability to survive any short-term challenge was never in question, the erosion of popular support for authoritarian rule surely weighed heavily in the minds of those responsible for initiating the transition to democracy. Rapid economic growth had modified somewhat the composition of the franquist coalition, without seriously eroding its commitment to authoritarian rule. For example, an important sector of the Catholic Church began to distance itself from the franquist regime in the 1960s, responding to changes in both the domestic and international environment. This loss, however, was more than compensated for by the rise of the Opus Dei technocrats, a group of economically liberal but politically authoritar-

536   COMPARATIVE POLITICAL STUDIES / January 1987

ian Catholics.[15] This shift in the franquist elite directly contributed to Spain's economic liberalization in the 1960s, and was initially accompanied by a small and temporary move toward political liberalization. The more technocratic orientation of Spanish cabinets in the 1960s and early 1970s, however, did not lead to a democratization of the regime, even in the context of spectacular economic growth, and even after the Spain's southern European neighbors (Portugal and Greece) experienced democratic transitions.

Macro-level structural factors played a much larger role as after transition through transaction was initiated. Mass support for democratization provided an invaluable prop for the transition's leaders, in both the reformist franquist sector and the democratic opposition. As will be argued below, both franquist reformists and opposition elites stood much to lose by embracing the contradictory and counterintuitive strategy of transition through transaction. Widespread popular enthusiasm for the Suárez strategy helped allay their reticence. As these same leaders attempted to consolidate the transition to democracy, by writing a new constitution, by reaching accords on the major socioeconomic issues facing post-Franco Spain, and by building a new party system, the importance of macro-level structural changes became even more apparent. The presence of a large middle class, unwilling to embrace political extremism of any type, clearly facilitated the writing and approval of a consensual constitution, agreement on consociational arrangements for the resolution of major economic issues, and the establishment of a moderate party system capable of peaceful alternation.

However, rather than focusing on long-standing democratic intentions, direct challenges to authoritarian rule, or the changing socioeconomic context (all of which are important but hardly crucial), the initiation of transition through transaction in Spain is best understood with reference to the internal political dynamics of the franquist coalition. During Franco's life, a diverse set of interests were kept in balance by the dictator's political skill, power, and charisma. The "families" of franquism (the Church, the National Movement, the Opus Dei, the monarchists, the military) differed considerably on economic, social, and political policy.[16] They had diverse views of how Spain's authoritarian system should be adapted to post-Franco reality. As long as Franco retained an active and direct role in politics—and this was the case for most of his life—these intrafamilia disputes were of little consequence. Even in the early 1970s, when a moribund Franco began to transfer some of his power to his trusted colleague, President Luis Carrero Blanco, the authoritarian coalition remained essentially intact.[17]

Carrero's assassination in 1973 threw the regime into a serious political crisis. With Franco ailing, and with the elimination of franquism's guardian, the authoritarian coalition began to unravel. Different families, and different factions and individuals within families, began to struggle for control of the transition. Transition through transaction was initiated out of the internal political struggle of the franquist coalition. The outcome of this struggle was determined more by *virtu* and *fortuna* than any necessity rooted in macro-level changes in the economic, social, cultural, or international environment.

It is easy enough to demonstrate that transition through transaction might *not* have been the result of the internal political struggle of the franquist regime. The first response by franquist elites to the death of Franco and the coronation of King Juan Carlos was not to implement transition through transaction. Rather, the King's first president (also Franco's last president), Carlos Arias Navarro, attempted to implement some liberal reforms without altering the authoritarian basis of the regime. While his plan enjoyed considerable initial support, it failed for a number of reasons.

Most important, Arias lacked the skill and will to initiate reform, even a plan as timid as his own. His attachment to his thoroughly franquist past, his close personal friendship with Franco, his deep-seated distrust of democratic politics, and his personal vacillations, all handicapped his reform program. Arias lacked the will and skill to impose his reform over the resistance of hardliners, and he was unable to convince a skeptical democratic opposition of his sincerity. At the same time, Arias was unable to build a solid coalition in support of his project. His proposals (combined with his government's intransigent behavior) alienated the opposition and incited the regime right. He could not even maintain intact his own government, which was seriously split over the pace and extent of political reform.

Arias's failure led to his removal, but more important, it discredited the option of a *democracia a la española*. Arias's successor, Adolfo Suárez, would have stood a far better chance of initiating a mild reform of franquism, similar to the Arias plan. By the time Suárez was appointed, however, the reformist option was exhausted, the political climate of the country was tense, and both the democratic opposition and regime right were becoming impatient.

538   COMPARATIVE POLITICAL STUDIES / January 1987

It was in this context of increasing tension and impatience that King Juan Carlos appointed a relative political unknown to the presidency, Adolfo Suárez. It is very likely that the choice of Suárez was largely motivated by the King's desire to speed up the democratic reform.[18] Juan Carlos no doubt realized that a prolonged failure to democratize the franquist system would discredit the new monarchy. To the extent that some future Spanish system would be democratic (the odds of which were perceived as being high), the monarchy's existence would require that the King identify himself (and the institution he represented) with democratization. It is worth recalling that the Bourbon monarchy in Spain had an inauspicious reputation. The Bourbons presided over the calamitous decline of Spain's empire, and the monarchy was directly implicated in the Primo de Rivera dictatorship (1923-1930). Franco's "restoration" of the monarchy in 1947 identified the institution with authoritarianism even further. For most members of the democratic opposition, the ability of the monarchy to coexist with democratic rule was seriously doubted.

It was therefore in the King's best interest to break the impasse created by the Arias government. Conceivably, Juan Carlos could have opted for an equally authoritarian but more competent successor to Arias. It seems likely that Spanish authoritarianism, with some further reforms, could have sustained itself for an extended period. In fact, the surprise appointment of the former leader of the National Movement led many Spaniards to suspect that Juan Carlos *had* opted for such a strategy.

Instead, the young monarch gambled on a democratic future for Spain, although he left it to his new president to bring about such a difficult and risky transition. Given this choice, the king understood that the institution of the monarchy must identify itself with the transition process, were it to survive the transition.

THE IMPLEMENTATION OF
TRANSITION THROUGH TRANSACTION

As the failure of the Arias reform illustrated, the desire to enact democratic change does not ensure successful implementation. Leaders of an authoritarian regime face numerous obstacles when attempting to implement transition through transaction. Nevertheless, Suárez fulfilled three conditions that help to explain how he disproved almost unanimous predictions of failure.

First, *a degree of support or toleration for political reform was mustered from the most powerful members of the authoritarian coalition.* In transition through transaction, a coalition of regime forces favoring (or at least tolerating) democratic change must be cultivated. In Spain, this meant that the military hierarchy, as well as the most powerful political leaders within the franquist system, had to be convinced to support democratization.

Suárez worked methodically and diligently to satisfy this condition. Immediately after his appointment, he initiated an extensive series of contacts with virtually all representatives of regime factions and opposition groups. Within the regime, Suárez reassured the military of limits to the reform—albeit in ambiguous and easily betrayed terms— and he convinced important regime elites to support his project as the best solution possible to the succession crisis. By respecting the legal framework of franquism, and by adhering to the institutional rules of authoritarianism, Suárez and the King were able to win the initial support, or at least the benefit of the doubt, of most of the franquist elite.

It is imperative to note that the presence and behavior of King Juan Carlos was paramount to Suárez's ability to gain support within the regime. For regime supporters, the King embodied the legitimacy of the franquist system. Even the most hardline franquists were hesitant to oppose Franco's hand picked successor, since opposition to the monarch would be tantamount to an admission that the *Caudillo* had erred. In fact, many hardliners eventually came to view the appointment of Juan Carlos as a mistake, but only after Suárez's reform had reached an advanced stage. Like Suárez, the monarch played his role to perfection by constantly reassuring the regime right, in word and in deed, that he would continue to act as the guardian of franquism. His strict participation in franquist ritual, his deferential treatment of franquist elite, and his incessant assurances that there would be no attempt to wipe the slate clean, contributed immensely to Suárez's success. While the presence of such an exceptional head of state is not necessary for successful transitions through transaction, there can be no question that these transitions are far more difficult without such well respected and talented leaders.[19]

Second, *the democratic opposition, or at least sectors of it, had to be convinced to participate in the resulting system.* In transitions through transaction, opposition leaders must somehow be assured that they will have a role to play in the future system, and that they will enjoy

540   COMPARATIVE POLITICAL STUDIES / January 1987

increasing freedom to operate. In the Spanish case, this requirement entailed winning the confidence of the disparate opposition groups, some of which were highly radicalized and hostile toward regime leaders. Moreover, this confidence had to be obtained while the entire franquist apparatus, including the security forces, remained intact. In fact, the independent behavior of the security forces was a constant source of tension between the regime and opposition.

Nevertheless, Suárez quickly won the opposition's admiration and respect for his willingness to dialogue and for his flexibility. The difference between Arias and Suárez was immediately evident to opposition leaders, and they soon indicated their satisfaction with the improvement.[20] Suárez's ability to push his Political Reform Law through the franquist system encouraged them to weaken their opposition to the principle of transition through transaction. By the end of 1976, many opposition leaders had come to accept the Suárez reform as the only possible route to democracy. This change in the opposition's posture was neither easy nor complete, but the thawing of regime-opposition relations gave Suárez the momentum necessary to complete the reform.

Suárez's personal attributes were uniquely appropriate for the task of convincing key sectors of the franquist regime and the democratic opposition to accept transition through transaction. For many franquists, Suárez's credentials as leader of the National Movement, his career in the franquist bureaucracy, and his experience in the Cabinet under Arias, all made him appear a trustworthy ally. For opposition democrats, Suárez's youth, his ability to dialogue with individuals of diverse ideological persuasion, and his modern political style, eventually convinced the opposition that, unlike Arias, Suárez was more a man of the future than a politician of the past. Most important, Suárez had no personal ties to the Spanish Civil War or the violent origins of the franquist regime. He therefore faced opposition elites not as a regime founder, but as a young franquist career bureaucrat. In fact, Suárez felt far more comfortable dealing with his generational peers than with most of his colleagues in the franquist regime.[21]

Opposition elites also contributed a great deal to the successful implementation of transition through transaction. A more intractable and less prudent opposition might have undermined Suárez's effort. For example, Carrillo's attempt to force the PCE's legalization, by appearing suddenly in Madrid, almost had disastrous consequences for the entire reform project. Carrillo apparently learned this lesson well since his party never again attempted to use provocation to exact concessions from the Suárez government. A more confrontational attitude by the opposition, in reaction to the massacre of leftist labor lawyers in February 1977, could have had similar consequences. Refusal on the part of the PSOE to participate in the first democratic elections could have imperilled the transition. A hostile campaign against the monarchy, or against Suárez himself, would surely have alarmed the franquist right and sectors of the military. A more triumphal reaction by democratic forces to the legalization of the Communist Party, or the dismantling of the National Movement and Syndical Organization, could have endangered Suárez's reform at delicate moments.

The ability of opposition elites, regardless of ideological persuasion, to act responsibly in a difficult environment had several explanations. First, opposition elites were well aware of the dangers entailed by the failure of the Suárez reform. After all, many of them had suffered under authoritarian rule. The opposition was aware that a popular insurrection to topple the regime was extremely unlikely. While on the eve of Franco's death much of the opposition adhered to the notion of a *ruptura democrática*, many opposition leaders acknowledged the need for an alliance with reformist sectors of the regime. Nevertheless, opposition leaders were constantly challenged by the fear that they might be outflanked by radical groups who could successfully accuse them of collaborationism, and by making such accusations gain support among newly politicized sectors.

Third, and directly related to the first two conditions, regime leaders had to *maintain enough control* over the political situation to allow for a rapid yet orderly transition. The Spanish leadership had to be able to resist pressure from the regime right for an authoritarian involution, and calls from the leftist opposition for a democratic break. This required a delicate equilibrium between an adherence to the basic rules of the authoritarian regime and a well-planned and incrementally implemented set of democratic reforms. In discussing the general dilemmas facing leaders of transitions through transaction, O'Donnell (1979a: 30) provides an almost exact description of Suárez's difficult situation during the Spanish transition:

> In these circumstances, it is evident that the demands on the quality of political leadership are extraordinarily severe. There is not only the problem of deciding at critical junctures which are the fundamental issues

and adversaries, but also of being able to convince followers and
opponents that the leaders' tactical flexibility is only an instrument which
is guided by a firm sense of direction toward democratization.

Between July 1976 and June 1977, Suárez implemented key aspects of
his reform plan. While not every facet of the reform was foreseen ahead
of time, and although Suárez appears to have improvised a great deal,
the reforms were surprisingly well staggered and timed. A simple
chronology of the major highlights of the reform illustrates this point.
The reform began with the limited amnesties in the summer of 1976, and
continued through the constitutional reform of November, the referendum in December, the legalization of most political parties in early
1977, the legalization of the PCE in April, and the dismantling of
important franquist institutions (notably the National Movement and
the Sindical Organization) in May. The latter reforms provoked open
hostility from sectors of the military and the right that had previously
tolerated Suárez's plan. However, by that time, Suárez had gained an
important popular mandate, and a crucial vote of confidence from the
opposition. In addition, a significant sector of the franquist right was
busy preparing for elections that it (mistakenly) hoped to win.

CONCLUSION

The first section of this article presented a fourfold typology of
transitions from authoritarian to democratic rule. The dynamics of, and
conditions for, each type of democratic transition can be expected to
differ considerably. A brief examination of the Spanish transition to
democracy, a rare case of transition through transaction, suggests that
this form of democratization requires some particularly demanding
conditions for its initiation and implementation.

The long-term conditions for the initiation of transition through
transaction were first, a serious succession crisis, created by the death of
the regime's only charismatic leader, and second, a lack of consensus
concerning the appropriate solution to the crisis. More proximate
conditions included the widely perceived exhaustion of a more limited
reform of franquism after Arias's failure, and Juan Carlos's decision to
break the resulting deadlock by attempting to endow the monarchy with
a new democratic legitimacy. The most direct conditions for the

initiation of transition through transaction were the political will and skill of Adolfo Suárez. Suárez designed the complex strategy of transition through transaction, despite widespread skepticism. He understood *why* it was important that the franquist regime initiate the transition to democracy. Moreover, he understood *how* the franquist regime could produce such a transition.

This article has highlighted three conditions for the successful implementation of transition through transaction. First, Suárez, with the support of the king, was able to garner support for demoncratization from a wide range of regime forces. Second, most of the democratic opposition was persuaded to participate in the Suárez reform. Third, Suárez's government was able to maintain significant control over the political situation to allow for rapid but orderly transition.

When considering the likelihood for the initiation of transition through transaction in other authoritarian regimes, the long-term conditions do not appear overly restrictive. Succession crises plague all authoritarian regimes, although they are especially devastating when a single ruler has dominated the regime for so long. The more proximate conditions in the Spanish case are less likely to be replicated elsewhere. While leaders who succeed a long-lived authoritarian ruler may often attempt to relegitimate their rule through political reform, democratization appears an unlikely outcome. Limited reform, much like that of Caetano in Portugal, or Arias in Spain, would appear to be more likely.

Where succeeding leadership brings to power a new generation of leaders, especially where the younger generation is not directly linked to the establishment of authoritarian rule, the prospects for the initiation of transition through transaction are increased. In Spain, the combination of the more common long-term conditions, and the more unusual proximate conditions, facilitated the initiation of transactive democratization.

The successful implementation of transition through transaction in Spain also had macro- and micro-level conditions. Most generally, and paradoxically, the absence of direct threats to the continuation of authoritarian rule encouraged the military to accept Suárez's plan. Had the regime's control over the transition been seriously challenged, the military's trust in Suárez's ability to limit the reform would have diminished. Likewise, the overwhelming superiority of the regime's strength, compared with that of the opposition forces, made it easier for the opposition to accept transition through transaction. Had the prospects for a successful transition through rupture been greater, the incentive to accept the Suárez plan would have declined. The implication for other political systems, then, is that transition through transaction is likely to be successfully implemented from relatively strong and secure authoritarian regimes, and not in regimes that fear for their very survival. In this respect, the contrast with transitions through rupture could not be greater.

It is often noted, quite correctly, that there was an important reservoir of popular support for democratic rule. Suárez drew on this reservoir to build momentum for his leadership, to carry him through some of the most difficult moments of the reform's implementation, and to facilitate the consolidation of transition through transaction. Nevertheless, the presence of this widespread desire for democratic rule—no doubt the product of economic growth and affluence, increased exposure to Western democracies, a general fatigue with authoritarian rule, and a general desire for change—does not explain the implementation of transition through transaction, even if it indirectly contributed to it.

At the micro-political level, the remarkable skill of political elites was an important condition for the successful implementation of transition through transaction. Most important were the actions of Adolfo Suárez. I have already alluded to his innate qualities, including his professional and generational credentials. Equally important, he possessed the ability to convince the regime right, at least initially, of his desire to protect the essence of authoritarian rule. He was willing and able to gain the trust and confidence, and eventually the support, of the democratic opposition. Many other successors to Arias might have initiated a transition through transaction, but it is difficult to imagine its successful implementation under less talented leadership. In short, Suárez possessed the skill to manage the many complexities of transition through transaction.

Likewise, the leaders of the democratic opposition performed an important role in the implementation of transition through transaction. Their ability to eschew ideological rigidity, and to embrace the politics of moderation and compromise, was by no means inevitable. In the case of the most important opposition force, the PSOE, a generational shift in the top leadership—similar in many ways to the change in government—undoubtedly facilitated the ability to embrace transition through transaction.

The comparative implications of this emphasis on the role of leadership are clear. Other authoritarian regimes may experience the initiation of transition through transaction. Some may even enjoy the presence of favorable macro-level conditions for the implementation of transition through transaction. Very few are likely to have, in addition, exceptionally skilled leaders in the regime and opposition. The Spanish case reminds us that, in the end, it is up to political elites to square the circle of transition through transaction.

NOTES

1. Some examples of the recent comparative works on the topic of transitions to democracy are O'Donnell et al. (1986); Herz (1982); Huntington (1984); Linz (1981); Bruneau (1983); Pridham (1984); Viola and Mainwaring (1985); Share and Mainwaring (1986); Luna (1983); Orrego Vicuña (1985).

2. For an overview, see Chilcote (1981: 271-312) and Packenham (1973: 195-241).

3. Among the few examples are Dahl (1971: 33-47) and Schmitter (1979).

4. An important treatment of this matter is Viola and Mainwaring (1985).

5. A more detailed analysis of this typology is Share (1984: chap. 1).

6. The concept of backward and forward legitimation is developed in Di Palma (1980a: 132-145).

7. For a discussion of why revolutions are less likely to produce democratic regimes, see Huntington (1984: 212). He states that "democratic regimes that last have seldom, if ever, been initiated by popular action. Almost always, democracy has come as much from the top down as from the bottom up; it is as likely to be the product of oligarchy as of protest against oligarchy."

8. This should not obscure the fact that revolutions may produce regimes far more democratic than their predecessors, even while failing to meet our initial standards of democracy.

9. For an recent example of concern about the prospects for what we have called transition through transaction, see the editorial article "On Negotiating Democratic Transition" in *Third World Quarterly* 2 (April 1985), xii-xvi.

10. The term "transition through transaction" was first employed by Di Palma (1980b: 166). Di Palma uses the term to denote a "syncretic" form of transition. Its usage here connotes negotiation between authoritarian and opposition elites. For a more detailed and comparative discussion of the conditions for transition through transaction, see Share and Mainwaring (1986).

11. Juan Linz's discussion of the importance of agenda setting is revelant to this point. See Linz (1978: 41-43).

12. A particularly provocative analysis of the problems confronting the consolidation of parliamentary democracy after authoritarian rule is Gunther (1985) and Gunther et al. (1986).

546   COMPARATIVE POLITICAL STUDIES / January 1987

13. See Share (1984) for a more detailed and documented argument.

14. On the growth of working-class and student opposition see Maravall (1978). On the organized democratic opposition see Tussell (1976).

15. The Sociedad Sacerdotal de la Santa Cruz (Opus Dei) is a secular institute of the Roman Catholic Church. This worldwide lay organization is centered in Rome, with branches in over 70 countries. In Spain, the Opus Dei technocrats became especially prominent in the spheres of government, education (especially higher education), and business. For an overview see Ynfante (1970).

16. For a description of the families of franquism, see Linz (1979).

17. A major exception was the franquist coalition's loss of the Catholic Church as a loyal member. By 1973 the Spanish Church had become seriously split between staunch franquists, Opus Dei technocrats, and progressives.

18. There are few published works concerning the attitudes and motivations of Juan Carlos during the transition. Among the most provocative are Bardavío (1979) and Alba (1981).

19. It is no coincidence that the two forms of consensual transition outlined in the first section of this article, incremental transition and transition through transaction, both appear to be associated with the institution of the monarchy. In such cases as the United Kingdom, Sweden, and Spain, the monarch has played a key role as "legitimator" of democratic change and "guarantor" of vestiges of the weakened authoritarian past. In the absence of a monarch, respected elder statesmen like Tancredo Neves in Brazil may be able to perform a similar function.

20. There is ample evidence that the opposition was dismayed by the King's selection of Suárez. For examples of the widespread skepticism, see Morán (1979: 306).

21. Interviews with Suárez's closest aides, conducted during 1981 and 1982, confirmed that Suárez was far more uncomfortable dealing with pressures from the regime right than with the forces of the left.

REFERENCES

ALBA, V. (1981) La soledad del Rey. Barcelona: Planeta.

BARDAVIO, J. (1979) Los silencios del Rey. Madrid: Strips.

BRUNEAU, T. (1983) "Transitions from authoritarian regimes: the contrasting cases of Brazil and Portugual," in F. Eidlin (ed.) Constitutional Democracy. Boulder, CO: Westview.

CHILCOTE, R. (1981) Theories of Comparative Politics: The Search For a Paradigm. Boulder, CO: Westview.

DAHL, R. (1971) Polyarchy. New Haven, CT: Yale Univ. Press.

DI PALMA, G. (1980a) "Derecha, izquierda o centro? Sobre la legitimación de los partidos y coaliciones en el sur de Europa." Revista del Departamento de Derecho Político, 6.

DI PALMA, G. (1980b) "Founding coalitions in Southern Europe: legitimacy and hegemony." Government and Opposition 2.

GUNTHER, R. (1985) "Democratization and party building: contradictions and conflicts facing party elites in the Spanish transition to democracy." Presented at the 1985

Annual Meeting of the American Political Science Association, New Orleans, August 29-September 11.

GUNTHER, R., G. SANI, and G. SHABAD (1986) Spain after Franco: the making of a competitive party system. Berkeley: Univ. of California Press.

HERZ, J. [ed.] (1982) Dictatorship to Democracy. Westport, CT: Greenwood.

HUNTINGTON, S. (1984) "Will more countries become democratic?" Pol. Sci. Q. 9.

LINZ, J. (1978) Crisis, Breakdown and Reequilibration. Volume one of J. Linz and A. Stepan (eds.) The Breakdown of Democratic Regimes. Baltimore: Johns Hopkins Univ. Press.

LINZ, J. (1979) "Spain: an authoritarian regime," in S. Payne (ed.) Politics and Society in Twentieth Century Spain. New York: New Viewpoints.

LINZ, J. (1981) "Some comparative thoughts on the transition to democracy in Portugal and Spain," in J. Braga de Macedo and S. Serfaty (eds.) Portugal Since the Revolution: Economic and Political Perspectives. Boulder, CO: Westview.

LUNA, F. (1983) Golpes militares y salidas electorales. Buenos Aires: Editoriales Sudamericana.

MARAVALL, J. (1978) Dictadura y disentimiento político: obreros y estudiantes bajo el franquismo. Madrid: Alfaguara.

MORAN, G. (1979) Adolfo Suárez: Historia de una ambición. Barcelona: Planeta.

O'DONNELL, G. (1979a) "Tensions in the bureaucratic-authoritarian state and the question of democracy," in D. Collier (ed.) The New Authoritarianism in Latin America. Princeton, NJ: Princeton Univ. Press.

O'DONNELL, G. (1979b) "Notes for the study of processes of democratization from the bureaucratic authoritarian regime." Delivered at a workshop on "Prospects for Democracy: Transitions from Authoritarian Rule." Washington, DC: Woodrow Wilson International Center for Scholars.

O'DONNELL, G., P. SCHMITTER, and L. WHITEHEAD [eds.] (1986) Transitions from Authoritarian Rule: Southern Europe and Latin America. Baltimore: Johns Hopkins Press.

ORREGO VICUÑA, F. [ed.] (1985) Transición a la democracia en America Latina. Buenos Aires: Grupo Editor Latinoamericano.

PACKENHAM, R. (1973) Liberal America and the Third World. Princeton, NJ: Princeton Univ. Press.

PRIDHAM, G. (1984) "The new Mediterranean democracies: regime transitions in Spain, Greece and Portugal." Special Issue of West European Politics 2.

PRZEWORSKI, A. (1979) "Notes on the logic of transitions to democracy." Delivered at a workshop on "Prospects for Democracy: Transitions from Authoritarian Rule." Washington, DC: Woodrow Wilson International Center for Scholars.

RUSTOW, D. (1970) "Transitions to democracy: towards a dynamic model." Comparative Politics 2.

SARTORI, G. (1976) Parties and Party Systems. Cambridge: Cambridge Univ. Press.

SCHMITTER, P. (1979) "Speculations about the prospective demise of authoritarian regimes and its possible consequences." Delivered at a workshop on "Prospects for Democracy: Transitions from Authoritarian Rule." Washington, DC: Woodrow Wilson Center for International Center for Scholars.

SHARE, D. (1983) "Transition through transaction: the politics of democratization in Spain, 1975-1977." Ph.D. dissertation, Stanford University.

SHARE, D. (1984) "Democratization in Spain: searching for explanations." Presented at the Ninth Annual European Studies Conference, Omaha, University of Nebraska at Omaha.

SHARE, D. and S. MAINWARING (1986) "Transitions through transaction: democratization in Brazil and Spain," in W. Selcher (ed.) Political Liberalization in Brazil. Boulder, CO: Westview.

TUSSELL, J. (1976) La oposición democrática al franquismo. Barcelona: Planeta.

VIOLA, E. and S. MAINWARING (1985) "Transitions to democracy: Brazil and Argentina in the 1980s." J. of Int. Affairs 38.

YNFANTE, J. (1970) La prodigiosa aventura del Opus Dei. Madrid: Ruedo Ibérico.

Donald Share received his Ph.D. in political science from Stanford University. He is currently Assistant Professor of Politics and Government at the University of Puget Sound. His publications include The Making of Spanish Democracy *(Praeger Publishers, 1986) and "Two Transitions: Democratisation and the Evolution of the Spanish Socialist Left" in* West European Politics *(January 1985).*

[13]

Democratising the Military: Lessons from Mediterranean Europe

CONSTANTINE P. DANOPOULOS

This article analyses the factors and processes involved in democratizing the armed forces of Spain, Greece and Portugal in the 1970s and 1980s. After a brief comparative review of the history of civil-military relations in the three countries, the article examines the role of societal, institutional (military professional) and international factors in the democratisation process. The article concludes that military professionalism can be a stimulant to intervention and de-intervention, depending on societal considerations and the perceptions of the military at a given time. Explanations accounting for military democratisation can be found at the level of value-congruency between society (including the international arena) and the armed forces.

Beginning with the mid-1970s, an increasing number of states governed by military or other authoritarian regimes[1] began experimenting with civilian rule and pluralistic, competitive politics. Academics and journalists interested in the politics of the changing societies of the Third World responded with an ever proliferating number of analysing why the military, which by and large had been governing these nations, would decide to leave the levers of authority and allow for civilian rule and even democratisation.[2] Recent events in Eastern Europe – particularly in the Soviet Union, Hungary and Poland – have increased scholarly interest in the causes of democratisation to new heights.

Drawing firm conclusions about the eventual fate of the newly opened East European regimes is risky, for the situation there is still fluid, and democratisation of communist regimes is without precedent. Civilian rule and democratisation in the developing world, on the other hand, have had a much longer history and are not without precedent. By and large, scholars and other observers are pessimistic regarding the long-term fate of civilian rule and the future of democracy in the Third World.[3] The overwhelming majority of successor regimes (those which followed the military) face difficult problems and have yet to cloak themselves with a mantle of legitimacy,[4] and consolidate democratic rule. Consolidation occurs when all social groups, including the military, repudiate the use of

West European Politics, Vol. 14, No. 4 (Oct. 1991), pp. 25–41
PUBLISHED BY FRANK CASS, LONDON

illegal means to achieve political authority. Under the circumstances, as Claude Welch states, the armed forces 'will continue to play central roles' in the politics of Third World countries 'for several decades to come'.[5]

Unlike their counterparts in Africa, Latin America, Asia, and the Middle East, the three Mediterranean countries (Spain, Portugal and Greece) that made transitions from authoritarian to civilian-dominated and democratic regimes in the mid-1970s present a different picture. Although some would argue that in terms of economic development, social composition, history, and geographic location Spain, Portugal and Greece cannot be considered typical Third World countries, scholars agree that the still new, democratic and civilian-dominated regimes in these countries have become consolidated and legitimised.[6]

There is little doubt that the armed forces have played a major role in maintaining and consolidating democracy in Mediterranean Europe. In the case of Portugal the military initiated the democratisation of the nation's political life by overthrowing the authoritarian Salazarist regime of *Estado Novo* (New State) in 1974. The Spanish armed forces reacted with some trepidation to the efforts of the Adolfo Suarez government to democratise the country's political life, following the death of General Francisco Franco in 1975, but have come to accept the new order and the dominance of the civilian leadership. Finally, the Greek military withdrew to the barracks in 1974 after a disastrous seven-year (1967–74) praetorian rule which included the Cyprus debacle. The Greek armed forces, like those of Spain and Portugal, now concentrate their efforts on their military mission and are content to leave politics to the constitutional authorities.

The aim of this article is to identify and analyse those factors that contributed to the making of a democratic-minded military in Spain, Portugal and Greece since the mid-1970s, when these nations moved away from authoritarian politics and opted for western-style liberal democracy. In order better to understand the military's changing role a brief history of civil-military relation in these societies is relevant.

HISTORICAL ANTECEDENTS

Mediterranean or Southern Europe countries contrast sharply in terms of the level of economic development, social mobility, cultural characteristics and political history with their northern counterparts. Whereas the north blossomed economically and took the lead in the development and con-solidation of democratic institutions, the south – and especially Spain, Portugal and Greece – remained underdeveloped, rural, technologically backward and isolated. Politically, Mediterranean European countries lacked participatory ethos, effective political parties and autonomous

DEMOCRATISING THE MILITARY: MEDITERRANEAN EUROPE   27

social groups. The mode of politics oscillated between authoritarianism and instability, although some feeble attempts were made in all three countries to introduce republican, participatory institutions.

In these politically fragmented societies political parties, lacking effective organisational structures and programmes, used the military as a stepping stone to advance their positions and aims. For much of the nineteenth century the armed forces of Spain, Portugal and Greece intervened in politics, either at the behest of political parties, social groups or the monarchies, or to prevent total anarchy. By and large military interventions were anti-absolutist and in favour of constitutionalism. This continued in the first three decades of the twentieth century, although the armies of all three nations displayed more independence and corporate spirit than in past, but also showed signs of increasing politicisation and factionalism.

The early decades of the last century intensified the economic and political decline of the Iberian peninsula. The loss of vast colonial holdings in South America accelerated these difficulties and generated political divisions in both Spain and Portugal between those who supported absolutism and the proponents of a constitutional monarchy. In time, the republican element also entered the picture, further complicating the political landscape. In this rather unstable and often charged atmosphere the largely aristocratic-based Spanish and Portuguese armies made their debut in their nations' political arenas with varying degrees of involvement. Between 1820 and 1850, the Portuguese military played 'an important role in high politics' to be followed by the 'relatively quiescent period of 1850–1891'.[7] But as the monarchy lost its effectiveness, a new era of *pronunciamentos* occurred in which the military sought to check the ever-more vocal forces of republicanism.

The First Portuguese Republic (1910–26) – a product of a largely civilian-inspired insurrection – desperately sought to check the military's influence by establishing a people's militia to act as a counter-weight to the distrusted regular army. Economic difficulties, political instability and disregard for the military's corporate interests[8] (such as equipment and uniforms) encouraged 'officers to protest and eventually plot the military overthrow of the First Republic' in 1926.[9] Lack of effective leadership and political divisions forced the rebels in 1928 to turn over the reins of leadership to Antonio de Oliveira Salazar, professor of economics in Portugal's main university at Coimbra. Within four years Salazar, taking advantage of divisions within the army, established a personal, corporatist and authoritarian dictatorship (*Estado Novo*) which lasted until 1974, when the Armed Forces Movement (MFA) overthrew the dinosauric Salazarist structure.

Spain suffered similar, if not more intense, shocks. Economic difficulties and political divisions were compounded by foreign interference, regionalism and class struggle between the landed gentry and the landless peasantry. As absolutism, constitutional monarchy, and republicanism took turns at the helm, a political void was created which was filled by the Spanish Army. Thus, the latter eventually came to occupy a 'privileged position'[10] in the nation's political landscape. A tradition of political *pronunciamentos* was initiated in 1820 when a group of liberal officers forced King Ferdinand VII to accept a constitution and 'became the customary way of changing governments' that continued into the twentieth century.[11] This interventionist but no-direct-rule disposition of the Spanish military changed in 1923. When the Cortes sought to investigate the Army's dismal failure to annex Morocco as well as the Army-Palace collusion, the military responded with General Miguel Primo de Rivera's *coup d'état* which imposed a pure military dictatorship (1923–29), the first in Spain's history.

Captive of the increasingly conservative Army and the Catholic Church, the Rivera dictatorship was unable to heal the wounds of Spanish society. Regionalism intensified, as did the rift between social classes. Supporting the unpopular dictatorship caused the monarchy to lose its legitimacy, and culminated in its replacement in 1931 by the liberal Second Republic (1931–36). Besieged by internal weaknesses and a less than favourable international environment, the Second Republic was unable to deal with Spain's problems. The rift between the conservative forces (backed by the landed aristocracy, the church and the financial and industrial elites) and the liberal republican camp (representing the popular strata) became wider than ever. On 17 July 1936, units of the Army, led by the Spanish Legion and those serving in Morocco, rose up against the republican government. Within days the bloody Spanish Civil War (1936–39) was under way, culminating in the republican forces' defeat and the inauguration of the Francoist dictatorship that lasted until the general's death in 1975.

In spite of the fact that the *Estado Novo* and the Francoist regimes owed their origin and stay in power to the support of the military, and despite General Franco's background, neither regime could be called a military dictatorship. Suspicious and even contemptuous of the military mind, Salazar kept aloof from personal involvement with officers but manipulated the armed forces by allowing ideological proclivities to surface and relying on his loyal paramilitary units to monitor and check potential threats against his regime. Salazar laboured long and hard to keep the officer corps happy by procuring modern weapons, providing relatively high budgetary appropriations, and securing lucrative positions for retired officers in the state apparatus or in major corporations. Finally, Salazar personally made all promotion decisions, promoting officers with the proper ideological credentials and loyalty to himself and his *Estado Novo*.[12]

DEMOCRATISING THE MILITARY: MEDITERRANEAN EUROPE 29

Franco's treatment of the military bore similarities with Salazar's, but differed in important respects. A military man himself, the Spanish *Caudillo* formed closer personal friendship with his colleagues, purged the armed forces of all non-Francoists, refused to allocate high defense appropriations[13] but made sure that officers received hefty salaries, and made each branch (army, navy, air force) autonomous. During his rule Spain had no ministry of defence responsible for making and coordinating security policy. Instead, each branch reported separately to Franco with no civilian involvement. To prevent hierarchical 'bottlenecks' Franco simplified promotion and retirement requirements and made sure high officers were well compensated and highly respected during service and in retirement.[14]

While the military of both countries were responsible for bringing about and maintaining the Salazarist and Francoist structures, the two officers corps parted company as far as their devotion was concerned in the last stages of these regimes. Salazar's and his successor's determination to retain by force Portugal's colonial presence in Africa helped to politicise and radicalise the nation's armed forces, diminished their social and professional standing, and paved the way for the toppling of the *Estado Novo* by the MFA in 1974. After a couple of years of uncertainty, the Portuguese military played a key role in promoting and maintaining democracy in their country.

In contrast the Spanish armed forces remained loyal to Franco until his death and may be said to have supported his successor because of their devotion to the *Caudillo*'s chosen heir, King Juan Carlos I. Unlike Salazar, Franco was aware of the dangers of prolonged military commitments to no-win situations, and he quickly negotiated Spain's disengagement from the Sahara in the mid-1970s.

If one excludes the problems connected with colonialism and the fact that the republican element came into the equation much later, Greece's economic and political map and the Army's role have had remarkable similarities to those of Portugal and Spain. Economic backwardness, political instability, foreign interference, and a clash between the indigenous and Europeanised elites dominated Greek society in most of the previous century. Foreign policy disagreements and the republican-royalist split followed by the bloody civil war (1946–49), helped to create political instability and provided the background for repeated military intervention, both direct and indirect. However, until the 21 April 1967 *coup d'état* and the seven-year rule that followed, the Greek military's involvements were similar to those of Spain and Portugal. The Army intervened as a surrogate for political groups or the monarchy.[15]

The Fascist Metaxas dictatorship (1936–41) followed by World War II,

the civil war, and subsequent American involvement in Greek affairs
provided the backdrop for a thorough purge of all centrist, neutralist, or
communist officers. As a result, the Greek military became a homogeneous,
die-hard, right-wing organisation no longer 'reflecting the contradictions
of the political society'.[16] Viewing Greece as 'merely one aspect of a
considerably more elaborate picture involving the future of the Middle
East',[17] and concerned with the inability of Greek political elites to work
out their personal differences, the US provided the military with sophisticated training and support – transforming it into 'an independent political
force within the country'.[18] With a brief centrist interlude (1964–65),
Greece was governed by the nation's conservative political forces from
1952 until 1967. Behind the parliamentary facade stood the Palace, and
behind the Palace the military establishment and its patrons.

In the early 1960s the ruling coalition came under attack from the rising
middle class, those who had not benefited from the economic activity
of the past decade. As a result, the political system suffered legitimacy
deficiency. The more reactionary elements and the anti-communist military
perceived these changes as harmful to the moral fabric of Greek society
and sought to arrest them by supporting the colonels' repressive military
dictatorship. All these together with a sluggish economy, social unrest,
political instability, and concern about Greece's future role in NATO
prompted a band of junior officers to stage a coup, on 21 April 1967,
thus sealing Greece's experiment with 'parliamentary democracy'.[19]

Unlike previous interventions, the 1967 coup and the seven-year rule
that followed represented an effort by the Greek military's more reactionary
elements to remake the nation's society in their own image and establish a
political framework that would ensure the armed forces' primacy. But the
ineffective and brutal colonels failed dismally. In the face of a worsening
economy, social agitation, divisions within the military, and finally, the
tragic outcome of the Cyprus adventure, the colonels' regime collapsed.[20]
The civilians, brought back in July 1974, established a pluralist parliamentary regime and have been governing Greece ever since.

DEMOCRATISING THE MILITARY

Democracy is an elusive concept and has been invoked and even abused
by pluralist, authoritarian and totalitarian regimes, especially in the last
five or six decades. Social scientists are increasingly equating democracy not
with a particular governmental structure, but rather with the procedures,
methods and the means employed in the process of governance. In this
light the definition utilised by O'Donnell and Schmitter seems most appropriate. They define democracy in terms of 'procedural minimums'

DEMOCRATISING THE MILITARY: MEDITERRANEAN EUROPE   31

which include: secret balloting, universal adult suffrage, regular elections, partisan competition, associational recognition and access, and executive accountability.[21]

This definition of democracy, or any other for that matter, is of little help when it comes to understanding complex and hierarchically structured organisations. Its usefulness and applicability become even more problematic in the context of military organisations, which by the very nature of the profession, thrive on the command and obey principle. There are no armies that are commanded by officers elected through secret ballots by enlisted men and fellow officers. Even during the height of the Portuguese revolution in the mid-1970s the idea of using 'democratic means' to fill top military positions, advocated by some extreme left-wing elements within the MFA, was rejected out of hand by the leftist-leaning Prime Minister General Vasco Goncalves.

Instead, when referring to the democracy and democratisation of the military, we invoke the attitudes held by officers corps towards pluralism and acceptance of and devotion to the values, the basic legal structures, and leadership selection procedures employed in their society. In order for the armed forces to live with the 'rough and tumble' that often characterise democratic processes, there must be a consensus in the beliefs of political groups and the military that the existing political institutions and processes are the most appropriate ones for their society.

The values and beliefs of the military do not exist in a vacuum; instead, they are the sum of general societal or environmental adaptations (including international factors), perceived by the military, as well as internal or organisational socialisation procedures, or what Abrahamsson refers to as military professionalisation.[22] The latter is a dynamic process, depends on prevailing societal and organisational adaptations, and it responsible for rendering the military conscious of, and ready to, defend its corporate interests when threatened by adverse systemic or political adaptations.[23] By the same token, professionalisation also disposes the armed forces to defend the existing political order when they perceive the actions and values of the political society are incongruent with the well-being and interests of their organisation and the larger society of which they are an integral part. Thus, to understand how the armed forces of Spain, Portugal, and Greece transformed themselves from supporters, if not the instigators of authoritarian (and in the case of Greece praetorian) regimes, to the defenders, if not the stimulators, of democracy one would have to look at both societal and internal (organisational) adaptations.

SOCIETAL

The three Mediterranean societies underwent significant economic and social transformations in the post-World War II era which eventually made possible the emergence of forces and attitudes supportive of pluralist political frameworks in those countries. In spite of efforts to isolate their economies through protective tariffs and quotas, rapidly changing economic conditions and domestic pressures forced the 1950s governments of Spain, Portugal and Greece to internationalise their economies through foreign investment and technology transfer, emigration and tourism. These led to 'a decline in the relative importance of agriculture and a massive shift of employment to industry and services';[24] tied the economies of these countries to those of Western Europe and the United States; established closer contacts between citizens of Southern Europe with their more affluent counterparts in the north; and eventually led political and economic elites to join the European Economic Community (EEC).

These changes stimulated participation, mobility, greater awareness and political consciousness; promoted urbanisation; led to social and political diversity; provoked a proliferation of the number of professional groups and associations; expanded the functions of the state; and brought about a closer identification and dependence between the individual and the state. In Greece, where the political system formally maintained the trappings of political participation throughout the 1950s, such developments prompted Greek society's more reactionary segments, led by the colonels, to stage the 1967 dictatorship in an effort to forestall the ever increasing demands for greater participation in governance.[25]

Thirst for greater political participation under the oppressive and extremely closed *Estado Novo* first became known in 1958 when General Delgado, running as the 'opposition' candidate for the presidency of the republic, in spite of massive vote manipulation, came within striking distance of defeating Salazar's official candidate. In the early 1970s the Society for Economic and Social Development (SEDES) – representing young lawyers, economists, engineers and even some large businesses – was organised 'to increase the level of public involvement in discussions of the major social and economic issues facing Portugal'.[26] SEDES and other similar groups were tapped by the MFA to play a major role in the 1974 revolution and became the backbone in the pluralist political system that subsequently emerged in that country.

The Spanish political landscape displayed remarkably similar characteristics, although little is known about political attitudes in Spain from the end of civil war until the mid-1960s. Strong measures of repression by the Franco regime, coupled with devotion to efforts to rebuilt their lives and

DEMOCRATISING THE MILITARY: MEDITERRANEAN EUROPE   33

a strong wave of consumerism, left Spaniards little room for political activity. However, as Franco's health began to decline in the mid-1960s, and with the designation of Prince Juan Carlos in 1969 as the *Caudillo*'s successor, political opinions began to emerge. The first real effort to gauge public opinion attitudes regarding political questions took place in 1970. The results of that survey showed very strong support for pluralism and democracy among the young and well educated. Armando de Miguel, who interpreted the results of the survey, wrote that 'in almost every group, except high school students and labourers, the majority predilection for pluralist solutions (two or more parties) is overwhelming'.[27]

Post-dictatorship popular sentiments in the three Mediterranean countries in favour of democracy are strong and growing. In Spain the percentage of those supporting democratic representation rose from 35 per cent in 1966 to 76 per cent in 1979. Public approval for competitive political parties shot up from a low of 3 per cent in 1971 to 67 per cent in 1976, whilst the rate of those against having political parties dropped from 34 per cent in 1973 to a mere 3 per cent in 1976.[28] The Greek scene reflects similar sentiments. For example, a May 1986 poll showed that 90 per cent of the Greeks have trust in Parliament, 67 and 68 per cent trust in the President of the Republic and the Prime Minister respectively, and 77 per cent have confidence in individual members of parliament.[29] Another survey found that the Greeks are generally satisfied with the way democracy works in their country at a higher rate than in Belgium, France, the Netherlands, and even the United Kingdom.[30] Democratic institutions and pluralism in Portugal also seem to enjoy widespread support. For example, the percentage of the Portuguese who favour a multi-party system went up from 26 per cent in 1978 to 40 per cent in 1984, whilst support for a no-party state remains less than 7 per cent.[31] Finally, it should be stated that voter turnout averages about 75 per cent in each country.

This consensus for democracy was further aided by the behaviour of the political leadership in each country. The restrictive policies of post-civil war governments in Greece and the exclusionary policies of the colonels' dictatorship and its counterparts in Portugal and Spain encouraged the political forces who found themselves at the fringes, or even in exile, to adopt moderate and conciliatory positions, once out of the political wilderness. This was true for liberal or democratic socialist politicians, most of whom had contracts and received support from western democracies, as well as communists. Moscow's decision to stay clear of the West's sphere of influence and domestic political realities forced the Communist Party of Spain to join the Eurocommunist movement; prevailed upon its Greek counterpart to accept the ballot box as the only avenue to political power and eventually to form an electoral alliance with its erstwhile enemies, the conservatives; and rendered the doctrinaire but 'impoverished' Portuguese Communists of Alvaro Cunhal impotent or unwilling to help their friends in the MFA to seize power in the November 1975 abortive coup.[32]

Armed with broad and strong-based popular support in favour of pluralism and democracy, the regimes that succeeded the Francoist and Salazarist structures and the colonels' junta in Greece moved cautiously and without recriminating spirit against the military and other supporters of the replaced dictatorial regimes. If one excludes the trial which resulted in the jailing of the coup leaders in Greece and a limited purging of elements with ties to the colonels and the *Estado Novo*, 'purification' was kept to a minimum in all three countries. Instead, the Karamanlis, Suarez, and Soares governments and their successors worked towards national reconciliation and building participatory, pluralist structures within which social groups, including the military, would have a voice in the making of national policies.

Slowly but steadily, civilian leaders took steps to confine the armed forces to military-related responsibilities and to establish the proper decision-making structures that would allow for military input in matters relating to defence, but would also ensure the supremacy of the elected, constitutional authorities. By allowing for freedom of expression, assembly, and other civil liberties, the Greek, Spanish and Portuguese regimes which succeeded the dictatorships severely curtailed and even disbanded paramilitary and other surveillance units, most of which were directly or indirectly linked to the military. These changes helped re-direct the role of the armed forces in the three countries from that of internal security, and in the case of Portugal fighting a no-win guerrilla war in Africa, to that of defending the state against possible external attacks. The officer corps were involved in these role re-definition decisions[33] and seem to have approved of them, with the military displaying a general reluctance to become involved in traditional constabulary functions.[34]

In addition, successor regimes in all three countries took steps to bring the military under the control of the civilian constitutional authorities. The Karamanlis government in Greece that replaced the fallen junta abolished measures which the praetorian regimes had enacted and which were designed to deprive the minister of defence and the chiefs of the three services of any autonomy. Instead, the Chief of the Armed Forces, a post created by the colonels, had been given ultimate responsibility on personnel decisions, jurisdiction over bureaus and agencies related to national defence, and a decisive voice in matters of budgetary appropriations. Act 660 did away with the junta's innovations, established the Supreme Council of National Defense (ASEA) – consisting of the prime minister, the minister of defence and other key ministers as well as the chief of the general staff

DEMOCRATISING THE MILITARY: MEDITERRANEAN EUROPE   35

and chiefs of each of the three services − and made it responsible for national defence matters. ASEA decisions 'are based on the suggestions of the minister of defence, who in turn is advised ... and influenced by his military advisers, i.e., the chiefs of staff'.[35]

In Spain, the military had not suffered the humiliation that its Greek counterparts had, and it was in better position to influence the process of establishing civilian supremacy. Yet Franco's background and personal relationship with the military had established him as the guardian of the institution's interests with all the reverence accorded to a legitimate ruler, and more. This special relationship was transferred to the *Caudillo*'s chosen successor, King Juan Carlos, and served successor governments well in their efforts to bring the military under the control of the civilian authorities, and to also thwart coup activities on the part of recalcitrant officers. The Suarez government moved prudently. It first sought and obtained 'the collaboration of prestigious military elements who were mainly concerned about the future of the armed forces, rather than confirmed democrats'. The latter may have been objectionable to the armed forces.[36] Then the government secured the consolidation of the three service ministries into a single ministry of national defence; established a joint chief of staff to bring about greater coordination between the three services; and appointed General Gutierrez Mellado, a reformist officer with good connections to the Franco regime, a minister of defence and vice premier. These reforms were accomplished with the 'collaboration' of the military[37] and, as Rafael Bañon has correctly pointed out, amounted to a 'recognition' by the civilian authorities of the armed forces' 'rights to advise and give opinions' on issues relating to their professional mission and to 'influence the process of defence decision making'.[38]

The Portuguese situation represented a different set of circumstances, and establishing civilian supremacy was slower in coming. Having overthrown the *Estado Novo* and taken the lead in establishing a liberal parliamentary regime in Portugal, many officers perceived the MFA as the guarantor of democracy in their country. Represented by the Council of the Revolution, the MFA sought to 'supervise the political system and to provide for the continuing progressive orientation of the [new] regime despite the political parties'.[39] This lasted until 1982 when the Portuguese parliament, 'in a rare display of unity, all non-communist parties combined to abolish' the Council, which they saw as an obstacle to establishing civilian supremacy over the military.[40] In spite of the 1982 appointment of a civilian to run the defence military for the first time since the late 1920s, and placing appointment and transfer of military personnel into the hands of the civilian-dominated Superior Council of National Defence, the Portuguese armed forces still retain influence in matters related to their profession which 'is a tacit admission that the military cannot be ignored'.[41] In other words, establishing civilian supremacy in all three countries has been accomplished and maintained with the armed forces participating in the process. And, as Welch has correctly pointed out, the military's consistent but limited participation in politics is one of the important factors that keeps the armed forces in the barracks.[42]

Finally, the constitutional authorities in all three countries took steps to strengthen their military's professional self-image. Such measures have included not interfering with the armed forces' internal affairs; joining the EEC where the principle of civilian supremacy is beyond question; reforming the curriculae of service academies; improving professional preparedness and emphasising devotion to the Clausewitizian maxim that 'the subordination of the political point of view to the military would be contrary to common sense';[43] modernising military equipment, training, and other war material (and in the case of Spain, joining NATO); and providing the military with healthy defence budgets.

Continuing disagreements with Turkey over the Aegean and Cyprus have caused post-disengagement Greek cabinets to spend nearly one quarter of total government spending on defence. Spanish military appropriations between 1977 and 1982 have realized a net increase of more than 33 per cent.[44] Ostensibly, military expenditures in Portugal relative to other countries have fallen dramatically since 1974, from 22nd place in terms of per capita public expenditures for defence (out of 132 countries) to 59th in 1986. However, these figures are misleading, since the number of men in uniform has dropped from 218,000 in 1974 to fewer than 100,000 in 1987.[45] And although recent governments have refused to increase officers' salaries, the Portuguese parliament regularly but incrementally allocates additional resources for defence outside the general budget.[46]

In sum, societal considerations have played a major part in instilling a 'democratic' mentality in the Spanish, Greek, and Portuguese military. Without popular support for pluralism and democracy it is doubtful whether the new democratic regimes in these countries would have been able to consolidate their rule and weather challenges from recalcitrant military elements.

THE ROLE OF THE MILITARY

The role of the armed forces in establishing and consolidating democracy should not be overlooked. Given its overwhelming power in relation to other social groups, the military is usually in a position to topple governments. Indeed, Greek and Spanish military units tried to bring down the newly established democratic regimes on several occasions in each country.[47]

DEMOCRATISING THE MILITARY: MEDITERRANEAN EUROPE 37

The plots did not succeed because the majority of officers remained loyal to the elected governments. Why did the armed forces, which supported the pre-1974/75 authoritarian regimes, transform themselves into supporters of democracy and pluralistic politics?

Historical antecedents regarding the role of the military in these societies were instrumental. As stated earlier, the different regimes that governed Spain, Portugal, and Greece from the early 1800s, with a few exceptions, were not military dictatorships, and the armed forces generally intervened in these countries in favour of constitutionalism. Moreover, the Salazar and Franco dictatorial regimes took pains to adhere to their own self-serving constitutions.[48] Though a mockery by democratic standards and formalistic in nature, these factors facilitated a rather strong loyalty to legality on the military's part and served the recently established democratic governments in these countries relatively well.

In addition, the considerable economic modernisation and development these societies experienced during the 1950s and 1960s also affected the officer corps, with young and better educated officers taking the lead plotting against the colonels, the *Estado Novo*, and to a lesser extent the Francoist regime. It is no accident that the MFA consisted almost exclusively of younger men, and it become known as the 'revolution of the Captains'. These young officers had borne the brunt of the fighting against the rebels in Portugal's African colonies. During the tumultuous days of the Portuguese revolution and after, these young officers replaced their more senior colleagues who had close ties to the Salazarist structure. The younger officers became the main proponents of democratisation. Young officers also played a major role in convincing their senior colleagues to replace the battered junta in July 1974 following the Cyprus debacle.

Finally, the need by the authoritarian regimes to maintain huge armies, mainly for domestic security purposes, necessitated a large officer corps. The latter forced these regimes to lower admission requirements to service academies and often to recruit officer trainees from poor social classes. In time, these practices diversified the military hierarchies, thus creating officer corps that reflected their societies' socio-economic composition. When democratisation came in Spain, Portugal, and Greece portions of the military could sociologically identify with many of the groups that advocated greater participation and pluralism.

In sum, tradition, socio-economic developments in the post-World War II period and their spin-offs, coupled with the societal changes analysed above, generated and supported values within the military in line with those espoused by the majority of their fellow citizens.

SUMMARY AND CONCLUSIONS

This article set out to identify and analyse the mechanisms employed by the recently established democracies in Spain, Portugal and Greece to instill in their armed forces the values of pluralism and the sanctity of democratic institutions. Following a brief examination of the relevant historical data, it was argued that the behaviour and the values of the military are related to societal and organisational adaptations operating in a society at a given time. It was concluded that the economic development and economic internationalisation which Spain, Portugal and Greece experienced in the post-world War II era generated social and political diversification and pluralist tendencies in these societies which eventually translated into consensus in favour of democratisation and participatory politics. When democracy came to the countries of Mediterranean Europe it did not represent a formalistic structure implanted from above, but an inevitable result of social, political and economic adaptations in these societies.

The military establishments were not immune to these developments. Historical experiences, coupled with diversification in the military recruitment bases, and willingness on the part of the civilian leadership to allow for military participation in policy decision, as well as to satisfy the armed forces' needs, sufficed to convince the officer corps in these countries that supporting the new democratic regimes constituted the best way to protect their integrity and professional interest. What emerged, therefore, was a congruence in the values, beliefs and interests between the civilian society and the military.

The vehicle which made this convergence possible was the dynamic and dualistic nature of military professionalism, defined as the sum of societal and organisational adaptations. The foregoing analysis and conclusions based on the Spanish, Portuguese and Greek experiences with respect to the military's role in the process and consolidation of democracy in these countries challenge some long-held theories regarding the effects of professionalism. Military professionalism is seen by some as the instigating factor that leads the armed forces to intervene;[49] and also by others, especially Samuel P. Huntington, as the agent that sets the officer corps apart from society, instills the principle of civilian supremacy, and renders them 'politically sterile and neutral' servants of the lawful authorities.[50]

Southern European experiences confirm the theory that professionalism is a stimulant to intervention but also indicate that it can be a stimulant to de-intervention and democratisation, depending on societal considerations and the military's perceptions at a given time. What professionalism does not do is to set the armed forces apart from society. Huntington's theory

DEMOCRATISING THE MILITARY: MEDITERRANEAN EUROPE   **39**

that professionalism instills the principle of civilfian supremacy in the military is half right, but for the wrong reasons. Instead, explanations accounting for military democratisation can be found at the level of value-congruency between society and the armed forces.

NOTES

1. Juan J. Linz, widely recognised as the foremost authority an authoritarianism, defines an authoritarian regime as a political system 'with limited, not responsible, political pluralism: without elaborate and guiding ideology (but with distinctive mentalities); without intensive not extensive political mobilization (except some point in [its development]: which a leader (or occasionally a small group) exercises power within formally ill-defined limits but actually quite predictable ones. See his 'An Authoritarian Regime: Spain', in Stanley G. Payne (ed.), *Politics and Society in Twentieth Century Spain* (New York: New Viewpoints, 1976), p. 165.
2. The literature here is proliferating rapidly. Among others see Guillermo O'Donnell, Philippe C. Schmitter, and Lawrence Whitehead (eds.), *Transitions from Authoritarian Rule – Prospects for Democracy* (Baltimore: The Johns Hopkins University Press, 1986); Constantine P. Danopoulos (ed.), *The Decline of Military Regimes – The Civilian Influence* (Boulder, CO: Westview Press, 1988); Constantine P. Danopoulos (ed.), *Military Disengagement from Politics* (London: Routledge, 1988); Louis W. Goodman, Johanna S. R. Mendleson and Juan Rial (eds.), *The Military and Democracy – The Future of Civil-Military Relations in Latin America* (Lexington, MA: D.C. Heath and Company, 1990); and Constantine P. Danopoulos (ed.), *From Military to Civilian Rule* (London: Routledge, 1991).
3. Among others see Claude E. Welch, Jr., *No Farewell to Arms? Military Disengagement from Politics in Africa and Latin America* (Boulder, CO: Westview Press, 1987), p. 204; Talukder Maniruzzaman, *Military Withdrawal from Politics – A Comparative Perspective* (Cambridge, MA: Ballinger Publishing Company, 1987), pp. 215–216; Samuel P. Huntington, 'Will More Countries Become Democratic?,' *Political Science Quarterly*, Vol. 99: 2 (Summer, 1984), pp. 193–218; Ulf Sundhaussen, 'Military Withdrawal From Government Responsibility', *Armed Forces and Society*, Vol. 10, No. 4 (Summer, 1984), p. 557; and Constantine P. Danopoulos (ed.), *Civilian Rule in the Developing World* (Boulder, CO: Westview Press), forthcoming.
4. Legitimacy is defined as 'the capacity of a system to engender and maintain the belief that the existing political institutions are the most appropriate ones for the society'. See Seymor Martin Lipset, *Political Man: The Social Basis of Politics* (Garden City, NY: Doubleday, 1960), p. 77.
5. Welch, *No Farewell to Arms?*, op. cit., p. 204.
6. See a collection of essays edited by Geoffrey Pridham, *The New Mediterranean Democracies* (London: Frank Cass, 1984); and Constantine P. Danopoulos, 'Farewell to Man on Horseback – Intervention and Civilian Rule in Modern Greece' in Danopoulos (ed.), *From Military to Civilian Rule*, op. cit.; and Danopoulos, 'Intervencion y Gobierno Militar en la Gracia Moderna,' a paper presented in a conference on *La inauguracion y la Consolidacion de la democracia: Experiencias para Chile*, Santiago, Chile, 10–11 August 1989.
7. Douglas L. Wheeler, 'The Military and the Portuguese Dictatorship, 1926–1974: The Honor of the Army', in Lawrence S. Graham and Harry M. Makler (eds.), *Contemporary Portugal – The Revolution and its Antecedents* (Austin: University of Texas Press, 1979), p. 192.
8. Ibid., p. 194.

9. Eric A. Nordlinger states that the military corporate interests include adequate budgetary support, institutional autonomy and exclusiveness, protection against encroachments from rival institutions, and the survival and viability of the military as a social institution. Tempering with these triggers powerful interventionist motives. See his *Soldiers in Politics — Military Coups and Governments* (Englewood Cliffs, NJ: Prentice-Hall, 1977), pp. 65–78.

10. Pedro Vilanova, 'Spain: The Army and the Transition', in David S. Bell (ed.), *Democratic Politics in Spain: Spanish Politics after Franco* (New York: St. Martin's Press, 1983), p. 149.

11. Hugh Thomas, *The Spanish Civil War* (New York: Harper and Row, 1961), p. 13; and Donald Share, *The Making of Spanish Democracy* (New York: Praeger, 1986), p. 9.

12. For details see Howard Wiarda, *Corporatism and Development: The Portuguese Experience* (Amherst: University of Massachusetts, 1977), p. 297; Wheeler, 'The Military and the Portuguese Dictatorship', op. cit., pp. 199–201; and Robert Harvey, *Portugal: Birth of a Democracy* (New York: St. Martin's Press, 1978), pp. 10–11.

13. For statistics regarding defence appropriations in Spain see Carolyn P. Boyd and James M. Boyden, 'The Armed Forces and the Transition to Democracy in Spain', in Thomas D. Lancaster and Gary Prevost (eds.), *Politics and Change in Spain* (New York: Praeger, 1985), p. 98.

14. For more details see M. G. Garcia, 'The Armed Forces: Poor Relations with the Franco Regime', in Paul Preston (ed.), *Spain in Crisis — The Evolution and Decline of the Franco Regime* (New York: Barnes and Noble, 1976); Boyed and Boyden, 'The Armed Forces in Spain', op. cit.

15. The 1909 intervention, which resulted in the coming to power of a new political elite, is generally regarded as the only time prior to 1967 that the Greek military acted independently. However, the military ruled for a very short time and invited Eleftherios Venizelos, the Cretan leader, to take over the government. For more details see S. Victor Papacosma, *The Military in Greek Politics; the 1909 Coup d'Etat* (Kent, OH: Kent State University Press, 1977).

16. Nicos C. Alivizatos, 'The Greek Army in the Late Forties: Towards an Institutional Autonomy', *Journal of the Hellenic Diaspora*, Vol. 5, No. 3 (Fall 1978), p. 37.

17. Lawrence S. Wittner, *American Intervention in Greece, 1943–1949* (New York: Columbia University Press, 1982), p. 53.

18. Yiannis P. Roubatis, 'The United States and the Operational Responsibilities of the Greek Armed Forces, 1947–1987', *Journal of the Hellenic Diaspora*, Vol. 6, No. 2 (Spring 1979), p. 55.

19. For more details see Constantine P. Danopoulos, *Warriors and Politicians in Modern Greece* (Chapel Hill: Documentary Publications, 1984), Ch. 2.

20. For more details see Constantine P. Danopoulos, 'Military Professionalism and Regime Legitimacy in Greece, 1967–1974', *Political Science Quarterly*, Vol. 98, No. 3 (Gall 1983); and 'The Greek Military and the Cyprus Question — Origins and Goals', *Journal of Political and Military Sociology* (Fall 1982).

21. O'Donnell and Schmitter, *Transitions From Authoritarian Rule*, op. cit., p. 8.

22. Military professionalisation is defined here in terms of (1) specialised theoretical knowledge accompanied by methods and devices for application; (2) responsibility, grounded on a set of ethical rules; and (3) a high degree of corporateness, deriving from common training and devotion to specific doctrines and customs. See Bengt Abrahamsson, *Military Professionalization and Political Power*, op. cit., p. 15.

23. Ibid.

24. Allan M. Williams, 'Introduction', in Allan Williams (ed.), *Southern Europe Transformed* (London: Harper and Row, 1984), p. 8. See also Glenda G. Rosenthal, *The Mediterranean Basin — Its Political Economy and Changing International Relations* (London: Butterworth Scientific, 1982).

25. The impact of high degrees of socio-economic development leads to these adaptations. See Samuel P. Huntington and Joan N. Nelson, *No Easy Choice: Political Participation in Developing Countries* (Cambridge: Harvard University Press, 1976), pp. 43–45.

26. Walter C. Opello, Jr., *Portugal's Political Development – A Comparative Perspective* (Boulder, CO: Westview Press, 1985), p. 94.
27. Armado de Miguel, 'Spanish Political Attitudes, 1970', in Payne (ed.), *Politics and Society in Spain*, op. cit., p. 225.
28. Rafael Lopez-Pintor, 'Mass and Elite Perspectives in the Process of Transition to Democracy', in Enrique A. Baloyra (ed.), *Comparing New Democracies – Transition and Consolidation in Mediterranean Europe and the Southern Cone* (Boulder, CO: Westview Press, 1987), pp. 90–91.
29. 'Trust in Values/Political and Social Institutions (Greece)', in *World Opinion Update*, Vol. X, No. 5 (May 1986), pp. 52–53.
30. Cited in Jürg Steiner, *European Democracies* (New York: Longman, 1986), p. 247.
31. Thomas C. Bruneau and Alex MacLeod, *Politics in Contemporary Portugal – Parties and the Consolidation of Democracy* (Boulder, CO: Lynne Riemer Publishers, 1986), pp. 33–35.
32. See David S. Bell, 'The Spanish Communist Party in the Transition', in Bell (ed.), *Democratic Politics in Spain*, op. cit.; Danopoulos, 'Farewell to Man on Horseback', op. cit.; and Coral Bell, *The Diplomacy of Detente: The Kissinger Era* (New York: St. Martin's Press, 1977), pp. 161–167.
33. See Rafael Bañon, 'The Spanish Military Reform and Modernization for the New Strategic Thinking', a paper presented at the Institute for Defense Analyses, Washington, DC, 5 October 1988; Fernando Rodrigo, 'A Democratic Strategy Toward the Military: Spain 1975–1979' in Danopoulos (ed.), *From Military to Civilian Rule*, op. cit.; and Danopoulos, 'Democratization by Golpe: The Experience of Modern Portugal', in Danopoulos (ed.), *Military Disengagement*, op. cit.
34. Morris Janowitz, *The Military in the Political Development of New Nations* (Chicago: The University of Chicago Press, 1964), p. 37.
35. Thanos Veremis, 'Security Considerations and Civil-Military Relations in Post-war Greece', in Richard Clogg (ed.), *Greece in the 1980s* (New York: St. Martin's Press, 1983), p. 180.
36. Rodrigo, 'A Democratic Strategy', op. cit., p. 2.
37. Ibid., p. 5.
38. Bañon, 'The Spanish Military', op. cit., pp. 9–10.
39. Thomas C. Bruneau, *Politics and Nationhood – Post-Revolutionary Portugal* (New York: Praeger, 1984), p. 103.
40. Tom Gallagher, 'Democracy in Portugal Since 1974', *Parliamentary Affairs*, Vol. 38, No. 2 (Spring 1985), p. 204.
41. Bruneau and MacLeod, *Politics in Portugal*, op. cit., p. 13.
42. Welch, *No Farewell to Arms?* op. cit., p. 13.
43. Karl Maria von Clausewitz, *On War* (London: Routledge and Kegan Paul, 1966), Vol. III, p. 424.
44. Bañon, 'The Spanish Military', op. cit.
45. Rugh Leger Sivard, *World Military and Social Expenditures* (Washington DC: World Priorities, 1974 and 1987–88).
46. This information was related to the author by a retired Portuguese air force general in October 1987.
47. Greece experienced several plots in 1975 and 1982. In Spain a plot was uncovered in 1978 before it had a chance to hatch and there another major coup attempt on 23 February 1981.
48. Salazar would always submit his resignation following each and every election, only to be religiously re-appointed to his post by the president of the republic.
49. For this view see Amos Perlmutter, *The Military and Politics in Modern Times* (New Haven, CT: Yale University Press, 1977); Abrahamsson, *Military Professionalization*, op. cit.; Nordlinger, *Soldiers in Politics*, op. cit.; Claude E. Welch, Jr., and Arthur K. Smith, *Military Role and Rule* (Belmont: Duxbury Press, 1974); and Danopoulos, *Warriors and Politicians*, op. cit.
50. The main proponent of this view is Samuel P. Huntington, *The Soldier and the State* (New York: Random House, 1962), p. 84.

Latin America

[14]

Dilemmas of Democratization in Latin America

Terry Lynn Karl

The demise of authoritarian rule in Argentina, Bolivia, Brazil, Chile, Ecuador, Peru, and Uruguay, when combined with efforts at political liberalization in Mexico and the recent election of civilian presidents in Guatemala, El Salvador, Honduras, and Nicaragua, represents a political watershed in Latin America. This wave of regime changes in the 1980s places a number of questions on the intellectual and political agenda for the continent. Will these newly emergent and fragile democracies in South America be able to survive, especially in the context of the worst economic recession since the 1930s? Can the liberalization of authoritarian rule in Central America and the possible prospect of honest competitive elections in Mexico be transformed into genuine democratic transitions? Will previously consolidated political democracies such as Venezuela and Costa Rica be able to extend the basic principles of citizenship into economic and social realms, or will they be "deconsolidated" by this challenge and revert to a sole preoccupation with survivability?[1]

Behind such questions lies a central concern expressed by Dankwart A. Rustow almost twenty years ago: "What conditions make democracy possible and what conditions make it thrive?"[2] This article addresses Rustow's query by arguing the following. First, the manner in which theorists of comparative politics have sought to understand democracy in developing countries has changed as the once-dominant search for prerequisites of democracy has given way to a more process-oriented emphasis on contingent choice. Having undergone this evolution, theorists should now develop an interactive approach that seeks explicitly to relate structural constraints to the shaping of contingent choice. Second, it is no longer adequate to examine regime transitions writ large, that is, from the general category of authoritarian rule to that of democracy. Such broad-gauged efforts must be complemented by the identification of different types of democracy that emerge from distinctive modes of regime transition as well as an analysis of their potential political, economic, and social consequences. Before these issues and their implications for the study of Latin America can be addressed, however, a definition of democracy must be established.

Defining Democracy

Defining democracy is no simple task because the resolution of a number of disputes over both its prospects and evaluation rests on how the term itself is operationalized. If, for example, democracy is defined in a Schumpeterian manner as a polity that permits the choice between elites by citizens voting in regular and competitive elections, the militarized countries of Central America could be classified as political democracies by many scholars, just as they are (with the exception of Sandinista Nicaragua) by U.S. policymakers.[3] But if the definition is expanded to include a wider range of political conditions—from lack of

1

restrictions on citizen expression, to the absence of discrimination against particular political parties, to freedom of association for all interests, to civilian control over the military—these same countries (with the exception of Costa Rica) could scarcely be classified under this rubric.

The problem is compounded when a number of substantive properties—such as the predominance of institutions that faithfully translate individual preferences into public policy through majoritarian rule, the incorporation of an ever-increasing proportion of the population into the process of decision making, and the continuous improvement of economic equity through the actions of governing institutions—are included either as components or empirical correlates of democratic rule.[4] Approaches that stipulate socioeconomic advances for the majority of the population and active involvement by subordinate classes united in autonomous popular organizations as defining conditions intrinsic to democracy are hard-pressed to find "actual" democratic regimes to study. Often they are incapable of identifying significant, if incomplete, changes towards democratization in the political realm. Moreover, they are cut off from investigating empirically the hypothetical relationship between competitive political forms and progressive economic outcomes because this important issue is assumed away by the very definition of regime type. While these substantive properties are ethically desirable to most democrats, such conceptual breadth renders the definition of democracy virtually meaningless for practical application.[5]

For these reasons, I will settle for a middle-range specification of democracy. It is defined as "a set of institutions that permits the entire adult population to act as citizens by choosing their leading decision makers in competitive, fair, and regularly scheduled elections which are held in the context of the rule of law, guarantees for political freedom, and limited military prerogatives." Specified in this manner, democracy is a political concept involving several dimensions: (1) contestation over policy and political competition for office; (2) participation of the citizenry through partisan, associational, and other forms of collective action; (3) accountability of rulers to the ruled through mechanisms of representation and the rule of law; and (4) civilian control over the military. It is this latter dimension, so important in the Latin American context, which sets my definition apart from Robert Dahl's classic notion of a "procedural minimum."[6] A middle-range definition of this sort avoids the Scylla of an overly narrow reliance on the mere presence of elections without concomitant changes in civil-military relations and the Charybdis of an overly broad assumption of social and economic equality. While perhaps less than fully satisfactory from a normative perspective, it has the advantage of permitting a systematic and objective investigation of the relationship between democratic political forms and the long-range pursuit of equity.

The Futile Search for Democratic Preconditions

If the questions raised by democratization remain relatively unchanged from the past, the answers that are offered today come from a different direction. This becomes evident through a brief comparison of the divergent theories about the origins of democratic regimes that have dominated the study of Latin America. The scholarship that preceded the new

Terry Lynn Karl

wave of democratization in the 1980s argued that a number of preconditions were necessary for the emergence of a stable democratic polity.

First, a certain degree of wealth or, better said, level of capitalist development was considered a prerequisite of democracy. Market economies in themselves were not enough; a country had to cross (and remain beyond) a minimum threshold of economic performance before political competition could be institutionalized. "The more well-to-do a nation," Seymour Martin Lipset claimed, "the greater the chances that it will sustain democracy."[7] A wealthy economy made possible higher levels of literacy, education, urbanization, and mass media exposure, or so the logic went, while also providing resources to mitigate the tensions produced by political conflict.[8]

A second set of preconditions that underlay traditional approaches to democracy was derived from the concept of political culture, that is, the system of beliefs and values in which political action is embedded and given meaning. The prevalence of certain values and beliefs over others was said to be more conducive to the emergence of democracy. Thus, for example, Protestantism allegedly enhanced the prospects for democracy in Europe while Catholicism, with its tradition of hierarchy and intolerance, was posited to have the opposite effect in Latin America.[9] Although arguments based only on the link between different religious systems and experiences with democracy have been dismissed by most scholars, more sophisticated claims sought to identify political cultures characterized by a high degree of mutual trust among members of society, a willingness to tolerate diversity, and a tradition of accommodation or compromise because such cultures were considered necessary for the subsequent development of democratic institutions. That a "civic culture" of this sort necessarily rested on a widely differentiated and articulated social structure with relatively autonomous social classes, occupational sectors, and ethnic, religious, or regional groups was an unspoken assumption. In other words, a prodemocratic consensus and set of values was considered the main prerequisite of political democracy.[10]

Third, specific domestic historical conditions and configurations were said to be prerequisites of democracy. Theorists of "crises and sequences" argued that the order in which various crises of modernization appeared and were settled determined whether economic and social transformations were conducive to the development of democracy. Democratic regimes were more likely to emerge if problems of national identity were resolved prior to the establishment of a central government and if both of these events preceded the formation of mass parties.[11]

In a different, yet still historically grounded vein, Barrington Moore, Jr. contended that democracies were more likely to appear where the social and economic power of the landed aristocracy was in decline relative to that of the bourgeoisie and where labor-repressive agriculture was not the dominant mode of production. When this occurred as a result of the commercialization of agriculture that transformed a traditional peasantry into either a class of small farmers or a rural proletariat, the prognosis for democracy was strong indeed.[12] A version of Moore's approach has been used to explain the different political trajectories in Central America. Specifically, democracy is said to have emerged in Costa Rica due to the creation of a yeoman farmer class, while the persistence of authoritarian rule in Guatemala and El Salvador is attributed to the continued dominance of the landed aristocracy.[13]

Finally, some scholars treated external influences as another set of preconditions on the grounds that these could be decisive in determining whether a polity became democratic or

3

Comparative Politics   October 1990

authoritarian. Dependency theorists in Latin America and the United States contended that the continent's particular insertion into the international market made democratization especially problematic at more advanced stages of import-substituting capitalist development and even enhanced the necessity for authoritarian rule under specific circumstances. In a logic that ran counter to Lipset's "optimistic equation," both Guillermo O'Donnell and Fernando Henrique Cardoso argued that, as dependent economies became more complex, more penetrated by foreign capital and technology, and more reliant upon low wages to maintain their competitive advantage in the international economy, professional militaries, technocrats, and state managers moved to the forefront of the decision-making process, forcibly replacing unruly, "populist" parties and trade unions in order to establish a supposedly more efficient form of rule.[14]

Inversely, using an argument based on external influences of a qualitatively different sort, proponents of an aggressive U.S. foreign policy towards the region declared that the rise and decline of democracy was directly related to the rise and decline of the global power of the United States rather than to market mechanisms or accumulation processes. In Samuel Huntington's view, the dramatic increase in authoritarian rule during the 1960s and 1970s was a direct reflection of the waning of U.S. influence. Specifically, it was due to the decreased effectiveness of efforts by U.S. officials to promote democracy as a successful model of development. Concomitantly, he argued, the spate of democratic transitions in the 1980s could be credited to the Reagan administration's renewed effort to "restore American power" through the rollback of revolutions and the promotion of electoral reforms. This position, so ideologically convenient for policymakers, located the roots of democracy outside Latin America.[15]

The experience of Latin American countries in the 1980s challenged all of these presumptions about preconditions. The hypothetical association between wealth and democracy might be called upon to "explain" the transition to democracy in Brazil after a protracted economic boom, but it could hardly account for the case of Peru, whose transition was characterized by stagnant growth rates, extreme foreign debt, persistent balance of payments problems, and a regressive distribution of income. Nor could it explain the anomaly of Argentina, where relatively high levels of per capita GDP were persistently accompanied by authoritarian rule. If the political cultures of Argentina, Uruguay, and Brazil all tolerated, admittedly to varying degrees, the practice of official state terror and widespread violations of human rights, how could they suddenly become sufficiently "civic" and "tolerant" to support a democratic outcome? As the Catholic church took an increasingly active role in opposing authoritarian rule, especially in Brazil, Chile, Peru, Central America, and Panama, the argument about the so-called "anti-democratic bias" of Catholicism became increasingly implausible.[16]

The predictability of approaches emphasizing the influence of the international system fared little better. While the manner of a country's insertion into the world capitalist economy is now considered essential in explaining its subsequent political and economic development, as dependency theorists claimed, criticisms of other scholars plus the democratic transitions in Brazil and Chile demonstrated that there was no direct or inevitable correlation between capital deepening and authoritarian rule.[17] The general trends towards recession in export earnings, debt crises, diminishing U.S. support for human rights, and the frequent resort to military instruments under the foreign policy of the Reagan administration

4

Terry Lynn Karl

boded ill for the emergence of democracies in the 1980s, yet emerge they did. The pattern of their appearance presented an undeniable challenge to Huntington's thesis linking democratization with the rise of U.S. power. In the southern cone, where influence from the north is not especially high, military rulers generally made way for civilian authority. In Central America, Panama, and Haiti, where the overriding historical role of the U.S. is indisputable, militaries either permitted elections to occur without limiting their own prerogatives, or they refused to leave power altogether. Indeed, where the decline in U.S. hegemony was greatest, democracy seemed to appear even though dictatorship "should" have been the more appropriate response!

These anomalies suggest the pressing need for important revisions, even reversals, in the way democratization in contemporary Latin America is understood. First, there may be no single precondition that is sufficient to produce such an outcome. The search for causes rooted in economic, social, cultural/psychological, or international factors has not yielded a general law of democratization, nor is it likely to do so in the near future despite the proliferation of new cases.[18] Thus, the search for a set of identical conditions that can account for the presence or absence of democratic regimes should probably be abandoned and replaced by more modest efforts to derive a contextually bounded approach to the study of democratization.

Second, what the literature has considered in the past to be the preconditions of democracy may be better conceived in the future as the outcomes of democracy. Patterns of greater economic growth and more equitable income distribution, higher levels of literacy and education, and increases in social communication and media exposure may be better treated as the products of stable democratic processes rather than as the prerequisites of its existence. A "civic" political culture characterized by high levels of mutual trust, a willingness to tolerate diversity of opinion, and a propensity for accommodation and compromise could be the result of the protracted functioning of democratic institutions that generate appropriate values and beliefs rather than a set of cultural obstacles that must be initially overcome. There is evidence for this contention in the fact that most democracies in Europe and Latin America's oldest democracy in Costa Rica have emerged from quite "uncivic" warfare. In other words, what have been emphasized as independent variables in the past might be more fruitfully conceived as dependent variables in the future.

From Contingent Choice to Structured Contingency

The failure to identify clear prerequisites, plus the hunch that much of what had been thought to produce democracy should be considered as its product, has caused theorists of comparative politics to shift their attention to the strategic calculations, unfolding processes, and sequential patterns that are involved in moving from one type of political regime to another, especially under conditions of nonviolence, gradualism, and social continuity. For Guillermo O'Donnell and Philippe Schmitter, democratization is understood as a historical process with analytically distinct, if empirically overlapping, stages of transition, consolidation, persistence, and eventual deconsolidation.[19] A variety of actors with different followings, preferences, calculations, resources, and time horizons come to the fore during these successive stages. For example, elite factions and social movements seem to play the

5

Comparative Politics   October 1990

key roles in bringing about the demise of authoritarian rule; political parties move to center stage during the transition itself; and business associations, trade unions, and state agencies become major determinants of the type of democracy that is eventually consolidated.[20]

What differentiates these stages above all, as Adam Przeworski points out, is the degree of uncertainty which prevails at each moment. During regime transitions, all political calculations and interactions are highly uncertain. Actors find it difficult to know what their interests are, who their supporters will be, and which groups will be their allies or opponents. The armed forces and the civilian supporters of the incumbent authoritarian regime are characteristically divided between "hard-line" and "soft-line" factions. Political parties emerge as privileged in this context because, despite their divisions over strategies and their uncertainties about partisan identities, the logic of electoral competition focuses public attention on them and compels them to appeal to the widest possible clientele. The only certainty is that "founding elections" will eliminate those who make important miscalculations.

The absence of predictable "rules of the game" during a regime transition expands the boundaries of contingent choice. Indeed, the dynamics of the transition revolve around strategic interactions and tentative arrangements between actors with uncertain power resources aimed at defining who will legitimately be entitled to play in the political game, what criteria will determine the winners and losers, and what limits will be placed on the issues at stake. From this perspective, regime consolidation occurs when contending social classes and political groups come to accept some set of formal rules or informal understandings that determine "who gets what, where, when, and how" from politics. In so doing, they settle into predictable positions and legitimate behaviors by competing according to mutually acceptable rules. Electoral outcomes may still be uncertain with regard to person or party, but in consolidated democracies they are firmly surrounded by normative limits and established patterns of power distribution.

The notion of contingency (meaning that outcomes depend less on objective conditions than subjective rules surrounding strategic choice) has the advantage of stressing collective decisions and political interactions that have largely been underemphasized in the search for preconditions. But this understanding of democracy has the danger of descending into excessive voluntarism if it is not explicitly placed within a framework of structural-historical constraints. Even in the midst of the tremendous uncertainty provoked by a regime transition, where constraints appear to be most relaxed and where a wide range of outcomes appears to be possible, the decisions made by various actors respond to and are conditioned by the types of socioeconomic structures and political institutions already present. These can be decisive in that they may either restrict or enhance the options available to different political actors attempting to construct democracy.

For example, certain social structures seem to make the emergence of political democracy highly improbable; inversely, it is reasonable to presume that their absence may make accommodative strategies more viable and reinforce the position of democratic actors. Political democracies have lasted only in countries where the landed class, generally the most recalcitrant of interests, has played a secondary role in the export economy, for example Venezuela and Chile, or where non-labor-repressive agriculture has predominated, for example Costa Rica, Argentina, and Uruguay. Thus the survivability of political democracy does seem to depend on a structural space defined in part by the absence of a

6

Terry Lynn Karl

strong landowner elite engaged in labor-repressive agriculture or its subordination to interests tied to other economic activities.[21]

The cases of Venezuela and Chile better make the point. In Venezuela, dependence upon petroleum as the leading source of foreign exchange had the (unintended) effect of hastening the decline of that country's already stagnant agriculture and, with it, the landowning elite. Faced with overvalued exchange rates that hurt agro-exports and abundant foreign reserves for importing cheap foodstuffs, landowners sold their property to oil companies and converted themselves into a commercial and financial urban bourgeoisie. This largely voluntary self-liquidation removed the incentive for them to commercialize rural areas, to subordinate the peasantry through repressive means, and eventually to maintain authoritarian rule. It also removed the social base for an antisystem party of the right. Thus, actors designing pact-making strategies in Venezuela during the regime transition in 1958 did not face powerfully organized antidemocratic rural elites.[22] Social dynamics in Chile, though different, had the same effect. Conservative elements based in a system of labor-repressive agriculture eventually supported the expansion of the suffrage in the nineteenth century as a means of combating the rising power of industrialists and *capas medias*, who were tied to the state and supported by revenues from copper.[23] In effect, the social impact of the dominant presence of mineral exports meant that, when compared to the cases of Central America, both Venezuela and Chile were able to institutionalize democratic agreements with relative ease.

These cases illustrate the limits, as well as the opportunities, that social structures place upon contingent choice. If the focus in explaining the emergence of democracy had been solely on the forging of institutional compromises, that is, conceptualizing the establishment of democracy as only the product of strategic interactions, the pact-making that characterized the Venezuelan transition and the gradual expansion of the suffrage in Chile would appear to be simply the result of skilful bargaining by astute political leaders.[24] Instead, by focusing on the internal social dynamics produced by a mineral-based insertion into the international economy, it becomes evident how oil- or copper-induced structural change makes such "statecraft" possible. This is not to argue that individual decisions made at particular points in time or all observable political outcomes can be specifically and neatly linked to preexisting structures, but it is claimed that historically created structures, while not determining which one of a limited set of alternatives political actors may choose, are "confining conditions" that restrict or in some cases enhance the choices available to them. In other words, structural and institutional constraints determine the range of options available to decision makers and may even predispose them to choose a specific option.

What is called for, then, is a path-dependent approach which clarifies how broad structural changes shape particular regime transitions in ways that may be especially conducive to (or especially obstructive of) democratization. This needs to be combined with an analysis of how such structural changes become embodied in political institutions and rules which subsequently mold the preferences and capacities of individuals during and after regime changes. In this way, it should be possible to demonstrate how the range of options available to decision makers at a given point in time is a function of structures put in place in an earlier period and, concomitantly, how such decisions are conditioned by institutions established in the past. The advantages of this method are evident when compared to a structural approach alone, which leads to excessively deterministic conclusions about the

7

Comparative Politics   October 1990

origins and prospects of democracy, or to a sole focus on contingency, which produces overly voluntaristic interpretations.[25]

Modes of Transition to Democracy

Once the links between structures, institutions, and contingent choice are articulated, it becomes apparent that the arrangements made by key political actors during a regime transition establish new rules, roles, and behavioral patterns which may or may not represent an important rupture with the past. These, in turn, eventually become the 'institutions shaping the prospects for regime consolidation in the future. Electoral laws, once adopted, encourage some interests to enter the political arena and discourage others. Certain models of economic development, once initiated through some form of compromise between capital and labor, systematically favor some groups over others in patterns that become difficult to change. Accords between political parties and the armed forces set out the initial parameters of civilian and military spheres. Thus, what at the time may appear to be temporary agreements often become persistent barriers to change, barriers that can even scar a new regime with a permanent "birth defect."

These observations have important implications for studying democracy in Latin America. Rather than engage in what may be a futile search for new preconditions, they suggest that scholars would do well to concentrate on several tasks: (1) clarifying how the mode of regime transition (itself conditioned by the breakdown of authoritarian rule) sets the context within which strategic interactions can take place; (2) examining how these interactions, in turn, help to determine whether political democracy will emerge and survive; and (3) analyzing what type of democracy will eventually be institutionalized.

Thus, it is important to begin to distinguish between possible modes of transition to democracy. First, we can differentiate cases in which democracies are the outcome of a strategy based primarily on overt force from those in which democracies arise from compromise. This has been displayed on the horizontal axis in Figure 1. Second, we can distinguish between transitions in which incumbent ruling groups, no matter how weakened, are still ascendant in relation to mass actors and those in which mass actors have gained the upper hand, even temporarily, vis-à-vis those dominant elites. This can be seen on the vertical axis in Figure 1. The cross tabulation of these distinctions produces four ideal types of democratic transition: reform, revolution, imposition, and pact.

Latin America, at one time or another, has experienced all four modes of transition. To date, however, *no* stable political democracy has resulted from regime transitions in which mass actors have gained control, even momentarily, over traditional ruling classes. Efforts at reform from below, which have been characterized by unrestricted contestation and participation, have met with subversive opposition from unsuppressed traditional elites, as the cases of Argentina (1946–1951), Guatemala (1946–1954), and Chile (1970–1973) demonstrate.[26] Revolutions generally produce stable forms of governance (Bolivia is an obvious exception), but such forms have not yet evolved into democratic patterns of fair competition, unrestricted contestation, rotation in power, and free associability, although developments in Nicaragua and Mexico may soon challenge this assertion.[27]

Thus far, the most frequently encountered types of transition, and the ones which have

Terry Lynn Karl

Figure 1 Modes of Transition to Democracy

STRATEGIES OF TRANSITION

	Compromise	Force
Elite Ascendant	PACT	IMPOSITION
Mass Ascendant	REFORM	REVOLUTION

RELATIVE
ACTOR
STRENGTH

most often resulted in the implantation of a political democracy, are "transitions from above." Here traditional rulers remain in control, even if pressured from below, and successfully use strategies of either compromise or force—or some mix of the two—to retain at least part of their power.

Of these two modes of transition, democratization by pure imposition is the least common in Latin America—unless we incorporate cases in which force or the threat of force is applied by foreign as well as domestic actors. This is not the case for both Europe and Asia, where democratization through imposition often followed in the wake of World War II. In Figure 2, the cell labeled imposition includes Brazil and Ecuador, where the military used its dominant position to establish unilaterally the rules for civilian governance. Cases on the margin include Costa Rica (where in 1948 an opposition party militarily defeated the governing party but then participated in pact-making to lay the foundation for stable democratic rule), Venezuela (1945–48) and Peru (where the military's control over the timing and shape of the transition was strongly influenced by a mass popular movement),[28] and Chile (where the military's unilateralism was curbed somewhat by its defeat in the 1988 plebiscite).[29]

Where democracies that have endured for a respectable length of time appear to cluster is in the cell defined by relatively strong elite actors who engage in strategies of compromise, as Figure 2 demonstrates. This cell includes the cases of Venezuela (1958–), Colombia (1958–), the recent redemocratization in Uruguay (1984–), and Chile (1932–1970).[30] What unites all of these diverse cases, except Chile, is the presence of foundational *pacts,* that is, explicit (though not always public) agreements between contending actors, which define the rules of governance on the basis of mutual guarantees for the "vital interests" of those involved. Chile appears to be an exception because there was no explicit pact or agreement among elites in 1932, when the democratic regime was simply "restored" on the basis of preexisting constitutional rules left over from the first democratic transition in 1874. While

9

Comparative Politics   October 1990

Figure 2 Modes of Transition to Democracy in Latin America

Compromise   –   Force

            PACT   IMPOSITION

Venezuela (1958-)   Costa Rica (1948-)   Brazil (1974-)

Colombia (1958-)   Ecuador (1976-)

Uruguay (1984-)   Mexico (1988-)*

     – – – – – – –   – – – – – – – –

                                            Guatemala (1984-)*
  Chile (1932-1970)
                                            El Salvador (1982)*
                        Chile (1988-)

                                            Peru (1978-)

                                            Venezuela (1945-48)
                  Argentina (1983-)

          REFORM   REVOLUTION

Argentina (1946-1951),   Mexico (1910-1929)*

Guatemala (1946-1954)   Bolivia (1952-)

Chile (1970-1973)**   Nicaragua (1979-)*

---

*   These cases cannot be considered democracies in the
      definition used here. They are included because they are
      in periods of transformation and thus illustrate possible
      modes of transition in the future.
**   See footnote 26.

---

the Chilean case suggests that elite-based democracies can be established in the absence of foundational pacts, this may be more difficult in the contemporary period, which is characterized by more developed organized interests, the presence of mass politics, stronger military capabilities, and a tighter integration into the international market. Under such conditions, *pactismo* may prove to be essential.[31]

Foundational pacts are well exemplified by the case of Venezuela. Here a series of agreements negotiated by the military, economic, and party leaders rested on explicit

10

Terry Lynn Karl

institutional arrangements.[32] The military agreed to leave power and to accept a new role as an "apolitical, obedient, and nondeliberative body" in exchange for an amnesty for abuses committed during authoritarian rule and a guaranteed improvement of the economic situation of officers. Political parties agreed to respect the electoral process and share power in a manner commensurate with the voting results. They also accepted a "prolonged political truce" aimed at depersonalizing debate and facilitating consultation and coalitions. Capitalists agreed to accept legal trade unions and collective bargaining in exchange for significant state subsidies, guarantees against expropriation or socializing property, and promises of labor peace from workers' representatives. This arrangement changed what could have become potentially explosive issues of national debate into established parameters by removing them from the electoral arena.

The foundational pacts underlying some new democracies have several essential components. First, they are necessarily comprehensive and inclusive of virtually all politically significant actors. Indeed, because pacts are negotiated compromises in which contending forces agree to forego their capacity to harm each other by extending guarantees not to threaten each other's vital interests, they are successful only when they include all significantly threatening interests. Thus, the typical foundational pact is actually a series of agreements that are interlocking and dependent upon each other; it necessarily includes an agreement between the military and civilians over the conditions for establishing civilian rule, an agreement between political parties to compete under the new rules of governance, and a "social contract" between state agencies, business associations, and trade unions regarding property rights, market arrangements, and the distribution of benefits.

Second, while such pacts are both substantive (about the main tenets of policy) and procedural (about the rules of policymaking), they initially emphasize rulemaking because "bargaining about bargaining" is the first and most important stage in the process of compromise. Only after all contending forces have agreed to bargain over their differences can the power-sharing which leads to consensual governance result. This initial bargain can begin to lay the basis for mutual trust if only by building up reserves of familiarity between opposing groups. Subsequently, the very decision to enter into a pact can create a habit of pact making and an accommodative political style based on a "pact to make pacts."

Such foundational pacts must be differentiated from smaller, more partial "managerial" accords.[33] These include the neofunctional arrangements frequently found in social democratic polities in Europe, for example, the annual corporatist negotiations among capital, labor, and the state in postwar Austria for setting wages and social policy, as well as the frequent mini-accords hammered out between political opponents in Latin America. Unlike foundational pacts, managerial accords are partial rather than comprehensive, exclusionary rather than inclusionary, and substantively oriented rather than rule making in content. These characteristics of comprehensiveness, inclusion, and rule making are critical in identifying the presence of a foundational pact. They help distinguish between basic agreements, like those present in Venezuela in 1958, and more transitory political deals, like the Pact of Apaneca which was forged in El Salvador in 1983 between the Christian Democratic Party and ARENA.[34]

Finally, these pacts serve to ensure survivability because, although they are inclusionary, they are simultaneously aimed at restricting the scope of representation in order to reassure traditional dominant classes that their vital interests will be respected. In essence, they are

11

Comparative Politics   October 1990

antidemocratic mechanisms, bargained by elites, which seek to create a deliberate socioeconomic and political contract that demobilizes emerging mass actors while delineating the extent to which all actors can participate or wield power in the future. They may accomplish this task by restricting contestation (as Colombian parties did in 1958 by agreeing to alternate in power regardless of the outcome of elections), by restricting the policy agenda itself (as Venezuelan parties did in 1958 by agreeing to implement the same economic program), or by restricting the franchise (as Chilean elites did beginning with the electoral law of 1874). Regardless of which strategic option is chosen, the net effect of these options is the same: the nature and parameters of the initial democracy that results is markedly circumscribed.

Types of Democracies and Their Prospects in the Contemporary Period

What are the implications of this excursus into preconditions and modes of transition for the prospects of democratization in contemporary Latin America? To begin with, the notion of unfolding processes and sequences from regime breakdown to transition to consolidation and persistence is fundamental in understanding the two concurrent realities of democratization in Latin America today. On the one hand, most of the newly emergent civilian or militarized civilian regimes—Argentina, Chile, Peru, Ecuador, Guatemala, Honduras, El Salvador, and Nicaragua—face the overwhelming problem of sheer survivability. What threatens their survival is the omnipresent specter of a military coup, a coup which may be provoked by intense partisan political disagreements, by the inability of political parties to manage the current profound economic crisis of the region, by the actions of antisystem elites, by a mass mobilization of labor, peasants, or the urban poor that escapes the control of traditional dominant classes, by the actions of a foreign power, or by threats to the vital corporate interests of the military itself. Significant uncertainty over the rules of the game still prevail in these fragile democracies.

What becomes important in maintaining civilian rule is to find mechanisms—other than rigged or unpredictable elections—that can limit this uncertainty, especially by reducing incentives for civilians on the losing end to appeal to the military for salvation. This suggests that there are two critical tasks initially facing Latin American democratizers: first, to arrive at a sufficiently strong consensus about the rules of the game (including institutional formalities guaranteeing respect for certain crucial but minoritarian concerns) so that no major elite is tempted to call upon the military to protect its vital interests and, second, to begin to design conscious strategies for the establishment of qualitatively new civil-military relations appropriate to future stable civilian rule. This is probably easier to accomplish in the more developed regions of the continent, where the armed forces have learned the importance of cooperating with capitalist and managerial elites, than in the less developed ones (Bolivia, Central America, and the Caribbean), where the military still retains relatively confident notions of its ability to manage the economy and polity or is simply too corrupt to worry about such matters.[35]

On the other hand, other types of democracies in the region—Venezuela, Costa Rica, and, more recently, Brazil and Uruguay—are relatively consolidated in that actors are not so preoccupied by the overriding concern with survivability. Rather, the challenge that

12

Terry Lynn Karl

confronts most of these polities (and that will certainly confront newer democracies as preoccupation with mere survivability recedes) is providing some new and better resolution to the ancient question of *cui bono*. This issue of "who benefits" from democracy is singularly problematic in Latin America, where the pattern of dependent capitalist development has been especially ruthless in its historic patterns of exploitation.[36] This means that the extension of citizenship and equal political rights must take place in a context of extreme inequality, which is unparalleled even in Africa or Asia.[37] It must also take place during *la decada perdida*, that is to say, in the midst of the most severe and prolonged economic crisis since the Depression.[38]

The relationship between the problematics of survivability and *cui bono* may well represent the central dilemma of democratization in Latin America. The choices taken by key political actors to ensure the survivability of a fragile democracy—the compromises they make, the agreements they enter into—will necessarily and even irrevocably affect who gains and who loses during the consolidation of a new regime. Subsequent "populist" decisions to redistribute gains without regard for losses may affect the durability of the regime itself, regardless of how consolidated it may appear to be. At the same time, decisions *not* to redistribute or inaction on this front may also influence regime durability because the commitment to democracy in part rests on the widely held (if sometimes inaccurate) conviction that economic benefits will be more fairly distributed or the welfare of the general population improved under this type of polity. Hence the current concern with both survivability and "who benefits" merely underlines the significance of choices made during the founding moments of democracies and highlights some potential relationships between political democracy and economic outcomes for future research. It also produces some not-so-promising scenarios for the emergence of different types of democracies.

First, political democracy in Latin America may be rooted in a fundamental paradox: the very modes of transition that appear to enhance initial survivability by limiting unpredictability may preclude the future democratic self-transformation of the economy or polity further down the road. Ironically, the conditions that permit democracies to persist in the short run may constrain their potential for resolving the enormous problems of poverty and inequality that continue to characterize the continent. Indeed, it is reasonable to hypothesize that what occurs in the phase of transition or early consolidation may involve a significant trade-off between some form of political democracy, on the one hand, and equity, on the other. Thus, even as these democracies guarantee a greater respect for law and human dignity when compared to their authoritarian predecessors, they may be unable to carry out substantive reforms that address the lot of their poorest citizens. If this scenario should occur, they would become the victims of their successful consolidation, and the democratic transitions of the 1980s that survive could prove to be the "frozen" democracies of the 1990s.

Second, while this may be the central dilemma of elite-ascendant processes of democratization, there may be important differences between countries like Uruguay, a pacted transition, and Brazil, a unilaterally imposed transition. Pacted democracies, whatever their defects, have been honed through compromise between at least two powerful contending elites. Thus, their institutions should reflect some flexibility for future bargaining and revision over existing rules. In Uruguay, for example, while the agreed-upon rules made it very difficult to challenge agreements between the military and the parties on the issue of amnesty for crimes committed during authoritarian rule, the left opposition, excluded from this agreement, was nevertheless able to force the convocation of a plebiscite on this major issue, which it subsequently lost. It is difficult to imagine that anything similar could occur in Brazil. Because the military exerted almost complete control over the transition, it never curtailed its own prerogatives nor fully agreed to the principle of civilian control, and it has not been compelled to adopt institutional rules reflecting the need for compromise.

The contrast between the cases of Uruguay and Brazil raises a hypothesis that merits investigation: to the extent that transitions are unilaterally imposed by armed forces who are not compelled to enter into compromises, they threaten to evolve into civilian governments controlled by authoritarian elements who are unlikely to push for greater participation, accountability, or equity for the majority of their citizens. Paradoxically, in other words, the heritage left by "successful" authoritarian experiences, that is, those characterized by relatively moderate levels of repression and economic success which has left the military establishment relatively intact, may prove to be the major obstacle to future democratic self-transformation.[39] This danger exists, albeit to a lesser extent, in civilian-directed unilateral transitions, for example, Mexico, because the institutional rules that are imposed are likely to favor incumbents and permit less scope for contestation.

Third, the attempt to assess possible consequences of various modes of transition is most problematic where strong elements of imposition, compromise, and reform are simultaneously present, that is to say, where neither incumbent elites nor newly ascendant power contenders are clearly in control and where the armed forces are relatively intact. This is currently the case in Argentina and Peru, as Figure 2 demonstrates. Given the Argentinean military's defeat in the Falklands/Malvinas war, the high level of mass mobilization during the transition, and the absence of pacts between civilian authority and the armed forces, on the one hand, and trade unions and employers, on the other, Argentina combines elements of several modes of transition. Such a mixed scenario, while perhaps holding out the greatest hope for political democracy and economic equity, may render a consistent strategy of any type ineffectual and thus lead to the repetition of Argentina's persistent failure to consolidate any type of regime. The prospects for failure are even greater in Peru. Given the absence of explicit agreements between the leading political parties, the possibility of mass mobilizations in the midst of economic depression, the presence of an armed insurgency, and a unified military, Peru is currently the most fragile democracy in South America.

Fourth, because political democracies generally arise from a compromise between contending organized elites that are unable to impose their will unilaterally or the unilateral action of one dominant group, usually the armed forces, this does not bode well for democratization in situations in which the armed forces are inextricably tied to the interests of a dominant (and antidemocratic) agrarian class. Guatemala and El Salvador in particular are characterized by a landowning elite whose privileged position is based on labor-repressive agriculture and on a virtual partnership with the armed forces, thereby making it unlikely that their militaries (as currently constituted) will tolerate comprehensive political competitiveness, civil liberties, or accountability. Regardless of the profound differences between these two Central American countries, the extraordinary pressure of U.S. intervention as well as international diffusion means that, at minimum, they can be expected to adhere to "electoralism," meaning the regularized holding of elections, even as

14

Terry Lynn Karl

they continue to restrict the other political rights and opportunities of their citizens. This hybrid mix of electoral forms and authoritarianism, which has been dubbed "electocratic rule" by one observer,[40] is likely to emerge in other developing areas wherever the spread of elections under foreign inspiration either precedes or is intended to coopt strong domestic pressures for democratization.

These observations can be distilled into types of democracies, which, at least initially, are largely shaped by the mode of transition in Latin America, as Figure 3 illustrates. They suggest that democratization by imposition is likely to yield conservative democracies that can not or will not address equity issues. To the extent that imposition originates from outside, however, the result is likely to be some form of electoral authoritarian rule, which can not be considered democracy at all. Pacted transitions are likely to produce corporatist or consociational democracies in which party competition is regulated to varying degrees determined, in part, by the nature of foundational bargains. Transition through reform is likely to bring about competitive democracies, whose political fragility paves the way for an eventual return to authoritarianism. Finally, revolutionary transitions tend to result in one-party dominant democracies, where competition is also regulated. These types are characterized by different mixes and varying degrees of the chief dimensions of democracy: contestation, participation, accountability, and civilian control over the military.

Such predictions are discouraging, but they may be offset by more hopeful observations that affect the contingent choices of contemporary democratizers. On the one hand, the Cold War features of the international system have changed remarkably, and this may offer new opportunities for the reformist mode of transition in Latin America. The failure of two of the three cases cited in this category, Guatemala (1946–1954) and Chile (1970–1973), was profoundly affected by U.S. intervention, motivated in large part by the ideological identification of mass-based reforms with the spread of Soviet influence in the western

Figure 3 Modes of Transition and Types of Democracy

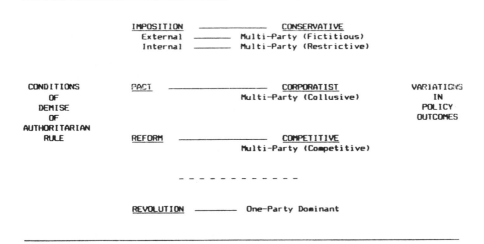

Comparative Politics   October 1990

hemisphere. U.S. intervention against peasant-based movements in Central America has been justified in the same manner. To the extent that the global state system loses its "bipolarity," the credibility of such accusations becomes increasingly difficult to sustain, thus potentially creating more space for mass ascendant political movements. The fact that this mode of transition failed in the past in Latin America does not mean that it will not succeed in the future.[41]

On the other hand, this discussion of modes of transition and varying probabilities for survival has not presumed that democracies will benefit from superior economic performance, which is fortunate given the state of contemporary Latin American economies. Most observers assume that crises in growth, employment, foreign exchange earnings, and debt repayments necessarily bode ill for the consolidation of democratic rule, and few would question the long-run value of an increasing resource base for stability. But austerity may have some perverse advantages, at least for initial survivability. In the context of the terrible economic conditions of the 1980s, the exhaustion of utopian ideologies and even of rival policy prescriptions has become painfully evident. Neither the extreme right nor the extreme left has a plausible alternative system to offer—to themselves or to mass publics. Though populism, driven by diffuse popular expectations and *desencanto* with the rewards of compromised democracy, is always a possibility—witness the experience of Peru and the recent elections in Argentina—it can not deliver the immediate rewards that have been its sustenance in the past.

To the extent that this situation diminishes both the expected benefits and rewards from antisystem activity, it enhances the likelihood of democracies to endure. This suggests a possible hypothesis for future exploration. The relationship between democratization and economic performance, rather than rising or falling in tandem, may be parabolic. Conditions to strike bargains may be most favorable in the midst of protracted austerity, as well as in the midst of sustained plenty. They may be worse when the economy is going through stop-and-go cycles or being hit with sudden windfalls or scarcities. If true, this provides a ray of hope for the otherwise unpromising decade ahead.

Finally, there is no a priori reason why one type of democracy can not be transformed into another, that is to say, why electoral authoritarian regimes, for example, can not evolve into conservative or competitive democracies, or corporatist democracies into more competitive ones. Given the frequency of *pactismo* and the gravity of the equity problem in Latin America, the latter scenario is especially important. While pacted transitions establish an improvisational institutional framework of governance that may become a semipermanent barrier to change, this framework is subject to further modification in the future. Such modification may be brought about preemptively when some ruling groups, having experienced the advantages of democratic rule, become more inclined over time to seek to accommodate potential pressures from below rather than suppress them, or it may occur through the direct pressure of organized social groups.[42] In either case, democratization can prove to be an ongoing process of renewal.

The notion that one type of democracy may gradually evolve into a qualitatively different type suggests that the dynamics of democratic consolidation must differ in important ways from the transition if "freezing" is to be avoided. Because the overriding goal of the transition is to reach some broad social consensus about the goals of society and the acceptable means to achieve them, successful transitions are necessarily characterized by

16

Terry Lynn Karl

accommodation and compromise. But if this emphasis on caution becomes an *overriding* political norm during consolidation, democracies may find it difficult to demonstrate that they are better than their predecessors at resolving fundamental social and economic problems. Thus, consolidation, if it is to be successful, should require skills and commitments from leading actors which are qualitatively different from those exhibited during the transition. In this latter phase, these actors must demonstrate the ability to differentiate political forces rather than to draw them all into a grand coalition, the capacity to define and channel competing political projects rather than seek to keep potentially divisive reforms off the agenda, and the willingness to tackle incremental reforms, especially in the domains of the economy and civil-military relations, rather than defer them to some later date. If the cycle of regime change that has plagued Latin America is to be broken and replaced by an era of protracted democratic rule, democratizers must learn to divide as well as to unite and to raise hopes as well as to dampen expectations.

NOTES

This article was originally presented at the Conference on Latin America at the Threshold of the 1990s, sponsored by the Institute of Latin America of the Chinese Academy of Social Sciences and the Ford Foundation and held in Beijing on June 8–16, 1988. The author wishes to thank Ken Erickson, Richard Fagen, Samuel Valenzuela, an anonymous reviewer, and, most especially, Philippe Schmitter.

1. These questions underlie a number of new studies on democracy. See, for example, Guillermo O'Donnell, Philippe Schmitter, and Laurence Whitehead, eds., *Transitions from Authoritarian Rule*, 4 vols. (Baltimore: The Johns Hopkins University Press, 1986); Paul W. Drake and Eduardo Silva, eds., *Elections and Democratization in Latin America, 1980–1985* (San Diego: Center for Iberian and Latin American Studies, University of California, 1986); Enrique A. Baloyra, *Comparing New Democracies: Transition and Consolidation in Mediterranean Europe and the Southern Cone* (Boulder: Westview Press, 1987); Carlos Huneeus, *Para Vivir La Democracia* (Santiago: Editorial Andante, 1987); and Larry Diamond, Juan J. Linz, and Seymour Martin Lipset, eds., *Democracy in Developing Countries*, 4 vols. (Boulder: Lynne Rienner Publishers, 1988–90).

2. See Dankwart A. Rustow, "Transitions to Democracy: Towards a Dynamic Model," *Comparative Politics*, 2 (April 1970).

3. This statement requires some qualification. J. A. Schumpeter defines democracy as "that institutional arrangement for arriving at political decisions in which individuals acquire the power to decide by means of a competitive struggle for the people's vote" in *Capitalism, Socialism and Democracy* (London: Geo. Allen and Unwin, 1943), p. 269. Under this definition the competition for leadership through free elections is the distinctive feature of democracy. But Schumpeter, unlike Jeane Kirkpatrick and other U.S. policymakers in the 1980s, considered civil liberties a necessary condition for the operation of democracy. Thus, it can not be assumed that he would have shared the current emphasis on the mere presence of elections, which I have elsewhere referred to as "electoralism," that is, "the faith that merely holding elections will channel political action into peaceful contests among elites and accord public legitimacy to the winners in these contests." See Terry Lynn Karl, "Imposing Consent? Electoralism versus Democratization in El Salvador," in Drake and Silva, eds. p. 34.

4. For an example of this approach, see Suzanne Jonas, "Elections and Transitions: The Guatemalan and Nicaraguan Case," in John Booth and Mitchell Seligson, eds., *Elections and Democracy in Central America* (Chapel Hill: University of North Carolina Press, 1989). Jonas and Stein argue against separating political democracy from socioeconomic equity and support "a broader view that meaningful 'transitions' to democracy' [in Central America] involve more sweeping social change on the scale of the major bourgeois and socialist revolutions historically." See Suzanne Jonas and Nancy Stein, "Democracy in Nicaragua," in Suzanne Jonas and Nancy Stein, eds., *Democracy in Latin America* (New York: Bergin and Garvey Publishers, 1990), p. 43.

5. In examining the problem of constructing institutions that can translate the preferences of majorities into public policy, for example, social choice theorists have demonstrated the difficulty of designing decision-making procedures that give equal weight to the preferences of all citizens and that permit the aggregation of these preferences into

17

governmental policies without violating any of the other basic tenets of democratic theory. See, for example, William H. Riker, *Liberalism versus Populism: A Confrontation between the Theory of Democracy and the Theory of Social Choice* (San Francisco: W. H. Freeman and Co., 1982), and the review by Jules Coleman and John Ferejohn, "Democracy and Social Choice," *Ethics*, 97 (October 1986). Theorists of democracy have long grappled with other dilemmas involving notions of social justice and equity. See, for example, Peter Bachrach, *The Theory of Democratic Elitism: A Critique* (Washington, D.C.: University Press of America, 1980); and Carole Pateman, *Participation and Democratic Theory* (Cambridge: Cambridge University Press, 1970).

6. I have drawn the first two dimensions and, to some extent, the third from Robert A. Dahl, *Polyarchy: Participation and Opposition* (New Haven: Yale University Press, 1971). But Dahl, like other democratic theorists, does not emphasize the establishment of civilian control over the military through the limitation of military prerogatives. Indeed, this dimension often appears to be an assumed condition or even an unstated prerequisite in other definitions of democracy. Alfred Stepan, *Rethinking Military Politics: Brazil and the Southern Cone* (Princeton: Princeton University Press, 1988), is an important corrective in this regard. Stepan defines the military's institutional prerogatives as "those areas where, whether challenged or not, the military as an institution assumes they have an acquired right or privilege, formal or informal, to exercise effective control over its internal governance, to play a role within extra-military areas within the state apparatus, or even to structure relationships between the state and political or civil society" (p. 93). The clear determination and limitation of these areas are a measure of civilian control and, in my view, are also a measure of democratization.

7. This formulation originally appeared in Seymour Martin Lipset, "Some Social Requisites of Democracy: Economic Development and Political Legitimacy," *American Political Science Review*, 53 (March 1959).

8. Some proponents of this view often measured the prospects for democracy by per capita gross domestic product, leading the occasional political observer to await the moment when a particular country would cross "the threshold" into democracy. This supposed threshold has varied from country to country. Spain's Lopez Redo once predicted that his country would not become democratic until it reached a per capita income of $2,000. More recently, Mitchell Seligson has argued that Central America needs to approach a per capita income of $250 (in 1957 dollars) and a literacy rate of over 50 percent as a necessary precondition for democratization. See James M. Malloy and Mitchell A. Seligson, eds., *Authoritarians and Democrats: Regime Transition in Latin America* (Pittsburgh: University of Pittsburgh Press, 1987), pp. 7–9.

9. For example, Howard Wiarda, "Toward a Framework for the Study of Political Change in the Iberic-Latin Tradition: The Corporative Model," in Howard Wiarda, ed., *Corporatism and National Development in Latin America* (Boulder: Westview, 1981), argued that Latin America possessed "a political culture and a sociopolitical order that at its core is essentially two-class, authoritarian, traditional, elitist, patrimonial, Catholic, stratified, hierarchical and corporate." A similar argument can be found in Richard N. Morse, "The Heritage of Latin America," in Howard Wiarda, ed., *Politics and Social Change in Latin America* (Amherst: University of Massachusetts Press, 1974).

10. The notion of "civic culture," first introduced by Gabriel Almond and Sidney Verba in *The Civic Culture* (Princeton: Princeton University Press, 1963), sought to analyze the relationship between the political attitudes of a population and the nature of its political system. It was the forerunner of the works on Latin America cited above.

11. This was the basic argument put forward by Leonard Binder et al., eds., *Crises and Sequences in Political Development* (Princeton: Princeton University Press, 1971), and by Eric Nordlinger, "Political Development, Time Sequences and Rates of Change," in Jason L. Finkle and Robert W. Gable, eds., *Political Development and Social Change*, 2nd ed. (New York: John Wiley, 1971).

12. See Barrington Moore, Jr., *Social Origins of Dictatorship and Democracy* (Boston: Beacon Press, 1966).

13. See John Weeks, "An Interpretation of the Central American Past," *Latin American Research Review*, 21 (1986); Enrique Baloyra-Herp, "Reactionary Despotism in Central America," *Journal of Latin American Studies*, 15 (1983); and Jeffrey Paige, "Coffee and Politics in Central America," in Richard Tardanico, ed., *Crisis in the Caribbean Basin* (Beverly Hills: Sage Publications, 1987). In a more recent work, Paige seeks to differentiate his argument from that of Moore. He correctly contends that there is no collision between an industrial bourgeoisie and a landed class in either Costa Rica, El Salvador, or Nicaragua and that the agrarian aristocracy has successfully transformed itself into a modern capitalist class, both conditions that belie Moore's argument. Nonetheless, in Guatemala and El Salvador a landed class continues to exercise domination, and the commercialization of agriculture has not replaced a labor-repressive mode of production, thus providing some important confirmation of Moore. See Jeffrey Paige, "The Social Origins of Dictatorship, Democracy and Socialist Revolution in Central America," paper presented at the Annual Meeting of the American Sociological Association, San Francisco, August 8, 1989.

14. See Guillermo O'Donnell, *Modernization and Bureaucratic-Authoritarianism* (Berkeley: University of

18

Terry Lynn Karl

California, Institute for International Studies, 1973), and Fernando Henrique Cardoso, "Associated-Dependent Development: Theoretical and Practical Implications," in Alfred Stepan, ed., *Authoritarian Brazil* (New Haven: Yale University Press, 1973), pp. 142–178.

15. See Samuel P. Huntington, "Will More Countries Become Democratic?," *Political Science Quarterly*, 99 (1984).

16. Furthermore, through the church's active promotion of "base communities," it could even be argued that contemporary Catholicism contributes to the creation of a uniquely democratic culture by encouraging participation among previously unorganized groups of the urban and rural poor. See Philip Oxhorn, "Bringing the Base Back In: The Democratization of Civil Society under the Chilean Authoritarian Regime" (Ph.D. diss., Harvard University, 1989).

17. For criticism of the O'Donnell hypothesis linking capital deepening to authoritarian rule, see David Collier, ed., *The New Authoritarianism in Latin America* (Princeton: Princeton University Press, 1979), and Karen Remmer and Gilbert Merkx, "Bureaucratic-Authoritarianism Revisited," *Latin American Research Review*, 17 (1982).

18. Albert Hirschman has even claimed that this search can be pernicious. In his view, to lay down strict preconditions for democracy—"dynamic growth *must* be resumed, income distribution *must* be improved, . . . political parties *must* show a cooperative spirit . . ."—may actually encourage the deconsolidation of existing democracies. Hirschman argues that this will almost certainly obstruct constructive thinking about the ways in which democracies may be formed, survive, and even become stronger in the face of and in spite of continuing adversity. See Albert Hirschman, "Dilemmas of Democratic Consolidation in Latin America," unpublished notes for the Sao Paulo Meeting on Democratic Consolidation in Latin America and Southern Europe, 1986.

19. See especially Guillermo O'Donnell and Philippe C. Schmitter, *Tentative Conclusions about Uncertain Transitions* (Baltimore: The Johns Hopkins University Press, 1986), Adam Przeworski, "Some Problems in the Study of the Transition to Democracy," in O'Donnell, Schmitter, and Whitehead, eds., vol. 3, and Adam Przeworski, "Democracy as a Contingent Outcome of Conflicts," in Rune Slagsted and Jon Elster, eds., *Constitutionalism and Democracy* (New York: Cambridge University Press, 1989).

20. See Philippe Schmitter, "Democratic Consolidation of Southern Europe," unpublished manuscript.

21. Evelyne Huber Stephens makes a similar observation in "Economic Development, Social Change and Political Contestation and Inclusion in South America," paper prepared for the Latin American Studies Association, New Orleans, 1988.

22. See Terry Lynn Karl, *The Paradox of Plenty: Oil Booms and Petro-States* (Berkeley: University of California Press, forthcoming), and "Petroleum and Political Pacts: The Transition to Democracy in Venezuela," *Latin American Research Review*, 22 (1986).

23. See Arturo Valenzuela and Samuel Valenzuela, "Los Origines de la Democracia: Reflexiones Teoricas sobre el Caso de Chile," *Estudios Publicos*, 12 (Spring 1983).

24. This is the general thrust of Daniel Levine's analysis of Venezuela, which attributes the emergence of a democratic regime primarily to statecraft and the ability of political actors to compromise. See Daniel Levine, "Venezuela since 1958: The Consolidation of Democratic Politics," in Juan Linz and Alfred Stepan, eds., *The Breakdown of Democratic Regimes: Latin America* (Baltimore: The Johns Hopkins University Press, 1978).

25. An approach of this sort treats regime changes as critical junctures and carries an implicit assumption of patterns of political change characterized by gradualism punctuated by sharp discontinuities. It has a long tradition in the study of politics, but it is especially important in recent work on the "new institutionalism." See, for example, J. G. March and J. P. Olson, "The New Institutionalism: Organizational Factors in Political Life," *American Political Science Review*, 78 (September 1984), 734–749, and Stephen D. Krasner, "Sovereignty: An Institutional Perspective," *Comparative Political Studies*, 21 (April 1988), 66–94. Krasner, though emphasizing political institutions alone rather than the combination of social structures and institutions, also argues that institutions established in the past constrain present choices, that the preferences of individual actors are conditioned by institutional structures, and that historical trajectories are path-dependent. The most recent comparative analysis of patterns of South American and Mexican development adopts a similar framework. Ruth Berins Collier and David Collier, *Shaping the Political Arena: Critical Junctures, the Labor Movement and Regime Dynamics in Latin America* (Princeton: Princeton University Press, forthcoming), is the most ambitious effort to utilize this sort of path-dependent approach. In their comparative analysis, they examine the different trajectories that result from the initial patterns of incorporation of the labor movement into political life.

26. Strictly speaking, the case of Chile from 1970 to 1973 is not an effort of regime transition from authoritarian rule in the sense considered here. Rather, it is better understood as an attempt to move from one type of democracy to another, that is, a move down the vertical scale of the classification scheme in Figure 1 towards a reformist democracy.

19

27. There are interesting moves in this direction in the processes taking place in both Nicaragua and Mexico. Nicaragua is the first revolutionary regime on the continent to hold national elections in which a number of political parties have been able to compete. In 1984, the traditional Liberal and Conservative parties and several small leftist parties competed with the FSLN and won almost 35 percent of the vote. In 1990, the UNO, a coalition of fourteen anti-Sandinista parties, defeated the Sandinistas, who promised to respect the mandate of the electorate. In Mexico, the PRI has begun to permit greater contestation at the municipal and regional level, but these elections are still characterized by numerous restrictions, fraud, and localized violence.

28. There is little information on the dynamics of regime transition in Costa Rica. See Jacobo Schifter, *La fase oculta de la guerra civil en Costa Rica* (San Jose: EDUCA, 1979), and Fabrice Edouard Lehoucq, "Explaining the Origins of Democratic Regimes: Costa Rica in Theoretical Perspective" (Ph.D. diss., Duke University, forthcoming), which applies the notion of democracy as a contingent institutional compromise to this case. On the transition in Peru, see Cynthia Sanborn, "Social Democracy and the Persistence of Populism in Peru" (Ph.D. diss., Harvard University, forthcoming).

29. Even where the military retained control over the transition, however, it systematically engaged in a process of consultation with civilian parties. See Anita Isaacs, "The Obstacles to Democratic Consolidation in Ecuador," paper presented to the Latin American Studies Association, San Juan, Puerto Rico, September 21–23, 1989; Francis Hagopian and Scott Mainwaring, "Democracy in Brazil: Origins, Problems and Prospects," *World Policy Journal* (Summer 1987), 485–514; and Manuel Antonio Garreton, "El Plebiscito de 1988 y la transicion a la democracia" (Santiago: FLACSO, 1988).

30. On these cases, see Charles G. Gillespie, "Uruguay's Transition from Collegial Military-Technocratic Rule," in O'Donnell, Schmitter, and Whitehead, eds.; Jonathan Hartlyn, "Democracy in Colombia: The Politics of Violence and Accommodation," in Diamond, Linz, and Lipset, eds., vol. 4; Alexander W. Wilde, "Conversations among Gentlemen: Oligarchical Democracy in Colombia," in Linz and Stepan, eds., *The Breakdown of Democratic Regimes;* Karl, "Petroleum and Political Pacts."

31. I am grateful to Samuel Valenzuela for this point. See Samuel Valenzuela, *Democratizacion via Reforma: La Expansion del Sufragio en Chile* (Buenos Aires: Ediciones IDES, 1985).

32. The roots of these arrangements can be found in the *Pacto de Punto Fijo* and the *Declaracion de Principios y Programa Minimo de Gobierno*, which were signed prior to the country's first elections by all contending presidential candidates. These agreements bound all signatories to the same basic political and economic program regardless of the electoral outcome. These pacts are described more fully in Karl, "Petroleum and Political Pacts."

33. This distinction was originally drawn by Philippe Schmitter in a conference on "Micro-Foundations of Democracy," University of Chicago, March 1988.

34. This agreement served primarily as a mechanism for partitioning state offices and establishing other temporary forms of power-sharing. Because it excluded powerful, well-organized forces on the left and was never aimed at establishing permanent rules of the game, it does not meet the criteria for a foundational pact.

35. I am grateful to an anonymous reviewer for this observation.

36. Most observers locate the roots of this exploitation in colonial and postcolonial landholding patterns that, slowly or abruptly, concentrated property ownership and dispossessed the majority. Specific social processes not conducive to democratization accompanied these landholding patterns. For example, unlike the reciprocal forms of feudalism which developed in Europe and which may have eventually contributed to widespread norms of reciprocity and community at the local level, the penetration of capitalism altered traditional clientelist relations between landlords and peasants in Latin America from a two-way to a one-way affair. As Paul Harrison, *Inside the Third World: The Anatomy of Poverty* (London: Penguin Books, 1979), p. 105, remarks, "in Latin America the peasant has only duties, the landowner rights." Such social relations have left little residue of notions of mutual obligation or reciprocity between the rich and the poor.

37. I am referring to indicators of inequality here, not absolute poverty. While most of southern Asia and Africa is far poorer than Latin America, their colonial past, patterns of land tenure, and relations of production are quite different. Parts of Asia that have experienced capitalist commercialization of agriculture are now beginning to approximate these same indicators of inequality, but Asia in general has not reached the regional scale of inequality that marks Latin America.

38. One statistic eloquently demonstrates the depth of the crisis. By 1987, Latin America's debt represented 46 percent of the region's GNP and more than four times the value of its exports. See IDB, *Economic and Social Progress in Latin America: 1988 Report* (Washington: Inter-American Development Bank, 1988), p. 541.

39. The notion that especially "successful" authoritarian regimes paradoxically may pose important obstacles for

20

Terry Lynn Karl

democratization can be found in Anita Isaacs, "Dancing with the People: The Politics of Military Rule in Ecuador, 1972–1979" (Ph.D. diss., Oxford University, 1986), and Guillermo O'Donnell, "Challenges to Democratization in Brazil," *World Policy Journal*, 5 (Spring 1988), 281–300.

40. I am grateful to Charles Call for this label.

41. There are important differences here, however, between South America and the Caribbean basin. Military interventions, which have been confined to this latter region in the past, predated the Cold War and are likely to continue after its demise. As the case of Panama shows, the rationale may simply change.

42. Paul Cammack has argued that a ruling coalition might make strategic concessions in its own long-term interest to help sustain democracy, especially after having experienced the failure of militaries to act as reliable allies. See Paul Cammack, "Democratization: A Review of the Issues," *Bulletin of Latin American Research*, 4 (1985), 39–46. There seems to be little evidence for this predicted behavior in the current period, however, and further democratization through mass pressure seems to be more likely.

21

[15]

LATIN AMERICA'S
FRAGILE DEMOCRACIES

Peter Hakim & Abraham F. Lowenthal

Peter Hakim is staff director of the Inter-American Dialogue. *Abraham F. Lowenthal* is executive director of the Inter-American Dialogue and professor of international relations at the University of Southern California in Los Angeles. Their essay draws in part on Chapter Four ("Democracy on Trial") of The Americas in a New World, *the 1990 report of the Inter-American Dialogue, and on an earlier draft that will appear in a forthcoming volume to be published by the National Defense University.*

The turn toward democracy in the Americas has been widely applauded in both the United States and Latin America. The Western Hemisphere, it is often said, is on the verge of becoming fully democratic for the first time in its history—with only Castro's Cuba now standing in the way. Some U.S. officials, present and former, give U.S. policy considerable credit for Latin America's democratic openings, while others think that the U.S. role was marginal at best. There is, however, little disagreement that the regional transition from authoritarian rule was spearheaded by Latin American opposition movements—parties, unions, women's groups, church officials, courageous political leaders, and plain citizens. And no one doubts that in recent years democratic politics has gained important ground throughout most of Latin America and the Caribbean.

Yet democracy in Latin America is far from robust. It is nowhere fully achieved, and it is perhaps most firmly established in those few countries where it was already deeply rooted and vibrant a generation ago. In most other nations, democracy is endangered by political and criminal violence, conflicts between civilian and military authorities, prolonged economic decline, and gross social and economic inequalities. Democratic institutions in much of Latin America remain weak—plagued by rampant corruption, political polarization, and growing public skepticism about government and politics. In some countries, democratic forms are still a facade; in others, they are precarious and vulnerable.

Latin American democracy today needs reinforcement, not premature celebration.

The Trend Toward Democracy

Latin America's democratic progress in the 1980s was real and significant, as encouraging in its way as the collapse of communist rule in Eastern and Central Europe. In country after country, military regimes and personalist dictatorships gave way to elected civilian governments. In the final months of the decade, Brazil held its first direct presidential elections since 1960 and Chile its first since 1970—thus bringing civilian presidents to office in every country of South America for the first time in a generation. Nicaragua's elections in February 1990 were the most open and competitive in that country's history, and elected civilian governments are today in place in every nation of Central America. At the beginning of 1991, Fidel Castro's regime in Cuba remains the only consolidated and unambiguously authoritarian government still ruling in Latin America.

Government office, if not always power, is now usually transferred peacefully from one elected president to another throughout Latin America. In recent years, incumbent administrations have yielded office to elected opponents in countries as diverse as Argentina, Bolivia, the Dominican Republic, Ecuador, Jamaica, Peru, and Uruguay—in some cases for the first time in memory. Not since 1928 had one democratically elected president succeeded another in Argentina before Carlos Menem replaced Raúl Alfonsín in 1989. In the face of economic crisis and terrorist threats, Peru has held three consecutive presidential elections for the first time in nearly a century. In economically traumatized Bolivia, frequent military coups have given way to three successive elections.

Even in countries where elections have remained flawed, important democratic gains have been registered. Although the balloting was marred by credible charges of fraud, Mexico held its most competitive presidential contest in more than a generation in 1988, and popular pressures are building for the further opening of Mexican politics. Despite severe restrictions on political participation in most Central American countries, elections have come to be accepted as the only legitimate route to office in that region. The 1989 presidential vote in Paraguay—called after a military coup ended Alfredo Stroessner's 35 years of dictatorial rule—was organized too hastily to be fairly contested; it did, however, allow opposition parties to campaign, express dissent, and begin mobilizing support. By nullifying Panama's national elections in 1989, General Manuel Antonio Noriega only underscored the massive popular repudiation of his regime. After several failed attempts to hold free elections in Haiti following the downfall of the Duvalier dynasty, an internationally supervised presidential vote finally took place in December 1990.

No longer is it commonly accepted that Latin America is somehow predisposed toward authoritarian rule, or that its culture is inherently antidemocratic. Year by year, it has become more evident that most Latin Americans embrace the fundamental democratic idea—that government authority must derive from the uncoerced consent of the majority, tested regularly through competitive and broadly participatory elections. It is striking that the commitment to building democracy has thus far even survived prolonged hyperinflation in Argentina, Bolivia, Brazil, and Peru; democratic institutions in many European nations in the 1920s and 1930s crumbled under similar circumstances.

It was not many years ago that self-proclaimed military "guardians" on the right and revolutionary "vanguards" on the left throughout Latin America openly expressed their disdain for democratic procedures—and could claim some significant following. In recent years, however, a wide spectrum of Latin American opinion has come to recognize the value of democracy: military officers and former guerrillas as well as intellectuals, corporate executives, small entrepreneurs, and religious leaders. But even as democratic ideals are now widely embraced, the practice of democracy remains very uneven across the region.

Costa Rica, Venezuela, Jamaica, and some of the smaller Caribbean countries have enjoyed uninterrupted democratic rule for more than a generation. Their political and civic institutions are relatively strong, human rights are respected, and civilian authorities exercise firm control over the armed forces. The prospects for sustaining vigorous democracy may be even more promising in Chile and Uruguay. Although they suffered years of military rule in the 1970s and 1980s and unsettling remnants from that period persist, the two countries boast long democratic traditions and solid representative institutions.

Elsewhere in the region, however, democracy is troubled—in some places, deeply so. The tasks of reinforcing and expanding democracy in the Hemisphere must begin with a sober appraisal of the severe challenges it faces.

Political Violence

In four countries—Colombia, Peru, Guatemala, and El Salvador—governments face insurgent threats to their effective control of national territory. Each of them confronts a vicious cycle of violence and counterviolence that, to varying degrees and in different ways, is undermining the institutions, procedures, and values essential to democracy. As long as the violence continues, democratic practice will remain truncated and precarious. The armed forces will intrude in political decisions, the authority of civilian leaders and institutions will be compromised, economic progress will be blocked, politics will remain polarized, and human rights abuses will persist at levels that destroy confidence in the democratic process.

Colombia continues to suffer repeated outbreaks of intense insurgent violence even as guerrilla activity overall has declined in the past several years. Sustained negotiating efforts by successive Colombian governments have led several guerrilla groups to stop fighting and enter politics. Two significant groups, however, continue to do battle, and the government has not been able to guarantee the security of the former guerrilla leaders who have become active politically within the democratic system. Nearly a thousand of them have been murdered in the past three years, including two presidential aspirants and scores of mayoral candidates. Their deaths, along with the kidnapping of many prominent citizens and the gangland-style killing of the leading candidate for president in the 1990 election, reflect the pervasive insecurity that besets Colombia. But insurgent movements are by no means the only menace to democratic politics in Colombia. A greater danger may come from the relentless violence of criminal drug organizations and paramilitary groups—often condoned or tolerated by national security forces—that operate in complex and shifting alliances with each other and with the remaining guerrilla fighters.

As devastating as the violence has been, Colombia's political institutions continue to demonstrate resilience and flexibility. The country's political leaders and most citizens remain committed to democratic rule, and the constitutional reform process now underway may strengthen that commitment. But democratic politics is being severely tested in Colombia, and its survival cannot be guaranteed.

El Salvador and Guatemala, in contrast to Colombia, lack established democratic institutions and traditions. After decades of almost uninterrupted military rule, elected civilian governments came to office in both nations in the mid-1980s amid prolonged guerrilla insurgencies. Since then, national and local elections have become somewhat more competitive, and have gained a significant measure of international approval. In neither country, however, are all major political constituencies represented at the polls, nor has democratic practice extended much beyond periodic and restricted elections. Civilian leaders have failed either to establish control over the armed forces or to end the violence that wracks both societies.

During the past decade of civil war in El Salvador, some 70,000 persons have died and hundreds of thousands have been displaced from their homes. Both the guerrillas and state security forces have been guilty of assassinations, random killings of citizens, and cruel violations of basic human rights. Neither side is now able to prevail by force of arms. The insurgent forces control large expanses of territory, but have little prospect of military victory. The army commands sufficient firepower to contain the guerrilla advances, but not to force their surrender.

The grim prospect of a destructive military stalemate, combined with the tempering of ideological passions both domestically and internationally following the end of the Cold War, may finally be propelling El Salvador toward peace. After a year of slow progress, UN-mediated negotiations supported by both the United States and the Soviet Union have in recent months produced some significant agreements between the guerrillas and the government that could well point the way toward a settlement. The obstacles to peace are still formidable, however. It is by no means clear yet whether the intransigence of hardliners on both sides can be overcome and the necessary compromises achieved. And even if a peace settlement is reached, the long years of fighting are bound to leave behind a bitter legacy of mistrust and division, making the task of building stable democracy daunting.

In Guatemala, more than 35 years of guerrilla violence and counterinsurgency have claimed the lives of over 100,000 civilians, while many thousands of others have been imprisoned, tortured, or displaced from their homes. By 1986, when the first civilian president in a generation came to office, the army controlled most of the countryside and appeared to have routed the guerrillas. But in the past two years, the rebels have regrouped their forces and resisted efforts to dislodge them from their strongholds. In recent months the guerrillas and the government have begun unprecedented face-to-face negotiations, but a peace settlement still appears a long way off, if it is possible at all.

The insurgency in Guatemala does not challenge governmental control, nor is it the central focus of national politics. But it has led to the persistent involvement of the armed forces in Guatemalan politics and to their continued repressive tactics in rural areas. The war is fueled by bitter ethnic and class divisions, which in themselves are a major obstruction to democratic progress. Electoral politics has meant little for Guatemala's impoverished indigenous majority, which has long been dominated by an urban minority of European ancestry. The 1990-91 elections, which were tarnished by violence among competing political parties, promise no immediate change. A profound process of national reform will be necessary to end the violence in Guatemala.

The Shining Path and Tupac Amaru insurgencies in Peru have become entrenched and virulent. With no apparent external support, the Shining Path has spread gradually through much of Peru since 1980. In the past five years, it has demonstrated a growing capacity to mobilize rural and urban support, disrupt the country's economy, intimidate local government officials, and inflict violence on a large scale. The Tupac Amaru movement is less powerful, but its targeted violence is also severely weakening the Peruvian state. Neither group has shown any inclination so far to enter peace negotiations with the government.

Some 20,000 deaths in Peru during the past ten years have been attributed to the guerrilla groups and the military forces battling them, and the killing is expanding. Both sides engage in pervasive human rights abuses. More than half of Peru's population has been placed under one form or another of emergency military rule. Democratic practice is more and more restricted to Peru's urban centers, and even there it is threatened.

The drug trade adds to the violence in Peru and complicates government efforts to control the guerrillas. The Shining Path finances itself partly by taxing drug traffickers and protecting peasant coca growers. Despite intense pressure from Washington, successive Peruvian governments have been reluctant to engage the army in the fight against the narcotics network because they are concerned that intensifying and militarizing the antidrug campaign will produce new recruits for the insurgents and expand the influence of the armed forces. President Fujimori has recently accepted U.S. support for such a military effort, but only as a condition for desperately needed economic assistance.

The Peruvian government is still freely elected, but it operates under restrictive and repressive conditions and with decreasing authority. Peru today is battling against national disintegration and mounting despair.

Strong Armies and Fragile Polities

Even where insurgents do not threaten, democratic rule is often challenged by armed forces that are not effectively subordinated to civilian control. Civil-military relations vary considerably from country to country in Latin America, but they remain troublesome nearly everywhere and are a source of serious tension in many nations. Constitutional democracy requires that all military forces be subordinate to the effective professional and political direction of elected civilian authorities. Today only a handful of Latin American countries—Costa Rica, Mexico, Venezuela, and the Commonwealth nations of the Caribbean—fully meet that basic condition.

In Guatemala and El Salvador, the military virtually defines the extent of civilian authority and influences most aspects of government policy. The armed forces of Bolivia, Ecuador, Honduras, Nicaragua, and Peru retain so much institutional autonomy that they are at best "conditionally subordinate" to civilian officials. Panama's security forces remain an active threat to democratic rule, despite the cashiering of more than 400 senior officials during a year-and-a-half-long effort to turn the army into a civilian-run police force. In Argentina, the armed forces have repeatedly confronted civilian authorities in the past several years, with debilitating effects on democratic institutions. Brazil has avoided such confrontations, but to some extent by making preemptive concessions to the military. In Haiti, military elements have operated for years as a rogue force. The army's move late in 1990 to prevent a coup by Duvalier loyalists, coupled with the new president's dismissal of most senior commanders, may point the way to a more responsible military, but hardly one that is securely under civilian direction.

In Chile and Uruguay, where civilians had seemed firmly in control until the armed coups of the early 1970s, military regimes have left a legacy of unresolved civil-military conflicts, some of them embedded in law. Chile's civil government operates within a series of legal restraints imposed by the armed forces before they left power. Former dictator Augusto Pinochet is still commander of the army and cannot legally be removed by Chile's elected president. Although the civilian governments of both Uruguay and Chile are gradually and skillfully asserting greater authority over their armed forces, the military's influence on policy remains strong in both nations.

Although direct military rule is now exceptional in Latin America, extensive military influence undermines the authority of elected civilian leaders, and the deterrents to further military intervention are still weak throughout the region. Until the armed forces are fully subordinate to elected civilian authority, democracy will remain at risk. In some places, armies may again seize power in the 1990s, but even where they do not, they will remain a significant obstacle to democratic advance.

Political violence and military incursions into politics are not the only obstacles to consolidating Latin American democracy. Effective democratic practice requires structured and dependable institutions, accepted rules of political conduct, and established judicial procedures. In their absence, politics can become personalized and erratic.

Legislatures and judicial systems in much of Latin America still lack the autonomy, stature, resources, and competence needed to carry out all of their constitutional functions fully. Courts are overburdened and their proceedings, both criminal and civil, are routinely delayed for years. Judges are, for the most part, poorly trained and paid, and they lack the funding to conduct investigations and administer justice effectively. In many places, judicial decisions are heavily influenced by political considerations, intimidation, or outright corruption.

Legislative systems face similar problems. Presidents, frustrated by delay and indecision, frequently resort to exceptional procedures to bypass the legislative process. In doing so, they debase the formal institutions of government, compromise legal norms, and undercut democratic legitimacy. This is especially troubling because there has been evidence in several countries—Brazil, Argentina, and Uruguay among them—that democratic institutions grow stronger when they are respected by all major political actors.

Except in a few nations, notably Chile and Uruguay, political parties in many countries of Latin America and the Caribbean have long lacked effective ties to regular constituencies and are often little more than vehicles for contesting elections and distributing patronage. They rarely offer coherent programs and are frequently manipulated to serve the personal ambitions of their leaders. For example Ecuador, with its array of small parties of constantly shifting loyalties, is plagued by these problems. So is the Dominican Republic, where old-fashioned *caudillismo* is combined with political opportunism. Democratic practice under such conditions is incomplete and crisis-prone.

Where political parties are weak, the media, particularly television, often exert a great and immediate influence on political choice, and sharp swings of public opinion are common. These factors contributed to the quick rise from obscurity to prominence and the subsequent election of independent presidential candidates without national party affiliation in Brazil and Peru. In both countries it has been difficult for the new and inexperienced presidents to govern without the organized support needed to forge legislative majorities and mobilize popular backing on policy issues.

Democracy in Latin America is also hampered by the lack of sustained citizen participation in political life. Although the waning of authoritarian rule sparked the emergence and growth of voluntary organizations in country after country, most nations of the region still lack a vigorous array of nongovernmental institutions through which the demands of ordinary people can be expressed, mediated, and consistently brought to the attention of authorities. In much of the region, trade unions, business groups, professional organizations, and civic associations remain weak and fragmented, and are too narrowly based to play effective political roles. In many countries, the press represents only a limited range of opinions, and does not serve as an effective check on corruption or the abuse of power.

Even in those nations with relatively strong political and judicial institutions, democratic governance is threatened when citizens stop participating actively in political life because of disillusionment, apathy, or a sense that they have been unfairly excluded or disadvantaged. Throughout much of Latin America today there is a growing distrust of politics. That voters in so many countries are casting their ballots for political newcomers reflects, in part, their low regard for established democratic leaders as well as their frustration with continued economic and social deterioration. Even more troubling, abstention from elections and skepticism about their significance are sharply on the rise. In some countries, growing emigration by professionals, entrepreneurs, and students is another manifestation of deep disaffection.

Economic Crisis

Each of these threats to democratic governance in Latin America—political violence, military incursions into politics, fragile institutions, and alienated citizens—has been greatly exacerbated by the region's economic crisis.

Since the debt crisis struck in 1982, the region has been mired in depression, its deepest and most prolonged ever. Per capita income has fallen by more than 10 percent for the region as a whole, and some countries have fared much worse—for example, in Peru, Argentina, and Nicaragua, per capita income has plunged 25 percent or more. In only two countries, Chile and Colombia, have living standards improved over the past ten years, though by very small amounts.

The cumulative effects of eight years of depression now pose severe obstacles to economic recovery and renewed growth:

- Latin America's debt burdens are enormous. Its aggregate debt today exceeds $420 billion, $100 billion greater than in 1982. Each year, Latin America pays out about $25 billion more in interest and principal than it obtains in new loans. That net outflow—amounting to 3 percent of the region's total output and more than 20 percent of its exports—deprives Latin American countries of the resources needed for investment and crucial imports. It also keeps budget deficits high, fuels inflation, and saps investor confidence.

- Record levels of inflation plague many countries. The average annual rate of inflation exceeded 1,000 percent for Latin America in 1990, more than 10 times higher than in 1982. Four countries—Brazil, Argentina, Peru, and Nicaragua—have been battling hyperinflation. Only Mexico, Costa Rica, and Bolivia have substantially reduced inflation from 1982 levels.

- Eight years of low investment—averaging some 16 percent of Gross Domestic Product (GDP) compared to 22 percent during the 1970s—have left Latin American industry with deteriorating physical plants, outdated technologies, and a lagging ability to compete internationally.

- More people than ever are trapped in poverty. Unemployment and underemployment are widespread in nearly every country. Wages have deteriorated badly, by 50 percent or more in some places. The quality of housing, medical care, and education has steadily worsened. Crime rates have surged. Life has gotten much harder in Latin America, and women and children are suffering the most.

- All of these economic ills have produced a devastating loss of confidence. Large numbers of people from all classes are leaving the region. Few countries are able to attract foreign investment, while domestic capital flight continues to drain resources. In country after country, economic distress has eroded the credibility of national leaders and reduced their capacity to govern.

Austerity has seemingly become a permanent fact of life in much of the region. In only a few countries are there solid prospects for sustained economic improvement anytime soon. Economic adversity is threatening Latin American democracy in several ways.

Worsening economic conditions help to sustain the Shining Path and other insurgencies. In some countries, economic "shock" treatments to halt rampant inflation have provoked outbreaks of violence. In Venezuela, more than 300 people died in riots protesting rises in the price of staple products. Food riots in Argentina contributed to President Alfonsín's decision to transfer power to President-elect Menem six months before the end of his constitutional term. Social and economic reversals were a main cause of Trinidad's violent uprising in July 1990. Other outbursts have occurred in Brazil and the Dominican Republic, and they can be expected elsewhere. In some places where large-scale group violence has not erupted, street crime and a pervasive sense of personal insecurity have become widespread, producing demands for order that are sometimes pursued at the expense of law.

Democratically elected leaders who have failed to stem economic decline have lost support and authority, thereby making it harder for them to institute and sustain the painful adjustments required for economic improvement. "Stop-and-go" policies, in turn, further damage economic performance and intensify political instability. In recent years, incumbent parties have only very rarely been able to retain office for more than one term. As one democratic leader after another loses support, the credibility of democratic rule itself is endangered.

Programs of market-oriented economic liberalization have become politically divisive. Even though such reforms have been widely adopted throughout Latin America and the Caribbean, they continue to face stiff resistance from many quarters. Economic reform programs in some countries have further concentrated income and wealth, and thus widened the already large gap between the rich and the poor. Social cohesion and political stability are put at risk as class divisions deepen.

If market strategies are unable to restore growth soon and to address such fundamental problems as poverty and inequity, advocates of alternative economic approaches are likely to gain increasing electoral strength. Politics then may become more polarized, and calls may intensify for restrictions to block opponents of current policies from power. In some countries, Argentina and Mexico among them, governments already seem tempted to circumvent or distort democratic processes in order to overcome opposition to their economic policies.

Requisites for Democratic Consolidation

It is not easy to make democracy work. Presidents must be strong enough to lead and command respect, but their power cannot be absolute. Legislatures must have the authority to curb executive power, but they must also be ready to cooperate and accept reasonable compromise. Courts must be independent, bound only to the rule of law. Political parties must be more than vehicles for protest or for winning elections; they must be able to represent their supporters effectively and formulate program and policy alternatives. It is proper for interest groups to serve their special constituencies, but they must also respect the rights and interests of others. Leaders and citizens alike must be willing to live with uncertainty and to accept unfavorable political outcomes that result from democratic procedures. Democracy draws its strength from a politically active populace and a multiplicity of representative institutions operating within legal and constitutional norms. Only a handful of Latin American countries can yet meet these standards.

With few exceptions, the countries of Latin America have achieved the first critical stage in the transition to democracy. Throughout the region, authoritarian regimes have yielded to elected governments. But elections—even where they are fully free and fair and are scheduled on a regular basis—are not enough by themselves to produce or sustain democratic rule. Few nations have yet managed to develop strong representative institutions that can maintain the rule of law, protect the rights of all citizens, effectively respond to popular demands, and give ordinary people a continuing, active voice in public policy decisions. Almost everywhere, progress toward meeting these and other vital requirements of democracy has been slow and painful, and some countries have, in fact, regressed in recent years.

For democratic institutions to take firm root and flourish in Latin America, four difficult challenges must be met.

First, the region's remaining internal wars must be ended. Democratic politics cannot thrive in settings where civil strife divides societies, expands the political role of armies, retards economic progress, and produces gross human rights abuses.

Second, the armed forces must be more effectively subordinated to the political control of civilian governments. In many nations this will require a profound rethinking of the mission and purposes of the military.

Third, many countries of the region have yet to curtail pervasive violations of human rights. Democratic practice and the rule of law cannot be consolidated unless the rights of political dissidents, minorities, and other vulnerable groups are respected and protected.

Finally, only a handful of nations have been able to restore economic stability and growth and to create opportunities for disadvantaged groups. Democratic institutions cannot thrive under conditions of prolonged economic hardship—when millions of citizens must survive without jobs, adequate shelter and nutrition, basic education, or much hope for the future.

Each of these challenges is daunting, even for those nations where democracy has begun to take root. They are not impossible to overcome, however. Acting individually and in concert, there is much that the countries of the Americas can do to protect, strengthen, and extend democratic politics in the 1990s.

Internal Wars

Direct negotiation between the warring parties is the best way to end Latin America's ongoing insurgencies. Nicaragua's decade-long war was resolved by a negotiated settlement, and the government and guerrillas now appear close to agreement in El Salvador. Negotiating efforts in Colombia have not yet stopped all guerrilla violence, but they have led several insurgent groups to lay down their arms and begin to compete politically.

A settlement can only be achieved, of course, when both sides—the guerrillas and the government forces—are prepared to make significant concessions for peace. But negotiations have a far greater chance of succeeding when they have the sustained and unambiguous support of many countries both within and outside the Hemisphere, including the external backers of the combatants. Peacemaking efforts by the UN and the Organization of American States can also play a vital role—as they did in Nicaragua and are doing in El Salvador.

Only the insurgencies in Peru now seem immune to a negotiated solution. The Peruvian government should keep open the future possibility of negotiations, but the immediate need is to design and implement a more effective strategy for combatting the guerrillas. Such a strategy must include far greater attention to remedying the economic deprivation and social injustice that are fueling the violence—and this, in turn, will require external financial aid, given Peru's desperate shortage of resources. It is also imperative that the armed forces stop their massive abuse of human rights, which adds both to the violence and to the appeal of the guerrillas. Destroying democratic values is no way to protect democracy.

Civil-Military Relations

There is no ready-made formula that civilian authorities can adopt to establish control over their armed forces. That task will remain difficult as long as civilian governments are weak and imbalances persist between fragile political institutions and strong military establishments. Lasting changes in civil-military relations will require basic shifts in the attitudes of Latin American officers that may well take a generation or longer to achieve.

Democratic leaders must maintain open communications with the armed forces, persistently seeking to build mutual confidence and to define an appropriate and agreed-upon mission for the military. They must also at times stand up to military officials and reject their intrusions into political affairs. It is crucial, in turn, for civilian politicians to resist the temptation to call on the armed forces to mediate political conflicts, endorse partisan causes, or promote particular candidates for office.

Military assistance programs from abroad must be designed to reinforce civilian control of the armed forces. Care must be taken not to aggravate the current imbalances between civilian and military institutions. Training programs in military strategy and other defense issues, like those offered at the Inter-American Defense College in Washington, should incorporate many more civilian participants in an effort to build civilian competence in Latin America to manage national security policy. In addition, the United States and other nations should make sure that efforts to fight the narcotics trade in places like Peru, Colombia, and Bolivia do not enmesh armies in political tasks and undercut civilian authority.

Human Rights

All nations of the Hemisphere, individually and together, can and must work harder to strengthen safeguards against human rights abuses. Stronger internal measures are urgently needed in many countries, some of which clearly require, in the first instance, stronger civilian control over military and police forces. National human rights offices, such as the one recently established in Mexico, can play an effective role in investigating, publicizing, and redressing violations—but they must be granted the authority, independence, and resources necessary to carry out their functions.

Latin American and U.S. leaders should also take action to broaden the mandate and expand the resources of the three official inter-American institutions responsible for protecting human rights (i.e., the Inter-American Commission, Court, and Institute), all of which are making significant contributions. The network of nongovernmental organizations that professionally and objectively monitor human rights should also be supported. Democratic governments should not provide economic or military assistance to regimes that systematically violate basic human rights.

Wherever there is the danger that national elections will be marred by fraud, manipulation, or violence, the inter-American community should stand ready to provide electoral monitors and other needed assistance. When such assistance is made available on a multilateral basis with respect for the host nation's sovereignty and laws, it can build confidence in the electoral process and increase prospects that the outcome will be accepted as fair by all parties. In 1990 alone, internationally monitored elections in Nicaragua, Chile, and Haiti constituted decisive steps toward political opening in those countries.

Economic recovery

The resumption of economic growth, combined with concrete measures to alleviate poverty and inequity, would contribute most to restoring confidence in democratic rule in Latin America. The task of economic recovery is largely up to each country—and most of the region's countries are struggling to restructure their economies and make them more productive. They are taking action to curtail budget deficits and bring inflation under control, giving new emphasis to extending trade and foreign investment, and turning toward markets and private enterprise.

The countries of Latin America, however, still need help from outside. External debt burdens continue to frustrate economic recovery and growth in all but a few countries of the region. The recent agreement among the United States and other industrial countries to slash Poland's debt was based on that country's enormous needs, its determined efforts to restructure its economy along market lines, and its commitment to building democracy. Most nations of Latin America meet all three criteria and deserve the same relief that was extended to Poland.

Perhaps even more than debt relief, Latin America requires open markets for its products and access to investment capital. The United States and other industrial countries should redouble their efforts to achieve a successful conclusion to the Uruguay Round of GATT negotiations, and Washington should move forward with its declared intention to strengthen hemispheric trade links. Even under the best of international circumstances, however, no Latin American country will be able to recover its economic vitality and address the needs of its people unless it takes the necessary measures to put its own house in order.

The hard fact is that it will take years of struggle to secure democratic stability in most countries of Latin America. There will be setbacks—even outright failures—in some places. Even where progress is made, democratic institutions will remain vulnerable for decades to come. The democratic idea has been gaining important ground in the Western Hemisphere, as in other regions of the world, but vigorous and consolidated democratic rule is still to be achieved. That is the challenge of the 1990s.

NOTES

The authors gratefully acknowledge the helpful comments on earlier drafts of Bruce Bagley, Julio Cotler, Liliana De Riz, Samuel Fitch, Manuel Antonio Garretón, J.A. Guilhon Albuquerque, Frances Hagopian, Jonathan Hartlyn, Bolívar Lamounier, Scott Mainwaring, Cynthia McClintock, Gabriel Murillo, Kenneth Sharpe, and Francisco Weffort.

[16]

Political Studies (1992), XL, Special Issue, 146–159

The Alternatives to 'Liberal Democracy': a Latin American Perspective

LAURENCE WHITEHEAD

Although *some* conventional liberal democratic regimes are likely to become consolidated in Latin America, the dominant pattern is better understood as 'democracy by default', and in a few cases little more than 'facade democracy' is to be expected. This paper reviews the major factors accounting for the fragility, instability and policy ineffectiveness of many of these new regimes. Although current fiscal crises lend some plausibility to the 'neo-liberal' analyses of democratization, the paper argues that in the longer run consolidated democracies will tend to develop a range of 'social democratic', participatory and interventionist features that are at variance with the neo-liberal model. Latin American nation-states are relatively well integrated and contain a stock of human and social resources that should favour constitutional outcomes, so that although many of these new democracies will remain provisional and incomplete for the time being, they possess the potential for subsequent extension and entrenchment.

There is one good reason for using Latin American evidence to document general arguments in comparative politics, and one bad reason. The *good* reason is that the subcontinent offers a sufficiently wide array of well-elaborated political structures and experiments to provide fertile ground for systematic comparative analysis. (For example, there is at least one long-standing 'model' liberal democracy – Costa Rica; one 'model' communist state – Cuba; one neocolonial democracy – Puerto Rico; one counter-insurgency regime – Guatemala; and a large range of intermediate political forms, many of them insecure and contested.) The *bad* reason is that observers from other regions have sometimes invoked stylized or even stereotypal images of Latin American politics to illustrate – or dramatize – arguments that would not be regarded as solid if applied to better-known (more 'serious') political processes.

With regard to liberal democracy and its alternatives, Latin American experience can be particularly rich and rewarding for comparativists, but only if they guard against the danger mentioned. The subcontinent contains 20 republics, nearly all with a century or more of independent political existence. (Moreover, it is becoming increasingly fruitful to add the various newer island states of the Caribbean, and to make select extra-regional comparisons with, for example, Spain, Portugal and the Philippines.) These 20 republics are all in a sense 'children of the French revolution' and their political history is impregnated with references to European and North American influences and parallels. They were in the vanguard of international liberalism when they repudiated monarchism, aristocracy and slavery in the past century, and at least in theory their governments have long rested on the principle of popular

0032–3217/92/Special Issue/146–14/$03.00 © 1992 *Political Studies* sovereignty.[1] However, these early experiments with an oligarchic[2] form of liberal democracy (often closely associated with efforts to reassure foreign investors and to strengthen market economies) produced very varied results. The region offers every kind of example: slow but steady progress; rapid advance followed by abrupt reversal; gradual disintegration; spectacular downfall; and equally spectacular emergence out of apparently overwhelming adversity. It is a central and ongoing question of political debate in nearly all of these countries which of these characterizations applies to which periods, and why. These debates are so intense and heartfelt because they express an almost permanent sense of insecurity and uncertainty about the solidity and relative performance of the various regimes in question.

These Latin American debates about the nature of democracy in what many would call peripheral and dependent societies, about the erratic history of liberalism and constitutionalism in the region, and about the limited advantages and uncertain prospects of this type of political regime, all raise questions that are of far more than purely regional interest. Indeed it may be a salutary corrective to some of the more static and complacent versions of democratic theory (for example in the Anglo-Saxon contractarian tradition) to re-examine implicit assumptions concerning the natural or inevitably superior nature of liberal democracy within a setting where such claims also require persuasive demonstration. It is not possible in this brief paper to do justice to the complex and controversial Latin American-based discussions on these themes,[3] and indeed what non-regionalists initially require are some brief unhedged judgements that may teeter on the brink of stereotyping, despite the disclaimer

---

[1] François-Xavier Guerra is currently disinterring much neglected evidence on the nature and importance of the formal systems of political representation that operated during the nineteenth century. See his 'Les Avatars de la représentation en Amérique Latine au 19eme siécle' in Georges Couffignal (ed.), *Réinventer la Démocratie* (Paris, Presses de la Fondation Nationale des Sciences Politiques, 1992). For an alternative view see G. Dealy 'The tradition of monistic democracy in Latin America', *Journal of the History of Ideas*, 35 (Oct.–Dec. 1974).

[2] 'Oligarchic' forms of electoral represenation were widespread in Latin America in the late nineteenth and early twentieth centuries. Export-led growth encouraged the establishment of constitutional regimes which could be relied on to honour contracts with foreign traders and investors. Local power was highly concentrated in the hand of a property-owing elite (usually of exporters) and a very restricted franchise ensured that such 'oligarchs' were well represented in national assemblies. For an illuminating case study of this oligarchic electoral system, which also includes a comparative discussion, see Michael J. Gonzales, 'Planters and politics in Peru', *Journal of Latin American Studies*, 23:3 (Oct. 1991).

[3] Major reference points include G. O'Donnell, P. Schmitter and L. Whitehead (eds), *Transitions from Authoritarian Rule: Prospects for Democracy* (Baltimore, Johns Hopkins University Press, 1986); L. Diamond, J. Linz and S. M. Lipset (eds), *Democracy in Developing Countries: Latin America* (London, Adamantine Press, 1989); B. Stallings and R. Kaufman (eds), *Debt and Democracy in Latin America* (London, Westview Press, 1989); R. Pastor (ed.), *Democracy in the Americas: Stopping the Pendulum* (New York, Homes & Meier, 1989); Giuseppe di Palma, *To Craft Democracies* (Berkeley, California University Press, 1990); A. F. Lowenthal (ed.), *Exporting Democracy: the United States and Latin America* (Baltimore, Johns Hopkins University Press, 1991). In addition to these widely disseminated publications there is an explosion of literature with more restricted circulation, some of it very worthwhile. Illustrative examples include *Quel Avenir Pour la Démocratie en Amérique Latine?* (Paris, Editions du CNRS, 1989); F. W. Reis and G. O'Donnell (eds), *A democracia no Brasil: dilemas e perspectivas* (Sao Paulo, Vértice, 1988); Carlos Strasser, *Para Una Teoria de la Democracia Posible* (Buenos Aires, Grupo Editor, Latinoamericano, 2 vols, 1990, 1991); and some of the 40 or so *cuadernos de CAPEL* published since 1985 by the Comite de Asesoria y Promoción Electoral of the Inter-American Institute of Human Rights, San José, Costa Rica, such as No. 23, *La Constitución Norteamericana y su Influencia en Latino América*, and No. 24, *La Constitución de Cádiz y su Influencia en América*.

above. The obvious (oversimplified) questions include: why has there been such a sustained swing towards democratic forms of governance in the region over the past 20 years? Are the old alternatives to liberal democracy really finished, or just in abeyance? What *kind* of democracy is emerging – how consolidated, how participatory, how efficient, and so on? For example, is the real alternative to stable liberal democracy unstable populist democracy? How restrictive are the conditions under which the latter can evolve toward the former? Answers to these regional questions should provide evidence helping to address, and perhaps to reformulate, some of the general ideals about liberal democracy elaborated elsewhere in this volume.

First, why has the region seen a strong move to democratic forms of government since the mid-1970s? What follows are broad-brush tendency statements, without all the necessary qualifications and exceptions. The 1980s witnessed the latest in a succession of democratizing 'waves' that punctuate the history of the region (as indeed they also punctuate European history). 1944–8 and 1955–62 were also powerful movements – the first cut short by the cold war and the second by the aftershocks of the Cuban revolution. Neither had the breadth or momentum of the past decade. Any explanation must be multi-causal and here there is only space to list the factors without properly weighting them. For one thing, neither the cold war nor the Cuban revolution intervened to cut short the process. (The Nicaraguan revolution may arguably have produced some such effect in Central America, but not more generally.) For another, the business interests and foreign investors who had rallied to authoritarian military regimes in the 1960s began to see these overly statist and apparently un-accountable governments as a source of danger rather than of protection, so they withdrew their support. (There were several sources of danger here: uncontrollable military expenditure and disrespect for private enterprise; counterproductive and indiscriminate use of repression and censorship; inability to institutionalize a smooth succession, and so on.) On the economic front, unrestricted sovereign lending surged and then went into reverse, leaving overconfident authoritarian regimes suddenly responsible for unmanageable fiscal crises. But perhaps a more sophisticated political explanation is required here. In most countries authoritarian rule was sufficiently durable and successful to 'sober up' or 'deradicalize' the opposition. A return to democracy no longer seemed so dangerous, because the opponents of military rule had learnt a severe lesson. The same idea can be expressed in different terms by saying that democratization was the product of a stalemate. Reformist, populist or socialist projects had been attempted and had failed; reactionary authoritarian projects had also been attempted and had also failed. All the main contenders for power were therefore forced to conclude that they would do better by settling for a 'second-best' outcome – a framework of rules within which they could compete without facing persecution, although without much hope of implementing their full programmes. In such circumstances, of course, many political contenders will have some non-democratic antecedents, and so risk the suspicion (which may initially be justified) that their new-found espousal of democracy is merely instrumental and insincere. Provisional democratic credentials have to be fairly readily available, if broad-based democratization is to proceed, although final judgements can only be made *post-mortem*. The current catchphrase for this idea is 'democracy by default' and it is said to apply almost throughout South America. Note that it implies a lowering of popular expectations of what can be achieved through political action, and therefore favours neo-liberal (or at least low participation) forms of electoral politics. Note also that it applies best to South America, rather than to Mexico, or the Caribbean. The Central American cases are also more complex, because there the alternative to accepting some democratic forms was the continuation of a possibly regional civil war, with the associated risks of external intervention.[4] In addition to the lessons learnt from these experiences of internal political statements, in the past decade there has also been a powerful international 'contagion' effect at work, which has reinforced the movement towards at least formal observance of democratic processes throughout the subcontinent. Another contributory factor has been the support provided increasingly from outside Latin America – by the party internationals, the Catholic Church, the European Community and such US-funded agencies as the National Endowment for Democracy. In general the literature analysing democratization in contemporary Latin America has rated such international factors as of secondary importance, but the transformation of Eastern Europe and developments in Nicaragua and Panama (and prospectively in Cuba) indicate the need for some reconsideration of this view.[5]

Notwithstanding the force of the current democratizing wave, a doubt remains. Are the old alternatives to liberal democracy really vanquished, or just in abeyance? Here we shall try to tackle this question *before* examining the durability, effectiveness, and so on of the new democratic regimes. This procedure may seem odd, particularly given the stress on 'democracy by default' in the previous section. The default could end, new totalizing projects with a capacity for mobilizing the transforming society may rally support, and if so these fragile democracies would seem poorly placed to resist the challenge. However, the procedure adopted here makes sense if one distinguishes between two types of alternative to fully consolidated and effective liberal democracy.

The first type are explicitly anti-democratic. They rest on explicit critiques of the inadequacies (either universal or local) of liberal democracy, and they offer more or less coherent and comprehensive alternative images of the social and political order. Communism was certainly of this kind. One variant survives in Cuba, and another continues to display considerable military strength in much of Peru. But even so it is pretty apparent that the Cuban model has been ideologically vanquished, delegitimized as well as materially crippled by the evaporation of communism in the Soviet Union. The liquidation of Cuban influence in Africa and Central America confirms the eclipse of this explicit alternative to liberal democracy, which is becoming increasingly anachronistic and unviable. This alternative is no longer real in Latin America, and it is doubtful whether it can ever be resurrected in any central role. The other well-elaborated regional alternative might be loosely called 'fascism',[6] and has more recently been known in the guise of 'national security ideology'. Here too there is only space for a sweeping generalization on a subject that merits more care. In the absence of a credible communist threat, and in view of the lamentable record of these movements when in power, it is plausible to assert that their day has passed.

---

[4] This argument was developed in G. Di Palma and L. Whitehead (eds), *The Central American Impasse* (London, Croom Helm, 1986). See also Lowenthal, *Exporting Democracy*.

[5] For example, see L. Whitehead, 'The international dimension of democratisation: a survey of the alternatives' (paper presented at the XVth World Congress of the International Political Science Association in Buenos Aires, July 1991).

[6] See in particular H. Trindade, 'La question du fascisme en Amérique latine', *Revue Française de Sciences Politique*, No. 2 (1983) and H. Trindade, *La Tentation Fasciste au Brésil* (Paris, Editions de la Maison des Sciences de l'Homme, 1988).

150   *Alternatives to Liberal Democracy: a Latin American Perspective*

(Even at their strongest the national security regimes were not quite the systematic alternatives to liberal democracy that they appeared – they were mostly 'regimes of *exception*'[7], meaning that they envisaged an eventual return to more normal forms of politics, once the circumstances precipitating their installation had been overcome.) Does this exhaust the range of explicitly anti-democratic possibilities? Not entirely – there was clerical corporatism for a while, and some of the simpler forms of personal and military rule (Stroessner's patrimonial regime in Paraguay, 1954–89, for example) were almost explicit about their repudiation of liberal values. My assessment, however, is that in future the regional democratic consensus will probably be robust enough to discourage the re-emergence of new movements of this type. The apparent failure of current attempts to salvage a 'duvalieriste' form of government in Haiti lends some support to this view. More ambitiously, a case could also be argued that this applies not only to Latin America but also to much of the rest of the world, where other forms of illiberal legitimation such as white minority rule, and perhaps Islamic fundamentalism, are potentially available. Certainly in Latin America, instead of rallying to explicitly anti-democratic alternatives, I would expect those threatened by liberal values to react (as the Mexican authorities have done so successfully) by paying them lip-service while seeking to resist their full implementation.

This, then, is the second alternative to fully consolidated liberal democracy, which is clearly more insidious, and also more ambiguous in sign. The Latin American literature on 'facade'[8] democracies (compare with the Portuguese phrase *para os ingleses ver*, which refers to the old habit of holding elections 'for the English to look at') should be taken seriously, but there is also force to the counter-argument that once a governing elite accepts the theoretical hegemony of liberal institutions, once it pays lip-service to popular sovereignty expressed through open elections, a process of habituation is set in motion which tends over time to turn the 'facades' into more real structures. The question of civilian control over the military provides a pertinent illustration. Although the jury on this is still out, there is an accumulation of evidence that many fragile new democracies which initially just *pretended* to subordinate the armed forces to the rule of law are gradually progressing towards a more genuine supremacy of constitutional norms.

So what kind(s) of democratic regimes can we expect to survive in Latin America (and perhaps also in other parts of the third world and the ex-communist world) – how consolidated, how liberal, how effective at governing, how capable of democratizing society at large? The references to my comments 'democracy by default' and 'facade democracy' already indicate some reasons for doubting that the general outcome will be fully consolidated, liberal and effective democracy. But before elaborating on the less prepossessing outcomes that may seem more probable, one should warn against undifferentiated pessimism (what Hirschman calls 'fracasomania'[9]). Costa Rica and the islands of the

---

[7] See A. Rouquié, 'Demilitarization and the institutionalization of military-dominated politics in Latin America', in G. O'Donnell, P. Schmitter and L. Whitehead (eds), *Transitions from Authoritarian Rule* (Baltimore, Johns Hopkins University Press, 1986).

[8] See, for example, L. Maira in di Palma and Whitehead (eds), *The Central American Impasse*. See also Edward Herman and Frank Brodhead (eds), *Demonstration Elections: US Staged Elections in the Dominican Republic, Vietnam and El Salvador* (Boston, South End Press, 1984).

[9] A. Hirschman, 'The search for paradigms as a hindrance to understanding', in A. Hirschman, *A Bias for Hope: Essays on Development and Latin America* (New Haven, CT, Yale University Press,

Commonwealth Caribbean are remarkably solid liberal democracies which have survived some impressive historical and geographical adversities. In a more qualified way, Venezuela and Puerto Rico also have strong claims to success. A reasonable 'tendency statement' would be that both in Latin America and in Eastern Europe there will be further such success stories in the next few years – not necessarily the ones that seem most obvious today. However, since it may reasonably be doubted that these will be the norm, the rest of this essay will concentrate on a range of intermediate possibilities: impotent, bankrupt and socially explosive democracies, 'unstable populism'; neo-liberal 'depoliticized democracies'; and internationally dependent or insecure democracies.

It is very difficult briefly to outline the main characteristics of 'unstable populist democracy' or to indicate the reasons for its likely prevalence, without falling into the negative stereotyping mentioned at the outset.[10] These can easily be perceived as 'unserious' democracies, frivolous imitations of political arrangements that properly developed elsewhere, closer to home. My objection to this perspective is twofold. It fails to do justice to the historical traditions and social forces that tend to generate Latin America's distinctive forms of political expression, and it reinforces a sense of complacency about the nature of democratic institutions in Western Europe and North America that is usually unjustified by the comparative record, and that in any case hinders genuinely detached understanding.

That said, there is a growing body of opinion within Latin America which argues that many of the emerging new democracies are showing little tendency to 'consolidate' or to 'institutionalize' according to the (supposedly) classical pattern. Instead, what we may find is highly presidentialist forms of government, in which some flamboyant individual leader emerges almost from nowhere, captures the majority vote on the basis of the vaguest of slogans and the loosest of commitments, and then proceeds to govern arbitrarily without restraint from party structures, parliamentary processes, legal or bureaucratic norms, until popular support is exhausted and another equally ill-prepared and erratic takes his place. Several terms have been proposed to analyse these recurrent patterns – 'deligative democracy' and *movimentismo* are among the most current. In my opinion none are as evocative as the term coined by the Venezuelan writer Valenilla Lanz over 60 years ago – '*Cesarismo democrático*'.[11] In any case, identifying such a political morphology is only the beginning of an analysis. We then need an explanation of the reasons why it reproduces itself so effectively, and whether over the longer term it is likely to break down, to stabilize, or to evolve into a more institutionalized structure.

These are the central issues in debate among Latin American political scientists today. In different countries the emphasis shifts from one aspect of the problem to another but the central cluster of issues remains the same. (For example, in some countries the party structures are quite strong and the question becomes how to

1971).
[10] For a political analysis of Brazilian democracy which is consistent with this label, but which is not easily dismissed as an instance of negative stereotyping, see Bolívar Lamounier (ed.), *De Geisel a Collor: o Balanço da Transição* (Sao Paulo, IDESP, 1990). For an economic interpretation focusing on the spectacular cases of Chile and Peru, see R. Dornbusch and S. Edwards, 'Macro-economic populism', *Journal of Development Economics*, 32 (1990).
[11] Guillermo O'Donnel and Giorgio Alberti are respectively refining these terms for a forthcoming conference at the European Centre for the Study of Democratisation in Forlì. See also Laureano Valenilla Lanz, *Césarismo Democrático: Estudio Sobre las Bases Sociológicas de la Constitución Efectiva de Venezuela* (Caracas, Tipografia Garrido, 4th edn, 1961).

152   *Alternatives to Liberal Democracy: a Latin American Perspective*

overcome their rigidity; in others the central problem may seem to be administrative corruption, or the failure of the legal system rather than erratic political leadership; in still others the fiscal crisis and the consequent collapse of state patronage may take centre stage. But in fact these are all interrelated, and when progress is made on one front another item from the same cluster typically comes to the fore.) One influential current of opinion (not shared by this author) regards presidentialism as the heart of the problem and recommends parliamentarism as the indispensable solution. Others argue, by contrast, that a switch to parliamentarism could well result in a policy paralysis that might only be overcome by extra-constitutional means.[12]

Another current of interpretation stresses the acute social inequality, insecurity and loss of welfare that has accompanied democratization, arguing that in these conditions popular frustration or desperation can be expected to destabilize any institutional order. Of course the masses vote for demagogic saviours, since responsible politicians offer them no hope. Although this argument has been bolstered by the outcome of several recent elections, in which outsiders with no real party support or political track record have been swept to victory in anti-political campaigns (such as Fujimori in Peru), it rests on various dubious assumptions, such as that the public attributes social distress to democracy, when in fact they may understand that the two are separate; and it denigrates the activities of political bargaining and persuasion that characterize the democratic process. A third, neo-liberal, line of thought will be discussed in the next section.

In summary then, my own position is that while *some* of these fragile and unstable regimes may gradually develop into consolidated, liberal and well-institutionalized regimes of the West European kind, and a *few* may visibly break down (through armed conflict, extreme social unrest, followed by new 'regimes of exception'), the range of conditions just enumerated is sufficiently widespread and entrenched to make probable a more or less indefinite continuation of the present political forms in more than a few countries. Even where progress towards consolidation is most notable, the prospects of relapse into 'unstable populism' remain very real. Even where 'regimes of exception' are once again attempted they are likely to prove temporary interruptions.

The strongest challenge to this position comes from what may loosely be labelled the 'neo-liberal' school of thought. Curiously, this vigorously anti-Marxist body of analysis is often characterized by a crude economic determinism of the type we used to associate with vulgar Marxism (a point I have elaborated in relation to the most influential statement of the neo-liberal case, Hernando de Soto's *The Other Path*[13]). However, the more sophisticated versions of this

---

[12] Juan Linz is the most influential advocate of parliamentarism: see J. Linz, 'The perils of presidentialism', *The Journal of Democracy*, I: 1 (Winter 1990). His ideas have been taken up in quite a few South American republics: see, for example, the Argentine Consejo para la Consolidación de la Democracia, *Presidencialismo vs Parlamentarismo* (Buenos Aires, Editorial Universitaria de Buenos Aires, 1988). The same articles by Linz and Lijphart also appear in Bolivar Lamounier (ed.), *A Opçao Parlamentarista* (Sao Paulo, IDESP, 1991), although in clear contradiction to the Linz thesis, Brazilian self-declared parliamentarists accept the inevitability of a directly elected presidency. For a healthy corrective to this Brazilian academic consensus see Renato Lessa, 'Constrangimentos a toda reforma institucional futura' (paper presented at the XVth Annual Conference of ANPOCS, Caxambú, Mina Gerais, Oct. 1991).

[13] Hernando de Soto, *The Other Path: the Invisible Revolution in the Third World* (London, I.B. Tauris, 1989). First published in Lima, the title explicitly contrasts neo-liberalism to the 'Shining Path' pursued by Peru's maoist insurgents. In 'Algunas reflexiones sobre "el Estado" y el sector

argument require careful consideration, particularly since, rightly or wrongly, neo-liberal ideas are being used to shape strategies of democratization in an increasing number of countries.

Their central claim is that what may be called 'populist democracies' are economically irrational: they violate property rights and therefore essential human freedoms; for that reason they are not only inefficient but also in a profounder sense undemocratic; and that by extending the scope of 'market' systems of allocation and by rolling back the state the social underpinnings of this 'politicized' or 'rent-seeking' economy can be dismantled.[14] Their preferred economic reforms – monetary stabilization, privatization, the enhancement of private property rights and 'openness' – will also in due course provide the social foundations for consolidated liberal democracy. If they are right then Latin America is in the process of escaping from an unstable, poorly institutionalized and economically and socially unsuccessful present, and can within a decade or so construct fairly well consolidated conventional liberal capitalist democracies – as Chile has already done.

There is only space here for very brief and inadequate comments on this line of argument. First, it must be conceded that in certain cases something like this is likely to happen, although it is far from clear that this will be the *general* outcome; even when neo-liberal success seems most complete (as in contemporary Chile), a detailed observer can expect to find substantial and potentially destabilizing counter-currents. Secondly, the neo-liberal strategy holds up the offer of a fully consolidated liberal democratic end-state, but in order to reach that condition it typically condones a considerable amount of interim illiberalism. Trade unionists, public employees, pensioners, the unemployed and so on may be tempted to use their democratic rights to oppose neo-liberal policy prescriptions. If so the theory will represent their actions as illegitimate ('rent-seeking' and so on) and so may justify repression. 'Depoliticization' of the economy may only be achievable if economic policy-makers are insulated from social feedback, if media criticism is restrained, and if resistance to the new patterns of property ownership is met with the full force of bourgeois (not necessarily democratic) law. Of course, once neo-liberal theorists have condoned such *means* to achieve their allegedly democratic *ends*, the old, old question arises as to how, if at all, they are eventually to free themselves from the instruments they have used. The ideological and intolerant *style* of neo-liberal policy-making is well illustrated by the fact that whenever the observable results fall short of what was promised by the theory, the typical response has not been to reconsider the doctrine but to prescribe a stronger dose of the same medicine. Thirdly, then, we must enquire what *kind* of a democracy would in due course be stabilized and consolidated if the neo-liberal programme met with complete success – in what sense would it be democratic at all?[15] Certainly *participatory* democracy tends to clash with the

informal', *Revista Mexicana de Sociologia* (1990), I argue that de Soto's analysis borrows from vulgar Marxism, merely substituting the informal sector for the proletariat, and 'the state' for 'the bourgeoisie'.

[14] See, for example, A. Krueger, 'The political economy of the rent-seeking society', *American Economic Review*, 64:3 (1974); R. Findlay and J. D. Wilson, 'The political economy of leviathan', in A. Razin and E. Sadka (eds), *Economic Policy in Theory and Practice* (New York, Macmillan, 1987); Deepak Lal, 'The political economy of economic liberalization', *World Bank Economic Review* (Jan. 1987).

[15] 'Unfortunately, liberal democracy can mean either . . . freedom of the stronger to do down the weaker by following market rules; or it can mean equal effective freedom of all to use and develop their capacities. The latter freedom is inconsistent with the former'. C. B. Macpherson, *The Life and*

154   *Alternatives to Liberal Democracy: a Latin American Perspective*

ideal of a 'depoliticized' market system, and far from advancing such causes as women's rights, racial equality or a social rights conception of citizenship, the neo-liberal model tends to dismantle whatever protections may previously have existed.[16]

There is nevertheless a major weakness in all these criticisms of the neo-liberal route to democracy. At least it offers the possibility of eventually arriving at a stable viable liberal regime. The alternative of permanent crisis and insecurity under 'unstable populism' seems unable to offer any such prospect. In fact it is the poorest, the most vulnerable, the racially subordinate and so forth who suffer most under erratic populism, despite intermittent rhetoric in their favour. Paulo Sergio Pinheiro, for example, has shown that the return to democracy in Brazil has been accompanied by a marked deterioration in that country's human rights performance.[17] True, the police no longer torture articulate middle-class dissidents, but instead the residential areas of the main cities bribe them to murder street children. Examples like this can be multiplied, particularly with reference to the countryside.[18] Most of the now quite abundant literature criticizing Latin America's democratization as elitist and unconnected with the lived experience of the mass of the population (the 'social movements' perspective) fails to distinguish adequately between neo-liberal and paternalist (or clientelist) strategies of democratization. Both may be opposed to autonomous participation from below, but only the neo-liberal strategy (extending the role of the market) seems capable of leading to regime consolidation. Here there is a paradox. Current Latin American experience can be invoked to argue that the only path to democratic 'consolidation' (a stable, durable and effective regime) is through sustained implementation of drastic 'neo-liberal' market reforms. In the absence of such reforms fragile 'populist' democracies will remain unstable, ineffective and indeed incoherent, lacking all the 'credibility' needed for responsible governance. The paradox is that what can be consolidated by these means would seem to exclude many of the features commonly associated with full liberal democracy (high participation, authentic political choice, extensive citizenship rights). Where a more ambitious – authentic – vision of democratization is attempted it would seem that nothing can be consolidated. The choice would be between a stunted version of liberal democracy that works, or a generous vision of social democracy that remains a mirage (the Chilean Constitution of 1980 versus the Brazilian Constitution of 1988).

Like most dichotomies this contrast, though real, is too stark. It can be softened by separating out the effect of fiscal crisis, and by viewing regime consolidation as a long-term and non-linear process. Democratization and fiscal crisis broadly coincided during the 1980s (although a good case can be made that these were quite separate processes that just happened to interact, and were not

Times of Liberal Democracy (Oxford, Oxford University Press, 1979), p. 1.

[16] Although Paul Cammack overstates his case he has a point in arguing that 'the accepted principles of liberal democracy and current practice of liberal economic doctrines stand in flagrant contradiction to the two central strategies – cooptation and repression – upon which Latin American democracy generally continues to depend'; see P. Cammack, 'Democracy and development in Latin America', *The Journal of International Development*, 3:5 (1991), p. 550.

[17] P. S. Pinheiro, 'The legacy of authoritarianism in democratic Brazil' (paper presented at the XVth World Congress of the International Political Science Association in Buenos Aires, July 1991).

[18] J. Fox (ed.), *The Challenge of Rural Democratization: Perspectives from Latin America and the Philippines* (London, Frank Cass, 1990).

necessarily connected). When fiscal crisis reaches the point of catharsis (as in Bolivia in 1985, Argentina in 1989, Brazil perhaps in the near future), the government – whether democratic or otherwise – faces a choice between accepting paralysis and impotence in virtually all spheres of public activity, or cutting back/discontinuing large areas of previous responsibility in order to achieve a minimum degree of efficacy in high-priority areas. What recent experiences of fiscal crisis seem to be demonstrating is that the political costs of abandoning unrealistic promises of state assistance and interventionism are less prohibitive than they seem, because public expectations of government are violently lowered by the spectre of hyper-inflation. Thus, after a certain 'threshold of crisis' has been passed it is possible for democratic politicians to achieve surprisingly dramatic gains in authority, credibility, and even in electoral support, by promising and attempting much less than before. The secret of success is to demonstrate that the limited tasks remaining on the public agenda really are achievable ('neo-liberal effectiveness'), and also perhaps to keep open the hope of some future prospect of re-enlarging the agenda. The second element is more debatable than the first, and in its absence fiscal crisis would simply inaugurate the new era of immutable neo-liberal democracies desired by the right. But the survival of so many fragile democracies in Latin America is not merely due to the absence of explicit alternatives; it also derives from the hope that in the end these regimes will start fulfilling some of their promises. Democratic procedures must be analytically distinguished from substantive outcomes, but there is always a link between the two. It is provided by the fact that under democratic rules the electorate's future options are not foreclosed. In the short run the experience of fiscal crisis may have reduced popular expectations of public policy so low that the right's paradise of *laissez-faire* seems within reach, but if the consolidation of democracy takes a generation or more, by the time the process is complete the electorate will have overcome that trauma, and the choice between 'neo-liberal' and 'social democratic' alternatives can be taken at least partly on its merits.

   In consequence there is scope for further work focusing on the conditions that would have to be met in order to reconcile political democratization with economic efficiency and social participation. As social democratic theorists have long argued (for example Schumpeter), such conditions are highly restrictive. In theory it may be possible to devise paths to consolidated social democracy that bypass the inequities of neo-liberalism and the irresponsibility of populism, but no one in contemporary Latin America has yet discovered how to do it in practice (despite the efforts of many very talented advisers). Reasons for pursuing this enquiry may be partly ethical but can also be grounded in some arguments from 'realism'. The consolidation of any type of democratic regime takes a generation or more, so the neo-liberals are at least right not to despair at the first setbacks. The key requirement seems to me a mutually reinforcing process by which both economic and political expectations are stabilized and brought into line with underlying material and institutional possibilities.[19] Market discipline provides one variant of this process that must to some extent be accepted, but in contrast to the neo-liberal perspective others see considerable need and some scope for democratic *political* processes of persuasion, organization, education and

---

[19] L. Whitehead, 'Democratization and disinflation: a comparative approach', in J. Nelson (ed.), *Fragile Coalitions: The Politics of Economic Adjustment* (Washington, Overseas Development Institute, 1989).

compensation. Lest this sounds like the illusion of the 'socialist third way' recently condemned by Ralf Dahrendorf,[20] one could comment that (a) the neo-liberal model may also be an illusion, in which case we are all floundering; (b) such attempts should not be viewed as a blueprint, but a political method – the policy contents must emerge from a process of democratic consultation; and (c) Dahrendorf's strongest criticism of social democracy was that it entered into crisis as a result of its own success. In Latin America (and other new democracies) this kind of objection lies far in the future. In present social conditions a *viable* programme of social democracy could potentially attract a large popular majority.

Of course it must be acknowledged that even in the prosperous and stable democracies of Western Europe there are powerful constraints on the extent to which 'viable' forms of social democracy can stray if not from dogmatic neo-liberal models, then at least from the broader confines of liberal capitalist democracy. One major source of constraint arises from the differentiation of identities and the conflicts of interest that come to divide the beneficiaries of the European welfare state as it ages. Similarly in Latin America, even though welfare provision has never been anything like universal, the system has aged badly and its support coalition (partly providers of welfare, partly beneficiaries and partly aspirants to membership) has become very fragmented. In addition, most Latin American societies are characterized by extremes of heterogeneity (regional, ethnic, linguistic and gender as well as class based), which gravely weaken the constituency in favour of universalistic welfare policies even when the resources for this are available. The second major source of constraint on European social democracy, the requirements of capital accumulation in a market economy, are of course far more acute in post-debt-crisis Latin America. In consequence, loosely 'social democratic' alternatives to neo-liberalism in Latin America will face simultaneous fire from two fronts. On the one hand they will be criticized as hopelessly over-optimistic given the weak productive base, and on the other they will be faulted as far too cautious and gradual given the rawness of existing social inequalities. Thus the potential popular majority for a viable form of social democracy is likely to prove large but volatile. This will not entirely preclude the development of more participatory and welfare-orientated alternatives to *laissez-faire*, but it means that any such process will probably be slow, troubled, and vulnerable to clientelistic distortions.

Such constraints are reinforced by the growing internationalization of economic processes. Social democracy is associated with Keynesian demand management in a single, partially insulated nation-state. Inflation and the fiscal crisis has eliminated whatever scope there was for Keynesianism, and the ultra-protected and inward-looking economies of individual Latin American countries are now destined for integration in the world market under regimes of greatly increased economic openess. This argument has considerable force but should not be applied mechanistically. The internationalization of the Mexican economy is a very different process from that of Bolivia; the geopolitical context often counts for a great deal (for example, Costa Rica's pivotal role in stabilizing liberal principles in Central America); and when a degree of economic success is achieved, the scope for autonomous policy choice tends to expand once more. In any case, 'internationalization' is more complex and ambiguous in sign than is often recognized. Perhaps during the 1980s its main manifestation was the

[20] R. Dahrendorf, *Reflections on the Revolution in Europe* (London, Chatto & Windus, 1990).

uncontrolled movement of private capital between nations, which reduced the policy autonomy of all governments and strengthened the political bargaining power of capitalists. But during the 1990s the uncontrolled international migration of labour may well prove equally relentless, with consequences for economic management (and for the stability of democratic institutions) that are quite distinct. Despite these imponderables, both theory and evidence still suggest to me that in the longer run, even in a very liberal international economic order (which is by no means assured), there ought to remain a substantial area of political discretion open to the governments of well-consolidated democracies.[21]

One very significant fact about Latin America, which may differentiate the subcontinent from most of the other new democracies currently under construction, is that it has a very long history of more or less stable frontiers. By international standards it has long been a 'zone of peace', and within nearly all republics the process of national integration has advanced to such a point that secession, partition or annexation of territory is unlikely. Many other states are attempting to democratize at the same time as they establish new national identities – a far more conflict-ridden enterprise.[22]

Another important feature of Latin American democratizations is that for the most part they proceeded by negotiation ('pact') rather than rupture. Consequently they were slow to unfold, taking years or even decades, whereas the post-Berlin democratizations are occurring overnight and sweeping away many of the institutional structures which went before.

A third generalization is that Latin American democratizations occurred in long-established but poorly functioning market economies. By contrast, many of the most recent regime changes are occurring in countries where market principles of allocation have to be established from scratch, rather than merely reformed. There are pluses and minuses to this contrast. It might be helpful to draw on a stock of expertise in commercial law, accountancy, international

---

[21] D. Held, 'Democracy, the nation-state and the global system', *Economy and Society*, 20:2 (May 1991). His article in this volume (pp. 10–39) raises broader theoretical issues about the impact of 'globalization' (understood to mean much more than just the intensification of international economic exchanges) and such central concepts of democratic theory as 'constituency', 'accountability', and 'participation'. Such issues acquire a sharp focus in contemporary Latin America where, for example, a Panamanian citizen's right to choose his own president is likely to seem a poor substitute for participation in US politics, where the key decisions affecting Panama are really taken. The Puerto Ricans have taken this reasoning to its logical conclusion: 'What US efforts at democracy promotion in the Caribbean basin seem to assume is that democratisation can be a *substitute* for what Washington regards as unacceptable or impractical assertions of national sovereignty'. See L. Whitehead, 'The imposition of democracy', in A. F. Lowenthal (ed.), *Exporting Democracy: The United States and Latin America* (Baltimore, Johns Hopkins University Press, 1991), p. 257. Even Mexican politicians may now devote as much attention to wooing US opinion as that of their home electorate: see L. Whitehead, 'Mexico and the "hegemony" of the United States', in R. Roett (ed.), *Mexico's External Relations in the 1990s* (New York, Lynne Riener, 1991). Nevertheless, Held's general point holds true for Latin America that 'the degree to which the modern state enjoys "autonomy" under various conditions is under-explored' and requires careful specification before one rules out the possibility of national democracies within a global liberal system.

[22] Adam Przeworski, *Democracy and the Market: Political and Economic Reforms in Eastern Europe and Latin America* (Cambridge, Cambridge University Press, 1991), p. 190, identified 'geography' as Eastern Europe's main hope of escaping the fate of the Latin American democracies ('the politics, the economics, and the culture of poor capitalism'). But he does not rate that hope very highly, nor does he specify with any precision the dynamics of the contrast, nor consider the possibility that Latin America's 'geography' could save that region from the fate of the East European democracies.

commerce and so on, but since market institutions have for so long worked so badly in Latin America it may be hard to eradicate their entrenched vices. The East Europeans have both less experience and fewer preconceptions. It could therefore be argued that it will be easier to promote modern capitalism in that setting than in a subcontinent where the elites have learnt the attractions of a primitive variant. On the other hand, Burke's flowery phrases about the legacy of failed revolutionary experiments acquire a chilling new resonance as the situation in parts of Eastern Europe continues to degenerate.[23]

Finally, Latin America is notorious for the extravagance of its social inequalities, perhaps more extreme than anywhere else in the world. It has been argued that this provides the key to the region's stability and lack of institutionalization. More egalitarian societies (for example, those accustomed to universal education and healthcare) might provide a more promising setting for social democratic consolidation. However, the counter-argument would be that in many ex-communist countries the explosion of inequalities likely to accompany marketization will generate more unrest and resistance than the mere continuance of long-lived injustices in a climate of greater freedom. This article has stressed 'democracy by default' as the central feature of the Latin American experience, and has commented on the way social expectations have been (and must be) lowered if these fragile democracies are to consolidate. Both these points would tend to lend credence to the counter-argument just stated.

Overall, then, it is difficult to find good arguments that the prospects for consolidated and participatory democracy are better in Eastern Europe than in the Latin subcontinent. Within Latin America quite a variety of political regimes may continue to be found. Explicitly anti-democratic ideologies and systems of government are in headlong retreat and seem unlikely to return. A few fully consolidated, reasonably autonomous and conventionally 'liberal' democracies may well emerge. But at least for the near future the norm will be a more provisional and unsatisfactory form of constitutional rule – 'democracy by default'. The limitations on these democracies will vary from country to country: restrictions on national sovereignty; curtailment of political choice by market mechanisms; 'facade' arrangements intended to project an external image of pluralism without disturbing traditional power relations; the persistence of undemocratic structures in rural areas; policy paralysis derived from fiscal crisis; misguided design of institutional arrangements; a fragmented civil society incapable of generating legitimacy or social consensus (and the list could be extended further). Thus most Latin American democracies are likely to remain provisional, incomplete and unconsolidated, at least for the next few years. This should not be considered particularly surprising or shocking, however. The consolidation of democracy is a process that must take at least a generation or longer. So long as the framework of representative institutions is kept intact the prospect remains open that a future government, under pressure from the citizenry, will rectify the omissions, correct the errors or enlarge the rights as required to complete democratization. Whether the outcome of such a process should be called a 'liberal democracy' will be an enduring source of controversy,

---

[23] '. . . if commerce and the arts should be lost in an experiment to try how well a state may stand without these old fundamental principles, what sort of a thing must be a nation of gross, stupid, ferocious, and at the same time poor and sordid barbarians'; see Edmund Burke, *Reflections on the Revolution in France* (Harmondsworth, Pelican, 1973 edn), p. 174. Compare A. C. Copetas, *Bear Hunting with Politburo* (New York, Simon & Schuster, 1991).

since rival projects are likely to compete for the same label. Given the liberal and republican traditions of Latin America, and the influence of the US and Europe, the label is likely to be viewed positively (in contrast to, say, the Islamic world), even if the contents prove idiosyncratic.

[17]

Political Studies (1991), XXXIX, 363–368

Transitions from Authoritarian Rule: Lessons from Latin America

JEAN GRUGEL

Instituto Universitario Ortega y Gasset, Madrid

> You yourself were only . . . the tremor of some taciturn lips . . . a comic
> tyrant who never knew where the reverse side of the coin was . . . clinging to
> his fear . . . and alien forever more to the music of liberation and the rockets
> of jubilation and the bells of glory that announced to the world the good news
> that the uncountable time of eternity had come to an end.[1]

Until the social and political upheavals of the USSR and Eastern Europe, the
academic debate on transitions from authoritarian rule was dominated by the
experiences of regime transformation in Latin America and Southern Europe.
Gabriel Garcia Marquez, Latin America's best-known writer, captured perfectly
the general spirit of hope and goodwill that accompanies the collapse of a long
and bloody dictatorship at the end of *The Autumn of the Patriarch*. However, our
understanding of the mechanisms of regime transformation is still far from
complete, so attention will be concentrated on where the theories of transition
remain deficient. In particular, the complex relationship between opposition to
the authoritarian regime, and the transition and the post-authoritarian society,
remains a grey area. Using the example of Chile, I will argue that we need to
recast the debate in a way which permits a clearer analysis of different forms of
opposition and their articulation.

Theories of Transition: a Top-down Bias in the Literature

Transitions are understood to last differing lengths of time and end in very
different sorts of political systems.[2] They are temporary and usually confused
affairs. The term suggests the creation of new political spaces and a growing
dispersion of power. In Latin American studies it has been taken to imply civilian
rule without the promise of redistribution or a more just social order, at least in
the short term. Overall in Latin America, democratization has been about
building systems of political domination based on only formal and hence limited
popular participation and on some accommodation with the authoritarian order,
such as a military veto on the issue of trials for human rights abuses.

The initial vulnerability of the authoritarian regime which may lead to

---

[1] Gabriel Garcia Marquez, *The Autumn of the Patriarch* (London, Picador, 1976), p. 206.
[2] In the literature on transition in English, G. O'Donnell, P. Schmitter and L. Whitehead (eds),
Transitions from Authoritarian Rule (4 vols) (London, Johns Hopkins University Press, 1986) merits
particular attention.

attempts at opening up the system often appears economic in character, whether the consequence of an abrupt crisis or the negative impact of a longer-term economic restructuring. Although the crisis may not immediately appear to be terminal, open opposition emerges which the regime is no longer able to hide, repress or contain. In fact, the real cause of regime vulnerability is not the economic crisis itself but other factors which make it impossible for the regime to respond adequately. These factors would seem to be primarily political.

Stepan suggests that there are two main types of present day transition: where the office-holders initiate steps towards power-sharing and where the opposition forces the transition.[3] However, the difference between the two is only one of degree. In both the composition and effectiveness (or ineffectiveness) of the opposition will play a role in determining the outcome. One way in which a limited space for some opposition groups within the system is created is by attempts to institutionalize the authoritarian regime. These groups may come either from dissatisfied ex-regime supporters or from among groups previously excluded from power but not usually among the most actively expressed. They form a legitimate opposition within the regime. Though they initially appear to have no teeth, they can become ferocious opponents in moments of crisis; Brazil after 1982 is an example of this. However, this is hardly a full explanation of the factors that prompt legitimation of some opposition groups and by no means exhausts the possibilities of opposition under military regimes. Consequently, it fails to recognize the multi-class and multi-layered opposition which actually occurs.

Opposition to authoritarian rule may come from several different groups in society and be expressed in different ways. The groups which form the legitimized opposition should not be thought to comprise the whole spectrum of the opposition, nor to constitute necessarily the most effective opposition. Achieving some form of legitimation from the authoritarian regime does not necessarily signify successful opposition and exclusion of unsuccessful opposition. Indeed, the decision to legitimize some opposition groups can be a response to a much greater threat for the survival of the regime: the organization of previously excluded popular sectors, for example, organized in community-based associations, peasant organizations, and single-issue groups such as the Mothers of Disappeared People.

Nevertheless, there is on the whole a tendency in the literature to focus too heavily on formal opposition from parties and even trade unions. These models of democratization make it difficult to take into account sufficiently the strength of popular organizations and protest. In Latin America at least, even before the establishment of authoritarian regimes, the political system operated to exclude rather than channel and represent popular participation inside parties and even trade unions. By seeing parties or political elites as the main agents of the transition, theories which focus on top-down factors inevitably tend to downplay or even miss the role of popular organizations. As a result, the interaction between levels of opposition is lost or not fully drawn out. Analyses run the risk of becoming static. A *de facto* separation of a political class from within the

---

[3] A. Stepan, 'Patterns towards redemocratization: theoretical and comparative perspectives', in G. O'Donnell, P. Schmitter and L. Whitehead (eds), *Transitions from Authoritarian Rule. Vol. 3. Comparative Perspectives* (London, Johns Hopkins University Press, 1986), pp. 64–84.

opposition is implied, composed of politicians, high-ranking party members and intellectuals from the rest of civil society. There is an implicit assumption that these groups act autonomously, almost without reference to other social forces. The result of focusing on top-down factors is a tendency not to distinguish between mass opposition and elite or party opposition and hence to miss the interaction between the two. The importance of this has not always been sufficiently stressed. To exercise some influence over the pace, timing and content of a transition from authoritarian rule, popular sectors need not have directly transformed the system themselves. The existence and growth of popular organizations can act as a catalyst for its transformation by provoking a change in military–civil relations and forcing the dictatorship into making some concessions.

It would be helpful if the literature distinguished explicitly between transition in those countries which have enjoyed a strong democratic tradition prior to authoritarianism and those which have not.[4] Clearly, the resurrection of civil society during the transitional stage means that opposition in the former is altogether more complex. A move away from top-down theorizing is evident in the work of Schmitter and O'Donnell.[5] They distinguish between democratization where *notables* from within the regime and from the ranks of the opposition play a dominant role during the transition (they draw in particular on the Brazilian case) and cases where *pacts*, generally between opposition groups with opposing class interests, are made (Spain is the best example). Pact-making occurs either in a weak civil society and especially with a weak popular sector or conversely when high levels of participation, social organization and political activation exist.

However, this approach still does not go far enough. More should be said about the articulation of opposition both before and during the transition from different, perhaps even competing, groups which may not be expressed as formal alliances or pacts. We should also identify possible channels of popular participation in the opposition outside the arena of formal or party opposition. Because many people in Latin America, alienated and repressed by authoritarianism, are nonetheless unable to participate in politics as members of formal organizations, we should examine the impact of community or neighbourhood-based non-party opposition. I am not suggesting that extraparty, mobilizational opposition is significant in all authoritarian regimes, but there is a need to establish when and under what circumstances it becomes a key factor. Is it that contradictions within the authoritarian state generate widespread popular protest or does it stem from tensions within the opposition bloc as a whole?

It is possible to see the transition to civilian rule in Latin America as the

---

[4] This distinction was made by Machiavelli: 'He who becomes master of a city accustomed to freedom and does not destroy it, may expect to be destroyed by it, for in rebellion it has always been the watchword of liberty and its ancient privileges as a rallying point, which neither time nor benefits will ever cause it to forget. And whatever you may do or provide against, they never forget that name or their privileges'. N. Machiavelli, *The Prince* (Harmondsworth, Penguin, 1974), p. 48. I would like to thank a reviewer of an earlier version of this article for pointing out the appropriateness of this quotation.

[5] G. O'Donnell and P. Schmitter 'Negotiating (and renegotiating) pacts', in G. O'Donnell, P. Schmitter and L. Whitehead (eds), *Transitions from Authoritarian Rule: Vol. 4. Tentative Conclusions About Uncertain Democracies* (London, John Hopkins University Press, 1986), pp. 37–47.

restoration of bourgeois hegemony.[6] Transitions will almost inevitably take place within the context of an emerging consensus in civil society over issues like civil liberties, moderation and the need for compromise. This consensus extends to the parties of the left, previously hostile to political models they have historically dismissed as 'bourgeois democracy'. During the transition, formal or party opposition groups, from which elements forming the basis of the post-authoritarian elite are drawn, need to constrain extra-party movements and protests in order to establish a political model which will guarantee bourgeois hegemony. That they have been successful so far in Latin America should not lead us to ignore the dynamic relationship which develops between bourgeois and popular opposition in the period leading up to and during the transition. The transition in Chile has emerged out of this interplay between bourgeois and popular opposition.

The Opposition in the Transition in Chile

An exclusively top-down focus is particularly inappropriate for analysing Chile. Perhaps more than elsewhere in Latin America, Chile's popular sectors proved themselves capable of pressurizing the authoritarian regime to the point of compelling it to make major concessions and forced the tempo of opposition politics. The Chilean example illustrates both the complexity of opposition to authoritarianism in societies with a previously strong democratic culture and the importance of identifying distinct forms of opposition politics and the interaction between them.

The transition in Chile is informed by the following cleavages: authoritarianism v. democracy; left v. right; party control v. mobilization pressures. They divided civil society and hence the opposition and bear witness to the intricate political affiliations and the ideological divisions which ripped the country apart in 1973. In the period 1973–89, when the opposition candidate won the presidential elections, it is useful to distinguish broadly between party or elite group opposition and mass, popular or extra-party opposition; legitimate and illegitimate opposition; and groups which favour negotiation with the regime and those which have favoured mobilization against it. These categories were not rigidly separated in that overlaps and even merging between categories was possible. Indeed, more and more groups were steadily incorporated into the 'legitimate' opposition after 1983. But the typology makes possible the identification of the various forms of opposition struggle, the consequent differences in strategies and tactics, and hence in the responses of the dictatorship.

The emergence of party-based opposition to the dictatorship has been well documented.[7] Less attention has been paid to non-party opposition, on the assumption that popular movements have been weakened by repression, by their isolation from the parties during the period of clandestinity and the restructuring

---

[6] P. Cammack, 'Democratisation: a review of the issues', *Bulletin of Latin American Research*, 4:2 (1985), 39–46.

[7] On opposition in Chile see A. Angell and B. Pollack, 'The Chilean elections of 1989 and the politics of the transition to democracy', *Bulletin of Latin American Research*, 9:1 (1990), 1–24; International Commission of the Latin American Studies Association, *The Chilean Plebiscite: First Step towards Democratisation* (1989); B. Pollack, 'The dilemmas facing the Chilean left', *Journal of Communist Studies*, 5:2 (June 1989).

of the Chilean economy leading to deindustrialization.[8] However, the emergence of significant extra-party opposition at critical moments in the authoritarian regime should be expected given Chile's long-standing tradition of participatory organizations, populist coalitions and *frentes* outside the party system and at times in opposition to it.[9]

In fact, this tendency became more marked after 1973 because opposition was forced underground and party cadres destroyed. A feature of politics under the dictatorship has been the proliferation of organizations which represent informal sector workers, shanty-town dwellers, those living in *carpamentos* (illegally occupied land) or poor women. The growing organizational capacity of these groups was illustrated by the First Metropolitan Congress of *pobladores* (shanty-town dwellers) in 1986. The working class also participated in the protests less in the form of strikes and stoppages, the traditional form of working-class activism before 1973, and more in street and neighbourhood activities, sometimes rendering whole areas of the capital Santiago no-go areas for 24 hours at a time. Thus, the organizations of the popular sectors occupied a central position in the development of opposition to the dictatorship.

The sudden eruption of street and neighbourhood protests in 1983 in the wake of Chile's severe economic crisis indicated the politicization of popular sectors and signalled the revitalization of the opposition. Although the protests failed in their primary aim of dislodging Pinochet, their importance should not be minimized. They galvanized the political parties into activity and away from internecine struggles, as well as forcing significant concessions from the regime. They also pointed to a resurgence of militancy and new forms of activism from a working class which had suffered a series of defeats since 1973. In relation to a history of the opposition under Pinochet, 1983 marks the turning point, thanks in no small measure to popular activity.

The Chilean opposition was transformed in the period 1983–87 by the resurgence of the party system. The dictatorship responded shrewdly, accepting the reactivation of the party system and conferring *de facto* legitimization on some civilian groups during the period, while repressing others. As a result, after the protests of 1983 had failed directly to overthrow Pinochet, two different options were considered by the party-based opposition: negotiation with the regime or support for mobilization against it. These strategies eventually came to be regarded as contradictory. Of the political parties, only the relatively powerful Communist Party consistently supported mass mobilization until the plebiscite of 1988. Negotiation with the regime was the preferred option of the centre-right, the centre parties, and eventually most of the Socialists.

The consensus within the party-based opposition around negotiation is best illustrated in relation to the 1988 plebiscite. Initially, the plebiscite had posed a serious ideological and tactical dilemma for the parties. Participation could be read as legitimating authoritarian elections and even the regime itself. This issue was most difficult for the left to resolve. In order to take part, the left had

---

[8] See M. Garreton, 'The political evolution of the Chilean military regime and problems in the transition to democracy' in G. O'Donnell, P. Schmitter and L. Whitehead (eds), *Transitions from Authoritarian Rule: Vol. 2. Latin America* (London, Johns Hopkins University Press, 1986).

[9] See A. Angell, 'Some problems in the interpretation of recent Chilean history', *Bulletin of Latin American Research*, 7:1 (1988).

368   *Research Note*

decisively to jettison mobilizational and confrontational tactics so as to reach an agreement with right and centre parties and to allay the suspicions of potential centre-right voters. This in turn increased the likelihood that politicians from the centre or democratic right would control the transition. It was the transformation of the strategies and tactics of the left which made the unity of the opposition possible during the plebiscite and which prepared the defeat of Pinochet. Opposition unity revealed the hollowness of the claim that only the dictatorship stood between the country and chaos. The success of the opposition campaign has strengthened the rebirth of the party system. As a result of this focus, the left has come to see its role as central in assuring the successful reintroduction of representative democracy and of the party system.

As the literature on transition currently stands, the top-down focus implies a greater emphasis on the gradual development of unity of the political parties around negotiation, the plebiscite and the election of December 1989. The top-down approach fails to draw sufficient attention to the significance of the role played by all sectors of the opposition because it has yet to define anything other than a generally negative role for mobilized popular sectors in Latin America. This is in spite of some excellent scholarship in Chile and outside on the growth of popular organizations during the dictatorship.[10] Popular protest is seen as dividing the opposition and hardening the regime, but to read the Chilean transition in this way means missing the dynamic contribution of popular protest, particularly in the period 1983–86. It also overlooks the vital importance of mass participation in the plebiscite and the election campaign, which opened up the democratic possibilities beyond the strict bounds of the 1980 constitution. Hence this approach does not offer an exhaustive analysis of opposition nor of the articulation between forms of opposition.

There is one other possible consequence of the top-down focus: because the role of popular protest in the opposition is ignored or undervalued, it could imply that popular organizations can simply be deactivated during the transition and in the post-authoritarian society. However, in countries like Chile with a long history of democratic and participatory politics this is unlikely to be the case. More than anything else perhaps, this marks Chile out from other Latin American countries which have recently experienced transitions. Yet if the democratic forces themselves err in their analysis of the transition and see the non-party, popular organizations as weak because they failed directly to oust Pinochet, rather than strong because they forced the pace of the transition, any analyses of post-authoritarian social forces will be correspondingly skewed.

In conclusion, a detailed analysis of opposition to authoritarian regimes in transition theories means that the opposition cannot be treated as one unified bloc. Nor should we deal only with supposedly 'successful' opposition, the groups which directly benefit from regime concessions and find themselves to some degree legitimated by the regime. As in Chile, these concessions may in fact have been won by other opposition groups. Transition theory must therefore incorporate and elaborate upon possible inputs from popular sectors on transition from authoritarian rule if it is to be able to speculate upon their possible roles in a post-authoritarian society.

[10] See for example F. Leiva and J. Petras, 'Chile's poor in the struggle for democracy', *Latin American Perspectives*, 13:4 (1986), 5–25.

Eastern Europe

[18]

B.J.Pol.S. **21**, 285–313
Printed in Great Britain

285

Democratization Processes in East Central Europe: A Theoretical Reconsideration

GRZEGORZ EKIERT*

This article explores various dimensions of the issue of transition to democracy in East Central Europe, focusing on the question of how past experiences shape the process of political change and on the limits of democratization in the region. The first part reviews scholarly debates on the relationship between the political crisis and processes of democratization in the region, arguing that new analytical categories are needed to account for different dimensions of the current transition process. The second part proposes a new framework for analysing changing relations between the party–state and society across time and in different state-socialist societies. The third part examines some recent political developments in countries of the region in order to identify those factors that may contribute to or impede a possibility of the transition to democracy in these countries. It concludes that in all East Central European countries the rapid collapse of party–states and the multidimensional social, political and economic crisis has initiated a parallel process of diminution of power of both the state and civil society, which may significantly endanger the transition to a democratic political order.

How well we know all this! How often we have witnessed it in our part of the world! The machine that worked for years to apparent perfection, faultlessly, without a hitch, falls apart overnight. The system that seemed likely to reign unchanged, world without end, since nothing could call its power in question amid all those unanimous votes and elections, is shattered without warning. And, to our amazement, we find that everything was quite otherwise than we had thought.

Vaclav Havel, *Letter to Dr Gustav Husak* (1975)

The little anticipated social, economic and political upheaval that swept Soviet-dominated East Central Europe in 1989 poses a fascinating intellectual challenge to social scientists and policy makers. Among the questions generated by the present momentous processes of change in the region the problem of transition towards democracy is the most interesting both theoretically and politically. This article explores various dimensions of the issue of democratization in East Central Europe. It focuses on the deeply rooted conditions which contributed to the sudden breakdown of state-socialism and probes possible limits to democratization in the region.[1]

* Department of Government, Harvard University. I would like to thank Daniel Bell, Michael Bernhard, Ellen Comisso, Samuel Huntington, Theda Skocpol, Houchang Chehabi, Carlos Forment, Jeff Goodwin, John Hall, Jan Kubik, Tony Levitas, Anna Seleny, Mustafa Emirbayer, Andrew Walder, Jeff Weintraub and all members of the CROPSO seminar at Harvard University for their comments on countless earlier versions of this article and their encouragement in my effort to follow the rapidly unfolding events in Eastern Europe. Special thanks are due to the referees and to the Editor of this *Journal*, Ivor Crewe.

[1] In addressing the issue of democratization, however, I do not speculate about the possible future shape of post-communist societies, agreeing with Comisso that the 'basic task of our field is not so much ... to predict what socialist societies may be in transition to but ... to illuminate some of the fundamental relationships among political, economic, and social variables that are vital to an understanding of all contemporary states and the emerging international order' (E. Comisso, 'Where Have We Been and Where Are We Going? Analyzing the Politics of Socialism in the 1990s' (paper presented at the annual meeting of the Midwest Political Science Association, 1989, p. 2).

286   EKIERT

Although East Central European state-socialist regimes experienced often surprising political instability in the past, we must resist, in my view, the temptation to characterize the social unrest, collective protest and political instability which occurred in the region after the Second World War simply as an inexorable and cumulative process of change leading to democracy.[2] We must also reject the popular notion that the history of East Central Europe began in 1985 with Gorbachev's ascension to power and culminated in 1989 when the Soviet Union decided to remove external guarantees of political order in the dependent countries of the region.

Despite many similarities, the instances of mass protest and social unrest which have occurred in different state-socialist countries do not necessarily form a single historical pattern or trend. While cases of political instability during the transition to and within the post-Stalinist period can be described as a crisis in state-socialism,[3] after the late 1970s countries in the region entered a radically new state of development which can be characterized as a crisis of state-socialism itself. This new transitory phase was shaped by six distinct but none the less interconnected processes: (1) a profound identity crisis within communist parties and the collapse of the Marxist-Leninist 'state-idea'.[4] This process was reflected in the corruption of the party ethos,[5] the disintegration of official political discourse and the transition from legitimation claims based on Marxist-Leninist ideology to ones based on a pseudo-*realpolitik* with strong nationalistic underpinnings; (2) the gradual disintegration of the auxiliary institutions of the party-state, such as trade unions, and professional and youth organizations which had constituted the 'organizational weapon' of state-socialism, serving as 'transmission belts', closing down political space and

[2] Arato, for example, argues that the three most important crises in the region, i.e. the Hungarian revolution (1956), the Prague Spring (1968) and Poland's self-limiting revolution (1980), represent successive attempts to democratize state-socialist regimes. He sees each of these crises as a macro-historical experiment in society's struggle for democratization, claiming that opposition forces changed their strategies from popular revolution in the Hungarian case, to reform from above in the case of Czechoslovakia and, finally, to reform from below in Poland. However, if the notion of three distinct strategies is historically correct, the meaning of democratization and the goals of collective actors in these cases are different. See A. Arato, 'Some Perspectives of Democratization in East Central Europe', *Journal of International Affairs*, 38 (1985), 321–35.

[3] J. Staniszkis argues that these early instances of crisis reproduced the existing type of domination by correcting deficiencies in the redistributive role of the state. At the same time party-states in the region were able to preserve their ideological vigour and political initiative; moreover, they were able to utilize existing reserves provided by extensive economic development and to extend margins of political relaxation within the existing institutional system (J. Staniszkis, *Ontologia Socializmu* (Warsaw: In Plus, 1989), p. 12).

[4] According to P. Abrams the state-idea not only gives directions to the state's policies and influences the state's institutional design but also serves as a tool of legitimation and self-legitimation for ruling elites (see P. Abrams, 'Notes on the Difficulties of Studying the State', *Journal of Historical Sociology*, 1 (1988), 58–90, p. 79).

[5] See K. Jowitt, 'Soviet Neotraditionalism: The Political Corruption of a Leninist Regime', *Soviet Studies*, 35 (1983), 275–98.

insuring political stability; (3) the failure of centrally planned economies, result-ing in economic stagnation, the collapse of the consumer market and severe financial crises on the domestic level as well as the erosion of regional economic institutions; (4) the emancipation of a vigorous second economy reflected in the explosive growth of the black market and of semi-legal and legal private enterprises; (5) the formation of a distinct political society comprising a wide variety of independent social and political movements and organizations; and (6) the relaxation of geopolitical constraints and the granting of increased auton-omy to the party-states in the region by the Soviet Union, itself plagued by economic and political crises. These processes unfolded with varying speed and intensity in different countries; accordingly they produced different con-ditions in which the decomposition of traditional forms of communist power could take place when external guarantees of political order were removed by the dominant regional power.[6]

One can distinguish three characteristic patterns in the beginning of the politi-cal transition in the region. In Poland and Hungary there were negotiated openings in which preliminary pacts between the party-state and opposition forces were established, stipulating the manner and extent of political change. In East Germany and Czechoslovakia rapid political mobilization, or what O'Donnell and Schmitter call 'popular upsurge',[7] forced within a short period of time some significant political concessions. And, finally, in Romania a full-blown revolution paved the way for political transition.

The first stage of the transition process which all the countries in East Central Europe entered in 1989 was characterized by the rapid disintegration of existing political institutions, the further aggravation of economic dislocations, the pro-liferation of various political movements breaking into the political arena and the establishment of transitory power arrangements in which opposition forces acquired varying degrees of access to the official political process and institu-tions. Although the democratic elections which took place in all countries of the region in 1990 established foundations for a democratic system, the consoli-dation of a functioning democratic political order is only one possible outcome of the political transition under way in the region. There are three other possi-bilities. The first is the reversal of present developments and a return to the one-party state with a centrally controlled economy. The second is the anarch-ization of the polity and the economy and a prolonged period of political instability which, in an extreme form, especially when aggravated by ethnic and/or religious cleavages, may turn into what Kis terms the 'Lebanonization

---

[6] This crucial role of geopolitical constraints sets the transitions in East Central Europe apart from most other cases of democratization which have occurred in the last two decades in Southern Europe and Latin America (see L. Whitehead, 'International Aspects of Democratization', in G. O'Donnell, P. C. Schmitter and L. Whitehead, eds, *Transitions from Authoritarian Rule: Prospects for Democracy* (Baltimore, Md: Johns Hopkins University Press, 1986), pp. 3–47).

[7] G. O'Donnell and P. C. Schmitter, *Transitions from Authoritarian Rule: Tentative Conclusions about Uncertain Democracies* (Baltimore, Md: Johns Hopkins University Press, 1986), pp. 53–6.

288   EKIERT

of Eastern Europe'.[8] Finally, a third possibility is the formation of new non-democratic political regimes.

I would suggest that while East Central European state-socialist regimes have already travelled a long way from their Stalinist pasts, a fact which makes the return to traditional state-socialism a highly unlikely possibility, the rise of Western-type democratic regimes in the region is also very uncertain. In my view, a transition towards another type of non-democratic political arrangement is more likely than genuine democratization, given the complexity of the current economic, political and social crisis in the region, as well as certain aspects of its political culture and traditions. The tasks facing new democratically elected governments are so enormous and the required shock treatment of ailing economies so drastic, that some form of coercive policies may be necessary in order to accomplish a fundamental restructuring of political and economic systems.[9] In this respect, East Central European countries find themselves in a much more difficult position than the Southern European regimes which underwent the process of democratization in the 1970s.

Studies of transitions from authoritarianism to democracy in Latin America and Southern Europe can shed light on the East Central European case. These studies clearly suggest that a rapid decomposition of state power, especially when aggravated by serious economic decline, is hardly conducive to the establishment of viable democratic regimes. Stepan points out, for example, in his analysis of the relationship of state and civil society in Latin American countries, that this relationship does not always present itself as a zero-sum game. It is quite likely that in some cases 'the state's capacity to structure outcomes may decline while the opposition's capacity to act in concert also declines'.[10] There is also the possibility that the power of both the state and civil society may grow simultaneously. It can be argued that only the latter pattern of development can bring about a consistent and successful process of democratization.

Applying Stepan's framework to East Central Europe, it should be stressed that the rapid disintegration of party-states in the region produced a power vacuum which has been hastily permeated by highly fragmented political forces. These new political actors have hardly been able, as the East German and Hungarian examples show, to form an effective political alliance. Even in Poland, the only country where a strong all-inclusive political alliance of oppos-

---

[8] J. Kis, 'Not with Them, Not with Us', *Uncaptive Minds*, 2, no. 4 (1989), 33–4.

[9] M. Mann makes a similar point in his analysis of state power. He argues that when the 'infrastructural power' of the state, that is, 'the capacity of the state to penetrate civil society and implement logistically political decisions', is weak, the most likely alternative is the resort to 'despotic power' – to state actions undertaken 'without routine institutionalized negotiation with civil society' (M. Mann, 'The Autonomous Power of the State: Its Origin, Mechanisms, and Results', *Archives Européennes de Sociologie*, 25 (1984), 185–214, pp. 188–90).

[10] A. Stepan, 'State Power and the Strength of Civil Society in the Southern Cone of Latin America', in P. B. Evans, D. Rueschemeyer and T. Skocpol, eds, *Bringing the State Back In* (Cambridge: Cambridge University Press, 1985), pp. 317–43, at p. 318.

ition forces was in place, the process of political fragmentation has become clearly visible in 1990. This situation hints at the possibility of a parallel diminution in the power of both the state and the newly constituted civil society which is likely to hinder successful democratization. The likelihood of such a direction of political change in the region suggests that the general notion of a unilinear transition of state-socialist regimes towards democracy – a derivative of modernization theory, which assumed zero-sum relations between the state and civil society – cannot be maintained. The barriers to democratization in East Central Europe are more complex and formidable than most scholars have previously recognized.

The aim of this article is to investigate the relationship between the state and society under state-socialism and the barriers to democratization. It begins by reviewing scholarly debates about the relationship between the political crisis in the region and processes of democratization; it argues that new analytical categories are needed to account for the present spectacular situation. Secondly, it proposes a framework which offers a more effective tool for analysing the changing relations between the party-state and civil society across time and in various state-socialist societies. And thirdly, it examines some recent political and economic developments in countries of the region in order to identify those processes that may contribute to a potential transition to political democracy, and those which are more likely to impede progressive political change.

I. DEBATES ON THE PROSPECTS FOR DEMOCRATIZATION IN EAST CENTRAL EUROPE

In the 1980s debates in the field of East European studies on the prospects for democratization of state-socialist regimes were centred around the concept of corporatism and the dichotomy between the 'state' and 'civil society'. The new application of classical categories in these debates reflected not only an attempt to grasp conceptually the meaning of fundamental changes under way in some state-socialist societies, but also, as Ash suggests, revealed the collapse of established concepts and analytical categories through which scholars had made sense of East Central European developments during the previous four decades.[11] These debates departed radically from the two previous attempts to address the issue of democratization in state-socialist regimes. The first debate was prompted by the process of de-Stalinization in the 1950s and was entirely framed by the concept of totalitarianism. The second debate, inspired by the changes occurring in East Central Europe after the mid-1960s, resulted in the rejection of the concept of totalitarianism and relied instead on the notion

[11] T. Garton Ash, 'The Empire in Decay', *New York Review of Books*, 35, no. 14 (1988), 53–60, p. 53.

290   EKIERT

of modernization and on a structural-functional approach adopted from the broader field of comparative politics.

The Issue of Democratization in the Totalitarian Approach

The first debate in East European studies on the meaning and effects of de-Stalinization was analytically centred around a pair of dichotomies understood in apparently Manichaean fashion. The first was a distinction between two types of institutional system – namely, totalitarianism and democracy – which underscored the fundamental rupture between Soviet-imposed regimes in East Central Europe and traditional Western democracies. The second was a distinction between forms of ideology – the nationalism which had traditionally been powerful in these countries and the imported, totalitarian ideology imposed by the Soviet Union after the Second World War.

According to scholars representing the totalitarian approach, the wave of social unrest and political instability that swept the entire Soviet bloc and culminated in 1956 with the Hungarian revolution and the Polish October was caused by the ideologically motivated policies of Stalinist regimes that violated the national interests, traditions and values of their societies. The uncompromising and alien character of the communist ideology which guided the behaviour of political elites in the region was held responsible for the economic and political crisis, the resurgence of national aspirations and the subsequent collapse of Stalinist regimes in some countries and the chaos of de-Stalinization policies in the region in general.[12] As Fletcher pointed out, 'overriding all other issues and welding them together into a single explosive mass, was the feeling of outraged national pride. Nationalism became the common denominator of East European resistance to communism'.[13] Similarly, Vali, interpreting the Hungarian revolution, claimed that 'nationalism ... is the most persuasive motivating force which engenders antagonism towards the main facets of Soviet-communist rule.'[14] Accordingly, the Soviet actions in the region during the 1950s were interpreted as a desperate attempt to resist the corroding influence of nationalism. As Brzezinski stated it, 'maintaining a balance between ideological unity and a recognition of domestic diversity is an intricate operation and has shaped much of the history of the formation of the Communist camp and of the relations among its members.'[15]

The hopes for a democratic transition in East Central Europe which emerged from the breakdown of Stalinism were dashed by the Soviet military invasion

[12] Describing the collapse of totalitarian policies, Brzezinski argued that, 'even totalitarian ideologies, dogmatic almost by definition, must respond in some measure to domestic aspirations and must reflect the existing reality, even while striving to change it altogether' (Z. K. Brzezinski, *The Soviet Bloc: Unity and Conflict* (Cambridge, Mass.: Harvard University Press, 1967), p. 139).

[13] G. Fletcher, 'Against the Stream', in T. Aczel, ed., *Ten Years After* (London: MacGibbon & Kee, 1966), pp. 32–58, at p. 56.

[14] F. C. Vali, 'The Regime and the Nation', in Aczel, *Ten Years After*, pp. 137–53, at p. 152.

[15] Brzezinski, *The Soviet Bloc*, p. 493.

of Hungary and by the return to more orthodox policies in Poland. Scholars concluded that de-Stalinization would not result in any significant changes in the dictatorial character of state-socialist regimes, and that the head-on clash of antagonistic ideologies had petered out. A diluted form of communist doctrine, supplemented by nationalist elements, presented itself as a working compromise between Marxist principles and the requirements of national beliefs. It was precisely this alleged compromise of two dominant ideologies which prompted many scholars to claim that state-socialist regimes cannot be truly modernized, liberalized and democratized.[16] Some commentators such as Fletcher argued that concessions forced by the opposition during the 1950s even strengthened the totalitarian character of state-socialist regimes by removing their most self-destructive but not quite indispensable features and practices. Developments in post-Stalinist political regimes, however, were too significant to be dismissed completely. Fletcher, for instance, admitted in 1966 that 'the central development of the past ten years has been the continuing retreat of totalitarianism', even as he pointed out that 'this has been by no means a rectilinear process', and warned that 'Communism ... has shown itself to be vicious, cunning and tenacious in decline'.[17]

The Issue of Democratization in the Modernization/Pluralist Approach

In the mid-1960s increasingly heterogeneous and pragmatic patterns of politics, both domestic and regional, emerged in East Central Europe and greatly undermined the premises of the totalitarian framework. Important developments at the level of theory led to a questioning of this approach as well. The Manichaean and pessimistic outlook of earlier debates was thus slowly replaced by a more optimistic perspective. Scholars noted the liberalizing trends in state-socialist regimes, as expressed in the decline of political terror, increasing popular participation at the local level, the inclusion of experts in the decision-making process, the improvement of living standards, and the expansion of social welfare benefits. Traditional analytical categories and dichotomies were also replaced by concepts imported from comparative sociology and politics. The nature of state-socialist regimes and the character and direction of social and political change were reassessed, and the whole explanatory enterprise was reconstructed on fundamentally different assumptions.

The rethinking of basic concepts took place at several levels. For instance, the notion of ideology as an exclusive propelling agent of historical transformation in state-socialist societies was replaced by a structural-functionalist

---

[16] After the breakdown of Stalinism there were significant political differences between the countries of the region but, according to Brzezinski, 'the new diversity was primarily a function of the diverging national interests of various communist regimes once the initial totalitarian revolution, common to all of them, had run its course' (Brzezinski, *The Soviet Bloc*, pp. 266–7).

[17] Fletcher, 'Against the Stream', p. 56.

292   EKIERT

approach to the conceptualization of political structure and processes.[18] The notion of economic and political modernization, as applicable to societies everywhere and as producing similar effects regardless of the type of political institutions, undermined the notion of the economic and political uniqueness of state-socialist regimes. The presumed causal relationship between economic development, socio-cultural modernization and the structural transformation of the political system allowed scholars to predict evolutionary, linear changes which would involve growing political equality, differentiation of political institutions and the expansion of popular participation in the political process.

From the point of view of this new approach, state-socialist regimes, instead of being considered unique political organizations, came to be regarded as a political form easily fitting on a general continuum of political systems. The very opposition between totalitarianism and democracy was questioned. As Huntington argued in his influential book:

the most important political distinction among countries concerns not their form of government but their degree of government. The differences between democracy and dictatorship are less than the differences between those countries whose politics embodies consensus, community, legitimacy, organization, effectiveness, stability, and those countries whose politics is deficient in these qualities. Communist totalitarian states and Western liberal states both belong generally in the category of effective rather than debile political systems.[19]

Similarly, the dominant role assigned to the conflict of ideologies was replaced by an emphasis on the competition for influence and resources between different groups and elites where the top political leadership played the role of political broker, reconciling major institutional interests within the system. New labels such as 'pluralism', 'welfare state authoritarianism' (Breslauer) or 'institutional pluralism' (Hough) succeeded the notion of totalitarianism. Modernization theory constructed an optimistic scenario of progressive and inevitable liberalization and a likely transition towards democracy. This change was assured, assumed scholars, by the inexorable logic of economic development and institutional pluralization which, sooner or later, would transform state-socialist regimes into advanced industrial societies. Convergence theory gave further credibility to the notion of an imminent fusion of antithetical political systems. It was argued that in the East, the economy would become more market-oriented and individual rights would be extended, while in the West there would be more state control over the economy.

In this debate, in contrast to the previous one where scholars had assumed

---

[18] See V. Nee and D. Stark, 'Toward an Institutional Analysis of State-Socialism', in V. Nee and D. Stark, eds, *Remaking the Economic Institutions of Socialism* (Stanford, Calif.: Stanford University Press, 1989), pp. 3–8.

[19] S. P. Huntington, *Political Order in Changing Societies* (New Haven, Conn.: Yale University Press, 1968), p. 1.

a common-sense idea of democratization, most scholars[20] used the notion of liberalization to describe gradual changes in the relationship between the party-state and society. 'Liberalization' was understood as a process correlative to and resulting necessarily from a more general process of modernization. According to Korbonski, a liberalized state-socialist regime entails a 'measure of pluralism, a degree of political and economic decentralization, and an opportunity for free expression by the participants'.[21] The level of liberalization achieved was assessed differently for various countries and in various time-periods, with peaks occurring during the Prague Spring, the Polish October and post-1968 Hungary.

Paradoxically, however, while the notion of democratization had at least some common intuitive meaning based on particular institutional guarantees and political principles, the notion of liberalization used by many scholars remained vague. As applied to state-socialist regimes, liberalization did not imply any extension of individual and collective liberties or institutional changes, and referred mainly to some modifications in the political and economic practices of the rulers. Therefore, it is probably more accurate to describe the relatively more tolerant political practices of post-Stalinist state-socialist regimes as a process of 'humanization'[22] which, although irreversible, might not have necessarily led to genuine political liberalization and democratization. In short, social analyses based on the notion of modernization assumed that the process of social change in East Central Europe would result in the emergence of liberalized or modernized state-socialist regimes, which, while not possessing authentic democratic institutions and guarantees of civil rights, would nevertheless allow the limited pluralism required by modern technology and modern systems of production.

The Issue of Democratization in the Corporatist Approach

In the second half of the 1970s, creeping economic stagnation, financial crisis and a decline of living standards affected all state-socialist societies, and in some countries created a highly explosive situation. These developments clearly

[20] See A. Korbonski, 'Liberalization Processes', in C. Mesa-Logo and C. Beck, eds, *Comparative Socialist Systems* (Pittsburgh, Pa: University of Pittsburgh Center for International Studies, 1975), pp. 192–214; A. Korbonski, 'Comparing Liberalization Processes in Eastern Europe: A Preliminary Analysis', *Comparative Politics*, 4 (1972), 231–49; R. D. Little, ed., *Liberalization in the USSR: Façade or Reality* (Lexington, Mass.: D. C. Heath, 1968); K. Jowitt, 'The Concepts of Liberalization, Integration, and Rationalization in the Context of Eastern European Development', *Studies in Comparative Communism*, 4 (1971), 79–92.

[21] Korbonski, 'Liberalization Processes', p. 194.

[22] According to Lamentowicz, humanization is an easily detectable process in the development of state-socialist regimes: 'no new rights are won by the non-ruling groups but the style of ruling becomes more sensitive, more humane and, sometimes, more responsive to basic needs'. This process also involves limitation of 'the scope and the level of the unpredictability of repressive measures' (W. Lamentowicz, 'Eastern Europe and the Emergence of Civil Society: Starting Point of a Long Process' (paper presented at the annual meeting of the ASA in Atlanta, 1988, p. 15).

294   EKIERT

undermined expectations of increasing pluralization, liberalization and market-
oriented modernization, and prompted some scholars to look for a new conceptual framework.[23] The concept of corporatism, revived in the social sciences
in the 1970s, presented an ideal framework for capturing the seemingly paradoxical mixture of progressive and liberalizing trends on the one hand, and
regressive and anti-democratic practices characteristic of post-Stalinist state-
socialist regimes on the other. The concept of corporatism also provided a
common ground for a discussion of contrasts and similarities between pluralist
and state-socialist regimes as well as traditional authoritarian regimes. The
corporatist model was most successfully applied to the analysis of political
processes in the 1970s. Bunce and Echols used it to analyse political practices
in the Soviet Union, claiming that 'corporatism will provide us with a more
accurate and more complete description of the politics of the Brezhnev era'.[24]
Similarly, Chirot and Staniszkis used the concept to analyse political processes
in Romania and Poland in the 1970s.[25]

Chirot's analysis specifically directs attention to the development of corporatist institutions in Romania. He argues that 'communist Romania never set
out to create a corporatist structure; it has only evolved one rather imperfectly,
over time, because this was the only way of solving organizational problems'.[26]
Thus, similarly to the modernization approach, he sees the creation of corporatist institutions in a reductionist way as a response to 'immediate economic
and political problems'. He does not share the optimism of the modernization
approach, however, regarding the possibility of a transition towards a more
democratic type of political regime in East Central Europe.

According to Chirot, the corporatist order clearly excludes genuine democratization by virtue of its specific mechanism for constructing and articulating

---

[23] Nee and Stark point to another motive behind this shift of perspective, namely, 'the lack
of fit between the analytical problem constructed by the competing theories and those faced in
societies themselves'. They argue that 'modernization theory misuses the comparative method
and consequently produces inadequate understanding of the distinctive features of the economic
institutions of socialism. [Also] by limiting its examination of interest groups only to elite actors
in or around official circles, modernization/pluralist theory unnecessarily restricts our analytical
field of vision and precludes the possibility that social groups outside the state play a role in
shaping society' (Nee and Stark, 'Toward an Institutional Analysis of State Socialism', pp. 7–8).
[24] V. Bunce and J. M. Echols, 'Soviet Politics in the Brezhnev Era: "Pluralism" or "Corporatism?" ', in D. R. Kelly, ed., *Soviet Politics in the Brezhnev Era* (New York: Praeger, 1980),
pp. 1–26, at p. 3.
[25] It can be argued that the popularity of the concept of corporatism stems in part from its
tempting ambiguity. As Williamson points out, 'Corporatism remains an ambiguous concept in
the political vocabulary, encompassing a wide range of all too often imprecise definition'. His
reconstruction of core dimensions or a general model of corporatism clearly casts doubt on its
applicability to state-socialist regimes (P. J. Williamson, *Varieties of Corporatism* (Cambridge:
Cambridge University Press, 1985), p. 3).
[26] D. Chirot, 'The Corporatist Model and Socialism', *Theory and Society*, 2 (1980), 363–81,
p. 373.

collective interests. He also claims that there is an inherent contradiction between a gradual corporatization of social institutions in state-socialist regimes and the monopolistic role of the Communist party. The party, endangered by the development of corporate institutions, periodically attempts to reassert its absolute control and to 'disorganize emergent corporate challengers'. The inherently non-democratic character of the corporatist order and its encroachment on the party's monopoly therefore make prospects for the democratization of state-socialist regimes rather unlikely. Chirot contends that 'there will be no gradual move toward a parliamentary, party-based democracy on the Western model, but rather toward decentralization of the corporate structure and toward a more poly-centric corporatism. The Party will become relatively weaker and elites in various key functionally defined sectors of the society and economy will gain'.[27] Thus, the relative autonomy of corporate institutions, and pacts between them and the Communist party, aiming at rationalization of the economy, will be the most likely effect of changes in state socialism.

Staniszkis, in her application of the concept of corporatism, does not focus on officially functioning institutional structures, but rather on semi-institutionalized forms of interest articulation which have taken the shape of corporatist networks of relations between the party-state and society. She argues that in Poland,

the corporatist structure of interest representation was authoritatively recognized but not legalized as a part of the political process. Corporatist groups, owing to their semi-legal participation in politics, did not have any specialized political apparatus, and their impact on politics was more a result of the style of the particular ruling team than of lasting institutional arrangement.[28]

This situation rapidly changed after the conclusion of workers' strikes in 1980. Staniszkis claims that it was precisely 'the social cost of corporatism, i.e., social differentiation, the corrosion of law, demoralization, and frustrations at the executive power apparatus, [that] led to the explosion of August 1980.'[29] Consequently, as the result of mass protests, a new institutional representation of interests was formed with a distinctive class basis and a 'class, rather than corporatist, form of interest representation'.[30] The emergence of the Solidarity movement heralded the end of Poland's imperfect corporatism. Society organized in a powerful social movement rejected corporatism as a political project and as an immoral practice in political life. Even the imposition of martial

[27] Chirot, 'The Corporatist Model and Socialism', pp. 376–7.
[28] J. Staniszkis, *Poland's Self-limiting Revolution* (Princeton, Conn.: Princeton University Press, 1984), p. 39.
[29] J. Staniszkis, 'Martial Law in Poland', *Telos*, 54 (1982/83), 87–100, p. 93.
[30] Staniszkis, *Poland's Self-Limiting Revolution*, p. 40.

law, according to Staniszkis, made the return to corporatist techniques barely possible. It can indeed be argued that the 1980 August Agreements signed by the Polish government with the striking workers were the high point and, at the same time, the final defeat of corporatist practices in Poland.[31] In fact, in the 1980s the political opposition, both in Poland and Hungary, rejected the idea of corporatist pacts with the party–state and demanded genuine democratic institutions. Similarly, although for different reasons, the party–states themselves were not able to overcome their internal splits to reformulate the Communist party's political role, and to muster resources necessary for creating viable, autonomous and legal corporate institutions.

As Ost points out in his recent article, however, the situation in Poland may be pointing to an inevitable corporatist solution. The extraordinary agreement legalizing the opposition in the spring of 1989 and the subsequent constitution of the first non-communist government in four decades might seem to be a step in this direction.[32] But already at the beginning of 1989 it was clear that the corporatist solution in East Central Europe was blocked by powerful political obstacles. Firstly, as Cox points out, 'corporatism requires a close affinity of interest and collaboration' between organized and powerful organizations and the state.[33] But in Poland, as the editorial of Solidarity's paper *News* emphasized, 'the necessity of an agreement [stemmed] not from a genuine rapprochement between the two sides but rather from the horrific prospect of a national catastrophe'.[34] This assessment represents a rather peculiar example of an affinity of interests. Moreover, the Polish opposition, by adopting a decentralized and diversified model of 'underground society'[35] after martial law, made the construction of a coherent system of political representation with a commonly accepted programme very unlikely. Generational change and the radicalization of young workers and students, so clearly detectable in the waves of strikes and protests before the 'round-table' negotiations in 1989, and even after the agreements were signed, further underscored the difficulties in reconciling the interests of diverse social groups and movements by the oppositional elites. Although the Solidarity movement has re-emerged as an umbrella organization uniting all oppositional forces, tensions have been grow-

---

[31]   Staniszkis, 'Martial Law in Poland', p. 97.

[32]   D. Ost, 'Towards a Corporatist Solution in Eastern Europe: The Case of Poland', *East European Politics and Societies*, 3 (1989), 152–74. Ost describes the likely corporatist solution in Poland as neo-corporatism or, following Schmitter, as societal corporatism. However, the notion of societal corporatism contradicts the very notion of corporatism itself because the latter's *sine qua non* is the strong state able to control and create interest groups.

[33]   A. Cox, 'Corporatism as Reductionism: The Analytic Limits of the Corporatist Thesis', *Government and Opposition*, 16 (1981), 78–96, p. 85.

[34]   'An accord or only a contract', *News Solidarność*, No. 130, 16–31 March 1989.

[35]   See D. Ost, 'Poland Revisited', *Poland Watch*, 7 (1985), 75–96.

ing rapidly between its trade-unionist and political components as well as between various political programmes and tendencies.[36]

A similar situation developed in Hungary in 1989. As Kis put it 'incipient pluralism [was] not born out of a social contract; it [was] the child of the breakdown of authority. There [were] no rules regulating the activity of the emerging organizations; they simply [tried] to break into the political arena'.[37] The Hungarian opposition, in spite of astonishing political events during the summer and autumn of 1989, was still much weaker and more fragmented than its Polish counterpart. Its social base was primarily restricted to the urban middle class and, unlike Solidarity, it was not a mass political movement.[38] The fragmented character of the Hungarian political opposition was apparent during the negotiations between new political parties and the party–state in the autumn of 1989, when some parties refused to sign the agreement, as well as during the electoral campaign of 1990. The elections, however, quite unexpectedly generated a strong majority for one party in the new parliament.[39]

A second obstacle to the corporatist solution in East Central Europe was the state's inability to grant representational monopoly and to control interest groups. Paradoxically, the party–states of Poland and Hungary were too weak and too divided to be able to control political mobilization from below and to impose the conditions of a corporatist solution.[40] Although the Polish regime invested considerable energy in an attempt to create the so-called 'intra-systemic opposition'[41] and state-controlled trade unions were conceived as partners in a corporatist pact, these efforts clearly failed and the regime was finally forced to legalize independent opposition movements and to surrender its monopoly of power. In other countries of the region the spectacular collapse of party–states in the second half of 1989 dramatically confirmed the weakness

---

[36] See, for example, Z. Bauman, 'Poland: On its Own', *Telos*, 79 (1989), 47–63; D. Ost, 'The Transformation of Solidarity and the Future of Central Europe', *Telos*, 79 (1989), 63–95; J. Staniszkis, 'The Obsolescence of Solidarity', *Telos*, 80 (1989), 37–51.

[37] J. Kis, 'Turning Point in Hungary', *Dissent*, Spring (1989), 235–41, p. 241.

[38] See Kis, 'Not with Them, Not with Us'.

[39] Despite indications to the contrary, Hungary's complicated electoral system produced a clear result. The Democratic Forum won 165 seats out of 386 and together with the Smallholders (43 seats) and the Christian Democrats (21 seats) has a safe majority in the Parliament.

[40] As Kis points out in his analysis of Hungarian reform at the end of the 1980s, 'the leadership and its apparatuses have never been so indecisive as to which elements of the regime are to be treated as untouchable and which permanent and which can be open to transformation' (Kis, 'Turning Point in Hungary', p. 238). Moreover, already at the beginning of the 1980s political initiative had shifted outside the space controlled by the regime. Urban, an official spokesman for the Polish regime, openly acknowledged this change in his confidential letter to the first secretary of the party written in 1981. In this letter he contended that 'we are facing disaster, since in my opinion the time has already passed when PZPR could effect a renewal, remodel the system of government, advance a programme, and obtain the acceptance and support of society' (J. Urban, 'Letter to the First Secretary', *Uncaptive Minds*, 1, no. 4 (1988), 3).

[41] For the notion of 'intra-systemic opposition' see J. J. Wiatr, 'Intra-system Opposition', *Polish Perspectives*, 31, no. 3 (1988), 9–15.

298   EKIERT

of the state and its inability not only to impose a corporatist solution but
even to secure an ordered process of transition.

II. CIVIL SOCIETY, POLITICAL SOCIETY AND THE STATE

The most recent post-Solidarity debate on the prospects for a democratic transition in East Central Europe combined many of the insights from the debates
of the last four decades. On the one hand, the experiences of martial law in
Poland reinforced the fatalistic view that no significant political transformation
is possible.[42] Another, even more bleak view, suggested that the ideological
vacuum left by the collapse of Marxist-Leninist ideology, together with profound economic crisis, were likely to cause a regress to the disreputable nationalistic and authoritarian past.[43] Some students of state-socialist regimes, on
the other hand, saw distinctively new potentials for democratic transition. These
more optimistic approaches were not exclusively influenced by the reformist
drive in the Soviet Union started by Gorbachev in 1985, but rather by domestic
developments in several countries of the region. The formation and growing
influence of a new kind of political opposition in Czechoslovakia and Hungary,
as well as the experiences of the Polish self-limiting revolution and post-
Solidarity political struggles, pointed, in the view of some scholars, to a more
general political process in East Central Europe. According to Arato and Cohen,

---

[42] Feher and Heller clearly represent this point of view when they argue in their recent
book that 'contemporary Soviet totalitarianism, which had left its revolutionary birth-pangs behind,
is an entirely conservative society, a legitimized and at least for the time being, a well-functioning
one. Unfortunately, all hopes of a near collapse of this social structure seem as misguided as
hopes for its eventual thoroughgoing social reform. This does not, of course, exclude changes
within the framework of the existing structures, for no society can be completely static' (F. Feher
and A. Heller, *Eastern Left, Western Left: Totalitarianism, Freedom and Democracy* (Atlantic
Highlands, NJ: Humanities Press International, 1987), p. 250; see also F. Feher, 'Inherent Weakness
and Unfounded Optimism', *Society*, 25, no. 4 (1988), 19–22; and A. Heller, 'Can Communist
Regimes Be Reformed?', *Society*, 25, no. 4 (1988), 22–4). A similar idea can be found in Garton
Ash's metaphor of the 'Ottomanization of the Soviet empire'. Garton Ash not only emphasizes
the continued existence of geopolitical obstacles to democratization, but also stresses the fact
that 'socialism has created in all the East European states an array of domestic barriers against
the transformation to liberal democracy . . . These barriers lie not only in the system of politbureauc-
ratic dictatorship . . . and not merely in the character of interests of the nomenclature ruling class,
but also in the interests, attitudes, and fears of many of the ruled' (T. Garton Ash, 'Reform
or Revolution?', *New York Review of Books*, 35, no. 16 (1988), 47–56, p. 56).

[43] This point of view is represented by Chirot, who, in projecting a likely scenario of Romanian
developments for the whole region, predicts the formation of a new sort of fascism in a form
of xenophobic, anti-rational nationalism (D. Chirot, 'Ideology and Legitimacy in Eastern Europe',
States and Social Structures Newsletter, 4 (1987), 1–4). Such a possibility seems, however, rather
unlikely unless there is a sufficient external threat to mobilize nationalistic fervour.

these changes amounted to nothing less than 'the creation of a post-bourgeois, democratic, civil society'.[44]

In the 1980s the idea of a rebirth of civil society and the old theme of a conflict between the state and civil society invaded the theoretical discourse of East European studies.[45] As Pelczynski observed, 'the subsumption of the history of Polish dissent, and Solidarity in particular, under the category of civil society is a truly remarkable intellectual development'. Few social and political concepts, however, as he noted, 'have travelled so far in their life and changed their meaning so much'.[46] There are two problems with the use of the concept of civil society in recent scholarship on state-socialist regimes. The first involves the specific meaning of this classic and highly contested concept: in its original Lockean or Hegelian definition it is hardly able to account for the complex political and social relations of modern societies.[47] The second is the concept of civil society used by contemporary students of state-socialist societies, who conflate two quite different phenomena. As Garton Ash points out, 'civil society' is used to describe:

(A) the entire range of social associations, ties, and activities independent of the state, from glee clubs to Charter 77, from samizdat to breviaries and from private farmers to homosexuals; (B) more narrowly, and more politically, the products of the strategy of 'social self-organization' which was, broadly speaking, adopted by the democratic opposition in Poland, Hungary and Czechoslovakia in the mid to late 1970s. For them,

---

[44] A. Arato and J. Cohen, 'Social Movements, Civil Society, and the Problems of Sovereignty', *Praxis International*, 4 (1984), 266–83. It should be noted, however, that most recent developments in the region and the abrupt collapse of one-party regimes caught the majority of experts by surprise.

[45] The state–civil society distinction was initially employed to analyse the phenomenon of the Polish self-limiting revolution (see A. Arato, 'Civil Society against the State: Poland 1980–81', *Telos*, 47 (1981), 23–47; A. Arato, 'Empire vs Civil Society: Poland 1981–82', *Telos*, 50 (1981/82), 19–48; Arato and Cohen, 'Social Movements, Civil Society, and the Problem of Sovereignty'; Z. A. Pelczynski, 'Solidarity and "The Rebirth of Civil Society"', in J. Keane, ed., *Civil Society and the State* (London: Verso, 1988), pp. 361–81)) and the new opposition movements in East Central Europe (see J. Rupnik, 'Dissent in Poland, 1968–78: The End of Revisionism and the Rebirth of the Civil Society', in R. L. Tokes, ed., *Opposition in Eastern Europe* (Baltimore, Md: Johns Hopkins University Press, 1979), pp. 60–112; I. Szelenyi, 'Socialist Opposition in Eastern Europe: Dilemmas and Perspectives', in Tokes, *Opposition in Eastern Europe*; V. Havel *et al.*, *The Power of the Powerless: Citizens against the State in Central-Eastern Europe* (Armonk, NJ: Sharpe, 1985); H. G. Skilling, *Samizdat and an Independent Society in Central and Eastern Europe* (Basingstoke: Macmillan, 1988); and T. R. Judt, 'The Dilemmas of Dissidence: The Politics of Opposition in East-Central Europe', *East European Politics and Societies*, 2 (1988), 185–241)). But more recently the notion has been extended to all aspects of independent or semi-independent social life under state-socialist regimes and has even been applied to some aspects of the reform in the Soviet Union (see J. P. Scanlan, 'Reforms and Civil Society in the USSR', *Problems of Communism*, 37, no. 2 (1988), 41–7; F. S. Starr, 'Soviet Union: A Civil Society', *Foreign Policy*, 70 (1988), 26–41).

[46] Pelczynski, 'Solidarity and the "Rebirth of Civil Society"', p. 363.

[47] The conceptual difficulties generated by this classical distinction are aptly analysed by Keane in *Civil Society and the State*, pp. 1–33.

300   EKIERT

the reconstitution of 'civil society' was both an end in itself and a means to political change, including, eventually, change in the nature of the state.[48]

To construct analytical categories which can account for present political developments in East Central Europe, it is necessary to reformulate the traditional distinction between the state and civil society and to define more precisely the social and political phenomena these categories are meant to describe. The first step in such a reformulation would be the substitution of a highly unclear and contested notion of civil society with two separate categories: firstly, the notion of domestic society,[49] which includes the whole range of primary and secondary social groups within society; and, secondly, the category of political society which may be derived from Alexis de Tocqueville and which embraces the entirety of voluntary associations and social movements in an active political community.[50] In this more complex distinction, the state as the apparatus of domination represents the domain of coercive power and administrative mechanisms of control; domestic society represents the domain of purposeful action restricted to the private sphere and organized in terms of material needs and self-interests; and political society, as Forment puts it, refers to

a place or realm where people congregate to debate and act on the burning, public issues of the day. Institutionally located somewhere between the state . . . and the market . . . political society has a distinct existence of its own. In political society, collective activity is organized around the principle of solidarity, and is expressed usually in terms of public debate and participation.[51]

To put it in more aphoristic terms, one may paraphrase Touraine by saying that political society is limited on one side by *Homo Oeconomicus* and, on the other, by Big Brother.[52] This distinction between domestic society, political society and the state allows us not only to account for the various dimensions of the relations between the state and society overlooked by past approaches, but also to identify new socio-political changes and processes in the region which shaped patterns of collapse in state-socialist regimes and to discern the contours of the current transition process.

[48] T Garton Ash, 'The Opposition', *New York Review of Books*, 35, no. 15 (1988), 3–6, p. 3.

[49] For the lack of a better term I borrowed this notion from the Spanish Jesuit Francisco Suares, who in his *Tractatus de legibus ac Deo legislatore* (1612) points out that 'human society is twofold: imperfect, or domestic; and perfect, or political' (cited in M. Curtis, ed., *The Great Political Theories* (New York: Avon Books, 1961), p. 288).

[50] I owe the idea of the importance of the concept of political society in Tocqueville and its possible application to state-socialist regimes to Jeff Weintraub. See J. Weintraub, 'Tocqueville's Conception of Political Society' (unpublished manuscript, 1986).

[51] C. A. Forment, 'Socio-Historical Models of Spanish American Democratization: A Review and a Reformulation' (Harvard University, CROPSO Working Paper Series, No. 0015, 1988), p. 21.

[52] A. Touraine, 'An Introduction to the Study of Social Movements', *Social Research*, 52 (1985), 742–89, p. 763.

Democratization Processes in East Central Europe 301

The Party–State Against Society: The Struggle for Political Space

Historical stages in the development of Soviet-type regimes in East Central Europe can be consistently categorized on the basis of relations between the party–state, domestic society and political society. One can distinguish four characteristic periods; firstly, the period of the imposition of Soviet-type regimes, accomplished by 1948, during which the polymorphic party–state was created and traditional political society was completely destroyed; secondly the period of Stalinization, lasting until the mid-1950s, which may be characterized as a full-blown assault on domestic society in the attempt to penetrate primary social ties and to politicize the entire network of social relations;[53] thirdly, the post-Stalinist period, which first ended in Poland with the formation of the Solidarity movement, where a 'pact of nonaggression' between the party–state and domestic society was established and where domestic society 'resocialized' the party–state from below; fourthly, the post-communist period, characterized by the reconstitution of a new political society, the identity crisis and institutional decay of the party–state, the dissolution of the official political discourse and the disintegration of the centrally planned economy.

The destruction of traditional political society in the countries of East Central Europe was accomplished by terroristic political means employed by the Communists under the umbrella of the Soviet army and police during the first years after the war.[54] Democratic institutions were dismantled, social organizations destroyed, trade unions incorporated into the state, and autonomous economic and political actors annihilated. The destruction of political society was further facilitated by the nationalization of the economy, the massive industrialization drive, mass migrations of the population and the opening of channels of social mobility through which social categories hitherto excluded from the polity (mainly the peasants) moved rapidly upwards to establish the ruling stratum of the new regime.

In this context, let me propose a hypothesis which could highlight differences in the level of terror and repression in different state-socialist countries during the imposition and consolidation of state-socialist regimes. It has been argued that Poland was a remarkable exception during this period because repression was relatively mild compared to other countries. This puzzle can be explained

---

[53] For a concise analysis of Stalinization policies in Hungary see E. Hankiss, 'Demobilization, Self-Mobilization, and Quasi-Mobilization in Hungary, 1948–1987', *East European Politics and Societies*, 3 (1989), 105–52.

[54] See T. T. Hammond, ed., *The Anatomy of Communist Takeovers* (New Haven, Conn.: Yale University Press, 1975) and B. Szajkowski, *The Establishment of Marxist Regimes* (London: Butterworth Scientific, 1982). This process of destruction was described by the infamous Hungarian leader Rakosi as 'salami tactics'. In Hungary the Communist party first entered into a coalition with the Smallholders, Peasants and Social Democratic parties in order to annihilate the conservatives. It then crushed the Smallholders party with the help of the remaining two parties. In the next step the Communists suborned the Peasants party and absorbed the Social Democrats, annihilating those parties' leadership. In the course of this manœuvering, politicians were bribed, intimidated, imprisoned, driven into exile or killed.

302   EKIERT

by the fact that Poland emerged from the war with its political and intellectual elites almost totally wiped out. Moreover, the social categories which formed the basis of pre-war political society (the intelligentsia, landowners, petty-bourgeoisie and bourgeoisie) were also effectively eliminated during the war. All other countries in the region survived the war with significantly smaller demographic losses and with a significant part of their pre-war professional, political and bureaucratic elites intact.[55] This difference is clearly detectable in political developments before 1948 in Hungary and Czechoslovakia, where the Communist party faced more effective and organized legal political opposition. Another indication of the importance of the absence of traditional political society in Poland was the 1956 transition to the post-Stalinist period. During the Hungarian revolution traditional political society was reborn within a few days, including all the political parties, associations and organizations suppressed by the Communists after the war. In Poland only the Catholic Church was able to recover from Stalinist suppression, and the absence of non-Communist political forces made the political crisis and transition from Stalinism far less dangerous and more controllable.

It can be argued that various important political processes in the post-Stalinist period in East Central Europe, such as the Polish October in 1956, Kadar's stabilization policies in Hungary after the revolution, the Prague Spring and its aftermath, were based on and reflected a fundamentally similar relationship between the state and society. This relationship could be characterized as one in which the state 'signed' an implicit pact of non-aggression with domestic society, allowing citizens to pursue (within limits) private and egoistic ends in exchange for withdrawal from public life and politics.[56] Thus the absence of political society h ●, been a crucial condition of stability in Soviet-type regimes in the post-Stalinist period. However, the elimination of political society and the achievement of an accommodation between the party–state and domestic

---

[55] Kovacs and Orkeny estimate that Poland lost 77 per cent of her professionals, businessmen and civil servants during the war. By comparison in Hungary losses in these groups were only about 10 per cent, and the situation was similar in other countries (M. M. Kovacs and A. Orkeny, 'Promoted Cadres and Professionals in Post-War Hungary', in R. Andorka and L. Bertalan, eds, *Economy and Society in Hungary* (Budapest: Hungarian Sociological Association, 1986), pp. 139–53). See also A. Gella, *Development of Class Structure in Eastern Europe: Poland and Her Southern Neighbors* (Albany: State University of New York Press, 1989), pp. 167–202.

[56] This implicit social pact between the party–state and society has sometimes been called a 'new social contract' (see A. J. Liehm, 'The Intellectuals on the New Social Contract', *Telos*, 23 (1975), 156–64 and A. J. Liehm, 'The New Social Contract and the Parallel Polity', in J. L. Curry, ed., *Dissent in Eastern Europe* (New York: Praeger, 1983), pp. 173–82). However, the idea of a social contract may be highly misleading in the context of state-socialist regimes and this relationship is better described, following Pakulski, as an example of relations based on 'conditional tolerance' (J. Pakulski, 'Legitimacy and Mass Compliance: Reflections on Max Weber and Soviet-Type Societies', *British Journal of Political Science*, 16 (1986), 35–56; see also G. Ekiert, 'Conditions of Political Obedience and Stability in State-Socialist Societies: The Inapplicability of Weber's Concept of Legitimacy' (Harvard University, CROPSO Working Paper Series, No. 0005, 1987)).

society had unexpected consequences which created a sort of permanent crisis of post-Stalinist state-socialist regimes.

After the destruction by the Communists of old political and social movements, traditional political institutions and intellectual elites, democratic civic culture and traditions, and following a thorough rebuilding of the social structure, the party–state apparatus became infused with the norms, values and patterns of behaviour characteristic of domestic society. In all these countries domestic society resisted and survived the Stalinist assault and the party–state's attempt to politicize the entire network of social relations and to abolish the distinction between the private and the public. Silent popular resistance undermined this effort to make the private public and thus susceptible to political control. In fact, the Stalinist reconstruction of the social order through an expansion of state power did not extend the public sphere but rather negated it altogether. In the post-Stalinist period domestic society, benefiting from the more restrained and inclusive strategies and policies of the party–state, grew in strength and slowly colonized all aspects of official institutional relations. This process became noticeable in the 1960s and acutely apparent in the last two decades. For years, however, the narrow preoccupation of Western scholars with political elites and the political decision-making process, as well as with the reductionist character of models applied to state-socialist societies, resulted in an almost complete disregard for this phenomenon.

Consequences of the Truce Between the Party–State and Domestic Society

Only in recent years have some scholars explored the role of domestic society in shaping the official institutional practices of state-socialist regimes. It has become clear that the unintended consequences of the annihilation of political society, the negation of the public sphere and the accommodation between the party–state and domestic society produced the informal institutionalization of an elaborate and enormous system of clientelism and corruption.[57] It also established informal mechanisms of interest mediation and representation.[58]

There have been two characteristic results of this type of accommodation between the state and society. The first of these is a process which Hankiss describes as 'the resocialization from below of the state and party institutions'[59]

---

[57] See, for example, V. Shlapentokh, *Public and Private Life of the Soviet People* (Oxford: Oxford University Press, 1989); K. Simis, *USSR: The Corrupt Society* (New York: Simon & Schuster, 1982); A. Walder, *Communist Neo-Traditionalism: Work and Authority in Chinese Industry* (Berkeley: University of California Press, 1986); A. Z. Kamiński, 'Coercion, Corruption and Reform: State and Society in the Soviet-type Socialist Regimes', *Journal of Theoretical Politics*, 1 (1989), 77–102; Jowitt, 'Soviet Neotraditionalism: The Political Corruption of a Leninist Regime'; J. Tarkowski, 'Old and New Patterns of Corruption in Poland and the USSR', *Telos*, 80 (1989), 51–63.

[58] See Staniszkis, *Poland's Self-Limiting Revolution*, pp. 38–40.

[59] E. Hankiss, 'The "Second Society": Is There an Alternative Social Model Emerging in Contemporary Hungary?' *Social Research*, 55 (1988), 13–43, p. 31.

304   EKIERT

and Kaminski as 'the privatization of the state'.[60] Through this process 'bureaucratic relations' have been transformed into 'clientelistic networks' representing in a selective and arbitrary way certain social interests and distributing
privileges and resources in exchange for political compliance. The process of
'resocialization from below' resulted in the abandonment of political mobilization strategies, and the gradual legalization or toleration of certain types of
previously forbidden individual social and economic activities: for example,
household production and sale in the market or black market of foreign
currency and goods. These more permissive conditions generated a booming
second economy which secured the tolerated existence and expansion of
domestic society and established reciprocal relations between segments of domestic society and the ruling elites.

Secondly, this process of accommodation not only undermined the legal
and institutional framework of the party–state, but was also reinforced by
a state strategy described by Feher and Heller as the 'collective bribery of
the nation'.[61] Post-Stalinist regimes replaced the use of terror with a strategy
of de-politicizing different segments of the population considered to be essential
to maintaining political stability by offering privileges in exchange for a withdrawal from politics. The party–state targeted intellectuals,[62] professionals
and selected groups of highly concentrated and educated industrial workers
(miners, steel workers and shipyard workers) with higher salaries and special
privileges. Such practices caused the corrosion of law, demoralization and a
widespread sense of moral crisis in all segments of society. But these practices
also corrupted, as Jowitt points out, the ethos of the party and reduced its
ability to act as an agent of reform.[63]

It can be argued that the persistence and eventual toleration of domestic
society in state-socialist countries contributed significantly to the peculiar characteristics of their social and political orders. Contrary to popular belief about
the crushing force of Marxist-Leninist ideology and of modern processes of
industrialization and urbanization, during the Stalinist period (and, more
especially, the post-Stalinist period) the ways of thinking and acting peculiar
to the stage of development of domestic society in the region were transferred
to the political arena and combined with imported political traditions and
institutions. Szelenyi characterizes this process as 'silent revolution from below',

[60] A. Z. Kamiński, 'Uprywatnienie panstwa. O problemie korupcji w systemach post-rewolucyj-
nych', in M. Marody and A. Sułek, eds, Rzeczywistość polska i sposoby radzenia sobie z nia (Warsaw:
University of Warsaw, Institute of Sociology, 1987), pp. 137–59.

[61] F. Feher and A. Heller, Hungary 1956 Revisited (London: Allen & Unwin, 1983), p. 147.

[62] G. Konrad and I. Szelenyi interpreted this development as leading to the formation of a
new dominant class in which the party bureaucrats and intellectuals were united as a more inclusive
ruling elite (G. Konrad and I. Szelenyi, The Intellectuals on the Road to Class Power (Brighton,
Sussex: Harvester, 1979). For a critique of their conclusion see J. Frentzel-Zagorska and K.
Zagorski, 'East European Intellectuals on the Road of Dissent: The Old Prophecy of a New
Class Re-examined', Politics and Society, 17 (1989), 89–113. See also M. Haraszti, The Velvet
Prison: Artists under State Socialism (New York: Basic Books, 1987).

[63] Jowitt, 'Soviet Neotraditionalism'.

Democratization Processes in East Central Europe   305

through which subordinate groups forced concessions from their bureaucratic rulers and sustained activities and aspirations rooted in enduring habits and dispositions.[64]

These particular features of East Central European domestic society which, in fact, reinforced the negation of the public sphere can be traced back to the economic backwardness of the region, the peasant tradition of these countries and their turbulent political history, in which a democratic political culture and a developed market economy had little chance to become well established and absorbed by the population.[65] For East Central European domestic society was never organized by the logic of a market system, but rather by a peculiar blend of etatist economic policies and a household type of production.[66] In short, the recent expansion of the second economy and domestic society should be seen as a result of a long process in which some elements of a historical legacy were reinforced in intended and unintended ways by the capacities and strategies of the party-state.

III. THE TRANSITION TO POST-COMMUNIST REGIMES IN EAST CENTRAL EUROPE

The breakdown of this post-Stalinist accommodation between the party–state and domestic society in the 1980s took place by means of two distinctive processes. The first is the rebirth and reassessment of traditional political and cultural values designed by intellectual elites as an attempt to defy dominant political institutions and to permeate the vacuum left by the collapse of Marxist-Leninist ideology and the dissolution of official political discourse.[67] This development can be described as the formation of a new political society and the creation of open public spaces.

The reconstitution of political society can be seen in three distinct dimensions

[64] I. Szelenyi, *Socialist Entrepreneurs: Embourgeoisement in Rural Hungary* (Madison: University of Wisconsin Press, 1988), p. 5.

[65] In a recent article J. Wasilewski analyses the impact of the social mobility of the peasant class in Poland after the war. He argues that the peasants were not only a majority of the population before the war but also the only social stratum which survived the war relatively intact and supplied the human material for the processes of industrialization, urbanization and the formation of new elites. As a result there was a significant 'ruralization' of cities, culture and political life. Thus social norms and values, styles of life and aspirations, cultural patterns and practices rooted in the Polish peasant tradition dominated the urban culture destroyed by the war and penetrated institutions of the party–state (J. Wasilewski, 'Społeczeństwo polskie, społeczeństwo chłopskie', *Studia Socjologiczne*, 3 (1986), 39–56).

[66] See J. Rothschild, *Return to Diversity: A Political History of East Central Europe Since World War II* (Oxford: Oxford University Press, 1989), pp. 20–3.

[67] For more detailed analysis of this process see R. Scruton, 'The New Right in Central Europe I: Czechoslovakia', *Political Studies*, 36 (1988), 449–63; R. Scruton, 'The New Right in Central Europe II: Poland and Hungary', *Political Studies*, 36 (1988), 638–53; J. Kubik, 'John Paul II's First Visit to Poland and the Collapse of the Official Marxist-Leninist Discourse' (Harvard University, CROPSO Working Paper Series, No. 0025, 1989); Judt, 'The Dilemmas of Dissidence'.

306   EKIERT

and in three separate organizational forms.[68] First was the revival of religion, which may be characterized as the shift from private to public religiosity.[69] This phenomenon involved not only the renewal of ecclesiastic institutions but, more importantly, the development of a wide range of lay institutions and associations which provided public space and support for various cultural, social and political activities. The second was a rapid development of critical cultural movements, youth subcultures and alternative way-of-life movements,[70] which often found institutional space on the fringes of official party–state institutions such as youth organizations. And finally, there was the eruption of political movements and organizations *sensu stricto*, which include modern single-issue movements, independent professional associations and trade unions, traditional political movements and embryonic political parties. The key to this process was the emergence of a new political discourse, new collective identities and new forms of social solidarity.

In the mid-1970s oppositional intellectuals in several countries developed a new political language and revived old political and cultural traditions which allowed different political actors within society to build new all-inclusive identities, monopolize political initiative and win public support. This new political discourse decoupled social analysis from traditional Marxist language and was built around concepts of human and political rights, legality, individual responsibility, personal rights and neo-evolutionism. These ideas, according to Scruton, 'constitute[d] a decisive reaction against the previously accepted alternative of "socialism with a human face"'.[71] The redefinition of political language facilitated an intellectual reconciliation between various opposition movements and the Church, and revindicated progressive national traditions.[72]

Only in Poland, however, was the development of new political society fully realized. Solidarity was a mass movement with developed organization, symbols and collective identity, which enjoyed wide-ranging social support. For years it had an extensive underground network and an institutional basis through its co-operation with the Church. In Czechoslovakia, groups gathered around Charter 77 were not able to establish any significant links to important segments

[68] See Hankiss, 'The "Second Society" ', p. 29.

[69] See, for example, P. Ramet, 'Religious Ferment in Eastern Europe', *Survey*, 28 (1984), 87–117; K. Cordell, 'The Role of the Evangelical Church in the GDR', *Government and Opposition*, 25 (1990), 48–60; and also the interview with father Vaclav Maly ('Not a Prophet but an Optimist', *Uncaptive Minds*, 1, no. 4 (1988), 37–41).

[70] See Z. Rykowski and J. Wertenstein-Żuławski, eds, *Wybrane zagadnienia spontanicznej kultury młodzieżowej w Polsce* (Warsaw, 1986); A. Bozoki, 'Critical Movements and Ideologies in Hungary', *Sudosteuropa*, 37 (1988), 377–87; T. W. Ryback, *Rock around the Bloc: A History of Rock Music in Eastern Europe* (New York: Oxford University Press, 1990).

[71] Scruton, 'The New Right in Central Europe I', p. 461.

[72] The fusion of the new political discourse with the traditional identities and historical experiences of these nations is likely to produce different results. Szelenyi compares Polish and Hungarian roads to civil society, arguing that the self-organization of society in Hungary finds its expression in the economy while in Poland this self-organization by-passes the economy and is expressed within the polity (see Szelenyi, 'Eastern Europe in an Epoch of Transition').

Democratization Processes in East Central Europe 307

of the population or to pragmatic elements inside the party–state, nor to build a mass opposition movement.[73] Yet in recent years there was growing political unrest, a multiplication of small independent groups, and a significant revival of the Catholic Church and religion. Similarly, in East Germany, where the Lutheran Church played an instrumental role in supporting embryonic political opposition, independent political society was very weak, comprising small, decentralized activist groups associated with particular churches. In less repressive Hungary, despite increasing political mobilization, new and revived oppositional political movements and groups were also weak and fragmented. But in contrast to Czechoslovakia, East Germany and Poland, Hungarian opposition was reinforced by reformist drive from above, initiated by pragmatic segments of the ruling elite. The Hungarian round-table negotiations, started by the state reflected acceptance of the inevitability of fundamental political change and served as an example of political action from above which benefited and legitimized both the reformist faction within the ruling elite and the opposition movements which were invited to participate.[74]

It was inevitable that in the relaxed political climate in Europe at the end of the 1980s political society in all these countries, representing the realm of public activity outside the structures of the party–state, would strive to institutionalize itself. Logically, such institutionalization could have been accomplished either by a compromise with reformist sections of the party–state or by a conflict with the state in which coalitions would have been built between emerging political actors and significant segments of domestic society. The first strategy developed in Hungary and to a certain degree in Poland, while the second – institutionalization through confrontation – took place in all other countries where Communist parties did not, for a variety of reasons, have the room for political manœuvre which the Hungarian party enjoyed.

It can be argued, therefore, that the strength of an emerging political society and its relation to the party–state was crucial to the process leading to political opening and subsequent liberalization in the countries of East Central Europe. The events of 1989 show that where political society was stronger and pragmatic forces within the party–state were more influential, there were negotiated openings, as in the case of Poland and Hungary. A weaker political society and a more ineffective reformist faction within the party–state facilitated popular upsurge in East Germany and Czechoslovakia. The absence of even a rudimentary political society and the non-existence of pragmatic forces within the party elite, a testimony to the neo-patrimonial character of the party–state, resulted in a revolutionary upheaval in Romania.

---

[73] See J. Bugajski, *Czechoslovakia: Charter 77's Decade of Dissent* (Washington, DC: Praeger with the Center for Strategic Studies, 1987) and Skilling, *Samizdat and an Independent Society*, pp. 43–157.

[74] For a brief overview of independent opposition movements in Eastern Europe see Skilling, *Samizdat and Independent Society*, pp. 157–239 and J. Pehe, 'Annotated Survey of Independent Movements in Eastern Europe', *Radio Free Europe*, Background Report/100, Munich, 13 June 1989.

308   EKIERT

A second process shaping the situation in East Central Europe which often, but not necessarily, went together with the formation and institutionalization of political society, was the slow relaxation of ideological, political and organizational constraints through which the party–state kept in check, often unsuccessfully, the expansion of domestic society.[75] This process, reflected in the development of a second economy, was crucially important not only because it was a necessary element of the economic reform of state-socialism initiated by the state[76] or forced by political society, but also because it produced quite unexpected and unintended political and social consequences.

Studies of the effects of market reforms in the 1980s show a growing system of inequalities. Scholars in the 1970s assumed that social inequalities in state-socialist societies were exclusively generated by the central redistributive mechanism and could be corrected by the introduction of market mechanisms,[77] but by the 1980s Szelenyi and Manchin noticed that 'while market-oriented reform did indeed have some equalising effect, it also began to generate inequalities of its own; to some extent at least, the inequalities induced by redistribution and by the market began to reinforce, rather than to counteract, each other.'[78] Presenting carefully selected empirical examples, Szelenyi and Manchin showed that in Hungary there was a rapid accumulation of privileges and resources by the new entrepreneurial class, as well as by a significant faction of the cadre elite which learned how to exploit market opportunities. On the other hand, there was an accumulation of disadvantages among large segments of the population which did not have access either to the old redistributive system or to market-generated income. In addition, it should be noted that the economic crisis which affected all state-socialist economies and the significant slowdown of economic development were additional factors reinforcing these structurally generated inequalities.[79]

[75] See J. Rostowski, 'The Decay of Socialism and the Growth of Private Enterprise in Poland', *Soviet Studies*, 41 (1989), 194–214; A. Bloch, 'Entrepreneurialism in Poland and Hungary', *Telos*, 79 (1989), 95–108.

[76] Szelenyi argues that the opening of the second economy was a strategy pursued by the Hungarian regime over the last ten years. Although quite successful as a strategy, it was not able to solve the crisis of a centrally planned economy (see I. Szelenyi, 'Eastern Europe in an Epoch of Transition: Toward a Socialist Mixed Economy?', in Nee and Stark, *Remaking the Economic Institutions of Socialism*, pp. 208–33).

[77] See, for example, I. Szelenyi, 'Social Inequalities under State Socialist Redistributive Economies', *International Journal of Comparative Sociology*, 19 (1978), 61–87; for a comprehensive analysis of social inequalities under state-socialism see P. Kende and Z. Strmiska, eds, *Equality and Inequality in Eastern Europe* (Leamington Spa: Berg, 1987).

[78] I. Szelenyi and R. Manchin, 'Social Policy Under State Socialism: Market Redistribution and Social Inequalities in East European Socialist Societies', in M. Rein, G. Esping-Andersen and L. Rainwater, eds, *Stagnation and Renewal in Social Policy* (Armonk, NJ: Sharpe, 1987), pp. 102–39, at p. 102.

[79] Dye and Zeigler convincingly argue this point through the comparative study of inequality. They contend that there is 'no discernible relationship between socialism and equality. Rather, inequality is inextricably linked to low levels of economic development' (T. R. Dye and H. Zeigler, 'Socialism and Equality in Cross-National Perspective', *PS: Political Science and Politics*, 21 (1988), 45–57, p. 54).

This situation posed a danger and dilemmas for political reform movements in the region. Growing inequalities generated not only by the opening of the second economy but more importantly by attempts to establish a genuine market economy threatened to destroy tactical political alliances, symbolized by the Polish Solidarity movement, and to diminish the power of new political societies by increasing competition among sectional and group interests, unleashing demagogic populist tendencies and making an anti-market reform coalition possible. Scholars like Szelenyi and Manchin emphasize that reformist forces in East European countries remain quite unprepared to solve this problem and to design new institutional mechanisms which would counteract the growing accumulation of inequalities. This may undermine the whole political reform process and result in coalitions of conservative political forces within the old ruling elite and those groups that do not benefit directly from the relaxation of economic policies. Poland provides the best example of this problem. The lack of a new consistent social policy was evident not only in the 1980s but even after the introduction of a full-scale marketization of the economy in 1990. In April 1990, facing a drastic decrease of living standards, economic recession and growing unemployment, the Polish Ministry of Labour admitted that 'we are not ready, either psychologically or organizationally, to confront the problem of unemployment'.[80]

These growing inequalities are reinforced by continuing economic decline, which produces severe dislocations and drastically affects the living standards of the population, as well as by radical marketization and austerity policies like those already introduced in Poland and Hungary.[81] These policies involve the large-scale privatization of state-owned assets which will necessarily entail a massive redistribution of wealth. Although all state-socialist economies must move beyond the reformist strategies of the past in order to overcome the present economic stagnation,[82] it is inevitable that a radical transformation of the existing economic system will produce dramatic social and political tensions and significantly endanger prospects for democratization in the region.[83]

Thus, the developments leading to the recent upheaval in East Central Europe were not defined exclusively by the conflict between the party–state and political society over political concessions, institutionalization of opposition movements and democratic reforms. The picture is much more complex and includes

[80] See 'Jaka koniunktura – takie bezrobocie', *Gazeta Wyborcza*, 7–8 April 1990; see also the interview with Prof. Andrzej Tymowski, 'Jutro będzie za późno', *Trybuna*, 50, 10 April 1990.

[81] See J. Bugajski, 'Poland's Anti-Communist Manifesto', *Orbis*, 34 (1990), 109–21; J. Kornai, *The Road to a Free Economy* (New York: Norton, 1990); M. Wolnicki, 'Self-Government and Ownership in Poland', *Telos*, 80 (1989), 63–79.

[82] Szelenyi, 'Eastern Europe in the Epoch of Transition', p. 208.

[83] Szelenyi and Manchin make the point that 'the expansion of market forces and the re-emergence of a market-indexed system of inequalities has created such a complex system of social conflicts that economic reform will be able to continue only if it discovers how to counteract the inefficiencies and inequalities created by the market.' They persuasively claim that 'the unity of social and economic reform or no reform at all – these are the real alternatives facing Eastern Europe' (Szelenyi and Manchin, 'Social Policy under State Socialism', p. 136).

310   EKIERT

domestic society's drive for emancipation and for the freedom to pursue individual ends and interests at the expense of the collapsing party–state and socialist economy – a struggle in which it has been supported by many forces within the new political society. Also important have been the relationships between new political groups and domestic society,[84] and between the party–state and domestic society.[85] Paradoxically, various political forces within both political society and the party–state have looked to domestic society as an actual or potential ally. All this has set the stage for many possible coalitions, conflicts and cleavages, in both horizontal and vertical dimensions which may decisively shape the course of the transition from state-socialism.

IV. CONCLUSIONS – DILEMMAS OF DEMOCRATIZATION

The events of 1989 mark a turning point in the history of socialism in East Central Europe. The rapid collapse of political regimes which dominated the region for the last four decades is the culmination of a long process of economic, social and political decay, as well as the result of the still puzzling decline of Soviet imperial will. The transition from state-socialism in the region is shaped by the legacies of these four decades of political dictatorship and distorted economic development. Moreover, the polymorphous nature of state-socialist regimes characterized by the lack of a clear distinction between political and economic institutions requires the simultaneous and fundamental reconstitution of both political and economic systems. Thus the transition process in East Central Europe implies a parallel effort to establish new democratic institutions and to convert centrally planned and state-owned economies into free market economies. The interaction between the democratization of the polity and the marketization of the economy presents a specific problem and creates an additional dimension of conflicts and tensions which are largely

[84] By supporting and promoting private ownership, property rights and free exchange, neo-liberal and neo-conservative groups within political society desire to create a new social force which, as classical liberalism would have it, might serve as the foundation for a free political system. This potential alliance was designed to form an irresistible, democratic political force confronting the party–state and forcing political concessions. T. Syryjczyk, the new Polish Minister of Industry, stressed this point of view in arguing that 'the only guarantee of democracy is a middle class that prizes the notions of contract and property' (A. Applebaum, 'Polish Government appointees stress pragmatism, steer clear of ideology', *Boston Globe*, 10 September 1989).

[85] The state, by relaxing control over some dimensions of economic life and thus accommodating private interests and individualistic acquisitive drives in the economic sphere, hoped to protect its political domination. It sought to channel people's attention into the accumulation of goods and the struggle for economic survival and success. Such a policy could create an alliance for what Ash ironically calls 'a suitably Central European outcome of Socialism' – 'Capitalists and Communists, shoulder to shoulder against the proletariat' (Ash, 'Reform or Revolution?' p. 56). But, as Szelenyi and Manchin point out, it may also result in an alliance between anti-reformist groups within the state and party apparatus and pauperized sectors of domestic society, an outcome which could threaten any economic and political reforms (see Szelenyi and Manchin, 'Social Policy under State Socialism').

absent in classical transitions from authoritarian regimes.[86] Moreover, the democratization process in the region has been unfolding against the backdrop of an acute economic and social crisis, making newly elected democratic governments the administrators of social and economic catastrophe rather than the champions of freedom and prosperity.

The transition to democracy is likely to occur in situations in which the powers of the state and civil society simultaneously expand. In East Central Europe, however, given the immensity of change both in the polity and economy, it is more probable that the power of the state and civil society will simultaneously decline. Thus, in spite of the significant shift to democratic political procedures in these countries, the transition to an effective and functioning democratic system is still very much in doubt. While various generations of students of state socialist regimes have identified the barriers to democratization as solely political, especially geo-political, these barriers appear to be more complex, depending equally on the successful institutionalization of new mechanisms of interest mediation and on the effective restructuring of economic institutions. In recent years many scholars have pointed to a number of important factors which may impede the process of democratization in the region. Morawska has emphasized the destructive impact of the economic crisis, declining standards of living and anti-pluralist tendencies in Polish popular culture.[87] Other scholars have stressed the fragility of popular social support for any radical transformation of the economic system and the rather precarious position of major social strata *vis-à-vis* the state's reformist efforts.[88] Finally, Comisso has pointed to 'objective' factors built into the functioning of socialist economic institutions which in spite of political will can effectively block the transition towards a market economy.[89] The radical political change in the

[86] In his study dealing with transitions to democracy in Europe and Latin America, Adam Przeworski concludes that 'we cannot avoid the possibility that a transition to democracy can be made only at the cost of leaving economic relations intact, not only the structure of production but even the distribution of income' (A. Przeworski, 'Some Problems in the Study of the Transition to Democracy', in O'Donnell, Schmitter and Whitehead, eds, *Transitions from Authoritarian Rule*, pp. 47–64, at p. 63). I would suggest, however, that in Eastern Europe a fundamental reform both of allocation mechanisms and the structure of ownership constitutes a pivotal element in the transition from state-socialist regimes. The fusion of the state and the economy in state-socialism forces a thorough remaking of economic institutions. And while the new economies rising on the rubble of the state-owned and run economic system will differ in many respects, there will certainly not be a painless road to a market system.

[87] E. Morawska, 'On Barriers to Pluralism in Pluralist Poland', *Slavic Review*, 47 (1988), 627–42.

[88] See, for example, W. Adamski, I. Bielecki, K. Jasiewicz, L. Kolarska and A. Rychard, 'Konfliktorodne interesy i wartości a szanse zmian systemowych', *Studia Socjologiczne*, 2 (1987), 101–17; A. Smolar, 'Perspektywy Europy Środkowo-Wschodniej', *Aneks*, 50 (1988), 27–55; J. P. McGregor, 'Economic Reform and Polish Public Opinion', *Soviet Studies*, 41 (1989), 215–27; J. L. Curry, 'Psychological Barriers to Reform in Poland', *East European Politics and Societies*, 2 (1988), 484–510; Z. Bauman, 'Poland: On its Own', *Telos*, 79 (1989), 47–63.

[89] E. Comisso, 'Market Failures and Market Socialism: Economic Problems of the Transition', *East European Politics and Societies*, 2 (1988), 433–66.

312   EKIERT

domestic and geopolitical situation of East Central European countries, however, has greatly modified and expanded the scope of challenges and problems
to be solved and overcome.

This article has focused on the political dimension of the transition, suggesting
that in spite of the emergence of political society, which is the *sine qua non*
condition of democratization, the rapid collapse of one-party regimes, the growing diversification and fragmentation of social and political forces, the deepening disorganization of the economy and the unequal distribution of the cost
of reforms within society may diminish the power of civil society and make
a transition to democracy highly difficult.

The issue of a potential democratic transition in East Central Europe contains
two complementary dimensions which correspond to the two traditional notions
of democracy. The first dimension is the striving for the extension of citizenship
and for the creation of truly democratic institutions. Here we have recently
witnessed the most spectacular changes. On the one hand, the swift disintegration of one-party states has left a dangerous political vacuum, setting in
motion an often chaotic process of political change. On the other hand, the
restoration of individual and collective rights, as well as the opening of public
spaces, has triggered rapid political mobilization. As a result, the power vacuum
has been permeated by highly fragmented political forces prone to radicalization
not only around political and economic issues but also around ethnic and
religious cleavages.[90] Such a situation may result in prolonged political instability and lead to the establishment of weak and unstable coalition governments unable to carry on the radical reforms needed in all these countries.

The second dimension is the striving for social equality and the just distribution of national wealth. This dimension has always been critical to fuelling
social unrest in the region,[91] and here we have witnessed significant developments which are likely to change the political map of all East Central European
countries. The transition to free market economies involves, at least in the
short run, drastic measures resulting in the aggravation of economic dislocations

---

[90] This fragmentation of political forces was clearly reflected in elections held in all countries
in 1990. Local elections in Poland in May 1990, for example, were contested by 240 organizations,
including eighty political parties forming forty different coalitions. In Czechoslovakia, where thirty-
seven political parties exist, the elections were contested by twenty-two parties, movements and
coalitions. In Hungary the complex electoral procedure determined that among approximately
fifty political parties and movements only the six biggest parties were able to contest the second
round of elections. Although in Poland, Czechoslovakia and Romania front-like coalitions (Citizens' Committees, Civic Forum, National Salvation Front), won the elections this fact does not
secure political stability. These groups represent a loose association of political actors with different
political orientations and sooner or later will have to decide either to transform themselves into
a hegemonic political party or to split along major political lines.

[91] See, for example, J. M. Montias, 'Observations on Strikes, Riots and Other Disturbances',
in J. F. Triska and C. Gati, eds, *Blue-Collar Workers in Eastern Europe* (London: Allen & Unwin,
1981), pp. 173–87; A. Pravda, 'Industrial Workers: Patterns of Dissent, Opposition and Accommodation', in R. Tokes, ed., *Opposition in Eastern Europe* (London: Macmillan, 1979), pp. 209–62.

and hardship for large segments of the population.[92] The rhetoric of social justice, however, has been deeply engraved in people's minds in all state-socialist societies and therefore unemployment, decreasing living standards and new market-induced inequalities represent a potential source of conflict and division which may decisively modify the strength and capabilities of political actors and affect the extension of citizenship and the creation of truly democratic institutions.

This double nature of the democratization processes in state-socialist regimes is not likely to be transcended. Political or economic reforms alone will not automatically produce social justice, just as the quest for equality will not produce political and economic freedom. Therefore, genuine democratization will depend on conceptual and practical efforts to reconcile two traditional notions or dimensions of democracy. Without a new approach to the problem of social justice and political and economic freedom, the region is likely to experience a political, economic and cultural regress which has very few historical parallels.

What is required in all state-socialist regimes in order to overcome the present debilitating social and economic crisis is a revival of the state through the infusion of a civic culture, democratic institutions and the consolidation of the new political society, together with economic reforms. The latter must include a radical restoration of market mechanisms and radical social reforms which level the old and new inequalities produced respectively by the redistributive roles of the state and by the market. Such a complex process of reform will require constraints on domestic society and the restriction of the state's power and influence. It will require the creation of a balance between public and private life and between individual and public interests. The failure to address the problem of reform in all of these dimensions simultaneously may easily lead to the further aggravation of the crisis and subsequently to the re-establishment of new forms of dictatorial regimes in East Central Europe able to carry on a new process of 'primitive accumulation'.

[92] Poland's economic policies represent the most radical example of transition to a free market economy. The Solidarity-led government, confronted with hyperinflation and a virtual breakdown of the economy, opted for a harsh stabilization programme and a rapid restoration of the market and even rejected the idea of a mixed economy. As J. Beksiak, an economic adviser to Solidarity, put it, 'a socialist economy does not have any prospects for reform ... [and] people have to realize this once and for all' (J. Beksiak, 'Economic Crisis, Economic Reform', *Uncaptive Minds*, 2, no. 4 (1989), 14–16, p. 14).

[19]

Jnl Publ. Pol., **11**, 2, 133–151

The Transition to Democracy in Central Europe: A Comparative View

ATTILA ÁGH, *Political Science, University of Economics, Budapest**

ABSTRACT

The collapse of Communist regimes in Eastern Europe has also caused the collapse of old-fashioned studies of Communist systems that subscribed to a simple notion of totalitarian uniformity, or a static belief in the continuance of self-equilibrating cycles within socialist states. To understand what is happening in Central and Eastern Europe today we need to be discriminating in a choice of paradigms. European conceptions of democracy as having a socio-economic as well as political dimension are more relevant than formalist American definitions. Moreover, Europe, in the form of the European Community, is also a much more immediate influence than the United States upon what is happening in Central or Eastern Europe. The transition to democracy in Southern Europe provides encouraging models for ex-Soviet satellites. The failure of Latin American countries to democratize provides warnings, such as the risk that Presidential government can produce dictatorship or instability, a risk that is present in new democracies in Europe too.

All fundamental social changes require the rethinking of the whole conceptual framework in political science. Such is now the case with the democratic transition in Central and Eastern Europe. For too many authors nowadays the concepts of democracy and dictatorship (or authoritarian rule and totalitarianism) as well as the transition between them seem to be self-evident. In such a way the triumph over communism risks being at the same time a triumph of the simplistic views, e.g. in the form of Brzezinski's *The Grand Failure* or Fukuyama's 'end of history'.

Democracies and world systems are different and they change rather frequently. The postwar period has had a constant flow of transforma-

* Revised version of a paper presented at the first meeting of the US-Hungarian Roundtable in Political Science, San Francisco, August 23–29, 1990

134   *Attila Ágh*

tions in the democracies and also in the world systems with the emerging democracies. But such revolutionary changes in Central and Eastern Europe as the collapse of the state socialist regimes have been connected with the most radical change in the whole world system. Therefore it cannot be just another democratic transition. In fact, it is about the disappearance of the cold war as a world order in a 50-year cycle of the bipolar world system, and about the emergence of a post-cold war world order as globalized, multi-polar world system.

In a bipolar world the negative or positive ideal types of societies or polities are born from inimical images. The promotion of democracy means assisting an ally in the world struggle, which makes definition of democracy rather arbitrary. In an atmosphere of global confrontation there is no place for empathy for the societies and states on the other side of the great divide. There is no place even for their heterogeneity; therefore mainstream thinking produces stereotypes by homogenising all countries both in the free world and in the Soviet bloc. In such a way it creates 'strictly scientifically elaborated' concepts and preconditions not to understand the particular situations on the other side and not to be able to foresee the coming changes over there. Comparative communism did this by the sweeping overgeneralization of the 'World Marxist governments' from Albania to Vietnam (Szajkowski, 1981), albeit their heterogeneity proves to be enormous, even if we only take Eastern Europe from Albania to Poland.

All social changes shed a new light on the societies concerned and discover their hidden capacity for change, and by so doing they raise some doubts whether the previous concepts and analyses of stability and rigidity were correct. With all transitions the promotion of democracy gets a new meaning and functions. Now the period of the promotion of democracy against the global enemy has ended. The victory of the new democratic governments in Central Europe and the collapse of the Soviet external empire, with the erosion of the internal one, requires a new program in the promotion of democracy, but it is still missing. Political scientists, first of all comparativists, have to work out a new conceptual framework for democracy and dictatorship in a global context.

This paper tries to contribute to the new comparative studies revolution by generalising the experiences of Central Europe in a comparative perspective. It is based on the following:

   (i) Comparative communism as a separate discipline has come to an end; it has to be fitted into the new globally oriented comparative politics;
   (ii) In postwar history there are two global waves of democratiza-

tion, their comparative analysis may be the starting point for the new comparative politics;

(iii) The regional approach may solve the problem of overgeneralization in comparative politics by avoiding the dominant legalistic-formalistic approach;

(iv) The debate about presidentialism and parliamentarism has a direct relevance for the contemporary theory of democracy and dictatorship, if (a) the focus of the discussion is to be shifted from the formal to the substantive side of the old and new democracies and (b) the historical and structural role of parliamentarism during the democratic transition is put to the forefront.

This is a policy paper for comparative politics while it cannot deal with all the above mentioned problems in detail, by being based on the generalizations of previous studies and hopes to be a useful introduction to the dialogue.

I. *Comparative Communism Versus Comparative Politics*

The process of rethinking democracy and dictatorship, at least in Central Europe, cannot start without a reassessment of comparative communism. Comparative politics and comparative communism are twin disciplines produced by the Cold War, one for friends, one for enemies. But with the revolutionary transformations in Central and Eastern Europe, all the preconditions of comparative communism have dramatically changed. Communism itself has almost completely disappeared, and if comparative communism as a discipline survives for a short period it is only to deal with its own history compared to the real history of the countries and regions concerned. A final scientific excursion to the necropolis of comparative communism would show both the historical relevance of the accumulated knowledge in area studies and the rapidly changing ideological functions of comparative communism during its history, leading now, after the end of the global confrontation, to an end of ideology.

The whole conceptual framework of comparative communism has presupposed some overgeneralizations: homogeneity, rigidity, and stability of the communist system. In this comparative trap of over-generalizations, comparative communism has accepted the official ideology of the system to some extent, albeit from the reverse side, since the system has presented itself as all-embracing, homogeneous, stable and dynamic, and ruled by an exclusive Marxist ideology. This reversed image, in which the claimed positive features are turned to the opposite, is classically represented by the theory of totalitarianism, originating in the fight against Nazism and transferred immediately to the new enemy

136   *Attila Ágh*

in the first days of the Cold War. Through this theory and ideology, comparative communism studies became a prisoner of cold war, although there has been a constant fight for independence against the concept of totalitarianism since it appeared for the first time, in an elaborated way, in the work of Friedrich and Brzezinski (1956), summarising the essence of all totalitarian systems in those well known six features. Lovenduski and Woodall (1987) correctly stated thirty years later that 'the totalitarian checklist suffers from an overstatement of its case, in particular from the inability to reflect change'.

Totalitarianism has meant also a preference for some bigger countries and was, in fact, a Soviet-centric approach, although for the experts 'a temptation to overdraw on their knowledge of particular systems leads often to unfounded generalizations about others'. Lovenduski and Woodall also point out in their comparative textbook on East European systems that these systems have been victims not only of a negative ethnocentrism, i.e. Soviet-centrism, but also of positive ones, being compared directly to Western systems so many times by direct transfers of Western concepts and features from pluralism to legitimation theory, without any specification of regional and national differences, that is, without any account being taken of the applicability of Western concepts in Central and Eastern Europe (Lovenduski and Woodall, 1987: 7, 11).

We can see the same assessment of totalitarianism from the introductory chapters of almost all textbooks of comparative communism. Stephen White co-authored at least two introductory pieces about the comparative study of communist political systems and in the later version he states: 'The totalitarian paradigm which was still dominant in the 1950s came under increasing scrutiny as the 1960s advanced. By the 1980s it was probably fair to say that no alternative orthodoxy had become dominant, rather a plurality of approaches had become accepted as legitimate', including regional and more general case studies (White and Nelson, 1986, x). Not even the early stage of communism, such as classical Stalinism, had managed to reach the ideal of totalitarianism, with a real homogeneity of the whole socialist camp. In later history communist states have moved from a more concentrated power system to a more pluralistic one under internal pressure and resistance, and under the external pressure and demonstration effect of the Western democracies. Totalitarianism, as the reversed picture of ideal Stalinism, has remained the bogey or scarecrow of Western anticommunism.

White generalizes the history of comparative communism into two generations. The first generation literature was completely Soviet-centric and overpoliticized; relatively little attention was paid to the relationship between politics and society; finally this approach was more

The Transition to Democracy in Central Europe   137

speculative than empirically grounded on statistics and documents. The second generation literature, emerging from the mid-seventies, differs from the first in the following essential points:

(i) it reflects the widening of the geographical boundaries of commu-
     nism, with no single world model or center;
(ii) with the opening up of these societies, the statistical yearbooks
     and other data began to appear as a basis for empirically founded
     research;
(iii) closer links are formed with the parent disciplines, i.e. with com-
     parative politics and economics, and other fields of research, e.g.
     political culture and legal studies etc. (White, 1987: 220–221).

The most important achievement of the second generation literature, according to White, was the extension of the geographical boundaries. In my opinion, it was its grand failure, accepting world communism as a dynamic system. Its extension in space proved to be a crisis phenomenon of the core territories, i.e. compensation for the missing development of structural accommodation, resulting in the global crisis in the whole Eastern Europe and the Soviet Union from the early 1970s onwards. Consequently, second generation literature that is 'more broadly based, empirically better founded and theoretically more sophisticated' appears to be a comparative trap, assuming positive pros-pects for communism in a stable bipolar world, so to say, objectively accepting not only the existence but also the dynamism of world commu-nism, in its heterogeneity, yet not being able to realize its increasing erosion and the coming final crisis.

The prevailing idea of continuity and stability has evidently been based on the recurrence of small cycles in the history of state socialism in Central Europe. These short cycles, ten years or so, usually started with some liberalization efforts but after some time met the resistance of the hard core of the regime; therefore, they led to conservative reactions and then to rearrangements or conservative restorations. As recurring crisis-cycles, these reform-cycles were the typical negative development pat-tern of state socialism in Central Europe, and provided a solid and reliable approach for comparative communism. The small cycle theory, had become a deeply embedded routine exercise of this discipline in the late 1980s. At the same time it was a very comfortable standpoint, since if nothing new happened in Central and Eastern Europe, the well known crisis cycle repeats itself, so nothing new is to be prepared for. The final crisis of communism has thus become the cause of the final crisis of comparative communism itself.

Until the late 1980s the small cycle theory explained major events in Central Europe. If the social tension deepened, it was easy to take this

138   *Attila Ágh*

phenomenon for the start of a new small cycle as most of experts of comparative communism thought just before the collapse and not for the end of the longer cycle of world communism. The pattern of recurring crisis was so widely accepted that this idea precluded the discovery of the real nature of the coming fundamental changes, although the 'native' experts in the countries concerned warned about the coming final crisis long ago. In the West the 'more of the same' cyclical approach dominated. Its stubborn continuity led area experts and comparativists to predict not the future, but the past, i.e. the repetition of the small cycles as before. For example:

I base this prediction on the fact that the current critical situation in the alliance is not unprecedented, and that Eastern Europe has faced worse crises before. Each of the previous crises was followed by some institutional changes accompanied by appeals, promises and exhortations from Moscow, and once the dust had settled things returned back to the normal *Schlamperei*, so characteristic of Communist systems in the region . . . I see little difference between the situations in 1988 and that twenty years ago, and hence I do not expect radical changes in Soviet relations with Eastern Europe, at least in the foreseeable future (Korbonski, 1989: 22).

This text is, in fact, the obituary of comparative communism in its second generation. It is true that comparative communism, with all of its theoretical and ideological weaknesses, has accumulated a large treasury of knowledge. But now, in the process of the final crisis it is high time to leave it behind, even in its promising and more sophisticated variant, the third generation literature of the late 1980s.

We have to realize that the more of the same approach was a very comfortable position for both politicians and political scientists. Therefore, during and after the 1989 revolutions a big resistance was felt among some Western experts to accept the new realities and to start the tiresome business of re-interpreting everything. With growing unease the slogan 'West is West, and East is East' again appeared, and later as another extreme position, the 'no-nonsense' approach emerged, stating that everything will be changed beyond recognition overnight. But the most important danger for comparative politics and Central European area studies is that the theory and ideology of totalitarianism returned with a vengeance. This simplified concept triumphs nowadays in social science, journalism and official declaration, both in the West and East, precluding the correct analysis of the real transition and the perspectives of new democracies.

Transitions never fit into previously well arranged rules and concepts, such as the rigidly closed alliance-systems and totalitarian theories. In the nicely arranged and regulated world generalized in the form of comparative politics versus comparative communism, some 'communist' countries like Hungary and Poland in the early 1980s began to move to the barren land of the in between, and felt themselves to be in the middle of nowhere. This sphere of nowhere has recently been extended to all formerly socialist countries, mostly to those which still resist changes, to the unsplendidly isolated China and Albania, themselves showing the first signs of the final crisis as well.

The study of world Marxist governments in the 1980s brought some meager results and missed the opportunity to grasp the real changes, because of the neglect of regional or even continental dissimilarities. This is why, in my opinion, the comparative revolution in this respect failed, since it was a doubtful exercise skating on the thin ice of global overgeneralizations about world communism (Ágh, 1990).

Comparative politics has had a series of revolutions and counter-revolutions (Mayer, 1989). Now we can afford some optimism that these fundamental changes in Central Europe may lead to a real comparative revolution by abolishing the Cold War type separation of comparative politics and comparative communism. To bridge the gap between the two, first of all, intensive cooperation of Western and native area experts is needed. But before suggesting the slogan, 'comparativists go East!', we have to state that the present rigid juxtaposition of democracy and dictatorship, which is an artificial and mostly ideologically motivated contrast, has to be overcome by shifting the focus of our research to transitions. In the comparative study of democractic transitions from authoritarian systems, Central Europe is a relevant case.

II. *Two Global Waves of Democratization*

Looking back at the postwar history of democratization from the standpoint of the Central European transitions in the early 1990s, what we see is not democracy but different democracies, and what is more, the processes of democratization, i.e. transitions to or changes in democracies. Not a theory of democracy but a series of discussions about democracies and transitions as a continuous flow of events and arguments. We can separate the first global wave of democratizations and its discussions in the early postwar period from the second one, starting from the mid-1970s, by an era of failures and breakdowns which makes it necessary to specify both periods in their major domestic and international characteristics.

Strangely enough, the real history of the first wave was written only after the beginning of the second one because this contrast removed false appearances and showed its actual achievements and limitations. The milestones for the presentation of the second wave were the works of Linz and Stepan (1989), with the central idea of breakdown, and of

140   *Attila Ágh*

O'Donnell et al. (1986), focused on transitions. They were, restricted to comparative politics and not extended to comparative communism, since the major effort for this extension could come only after the revolutionary changes in Central Europe in the late 1980s.

Early discussions about democracies and the promotion of democracy in the world were running parallel and closely interwoven, starting in the 1950s from the home-made American definition of democracy, designed for export to the Third World as well, to the outspoken statements of Huntington (1981, 1984) about the direct connection between the success of global democratization and the undisputed world hegemony of the United States.

By now the time has come to lay the foundations for a new paradigm of global democratizations by creating the small 'islands of theory' called for by Stanley Hoffman for the comparative politics (Wiarda, 1985: 209). These independent islands or suggestions make it possible to present a set of ideas about comparison between different regions in the democratic transitions before the big international projects, like the *Transitions* program of the Woodrow Wilson Center, are launched.

My small island of theory is built on the presumption that moves to democratization are first of all a function of the world system and not an exclusively domestic political formation. The existing democratic structures are special political organizations of the core countries, and postwar history has shown that stable democratization in other countries has been possible only by the extension of the core of the world system, i.e. the sphere of the economically successful and politically powerful countries. Democratization beyond the core may only be partial and superficial, fragile and transitory, because only these countries can afford the luxury of the two major features of democracy (Dahl, 1982), participation and competition, creating a pressure of demands by the whole population on the political system. Those countries which are unable to attain economic consolidation, being also politically weak and dependent, can reach at most the state of semi-democracies with the constant danger of sliding back to authoritarian rule. I admit, this may sound too deterministic but it seems to be supported by the postwar history of democratizations.

The major features of the first wave of democratization are the following:

(i)   Geographical extension of democracy in the early postwar period concerned only the West European core with some American efforts at liberalization in the Far East, and consisted of redemocratization of some countries after the war (France, Benelux states, etc.) and democratization of others (Germany and Italy);

The Transition to Democracy in Central Europe 141

(ii) Early democratization stopped at the Southern fringes of Europe (Spain, Portugal, Greece, Turkey) and at the same time an American dilemma emerged when faced with including allies that were dictatorships, and it was decided in favour of maintaining alliances;

(iii) As a result of West European democratizations, the rapid economic recovery and the accelerated European integration, a new contradiction was born between the American and European approach to democracy, as far as the domestic 'definition' and the international promotion of democracy are concerned.

The mainstream American approach to democracy can be characterized by the Schumpeterian idea of the procedural, formal or electoral democracy (Huntington, 1984). This goes well with the idea of the promotion of democracy in the world as a function of American foreign policy. The European approach is a substantive definition of democracy with a large body of social and political rights to help people exercise democracy. The promotion of democracy appears as a 'binding contract' between partner countries for implementing the same project of this substantive democracy. The contrast of the American and European approaches manifests itself in government policies as well as in theoretical deliberations. In the marketplace of international political science in the last decade we witnessed a process of the Europeanization of the major products of comparative politics.

In 'International Aspects of Democratization', Whitehead (1986: 39, 31, 35) contrasts the major features of the American and European approaches in much more detail: 'The United States has been the dominant power in the Western world and has taken over prime concern for the stability and the security of its alliance system'. As American power expanded round the world, Washington acquired direct interests in many areas where any attempt to promote genuine democracy would tend to prove quite destabilising. Consequently, American policy makers have learned to exercise great caution and discrimination in pursuing this objective, and have stretched the meaning of the term to embrace an extraordinary variety of friendly but repressive regimes. American political scientists have designed rationales to systematize this evolution (the emergence of the middle sectors was followed by crises of modernization, and most recently, the authoritarian/totalitarian dichotomy), but the more traditional view still retains its hold over significant sectors of American public opinion. The promotion of democracy as a foreign policy rhetoric may be seen from different angles but, Whitehead declares, as a result of the diverging foreign policy strategies in the recent period of the new transitions to democracy 'the

142   *Attila Ágh*

European sphere of influence looks better than the U.S. sphere',
although, he thinks, in the 1980s the American way of promoting
democracy was to a great extent Europeanized. The National Endowment for Democracy, established in 1983, 'apparently represents an
attempt to bring U.S. practice closer to the European pattern'.

The analyses of the *Transitions* (O'Donnell et al., 1986) were mostly
written from the standpoint of successful South European states, most of
all Spain. The European sphere of influence means that the Mediterranean region becomes part of the European integration process, so
Whitehead considers that 'U.S. support for democratization will be
viewed by all concerned as a superficial commitment, whereas in
Southern Europe the EEC could offer something more closely resembling a binding contract'. To complete the contrast, he also mentions
that 'European definitions of democracy seem to give more stress to
social and economic participation, whereas Americans give almost
exclusive emphasis to the electoral aspect' (Whitehead, 1986: 23–24,
17). I think myself that the American foreign policy has recently been
streamlined to the emerging needs of the multipolar world and particularly to a much more flexible approach in the promotion of Central and
East European democracies. Yet Central and Eastern Europe continue
to look first to some 'binding contract' from the EEC.

The now dominant American definitions of democracy reflect both the
uniqueness of the US development and the early postwar situation, with
not only American domination in the world but also in international
political science. The summary of the experiences of the new
democratizations by A. F. Lowenthal (O'Donnell et al., 1986: vol. 1, ix)
warns us against this simplification: 'All authoritarian regimes are not
equated with each other. No authoritarian regime is regarded as
monolithic, nor are the forces pushing for democratization so regarded.
Distinctions are drawn between democracy and polyarchy, between
democratization and liberalization, between transition and consolidation, between hard-liners and soft-liners or accommodationists within
the authoritarian coalition, and among maximalists, moderates and
opportunists in the coalitions supporting *abertura* (liberalization).'

This claim for a new approach to transitions or democratizations
expresses the spirit of the second wave and challenges the first wave
formulated in the American definitions of democracy. Although the list
of new terms of differentiations was collected in the Latin American and
Southern European transitions, it applies too well to the Central and
East European region. The most common mistakes of the Western
analyses of Central European transition are also listed there, i.e. the
neglect of the internal differentiation on both sides of the 'opening up'
(hard-liners and soft-liners in all political organizations), and what is

more, under the common label of totalitarianism all previous regimes are equated, and by that all transitions are considered to be essentially similar from Poland to Roumania.

Finally, the first global wave of democratizations may be qualified as the Cold War pattern of transitions, with unilateral US dominance in the Free World and in political science with an 'electoral' mode of democracy. After the failure of the Almondian modernization-cum-Westernization model, the stability of the political system came to the fore and this was widened with the newly emerging democracies to a theory of transitions. The second global wave of democratizations, qualifying as the Post Cold War pattern, began in Latin America and Southern Europe and was extended in the 1980s to Central Europe.

III. *The Central European Case: Regionalism or Globalising Formalism?*

The idea of transition has appeared as an intermediate system type between dictatorship and democracy, questioning the black-and-white contrast between them. But with the new type the issue of regionalism has also appeared. Instead of a contrast between perfect democracies and ideal dictatorships (totalitarianism), slowly a new contrast, that of different regions experiencing democracy began to appear in the late 1970s between the fragile democracies of Latin America and the consolidated ones in Southern Europe. Thus, the regional approach in its cultural, historical and socio-political complexity also emerged during the second wave of democratizations. It offers a theoretical alternative in comparative politics to the formalistic typologies moving only on the surface of socio-political reality, separating the legal-constitutional and other features from the regional and national complexity, and comparing remote countries and continents, thus neglecting the regional similarities in the deeper structures of the societies concerned. After the Latin American and Southern European 'studies' in comparative politics, Central Europe has again raised the issue of the regional approach as a *sine qua non* of the correct explanation or theorising about the transition to democracy.

After the modest Bucharest repeat of the Tienaamen massacre one year earlier, American newspapers discovered a 'split in Eastern Europe', although there was nothing to discover. Or it may be something new just for the Americans, since Central Europe and Eastern Europe proper (or the Balkan region in this case) have ever been very different, so any split between them might have taken place much before the discovery of the Americans. But in the whole postwar period the Westerners usually have operated with the misnomer of Eastern Europe, meaning the Soviet bloc or the external empire of the Soviet Union as a

144   *Attila Ágh*

military and political unit. This artificial creation of the Cold War appeared to be homogeneous with very small, similar and basically insignificant countries. In this Eastern Europe, evidently, it is just a waste of time to look for individual or regional differences. Although the official American foreign policy in this part of Europe allegedly was that of differentiation, it was not too much felt in theory or in practice.

No doubt there was a great effort by the Soviet Union to introduce political, social and economic homogeneity in their external empire, which was formulated in the so-called Brezhnev doctrine fixing the definition of socialism with its obligatory criteria for ideology and politics. This homogenization, however, was never able to reach the deep structures of societies and transform them. Westerners were too willing to accept the reinforced military and political unity for the all-embracing reality. The half-a-century long cycle of Sovietization in the external empire left behind a lesson of history that armies can harm a lot but they cannot liquidate centuries-old differences in state, economy and civil society between and within regions. The contrast is now bigger than ever between Central Europe (Hungary, Czechoslovakia, Poland and the North-Western part of Yugoslavia) and Eastern Europe proper (Roumania, Bulgaria, Albania, the South-Eastern part of Yugoslavia), and opens the possibility of an extending zone of emerging independent states in the Western part of the Soviet Union.

There have been a lot of debates about the coherence of Central and Eastern Europe and there will still be many, as has also been the case with Southern Europe. The question remains whether they are separate regions indeed, and if it is so, what are their major distinguishing features? The answer is not simple; still the regional approach seems to be more fruitful than a legal formalism that neglects the common regional features. I accept, on my side, that these regional similarities and common features, rooted in history and expressed in the relative same level of development, cannot and should not be overstretched. Thus, the study of democratic transitions offers itself as a test case for the reginal approach and vice versa. The regional approach, if it proves to be fruitful, may also be applied in other fields of comparative politics. Latin America, as such is too big and heterogeneous for a region, so it is considered here only as a general background of the analysis. The Latin American regional approach can be exemplified here by some major states (Brazil and Argentina, see O'Donnell, 1988), but Southern Europe, Central Europe and the latecomer, Eastern Europe, are certainly real regions on their own and they may offer a more solid foundation for comparative analysis in a regional approach.

The comparative analysis of Latin America and Southern Europe has been by and large accomplished in the Woodrow Wilson Center volumes on Transitions. The ambition of Central European political scientists is evidently, to extend it to their region, by focusing on three countries on each side, namely Spain, Portugal and Greece in Southern Europe and Hungary, Czechoslovakia and Poland in Central Europe, albeit the early comer Italy and the latecomer Turkey may enter the picture on the Southern side, and the early comer Austria and the latecomers Slovenia and Croatia cannot be neglected in Central Europe. This comparative endeavour is especially important for Hungarian political scientists, since the analysis and presentation of our democratic transition is, at the same time, also a test case for the maturity of the Hungarian political science, which has played a very significant and unparalleled role in the democratic transition (Ágh, 1990a).

Following the general models of *Transitions*, I have tried to extend it to Central Europe, using as the two major indicators the international system and the internal development patterns. I think that differences between the American and European approaches to the promotion of democracy abroad are largely responsible, indeed, for the divergence of democratizations between Latin America, with democracies fragile and unconsolidated, and Southern Europe, with an almost completely finished economic and political consolidation process. Thus, it is mostly from *longue durée* historical trends and the present international factors that the asymmetrical relations between major Latin American countries and the United States, and the symmetrical ones between the Mediterranean region and the Brussels-based European Community, have produced different transitions in the first two stages of their democratizations. It is not by chance, but because of this factor, that we have in Latin America a development pattern of recurring crisis, i.e. the constant historical move from dictatorship to democracy, and from democracy to dictatorship. In southern Europe, there is an evolutionary development from the mid-seventies after the long cycle of the authoritarian rule. An evolutionary and gradualist development started, progressing towards democratization by pacts in a peaceful way (*ruptura* or *reforma pactada*).

The same model with two major indicators gives a point of departure also for the analysis of Central Europe, which shows, in my opinion, a composite picture of both Latin America and Southern Europe. There was in Central Europe a long cycle of dictatorship for half a century, it is a general frame of reference of all historical and political analyses, and very similar to Southern Europe. Within this long cycle, however, we have a series of small cycles of reforms and conservative rearrangements, which makes Central Europe similar to the Latin American development pattern of recurring cycles with a constant move from liberal to conservative periods and vice versa. This development pattern in

146   *Attila Ágh*

Central Europe, again, was determined by the special international set-up, but this time much more closely and directly than in the other two cases, because of the direct involvement of the Soviet Union and the imperial nature of dependence. The whole internal structure and domestic development, from the security dimensions to cultural fields, was determined very strictly from outside by the external empire, and the reform cycles could move only within this framework, touching the 'walls' each time. The reform movements, even though very cautious, had really hit the 'walls' (1956, 1968, 1981) because the reform process had its inner dynamism and once started, it was almost impossible to stop it, even for those who initiated and led it. Due to its internal contradiction, the term 'reform' has turned out to be a misnomer, meaning originally the correction of the system but after having realized that this was impossible it has come to be used as a term for systematic change. The major conclusion of the reform politicians of Central Europe, at least in Hungary after 1956, 1968–71 and 1985–89 was that state socialism as a system cannot be reformed, it should be abolished.

After Latin America and Southern Europe, we can take Central Europe as the third stage of the second global wave of democratic transitions; Eastern Europe may be the fourth one. Latin America still has no consolidated democracies, Southern Europe has its success story in democratization, but the fate of Central Europe is still undecided; it can go either way. The 1990s will be a decade of chaos and uncertainty for Central Europe, and the future for Eastern Europe is much more problematic for a longer period. The decisive issue is whether Central Europe could become a part of the European integration process with its binding contracts, i.e. with growing intensive ties and substantial assistance by the advanced states to overcome the present economic crisis in a form like Marshall aid, using this term conditionally to indicate a parallel process of what is going on currently in East Germany. Can the three Central European countries become involved in European integration with its standards and safeguards in economic development and political democratization?

The first issue for the new democracies is how to promote equitable economic development which is at the same time democratically responsible, i.e. how to contain social unrest which could jeopardize democracy if it is identified with disorder and decreasing living standards. This decisive issue of the stabilization of new democracies is formulated by President Vaclav Havel in his statement; 'We have done away with the totalitarian system but we have yet to win democracy'. The Central European transition has had so far an evolutionary development pattern, it has been rather peaceful, moving by pacts, but the real similarity with Southern Europe can be only in transition, after the initial crisis

The Transition to Democracy in Central Europe 147

with a combination of the old and new socio-political systems, and finally in the third phase of the consolidation process, if we are involved in European integration.

If Central Europe is only marginally involved in European integration, then we can expect a protracted process of the deepening crisis with a possible return to the authoritarian rule in a development pattern similar to Latin America. The re-emergence of the right-wing dictatorship as a new edition of the traditional type in the period between the two world wars will be very likely, and some signs of preparations may be seen in all the three countries in extreme right, populist-nationalist movements, openly launching an anti-liberal campaign. This is why the 'Europeanization' of Central Europe could mean not only economic and political assistance but also a safeguard against the newly organized anti-liberal and anti-democratic movements and ideological tendencies, fixing the European standards of the liberal-democratic constitutional state for the new entrants, as was done for the countries of Southern Europe.

The second wave of democratizations has not ended yet and the preconditions now are present for its further dynamism. The world system has changed beyond recognition, using Karl Polányi's term, it is the period of the 'Great Transformation'. In these fundamental changes the Central European countries have played an enormous role by eroding the Soviet empire from inside. In a world system turning from bipolar to multipolar, the Post-Cold War generation of new democracies can consolidate. Since I consider democratization as a function of the extension of the core, it is possible only by a widening of Europe as an integrated unit (see Bunce, 1990: 428) which could be described by future historians as the extension of the West European core first to Northern, then to Southern, and lately to Central Europe in the long and painful process of the 1990s. In the risky and not predetermined process of democratization of Central Europe, the signs of the geographical limitations of the further extension can also be clearly seen in the case of Eastern Europe because of its strong state, undeveloped economy and weak civil society. Although no countries are happy with neighbours in permanent crisis, I guess that the countries of Eastern Europe have to wait for the third wave of global democratization. After this second wave a new period of breakdowns may start with the Balkanization of the Balkan and 'Africanization' of Latin America as new-old semi-peripheries (Castañeda, 1990).

This optimistic prediction for Central Europe may be criticized in several ways, both as a theoretical project and as a plan for action. It suggests that instead of a formal-legalistic typology of transition we need a regional and historical analysis of democratization, and also a regional

148   *Attila Ágh*

organization for cooperation to assist at the birth of the new democracies, such as the Pentagonale, linking Austria, Czechoslovakia, Hungary, Italy and Yugoslavia.

IV. *Presidential or Parliamentary System: The Direct Relevance of Recent Debates for Central Europe*

At first glance the recent debates of political science in the West, including that about presidentialism, seem to be far away from the current
problems of the democratic transition in Central Europe. Yet by raising
the issue of presidentialism and parliamentary systems in the process of
democratization, this particular debate touches upon the most controversial and timely question of transition.

The stability of the presidential system has been taken as given in
American political science without questioning its rationale and the
reason for its uniqueness. On the other side, the presidential systems
outside the US are not only very fragile but also conducive to dictatorships, especially in Latin America, being one of the political factors in
the recurring crisis development pattern (see Riggs, 1988; Schmitter, in
O'Donnell *et al.*, 1986: vol. 2, 9). This leads us to question the political
preconditions of consolidated democracy as well as to those of
democratic transition. Attending to the advantages of the parliamentary
system in the creation of a consensual mechanism instead of a
majoritarian dictatorship (cf. Rose, 1991) may help to discover the
secret of the proper political mechanism and devices for the consolidation of the democratic polity in Central Europe.

There is a paradox in the democratic transition for the countries in
deep economic troubles and widespread unrest, namely, the democratic
transition itself needs stability and governability as a concentrated
political effort to overcome the crisis and establish a new framework for
the economy and polity. This concentrated effort creates a need for a
power concentration in the hands of the new parties and political forces,
but this power concentration acts against the consolidation of the new
democracy itself and reproduces some forms of the previous
authoritarian rule. This is not a theoretical paradox but a living contradiction in the Central European countries. As Lijphart (1990) indicates the *Kanzlerdemokratie* resembles the presidential system, and it was
introduced by the new government in Hungary with the same model of
the positive non-confidence vote as exists in Germany but without a
German consolidated democracy. In Hungary it means a great concentration of power in the executive or in the government, and within
the government in the hands of the prime minister, acting as a *Chancellor*
with big personal power, being indeed a strong president, but we find

The Transition to Democracy in Central Europe 149

these pseudo-parliamentary and actual presidential systems in Poland and Czechoslovakia too, with illusions of the benevolent dictator. Within the emerging democratic-parliamentary framework we have a revolutionary aristocracy in power in Czechoslovakia with a new philosopher-King and a constitutionally unclear situation in Poland between the newly elected president, Lech Walesa, claiming full powers, and the old parliament elected two years ago in a semi-democratic way. I think, again, that the statement, that the foundations of democracy are weak in Eastern Europe is an overgeneralization, mixing as usual, Central and Eastern Europe (Bunce, 1990: 401), but the danger is real. With a deepening crisis, the parliamentary systems in Central Europe may turn out to be facades for presidentialism in a Latin American development pattern.

The word 'transition' can be the solution; parliaments may authorize governments and prime ministers to have some concentrated power to facilitate a surgical operation on the ailing economies, but only for a short period and under strict parliamentary control. The danger is, that these institutions may be transitory in character but because of the new elites the whole process of democratization could run into a blind alley. The new political class tries to stick to these transitory forms as final ones, not being ready to resign from a quasi-monopoly of power. Therefore, any power concentration in the democratic transition should be handled with extreme care and the parliament must be strengthened constitutionally against the executive, relying on the remnants and the traditions of the power concentration. We cannot be happy with any kind of emerging semi-democracy leading to hidden or open presidentialism. The danger of a presidential system is most imminent in Poland with the split in Solidarity and Walesa as President in a partnership with right-wing forces. The charisma and extreme popularity of President Havel is also not without a danger of becoming a benevolent dictator, and beyond this mixed blessing Slovakia has produced also strong right-wing extremism striving for the independence of Slovakia. The Hungarian case with *Kanzlerdemokratie* or a semi-presidential system is also very complicated. This is why the intensive interest of the Hungarian political scientists in the recent debates is not an academic luxury of experts but addresses the necessity of everyday politics.

In Central Europe we need a new type of democracy and not just a new democracy. The narrow definition of democracy as electoral or procedural may work in consolidated or well-established polities like the United States. As the West European case suggests, the new social movements have raised a demand for the 'new politics' with much wider rights for participation as the new challenge for democracy (see Rödel *et al.*, 1989). Democracy is, in one of its substantialist definition, a socio-

150   *Attila Ágh*

political framework for efficient conflict regulation (see Przeworski in
O'Donnell et al., vol. 1, 1986: 56). The establishment of an efficient
mechanism of conflict regulation and crisis management based on a
large national consensus and participatory rights is on the agenda of
current history in Central Europe.

   In the democratic transition of Central Europe a formalistic or procedural model of democracy would not work properly, even functionally,
and it would certainly alienate people from politics, which is an acute
danger. The peaceful revolution or transition has been a limited participation model, the population is tired, it has been exhausted by overwork
and an increasing economic burden. Any legal formalism without
meaningful participation would turn people against politics, even with
competitive parties and rival ideologies. The peoples of our countries
need a clear commitment of the new democratic state to all citizens to
make them able, by providing them with all the necessary social and
economic preconditions, to exercise fully their democratic political
rights. To avoid the separation of politics and people, participation is
now much more important than in the consolidated democracies.
Without a clear identification with the process of transition by doing it
themselves, the unsatisfied masses can sweep away the whole politics,
old and new, by outbursts of lawlessness, strikes and mass
manifestations.

   We are at a turning point. As it was written on the walls of Prague in
November 1989: 'Who, if not we? When, if not now!'

REFERENCES

Ágh, Attila (1990) Comparative Commission: Toward a Third Generation? *Studies in Comparative
    Communism*, Summer.
Ágh, Attila (1990a) The Emergence of the 'Science of Democracy' in Hungary and its Impact on the
    Democratic Transition. Barcelona: IPSA Conference on Democracy and the Development of
    Political Science, May.
Ash, Timothy Garton (1990) *We the People, The Revolution of '89*. Cambridge: Granta Books.
Bunce, Valerie (1990) The Struggle for Liberal Democracy in Eastern Europe. *World Policy Journal*.
    Summer, pp. 395–430.
Castañeda, Jorge G. (1990) Latin America and the End of the Cold War. *World Policy Journal*,
    Summer, pp. 469–492.
Dahl, Robert (1982) *Dilemmas of Pluralist Democracy, Autonomy vs. Control*. New Haven and London:
    Yale University Press.
Dawisha, Karen (1990) *Eastern Europe, Gorbachev and Reform*. Cambridge: Cambridge University
    Press.
di Palma, Giuseppe (1990) *To Craft Democracies: an Essay on Democratic Transitions*. Berkeley: Univer-
    sity of California Press.
Friedrich, C. J. and Brzezinski Z. (1967) *Totalitarian Dictatorship and Autocracy*. Cambridge: Harvard
    University Press.
Held, David (1987) *Models of Democracy*. Stanford: Stanford University Press.
Huntington, Samuel P. (1981) *American Politics, the Promise of Disharmony*. Cambridge: Harvard
    University Press.

The Transition to Democracy in Central Europe 151

Huntington, Samuel P. (1984) Will More Countries Become Democratic? *Political Science Quarterly*, Summer, pp. 193–218.

Korbonski, Andrzej (1989) Soviet-East European Relations in the 1980s: Continuity and Change, pp. 5–22. In Marco Carnovale and William C. Potter, eds., *Continuity and Change in Soviet-East European Relations, Implications for the West*. Boulder, Col.: Westview Press.

Lijphart, Arend (1990) *Presidentialism and Majoritarian Democracy: Theoretical Observations*. Paper for the APSA Annual Meeting, San Francisco.

Linz, Juan and Alfred Stepan (eds) (1978) *The Breakdown of Democratic Regimes*. Baltimore: John Hopkins University Press.

Lovenduski, Joni and Jean Woodall (1987) *Politics and Society in Eastern Europe*. London: Macmillan.

Mayer, Lawrence C. (1989) *Redefining Comparative Politics, Promise Versus Performance*. London: Sage Publications.

O'Donnell, Guillermo, Philippe C. Schmitter and Laurence Whitehead (eds) (1986) *Transitions from Authoritarian Rule, Vol. 1, Comparative Perspectives, Vol. 2 Southern Europe*. Baltimore: Johns Hopkins University Press, 1986.

O'Donnell, Guillermo (1988) Challenges to Democratization in Brazil. *World Policy Journal*, Spring, pp. 281–300.

Powell, G. Bingham (1982) *Contemporary Democracies*. Cambridge: Harvard University Press.

Prins, Gwyn (ed.) (1990) *Spring in Winter: the 1989 Revolutions*. Manchester: Manchester University Press.

Riggs, Fred W. (1988) The Survival of Presidentialism in America. *International Political Science Review* 9, 4, 247–781.

Rödel, Ulrich, Gunter Frankenberg and Helmut Dubiel (1989) *Die demokratische Frage*. Frankfurt am Main: Suhrkamp Verlag.

Rollo, J. M. C. et al. (1990) *The New Eastern Europe: Western Responses*. London: Pinter, for Royal Institute of International Affairs.

Rose, Richard (1991) Prime Ministers in Parliamentary Systems. *West European Politics*, 14, 2, 9–24.

Rupnik, Jacques (1989) *The Other Europe*. London: Weidenfeld and Nicolson.

Szajkowski, Bogdan (ed.) (1981) *Marxist Governments, A World Survey*. London: Macmillan, Vols. 1–3.

Tokés, Rufolk L. (1990) *From Post-Communism to Democracy: Party Politics and Free Elections in Hungary*. Berg Alfter: Konrad Adenauer Stiftung.

White, Stephen, John Gardner and George Schöpflin (1980) *Communist Political Systems: An Introduction*. London: Macmillan.

White, Stephen and Daniel Nelson (eds) (1986) *Communist Politics: A Reader*. London: Macmillan.

White, Stephen (1989) Comparative Communist Politics: Towards the Second Generation. *Studies in Comparative Communism*, Summer, pp. 209–212.

Wiarda, Howard J. (ed.) (1985) *New Directions in Comparative Politics*. Boulder: Westview Press.

[20]

Coexistence **27**: 245–267, 1990.
© 1990 *Kluwer Academic Publishers. Printed in the Netherlands.*

DEMOCRATIZATION IN EASTERN EUROPE

PAUL G. LEWIS

Open University, Milton Keynes, MK7 6AA, United Kingdom

Democratization: The global context

The political changes that swept over Eastern Europe in the second half of 1989 were striking in a number of respects. One was simply their rapidity. Significant political changes had begun to get under way during 1988 in Hungary, as Kadar was prised out of the leadership by an increasingly impatient party elite, and in Poland, where roundtable negotiations with a view to extending the parameters of trade union pluralism were agreed to by an embattled leadership following two waves of strikes. But with the conclusion of an agreement in Poland things began to move more quickly. Semi-free elections were held in June 1989 in which communist candidates sustained such a battering that plans for a pre-arranged, if reconstituted, communist-dominated government proved to be impossible to carry out and Eastern Europe saw in Poland the installation of its first non-communist prime minister since the 1940s. That, however, was barely the beginning and from October the established leadership crumbled in the German Democratic Republic, Bulgaria, Czechoslovakia and, finally, in Romania too.

A second aspect was their unexpectedness. While matters had begun to move more quickly in Hungary and Poland, and more significant change than had been seen for some years was clearly on the cards by the early summer of 1989, the reform process remained largely limited to those two East European countries — although they were increasingly accompanied in this by the great neighbour to the east, where Mikhail Gorbachev was assiduously applying his energies to inducing change within the moribund Soviet system. Relatively strong pressures for change, and a higher level of tolerance of such domestic deviation were, however, nothing new for those two countries. Persistent Polish instability had produced a greater tolerance for the unique domestic solutions devised to cope with them, while Hungary had pursued since 1968 the reform initiated with the New Economic Mechanism — although with varying degrees of enthusiasm. The collapse of communist East Germany — the Soviet advance post in Central Europe, the end of normalized Czechoslovakia — politically

246   *Paul G. Lewis*

frozen since the invasion of 1968, and the mass uprising against the nepotistic socialism of Ceausescu's Romania were a different matter and represented a sea change quite unforeseen until the tidal wave actually broke.

A third striking feature was the depth of their impact on the European settlement and, indeed, the global order that had been established in the wake of World War II following the emergence of the rivalry between the superpowers as the dominant fact of world politics in the second half of the twentieth century. The sharp division between capitalist democracy and communist dictatorship which had run through post-war Europe disappeared. The position and prospects of both parts of Europe were suddenly transformed by the removal of previously solid barriers. The withdrawal of the Soviet veto over change in Eastern Europe meant even more than this, though, and reflected both a fundamental reappraisal from the Soviet side of the superpower contest and a redefinition of the Soviet view of world capitalism. The Soviet decision not to maintain by force the "achievements of socialism" in Eastern Europe (i.e. the abandonment of the Brezhnev Doctrine) expressed a major change in the way the ideology and dynamics of world communism were interpreted and the acceptance of a new analysis about the nature of Leninist systems.

Not surprisingly, the implicit decision of the Soviet leadership to abandon the maintenance of communism in Eastern Europe by force and the collapse of Leninist regimes there was generally hailed as a rejection of Stalin's Cold War legacy and a major blow against political dictatorship. That much was certain. Less clear, though, were the implications of these developments for the ongoing political situation in Eastern Europe and the nature of the post-communist systems. One widely publicized view was that 1989 had seen a democratic revolution in Eastern Europe and that, with the removal of the Stalinist straitjacket, the region would see the emergence of more normal, less constrained social forms and the establishment of popularly based political regimes. A major process of democratization throughout the eastern part of Europe was understood to be in course. Such, indeed, was one option — although the nature of such a social normality and the form of the popular basis that the post-communist political regime might take were far from clear at this stage. On reflection, too, the political implications of the 1989 revolution were open to some question and the process of democratization that the demise of East European communism had set in motion required closer scrutiny.

At first glance, the changes in Eastern Europe seemed to accord with a broader process of political transformation that had been proceeding elsewhere on the globe. The democratization in the 1970s of states in the European southern tier (Portugal, Spain, Greece) appeared as a precursor in a different part of the same continent, while analogous changes in Latin America in more recent years suggested an equivalent process closer to the centre of influence of the other superpower. The process of democratization, in general terms, seemed to have made significant progress across the globe even before the developments in Eastern Europe. Sixteen states had moved towards democracy during the previous 10 years, it was calculated in 1985, while only six had moved in the reverse direction.[1] Awareness of what appears to be a secular trend, however, may tend to impose a spurious identity on the sequence of developments that has promoted the spread of democracy throughout different parts of the globe. A tendency towards loose generalization in this respect was noted before the recent East European developments. One problem was that, "attracted by extraordinary and liberating post-1973 changes from Greece to Argentina, much of the writing on democratization treats the process as one of redemocratization", an approach which in East European terms has some validity in the case of Czechoslovakia but little relevance to other countries.[2]

Another difference has been that of economic context. The reestablishment of democracy in Southern Europe, for example, took place following a period of striking economic growth and the influence of the long-lasting post-war boom provided a stable economic background for political change.[3] Taiwan and South Korea have taken steps towards democracy following the pursuit of successful strategies of economic growth under conditions of extensive modernization and social development.[4] The economic context of the 1989 overthrow of the East European regimes was very different, with the more taxing conditions of the 1980s supplementing the progressive collapse of the traditional command economy (although, in terms of the global economic environment and the problems posed by excessive levels of indebtedness, parallels with Latin America were easier to draw). It will indeed be clear, on a moment's reflection, that the establishment of democracy (in fact a fairly rare occurrence until recent times) has taken place in a variety of contexts and in a number of countries with very different social and historical circumstances.

Limited experience of political democracy in Eastern Europe and patchy development of a political culture nourished by patterns of sustained participation form part of the region's historical experience and condition contemporary prospects for democratization. Signs of the pluralization recognized as characteristic of modern democracy can be detected in the form taken by political developments during the communist period and in the steps taken towards democracy before the events of 1989. Hungary in 1956 saw the revival of formal party pluralism and the creation of workers' councils; during 1968 in Czechoslovakia pluralism

248   *Paul G. Lewis*

emerged within the communist party itself; while Poland during the Solidarity period and subsequent years witnessed the creation or strengthening of an alternative public sphere and the multiplication of autonomous social groupings. These strategies were in large part a response to the limitations placed on free political activity by the communist system — but they also drew on existing traditions and indigenous forms of political expression which encouraged the strengthening of particular patterns of political participation. The movement towards democracy in Eastern Europe has thus operated on several levels and progressed at a variable pace. It may be argued, however, that its common denominator has been the implicit struggle to democratize the political culture itself and that this experience is likely to provide a central theme of contemporary efforts to establish democracy in Eastern Europe.[5]

Democratization as incremental development and conflict resolution

The lifting of many of the formal limitations on the process of democratic change imposed by Soviet regional dominance, however, suggests that future patterns of democratization may have less specific characteristics and follow a more general pattern. While the East European changes were sudden and fundamental a related process had been in train in the Soviet Union, where *perestroika* had been pursued for several years — although a somewhat less far-reaching degree of change had actually been achieved there. This, too, began to prompt reference to established models of democratic change in the attempt to gauge the likely extent of political change and evaluate its propsects of success. One influential model of the democratization process has been that of Dankwart Rustow, expressed in his conceptualization of "Transitions to Democracy: Towards a Dynamic Model".[6] Rustow's model was based on his knowledge of Sweden and Turkey, but in fact had the capacity for considerable general applicability.

It had a number of components. The first was a background condition of national unity, the idea that the great majority of citizens had no doubt or mental reservations as to which political community they belonged to. the second condition was that the process of democratization was set off by a prolonged and inconclusive political struggle, a "hot family feud". A third phase begins when political leaders accept the existence of diversity within unity and prepare to institutionalize some crucial aspect of democratic procedure. The fourth, and final phase, is that of habituation — when people are forced to live with the decisions that have been made. Taken in sequence, it is suggested, these steps lead to the creation of a viable democracy which should have the capacity to create a lasting regime. This model has been applied to many situations since its original

formulation, including developments in the Soviet Union under the Gorbachev leadership. One commentary noted that it includes a number of
features which have relevance to the contemporary Soviet situation,
suggesting that the path of democratic development takes many forms and
that it passes through several phases; that democracy emerges from a
deep, protracted between radical and conservative forces in which even
non-democrats may be persuaded into the acceptance of alternative values
and forms of behaviour. Finally, that democracy has rarely been a primary
goal but has eventually been adopted as a means to another end.[7]

While, Breslauer admits, this congruence does not mean that the Soviet
Union will follow the same path or reach the end state occupied by
Western Europe, it does, he suggests, alert the academic community to the
probability of certain outcomes. The gradualism of the process alluded to
in Rustow's model is one prime lesson taken from this conceptualization
for Soviet developments, with the implication that the residual strength of
the Soviet bureaucratic dictatorship and protracted resistance on the part
of conservative forces do not necessarily rule out the prospect of democratic change. Not mentioned by Breslauer, however, is the background
condition of national unity — a critical factor as fissiparious tendencies
develop in the formerly monolithic Union and national sentiment rather
than commitment to democracy or perestroika gain the upper hand in
many republics. The question of to which political community the Soviet
citizen owes his or her prime allegiance is one that is far from resolved
and this must be perceived as a major obstacle to the smooth development
of the democratization process, at least in terms of the model proposed by
Rustow.

It is a factor which also appears in the East European context, although
it features more powerfully in some countries than others and does not
generally emerge in such acute form as in the Soviet Union. There the
contradiction between Soviet allegiance and national sentiment has become posed more and more sharply, while in Eastern Europe the nationality issue emerges less as a general crisis of identity and political authority
and more as a basis for discrete domestic and international conflicts.
It has, however, gained prominence in the GDR, Bulgaria and through
the long-lasting tensions within the Yugoslav federation, as well as in
Romanian-Hungarian relations. National conflict has still not been eliminated in relations between Czechs and Slovaks, and remains an issue in
Polish political life — although far less than in earlier periods. Nevertheless, while these developments have raised again the issue of political
culture identified as critical for East European developments, nationalism
and problems of conflict seem to pose less of a threat to democratization
in Eastern Europe than they currently do in the Soviet Union.

The emphasis on lengthy domestic struggle and gradualism found in

250   *Paul G. Lewis*

Rustow's model, and noted by Breslauer in the Soviet context, also suggests a certain contrast with the changes seen in Eastern Europe during 1989. The demise of most of the communist regimes there occurred unexpectedly and with great rapidity. In Poland Solidarity had to fight and survive underground for years before relegalization in 1989 — but the 1989 election brought a sweeping victory with the eventual installation of a Solidarity-led government when the ruling coalition fell apart. The Hungarian party resigned its leading role and resolved to reconstitute itself to avoid a similar electoral fate — but alternative forces encountered difficulties in the organization and mobilization of effective support, leaving the opposition in a state of some disarray prior to the elections of March 1990. The East German party quickly passed through a phase of attempting to rally and reform the forces of orthodoxy under Egon Krenz, but this too proved to be a brief interlude and the subsequent leadership soon found itself having to resign its monopolistic leading role.

Developments in Czechoslovakia ran even faster and, while an opposition (in the form of Charter 77) had an established existence and distinguished record, it was far smaller and more socially isolated than in Poland. Failures of party leadership and the collapse of party rule took place at a comparable pace in Bulgaria and Romania. Common factors in these developments were therefore the limited emergence of conflicts over power and the fact of regime collapse being caused primarily by the withdrawal of Soviet support. Political mobilization was of relatively short duration and the organization of opposition generally at a low level. While important, then, the role of opposition was hardly critical. It would not be generally appropriate, say, to repeat the observation derived from the experience of Taiwan, that "the analysis of democratization should focus on the origin and development of political opposition".[8] For such reasons Hungarian philosopher (and, later, leader of the Free Democrats) Janos Kis noted well before the final collapse of late 1989 that there was reason for fear as well as hope in the current situation. What he perceived in Hungary was not an ordered transition towards democracy but a less positive process: "the incipient pluralism is not born out of a social contract; it is the child of the breakdown of authority".[9]

East European developments stood, therefore, at some distance from the situation suggested by Rustow's model which proposed that the ingredients for democracy had to be assembled one at a time. The development of national unity, a prolonged and inclusive political struggle, the emergence of new elites, growing awareness of the benefits of compromise and mutual tolerance, and the eventual agreement on a democratic framework formed part of a lengthy process and interacted as links in a sequence which strengthened the incipient process of democratization.

These ingredients have not all been present in Eastern Europe and doubts may well be cast on the viability of processes there in the light of the Rustow model. While the proviso of national unity and secure political identity (if not the absence of ethnic conflict and the existence of uncertainty about the geographical extent of the national community) constituted less of problem than in the Soviet Union, the speed and spontaneous character of the regimes' collapse did not provide the conditions for the political integration and democratic development otherwise deemed necessary by the terms of the model.

Society and state in the establishment of democracy

The question of the presence and political influence of long-lasting domestic conflict recurs in another major view of the origins of democracy which has been referred to in recent discussion of *perestroika* and the process of democratization. Barrington Moore's influential work traced the origins of parliamentary democracy to the configuration of pre-modern social forces and the relations that had been established between lords and peasants, government forces and the bourgeoisie.[10] His argument, based on detailed historical analysis of developments in England, France and the United States, rested on a complex analytical account which was highly sensitive to the unique features of the historical evolution of different societies. Nevertheless, it is possible to identify the general argument that democracy emerged where a strong and independent bourgeoisie developed in opposition to the old regime and gained control over national policy, while a rough balance was maintained between the power of the landed upper classes and government bureaucracy, and the political influence of the peasantry was historically small or reduced either by the power of the lords or the impact of commercialization.

Although Moore had been at any earlier stage of his academic career a noted Soviet specialist, nothing like the same attention was paid in his work to developments in Tsarist Russia as to the steps taken towards modernity by England, France or the United States — or even in the same comparative detail to the roots of communist revolution in China, which appears as the model of the communist mode of modernization. To the extent that it does figure Russia is, of course, treated as an example of communist revolution rather than as a source of further insights into the democratic route to modern society. That, however, does not mean that Moore's understanding of the dynamics of democratic development have not been regarded as relevant to the subsequent development of Soviet or communist society. The gradualist conception of socialist economic devel-

252   *Paul G. Lewis*

opment incorporated in the NEP approach of the 1920s, for example, carried implications about the development of a domestic bourgeoisie and its eventual consequences for Soviet political development. The totalitarian solution adopted by Stalin was both a response and an alternative to this, and had decidedly negative implications for the development of democracy in the Soviet Union.

Moore's recognition of the critical consequences for subsequent social and political development of the way in which the modernizing state deals with the peasantry has also continued to receive the attention of those concerned with the trajectory of Soviet political development. The impact of Soviet collectivization in this respect has been linked with continuing discussion of the persistent weakness of the Soviet system and the drastic contemporary consequences of the coincidence of an impoverished civil society with a state formation which has come clearly to show strict limitations on its effectiveness. Reference to Moore's work and the issues it raised have continued to play a part in this debate, and the consequences of methods applied in the implementation of the collectivization campaign have been identified as the source of major structural impediments to the contemporary democratization of the Soviet and the process of *perestroika*.[11] The Soviet state, it has been argued, has great power but limited political capacity in terms of the effective exercise of that power.

The organizational structure which proved so successful in forming the Soviet state, providing the framework for its institutional development and enhancing its centralized power resources, has also proved to be a source of its weakness, as the coercive power built up by campaigns like that which fuelled the collectivization process proved to be much stronger in their prohibitive aspect and less effective in sustaining innovation and enabling functions. To the extent that the Stalinist model was successfully implanted in the other communist countries (a process that was obviously more effective in some East European countries than others) such problems may also be detected in their political processes. The effect of these developments were positive for strengthening the powers of state dictatorship but proved to be quite otherwise in furthering processes of change like the contemporary policy of *perestroika* and pursuit of democracy. It can, indeed, be argued that together with the role of civil society the effective power of the state also needs to be enhanced in the process of democratization. The different routes to the modern world which are identified in Moore's work seem to have been associated not just with processes encouraging the establishment either of democracy or dictatorship but also with the formation of states with radically different capacities for effective political action.

The emphasis placed by Moore on the political importance of an independent bourgeoisie in sustaining a civil society and supporting the development of parliamentary democracy (a perception shared, of course, with Karl Marx and one repeated with great frequency throughout the lands governed by Lenin and his followers) is one shared by many East Europeans as they enter the 1990s with the dual intention of building democratic regimes and establishing free market economies. It is one strengthened by the observation of developments in countries as diverse as Chile and Taiwan.[12] While the progression identified within the Marxist-Leninist tradition was one from bourgeois parliamentary democracy and market capitalism to socialist democracy and economic planning, an analogous sequence of developments is now identified for contemporary Eastern Europe — although in reverse order. This poses the considerable problem of how, after 40 years of state control of most of the economy and consistent discrimination against the bourgeoisie, such a middle class can be identified or assumed to be likely to emerge in the immediate future — as the contemporary pursuit of the market economy and various models of democratization seem to assume. Social conditions even in countries like Hungary and Poland, those most advanced in the process, and the value structures of their populations do not seem particularly likely to favour the development of such a group.[13]

The question of social formations emphasized in Moore's work, though, has overshadowed that of another theme linked to his outline of the different routes taken to the modern world which has equal importance and relevance to the issue of democratization in Eastern Europe — that of institutional development in the process of political modernization and the formation of modern states with an organizational infrastructure capable of meeting the diverse demands placed on them and the societies over which they claim authority. The issue of regime change was suddenly placed on the agenda in 1989 not because of opposition strength, the rise of new social groups or the mobilization of forces previously excluded from the political arena, but rather because of the increasingly clear evidence of the inefficacy of the established communist leadership in Eastern Europe associated with the growing awareness that they would no longer be able to compensate for domestic weakness with the resources and support of the Soviet Union.

The recourse to extensive foreign credits during the 1970s in Poland in preference to contemplating the prospect of effective reform, an option accepted also by the Hungarian leadership as the initial reform impetus faded in the years following the implementation of the New Economic Mechanism with somewhat less traumatic results, was a clear response to the recognition of leadership weakness and its lack of institutional capacity to implement policies of structural change.[14] Polish inability to make

254 *Paul G. Lewis*

structural reform initiatives and price realignments stick even under conditions of martial law was a further sign of the incapacity of the party-state complex during the 1980s, and the lack of take-off of a further "second stage of reform" in 1987 a final testament to government inca-pacity. This, of course, was not so much the consequence of national solutions to the peasant problem or a result of the application of the campaign method of collectivization (which faded in Poland at an early stage), but rather a failure of the overall Soviet model which proved even less effective under certain East European conditions than it had in the domestic context.

Developments in Eastern Europe do not fit particularly well, then, with either of these models of social and political development. The collapse of the authoritarian communist regimes did not take place under the pressure of internally generated forces, and democratization received little impetus from agreements reached between conflicting domestic groups or national political compromises. Neither, of course, did they follow the pattern of relations forming between major social groups and the shifting constella-tion of social forces that have been identified as underlying the emergence of parliamentary democracy. Further, to the extent that democracy has been seen as an attribute of modern society and democratization asso-ciated to at least some extent with the emergence of modern social formations, the inability of communist systems to meet the challenges of continuing change raises fundamental questions about their status as credible end-points on any route to the "modern world". The problem may be most appropriately cast in terms of democracy confronting not so much the legacy of communist dictatorship as the obstacles presented by communist traditionalism and the persistence of pre-modern political forms.

Modernization and the global economic context

Contemporary Eastern Europe is facing the challenge of modernization as much as that of democratization. This is one of the reasons why the global economic context has been so significant for the changes in Eastern Europe. Communist economies have encountered common problems in terms of stagnation and the obstacles to sustaining economic growth. The roots of the weak development impetus can be traced to the rigidity and sluggishness of the administered economy, restrictions on innovation and overall technological backwardness. East European problems, however, have been compounded by greater sensitivity to international economic pressures and in some cases by massive foreign debt. Lack of competitiveness on world markets, persistent problems in servicing foreign debt and increased economic pressure from the Soviet Union all played a part in worsening economic conditions in Eastern Europe, undermining political stability and reducing the leadership's capacity for manoeuvre.

Despite certain measures of Western economic assistance equivalent pressures are and will continue to be brought to bear on the post-communist regimes which, by virtue of their greater sensitivity to popular pressure, enhanced reliance on social support and more open character, are likely to encounter problems in coping with them as great as those experienced by their political predecessors. There will certainly be strong international economic influences exerted on the democratization process in Eastern Europe. In this respect the experience of Latin American countries is likely to prove to be of considerable relevance. While the major conclusion to be drawn from this experience in terms of political democratization and political development is broadly a positive one, there are also hard lessons to be learnt from the experiences of countries like Peru, which attempted to cut loose from the burden of foreign debt, about the ineluctability of global economic processes. The fate during the 1980s of Mexico, Bolivia and Chile, too, meant falls in living standards they thought "no government, democratic or otherwise, would ever willingly embrace".[15] In general, concludes Munck, "under conditions of dependent or dominated capitalism the advance of democracy is even more halting and problematic".[16]

Like the Latin American countries, and unlike Pacific states such as Taiwan and South Korea which have embraced processes of democratization in recent years, economic growth and development in Eastern Europe was sluggish in the 1980s. The problems of debt and relative economic weakness in Eastern Europe have been greatest in Poland and Hungary which, not coincidentally, have been to the fore in processes of reform and democratization. The legacy of the tradition of economic autarchy (economic development in one camp in line with the Stalinist principle of socialism in one country) exacerbated the problems of indebtedness that followed the unbalanced opening of the Eastern economies to international economic forces in the 1970s. While overall per capita foreign debt has been higher in Hungary than in Poland its economic impact in the latter country has been worsened by a low level of participation in patterns of foreign trade. Net debt in Poland in the early 1980s as a percentage of the value of exports to the West stood at 649, in contrast to a level of 267 in Hungary.[17] In 1985 the relative ratios were reported to stand at 506 and 259.[18]

This was comparable to the situation in Mexico during 1982, when its foreign debt was equivalent to 335 percent of its annual exports of goods

256   *Paul G. Lewis*

and services. Like the East European countries, Mexico did not derive
much benefit from involvement in world economic processes. This, again,
provided a contrast with more dynamic Asian economies. Between 1955
and 1980 Mexico's net import of goods and services, a measure of the
flow of resources to Mexico from the rest of the world, averaged one per
cent of its GDP while South Korea derived eight per cent from this
source. Low levels of integration with the world economy and the derivation of minor benefits from the exchanges that do take place clearly place
even greater pressure on the political system and impose further constraints on the democratization process. In 1988 the combined value of
imports and exports per head of population in Poland stood at $690, less
than the world average, below Hungary at $1828 and even less than the
more self-sufficient Soviet Union.[19] In the same year Poland, with a
population only slightly smaller than that of South Korea, exported barely
one quarter as many goods and services.[20]

The Polish experience was a notable example of a more general tendency that could be detected in terms of disengagement from global
economic processes and the uncoupling of the East from West European
economies during the post-war period. In 1937 the countries that later
became the European members of CMEA accounted for 20 per cent of
West European exports and 16 per cent of their imports. In 1987 the
equivalent levels were 5 and 4 per cent.[21] Such low levels of participation
in foreign trade processes clearly creates great problems for a country
with a large foreign debt and imposes tricky conditions on nations newly
embarking on the process of democratization. The influence of the international environment in such a situation will certainly be significant and it
is clear that prospects for the establishment of democracy will not be
decided by the play of domestic forces alone. The heritage of economic
autarchy has become increasingly burdensome as processes of economic
change and global interaction accelerated under the impetus of the postwar high-technology revolution, whose fundamental impact has been to
"render national borders, and thus national sovereignty, inconsequential
for many economic activities". Eastern Europe, it may be argued, has
fallen even further behind in this process than it did in the first Industrial
Revolution.[22]

Rather than the influence of domestic conflict and the effect of group
interaction, of critical importance for the situation in the more reform-
oriented countries of Eastern Europe have been the consequences of the
developmental path taken by the communist party-state and the difficulties
it then faced in coping with the demands of the global economic environment. Accelerating technological development and intensifying global
economic integration combine to produce a context of modernization that

is likely to have a profound influence on contemporary processes of political change and place established notions of democratization in a new light. The establishment of new regimes in the late twentieth century is increasingly understood to be conditioned by and to form part of more general processes of modernization. East Europeans themselves have shown just as much, if not more, interest in abandoning outdated Stalinist practices and joining what is perceived as the mainstream of modern European development as in building democratic institutions for their own sake. At issue is not just the question of autonomous development in relation to the importance of external influences on national political processes, but rather the character of those influences and the social framework within which internally- and externally-derived processes interact to produce a given political outcome.

From a viewpoint which takes account of the developments of the 1980s the nature of the modernity that came to prevail in the wake of communist revolution has increasingly come into question. Modernity can no longer be understood simply in terms of industrialization, as the experience of the East European countries — with economies trapped in a model overdetermined by Stalinist conceptions of the accelerated development of heavy industry — clearly shows. Recent developments suggest that the dimensions of international integration, involving the growing prominence of global connections, and modernity also stand in an increasingly close relationship. Modernization in the contemporary context may be usefully viewed in terms of the institutionalized capacity for response to the evolving imperatives of new technology and changing world market logics.[23] Openness to the influence of the international world of advanced science and technology itself increasingly appears to be a prerequisite for the effective development of democratic processes. Democratization as a process of domestic change thus also needs to be viewed both in relation to the international environment and with reference to the role it plays in the dynamics of modernization, a movement which itself increasingly takes on the form of a global process.

Modernization and the functions of democracy

In view of the significance of the problems of technological and economic development for the Eastern countries and their evident importance in the sequence of events that led up to the dramatic changes of 1989, it may therefore be argued that democratization is best treated not so much as an object of study in its own right but more as one element in a broader process of social development and modernization on a global scale. The

258   *Paul G. Lewis*

adoption of specific political forms and the institutionalization of particular governmental practices may be understood as an aspect of a process
whose dynamic is not expressed primarily in the political sphere. This
means that the prospects for further, substantial democratization in Eastern Europe depend not just on internal political forces but also on a range
of other factors which operate at a more general level. The establishment
of democratic institutions and processes may in this view be understood as
elements contributing to the success or otherwise of a broader process
and performing specific political functions for the transformation of the
system as a whole.

Democratization, for example, may more appropriately be seen as a
response to a general systemic crisis, as "an attempt to relegitimate the
system and its temporary need for shared sacrifice in order to retool
economically".[24] Democratization can be understood to operate in several
ways within this overall context and to perform a variety of political
functions for the modernization process. The fate of democracy in Eastern
Europe may be not so much dependent on the nature of group relations
within the region's states and their ability to produce a viable working
relationship as contingent on the functions it may be able to perform
within broader processes of modernization. To the extent that the transition to democracy can be presented at a process of institutionalizing
uncertainty, of subjecting all social and political interests to the prospect
of unknown outcomes, such a view may be more in keeping with contemporary prospects than deterministic accounts of the structured outcomes
of long-standing group relationships.[25] Contemporary prospects for democratization depend to a large extent on the capacity to seize existing
opportunities and take advantage of new openings — and therefore involve
to a significant degree factors which are contingent and conjunctural.

By no means the least important of these functions in contemporary
Eastern Europe is the legitimating role of the democratization process
within international relations. This provides critical support for programmes of economic recovery and a framework for the thoroughgoing
transformation of economic structures and processes. Pre-eminent among
the expectations of the new democracy in Eastern Europe must also be
the removal of the political direction of the economy, the elimination of
party-state control over the means of production and distribution, and the
opening up of the region to the influence of global economic processes.
Democratization means the introduction of greater political choice and
spells the end of the system of guaranteed single-party rule which underlay
the fusion of party and state and created conditions for the central
administration of, if not the totality, then at least a great range of political,
social and economic processes. The introduction of political choice severs

the connection of any one party with the apparatus of state and reduces opportunities for the political administration of social and economic processes.

Single-party rule and the political dominance of the economy were the core of the system which facilitated the imposition of a basic industrialization model but prevented progress beyond it, barring the way to full participation in the process of continuing modernization. The primacy of administrative coordination and bureaucratic control over economic processes restricted innovation, produced bottlenecks throughout the system and generally lowered efficiency. Democratization should, therefore, increase the level of exposure of the East European economies to leading technological processes and facilitate their integration with the mechanisms of the world economy. The withdrawal of the state from the economy and the separation of politics from economics is not, of course, synonymous with democratization. The relationship between capitalism and democracy has been contingent rather than one of logical entailment. Authoritarianism, capitalism and free-market economics are not an unknown combination, but this is not the mix envisaged for Eastern Europe (at least in public) either domestically or internationally. It has been common, further, for the liberal state to be associated with parliamentarism, while liberal democratic representation does seem to have been characteristic of certain stages of capital accumulation.[26]

The rapid integration of East Germany with the most dynamic force of European capitalism and the rigorous application of liberal economic principles in Poland, subsequently reflected also in developments in Hungary and Czechoslovakia, has already strengthened this association. The 35-member strong Conference on Security and Cooperation in Europe which ended in April 1990 formally recognized in its concluding document the relationship between political pluralism and market economics and emphasized that, while political pluralism was essential to sustain economic development, economic well-being was best achieved by market forces. This will, it has been noted, be a process that involves costs and penalties as well as bringing anticipated economic advantages. It is, as Hungarian writer Janos Kis recognized, "simply not possible simultaneously to meet the challenges of the world economy and to provide the population with administrative guarantees of a life without losses and conflicts".[27] Democratization should play a part in establishing structures and evolving policies that can help to cope with these pressures.

The introduction of a market economy, as Poles and Hungarians have become aware, carries the threat of inflation and unemployment and an enhanced risk of social conflict. Political institutions are therefore needed which can regulate and resolve such conflicts. Democratization will need

260   *Paul G. Lewis*

to encompass not just the creation of different forms of political organization but also the evolution of a new conception of politics — one that legitimates and tolerates conflict rather than equating the world of politics as one of rule and command, an association that put down strong roots under Stalinist socialism. The adoption of a new conception of political life was a critical factor in the process that set Taiwan on the course of democratization as it lost its membership of the United Nations and the patronage of powerful Western countries.[28] Similar processes will need to accompany democratization in Eastern Europe. Reluctance to contemplate a return to the stronger expression of political conflict was identified as an early weakness of the incipient Polish democracy.[29]

Six months after the installation of a Solidarity-led government the political honeymoon period was declared to be over and Polish democracy described as becalmed and drifting, the impetus of change fully dominated by the liberal economic programme of Finance Minister Balcerowicz. Opposition was absent from the parliament, while the social base of the Solidarity government camp and of the union itself was subject to increasing decomposition. To this extent more sceptical observers have already suggested that Poland had shown few signs of developing beyond the nursery school stage of democracy, while its population continued to define its attitude to the political leadership in terms of confidence and trust — rather than support for the government in terms of reason, interests and the imperatives of compromise.[30] Poland led the movement in Eastern Europe away from the orthodox communist-dominated form of election that had held sway since the 1940s and appeared to be the first to discover some of the problems involved in progressing beyond the first stages of democratization. But conditions elsewhere were not very different. The new Hungarian parties were internally divided, lacked national networks and constituencies, and had few funds or representatives of political stature. Their identities were imprecise and they were struggling to find their places in the political spectrum. This, of course, was hardly surprising — but progress out of the organizational confusion and conceptual poverty of late communism was slow and hesitation itself, it was suggested, could jeopardize the success of the transition towards democracy.[31]

Expectations of political development could be disappointed or met in surprising and perhaps unsatisfying ways. As Mark Frankland reported of the East Germans' experience of the March 1990 elections: "They thought they had discovered a new sort of politics in which citizens would participate in the management of their own affairs. What they have got is an election campaign masterminded by the political professionals of West Germany".[32] There exists at least a possible danger that, despite the historic transformations of 1989, real political achievements and social progress may fail to emerge under the new conditions, that "on the surface everything is accomplished; in reality, no substantial change takes place".[33] The elimination of political control over economic processes will produce conditions for the emergence of fresh tensions and new sources of social conflict, a development necessitating redefinition of the political process as one able to cope with such clashes and able to provide an arena accessible to contending interests. It is likely also to require the qualified but effective deployment of state resources, as recognition of the critical role of domestic and supranational economic factors is likely to reinforce the need for the judicious use of state power.

Tensions in the democratization process

But the democratization programme itself envisaged for Eastern Europe and the paths it is likely to follow may themselves involve certain contradictions and internal conflicts in terms of the variety of goals pursued. Some of these have already been hinted at, and there is no space here to survey the whole range of possible tensions and problems that might arise across a range of increasingly diverse countries. Here, just some of the critical political factors involved in the contemporary democratization process will be identified and their role in present developments outlined.

1. *The Role of the State.* The inauguration of free market processes, the establishment of capitalist structures and the separation of economic processes from politics, the leading edge of current East European developments, raise fundamental questions once it is recognized that such changes and radical innovations are hardly likely to come into existence spontaneously. Latin American experience has again been alluded to and the Brazilian case invoked to demonstrate the continuing need to develop and strengthen state structures under conditions imposed by the prevailing liberal ethic. The dogmatic pursuit of one principle was no better than the obsession with another and the liberal catechism, wrote Polish economist Ignacy Sachs, was no substitute for seeking "new forms of articulating the state, market and social sector" as a new version of the mixed economy.[34] The capacity and willingness of the East European state to intervene to the extent required, and the authority of nation states with respect to economic processes which are bound to have a major international and transnational dimension, evoke considerable uncertainties.

Some shifts and divergencies in terms of the relationship between economic liberalism and state authority were already becoming evident by

262   *Paul G. Lewis*

late spring 1990. Privatization and managerial buy-ins to nationalized
property assets were a major focus of this. Spontaneous privatization and
a boom in joint ventures had run ahead of programmed economic reform
in Hungary which, according to a wide-ranging *Economist* report, caused
considerable damage and "may have undermined support for liberalisation
in general". The Polish government, however, had been quick to recognize
the danger and insisted on consolidating property rights before much
privatization was pushed through — effective renationalization being
imposed as the first step with the state reasserting its ownership of enterprises before they are sold off.[35] This, however, attracted domestic criticism for departing from liberal capitalist principles and creating not so
much a private sector or market as a new administrative monopoly.[36]

2. *Political Culture and the Shallow Roots of Political Pluralism* suggest a
further tension, if not contradiction, in the combined liberal economic/
democratic political programme that has emerged for the development of
Eastern Europe. This involves consideration of the effects of economic
liberalism, the strengthening of market forces and the growing dimensions
of social inequality and impoverishment of major social groups that are
necessarily involved. Such a consequence may be regarded as a sign of
healthy competition, an indication that more productive forces and elements of the labour force are receiving appropriate levels of reward, and a
dimension of enhanced profitability and the greater efficiency of economic
processes. The resulting rise in levels of potential social and political
tension may, too, be accepted as a natural consequence of economic
change even if it does incur costs in other terms. The reformulation of
politics and establishment of new institutions which form part of the
democratization process are, of course, the natural complement and
counterbalance to this process, and may be regarded as a sufficient
response to the dangers of increased social tension.

    The likelihood of enhanced social conflict following the rigorous pur-
suit of the range of liberal policies now emerging, though, may be regarded as a source of potentially excessive demands on the emerging
framework of a post-communist politics which is already encountering a
full range of problems in its formative period. Only in Czechoslovakia
prior to World War II was there anything like an effective system of
parliamentary democracy sustained by a developed society with evident
attachment to pluralist values. The absence of such a heritage throughout
much of contemporary Eastern Europe undoubtedly hampers the development of political structures with sufficient complexity and the capacity
to cope with the political strains arising from extensive socio-economic
dislocation and growing social differentiation.

Coalitions and alliances which made a contribution to the downfall of the communist regime may no longer be sustainable and fragment with further consequences for social stability. Growing social differentiation could provide conditions for the articulation of new interests and sympathies which point the way to the formation of new groups in the political arena, including backlash movements and the emergence of a significant anti-reform coalition. Rather than contributing to the elimination of the economic inefficiencies and institutional rigidities engendered by the former communist regimes and assisting the formation of more advanced, productive systems, these currents may simply aggravate the existing crisis and block the emergence of solutions to it. Widespread reluctance to contemplate the stronger expression of political conflict was identified as an early weakness of the incipient Polish democracy, where a non-competitive political culture and the traditional emphasis on "solidarity in the fight with a common enemy" were seen as obstacles to political development.[37] In this context stabilization of the existing situation may well require the adoption of a programme of radical social reform that is incompatible with the liberal turn in economic policy seen in Poland and elsewhere.

3. *Weak Institutional Development.* A widespread hesitancy in Eastern Europe about the form to be taken by post-communist politics has hardly been surprising. The value and role of conventional party politics has been placed in question throughout the region by the rise of peaceful social movements and the success of their democratic demands.[38] Bronislaw Geremek, leader of the Solidarity-sponsored deputies of the Polish parliament, affirmed in early 1990 that Poland was the most advanced of the Central European countries along the path of authentic democratization, and that continuing restrictions on freedom should not be exaggerated. Obstacles to the development of political pluralism and a multi-party system were present, however, and grew more out of public hesitancy about the institution of the political party itself than the inherent limitations of the new political arrangements.[39] There was, further, an increasingly critical view taken by the public of Polish parliamentary bodies and the behaviour of their members. It was becoming more commonly felt that they were pursuing their own interests and becoming isolated from the electorate.[40]

Surveys on party options and preferences in Eastern Europe, further, have shown some significant differences between the different countries. Poles, like Hungarians and Soviet citizens, chose a social-democratic future for their country in preference to other political options and, like Hungarians, said they would vote for a social-democratic party rather than

264   *Paul G. Lewis*

any other if elections were imminent. Unlike Hungary and the Soviet Union, however, it was the party of the "don't knows" which had the greatest support in Poland while, in reference to the most favoured political party, as many as 60 per cent of Poles also held the view that social democracy was now more a matter of past history than a credible political option — an opinion expressed three times more frequently by Poles than Hungarians, for example.[41] Such perceptions underlay the lengthy discussion that has taken place in Poland about the status and most appropriate political form both of Solidarity-sponsored political forces, as well as that of the post-communist left. The value of maintaining the traditions of a political movement was counterposed to the advantages of interest articulation and clearer political expression that might be derived from a more fragmented organizational structure.

4. *Aspects of Political Participation* raise further questions, particularly in the context of the developments and potential conflicts in the situation outlined above. The consolidation of democratic practices (the habituation phase in terms of Rustow's model) requires a certain restraint on the part of major social groups — in particular of labour movements, which have played a central part in modern democratization processes and whose role is given even greater salience with the process of market formation and the activation of market forces. The ideal mix in terms of the labour movement's contribution to the democratization process is likely to be a combination of high labour and popular mobilization in the period leading to the break-up of authoritarian institutions, followed by the decline of that mobilization and the adoption of restraint when the political agenda shifts towards a democratization policy.[42] The lesson here appears still to be that delivered by Samuel Huntington, who warned against the dangers of insufficiently institutionalized participation and unchannelled political activity for political stability.[43]

The role of such movements currently remains the subject of speculation for most countries of Eastern Europe, although it has considerably more prominence in Poland. Up to early 1990 the situation was not unpromising in this respect. Membership of the trade union Solidarity, legalized in April 1989, was less than 2 million at the time of its congress in April 1990 in contrast to the rapid build-up to a membership of 9.5 million in 1980. A number of factors played a part in this. The regime-sponsored OPZZ, an umbrella union organization set up by the militarized party leadership in the early 1980s, retained a fair degree of autonomy and maintained a significant distance from the regime and its failed policies of economic reform in the mid-1980s. Its insistence on full wage-indexation for inflation and resistance to the deleterious consequences of the freer play of market forces for the industrial working classes helped it retain members' support. Lower levels of membership subscriptions also played a part, as Solidarity dues were pegged to wage levels and rose significantly during the inflation of the late 1980s.

In overall terms, the moderation of support for the trade union was not unwelcome as the Solidarity-sponsored government developed a radical economic programme favouring the operation of free market forces. Regimes which have pursued an exclusively market-oriented strategy can, notes Valenzuela, "only be characterized as harsh", citing Chile under Pinochet as an example — hardly an ideal model for the new Solidarity government.[44] The problems involved in combining democratization with a rigorous programme of structural change in the economy are clearly daunting. The possibility cannot be avoided, wrote Przeworski, that a transition to democracy can be made only at the cost of leaving economic relations intact. Indeed, he noted, the democratic system was consolidated in Belgium, Sweden, France and Great Britain only after organized workers were badly defeated in mass strikes and forced to adopt a docile posture.[45] Signs of internal opposition within the union and a growing tendency to strike action were evident, but the ambiguous organizational base of the Solidarity-led government remained reasonably solid for the first half-year of the post-communist government.

There was tolerance of the rigours of the first month of the economic programme, when the value of wages fell by 43 per cent in January 1990, but stability during such processes of economic change can hardly be assured. Such reserves are limited, their extent attributable to the resilience developed by Eastern European society to the lengthy dictatorship of the communist state, the rapidity of recent changes and the sheer degree of confusion produced, and to the extensive support and sympathy shown towards the new government. Signs of more active opposition to the Mazowiecki government and its economic programme surfaced with hunger-strikes and the paralysis of parts of the railway network in May 1990 in the run-up to local elections. The strikers, significantly, pro-claimed the autonomy of their action and separation from existing labour and political organizations. The unions initially showed restraint but the former communist OPZZ organization and a fraction within Solidarity, led by a rival of Lech Walesa committed to the defence of immediate worker interests, soon involved themselves in the action and publicly endorsed the strike. Only after this did Walesa intervene and persuade the strikers to call off their action in order to stabilize a situation that threatened to develop into a major political crisis.

In general terms then, democratization seems to demand the creation of conceptions of political activity different from those previously seen in

266   *Paul G. Lewis*

Eastern Europe as well new political institutions and channels of participation — but not competitive institutions that are too strong or
participation that is too enthusiastic. But higher levels of political participation clearly form part of the democratization process as a aspect of
the turn away from communist dictatorship and its exclusive pattern of
government. Sustained capitalist development, it has been argued, also
depends on vigorous and effective political participation for the process of
market-based development. Participation "within leading fields of interaction and then increasingly more and more arenas at every social level" is
essential if capitalist economic development is to be sustained.[46] Social
pressures as well as theoretical arguments thus support the drive for
enhanced political participation, although historical experience and the
dangers of political turmoil suggest that it may well prove to be a area of
further sensitivity in the democratization process.

Notes

1. *The Economist* (London), 8 June 1985.
2. E. Friedman, "Modernization and democratization in Leninist states: the case of China", *Studies in Comparative Communism* vol. 22, 2/3 (1989), p. 259.
3. G. Pridham, "Comparative perspectives on the new Mediterranean democracies", in *The New Mediterranean Democracies: Regime Transition in Spain, Greece and Por-tugal* (ed. G. Pridham), London: Frank Cass (1984), pp. 19—22.
4. T-J. Cheng, "Democratizing the quasi-Leninist regime in Taiwan", *World Politics* vol. 41, 4 (1989); J. Cotton, "From authoritarianism to democracy in South Korea", *Political Studies* vol. 37, 2 (1989).
5. A. Arato, "Some perspectives of democratization in East Central Europe", *Journal of International Affairs* vol. 38, 2 (1985), pp. 322—23.
6. *Comparative Politics*, vol. 2 (1970).
7. G. Breslauer, "Linking Gorbachev's domestic and foreign policies", *Journal of Interna-tional Affairs* vol. 42, 2 (1989).
8. T-J. Cheng, "Democratizing", p. 474.
9. J. Kis, "Turning point in Hungary", *Dissent* (Spring 1989), p. 241.
10. B. Moore, *Social Origins of Dictatorship and Democracy*, London: Allen Lane (1967).
11. D. Van Atta, "The USSR as a "weak state": agrarian origins of resistance to perestroika", *World Politics* vol. 42, 1 (1989), pp. 132—33.
12. P. Constable and A. Valenzuela, "Chile's return to democracy", *Foreign Affairs* vol. 68, 5 (1989—90), p. 170; Cheng, "Democratizing", p. 474.
13. E. Hankiss, "In search of a paradigm", *Daedalus* vol. 119, 1 (1990), p. 209; Z. Bauman, "Poland: on its own", *Telos* 79 (1989), pp. 55—57.
14. P. G. Lewis, "Institutionalisation and political change in Poland", in *The State in Socialist Society* (ed. N. Harding), London: Macmillan (1984); Kis, "Turning point".
15. "Of debt and democracy", *Economist*, 11 February 1989.
16. R. Munck, *Latin America: the Transition to Democracy*, London: Zed Books (1989), p. 20.

Democratization in Eastern Europe 267

17. K. Dawisha, *Eastern Europe, Gorbachev and Reform*, Cambridge University Press: 1988, p. 143.
18. J. Prybla, "The great malaise: economic crisis in Eastern Europe", in *The Uncertain Future: Gorbachev's Eastern Bloc* (ed. N. Kittrie and I. Volgyes), New York: Paragon House (1988), p. 77.
19. *Mały Rocznik Statystyczny 1989* (Warsaw), p. 400.
20. *Rzeczpospolita* (Warsaw), 9 November 1989.
21. *Tygodnik Solidarność* (Warsaw), 22 September 1989.
22. W. E. Griffith, "Central and Eastern Europe: the global context", in *Central and Eastern Europe: the Opening Curtain* (ed. W. E. Griffith), Boulder: Westview Press (1989), p. 2.
23. Friedman, "Modernization", pp. 251, 257.
24. Friedman, "Modernization", p. 252.
25. A. Przeworski, "Some problems in the study of the transition to democracy", in *Transitions From Authoritarian Rule, vol. 3: Comparative Perspectives* (ed. G. O'Donnell et al.), Baltimore: Johns Hopkins (1986), p. 58.
26. B. Jessop, "Capitalism and democracy: the best possible political shell?" in *Power and the State* (ed. G. Littlejohn et al.), London: Croom Helm (1978).
27. Kis, "Turning point", p. 238.
28. Cheng, "Democratizing", p. 484.
29. *Polityka* (Warsaw), 4 November 1989.
30. *Polityka*, 24 March 1990.
31. Hankiss, "In search", p. 206.
32. *The Observer* (London), 18 March 1990.
33. Kis, "Turning point", p. 237.
34. *Polityka*, 11 November 1989.
35. 28 April 1990.
36. *Polityka*, 24 March 1990.
37. *Polityka*, 4 November 1989.
38. A. G. Frank, "Revolution in Eastern Europe", *Third World Quarterly*, vol. 12, 2 (1990), p. 37.
39. *Rzeczpospolita* (Warsaw), 17 January 1990.
40. *Rzeczpospolita*, 3—4 March 1990.
41. *Liberation* (Paris), 19 February 1990.
42. J. Valenzuela, "Labor movements in transitions to democracy", *Comparative Politics* vol. 21, 4 (1989), p. 451.
43. *Political Order in Changing Societies*, New Haven: Yale University Press (1968).
44. Valenzuela, "Labor movements", p. 457.
45. "Some problems", p. 63.
46. G. Goodell, "The importance of political participation for sustained capitalist development", *Archives Europeens de Sociologie* vol 26 (1985), p. 94.

[21]

Journal of Theoretical Politics 5(2): 231–252 (1993)   © Sage Publications

THE 'COMPARATIVE REVOLUTION' AND THE TRANSITION IN CENTRAL AND SOUTHERN EUROPE

Attila Ágh

ABSTRACT

The Latin American, South European and, later, the Central and East European democratic transitions have led to a 'revolution' in comparative politics. Instead of the polar notions of democracy and dictatorship, different types of 'transitions' have emerged and democracy has appeared also as a function of the world-system. The paper suggests that there are four scenarios for Central and East European democratic transitions in their international context: (1) Sleeping Beauty (easy westernization); (2) Deepfreeze (return to the past); (3) Latin Americanization (falling back to the Third World); and (4) Fair Weather (Central Europe joins the European integration).

KEY WORDS • democratic transition • European integration • linkage politics • Central and Eastern Europe

Democratic Transitions – the First Step: Latin America

Since the late 1970s the democratic transitions in Latin America and later in southern Europe have given new impulse to the 'Comparative Revolution' in political science. Within this framework an important initiative was launched by the Woodrow Wilson International Center (Washington) in 1977 to study the parallel developments in Latin America and Southern Europe. These two regions have been connected by the same historical and cultural heritage, but also by very intensive economic and social ties. The result of this international effort in comparative research was a four-volume work published in 1986, *Transitions from Authoritarian Rule*. This book, still the most authoritative guide in the comparative research of democratic transitions, enables us to outline the major features of the democratic transitions of the two regions, Southern and Central Europe.

Although Latin America is not the focus of interest for many of us in these two European regions, it is an obligatory point of departure for all of us, because it is in this context that the most important achievements of the theory of transitions have been reached. 'Latin Americanization' of the comparative research of democratic transitions has been the cause of US concern; Latin American dominance is still felt in the relevant theories but the 'de-Latin-Americanization' of Southern and Central European research efforts begun only a few years ago has already led to some significant results.[1]

The Latin America-based Comparative Revolution has provided us with certain new findings which transform the body of political science research:

> (i) Instead of polar notions of 'democracy' and 'dictatorship', in fact only different types of transitions exist, the developed democracies are not 'perfect models' and the not-yet-democratic countries have some internal resources for democratization, they are not divided for ever. (ii) Democracy is not only a structure of the (national) polity but also, or even first of all, a function of the world-system; this is why the international factors in most cases are decisive in the emergence and consolidation of the new democracies. (iii) There are three major waves of the global democratization process, the first wave concerned the core countries of the world-system, the second wave came in some European countries after World War II and what we are witnessing is the third wave in its first step in Latin America, second step in Southern Europe and third step in Central Europe. (iv) The emergence and consolidation of the new democracies cannot be approached from a strictly deterministic-structuralist point of view, but in an open approach the 'crafting the democracy' has to be taken as a guiding line in the comparative theory of transitions (Di Palma, 1990).

Comparative Transitions: Latin America and Southern Europe

The similarities between Latin American and Southern European transitions in timing as well as in targets are very important, yet the contrasting features or dissimilarities dominate. In the whole transition 'package' (free market economy, human rights and the constitutional legal state) the differences between the two regions are not only big, but fundamental, both in domestic developments and in international setting.

1. Development Pattern – Cyclical or Evolutive?

There are marked differences in domestic development patterns between Latin America and Southern Europe. The development pattern is cyclical in Latin America, with fragile democracies moving in a recurrent crisis model, i.e. from authoritarian rule to democracy and vice versa. In Southern

---

1. After comparisons between Latin America and Southern Europe the first all-embracing analyses have appeared on the Southern European democratic transitions and consolidations – see U. Liebert and M. Cotta, eds (1990), Geoffrey Pridham, ed. (1990) and Geoffrey Pridham, ed. (1991). The above-mentioned editors in their recent papers have begun to extend their comparisons to Central and Eastern Europe, arguing that it is more fruitful than the comparison between Latin America and Southern Europe. I note here, at the very beginning, that the Latin American model, as it has been widely accepted in the comparative politics literature, means for me only the major trends embodied in the leading, trend-setter South American countries (e.g. Brazil and Argentina).

Europe there is an evolutionary development pattern with consolidated democracies, efficient social and political crisis management systems and no danger of a slide back into dictatorship. In their current history some Latin American countries have made both these transitions several times, because their democracies have always been socio-economically fragile and never sufficiently consolidated. The Southern European countries, however, have a long, unbroken history of authoritarian rule behind them, between the 1930s and 1970s, but their recent transitions have resulted in solid and stable democratic regimes, at least in Spain and Portugal, with economic prosperity. The pattern in Greece in some ways was close to the Latin American development pattern, but in the 1980s diverged completely from this course (see also Bonime-Blanc, 1987).

2. *International Setting – Dependence or Integration?*

In the world-system, or in the system of international relations, Latin American countries have traditionally belonged within the sphere of influence of the United States, through a complexity of economic, cultural, political and, sometimes, military dependence. The recent democratization of the Southern European countries has been accomplished, in turn, on the 'rimland' of European integration as an extension of the integration process to the Mediterranean region. Thus the role of the United States in the democratization process of Latin America has been ambiguous, i.e. the United States may have bolstered the process of political democratization in some Latin American countries, at least in the short run and to some extent (by the demonstration effect or through economic, political or military pressures). Because of economic dependence (and the lack of economic assistance for the new democracies) the role of the United States in the Latin American democratization process has in the long run been largely negative, though not supportive and facilitating enough for consolidation of the new democracies.

The successful and stable democratic transitions in the Southern European countries have taken place in an extremely favourable international setting, having been the new phase of the extension of the European integration process. The previous *asymmetrical* relations of dependence have become a new subregional and regional system of *symmetrical* relationships of interdependence, and integration has emerged. The external factor has proved to be the prime mover behind the democratization process from the initial crisis to consolidation. The European process of integration as the external driving force behind internal political democratization and economic liberalization has given at the same time the *standards* (norms and models of the European institutions) and the *safeguards* of the whole transition, securing and accelerating the evolutive character of their domestic developments.

These broad outlines demarcate the most essential features of the contrast between the Latin American and Southern European transitions, revealing the special character of the second step or stage within the third wave of the global democratization process in Spain, Portugal and Greece which has been, in fact, an obligatory introduction to the analysis of the developments in Central Europe. The significance of the direct involvement of the Western European countries in the democratization process of the Southern European countries, in my opinion, cannot be emphasized enough. Without their massive financial assistance and large-scale capital investment, solution of the debt-crisis and accomplishment of the structural changes in the national economies might not have been possible at all. The direct political assistance of the Western European states has also to be seen as a very important factor in the whole political democratization process. While Latin America has failed, Southern Europe has succeeded in the transition to democracy, above all because of the predominance of external factors in the transition, which will also determine the fate of further democratic transitions (see O'Donnell et al., 1986).

The European Community needed this Mediterranean extension to improve its own performance on a global scale and the Mediterranean needed Europe in order to overcome authoritarian rule and relative backwardness. In this historical bargain 'Europeanization' has not been an empty political slogan but a catch-up and effective safeguard against sliding back into authoritarian rule. Europeanization has also meant the reinforcement of the European tradition of parliamentary system with its leading role in the political transition. In Latin America, however, the US presidential system tradition has prevailed but without its supporting systems, i.e. without the proper 'checks and balances'. The presidential system has proved to be the 'king's way', that is, the easiest way for transition not just from authoritarian rule to democracy, but also from democracy to authoritarian rule.[2]

These descriptions of Latin American and Southern European developments may serve as predictions for the newly emerging democracies of Central Europe, since they offer two contrasting scenarios, two possible futures (see Linz, 1978).

---

2. I have described the alternatives of presidential and parliamentary systems in Ágh (1991b). Europeanization in Southern Europe clearly means the option for the parliamentary system. The same European 'craze' may be observed in the East Central European countries. Europeanization of the socio-political system into a structure comparable to the 'acquis communautaire' of the European Community will be an even bigger task than economic transformation. Our Institute, the Hungarian Centre for Democracy Studies, has dealt with this specific project very intensively.

Disintegrated Alliance: Central versus Eastern Europe

As a third step in the third wave of global democratizations, in the late 1980s a new region, the eastern half of Europe, began its long march towards democracy whilst posing a still unsolved problem for comparative politics. 'Eastern Europe' is a misnomer, a result of the splitting of Europe into two parts by the Cold War (usually referred to as the Yalta system), i.e. it is not an organic entity, neither geographically nor culturally, but a political and military unit or conglomerate imposed upon the region from outside by the eastern neighbourhood. This artificial Eastern Europe completely disappeared in the 1989 autumn revolutions ('Spring in Winter') after the 'Year of the Century'. The traditional and organic (subregional) structure of Europe has re-emerged: *Central Europe*, with Austria and parts of Italy on the western side and Hungary, Czechoslovakia, Poland and parts of Yugoslavia and Romania on the eastern side; and *Eastern Europe* proper, with Romania, Bulgaria, the eastern part of Yugoslavia, Albania – and possibly the Ukraine and Belorussia.[3]

For a historical study of comparative communism it may be relevant to analyse the *common* features of all state socialism in the eastern half of Europe, but for the current history of democratic transitions it is the *divergences* between these two regions that matter. Any attempt at homogenizing them would be seriously misleading. No doubt the whole of 'Eastern Europe' suffered from the alien, Stalinist type of modernization forced upon these countries from the outside by the Soviet Union. However, the regional differences were established enough to resist the pressures of the 'external empire' of the Soviet Union and its homogenizing effects. Central Europe has in many ways kept its western-like structures for the last forty years, since it has been much more developed historically than Eastern Europe proper. These differences are quite clear in the economy (industrialization) and in political life (constitutional state), but above all in the development of civil societies (with their organizations and political cultures). The deep structures of civil societies were effective resistance to the pressures of the authoritarian state in Central Europe during the postwar period (see Dawisha, 1990; Rusi, 1991).

---

3. Concerning the fundamental, revolutionary transformations in Central Europe we have had mostly impressionistic descriptions and not all-embracing theoretical analyses, such as those by T. G. Ash (1990), Gwyn Prins, ed. (1990) and Misha Glenny (1990), and only recently have we had more systematic analyses from Judy Batt (1991) and Hankiss (1990), for example. In order to have reliable documentation, the Political Science Department at the Budapest University of Economics has edited, so far, four thick volumes, one on each year of the transition (1988, 1989, 1990, 1991) in the form of a *Political Yearbook of Hungary* (Budapest: Aula Press, 1989, 1990, 1991, 1992), with my Introduction as a summary of the previous year. These Yearbooks contain comprehensive documentation and statistics, public opinion surveys and analyses from all fields of political life.

This time Central Europe, too, started the democratization process earlier than Eastern Europe. Central Europe is more likely to accomplish the democratic transition as well. It is against this background that the problem of the South European and Latin American scenarios emerges, the first one for Central Europe, the second for Eastern Europe. Not simply as 'predictions' but to some extent as 'descriptions', too. The Central European countries have gone through deep systemic changes and the political and socio-economic transformations (constitutional state and privatization-marketization) have reached the point of no return, i.e. they have become irreversible. The East European countries have not reached this point yet, they are facing further turmoil and destabilization, because no systemic change has yet taken place. Europeanization is the present of Central Europe in the 1990s and it is the future of Eastern Europe, hopefully, in the early 21st century (see Ágh, 1991a).

The test-case for West European intentions in the new global dynamism has arrived with the fundamental changes taking place in the eastern part of Europe and with the decomposition of the external empire. The two separate subregions and the states of the former Soviet Union as a third unit need totally different approaches in the crisis management process. The Central European countries require the same treatment as given to Southern Europe and, with a longer transition, can eventually be members of the European Community, whereas the Eastern European countries are looking to stabilize their ailing economies and troubled polities and the states of the former Soviet Union have to be placed into a new global world order.

It was not the 'Gorbachev factor' but the 'Spring in Winter' Revolutions of the Central (and Eastern) European countries that was the mortal blow to the postwar European order and, as a result, the whole Cold War period came to an end. The revolutions in the Central European nations, in fact, with their East European partners, became an event in 'world history'. These nations have been very active and instrumental in restructuring European security and political order. These small countries of Central Europe have been on a so-called 'forced-course development' historically, i.e. the external factors have always dominated over the internal ones. This development model applies most brutally and directly to the postwar period of the Stalinist type modernization. They belonged to the Soviet external empire which could not be liquidated without a major earthquake in Europe and its collapse led necessarily to the end of the postwar bipolar world order.

The Comparative Adventure: Southern versus Central Europe

At first glance it is risky to argue for parallel developments in Southern and Central Europe. It is too easy to refute this type of argument: the Central European countries are lagging behind in many ways. They started the democratic transition much later and their democratization has brought about much more change in Europe than that of the Southern European countries with their 'smooth' transitions within the same alliance system and by and large within the same system of socio-economic ties. The Central European countries had their Brezhnev doctrine to prevent them from joining Europe, the Southern European countries had their 'Atlantist' doctrine (Greece and Portugal as NATO members, Spain had become a member by the transition process) to be accepted militarily and politically, and catching up 'only' economically. Second, allegedly, even economically the Southern European countries were on the other side of the iron curtain. They were undeveloped market economies and the Central European countries were command economies, so for them economy and politics had to change in the same transition process.

These differences have been conceptualized in Western political science in the terms 'authoritarian' and 'totalitarian' regimes, first by H. Arendt (1973) and later in a more overpoliticized way by J. Kirkpatrick (1979), distinguishing allies and enemies in the underdeveloped world. This conceptual structure has recently been transferred to the analysis of the newly born democracies of Central Europe and it serves as a point of departure for the counter-argument against the parallel between Southern and Central European transitions.

Totalitarianism is a Cold War ideology based on the mutual enemy image, an ideological construction depicting 'ideal' communism with one centre of power and no change. It is true that 'real socialism' meant 'extensive' political and economic regimes with their efforts to subdue the whole of society. These efforts, however, were only very partially successful. In general, the theory of totalitarianism presupposes a static model of 'communist' society and gives no explanation for its recurring crises (Rupnik, 1989). The difference between 'authoritarianism' and 'totalitarianism' proves to be in most cases a journalistic oversimplification, as in the comparison between Southern and Central Europe. As far as the economy is concerned, the capitalist market economy was better developed in the Central European region in the prewar period than in the Southern European one. No doubt in the postwar period the Central European countries had a command economy system, but the political concentration of the economy and its management was also very high in Southern Europe with many features of 'command'. Consequently the contrast is big but not 'total'. In Southern Europe the transition was not reduced to the political sphere but that was the decisive process. In Central Europe, however, both the economy and politics need a radical and profound transformation, although in both spheres of society there have been positive historical traditions and antecedents.[4]

Southern Europe and Central Europe as two semi-peripheries of Western Europe had been developing in similar ways for centuries in their macro-structures and mega-trends. This close parallel came to an end only with the postwar arrangements. Even Central Europe was slightly more modern and better industrialized than Southern Europe until World War II. The fundamental change came in the postwar system splitting Europe into two parts. Southern Europe became integrated into the Western political and military, partially economic and social system, and Central Europe (with the exception of Austria (1955), and Finland (1948) was a similar case) into the Eastern one. Thus, external factors were responsible for the further divergences of these regions. These factors were relatively favourable for the Southern European countries in the early postwar period and extremely favourable in the 1970s and 1980s, at the time of their democratic transition. These same factors were brutally unfavourable for the Central European countries in the early postwar period, when they became members of the Soviet 'external Empire' and only turned more favourable in the late 1980s, when the external Empire collapsed. The homogenization efforts of the Empire in 'Eastern Europe' based on the Soviet model crippled Central Europe and deprived it of its previous organic western contacts for some decades. But now this negative external factor has disappeared and the similar features with the Southern European region have come to the fore, again, as a long-term historical tendency.

With all the differences in their economies, Central and Southern European countries reacted to the global crisis of the early 1970s in similar ways. Both regions failed to accomplish structural accommodations to meet the fundamentally changed world economy, which resulted in outdated industries and high unemployment and inflation rates: for the Southern European countries in the 1970s and for the Central European countries in the late 1980s. Southern Europe, in fact, was able to manage the crisis earlier and better because it became part of the European integration in the mld-1970s. Central Europe mismanaged it because of the paralysing effects of the external Empire, so the crisis turned deeper and deeper. With the assistance of Western Europe it is still manageable now, but only in a

---

4. For the joint task of transforming both the economy and the polity in Central Europe, see Claus Offe (1991). Against the widespread commonplace that Southern Europe had a perfect market economy even before the transition, Victor Pérez-Diaz asserts, unambiguously, that for 'Forty years of the authoritarian rule . . . the Spanish economy was a mixture of a market economy and state-controlled economy, and this affected all sectors . . . Spaniards, including, significantly, many industrialists, have always had very limited experience with the theory and practice of a free market economy' (in I. Scholten (ed.) 1987: 224).

longer and more painful process, through the 'valley of tears' (Dahrendorf, 1990: 77).

All in all, the parallel between Southern and Central Europe as subregions of Europe may be confirmed in three dimensions at least: (i) in their common historical traditions, long-term mega-trends and cultural similarities, (ii) in their failed structural accommodation to the global crisis and in the common need for Western assistance to get out of the socio-economic crisis, (iii) in both the common tradition of the parliamentary structures of the polity and the negotiated way of political transition. Let us consider first of all Spain and Hungary.

Central European Development Pattern: Evolutive (Southern European) or Cyclical (Latin American)?

The forced-course development in the postwar period accumulated a tremendous crisis potential in Central Europe. Since the general features of the 'socialist' society (in the economy, politics and ideology) had been fixed forcefully, i.e. by military means in the external Empire, from time to time the necessity for a minor correction or 'reform' arose. So within a longer cycle of dictatorship (a full Kondratieff cycle or 'long wave') the 'iron laws' of development were fixed by a very rigid structure. But there were shorter cycles as well; 'reform cycles' or cycles of recurrent crises between more liberal and more conservative regimes. Within the 40–50 years of the long cycle there were about 4 or 5 shorter cycles of 9–11 years, but at the end of the 1980s its crisis proved to be the 'final crisis' of the long cycle, itself.

The final crisis of the 1980s showed in a very short time that the internal and external resources of the 'State Socialist Project' had been exhausted completely, because the 'cannibalistic' modernization had sacrificed the resources of agriculture, environment, human capital and infrastructure on the altar of the 19th-century heavy industry. The whole economy came into a period of stagnation and disintegration. Even the external resources and safeguards of the reproduction of the 'State Socialist Project' had been exhausted by the rapid weakening of the 'Soviet Dis-Union' itself with its complex crisis. Finally, the growing debt crisis curtailed the further possibility of financing the 'dead industries' as 'open-air technological museums' by foreign resources as credits from the most advanced industrial countries.

Without the new massive credits and/or the 'brotherly assistance' of Soviet troops the previous long cycle ended with the latest shorter cycle in a form of the recurring socio-economic and political crisis. Thus, we are at the beginning of a new long cycle with its first shorter cycle. Nowadays the most important question is: which way to go, by the Latin American way of the recurrent crisis of the new type (right-wing populist dictatorships) or by the evolutionary way of the Southern European countries? We have started out on a new course, for better or worse, but certainly not repeating the previous pattern of short cycles in state socialism from socio-political reforms to conservative rearrangements. The 'systemic change' as socio-political transition has become irreversible. There is a chance now for Central Europe either to return to the very long historical trendlines ('longue durée') of rebuilding the West European structures in the Southern European way or, according to the Latin American scenario, to start the new type shorter cycle in a recurring crisis model.

All depends on the external factors again. If Central Europe could join the European integration and get assistance similar to that which Southern Europe got more than a decade ago, then the recent crisis could be resolved and the democratic transition completed during the 1990s. If the European Community is not ready to include Central Europe in the European integration process, step by step, i.e. through a long transition period and many transitory forms, then Central Europe may revert to 'authoritarian rule'; this time, however, not the well-known Stalinist type of dictatorship but the traditional, right-conservative type.

For Central Europe, the biggest historical burden now is that the 'State Socialist Project' has discredited the real left in these countries. The 'victory of the left' in the late 1940s was in fact suicide for the genuine left in the Central European countries, although most of its representatives did not realize it for a long time. The genuine left has survived until now merely as an undercurrent, first in the form of intra-party opposition, but later also as open democratic opposition. Anyway, given the fact that the left itself as democratic socialism has lost its credibility, the contrast between Southern and Central Europe appears here in the sharpest way. In Southern Europe the socialist and other leftist parties have proved to be the major driving forces behind the democratic transition and its consolidation has been a victory for them. In Central Europe, on the contrary, the democratic transition seems to be a defeat for the left; the socialist and leftist parties are weak and are on the defensive. The words 'socialism' and 'left' have become dirty words and taboos even for those who support them. This perverse character of the Central European democratization process, in my view, is the major obstacle for its dynamism and it has to be overcome in order to avoid the trap of the Latin Americanization scenario and to return to the Southern European parallel in a meaningful way.

The Central European countries themselves differ a lot in this respect. In Hungary, the most liberal version of state socialism allowed some opposition even within the ruling party. This was accompanied by some active parliamentary functions in political life, economic liberalism and entrepreneurship, and the weak independence of civil society appeared to some extent. In Czechoslovakia, and even in Poland, the whole historical process was more confrontational, so the left was completely discredited and excluded from the ruling parties. Therefore, Hungary began the democratic transition earlier and has been more evolutionary, fairly close to the Spanish model of negotiated revolution (*reforma pactada* versus *ruptura pactada*).[5]

Hungary provides the classical case for the analysis of peaceful and gradual transition to democracy in Central Europe, with Poland and Czechoslovakia offering other historical innovations and lessons on democratic transition.

The Life Expectancy of the New Democracies

Why do some democracies succeed while others fail? In seeking an answer to this problem G. Bingham Powell examines the comparative record of 'Contemporary Democracies' in terms of factors like: (i) voter participation and citizens' involvement, (ii) government stability and performance, (iii) strength of the party system, (iv) constitutional setting and rule of law, (v) managing violence, crises and sustaining democracy.

In the 29 countries which are working democracies in the postwar period, Powell offers a multifactor analysis taking all institutional, environmental and participatory aspects into consideration. He emphasizes, however, that a strong and stable system of the political parties is likely to play a key role in the sustainability of the contemporary democracies, i.e. in shaping the political performance of the democratic polity within the context of the social and cultural environment (Powell, 1982: 1–11, 201–18).

In the late 1980s the Central European countries began the second largest experiment with democratization in recent European history after the successful catch-up efforts of the Southern European nations. The basic issue of the sustainability of the democracies in Central Europe has to be raised, even if we cannot yet describe this democratization process in a well documented way. Yet, we may outline the major features of the Central European democracies and their chances for survival. Since the major criterion for Powell is the party system, we take this as the cornerstone for our short characterization of Central European developments, which always have to be approached in their international setting.

In the 1970s political science was aware of the potential fragility and vulnerability of the new democracies, even more so with the process of democratization, namely, that the eruption of mass discontent and violence

---

5. In Spring 1991 Hungary seemed to be getting closer again to the 'Spanish way' by suggesting having a 'Moncloa Pact' of the six parliamentary parties. The social pact is still far down the road, but the six parties negotiate from time to time.

can lead again to systemic change and to a return to authoritarian rule. In the 1990s, however, this approach returns with a vengeance in the case of the newly emerging democracies of Central Europe.

Although the long life-expectancy of the new democracy cannot be taken as given either, their return to the authoritarian rule, after a short experiment with democracy, would still be an unfounded prediction.

The milestones of the revolutionary transformations are: '1989' – 'annus mirabilis', the 'Year of Century', i.e. the year of collapse of the authoritarian regime, '1990' – 'annus miserabilis', the year of the new difficulties with the hope of short transition, '1991' – 'annus horribilis', the year of the new mass dissatisfactions and the danger of survival.

These milestones indicate the accelerated historical changes from the negative side as the cumulated troubles and difficulties facing the new democratic systems, in their recent past and future. It is a big question whether their party systems are ready for interest articulation and crisis management, i.e. whether they are able to overcome the recent, new crisis of the transition and can make the democratic process politically and constitutionally irreversible.

The centrality of the party system and of parliament comes from the fact that during the transition the parties have been the first actors to become organized within a parliamentary system. They take all the roles and functions which are played normally by civil societies (participation, citizens' involvement, local governments, etc.) or even by the government (managing the crisis by party-pacts, etc.). A very characteristic feature of Central European democratization is that the parties have an extreme dominance in the political process ('overparticization') and parliament is the only scene of the political drama ('overparliamentarization'). The party system in the Central European countries may be described as big fragmentation (except in Hungary), but also as the extreme volatility of voters and the almost completely missing identity and identification of parties. In Hungary, for example, the three governing parties and the three opposition parties showed quite the opposite results after six months. The Spring 1990 general elections were won by the incumbent governing parties, the Fall 1990 local government elections by the opposition parties.

Compared to Western Europe, the party systems in Central Europe are still relatively weak and suffer from all kinds of 'infantile disorder', although they are much stronger than in Eastern Europe. Again, the party system in Hungary is relatively more stable and better organized than in Poland or Czechoslovakia, where the new parties are just emerging from the unspecified opposition movements. The analysis of the Hungarian party system may offer a short explanation for the genetic defects of the democracy in Poland and Czechoslovakia as well. The common weaknesses of parties are the missing links to the social actors, i.e. from the lack of dialogue between the social

and political actors which would be the case in a developed liberal constitutional state with the process of interest articulation and aggregation. The
parties are still 'hovering' over the social and economic realities, they are not
yet articulated according to the relevant programmes and value systems,
which is the major reason for the missing party identities and party identifications (see Ágh, 1992a).

The major criteria for the different parties have been their relationship in
the transition process itself (radical or evolutionary). Their articulation has
been motivated by the main political subcultures and expressed not so much
by party programmes as by their fundamentally different political discourses. The relevant political discourses in Central Europe are the following
(they show, again, a close parallel with the Southern European countries):
(1) Traditionalist–legalist discourse – the language of the traditional
political class returning to power. (2) Populist–nationalist discourse – the
style of gentry messianistic nationalism and populism. (3) Literary–artistic
discourse – the self-identification of the traditional intelligentsia as the
substitute for the middle class. (4) Religious–church-oriented discourse –
the political communication of the elderly people and derelict regions.
(5) Rationalist–European discourse – the expression of the reform-process
tradition and the idea of 'Return to Europe'.

Comparative analysis of the Southern and Central European countries in
their democratic transition would show that there are particular social actors
and agencies behind these political discourses. Political subcultures such as
'organizing centres by communication' play a major role in the party formation process. The 'proto-parties' of Central Europe have gone well beyond
their social legitimation by the social actors and agencies, while not yet playing their own political role properly and efficiently. With 'overparticization'
and 'overparliamentarization' they have reached their limits and by increasing their delegitimation process they risk not only their own survival but also
that of the new democracies, not yet being capable themselves of successful
crisis management.

With so many weaknesses these parties also have some extra strength as
prime movers of the transition process. Even in the period of the initial crisis
the parties were the most rapidly changing elements of political life and
remain so in the second period, i.e. in the transition proper, where the
previous and recently emerging systems are present in a rather chaotic way.
The parties and the whole workings of parliaments are now showing the first
signs of sobriety and growing maturity. If they realize that they are important but not exclusive actors of the social and political transition, then the
likelihood of survival of the new democracies will be much greater. In the
second period, the construction of the new democracies begins necessarily
from above, as the general framework of the new polity (parliament,
constitution, party system), which makes the new regimes into an 'elite

democracy' with the new political class in the parties and parliaments. The progress in democratization leads towards the inclusion of the other social and political actors (organized interest associations) reaching, by this fundamental transformation, the bottom level of civil society, building a solid foundation there in political culture for the new democracies. Only the construction of this full-scale democracy to replace the present lopsided one can contain violence and popular dissatisfaction, giving people a voice and participation in the decision-making process. This is where the real democracy starts: in the third period as a consolidation of the new democracies with the 'innovation of the democratic tradition' (see Pérez-Diaz, 1990).

Four Scenarios of Linkage Politics

The political science literature about Central and Eastern Europe may be outlined in four basic scenarios, their conceptual frameworks completely different, as are their 'predictions' and consequences. The first two are, in fact, *repetition scenarios*, i.e. polarized images of the past projected into the future. The second two, in turn, are the real *transition scenarios*, containing genuine social change and conceptualizing the future in completely different directions. Finally, the first and fourth scenarios are, indeed, about Central Europe, the second and third about the whole of 'Eastern' Europe. All the scenarios as characterized below are coherent theoretically but appear very rarely in pure forms in the present jungle of theories and interpretations. The overwhelming majority of the analyses about Central (and Eastern) Europe usually combine the features of these competitive scenarios into one contradictory, narrative descriptive and/or theoretical-analytical framework. The four scenarios may be described as follows.

Sleeping Beauty (the Raped West)

The first scenario states that the western-style modernization process was brutally broken by the Soviet Conquest in Central Europe after World War II, i.e. Central Europe as a genuine part of the West was 'raped' by the Red Army. The Soviet external empire, that is, the region of small states in Central Europe (and in Eastern Europe), imposed alien roles and rules upon these nations, but it was unable to change the fundamentally western nature of their (civil) societies. This amounts to a definition of Central Europe, as suggested by Milan Kundera (1984), which has been the point of departure for the renewed discussions about the region in the 1980s. Central Europe has always been part of the West, but has suffered from time to time from eastern aggression. After 'easternization' with a new effort at 'westernization' this region is maintaining and restoring its character.

Obviously, nowadays, the latest eastern invasion is over, and Central Europe, again, so to speak, is automatically returning to the West. It is the story of the Sleeping Beauty being woken up by the Young Prince. The politicians as well as the peoples of Central European countries thought in late 1989 that the return to democracy and free market society could be resolved quickly and easily, 'overnight' by the pluralization and privatization programmes, without major pain and conflict but with significant western assistance. The western character of Central Europe will therefore be almost completely restored and these countries of East–Central Europe (Poland, Czecho-Slovakia and Hungary, perhaps also Crovenia, i.e. Croatia and Slovenia) will soon join the community of free European nations.

This is the great utopia of an easy transition and was common wisdom and belief everywhere, but most vehemently formulated and preached in Bohemia, in the Czech lands, offering for our external typology a Czech way of transition (contrasted even to Slovakia, the Czechs considering themselves the only real western nation in Central Europe). But when the initial euphoria was over by the mid-1990s, the disappointment became widespread and a counter-utopia came to the fore. As A. Motyl (1991) suggests: 'Slowly but inexorably, the euphoria of 1989 is giving way to the gloom of 1991. Transitions to democracy and markets in postcommunist Central Europe are not proceeding as smoothly as had been forecast' (p. 499).[6]

For the transition between the dominance of the two scenarios, it is important to note with Deborah Milenkovitch that 'In the space of seven months, the entire political landscape of East Central Europe had been fundamentally and irreversibly altered . . . Not surprisingly, ruling in postcommunist East Central Europe proved more difficult than taking power, and by the Summer of 1990, the euphoria of late 1989 had given way to a more sober view' (1991: 151–2, 158).

Deepfreeze (the Eternal East)

The second scenario reflects the mentality of the period of the Great Uncertainty after the collapse of the previous regime and before the consolidation

---

6. Walter Mead (1991) stated: The United States was 'ecstatic in contemplating the new order arising in what used to be communist Europe. The downfall of communism in the former satellites and the rise of reformers in the Soviet Union sent a wave of euphoria through Washington' with the simplistic slogan: 'Communism had made Eastern Europe poor; capitalism would make it rich – quickly. This was the easy wisdom with which neoliberal Washington greeted the changes in Europe.' Thus, the easy transition as a scenario was shared by the West: 'Washington supposed that beneath the communist overlay was a part of the world essentially identical to Western Europe. Once the heavy hand of the bureaucratic and conservative occupying power was removed, these countries could return to their democratic traditions' (pp. 395, 397).

of something completely new facing the unknown future. When the initial euphoria was over, everything became uncertain, including the past, not just the present and the future. The new regimes glorified the past, i.e. the inter-war period before 'communism' and even earlier historical times, without too much careful selection among historical traditions. At the same time, the contradictions of backward 'eastern' Europe seemed to return from the prewar period and before. Apparently, they were only deeply frozen by the 'communist' regime but not created by the occupying forces, since they proved to be too well known from previous historical periods. The past was glorious and shameful, glorious for the new conservative leaders in govern-ment and shameful for the liberal intelligentsia and press, and also for the West. It was even suggested by the western press that the Soviet oppression came from the same 'eternal' East European soil. Consequently, it was not alien at all for Central (and Eastern) Europe, as stated before, in revolu-tionary mood. Quite the contrary, these negative features expressed the real nature of the East European nations: century-old contradictions of state-led modernizations, hopeless emotional nationalisms, lack of democratic culture and free market behaviour.

Thus, instead of the programme 'return to Europe', the opposite, 'return to the past', came to the fore, i.e. all the demons of the past returned. *The Economist* formulated the verdict about central Europe with real western arrogance in its headline: 'The East is East, the West is West'. The Deep-freeze scenario, in fact, was not really 'home-made'. It reflected more the disillusionment of the West in its own unfounded expectations of the easy transition, although the natives shared the pessimism of this scenario without too strongly advocating its qualification, i.e. *quid pro quo* of Cen-tral Europe for Eastern Europe. The westerners seemingly were disappointed because of the slow pace of change and the newly emerging contradictions. Above all, it served them as a good excuse to turn away from the region to more burning issues in other parts of the world. This scenario has been very popular with the USA, thinking mostly, if not exclusively, of the superpower relations, and less interested in the small Central European nations with their idiosyncrasies than in issues of global crisis management. Consequently, they have a fetish about stability in the 'marginal' zones and have put for-ward, by withdrawing their previous commitments for assistance, an approach of damage limitation or a stand of benign neglect.

The greater part of the new western pessimism might have been connected with the decline and dissolution of the Soviet Union. As Motyl (1991) indicates: 'Of all reasons for pessimism, the condition of the Soviet Union is perhaps the most worrisome. . . . Economic collapse, social chaos, political ungovernability, and nationalist strife may all portend an event of great historical significance – the disintegration of a superpower.' The Soviet Dis-Union can have a destabilizing effect for the whole world, but first of all for its direct neighbours: 'a nervous nuclear-armed Russia might be more dangerous than a self-confident nuclear-armed Soviet Union, and the emergence of unstable post-Soviet states could upset Central Europe's delicate transition to democracy' (Motyl, 1991: 499).[7]

The essence of the damage limitation strategy for the West was the isolation of the Soviet Union either by putting it together with the unstable Central and Eastern European states into some 'quarantine' or by creating buffer zones to protect the West from any spillover effects across the borders. A good illustration of the first two scenarios is the famous speech of Z. Brzezinski ('Destinations: Strasbourg or Sarajevo?') which puts together the first polarized and overgeneralized scenario with the second one as alternatives. It reveals more about western simplifications than about the real contradictory nature of the Central European region. As Brzezinski sees it, the developments of the East may lead 'towards larger cooperation, broader integration, the emergence of more interdependent collaborative societies based on institutionalized democracy and workable free market system' or 'developments in the East will increasingly involve fragmentation, destabilization, social and economic tensions, political, perhaps ethnic and national collisions' (Brzezinski, 1991: 6).

Mead, in turn, criticizing the overoptimistic scenario in the West, has described its backlash in the terms of our second scenario but also points towards our third scenario: 'The roses are fading from this scenario, though Washington has still not come to grips with the real story in Eastern Europe. Despite some promising developments scattered here and there, the situation in the eight formerly communist countries . . . continues to worsen. This suggests that we should be thinking of much of the region as a European extension of the Third World' (Mead, 1991: 396). Yet, it is Yugoslavia which offers the best illustration of the second scenario, as well as of the external typology of transition patterns. It is true that Yugoslavia presents not only an excellent display of the 'return of the past' with 'demons' but also connects the second scenario with the third one. First, it is not just the revival of the 'old' nationalisms but the emergence of quite new contradictions as well. Second, by falling apart, Yugoslavia proves the existence of two different regions in the 'old', postwar Eastern Europe, namely Central Europe and Eastern Europe, rising and separating from each other: 'the forces pulling Yugoslavia apart are but local manifestations of traditional divisions that mark the entire region' (Comisso, 1991: 4). Yugoslavia has been a summary of the contradictions of the old 'eastern' Europe and it can be a real test case for the West in crisis management.

---

7. A good presentation of the essence of the second scenario is given by Gregory Treverton: 'The ethnic conflicts and the possibility of the erratic politics in Eastern Europe are reminiscent of the interwar period. So, too, is the prospect that the preeminent actor in the region will be Germany' (Treverton, 1991: 111).

Latin Americanization (the Extended South)

The third scenario is the real(istic) worst-case scenario, not the second one. The third scenario of Latin Americanization came into being in 1990 as a combination of the feeling 'abandoned by the West' with the shock of the domestic economic crisis in the context of the whole world system. Latin America is, of course, a huge continent. Latin Americanization as a tendency has been introduced into political science by the authors of *Transitions from Authoritarian Rule*, based on some big countries of South America (Brazil, Argentina, etc.) as the pattern of the recurring crisis: moving not only from authoritarian rule to democracy but also, after a time, from democracy back to authoritarian rule. The tendency towards Latin Americanization for the whole of Eastern Europe, however, appeared long before 1989 as a result of erroneous Soviet-type modernization. This threat was mentioned both in the western press (it is sufficient to mention again *The Economist*: NICs versus NUCs, i.e. the New Industrialized Countries versus the New Underdeveloped Countries) and in the public opinion of the countries concerned. This idea returned with a vengeance only in the 1990s as a new scenario and gained currency in the wide circles of population and opinion-makers when the situation began to deteriorate tragically.

Historically, it is true that Central Europe (with parts of Southern Europe) since the 16th century has always been the semi-periphery of the West European core, in this respect showing some parallel with the Latin American countries as well. The semi-peripheral status provides the possibility for joining the core as well as that of falling back to the real periphery. The genuine danger for Central Europe of becoming 'southernized' came in the 1980s with the growing foreign debt, increasing poverty and unemployment, and, as a result, with the marginalization among the (European) nations in per capita terms. After the decades of the 'cannibalistic' modernization (the eating up of resources by the old-fashioned heavy industries from the real development, i.e. human investments, etc.) some characteristic features of underdevelopment appeared in the postwar developments and these negative features began to dominate in the 1980s (again, more in Eastern Europe than in Central Europe, but even Central Europe could not escape).

In the actual socio-economic processes, Soviet type modernization meant a craze to create the late 19th-century model of heavy industry, all the resources of the nations being sacrificed for its development. Its results are now much worse than those of a lost war, since these pseudo-investments have mostly devoured the material and intellectual resources required for a possible take-off of the real development. Even in Hungary, with its modest progress in recent decades, the 'moment of truth' came in the late 1980s with decreasing real incomes and with erosion of the previously relatively strong middle strata. For Poland this Soviet-type modernization was even more disastrous, making Poland into the show-case of Latin Americanization, or the best illustration of our third scenario. The real danger of Latin Americanization has arisen in the most acute way in this growing poverty of the lower middle classes, i.e. the whole society splits into two parts, as 'two nations in one', namely into a Europeanized–modernized society and a provincialized–traditionalized one, according to the classical Latin American dual model.

In politics, Latin Americanization means that mass dissatisfaction due to economic hardship will prevail over democratization tendencies and some right-wing populist movements will pave the way back to authoritaritan rule. This populist upheaval can generate support for a strong president, a Latin American-type 'caudillo' (and his junta) against weak parliamentary regimes. The end of the story is well known, the stark choice is either Pinochet or Peron. Both versions, however, are only short-term 'solutions', in fact, they will lead to a deeper crisis. The earlier the West realizes this, the better. This sober reminder has been formulated by Milenkovitch with justification: 'The European Community and the United States must assess the interest they have in the success of this transformation (i.e. in the democratization of Central Europe – A.Á.). It is difficult to imagine that anyone's interests would be better served by a marginalization of these countries into the Pinochet–Peron dilemma' (Milenkovitch, 1991: 164). [8]

Fair Weather (the Promising North)

The fourth scenario is, again, optimistic, but this time only very cautiously. It accepts the 'in-between' situation in Central Europe by turning it into an advantage, namely into a historical explanation of European integration. Central Europe is different from the West, indeed, but so were the Nordic countries before they began their long march toward the core, finally succeeding in catching up with the most developed countries. The Nordic countries have overcome not only their relative backwardness but have invented a new social model in their welfare democracies which may be favourably compared with that of the West. The story has been repeated, *mutatis mutandis*, by Southern Europe, although in a different way. In fact, they have been involved in the European integration process as a 'promotion of democracy' by the members of the European Community. The Nordic way has always given theoretical aspirations to the Central European politicians and political scientists with its Social Democracy, basic community approach and active small states' policy. Nowadays, however, the South

---

8. The danger of Latin Americanization has been described by Adam Przeworski in much more detail (see Przeworski, 1991). I have elaborated these four scenarios also in international security matters (Ágh, 1992b).

European developments are more encouraging, the Mediterranean way of catching up from the recent past has provided even more aspirations for the Central European countries, first of all the so-called Spanish model of negotiated transition. The democratization programmes in Central Europe now revolve around the idea of this historical sequence: after such a long period of Bad Weather, i.e. unfavourable external circumstances, in our days, at last, there is Fair Weather, i.e. the international factors seem to be encouraging democratization and marketization.

Conclusion

All four scenarios contain moments of truth and reality, they are true and valid to greater or lesser extents. As I have tried to indicate, however, the first two scenarios have only analytical value, since there is no real possibility of a Great Leap or 'return to the past'. The second two are, indeed, open historical opportunities and no theoretical exercise could decide between them. The most decisive factor would be the international one, more precisely the readiness of the EC for a 'promotion of democracy' programme in Central Europe, as well. The Western countries may have a self-fulfilling prophecy by their benign neglect: what they consider to be 'South', will be 'South', no doubt, since the world economy is to some extent a 'hostile environment' and without major assistance it is almost impossible to manage the present socio-economic crisis.

On the other hand, the Fair Weather scenario presupposes, on the basis of western 'help for self-help' strategy, a very active structural accommodation and adjustment programme to the world economy and an intensive learning process, lacking almost completely in the three previous scenarios, by the political elites and populations alike. When most of our thinking and theories focus upon this fourth scenario in Central European countries, we have to be aware of the necessity of the fundamental domestic transformation instead of only passively waiting for western assistance. In order to avoid the abyss of Latin Americanization we have to couple macro-level democratization with micro-level political participation in a way that is parallel with the integration of our country to the EC. We have to integrate the citizens of our countries into their own societies substantially, i.e. to construct a substantial democracy instead of a formal one in the shape of electoralism according to which so-called free elections are the only criteria of democracy. We believe in Hungary that our country may be the best case for illustrating this fourth scenario, i.e. it offers the fourth model for our external typology. It is not a question of being 'ahead' of others, but of having gone through the long, smooth and negotiated transition, which has led to a 'parliamentary' democracy with distribution of powers, and not their concentration, as in the 'semi-presidential' systems of Poland and Czecho-Slovakia (see Ágh, 1992a).

REFERENCES

Ágh, Attila: (1991a) 'The Transition to Democracy in Central Europe: A Comparative View, *Journal of Public Policy* 11(2): 135-51.

Ágh, Attila (1991b) 'The Parliamentary Way to Democracy: The Case of Hungary', *Budapest Papers on Democratic Transition* (Hungarian Centre for Democracy Studies), vol. 1(2): 1-45.

Ágh, Attila (1992a) 'Reform Patterns in Central and Eastern Europe', *Budapest Papers on Democratic Transition* 2(1): 1-36.

Ágh, Attila (1992b) 'New Forms of Security and Cooperation in Central Europe', in C. Gasteyger (ed.) *Candidates for Integration. The Neutral and Central European Countries Facing the European Community.* Occasional Papers, Graduate Institute of International Studies, Geneva, 2: 60-81.

Arendt, Hannah (1973, first edition 1951) *The Origins of Totalitarianism.* San Diego and New York: Harcourt Brace Jovanovich.

Ash, Timothy Garton (1990) *We The People, The Revolution of 89.* Cambridge: Granta Books.

Batt, Judy (1991) *East Central Europa from Reform to Transformation.* London: Pinter.

Bonime-Blanc, Andrea (1987) *Spain's Transition to Democracy.* Boulder, CO: Westview Press.

Brzezinski, Zbigniew (1991) 'Destinations: Strasbourg or Sarajevo?' *Atlantish perspektief*, The Hague, No. 1.

Comisso, Ellen (1991) 'Political Coalitions, Economic Choices', *Journal of International Affairs*, Summer, vol. 45(1): 1-29.

Dahrendorf, Ralf (1990) *Reflections on the Revolution in Europe.* London: Chatto and Windus.

Dawisha, Karen (1990) *Eastern Europe, Gorbachev and Reform. The Great Challenge.* 2nd edn. Cambridge: Cambridge University Press.

Di Palma, Giuseppe (1990) *To Craft Democracies: An Essay on Democratic Transitions.* Berkeley, Los Angeles, Oxford: University of California Press.

Glenny, Misha (1990) *The Rebirth of History, Eastern Europe in the Age of Democracy.* London: Penguin.

Hankiss, Elemér (1990) *East European Alternatives.* Oxford: Clarendon Press.

Kirkpatrick, Jeanne (1979) 'Dictatorships and Double Standards', *Commentary.*

Kundera, Milan (1984) 'The Tragedy of Central Europe', *New York Review of Books*, 26 April.

Liebert, Ulrike and Maurizio Cotta, eds (1990) *Parliament and Democratic Consolidation in Southern Europe.* London: Pinter.

Linz, Juan J. (1978) *Crisis, Breakdown and Reequilibration* (in the series *The Breakdown of Democratic Regimes*). Baltimore, MD and London: Johns Hopkins University Press.

Mead, Walter R. (1991) 'Saul Among the Prophets: The Bush Administration and the New World Order', *World Policy Journal*, Summer, VIII(3): 375-420.

Milenkovitch, Deborah (1991) 'The Politics of Economic Transformation', *Journal of International Affairs*, Summer, 45(1): 161-4.

Motyl, Alexander J. (1991) 'Empire or Stability: The Case for Soviet Dissolution', *World Policy Journal*, Summer, VIII(3): 499-524.

O'Donnell, Guillermo et al., eds (1986) *Transitions from Authoritarian Rule.* Baltimore, MD and London: Johns Hopkins University Press.

Offe, Claus (1991) 'Das Dilemma der Gleichzeitigkeit, Demokratisierung und Marktwirtschaft in Osteuropa', *Merkur* (Klett-Cotta, Stuttgart) 505: 279–92.

Pérez-Diaz, Victor (1987) 'Economic Policies and Social Pacts in Spain During the Transition', in Ilja Scholten (ed.) *Political Stability and Neo-Corporatism*. London: Sage.

Pérez-Diaz, Victor (1990) *The Emergence of Democratic Spain and the 'Invention' of Democratic Tradition*. Working papers, Centro de Estudios Avanzados en Ciencies Sociales, Madrid, June, No. 1.

Powell, G. Bingham (1982) *Contemporary Democracies*. Cambridge, MA and London: Harvard University Press.

Pridham, Geoffrey, ed. (1990) *Securing Democracy: Political Parties and Democratic Consolidation in Southern Europe*. London and New York: Routledge.

Pridham, Geoffrey, ed. (1991) *Encouraging Democracy: The International Context of Regime Transition in Southern Europe*. London: Leicester University Press.

Prins, Gwyn, ed. (1990) *Spring in Winter. The 1989 Revolutions*. Manchester and New York: Manchester University Press.

Przeworski, Adam (1991) 'The "East" becomes the "South"? The "Autumn of People" and the Future of the Eastern Europe', *Political Science and Politics* XXIV(1): 20–4.

Ruprik, Jacques (1989) *The Other Europe*. London: Weidenfeld and Nicolson.

Rusi, Alpo M. (1991) *After the Cold War. Europe's New Political Architecture*. New York: Macmillan.

Treverton, Gregory (1991) 'A New European Security Order', *Journal of International Affairs* vol. 45(1): 91–112.

ATTILA ÁGH has held visiting professorships in Tanzania (Dar es Salaam 1978–80), India (Nehru University, 1983, 1985) and Austria (Institute of European Studies, 1988). In the 1980s he was Director of the Hungarian Institute for International Relations. Currently, Professor Ágh is Head of the Department of Political Science at the Budapest University of Economics and Director of the Hungarian Centre for Democracy Studies. ADDRESS: H-1093. Fövám tér 8. Budapest, Hungary.

Paper submitted 17 February 1992; accepted for publication 10 May 1992.

[22]

Political Studies (1993), XLI, 594–610

Civil-Military Relations in Comparative Perspective: East-Central and Southeastern Europe

Zoltan D. Barany

University of Texas at Austin

Any discussion of Eastern Europe should begin with the customary admonitions about the distinctiveness of each of the region's states.[1] Even during the four and a half decades of Soviet-imposed Communism – when similar economic and socio-political policies were forced on the region – differences among these countries remained very real and perceptible. Eastern Europe seemed most homogeneous until the death of Stalin, as petty dictators from Poland to Bulgaria obediently observed Moscow's desires. Not unexpectedly, as the extent of repression had waned, the political and economic development of these states reflected more and more disparities. The title of a volume examining the recent political history of Eastern Europe, *Return to Diversity*, is a precise summation of this phenomenon.[2] The profound differences in the nature of the 'revolutions' that marked the collapse of Communism and the variations in the subsequent transition processes serve as further proof of Eastern Europe's endless disparities.

Differences between the region's states are evident in every area of social, economic and political life. In the Communist era, these disparities were apparent even in civil-military relations, an area that was subjected to particularly strict control and unifying attempts by the Soviet Union, the Warsaw Pact and the individual states themselves. This paper examines civil-military relations in five of the six former non-Soviet Warsaw Pact (NSWP) countries: Bulgaria, Czechoslovakia, Hungary, Poland and Romania.[3] I aim to show that though during the Communist period there were important similarities in their party-army relations, significant deviations also existed. These differences have become all the more pronounced during and since the revolutions. My fundamental hypothesis is that while we should take the inherent uniqueness of

---

[1] This paper partially draws on earlier research published as 'Civil-military relations in communist systems: western models revisited', *Journal of Political and Military Sociology*, 19 (1991), 75–99; and 'East European armies in the transitions and beyond', *East European Quarterly*, 26, (1992), 1–30.

[2] Joseph Rothschild, *Return to Diversity: a Political History of East Central Europe since World War II* (New York, Oxford University Press, 1989).

[3] In this study East Germany is not discussed because German reunification made its post-1990 development far too different from that of the other former Warsaw Pact states.

these states as a given, there is sufficient empirical evidence to justify differentiation between East-Central Europe (Czechoslovakia, Hungary, and Poland) on the one hand, and Southeastern Europe (Bulgaria, Romania) on the other.[4]

This study, then, sets out to accomplish three objectives: to discuss the general characteristics of Communist civil-military relations and the most important disparities thereof between the region's states; to analyse the militaries' role in the revolutions of their states; and to examine developments of civil-military relations since then.

Civil-Military Relations in Communist Systems

The fundamental role of the armed forces in democratic societies is to defend the state from its external foes, while in Communist systems its crucial functions are external *and* internal. The external defensive and offensive roles of the Communist army are analogous to those of its democratic counterparts. Its domestic purpose, however, is to defend the Communist regime from its opponents within the system. Mao Zedong's axiom that 'power grows out of the barrel of a gun' illustrates well the crux of civil-military relations in Communist states.

During the decades of East European Communism civil-military relations were similar in many respects to those of the Soviet Union. After all, it was Moscow that imposed Communism on and demanded not only unconditional loyalty but also servile emulation of its 'proven' practices from the region. In fact, the pivotal difference between civil-military relations in the USSR and in Eastern Europe is that while the Soviet military was controlled by the independent *Soviet* Communist party, the East European parties were themselves controlled by Moscow. Consequently, the region's armies were governed by the given party but in the final analysis their supreme masters were foreign: the Soviet-dominated Warsaw Pact and, ultimately, the Kremlin. The satellite status of East European states detracted from the party's legitimacy and impaired its relations with the military as well as with the general population. Only one aspect of this inferior position was the occupation of most of these countries by the Soviet army.[5]

The peculiar attributes of the Soviet-type armed forces evolved largely as a result of their complex relationship with the Marxist-Leninist party. Ruling Communist parties maintain close ties with their armed forces out of necessity: they *need* the military to guarantee the very survival of the regime. In many cases

---

[4] A similar distinction was made by students of Communist military politics. The Northern Tier of the Warsaw Pact was taken to denote Czechoslovakia, East Germany and Poland; while the Southern Tier to include Bulgaria, Hungary and Romania. See A. Ross Johnson, Robert W. Dean, and Alexander Alexiev, *East European Military Establishments: The Warsaw Pact Northern Tier* (New York, Crane Russak, 1982); and Ivan Volgyes, *The Political Reliability of the Warsaw Pact Armies: The Southern Tier* (Durham, NC, Duke University Press, 1982). For a good primer on regional variances, see Volgyes 'Regional differences within the Warsaw Pact', *Orbis* (1982), 655–79. These efforts considered the region's states from doctrinal and geostrategic viewpoints. Thus Hungary was treated as a Southern Tier state. With the Warsaw Pact's demise it no longer seems necessary to maintain this division, therefore, Hungary is examined here as the East-Central European state it is.

[5] The Soviet Union militarily occupied Czechoslovakia (1968–91), Hungary (1945–91), Romania (1945–58). East Germany and Poland had played reluctant hosts to Soviet forces – whose withdrawal will be completed in 1994 and 1992, respectively – since 1945. The USSR did not deploy troops in Bulgaria.

(Albania, China, Cuba, Yugoslavia) the revolutionary army at first *was* the party.[6] The military in the party-state may be considered as a senior partner of the regime, although this is not an equal relationship. Rather, it is in many respects a tightly controlled interdependent alliance in which the party holds the trump cards. The party needs unfailingly loyal armed forces that can reliably discharge their important missions, the foremost of which is the defence of the Communist regime from its external *and* internal foes. The armed forces are the guardians of the hegemonial party's revolutionary-ideological heritage and play the traditional role as the defender of the homeland. In addition, the military acts as an agent of political socialization, offers assistance during natural disasters and in times of economic hardship. In turn, the army needs the party for the preservation and improvement of its material status and social prestige.

There are similarities and differences between the East European Communist parties' management of their militaries. To be sure, the overall structure of the party's political domination was quite similar across the region, after all, these states adopted the same Soviet *modus operandi*. This pattern included party organizations within the armed forces supervised by a separate department of the Central Committee, the Main Political Administration (MPA) with its own army of political officers, heavy doses of Marxist-Leninist indoctrination in all levels of the military-education system, etc. Through these and other mechanisms the parties intended to assure their political control over the armed forces. Apart from crises, the party-army relations appeared to be devoid of major tensions. The Commanders-in-Chief of the armed forces – insofar as this position was legally regulated at all – was none other than the leader of the Communist party.[7]

One of the primary constraints on the MPA's political-ideological work was the increasing professionalization of the military establishments, a phenomenon that was concomitant with the diminution of the political 'attentiveness' of career officers. As the technical and theoretical requirements of modern warfare increased, military education and training placed a premium on expertise while ideological rigour became somewhat de-emphasized.[8] Officers began to exhibit 'apolitical attitudes,' political work in the military had become superficial and routine: a plethora of articles and studies in all NSWP states decried these troubling phenomena at one time or another. The political elites of the NSWP armies attempted to counter this trend with periodic reorganizations and ideological campaigns (as in Poland 1957, 1970; and in Czechoslovakia in the post-1968 period, etc.) which nonetheless failed to yield to desired results.[9] In the southern tier of the WTO, however, this phenomenon was not so apparent as the Bulgarian and Romanian armed forces had not undergone the same level of professionalization as their northern neighbours.

While professional credentials and reputation had gradually become more important conditions for promotion in Eastern Europe's militaries, they never

---

[6] Daniel N. Nelson, *Romanian Politics in the Ceausescu Era* (New York, Gordon Breach, 1989), p. 132.

[7] See for instance, Michael Sadykiewicz and Louisa Vinton, 'Politicization in the Polish military', *Report on Eastern Europe*, March 30 (1990), p. 30.

[8] One of the best accounts of this development is Dale R. Herspring's *East German Civil-Military Relations* (New York, Praeger, 1973).

[9] For some studies that reach this conclusion, see Johnson *et al.*, *East European Military Establishments*; Volgyes, *The Political Reliability*; and J. Hacker, *Die Nationale Volksarmee der DDR im Rahmen des Warschauer Paktes* (München, Bernard and Grafe, 1980).

replaced political reliability as the *ultima ratio* of success. By the mid-1970s and certainly in the 1980s, political-ideological control over the military had become more subtle in Poland and Hungary and professional criteria were given more currency. In Czechoslovakia and in the two Balkan states, however, political control over the military (and society at large) remained quite rigid. The increasingly paranoid rule of President Nicolae Ceausescu portrayed any measure of domestic relaxation as a potentially fatal blow on Romanian Communism.

In times of political crises, however, the party's control appeared to dwindle. This phenomenon was clearly noticeable in Poland, where the post-1956 liberalization trend was reflected in the reduction of the Polish People's Army's (PPA) party apparatus and the previously high profile of political officers.[10] In the Czechoslovakia of the mid-1960s, one of the foci of the reform movement within the Czechoslovak People's Army (CSPA) was the issue of the Czechoslovak Communist Party's (CSCP) domination of the armed forces. Although MPAs had traditionally represented the conservative elements in NSWP militaries, an important exception was the CSPA's MPA which became the institutional locus of the movement to limit party control of the military before the invasion.[11]

Let us now turn our attention to the question of the extent of the party's co-optation of military personnel into political life. Did the military participate in politics or did it play the role of the passive bystander, particularly in crisis situations: in other words, how reliable were Eastern European armies in the domestic context? How did these crises affect the armed forces? In trying to answer these queries one quickly realizes that, again, no clear-cut pattern emerges.

In all NSWP states the representation of military personnel in the highest policy-making bodies was less extensive than in the USSR. Military presence on the Central Committee of the Soviet Communist Party, for instance, has averaged from 7% to 9% since 1972, while in Eastern Europe the corresponding figure is only about 3%.[12] Since the 1960s, all NSWP defence ministers were members of their Politburo – or in Romania's case, the Political Executive Committee – with the exception of Hungary. The Poland of the 1980s, where the imposition of martial law was accompanied by the creation of the Military Council of National Salvation (composed of 20 high-ranking officers), is of course, a special case. After the election of General Jaruzelski as the leader of the Polish United Workers' Party (PUWP) in October 1981, several military cadres were appointed to top political offices.

Without exception, the overwhelming majority of professional military personnel in the NSWP had been members of the Communist party. Party membership of professional cadres was the highest in the (East German) National People's Army (NPA) (99%),[13] up to 90% in the Romanian People's Army (RPA),[14] 82% in the Hungarian People's Army (HPA).[15] 80–83% in the

[10] See, for instance, Johnson *et al.*, *East European Military Establishments*, p. 24.
[11] Johnson *et al.*, *East European Military Establishments*, p. 146.
[12] Ivan Volgyes, 'Military politics of the Warsaw Pact armies', in Morris Janowitz (ed.), *Civil-Military Relations: Regional Perspectives* (Beverly Hills, CA, Sage, 1981), p. 198.
[13] Henry Krisch, 'German Democratic Republic', in Daniel N. Nelson (ed.), *Soviet Allies: the Warsaw Pact and the Issue of Reliability* (Boulder, CO, Westview, 1984), p. 170.
[14] Jonathan Eyal, 'Romania: between appearances and realities', in J. Eyal (ed.), *The Warsaw Pact and the Balkans: Moscow's Southern Flank* (London, Macmillan, 1989), p. 101.
[15] *Vasarnapi Hirek* (Budapest), September 17, 1989.

Bulgarian People's Army (BPA),[16] 80% in the PPA,[17] 75% in the CSPA.[18] These numbers should not be taken to denote genuine allegiance to Communist ideals as the military's role in the 1989 revolutions and their aftermath demonstrated. Instead, they reflect the realization by Eastern European officers that party membership – while it did not by itself assure promotion – was a necessary condition of advancement in the ranks.

In spite of the foregoing, evidence clearly indicates that the East European militaries failed to throw their support behind the Communist regimes in politically tense situations. In Czechoslovakia (1953, 1968), Hungary (1956), Poland (1956, 1970, 1976) the armed forces did not actively support the Communist system against its internal foes. In December 1981, the PPA was a reluctant participant in the repression of the Solidarity movement.[19] Some lessons are worth drawing from the lacklustre performance of the NSWP forces in domestic crises.

Actual experience shows that the armies were reluctant and even unwilling to discharge their most important function, that is, the repression of internal challenges to the Communist regime. In fact, evidence suggests that when possible, the party was disinclined to assign the 'dirty job' to the military and entrusted the security police units with them: the political elites of the region appear to have had far more confidence in the loyalty of the security troops and 'people's' (that is, the party's) militias who were often better trained, equipped and paid.[20]

One important reason for the military's success to sustain a measure of independence from the party was that these armies were based on conscription and drafted soldiers could not be trusted to support the party and fight against their own people. Aside from its obvious doubts about the army's performance, the party was concerned with popular attitudes toward the military as well. The armed forces' legitimacy as a national institution would have been further eroded if it had been considered by the public as the able agent of domestic repression.[21]

Conventional wisdom held that the military in a Communist system would support the 'status quo' and would be reluctant to actively interfere in politics. Nevertheless, the reformist attitudes of important segments (in fact the *majority* of the officer corps)[22] of the CSPA before and during the Prague Spring, and that of the PPA in 1956 mitigates this assumption. Thus in contrast with the militaries'

---

[16] Volgyes, *The Political Reliability*, p. 33.

[17] Sadykiewicz and Vinton, 'Politicization in the Polish military', p. 30.

[18] This is a 1977 figure, cited by Christopher D. Jones, 'The Czechoslovak armed forces', in Jeffrey Simon (ed.), *NATO-Warsaw Pact Force Mobilization* (Washington, DC, National Defense University Press, 1988), p. 229.

[19] For an excellent analysis of the Polish military's role in 1980–81, see Andrzej Korbonski's 'The dilemmas of civil-military relations in contemporary Poland', *Armed Forces and Society*, 8 (1981), 134–58.

[20] Even the reliability of these 'elite' units could be questioned, however. For instance, the fact that between 1970 and 1980 dozens of East German border guards emigrated illegally to the West should rouse scepticism concerning the reliability of East Berlin's elite troops. See, Ivan Sylvain, 'German Democratic Republic', in Teresa Rakowska-Harmstone *et al.*, *Warsaw Pact: The Question of Cohesion* (Ottawa: Operational Research Analysis Establishment Department of National Defence, 1984), p. 129.

[21] This phenomenon is particularly observable in Poland where the army's popularity remained consistently high, even during the Solidarity crisis of 1980–81. See Jerzy W. Wiatr, *The Soldier and the Nation: the Role of the Military in Polish Politics, 1918–1985* (Boulder, CO, Westview, 1988), pp. 151–2.

[22] Johnson *et al.*, *East European Military Establishments*, p. 170.

ZOLTAN D. BARANY   599

putative conservatism, the region's armies had at times displayed clearly reformist attitudes.

Other cases of military interference in politics are also noteworthy because they provide further support for the argument that East European armies did not shy away from political involvement. It appears that the Communist party's traditional fear of Bonapartism had not been irrational. In fact, the armed forces were implicated in several coups and coup attempts in Bulgaria, Czechoslovakia, Poland and Romania. In the 1960s there were two cabals in Bulgaria, a country where military putschism has had a long-standing tradition.[23] A coup attempt by some conservative officers in early 1969 in Czechoslovakia who allegedly conspired to overthrow the then-moderate regime of Gustav Husak was also rumoured. Some experts suggest, that this was the second coup attempt in Czechoslovakia within a year, for in early 1968 conservative officers attempted to utilize the CSPA to support Novotny's regime but were prevented from doing so by MPA Chief General Prchlik and officers loyal to him.[24] Robin Remington and others have argued that the imposition of martial law in Poland was a textbook case of coup d'etat.[25] In 1987 up to seven RPA officers were arrested on suspicion of plotting against President Ceausescu's regime.[26] In 1990, Romanian sources revealed that Ceausescu's ouster had actually been modeled on a plot to remove him from power in 1984.[27]

It is noteworthy that while all of the East-Central European states openly rebelled against Communist rule, this was not the case in the Balkans. The reason for this phenomenon may be found in a combination of (a) the unusually high level of repression and control over the population in Southeastern Europe; (b) the extremely strong security apparatus, especially in Romania; (c) the relative material well-being of the armed forces in Bulgaria; (d) lack of popular confidence in the potential success of a revolt, etc.

The Armies in the Revolutions

An examination of the East European armies' role in the revolutions of 1989 further supports our thesis that the military acted differently in the five states under consideration and a clear distinction can be made between the East-Central and the Southeastern European armies' positions. Thus, the spectrum of military activities extends from essential non-involvement (Hungary, Poland) to very limited action (Czechoslovakia), to a determinant role (Bulgaria and especially Romania).

The armed forces played the least active role in the revolutionary changes of the two countries where the liberalization process had begun long before 1989: Hungary and Poland. In the other NSWP states there were indications that the

---

[23] For excellent discussions of the Bulgarian coup attempts, see J. F. Brown, *Bulgaria under Communist Rule* (New York, Praeger, 1970), pp. 173–81; Volgyes, *The Political Reliability*, p. 33; Peter Gosztony, *Zur Geschichte der Europaeischen Volksarmeen* (Bonn-Bad Godesberg, Hochwacht, 1976), pp. 227–8; and J. L. Kerr, 'Dissidence in Bulgaria', RAD Background Report 156, *RFE Research*, July 10 (1978), 1–2.

[24] See for instance, Jiri Valenta and Condoleezza Rice, 'The Czechoslovak Army', in Jonathan R. Adelman (ed.), *Communist Armies in Politics* (Boulder, CO, Westview, 1982), pp. 140–1.

[25] See her excellent introduction to Wiatr, *The Soldier and the Nation*, pp. xiii–xiv.

[26] *The Daily Telegraph* (London), December 15, 1987. It is worth mentioning that this was the third time in 15 years that reports of an attempted coup or plots to stage one surfaced. There is little hard evidence to substantiate these stories, however.

[27] See Michael Shafir, 'New revelations of the military's role in Ceausescu's ouster,' *Report on Eastern Europe*, May 11 (1990), 24–7.

600   *Civil-Military Relations*

army might actively participate in the events. Curiously, as the regimes of the region fell one by one (Bulgaria, Czechoslovakia, Romania), the military's profile in the events correspondingly increased.

East-Central Europe

There is no evidence to suggest the Polish army's active opposition to the transition from post-Communism to democracy. Throughout the transition period that started in Poland during the summer of 1988, nothing indicated that the PPA would be involved in the political struggle that culminated in the PUWP's partial surrender of power to the Solidarity-led government in August 1989. With so many military men installed at the apex of political power in the post-1981 period the armed forces represented an area over which the regime wanted to maintain its control as long as feasible. Indeed, Communist Defence Minister Florian Siwicki remained the minister in charge of Tadeusz Mazowiecki's government, but the PPA's transition could not be thwarted for long. The PPA had assumed a detached role in Poland's political transition, witnessed by the fact that it remained a well-liked social institution, in popularity second only to the Catholic Church.[28] Although the majority of Polish officers were members of the Communist party, this fact, explained Siwicki, did not hurt Poland 'since the army always represented the interests of the entire nation'.[29] Some elements of military reform were already evident under Siwicki's tenure in the Mazowiecki government, such as the 'reexamination' of the MPA's functions in the PPA.

Neither did the HPA play an appreciable role in the political transitions of Hungary. Simultaneously with the party at large, the HPA's own Communist party organizations began to lose members in ever greater numbers starting in 1987. After mid-1989, HPA personnel began to take advantage of a law permitting them to join parties other than the Hungarian Socialist Workers' Party (HSWP). The military press published scores of articles discussing the politico-ideological decay in the armed forces, although authors frequently attempted to find remedy for the shortcomings in 'enhanced party (i.e. HSWP) discipline' and, especially, 'renewal'.[30]

The crucial question dividing the professional strata of the armed forces was the issue of party organizations within the military. Most of the army's leadership supported the HSWP's continued involvement in the HPA, while the majority of younger career soldiers wanted all political institutions out of it.[31] Even though top army leaders were generally reluctant to embrace the political transformation, throughout the process they continued to reassure the population that the HPA would remain calm and had absolutely no intention of political involvement.[32] Although few Hungarians believed such a possibility existed, the army certainly earned points by explicitly taking such an unambiguous stance.

[28] Some 80% of Poles sympathized with the armed forces in 1989. See *Sovetskaya kultura* (Moscow), May 25, 1989.

[29] *Zolnierz Wolnosci* (Warsaw), September 26, 1989, translated in *Foreign Broadcast Information Service-Eastern Europe* (hereafter *FBIS-EEU*), September 29, 1989, p. 50.

[30] See, for instance, Gyorgy Sandor, 'Mit jelenthet az ifjusagi mozgalom megujulasa?' *Hondvedsegi Szemle* (Budapest), 43 (1989), 1–13; and Sandor Faar, 'Az alapszervi munka megujitasarol', pp. 17–24 of the same issue.

[31] See for instance the disagreement between Generals Borsits and Krasznai on the one hand, and General Sebok on the other in *Otlet* (Budapest), September 9, 1989.

[32] See, for instance, *Magyar Hirlap* (Budapest), May 20, 1989.

Though the CSPA was not utilized in Czechoslovakia's domestic crisis, the CSCP resorted to the use of security troops against demonstrators on November 17, 1989 in Prague's Wenceslas Square. A few days later the CSCP General Secretary – and the Commander-in-Chief of the CSPA – ordered the People's Militia to march on the capital. In the end, the CSCP's 'private army' was not used against the protesters, probably because of the political leadership's opposition to the use of further force.[33] Some reports alleged that the militia itself refused to take action.[34] Defence Minister Milan Vaclavik publicly denied the army's involvement in the violent police repression of the demonstrators, and criticized attacks on the security forces for their efforts to observe 'the basic norms of the socialist state and to preserve order'. Although Vaclavik castigated demonstrators, he rejected rumours that paratroopers of the CSPA were deployed.[35] In mid-December 1989, the new Defence Minister, Miroslav Vacek, announced that the CSPA supported the democratization process, denounced reports of a potential coup by the army and stated that the military would not be used against the people.[36] Later that month, the CSCP's extraordinary congress disbanded the People's Militia.

Southeastern Europe

For outside observers, it appeared that the BPA had an almost symbiotic relationship with the Bulgarian Communist Party (BCP). The events of 1989 serve as convincing evidence that the BPA officers' loyalties were not to the party, let alone to its long-time leader Todor Zhivkov, but to the army as an institution and to its access to resources.[37] As a result of reductions in Bulgaria's military spending, professional soldiers had seen their relatively high living standards dwindle.[38] Consequently, their support for Zhivkov's removal had increased. Defence Minister Dobri Dzhurov was an important participant in the cabal – by virtue of his assurance to the BCP leader's foes that the BPA would neither support Zhivkov nor take action on its own – that unseated the party's leader in November 1989.[39] Dzhurov, a popular military leader who was also a powerful member of the BCP's Politburo, almost certainly enjoyed the tacit support of the Bulgarian armed forces.[40] Clearly, the high military leadership used its influence to induce the desired political outcome, and thereby fostered change rather than sustaining the status quo.

Following the November 1989 session of the BCP's Central Committee (at which Zhivkov was dethroned), the BPA began the process of democratization, a

[33] Jan Obrman, 'Changing conditions for the army and the police', *Report on Eastern Europe*, January 26, 1990, p. 14.

[34] See, for instance, Radio Vienna, 11:00 am, November 23, 1989, translated in *FBIS-EEU*, November 24, 1989, p. 17.

[35] Radio Prague (in English), November 23, 1989, 6:45 pm.

[36] Zoltan D. Barany, 'Non-Soviet Warsaw Pact forces in domestic context,' Internal report, *Radio Free Europe Research*, December 21, 1989, p. 1.

[37] See Daniel N. Nelson's 'WTO mobilization potential: a Bulgarian case study', *Defense Analysis*, 5, (1989), 31–44; and his 'The Bulgarian People's Army', in Jeffrey Simon (ed.), *NATO-Warsaw Pact Force Mobilization* (Washington, National Defense University Press, 1988), pp. 449–78.

[38] See, for instance, *Narodna Armiya* (Sofia), June 28, 1989, translated in *FBIS-EEU-89-125*, June 30, 1989, p. 15.

[39] Daniel N. Nelson, 'Political dynamics and the Bulgarian military', paper presented at the Force Mobilization Conference held at National Defense University, June 19–21, 1990, pp. 33–4.

[40] Duncan M. Perry, 'A new military lobby', *Report on Eastern Europe*, October 5, 1990, pp. 1–4.

term that was seemingly interpreted by BPA leaders quite liberally. While military leaders were 'delighted by the democratization process and glasnost', they were also careful to point out that 'the restructuring of Bulgaria is possible solely and exclusively within the framework of socialism'.[41] Furthermore, after the BCP had changed its name to Bulgarian Socialist Party (BSP) in November 1989, the BPA assured the 'new' party of its 'wholehearted support'.[42]

Nowhere in the region was the role of the armed forces in the collapse of the *ancien régime* as prominent as in Romania. It appears that before December 21, 1989, the Romanian People's Army (RPA) did carry out the orders of the higher military leadership to fire on demonstrators in Timisoara, Cluj, and Bucharest, although security troops played the major role in the crackdown.[43] After this date, however, the military refused to carry out orders, and its noncompliance essentially decided the fate of Ceausescu's regime. On the top level, it was Defence Minister Vasile Milea who refused to reinforce troops in Bucharest to defend the political leadership. He reportedly commented that he had searched in vain in the military regulations for a paragraph requiring 'the people's army to fire on the people'.[44] Milea was executed by Ceausescu loyalists on December 22.[45] In Bucharest, the soldiers 'threw down their weapons' and openly took the side of the protesters rather than follow orders issued by Ceausescu's supporters.[46]

According to General Stefan Guse, all RPA units were on the 'people's side', and the army took over the offices of the Ministry of Interior as early as December 22.[47] At least some of the RPA's generals joined the revolution reluctantly, and only after some of Romania's current leaders (e.g., President Ion Iliescu) appeared on national television and expressed their support for the uprising. Others could not be counted on to endorse the emerging National Salvation Front (NSF). As Silviu Brucan, a prominent member of the NSF said, 'we had always been sure of the army, but not of all generals'.[48]

Although some details about the RPA's role in the revolution may never be satisfactorily clarified, it appears clear that not all RPA troops and officers supported the revolution and not all Securitate units fought on the side of the pro Ceausescu forces.[49] Nonetheless, the vast majority of the army leadership backed the NSF after December 22, and following the cessation of hostilities assured Romanians that the army would 'never stage a coup d'etat'.[50]

A crucial question that begs an answer is, then, did the East European militaries fail to prop up the regimes when asked to, or did the moral fibre of the

[41] *Narodna Armiya* (Sofia), November 14, 1989, translated in *FBIS-EEU*, November 20, 1989, pp. 13–14.
[42] *Narodna Armiya*, November 25, 1989 translated in *FBIS-EEU*, December 4, 1989, pp. 8–9.
[43] See, for instance, George W. Price, 'The Romanian armed forces: the impact of the revolution of December 1989,' paper delivered at the Force Mobilization Conference, National Defense University, June 19–21, 1989, pp. 13–4.
[44] *Adevarul* (Bucharest), January 15, 1990, quoted by Radio Bucharest, January 15, 1990, 17:40 GMT.
[45] *Adevarul* (Bucharest), January 15, 1990, quoted by Radio Bucharest, January 15, 1990, 17:40 GMT.
[46] *Kyodo* (Tokyo), December 22, 1989, translated in *FBIS-EEU*, December 22, 1989, p. 66.
[47] Radio Bucharest, December 22, 1989, 1530 GMT, translated in *FBIS-EEU* of the same date, p. 74.
[48] See the interview with Brucan in *Le Monde* (Paris), December 29, 1989.
[49] Michael Shafir, 'The revolution: an initial assessment', *Report on Eastern Europe*, January 26, 1990, p. 40.
[50] See *La Repubblica* (Rome), January 2, 1990, translated in *FBIS-EEU*, January 5, 1990, p. 64; and *Nepszabadsag* (Budapest), January 9, 1990.

TABLE 1. East European Armed forces in the 1989 Revolutions

Armed Interference		
Not considered	Considered	Occurred
←		→
Bulgaria	Czechoslovakia	Romania
Hungary	East Germany	
Poland		

Political Interference		
Absent		Prominent
←		→
Czechoslovakia	East Germany	Bulgaria
Hungary		
Poland		Romania

regimes disintegrate so rapidly that the request was never made? The response in the cases of Hungary and Poland is unambiguous. Both states had gone through a protracted and gradual liberalization process which culminated in the Communist regime's voluntary surrender of its political power. Thus, the armed forces were not asked to play any role supportive of the Communist regime. In the case of Czechoslovakia, the emerging picture is more confusing. It seems that both the party and army leaderships considered the utilization of the military to aid the *ancien régime* but events unfolded rapidly and the Husak-Jakes leadership was replaced quickly and the new Communist leader Urbanek realized that not even the army could help to turn the tide. In any event, one might reasonably wonder whether or not the CSPA would have actively assisted Communist power.

We are facing a very different scenario in the Balkans. The Romanian political leadership requested military help to repress the swiftly multiplying demonstrations. At first, the RPA did heed this call but soon turned its weapons against its masters (as represented by the loyal Securitate troops). At least some of the reasons for this change of heart may be sought in: the RPA leaders' realization that this was a major crisis that could result in the demise of Ceausescu's regime (that neglected and humiliated the military for decades); the soldiers' fraternization with the demonstrators and the general population; a chance for the RPA to regain the respect of Romanians by engaging the Securitate in combat. In Bulgaria, the circumstances were drastically different. Defence Minister Dzhurov – probably together with the BPA's leadership – decided not to support Zhivkov's leadership but to transfer its loyalties to the reformist faction of the BCP. It seems that Dzhurov and his colleagues in the BPA's top ranks did not expect a wholesale change in the Bulgaria's political system; rather, they elected to strengthen the power of another group of Communists leaders from whom they anticipated improvement of their situation.

Table 1 recapitulates these disparities in the NSWP militaries' role in the collapse of Communism.

East European Armed Forces in Transition

Since late 1989, the political and military landscape of Eastern Europe has changed dramatically: the two Germanies are reunited (signifying also the demise of the NPA), the Warsaw Pact is dissolved, and the Soviet Army has already withdrawn from Czechoslovakia and Hungary and will soon leave eastern Germany and Poland. In the past two years, the East European armies themselves have become quite different. Although there are many similarities in the democratization processes these militaries have undergone, there are also profound disparities between them which may define their stances in the future.

Determining the appropriate role of the armed forces in the political superstructures of the region turned out to be a difficult task. After all, in these states even the line of command over the military was left unspecified in the constitutions and legal documents. A good illustration of this problem was inadvertently provided by Hungarian Prime Minister, Miklos Nemeth, who, when asked in July 1989 who the Commander-in-Chief of the armed forces was, answered that 'it is not possible at present to give an unequivocal reply to this'.[51] In every East European state under consideration post-revolution political and military leaders affirmed their goal to create a politically neutral or apolitical military that would be loyal to the constitution and not to any political organization. Disagreements occurred, however, even after the constitutional amendments settled the army's place in the political system.

The process of the military's depoliticization denotes the obliteration of all party mechanisms in the armed forces. This procedure includes the withdrawal of party organizations from the armed forces, the termination of the MPA and the abolition of the political officer positions, the elimination of political indoctrination from the curricula of military colleges. In short, it means putting an end to the party's control of the armed forces, preventing other political organizations from doing so by legal means, and ensuring the armies' political neutrality and freedom from ideological influences. The institutionalized ties between the parties and the armies were quickly dismantled on the national level. By March 1990 party organizations in the military were abolished in all of the NSWP states except for Poland where this was accomplished later in the year.[52]

The depoliticization of the East European military establishments was not as smooth a process as it may have seemed to outside observers. Not unexpectedly, senior officers were frequently critical of the political and military democratization and delayed reform processes.[53] Demands for speedier change were voiced in all NSWP states, not only by opposition groups and junior military cadres, but also by the new governments themselves. The underlying problem that most of the new rulers have had to contend with is that officers with extensive links to the Communist regimes are still in dominant positions in the armed forces, since they cannot be dismissed until replacements with comparable expertise can be found. In a region where military leaders often enjoyed decades-long tenures, changes in personnel also indicated the shifting winds in civil-military relations. The process of personnel transition served also as a reliable gauge of the democratization processes in Eastern Europe.

---

[51] Radio Budapest, July 1, 1989, 04:30 GMT.

[52] See Ivan Scipiades, 'Vissza a starthoz,' *Vilag*, March 1, 1990; and Radio Warsaw, August 8, 1990, 09:05 GMT.

[53] See, for instance, Daniel N. Nelson, 'Watching the Pact unravel,' *Bundesberichte für ostwissenschaftliche Studien* (Cologne), May 1992, pp. 4–5, 14.

ZOLTAN D. BARANY   605

It appears that the military's depoliticization has gone farthest in the states of East-Central Europe where the transition to democratization has been the most comprehensive. In the Balkans, however, just as questions remain about the extent of political transition, doubts about the armies' reform, are also to be entertained. To illustrate this point, I will highlight some of the differences between the post-revolution East-Central and Southeastern European armed forces in the balance of this section.

East-Central Europe

Although some steps still remain to be taken in the transformation of the Czecho-Slovak, Hungarian, and Polish armed forces these militaries have undergone comprehensive reforms. Although this process has had its ups and downs, difficulties usually originated in the lack of political and legislative experience. The best example of this phenomenon is a controversy that took place in Hungary. In April 1991, General Kalman Lorincz, the country's senior soldier, accused Defence Minister Fur of attempting to weaken President Arpad Goncz's constitutional position as commander-in-chief.[54] Clearly, the entire dispute was at least in part the result of the Hungarian defence establishment's complex organizational scheme – with a separate Ministry of Defence for policy and administration, and a Command of the Hungarian Army to oversee actual military activities – and the whole affair demonstrated well the potential problems that could be produced by deficient or ambiguous regulations.

Nonetheless, the depoliticization of the armed forces did not encounter any major problems in these states. In fact, in Poland it was Communist Defence Minister Siwicki who presided over the abolition of the military's party affiliations in the military. The termination of the MPAs, one of the most important aspects of depoliticization, was achieved differently. In Poland, first the 'Main Political Board' was renamed the 'Main Educational Board'. Amidst charges from reformers that the name change meant little more than just that, Defence Ministry officials in Warsaw altered the designation once more – this time to 'Educational Department'.[55] This organization is supposed to teach military history to soldiers and instill them with patriotism. Elsewhere (in Hungary, for example), MPAs were also transformed into teaching training institutions but their second lease of life expired shortly after the newly elected governments took office.

Reformist circles within and outside the armed forces were impatient with the pace of liberalization. Czechoslovak soldiers, for instance, called for the acceleration of reforms and the clarification of the army's role in the revolution. Czechoslovakia's Civic Forum criticized the army on numerous occasions for lagging behind in democratization. A *communiqué* confirmed that no deep structural or personnel changes took place, and that the armed forces were isolated from society and lacked public supervision.[56] To counter these adverse developments the Prague government established a General Inspectorate, subordinate to the Federal Assembly (parliament) but independent of the Federal Ministry of National Defence, to oversee military matters.[57] The

[54] *Nepszabadsag* (Budapest), April 1, 1991.
[55] *Tygodnik Solidarnosc*, April 20, 1990, translated in *FBIS-EEU*, April 27, 1990, pp. 37–9.
[56] *Mlada Fronta* (Prague), July 9, 1990.
[57] Prague Television Service, June 26, 1990, translated in *FBIS-EEU*, June 29, 1990, p. 14.

Forum's analysis of the problems is equally pertinent to the problems encountered in the other states of the region, particularly in the Balkans.

The national elections that were held in 1990 constituted major tests of the political neutrality of the region's armed forces. The East-Central European militaries passed the test well. Indeed, some soldiers in Czechoslovakia, for instance, protested the fact that soldiers could not be elected to legislative bodies as in the past, fearing that the new system will thus have negative effects on their interest representation.[58] There was no military interference in the election processes in the East-Central European states.

The governments of Czechoslovakia and Hungary selected civilian ministers of defence with little military expertise, while in Poland a well-respected naval officer was appointed. The smoothest changes occurred in Hungary and Poland. In Budapest, civilian Lajos Fur succeeded General Ferenc Karpati (May 1990), while in Poland Admiral Piotr Kolodziejczyk replaced General Siwicki (August 1990).[59] In Prague, shortly after the revolution, Defence Minister Milan Vaclavik was replaced by General Miroslav Vacek in Prime Minister Ladislav Adamec's short-lived cabinet. A commission investigating the CSPA's (and Vacek's) role in the 'velvet Revolution' disclosed that Vacek played an ambiguous role in November 1989. He was replaced by a civilian, Lubos Dobrovsky, in October 1990.

All East European armed forces have faced the dilemma of 'red' or 'expert' officers with the expertise necessary to run modern armies are usually tainted by their excessive affiliations with the past. In East-Central Europe many officers either resigned or expressed their allegiance to the new regime. Individuals who were unable to commit themselves to the democratic political order were often dismissed. In Hungary, for instance, by February 1990 more than 50 generals and 400 colonels were retired.[60] Many officers left military service for economic and some, no doubt, for political, reasons. The question of what to do with those officers who were active in the Communist parties was addressed by the new governments. The new regimes quickly came to the realization that 'it was impossible to dismiss the entire army' (after all, the majority of the officers were at least *pro forma* members of the Communist parties) and professional competence should be the decisive factor.[61]

Southeastern Europe

The changes affecting the militaries of the two Balkan states have been far less comprehensive than those of their former NSWP counterparts. Political and structural reforms in the Bulgarian and Romanian armed forces seem far less convincing. Military leaders in the Balkans were actively opposing the depoliticization of the armed forces, especially in Bulgaria where some of them insisted that the BCP's domination of the armed forces was the consequence 'of a long historical process', and expelling that party from the military might not be a wise policy.[62] Nonetheless, by late January 1990 party and Komsomol organizations were disbanded in the army.

[58] Radio Prague (in English), February 26, 1990, 11:00 GMT.
[59] The deputy ministers of defence, Bronislaw Komorowski and Janusz Onyszkiewicz, were civilians.
[60] *Magyar Hirlap*, February 24, 1990.
[61] *Magyar Nemzet* (Budapest), May 10, 1990.
[62] See, for instance, *Otchestven Front* (Sofia), January 4, 1990, translated in *FBIS-EEU*, January 23, 1990, pp. 13–5.

ZOLTAN D. BARANY   607

   The overt opposition of military personnel to the democratization of the army
was particularly prevalent in Bulgaria. The army's paper, *Narodna Armiya*,
published a series of articles that intended to limit the concept of 'genuine'
democracy to the BCP (and later, the BSP). A representative piece called for a
distinction between 'real democratization and glasnost', and for 'Communists,
including those in the army . . . [to] conduct an aggressive struggle for unmasking
the real face of the self-proclaimed "democrats" '.[63] These articles attempted to
disguise the design of some BPA circles that purported to monopolize the reform
process and portray themselves as the champions of change. In December 1990, a
veteran observer of the army bitterly reported that 'nothing has changed'.[64]
   In Romania, too, control over the military remains a contentious issue.
Opposition circles called a bill on the establishment, organization, and operation
of the country's Supreme Defence Council 'most disturbing . . . because it turns
the army into a gendarmerie', and puts it completely under the control of
President Iliescu's authoritarian regime.[65] The decree includes a cooperation
plan between the Ministries of Interior and Defence concerning such questions as
use of weapons and maintaining and restoring domestic order. The Iliescu
regime's opponents demanded in vain real depoliticization, the transfer of active
generals to the reserves, and for 'bringing Generals Stanculescu, Guse, and
Chitac before the military tribunal . . . not as witnesses but as persons responsible
for the . . . Timisoara massacre'.[66]
   In Southeastern Europe, the tense political situation often gave rise to rumours
of impending military coups and defence officials had to repeatedly deny any
military intent to intervene in political processes. In August 1990, military
authorities in Bucharest refuted rumours 'perpetrated by foreign news agencies'
that the army was poised to take power and establish a military dictatorship in
Romania.[67] In November 1990, Bulgarian Defence Minister Yordan Mutafchiev
offered firm verbal guarantees of the army's political neutrality in order to
counter speculations that it might take power.[68] Six months later, President
Zhelyu Zhelev expressed confidence in his minister's endorsement. He said that
while he saw no threat of a military coup he did not reject the possibility of things
getting 'complicated'.[69]
   In contrast to the rest of the region, Bulgaria's military became involved in
debates about defence issues prior to the June elections. In May, an official
organization, the 'Georgi Stoikov Rakovski' Legion was formed in Sofia to
promote democratization within the armed forces. Leaders of the Legion had
written to the political leadership on several occasions, expressing their anxiety
about political forces attempting to subvert the army.[70] The BPA leadership
threw its support to the BSP, although the Union of Democratic Forces appeared
to enjoy the backing of the lower ranks.[71] After the elections, charges that

   [63] *Narodna Armiya* (Sofia), December 12, 1989, translated in *FBIS-EEU*, March 14, 1990, pp. 8–
10.
   [64] *Narodna Armiya*, December 18, 1990, translated in *FBIS-EEU*, December 27, 1990, pp. 7–8.
   [65] See *Romania Libera* (Bucharest), December 6, 1990, translated in *FBIS-EEU*, January 11, 1991,
p. 32.
   [66] *Romania Libera*, November 18, 1990, translated in *FBIS-EEU*, December 3, 1990, p. 61.
   [67] Radio Bucharest, August 14, 1990, 17:00 GMT, translated in *FBIS-EEU*, of the same date,
p. 32.
   [68] *Duma* (Sofia), November 26, 1990.
   [69] BTA (Bulgarian wire service, in English), May 5, 1991 citing an interview published in the Sofia
daily, *ABC*.
   [70] Perry, 'A new military lobby', p. 2.
   [71] Nelson, 'Political dynamics and the Bulgarian military', pp. 29–31.

soldiers manipulated the voting procedure were rejected by army officials. The denial – which included a plea for public confidence in the army: 'The Bulgarian soldier has long . . . proved that he is incorruptible. Let us trust him!' – sounded eerily reminiscent of the Communist era.[72]

The role of the armed forces in politics is nowhere as unsettled in the region as in Romania, despite the military leadership's frequently stated intent to depoliticize the army, emphasizing that it was the defender of national interests and its function was not to serve as the support base for any particular regime, party, or government organization.[73] Army leaders have rejected any criticism targeting the armed forces and seem to consider the military as standing above criticism. Defence Minister Constantin Spiroiu's statement in September 1991 that 'any attack on the army is an attack against the country' illustrates this phenomenon well.[74]

The Romanian Army is the only former NSWP force to have seen action in the post-revolution era. In March 1990, the military stepped in to break up ethnic clashes between Hungarians and Romanians in the city of Tirgu-Mures. Despite constant appeals from besieged ethnic Hungarians, the army and the police let two days pass without making any attempt to protect them.[75] The armed forces' role in the clashes appeared to support one analyst's assertion that the Romanian 'military's loyalty is most clearly to the institutions of the state and not the people in the street'.[76]

The military apparently did not intervene in the anti-government protests of June 1990, in Bucharest. These demonstrations were bloodily suppressed by some 20,000 miners called in by President Ion Iliescu to help prop up his regime.[77] Although the army did not actively interfere with the widespread strikes of December 1990, it threatened to do so. On December 1, 1990. General Paul Cheler, Commander of the 'Transylvania' Army published a declaration promising that 'the army . . . will firmly retaliate and even open fire against all those who will disturb and will try to compromise our sacred national holiday'.[78]

In late September 1991 thousands of Jiu Valley miners went to Bucharest (for the fourth time in two years) to demonstrate against government policies and demand the resignation of Prime Minister Roman. The Romanian Army was once again an active participant in the events – that resulted in several deaths and over 200 injuries – although this time security and police forces played the more important role in restraining the violent protestors. In any event, the Ministry of Defence raised combat capability, distributed ammunition to all small units guarding public buildings, and took other precautionary measures. Following the crisis the 'perfect cooperation' between the ministries of Interior and Defence was lauded by government leaders.[79]

[72] *Narodna Armiya*, June 19, 1990, translated in *FBIS-EEU*, June 22, 1990, pp. 7–9.

[73] See Price, 'The Romanian armed forces', p. 32.

[74] *Curierul National* (Bucharest), September 19, 1991.

[75] Vladimir Socor, 'Forces of old resurface in Romania: the ethnic clashes in Tirgu-Mures', *Report on Eastern Europe*, April 13, 1990, p. 40.

[76] Nelson, 'Watching the Pact unravel', p. 19.

[77] There is at least one student leader on record saying that the army also participated in the massacre. See ROMPRESS (Bucharest), June 15, 1990, translated in *FBIS-EEU*, June 18, 1990, p. 70.

[78] *Unirea* (Alba Iulia), December 1, 1990, cited in *Romania Libera*, December 5, 1990, translated in *FBIS-EEU*, December 13, 1990, p. 41.

[79] Programul Unu Radio (Bucharest), 20:06 GMT, September 26, 1991; translated in *FBIS-EEU*, September 27, 1991, p. 32.

ZOLTAN D. BARANY   609

Shifts in personnel in the Balkan states came after protracted infighting in political and military circles. Dobri Dzhurov, a long-time occupant (since 1963) in Sofia's Ministry of Defence, was reluctant to step down. Opposition groups and news organizations demanded Dzhurov's resignation because of his extensive links to the Communist regime.[80] Although he was succeeded by General Yordan Mutafchiev in October 1990, Dzhurov remained an active member of Bulgaria's National Security Council and the Grand National Assembly's Commission on National Security. According to some charges originating in military circles, Dzhurov continues to interfere in the internal affairs of the Bulgarian Army.[81]

Personnel changes were stormiest in Romania. In December 1989, General Militaru was appointed to fill the seat of General Milea, who was executed a few days earlier. In February 1990, a Committee for Action to Democratize the Army (CADA) was formed by professional armed forces personnel. Its main demands were the acknowledgement of the true role of the RPA in the December uprising, the removal of compromised military officers and generals from the service, the appointment of a civilian, non-partisan defence minister and the depoliticization of the armed forces.[82] After a long standoff, CADA – aided by on-going demonstrations and political tension – achieved the dismissal of Defence Minister Militaru, who was replaced by General Victor Stanculescu, formerly the minister responsible for economic affairs in the NSF government and a deputy defence minister under Ceausescu. Not surprisingly, Stanculescu's appointment failed to appease CADA, whose members charged that he was implicated in the shooting of civilians in Timisoara.[83] Following continuous protests from both opposition and military circles, Stanculescu was finally replaced by General Spiroiu in May 1991. In the fall speculations concerning a power struggle between the army and the police – particularly in view of their activities in September 1991 – persisted.[84]

Conclusion

The 45-year long history of civil-military relations in the East European Communist states exposes the inability of Marxist-Leninist parties in this region to secure the loyalty of the armed forces. Although the degree of reliability of these armies varied across the region, in domestic emergencies they either shied away from turning against the regime's enemies or were never asked to perform. During the political transitions of 1989 this conclusion was once again supported by the NSWP armies' performance. By this time, some of the regimes (in Czechoslovakia and East Germany, for instance) lacked the confidence to utilize the armies in domestic crises, and counted on the militias to protect them. Furthermore, it is highly doubtful whether or not the armed forces would have supported the regimes, especially in the face of earlier evidence.

[80] See, for instance, *Demokratsiya* (Sofia), June 4, 1990, translated in *FBIS-EEU*, June 6, 1990, p. 7.
[81] See *Narodna Armiya*, December 18, 1990, translated in *FBIS-EEU*, December 27, 1990, pp. 7–8.
[82] See Paul Gafton, 'Armed forces seek to democratize,' *Report on Eastern Europe*, April 6, 1990, pp. 37–41.
[83] Reuter and AP dispatches (Timisoara), March 3, 1990.
[84] See, for instance, ORF Television Network (Vienna), 20:00 GMT, September 27, 1991; translated in *FBIS-EEU*, September 30, 1991, pp. 22–3.

In spite of the political indoctrination, socialization and generally better-than-average living standards, the majority of East European military personnel did not feel sufficiently allied with the regime to fight for it. One way to explain this phenomenon is to appreciate the armies' loss of social status in the Communist era. Although the military traditions among the East European countries are very different – recall Prussia's martial traditions on the one hand and the pusillanimity of Czechs and Slovaks (as shown in 1938, 1948, and 1968) on the other – during the interwar period the occupation of the military officer enjoyed a degree of prestige in all of these societies. Perhaps the most important reason for the loss of the armies' social esteem after the war was popular recognition that the armed forces served not national, but politico-ideological (i.e. Communist) and supranational (i.e. Soviet) interests. These and other problems resulted in acute recruitment difficulties at one time or another in all NSWP states.

The record of the East European armed forces in the transition period underscores the profound disparities between the region's states. The countries of East-Central Europe are well on the way to completing the democratization of their armed forces. These armies appear to be depoliticized and loyal to the constitutional order that is taking shape in their respective societies. The situation in the Balkans, where the armies have not made an unambiguous commitment to political democratization, and seem to be ill-prepared for a new democratic era, is quite different. The political life of the Balkans is still inundated by 'reform-Communist' elements some of whom played major parts in the pre-revolution regimes and replacing military cadres tightly connected with the Communists remains to be a neglected issue. In sum, then, just as the political transformation of East-Central Europe is more convincing and comprehensive than in Southeastern Europe, the depoliticization process of the armed forces in the former region has also been more assuring.

Naturally, one hopes that comprehensive political, economic, and military transformation will soon be completed in all of Eastern Europe. Given their historic and cultural disparities, their varying ethnic composition, and scores of other factors, one may well expect that the states of the region will cross the finish line in different ways and at different times. One does not need prophetic powers to predict that East-Central Europe will complete this process sooner and with fewer difficulties than the Balkans.

Part IV
The International Context
of Transition

[23]

DEMOCRATIC TRANSITION
AND THE
INTERNATIONAL ENVIRONMENT:
A RESEARCH AGENDA
Geoffrey   Pridham
CMS-OCCASIONAL PAPER No.1   February,1991

1. Introduction

The international context is the forgotten dimension of regime
transition.   In recent times, particularly since the Southern
European transitions of the mid/later 1970s, there has been a
remarkable growth in both theoretical and empirical work on
the causes, processes and outcomes of transition from
authoritarianism to liberal democracy.   But surprisingly this
has largely chosen to ignore international influences and
effects on such major political change, not to mention effects
in the opposite direction in terms of external policy
discontinuity or otherwise.

That the international environment is clearly a dimension of
some importance is demonstrated albeit in differing ways by
the three regional examples of Southern Europe, Latin America
and more recently Eastern Europe.   All these examples, as do
furthermore those of the postwar former Axis powers of Italy,
West Germany and Japan, reveal the direct impact or indirect
influence on democratisation of international organisations,
of one or other super-power or other states in the same region
and of non-governmental organisations.   In Southern Europe,
the most successful so far of these recent regional examples,
the simultaneous process of democratic transition in three
states - Spain, Greece and Portugal from 1974-75 - itself
argued for considering a common geopolitical environment in
helping to explain its achievement there.   Moreover, the
existence of the European Community as an integrative
organisation, and one which intensifies bilateral links
between actual and also prospective member states, reinforces
this argument, as does the pull of NATO membership to some
lesser extent.

Both other regional examples highlight especially the decisive
influence of the super-power relationship - with the USA and
the USSR in the Latin American and Eastern European cases
respectively.   Indeed, in the latter case, the systemic
reform policy of Gorbachev in the USSR has emerged as probably
the crucial independent variable, in stimulating not to
mention tolerating change in Eastern Europe during 1989-90;
while the embarcation on transition in rapid succession in the
Eastern block states strongly suggested some 'domino theory'
effect with an obvious transnational dynamic.

While the salience of the international context of democratic
transition may thus be generally recognised, analysing its
real impact or influence on this process is no easy task
either theoretically or empirically.   This is partly due to
the absence of adequate analytical tools and also problems of

1

2

evidence deriving from the confidential nature of some
political activity 'crossing the boundary' between countries.
Moreover, it cannot avoid the wider problem of different
disciplinary approaches and lack of cooperation between them
that is a leitmotiv of this paper. As a whole, the
theoretical and comparative literature that has a bearing on
the linkage between external conditions and domestic
developments is rather too bland and loose in its concerns,
but it does offer directions for research and it allows us to
develop further approaches for our focus on political system
change.

The problem of the disciplinary divide between international
affairs and comparative politics is one readily acknowledged
by both sides, especially those in international affairs.
There have been conceptual difficulties in overcoming
established assumptions - notably, about the role of the
nation-state (e.g. international relations work has
traditionally regarded the state as a unitary actor) - and
also intrinsic and vested interests of those working in both
sub-fields as being largely non-convergent (Clarke, 1986, pp3-
9; Panebianco, 1986, pp. 434-5).

More recently, there have been signs of perhaps a new phase in
disciplinary bridge-building, with possibly more chance of
this becoming a permanent and not merely a transitory concern
as with early work in international affairs on this area, e.g.
Hermann, Kegley and Rosenau (1987) and Boyd and Hopple (1987).
At the same time, there is greater acknowledgement on the part
of those in comparative politics of the need to take into
account the international dimension of political systems.
'Another flaw is its failure to give adequate consideration to
the way the world of international politics inevitably
impinges on any individual political system; foreign politics
shapes the behaviour not only of the political leaders of
other systems but also of their citizens' (Lawson, 1985, p.
82). This tendency is likely to encourage due attention to
'inner-directed' linkages (impact of the international system
on domestic structures) as well as 'outer-directed' linkages
(vice versa).   At the same time, recognition on the
international relations side of an increasingly interdependent
world has led some to argue, in the words of Hanrieder, that
there is 'a new international order which resembles in
important ways the domestic political systems prevalent in, the
industrialised non-communist part of the world; this leads to
the "domestication" of international politics' (Hanrieder,
1978, p.1276).

One of the main problems encountered by earlier work on
"linkage politics", as this concern has become known, was its
lack of specificity. Broad frameworks were formulated to
guide work along these lines, but they were too often loosely

constructed and open-ended. Some recent studies have however
admitted, as in Almond's 'interactive analytical model' in a
review article on "linkage politics", that 'the picture which
emerges... is one of a complex dynamic process which offers no
simple answers or solutions' (Almond, 1989, p. 257). However,
in reference to the work of the historian Otto Hintze, he
comments:

> 'It is very difficult to grapple with these factors in
> terms of general propositions and regularities. At any
> given time during the past several centuries there has
> been one central, international system, consisting of the
> interactions of the principal European states. Given
> variations in the political organisation of these states
> in a singular international environment, it was the
> course of least resistance to assume the international
> environment to be a constant vis-a-vis all states, or
> simply to extract the state from its international
> environment, and explain national political variation by
> internal economics, social structure and culture. It was
> the virtue of Hintze to attribute spatial and temporal
> variability to the international environment, and to find
> in these variations some significant part of the
> explanation of internal variation' (Almond, 1989, pp.
> 258-9).

The overall problem has been neatly summarised by Rosenau, an
early proponent of "linkage politics": 'Obviously the concept
of the salient environment [in the international system]
presents a number of empirical and theoretical challenges;
most notably, there is the empirical problem of tracing the
way in which changes in saliency occur and the theoretical
problem of formulating the relationship between different
genotypical societies and the kinds of environments that are
salient for them' (Rosenau, 1970, p. 372).

One simple way of responding to the above-mentioned problem of
specificity is simply to eschew grand-scale models for
"linkage politics" and to focus on area study concerns and/or
those issue-areas which, although perhaps peculiar to certain
countries or groups of them, nevertheless contain broader
implications for the analysis of political systems and hence
some potential for inductive theorising. As long ago as
1966, Rosenau bemoaned haphazardness in treating the
external/internal mix and argued for turning to issue-areas in
systematic enquiry: 'each area must be conceptualised at a
high enough level of abstraction to encompass a variety of
vertical systems, and each of the latter must in turn be
conceived as based on a continual processing of the values
that its structure is designed to allocate' (Rosenau, 1966, p.
77).

One such area is **regime change**, since this draws attention to
something more specific than vague "political change" and yet
is of basic importance. Furthermore, for the sake of
researching liberal democracies, this exercise may be confined
to the question of democratic transition rather than, say, the
opposite process from democracy to authoritarianism - a choice
which offers the added advantage of moving towards a more open
type of system, hence one where international constraints may
well be much more visible. There are other relevant reasons
for selecting this problem:

(a) it is likely to focus attention on the dynamics of
political change, this being particularly important since
earlier models of "linkage politics" tended towards a static
approach;

(b) it concentrates on a process in which political systems
may well be especially vulnerable to international influences,
given the uncertainty that is commonly seen as marking
democratic transition (O'Donnell, Schmitter and Whitehead,
1986, pt. IV, chap. 1);

(c) it also prompts interest in the temporal and spatial
dimension of the international environment;

(d) regime change automatically raises the question of foreign
and defence policy continuity or otherwise, i.e. one likely to
'provoke' international constraints;

(e) it highlights a number of specific problems relating to
system stability and international considerations, e.g. the
role of the military is directly concerned with external
affairs (defence policy), and yet a crucial test of the move
from authoritarianism to liberal democracy is its retraction
from politics;

(f) there is some connection here with the theme of
modernisation, seeing too that first attempts at partial
theories on "linkage politics" singled out the foreign
policies of modernising societies (Rosenau, 1966, p. 33);

(g) one may adapt or apply the work of a 'third party' school
of thinking, namely theories of regime transition, which
although not straddling the divide between international
affairs and comparative politics provide at any rate a
different angle of analysis;

(h) this problem presents a viable case-study of the actual
relationship between 'inner-directed' and 'outer-directed'
linkages , for in reality the two lines of enquiry cannot be
separated even though general theory has so far shown a
preference for one or the other.

5

separated even though general theory has so far shown a preference for one or the other.

As a whole, therefore, a theme like regime change allows a much sharper focus for relating problems of theory and practice in "linkage politics" than would the general question of international constraints and democratic regimes. The overall purpose of this paper, then, is to develop a comparative framework for assessing the importance of the international context of transitions to liberal democracy. We therefore start by assessing standing theoretical concerns and apply these in formulating this framework (see appendix).

This is all the more necessary since the theme of international influences in democratic transition is a largely unresearched area, and thus requires an approach developed from basic principles. This will be done by reviewing in turn theories of democratic transition, relevant approaches in the international affairs literature, lessons from the comparative analysis of political systems and indications from historical experience. The order is determined by the sequence of disciplinary concerns and the extent to which they overlap.

2. Theories of Democratic Transition and the International Context

Although theories of regime transition have, somewhat like comparative politics, focussed essentially on domestic political systems, they do allow us to develop different hypotheses for our line of enquiry. Thus, the international context is recognised as one of the conditioning variables of transition, although - it has to be admitted - this is more often assumed than incorporated adequately in theoretical work. Nevertheless, the very definition of democratic transition offers clues about the scope for international factors.

Broadly speaking, **democratic transition** runs from the point at which the previous authoritarian system begins to be dismantled, through the constituent phase of the new democracy to its inauguration and early operation. The initiation of transition may be explicit such as with a strategic decision by key political actors to embark on this process; it may even be marked visibly by a major event serving to redirect a country's politics, e.g. military defeat, death of the dictator. Or, less clearly, this process may be preceded or prepared by a phase of 'pre-transition' in which the outgoing regime disintegrates and the course is set for eventual regime change. Here, international factors may well highlight this phase in that the external environment may be either

6

like Western Europe) or promotive of democratisation through
cross-national socio-economic change of a modernising kind.
In the view of this study, democratic transition ends not
merely once the constitution is in place but also when the new
democracy begins to function with a popularly elected
government. In other words, the elites start to work the
system and to adjust accordingly.

Common to **definitions of democratic transition** is the emphasis
on its intrinsic uncertainty, making the process open or even
vulnerable to the impact of events as from the international
environment.   As Whitehead points out:

> 'After any transition from authoritarian rule the
> emergent democracy will be a regime in which not all
> significant political actors have impeccable democratic
> credentials, and where democratic rules of procedure have
> yet to be "internalised"by the society at large. Many
> established institutions have to be restructured, some
> demoted, some virtually created anew, to make them
> conform to democratic rather than authoritarian modes of
> governance. New and inexperienced political actors enter
> the stage, while long-established parties and interests
> find themselves required to compete on a quite different
> basis than before. The rules of competition are up for
> negotiation, the outcomes are uncertain and often quite
> unexpected, no-one is quite sure which elements of
> continuity remain in place... In short, the transition
> phase is often one of acute uncertainty and high anxiety
> for many social actors. Such uncertainty may be exciting
> and creative... but if it becomes too generally
> threatening, or if it lasts too long without any fruitful
> outcome, then the chances of an authoritarian relapse
> becomes very great' (Whitehead, 1988, pp. 6-7).

At this point, we should note there have been **two schools of
regime transition theory**: those called functionalist,
emphasising environmental factors and in particular the state
of socio-economic development; and others termed genetic,
stressing political variables and hence significant scope for
political actors and their strategic choices (Pridham, 1984
pp.1-29).   In the former case, the time-scale is obviously
longer, for functionalist theories have usually hypothesised
that the chances for democratisation in a given case depend
crucially on a fairly advanced level of socio-economic
development or modernisation.   Insofar as this explanation has
been based on one dominant cause of transition, it has been
criticised for being too deterministic.

However, theories which incorporate such environmental factors
and focus on their interaction with political choice and

action are rather more convincing. Clearly, in both schools of thinking there is room for external factors to come into play; while this very interaction is obviously similar to the concerns of "linkage politics". Here, we turn to various theories of democratic transition and group them according to their relevance to our theme.

Firstly, several early theories have dwelt on problems of **historical sequence and conditions;** and, inevitably, these present some scope for the international context. On the side of political choice, Rustow's 'dynamic model' for transitions to democracy noted 'major impulses from outside' towards democracy and that 'foreign influences are almost always present' (Rustow, 1970). His 'background condition' which 'must precede all the other phases of democratisation' is national unity, which immediately introduces an international dimension. Furthermore, Rustow's different phases of democratic transition allude to this same dimension. While his decision phase really concentrates on the domestic game (except in cases of foreign occupation) - notably, the formulation of a new constitution - his preparatory phase which precedes that ('a prolonged and inconclusive political struggle') and the eventual habituation phase ('process of Darwinian selectivity in favour of convinced democrats') leaves some room for international influences, even if they are strictly secondary, such as the external linkages utilised by domestic transition actors.

As to functionalist theories, Kirchheimer's thesis of 'confining conditions' in regime change, one specially applied to 'revolutionary breakthroughs', has a bearing on our theme. This underlined the dictates of socio-economic conditioning: 'what matters in this context is the interrelation between socio-economic conditioning and the discretionary element left to the decision of the regime... the social and economic frame of the particular society, then, lays down a conditioning perimeter within which the original choice has to be made and solutions have to be sought' (Kirchheimer, 1965, pp. 965, 966). He was referring to domestic conditions and structures, but this may well be extended to the regional frame of the international economy and constraints deriving from it, particularly where this frame - as in Western Europe - is moving along the path of transnational integration.

Secondly, more recent theoretical work has begun to pay attention to this question of **regional international contexts** and transnational organisations. For instance, Schmitter has commented:

> 'Why have the liberalisations/democratisations of
> Southern Europe got off to what seems to be a better and
> more reassuring start [than Latin America]? A partial

explanation is that the international context in that
part of the world and at this point of time is more
supportive of such an outcome... But such international
factors cannot be made to bear the entire explanation
burden... external factors tended to play an indirect and
usually marginal role, with the obvious exception of
those instances in which a foreign occupying power was
present' (O'Donnell, Schmitter and Whitehead, 1986, pp.
4-5).

Moreover, the political 'rhythm' in the replacement of regimes
at the national level is sometimes accelerated or deflected in
new directions by socio-economic trends, unexpected events,
cyclical disturbances and shifts at the international level,
e.g. war, terrorism, trade depressions, changes in
international allegiances (Schmitter, 1985, p. 64).
Similarly, Morlino has drawn attention to the need 'to treat
autonomously the possible role of international actors, at
least in two specific senses: the first sense could be
considered passive and mechanical - that the country belongs
to a geopolitical area already completely democratised, and
entry to supranational economic organisations which influence
the political forces of the country... the second modality of
influence by the international factor is more direct... the
possibility that in different but concrete ways (e.g. economic
aid to the government or to certain democratic forces,
diplomatic pressure from external actors) the internal
legitimation of the regime is helped'(Morlino, 1986, pp. 454-
5).

Thirdly, some work on democratic transition has sought to
identify **types of external actors** and hence specific forms of
international constraints on this process.   One direct effort
at relating comparative theory to practice is the essay on
'international aspects of democratisation' by Whitehead in
Transitions from Authoritarian Rule (1986) (O'Donnell,
Schmitter and Whitehead, pt. III, chap. 1). While agreeing
that domestic political forces operate with a high degree of
autonomy and that international factors are normally secondary
(at least they may be mildly supportive or destructive),
Whitehead notes that the unpredictability and uncertainty
characteristic of regime transition tends to encourage parties
engaged in it to enlist international support if only for
symbolic endorsement (Whitehead, 1986, pp. 4-5, 9). A
distinction should be drawn here between types of external
actors - different foreign governments, international or
integrative organisations, but also between governmental and
non-governmental agencies, such as transnational parties or
interest groups and the churches. In this sense, the question
of models of democracy, in the socio-economic as well as
political meaning of the term, becomes highlighted, given

that systemic and ideological variants invariably determine
the extent of its promotion from outside.

According to Whitehead, 'the boundary between exercising
legitimate external influence and improper intervention is far
more blurred than most governments are willing to admit'
(Whitehead, 1986, p.19). He comes to the conclusion there are
three components of the international 'promotion of
democracy': pressure on undemocratic governments to
democratise themselves; support for fledgling democracies that
are attempting to consolidate; and, the maintenance of a firm
stance against anti-democratic forces that threaten or
overthrow established democracies (Whitehead, 1986, p. 44).
Instruments for influencing this process can thus vary and may
be moral, economic, military and political and diplomatic -
or, indeed, one might add, some combination of these.

In the same volume, O'Donnell and Schmitter argue with respect
to opening up authoritarian regimes that

> 'ideological constraints at the international level have
> some effect on actor perceptions of the long-term
> viability of a given regime, and the negative impact of a
> downturn in the international economy can accelerate
> matters. Nevertheless, it seems to us fruitless to search
> for some international factor or context which can
> reliably compel authoritarian rulers to experiment with
> liberalisation, much less which can predictably cause
> their regimes to collapse' (O'Donnell, Schmitter and
> Whitehead, pt. IV, p.18).

Once more, international factors are viewed as secondary or
dependent variables, their influence or impact largely
conditional on opportunities presented by domestic
developments. Pasquino explores this point by concluding that
the international climate can provide the impetus for
transition, but that 'it cannot produce a successful
democratic outcome unless many other conditions are
simultaneously present' (Pasquino, 1986, p.70). Hence, the
interplay of international factors with domestic processes is
often crucial; and here national variation is likely.

Fourthly, transition theory has also focussed on **cause and
effect relationships**. Here, we are approaching more closely
the dynamics of the democratisation process. In Baloyra's
<u>Comparing New Democracies</u> (1987), Morlino suggests that the
international dimension in the move to democratic transition
has 'enormous potential relevance' and 'may be the crucial
"intervening variable" that accounts for the crisis and the
breakdown' (Morlino, 1987, p. 71). Baloyra himself refers to
direct causal factors in the external environment (e.g. the
impact of international economic disequilibria on regime

performance) as contributing to the deterioration rather than
breakdown of regimes, although in some cases external setbacks
- notably, military defeat - may precipitate events (Baloyra,
1987, pp.297-8). Baloyra goes on to schematise patterns of
democratic transition, underlining the importance of timing
and locus. He thus distinguishes between early-internal,
delayed-external, delayed-internal and late-external
variations in the sequence of events here. For example,
'delayed-external' refers to deterioration in the previous
regime, with the endgame precipitated by external factors that
produce the breakdown as well. This takes us back to the
'pre-transition' phase, marked among other things by the
'liberalisation' of authoritarianism.

But, as Morlino comments, there is a particular difficulty in
establishing causality:

> 'It is very difficult empirically to identify only one
> effective "cause". It is more realistic to frame
> hypotheses based on more than one of the reasons for
> crisis discussed herein. However, given the importance of
> the coercive factor, its determining impact on the
> outcome of the crisis, and the fact that these constitute
> the focus of military concern, the conflicts and the
> eventual isolation of the military from other political
> actors and from society weigh more heavily than other
> causes' (Morlino, 1987, p.72).

While he was generalising from the Portuguese democratic
transition (i.e. the impact of colonial war), whereby external
events may be decisive though not necessarily conclusive,
Morlino was mainly concerned with cause and effect in terms of
type of transition. As he has written elsewhere:

> 'Normally, the international factor has a notable
> influence on the modalities of the transition and on the
> type of new regime established. In fact, however, it is
> difficult on this question to go beyond a few general
> indications because the ways in which the international
> aspect is influential vary enormously, namely they are
> very different one from other. Formulating general
> hypotheses which are appropriate is really difficult, if
> not impossible' (Morlino, 1980, p.91).

Above all, this line of reasoning rejects treating the
international dimension as simply one 'cause' when analysing
democratic transition. In this same vein, the problem of
causes has been broached more directly by Falk in assessing
'the global setting and transition to democracy', recognising
again the complexity in the interplay between the external and
the internal:

11

'It is difficult to establish convincing causal linkages.
At the same time, the interaction between the global
setting and national political development involves a
plethora of elements difficult to assess in terms of
their relative importance. At the same time, the
clustering of regional and subregional tendencies toward
and away from democratisation lends substance to the
contention that the global setting is an important
element in any adequate account of the course of the
political development for any particular country' (Falk,
1981).

Elaborating on this global or regional setting, Falk presents
various ways for externally promoting democracy. These
include state actors agreeing to respect the dynamics of self-
determination by refraining from intervention,
demilitarisation initiatives on all levels - international and
other - as conducive to democratic potential, and the
selective easing of short-term economic burdens as encouraging
democratisation. He relates, for instance, such questions as
demilitarisation at the international level to the style of
opposition politics, which may in turn help to determine the
often crucial matter of consensus in the transition process.

As a whole, theories of democratic transition provide various
directions for examining the problem of international impacts
and constraints on democratising regimes. Above all, they
argue strongly for 'unscrambling' the international dimension,
for vague references to the 'international climate' as broadly
positive or negative do little to facilitate analysis. Then,
there emerges a convincing case for dividing the transition
process into sub-phases (e.g. pre-transition, inaugural,
intermediate, concluding) so far as the variable scope for the
impact of international factors is concerned. One may take
this point further by asking whether there is more potential
for 'inner-directed' than 'outer-directed' linkages in the
transition process or not. Moreover, in this respect, a basic
distinction should be drawn between the long-term and short-
term impact of international factors. The former may have a
pervasive albeit indirect effect, as with socio-economic
change in the external environment prior to transition; while
the latter's impact may be direct, as military defeat or
setback in helping to overturn an authoritarian regime or in
the form of external events during the sensitive transition
process. But generalisations here are difficult and rather
nationally variable.

Finally, a different distinction has to be made between
'power' and 'influence' with respect to international actors
impinging on regime change. Attention is really more on the
second. Indeed, Whitehead deliberately chooses the term

'influence' since internal forces possess a substantial degree
of autonomy, although 'when these are finely balanced external
actors may determine the outcome by weighing in on one side or
the other' (Whitehead, 1984, p.12). On the other hand, the
term 'power' may well be more apposite when referring to
democratic transitions taking place in countries under
(temporary) foreign occupation. On specifics, these theories
help to identify particular linkage mechanisms, such as the
role of the military but also other actors of a (party-)
political and economic kind. A significant variation on this
point would be how far major transition strategists in
individual countries purposefully or overtly include an
international component in their role of inaugurating and
establishing a new democracy.

The principal lesson from regime transition theory is
therefore the need to differentiate over the problem of the
international context of democratisation and to indicate ways
in which this may be pursued. At the same time, it is
apparent that, while external influences are as a rule
secondary to the role of domestic actors in the transition
process, the impact of the former should not be underrated and
at certain points it may be crucial.

3. International Affairs and Regime Change

Relevant approaches in the international affairs literature
have nowhere dwelt as such on the question of regime change or
transition in the meaning used in this study. Some work has
looked either more broadly at political change or different
types of political systems or more narrowly at 'regime change'
in the sense of governmental or leadership change within a
given system, although usually concerning the effect of regime
properties on the conduct of foreign policy (e.g. Boyd and
Hopple, 1987; Geller, 1985; and, Hermann, Kegley and Rosenau,
1987).   However, such approaches both complement the 'inner-
directed' focus of regime transition theory and - as we shall
see - of comparative politics, but also confirm some of the
conclusions from looking at the former.

This is all the more true of recent work, influenced it would
seem by Hanrieder's contention that

> 'a new convergence of international and domestic
> political processes is under way ...In some major
> respects, governments find it increasingly difficult, or
> meaningless, to distinguish between foreign policy and
> domestic policy. Nowhere is this more clearly visible and
> institutionalised than in the operations of regional
> international organisations that are endowed with some

measure of supranational authority, however limited...
But the fusion of domestic and foreign policy takes place
even in the absence of supranational processes; it
reflects a process in which the traditional boundaries
separating the nation-state from the environing
international system are becoming increasingly obscured
and permeable' (Hanrieder, 1978, p. 1280).

Again, these approaches are grouped and discussed by way of
developing the framework for this theme.

Firstly, there is the general notion of **'penetrated systems'**,
which featured in earlier work and has reappeared in some
recent studies. Originally, this notion formed part of
dependency theory in explaining the structural position of
developing states in the international system. It is perhaps
therefore less obviously applicable to say Western European
examples, although those in Southern Europe as 'semi-
peripheral' states would presumably count as in some respects
candidates for consideration. Moreover, the phenomenon of
interdependence suggests a degree of penetrated-ness, although
Rosenau was at pains to argue that 'penetration' involved more
than interdependence (Hermann, Kegley and Rosenau, 1987, p.
435).

For Rosenau, 'a penetrated system is one in which non-members
of a national society participate directly and
authoritatively, through actions taken jointly with the
society's members, in either the allocation of its values or
the mobilisation of support on behalf of its goals' (Rosenau,
1966, p.65). This involves a certain 'fusion of national and
international systems in certain kinds of issue-areas'
(Rosenau, 1966, p.53), although Rosenau recognised the need
for some differentiation as between those states where
penetration is well-developed and those where it is limited
(Rosenau, 1966, pp.70-1). He also noted that 'penetrated
systems' are not static: they come into being, develop and
disappear as capabilities, attitudes or circumstances change.
For Rosenau, penetrating agents could be either other states
or international organisations, where clearly a salient
example of the former would be the the USA in postwar Western
Europe.

The concept of 'penetrated systems' suffers, however, from
being too loose as a working definition. It is still not, for
instance, fully clear how this condition differs from a
'normal' degree of permeation of national systems by the
international environment, in line with Hanrieder's above-
quoted contention.

If applied to specific problems, the concept of 'penetrated
systems' has however some bearing on the question of regime

14

change. For instance, one question arising so far from the
discussion is: does democratic transition make regimes
especially vulnerable to international influences?   Thus, it
may be hypothesised a new regime is particularly concerned
with its own legitimation and eventual stabilisation, and to
this end seeks to harness direct support from outside
organisations or actors (e.g. economic aid from the IMF or
EC). Similarly, if regime transition is internally contested,
or there develops a struggle over systemic models to be
adopted, then domestic actors may well look to different even
rival outside powers.

That line of reasoning leads to two further points of
differentiation. The extent to which outside actors respond
will probably vary according to the geopolitical situation of
the country in transition. Also, it is conceivable that if
such 'penetration' is significant in regime transition then it
may become a formative influence on the new system, supporting
the argument that the mode of transition is a primary
determinant of regime consolidation.

Taking our Southern European examples, Italy is a notable
instance of this last point since the imprint of the Cold War
on its postwar transition to democracy - with intense
Left/Right polarisation - left long-lasting effects; while
Greece, a country with a history of foreign intervention,
demonstrates how much 'penetration' can enter the value system
and hence political culture. But this syndrome can have
either positive or negative consequences. The Greek democratic
transition from 1974 witnessed a reaction to this historical
tradition, as expressed concretely over American support for
the disgraced Colonels' regime. This recalls Deutsch's
suggestion that 'very often an external event will have only
limited effects on domestic affairs... but foreign events may
have an effect on the memories of people'(Deutsch, 1966,
p.25). Clearly, at this point, we move away from
generalisations to national-specific analysis.

Secondly, international affairs approaches have usefully
differentiated between **types of external environments** with
respect to linkages; and, in this sense, they enlarge on a
notion touched on by regime transition theory. For Rosenau, a
'linkage' is any recurrent sequence of behaviour that
originates in one system and is reacted to in another in an
output/input fashion, an approach akin to the functional
paradigms of Almond, Apter and Easton about political systems.
Rosenau was thus concerned with patterns rather than
'boundary-crossing' events with short-lived repercussions,
i.e. with the recurrence rather than the occurrence of events.
This does not of course accord strictly with the idea in
transition theory that well-timed events might have some
catalytic effect on authoritarian regime collapse. It is also

conceivable that some linkages might also be affected by
regime change itself, as we have noted above in the case of
Greece. But such problems only reveal the difference between
the broad scope of "linkage politics" approaches and the
specific concerns of transition theory.

Rosenau then sub-divides the domestic and international
environments and categorises different types of linkages
according to these - such as the contiguous ('any cluster of
polities that border geographically upon a given polity'), the
regional (entire regions), the Cold War or East/West blocs and
the organisational (international organisations) (Rosenau,
1969, pp.60-3). The intention is to 'curb the tendency to
regard polities as having undifferentiated external
environments', so making it 'difficult to presume that events
abroad operate as constants rather than as variables in the
functioning of polities' (Rosenau, 1969, pp.53-4).

Thus, we may suppose that certain external sub-environments
might come more into play than others over cases of regime
transition; and here, too, we need to consider a time-period
environment as undoubtedly conditioning their salience and
influence. Obviously, the Cold War environment of the later
1940s - when democratic transition occurred in Italy - was
considerably different from the context of detente when the
Iberian and Greek transitions took place.

A more elaborate attempt drawing on functional political
models is Brecher's framework of analysis for assessing
foreign policy systems (Brecher, 1972). He argues that it is
not sufficient to develop categories but necessary to identify
crucial variables and establish relationships among them
(Brecher, 1972, p.1). Brecher's research design involves
dividing inputs into the operational environment (external and
internal), communication (especially the media) and the
psychological environment (attitudinal prism, elite images),
the process into formulation and implementation and then
outputs simply defined as the substance of decisions (Brecher,
1972, p.3). The internal operational environment includes
political structure: type of political regime, character of
party system, civil-military relations of control, and the
extent of continuity and stability of the authority structures
in the system (Brecher, 1972, pp.8-9).

While these systemic features summarise familiar structures
that may undergo alteration with regime transition, other
variables among inputs relating to mode of communication and
elite outlooks highlight possible qualitative changes
accompanying the move to liberal democracy. For instance, the
psychological environment encompasses ideology and tradition
as well as personality factors, the last notably prominent in
authoritarian systems. As Brecher concludes, 'elite image is

the decisive input of a foreign policy system... the reason
for this pivotal role is that decision-makers act in
accordance with their perception of reality, not in response
to reality itself - image and reality may coincide or may
diverge' (Brecher, 1972, pp.11-12). This could apply to the
outlook of authoritarian rulers in the phase of 'pre-
transition', as not corresponding comfortably with the
changing external context (e.g. their systems become
increasingly regarded as anachronistic in Western Europe).
Equally, it may be said that transition actors, among other
things, adopt a different perception of reality, presumably
one which may coincide better with the international
environment - in this case, Rosenau's regional environment.

Thirdly, some recent work has pursued the question of **regime
fragmentation and vulnerability;** and, with this, of
constraints deriving from either internal or external
environments. Hagan, for example, presents in <u>New Directions
in the Study of Foreign Policy</u> (1987) an agenda for
comparative research on political influences, looking above
all at this very problem (Hagan, 1987). In measuring regime
characteristics, his dominant concern is with political
constraints, as when 'pronounced political divisions within a
regime and the occurrence of strong political pressures
threatening to remove the regime from power are likely to have
a broad impact on foreign policy' (Hagan, 1987, p.348).

In particular, Hagan's analysis turns on the role of
oppositions in influencing foreign policy, and he argues for
'integrating political explanations with those from other
theoretical perspectives in the field' in favour of
multivariate schemes for 'understanding the apparently complex
linkage between domestic politics and foreign policy' (Hagan,
1987, p. 363). Similarly, in another recent study, Geller has
focussed on regime coherence and its effect on foreign policy
behaviour (Geller, 1985). Constraints arise, notably with
certain levels of domestic strain, such as when internal
instability produces conflictual rather than cooperative
foreign policy.

This line of thinking prompts a number of different though
related enquiries into the problem of democratic transition.
Thus, as noted earlier, an internally contested transition, is
almost bound to be projected onto the international stage.
Partisan domestic actors will look to external agents for
support to protect given political and also perhaps economic
interests. Those agents will respond according to a
calculation about their chances for influence,`with national
or partisan interests in mind and behind those how far this
case is salient or essential on strategic grounds. We already

see here the scenario for some kind of interaction between
'outer-directed' and 'inner-directed' responses.

Other considerations arising over democratic transition refer
to the effective pursuit of foreign policy and also its
continuity. It is likely that the very process of transition
will entail a marked - and, at times, maybe exclusive -
concentration on domestic affairs, i.e. creating the new
regime, to the neglect of foreign policy. An active or
effective foreign policy is therefore unusual at this point of
time, when political elites become 'introspective'. On the
matter of continuity, a change of regime does present the
possibility of a break here, since leaders of a new liberal
democracy will probably show different priorities or at least
value judgements from their authoritarian predecessors.

Alternatively, embarking on transition might actually speed up
developments in an area of foreign policy, as when the
Portuguese revolution of 1974 led swiftly to de-colonisation;
or it might open the way for an overdue shift away from past
conditions, as when the move to democracy in Spain put an end
to that country's isolation during the Franco years. It
notably opened the way for Spain, as also Portugal and Greece,
to apply for EC membership, previously barred to these
countries because of their authoritarian regimes.

At the same time, constraints from the international
environment may act as a persistent pressure for continuity in
the face of domestic change or upheaval. This is most evident
in the existence of integrative international organisations
like the European Community. That is, integration has taken
place through a close and progressive interweaving of national
economies and regular and routine political relations as well
as a variety of transnational links, both multilateral and
bilateral. This induces various patterns of socialisation,
creates new networks and generally results in a growing
interaction between domestic and European-level actors.
However, the effects of this on new democracies is perhaps
more pertinent to their later consolidation than to the
immediate task of democratic transition.

In fact, one obvious and rather important omission in the
international affairs literature on external\domestic
"linkage" is the international economy. This is alluded to
by functionalist theories of regime transition, but it is
hardly incorporated in work dealing with political change.
One exception is again <u>New Directions in the Study of Foreign
Policy</u> (Hermann, Kegley and Rosenau, 1987), where Moon argues
for introducing political economy approaches in comparative
foreign policy studies not least because international
economic relations 'bear upon the distribution of economic
surplus within the nation' and as 'a broad range of policy

actions are undertaken to control transactions across national boundaries' (ibid, pp. 36, 41).

This does not help us particularly with regime transition, except perhaps by reminding us of the sometimes profound influence of international economic developments surrounding the transition period and serving to condition the prospects of a successful outcome. This point may either be expanded to refer to socio-economic modernisation pressures or contracted by noting the impact of certain interventions by international economic organisations - such as the International Monetary Fund (as in Portugal during transition) as well as the European Community.

In the case of modernisation pressures, one may of course refer back to 'pre-transition' and the onset of liberalisation (often economic before political) under authoritarian regimes. Such a change of policy direction is invariably made under some form of compulsion and is therefore somewhat defensive, notably as a strategy for maintaining (vulnerable) regime legitimacy. Depending on its timing, this move may become part of a process of authoritarian regime disintegration. Thus, the international economy may acquire an indirect influence both over the 'pre-transition' phase as well as the transition process itself, broadly seen. But political determinants (policy choice, strategies of transition actors) are crucial intermediary variables.

While the focus on the 'outer' direction of linkage action is still largely true of recent literature in international affairs, this has nevertheless moved some way towards handling a two-way effect. That is most evident with respect to international organisations and their 'influence and instrumentality' in providing constraints or policy opportunities. These indeed look at the 'inner direction' of linkages. For instance, Karns and Mingst hypothesise that 'the existence and outputs of IGOs [intergovernmental organisations] do make a difference in the behaviour of states, but that the impact varies along a series of different dimensions', depending on issue-areas and also individual states (Karns and Mingst, 1987, p. 455). In the latter respect, variables include the national attributes of a state, the nature of the domestic political system and the characteristics of the international organisation (Karns and Mingst, p.458). It is noted that IGOs 'are the institutional components of many regimes', for: 'IGOs can be treated as variables within a complex interdependence system that impinges on national governments; they provide opportunities for national decision-making at the same time that they add to the constraints under which states must operate' (Karns and Mingst, p. 457).

In conclusion, despite some difficulties in applying the broad
approaches of "linkage politics" to the particular process of
democratic transition, they do nonetheless offer new angles on
relevant linkages. In the view of Rosenau, we should be
looking for patterns whereby phenomena on one level impinge
recurrently on behaviour at the other. These usually amount
to constraints or opportunities, or maybe some complex
combination of both, although it is important to see these as
part of the transition dynamics and not simply as expressing a
certain structural configuration. While the focus is
undoubtedly on the present situation, it may however be
coloured by past associations; but, most of all, we are
talking about different kinds of actors both domestically and
externally, where clearly there is much scope for the
national-specific. Also, pace Rosenau, it should not be
forgotten that one-off external events - such as the 1974
Cyprus crisis in the Greek case - may help to provoke the
shift from 'pre-transition' to transition proper.
Furthermore, it is apparent that systems in transition are
indeed more subject to international influences than usual,
since transition to democracy is invariably regarded at the
time as not a 'normal' situation, even as an historical one.
This may well create a greater readiness for 'boundary-
crossing' activity, by external actors, depending on how the
situation evolves.

Referring to interaction between 'outer-directed' and 'inner-
directed' linkages, the international affairs literature
provides some clues given its predominant concern with the
first. One might adopt the idea of different kinds of
environments - as sub-divisions of the external and internal
environments - and view them as interacting themselves. But,
in so doing, we have still to answer the key question raised
by Gourevitch a decade ago:

> 'The international system, be it in an economic or
> politico-military form, is underdetermining. The
> environment may exert strong pulls but short of actual
> occupation, some leeway in the response to that
> environment remains. A country can face up to the
> competition or it can fail. Frequently more than one way
> to be successful exists. A purely international system
> argument relies on functional necessity to explain
> domestic outcomes; this is unsatisfactory, because
> functional requisites may not be fulfilled. Some variance
> in response to external environment is possible. The
> explanation of choice among the possibilities therefore
> requires some examination of domestic politics'
> (Gourevitch, 1978, p.900).

4. Comparative Politics and Regime Change

The value of applying approaches from comparative politics is
essentially to complement those outlined above in
international affairs; and, in particular, to elaborate on the
relative importance of the different domestic environments.
As Gourevitch noted more than a decade ago, in looking at the
international sources of domestic politics, 'the
comparativist's perspective has been neglected, that is, the
reasoning from the international system to domestic
structure'(Gourevitch, 1978, p.882).

Firstly, some attention has been given the **kinds of
international influences** that impinge on domestic political
development. One of the few comparative politics surveys to
pay attention to 'international influences on the state'
categorised these as threefold: ideas, economy and
organisation (Hague and Harrop, 1987, pp. 42-4). 'The level
of ideas is both the most fundamental and the most prosaic...
what happens in one country thereby alters the situation in
all others', referring to major historical events, although
this point is taken further in looking at 'the diffusion of
specific policies across nation-states' (Hague and Harrop,
p.42). This leads to discussion about how far systemic
trends, in particular the cross-national fertilisation of
values favouring democratisation, in a given area - such as
the move to democratic regimes in Latin America in the 1980s -
have a self-reinforcing dynamic. So far as Southern Europe is
concerned, this is an unresearched topic, although any
examination of the impact of the first case of authoritarian
collapse (Portugal, spring 1974) on later similar cases in
the mid-1970s is likely to show its effect as limited, with
domestic factors to the fore (O'Donnell, Schmitter and
Whitehead, 1986, Pt.1,pp.131-32).

The other two levels - the international economy,
international organisations - have already been mentioned
before. In the former instance, the question arises as to
whether 'semi-periphery' countries (a term applied also to
those in Southern Europe and their relationship with the
'core' of Western Europe) are particularly susceptible to the
influence of transnational actors, notably of an economic
kind. In a broader sense, the state of the international
economy is especially pertinent to the transitions to
democracy in the mid-1970s, since they occurred at the time of
the recession following the oil crisis. While this situation
seemed at first unfavourable for the prospects for these
transitions, as Tovias argues, it nevertheless contained
features which eventually proved supportive (Tovias, 1984,
pp.169-70). Above all, institutional networks for assistance

such as the EC and the international financial community
helped to cushion the oil shocks. Given Western concern for
political stability in the Mediterranean, these Southern
European regimes in transition were able to turn in effect a
weakness into a strength and with such international
assistance to 'postpone their day of reckoning with the
economic problems resulting from the oil crisis'
(Diamandouros, 1986,p.552).

Hence, we may hypothesise that the prospects for democratic
transition can be affected in a differentiated manner with
even positive and negative variables combining in one given
scenario. In other words, it cannot be assumed different
external sub-environments will necessarily harmonise in their
impact on regimes in transition.

A second line of approach is to utilise the **conventional
concerns of comparative politics**: structures, elites,
political parties and interest groups, issues and policies,
and even cleavages and political culture. Obviously, this
denotes various possible sources of reaction to influences or
impacts deriving from the external environment(s), similar to
Brecher's framework for unscrambling the internal operational
environment. An important empirical example of this approach
is Gourevitch's own <u>Politics in Hard Times</u> (Gourevitch,1986),
looking at why different countries make different choices in
response to world economic crisis. He tests this problem with
respect to both sectoral interests but also political
organisations and interest groups and other associations as
well as state structures. Gourevitch concludes that the power
of the variables changes over time and that their
relationships are not constant; and he argues for an eclectic,
dynamic and indeterminist treatment of the interaction of the
international context with the economy, society and the
political system (Gourevitch, 1986).

Thus, one may speak of actor-oriented or sectoral linkages in
the decision process, as with parties' transnational links and
of course those cultivated by different elite groups,
including economic ones, with outside actors.   These may have
a direct or indirect bearing on the transition process.   For
instance, political parties whether supportive of liberal
democracy or 'anti-system' may benefit from the support of an
external actor, whether a fraternal party or even a foreign
government. At a sensitive moment of decision, such an
external linkage may help to influence the balance of domestic
forces and thus affect the dynamics of regime change,
dependent no doubt on other variables favouring this
possibility. Indeed, in this respect, the systems analysis
model of Easton looking at 'gatekeepers' channelling demands
and support to political authorities can without difficulty be

extended to include pressures from the international environment.

Similarly, the question of cleavages should include an international dimension, namely whether and to what degree an international cleavage is salient, as for instance it undoubtedly was in the postwar Italian transition. Work on political culture has usually taken insufficient account of the influence of international problems; and, at least, there must be a strong case for looking at elite political culture in this sense over matters of regime transition.

Thirdly, some comparative work has focussed on problems relating in one way or other to **problems of regime change**. This is first of all true of a number of studies dealing with the importance of international factors in explaining revolutions and also political crises in regimes, usually by use of historical case-studies (Almond, 1989, pp.252-54). As Panebianco has commented, 'the principal modern revolutions have had as catalysts dynamics connected with political/international strategy interaction... it is rare for a political regime to collapse , even if afflicted by the absence of a dominant coalition, by grave problems of legitimacy and/or efficiency, without a change in the international conjuncture intervening' (Panebianco,1986, pp. 472-3). As historians will point out, the major international causes of regime breakdown are war and international economic crises, but there are other less dramatic ways in which this may happen, such as the impact of the international security environment and also significant developments in other countries (e.g. their own revolutions or regime transitions).

On another level of analysis, **theories of modernisation** are vaguely relevant to comparative approaches to regime change. This is partly because they are concerned among other things with pressures which arise from different degrees of development between states; and also, empirically speaking, as the Southern European countries have evidenced far-reaching socio-economic change in precisely the period leading up to and beyond their own experiences of democratic transition (Williams, 1984, chap.1). This at once presents the attractive theme of the interaction between socio-economic and political change or modernisation. And, as modernisation theories only emphasise, this must be considered as part of a global or international development.

However, modernisation is usually a complex process. As Black has pointed out, there are some ambiguities in applying the concept of modernity. In particular, it is important to avoid identifying modernisation automatically with the development of democratic institutions (Black, 1976, p.15). While there is evidence of some connection between technological change in society and democratic attitudes, nonetheless 'it is remarkably clear from recent history that no deterministic link exists' here (Black, 1976, p. 15). In other words, other factors which may not be easily categorised alongside this connection may also have an important influence.

From the foregoing, it is clear that by focussing on many of the same problems comparative politics is very complementary to "linkage politics" theory in international relations. Since together they combine both 'inner-directed' and 'outer-directed' linkages, it is essential, therefore, to marry their concerns. As Gourevitch put it, 'in using domestic structure as a variable in explaining foreign policy, we must explore the extent to which that structure itself derives from the exigencies of the international system' (Gourevitch, 1978, p.882). He was also critical of much of the literature on this point for stressing structural features of domestic systems 'regardless of the content of the interests seeking goals through public policy or the political orientation of the persons in control of the state machine' (Gourevitch, 1978, p.882). This reminds us of the approach of genetic theories of regime transition, but on this we can also draw some lessons from historical work.

5. Historical Experience and the International Context of Democratic Transition

From historical literature one usually expects new empirical insights into the kinds of questions so far raised. This is to some extent reinforced by most of the literature being in the form of country-studies. However, comparative history has produced some relevant results, and the first and in some cases the best studies of the **specific impact of the international environment on domestic politics** have come from historians in this field (Almond, 1989, p.239). In a review of this work, Almond came to the view 'that the penetration of domestic politics by the international environment is not only a matter of dramatic events but is a constant process at medium and lower levels of visibility, affecting political, economic and social stability in both positive and negative ways' (Almond, 1989, p.254).

The task here, as before, is to see how far such work has a bearing on our theme of regime change and especially the dynamics of the transition process. Primarily, this has more often than not dwelt on external constraints impinging on the internal characteristics of states. Thus, Hintze pursued a complex interplay between the international context, social and political structures, military technology and foreign

policy in interpreting the development of the European state
system, and drew conclusions about a relationship between
constitutional systems and geostrategic situations and
international power politics (Almond, 1989, pp.242-5). This
general approach, while perhaps tending to overstate the
impact of international power politics, serves to illustrate
abundantly the dynamics of the domestic/international
interplay in action. And such historical work might at least
help in avoiding the pitfalls of the circular reasoning
mentioned above by Gourevitch.

At a more basic level, historical analysis helps to identify
the actual salience and influence of international factors in
regime change. In doing so, one may adapt Almond's hypothesis
about the penetration of domestic politics. That is, a
distinction may be drawn between 'developments' (as continuous
or longer-term) and 'events' (one-off occurrences). This
departs from Rosenau's view of 'penetration', but the point
here is that the relatively brief period of democratic
transition - as an occasion of high uncertainty, to borrow a
phrase from transition theory - may indeed be particularly or
even temporarily open to the impact of outside events. What
therefore matters here is their timing. At the same time,
such 'events' may either be a culmination of 'developments';
or, perhaps more pertinent to our discussion, they may
interact with domestic developments in a way that instigates
the shift to democratisation.

The two Southern European transitions to democracy in 1974
demonstrate this argument in different ways. In July 1984,
the leaders of the Greek military junta were compelled by
their military defeat over Cyprus by the Turks to hand over
government to Karamanlis, who returned from exile. This seems
a fairly straightforward case of an outside event prompting
regime change, but in fact it was also a catalyst for change
following a prior process of disintegration of the Colonels'
regime. One may also note that international opinion had to
varying degrees been hostile to the military dictatorship,
although this was apparently not decisive in the collapse of
this regime; and it is in any case difficult to measure the
exact influence of that kind of environment. At the same
time, while the crisis over Cyprus led directly to the regime
change - it created a decisive opportunity - it was no
guarantee of a successful democratisation.

In the Portuguese case, we have a classic instance of the
corrosive effects of unsuccessful and increasingly unpopular
colonial wars on the domestic system. There was a direct
causal link between these wars and the military coup of 25
April 1974, as the (domestic) event which led to
democratisation, because of the radicalising influences of
their African experience on the middle-ranking officers who

led the coup. Equally, the subsequent domestic turbulence that marked the Portuguese democratic transition during 1974-76 suggested at first glance that international considerations withdrew from centre stage. But the course of events only showed there was quite some fluctuation in the interplay between domestic and international developments, a sequence perhaps best conveyed by close historical analysis. For instance, there were moments during the highly unstable year of 1975 when Western concern over Portuguese affairs was intense, being high on the NATO agenda and the subject of some covert intervention (Maxwell, 1986, p. 131).

As previously noted, there is considerable national variation between the different cases of democratic transition in this respect. Thus, the Spanish example tends to show that external factors were probably much less decisive in terms of influential transition events, although there is undoubtedly a case for considering how the international economic environment in the form of longer-term developments may have affected regime change. There is firstly an analytical and methodological problem in trying to evaluate such a relationship. But there may also be a simple problem of historical evidence if we are talking about the full story behind the impact of international influences.

Here, the difficulty is the lack of hard evidence on some aspects of the more recent transitions to democracy for reasons of official restrictions on archival sources. It is no surprise that the Italian postwar transition is the best documented so far as international influences are concerned. Some recently published research-based studies on the American role in immediate postwar Italy provide several insights into the transition process there, revealing in tortuous detail the interplay between American concerns and assumptions and Italian interests and calculations (Miller, 1986; Harper, 1986). Even so, historical evidence does not always satisfy. As Couloumbis has pointed in a discussion of U.S. influence in Greece and Turkey:

> 'Some insight into the covert aspects of contemporary affairs can be gained by reviewing historical works based on archival materials which have been declassified (usually 30 to 50 years after the fact). Even here, however, governments concerned with protecting their images rather than indiscriminately opening all data to public scrutiny, may decide never to release certain embarrassing "details" ' (Couloumbis, 1983-4, pp. 44-45).

Obviously, this concerns particular kinds of activities (notably, covert), but it has to be estimated how much such matters may really be relevant for the transition process.

Also, there are international 'events' which do not require
special inside information for assessing their importance.

In conclusion, historical experience teaches us a few familiar
or less familiar lessons. By and large, historical tools if
available allow for a more subtle appreciation of the
interaction between external and internal environments and
their components, as discussed in this paper.   Apart from
that, the historical approach emphasises once more the
importance of considering the international context with
reference to different time periods.

**6. A Framework for the International Context of Democratic
Transition: examples from Southern Europe**

From the preceding survey of different approaches in
transition theory, international affairs, comparative politics
and historical work, it is evident there is substantial scope
for empirical research on the international context of
democratic transition – a theme which fills an important gap
in the literature both on regime transition and also to some
extent on "linkage politics".   These different disciplinary
approaches have strongly influenced the framework, described
in the appendix to this paper.   Indeed, in many respects,
they are not only complementary; they also overlap or confirm
the importance of key variables.

The main analytical problem, however, is not establishing the
relevance of the international dimension of regime change.   It
is not even that of identifying explicit linkages, for the
literature surveyed contributes much in this way.   Rather, the
main problem is one of causality, of analysing what Almond has
called 'the complex dynamic process' of interaction between
international factors and domestic processes.

As noted earlier in this paper, the method of "linkage
politics" was an important development in confronting this
interaction, but it tended to produce broad schemes which
remained too open-ended for systematic analysis.   While the
kind of approaches discussed above generally run some risk of
producing an eclectic framework, nevertheless the particular
focus on democratic transition and hence a certain temporal
span facilitates thematic cohesion; and, again, its
application to a certain region makes for specificity.

As argued above, this framework merges the two directions of
"linkage politics": the 'outer' direction from the study of
international affairs; the 'inner' direction from the study of
comparative politics and also regime transition theory; while
historical work deals to some extent with both.   As such, the

framework is based on these two directions and their sub-environments. At the same time, the importance of background conditions as highlighted by both transition theory and historical work is recognised.   As such, there is therefore a strict orientation in this version of "linkage politics" but also sufficient flexibility for national variation, and indeed also temporal variation, taking account of Italy (later 1940s) and Turkey (1980s) as well as the three cases of transition in Iberia and Greece in the mid/later 1970s.

In looking at these cases, it is possible to identify general and specific conclusions concerning the importance of the international context for democratic transition in Southern Europe.   Common patterns of interaction between the external environment and domestic system change emerge notwithstanding national-specific experience, and even though our theme is indeed complex.   These results are best summarised with reference to the comparative framework outlined in the appendix; and they draw on contributions on the five countries and on different actors in the international environment in Geoffrey Pridham (ed.), Encouraging Democracy: the international context of regime transition in Southern Europe (Leicester University Press, 1991).

Looking at **introductory themes (A)**, the focus is rather more on longer-term developments relating both to the national-specific (historical background; system 'penetrated-ness') as well as to the common overall process of system change (phases of regime transition) than on the shorter-term dynamics of the transition process itself.   The first of these developments, as one would expect, is likely to highlight cross-national differences.   Some of the national studies reveal a greater emphasis than others on individual historical background as salient to our theme, such as those on Greece and Turkey in particular.   Indeed, Karaosmanoglu underlines Turkey's strong difference, if not separatedness, from the other countries in terms of historical and cultural, not to mention religious, evolution, while at the same time participating in the European states system.

Historical background invariably reveals the degrees of international 'penetration' of domestic systems, which may either be conducted by a foreign power (USA in postwar Greece, also in postwar Italy) or alternatively assume a less tangible form such as socio-economic pressures from the European environment, e.g. economic modernisation pressures in Spain; cultural modernisation pressures in Turkey.   It follows these external agents or developments are likely to exert a powerful influence on regime transition, by preparing the way for it (more so in the latter case) as well as through direct impact during the process itself (more so in the former case).

This is broadly suggested by the various national studies,
where Italy and Greece emerge as the most obvious cases of
'penetrated systems' in the sense defined by Rosenau: in both
countries external allegiances played a major part in
transition politics. But a difference is also evident: Greece
was an historically-determined case of 'penetration', as in a
different way is Turkey; while in postwar Italy such
'penetration' really only commenced with her regime transition
but then it subsequently influenced political attitudes in the
new system, not least because it formed one of the major
political cleavages between political parties. In mid-1970s
Portugal, 'penetration' was also situational rather than
historical but not so long-lasting as in the Italian case -
therefore, questioning her being such a clear-cut case of a
'penetrated system' in Rosenau's eyes.

As to phases of the transition process, our concern is with
placing this in a wider context. For instance, 'pre-
transition' developments when the authoritarian system in
question begins to disintegrate and eventually collapses or is
overthrown may link longer-term change with the immediate
'shift' to transition. This phase may overlap with the kind
of 'penetrative' pressures mentioned above, or at least
highlight their effects.   Whitehead suggests such ·
international pressures may interact with divisions within
authoritarian systems increasingly on the defensive; while
Pridham applies this to the role of European organisations in
'pre-transition'.   The latter found the decisive variable is
the scope or potential for interaction with domestic
conditions (such as oppositional activity, public response and
weaknesses or divisions within the regime); but, in general,
European organisations impinged rather more as a longer-term
pressure for regime change than as an immediate determinant of
the shift to democratisation.

External developments or events can also be decisive in the
inauguration phase of transition, notably in the Greek and
Portuguese cases, namely in providing the final stimulus to
system change.   As Opello reveals in his review of the
latter, it is how such occurrences interact with the dynamics
of a domestic situation open to system transformation.   On
balance, he sees the international context as more important
than the domestic in determining the actual process of
transition in Portugal.   But there is nothing deterministic in
this and the other cases about the impact of external
influences: the latter were 'confining conditions' but
domestic actors still exerted a choice in their course of
action and in its timing.

But 'transition events' may also contribute to the outcome of
the process, in securing the option of liberal democracy.   The
best single example from our five countries is the 1948

national election in Italy, when the clear-cut victory for the Christian Democrats (DC) both crystallised the pro-system direction of transition dynamics and clarified Italy's international allegiance to the West. Altogether, then, distinguishing between its different phases does facilitate any assessment of the overall rhythm of the transition process. Thus, we can identify key points of time when its evolution might have taken a different course and in turn measure here the likely impact of external factors.

Turning to **Inner-Directed Linkages (B)**, the common geopolitical environment of the Southern European transitions is emphasised by Segal, in reference to the Northern Mediterranean flank's strategic importance. This is largely confirmed by the national studies, although differences emerge between the E. Mediterranean cases – notably, Turkey – as more vulnerable to externally inspired destabilisation, and those in the W. Mediterranean (the Iberian countries). Italy is really in a separate sub-category, for her crucial geopolitical location in centre of the Mediterranean was enhanced by the then emerging Cold War in the later 1940s. Inevitably, one by-effect of geopolitical considerations was to lend an anti-Communist theme to regime transition in most of these cases, although to differing degrees.

The national cases taken together underline the relevance of different time contexts concerning the impact of the international environment. Indeed, the virtual contrast between the Cold War context of the Italian case and the detente context of the three transitions of the mid-1970s mattered considerably in one particular way. While the USA felt compelled as the postwar situation evolved to intervene in Italian domestic politics and to establish a client relationship with the main pro-West transition actor, the DC (see Leonardi); in the other cases, as Tovias shows, the same foreign power took a much less interventionist line a generation later precisely because the international situation allowed it, even though the same technique of a link with an internal transition actor was adopted. At the same time, the role of the USSR appeared as less of a threat notwithstanding moments, as over Portugal in 1975, when this seemed otherwise.

We can therefore start concluding on the influence of different external actors on the Southern European transitions. As to foreign power 'penetration' of democratisation, the USA gave a fairly clear top priority to strategic or global motives, as Tovias demonstrates. With Italy, this outside influence nevertheless had a decisive result in that alternative system options or international allegiances were effectively excluded, with liberal democracy the outcome. In the case of postwar Greece, there was a similar outcome following the crucial American role in the

victory of the Right in the Civil War, but the postwar system
that ensued lacked consensus and really failed to consolidate.
The restoration of parliamentary democracy after the interlude
of the Colonels' rule was however marked by a widespread
reaction against this American connection, discussed by Verney
and Couloumbis. Thus, foreign power 'penetration' can produce
both positive and negative impacts on regime change; and in
the Greek case this allowed the country in question to shuffle
off its subordinate link with the superpower.

In fact, the three transitions of the 1970s - as also the
Turkish transition in the 1980s - really featured the European
Community as the principal external actor.   The EC and its
networks had created an ambience with significant potential
for influencing internal change in a variety of ways, as the
chapters by Whitehead, Sidjanski and Pridham show. These
forms of influence ranged from moral support through economic
assistance to political leverage, and they were perhaps more
subtle than those exerted by a dominant foreign power.   They
tended to be multilateral rather than bilateral, although some
EC member states exercised a greater influence than others;
and they included both intangible consequences (like promoting
democratic values, as Whitehead and Pridham indicate) and more
direct effects, as in resolving the question of the
international allegiance of new democracies following the
upheaval of regime transition.   Again, Greece is a pertinent
case here for the conscious adoption by Karamanlis of the
European option provided a real alternative to the previous
status of US satellite.   Hence, a link became established
between external policy redirection and new system
reinforcement.

Socio-economic forms of external 'penetration' are less easy
to evaluate, whether seen as deriving from European
organisations or from broader developments.   As the example
of Spain demonstrates, economic modernisation occurring a
decade or more beforehand created its own pressures in favour
of political liberalisation and later democratisation.   In
Turkey, the internationalisation of the economy as well as
some specific forms of 'system penetration' through links with
Western Europe at different levels (e.g. military, also social
esp. over human rights) also opened the way for influences
promotive of democracy, these coming into play particularly
during the transition process.   Such interactive dynamics
involving on the one side economic change (modernisation) and
on the other political change (democratisation) is explored
comparatively by Sidjanski in his analysis of national
interest groups and their involvement in the EC network, this
both strengthening their own role as economic actors and in
turn promoting political pluralism in these countries
undergoing transition.

On examining **Outer-Directed Linkages (C)**, it becomes all the
more evident that eventually - as Whitehead argues -
disaggregating internal and external factors is somewhat
artificial, and that the boundary between them is blurred.
However, as a point of departure, the one-directional focus as
above assists in identifying relevant determinants of the
transition process.   Thus, the operational and domestic
environments in these countries both had important and fairly
early effects on their behaviour towards the international
environment.   That is, embarking on democratic transition
opened the way for a different political structure and
distribution of power and for new political elites, usually
with different views and expectations of this environment.
This in turn made it possible for external influences to
operate more openly and freely so far as these countries were
concerned.

Focussing on this outer-direction also tends to emphasise the
relevant short-term perspectives of the transition process.
So, while geopolitical and European pressures perhaps made
probable the outcome of liberal democracy, the intrinsic
uncertainty of transition as seen at the time only intensified
the way in which domestic actors, among other things, looked
outwards.   This was more apparent in the Italian and
Portuguese cases than say with Greece and Spain by virtue of
the systemic outcome of transition being contested or less
taken for granted in the former countries.

When we look at domestic actors, there is much evidence of
their 'boundary crossing' behaviour.   For example,
international support proved very desirable for democratic
oppositions during 'pre-transition' (Whitehead, Pridham).
Later, there are several notable examples of transition actors
(political figures, also political parties) incorporating
designedly an international dimension to their transition
strategies by looking to external allies to bolster their
internal positions, a clear case of this being Portugal
(Opello).   In general, parties are a prominent instance of
non-governmental organisations seeking outside reference
points in their struggle for both political power and also
system support.   This tendency was rather nationally variant.
It was strongest in the Iberian cases and for different
reasons less important in the others: the non-existence yet of
such transnational ideological links in the Italian
transition; reluctance over them or problems of identifying
the right links on the part of Greece and Turkey.

With non-political elites, the pattern was somewhat different.
Economic circles had an obvious interest motive in looking
outwards for commercial opportunities, whether or not they
consciously thought in terms of encouraging political system
change.   On specific matters, as Sidjanski explains, interest

groups sought to enhance their own legitimacy through closer
involvement in the European network.

As to military elites, any answer has to be rather national-
specific depending on their role in the previous authoritarian
system and the manner of transition, e.g. the latter served to
discredit the military particularly in postwar Italy but also
in Greece, while in Spain the consensual approach dissuaded
from any confrontation with them.   If there is a common
pattern, it is that international influences favouring the
military's retraction from politics also promote democratic
transition.   As Verney and Couloumbis show, the 'Turkish
factor' served to direct the military's attention away from
domestic politics in the transition period.   Similarly, in
post-Franco Spain, there was the belief that the military's
involvement in NATO would help to recondition their political
outlook to conform with the new democracy.

In **Conclusion (D)**, we are now in a better position to make an
overall assessment of the importance of the international
context for the Southern European transitions. By and large,
these comparative and national studies confirm this made a
significant difference both in generally promoting trends of
democratisation and in loading the dice in favour of
successful transition to liberal democracy. More
specifically, international influences also contributed in
important ways at crucial moments of the transition process,
as noted above.   Broadly speaking, these two conclusions are
more or less equivalent respectively to the functionalist and
genetic schools of regime transition theory. Taken together,
they present a convincing argument for not underrating the
international context in studies of regime transition; and it
has been in previous work on the Southern European cases.

7.Conclusion

Whether the international context is secondary to domestic
developments is less clear-cut than originally assumed at the
outset, as suggested in the theoretical or comparative
literature discussed earlier in this paper.

Southern European experience shows there are different
national cases and different kinds of external actors, with
different degrees of influence, as well as different time
contexts and different phases of transition. Despite
similarities of experience and common patterns to them, this
variation does make for some caution in generalising in any
such way about the relative value of internal and external
factors.   Overall, however, one can say that the external

environment did make a significant difference to the
democratic transitions in Southern Europe, in terms of
external actors - whether foreign powers or European
organisations - enjoying various mechanisms for influencing
developments in these countries and elites within them looking
outwards in their operation as transition actors.

Common patterns among contemporaneous transitions have of
course been highlighted all the more by the experience of
Eastern Europe from 1989. Here, we are talking many more
countries undergoing system change - both economic and
political - in the very same period. Clearly, too, there is
a common international environment whether we are referring to
the traditional relationship with the Soviet super-power, now
being abandoned in most cases, or the theme of the "return to
Europe" - namely, the development of new links with the
European Community and its member states, with the Federal
Republic of Germany at the forefront. There is a distinct
pattern, especially in the northern half of the area, of an
outer-directed concern with strengthening links with Western
Europe, whether economic or commercial, political or even
cultural. In certain cases, a future membership of the EC -
and maybe some halfway solution in the meantime - is presented
as an important component of these countries' successful
transitions to liberal democracy. At the same time, it is
already apparent there is significant cross-national variation
in the actual mode of transition and also to some extent in
the problems encountered by these new democracies.

Finally, it is clear from the examples of Southern Europe that
the focus here on democratic transition cannot exclude some
consideration of the subsequent process of democratic
consolidation. This is not merely because in given cases,
notably Italy, it is difficult to determine exactly when
transition actually ended. It is also necessary as some
effects of external actors or influences carry through well
into the consolidation period. This was notably true of the
impact of European organisations, especially the EC, as
Sidjanski and Pridham and certain national studies
demonstrate. The impact of European integration increases
with time, particularly with regard to its structural effects
on new member states and their economies, as distinct from the
politics of regime transition. On the other hand, some
decisions by external actors had, more obviously, an impact
during the transition process itself such as those taken by
the USA with regard to postwar Italy and perhaps by European
countries concerning Portugal in 1975.

34

(This occasional paper is a rewritten version of the author's introductory chapter in Geoffrey Pridham (ed.), Encouraging Democracy: the international context of regime transition in Southern Europe (Leicester University Press, 1991)

REFERENCES

Almond, G., 1989, Review article: the international-national connection, British Journal of Political Science, April: 237 -59

Baloyra, E. (ed.), Comparing New Democracies: transition and consolidation in Mediterranean Europe and the Southern Cone, Westview Press, Boulder

Black, C. (ed.), 1976, Comparative Modernization, Free Press, New York

Boyd, G., Hopple, G.,W.(ed.), 1987, Political Change and Foreign Policies, Frances Pinter, London

Brecher, M., 1972, The Foreign Policy System of Israel, Oxford University Press, London

Clarke, M., 1986, Foreign policy and comparative politics, Politics, October: 3-9

Couloumbis, T., 1983-84, Assessing the potential of US influence in Greece and Turkey: a theoretical perspective, Hellenic Review of International Relations: 27-50

Deutsch, K., 1966, External influences on the internal behaviour of states, in R.B. Farrell (ed.), Approaches to Comparative and International Politics, Northwestern University Press, Evanston: 5-26

Diamandouros, N. The Southern European NICs, International Organization, spring 1986: 547-56

Falk, R., 1981, The global setting and transition to democracy, Smithsonian Institution, Washington, paper

Geller, D., 1985, Domestic Factors in Foreign Policy, Schenkman Books, Cambridge, Mass.

Gourevitch, P., 1978, The second image reversed: the international sources of domestic politics, International Organisation, autumn: 881-911

Gourevitch,P., 1986, Politics in Hard Times: Comparative

35

Responses to International Economic Crises.Cornell Univer
sity Press,Ithaca.

Hagan, J., 1987, Regimes, political oppositions and the
comparative analysis of foreign policy, in C. Hermann, C.
Kegley and J. Rosenau (eds.), New Directions in the Study of
Foreign Policy, Allen & Unwin, Boston: 339-365

Hague, R., Harrop, M., 1987, Comparative Government and
Politics, Macmillan, Basingstoke

Hanrieder, W., 1978, Dissolving international politics:
reflections on the nation-state, American Political Science
Review, December: 1276-87

Harper, J., 1986, America and the Reconstruction of Italy,
1945-48, Cambridge University Press, Cambridge

Hermann, C., Kegley, C., Rosenau, J.(ed.), 1987, New
Directions in the Study of Foreign Policy, Allen & Unwin,
Boston

Karns, M, Mingst, K., 1987, International organisations and
foreign policy, in C. Hermann, C. Kegley, J. Rosenau (eds.),
New Directions in the Study of Foreign Policy, Allen & Unwin,
Boston: 454-74

Kirchheimer, O., 1965, Confining conditions and revolutionary
breakthroughs, American Political Science Review, December:
964-74

Lawson, K., 1985, The Human Polity, Houghton Mifflin, Boston

Maxwell, K., 1986, Regime overthrow and the prospects for
democratic transition in Portugal, in G. O'Donnell, P.
Schmitter, L. Whitehead (eds.), Transitions from Authoritarian
Rule, John Hopkins University Press, Baltimore: 109-37

Miller, J., The United States and Italy, 1940-50, University
of North Carolina Press, Chapel Hill

Morlino, L., 1980, Come cambiano i regimi politici, Franco
Angeli, Milan

Morlino, L., 1986, Consolidamento democratico: alcune ipotesi
esplicative, Rivista Italiana di Scienza Politica, December:
439-59

Morlino, L., 1987, Democratic establishments: a dimensional
analysis, in E. Baloyra (ed.), Comparing New Democracies,
Westview Press, Boulder: 53-78

36

O'Donnell, G., Schmitter, P., Whitehead, L. (eds.), 1986, Transitions from Authoritarian Rule: prospects for democracy, John Hopkins University Press, Baltimore

Panebianco, A., 1986, La dimensione internazionale dei processi politici, in G. Pasquino (ed.), Manuale di Scienza della Politica-tica,Il Mulino,Bologna:431-99

Pasquino, G., 1986, The demise of the first Fascist regimeand Italy's transition to democracy, in G. O'Donnell,P.Schmitter, L. Whitehead (eds.), Transitions from Authoritarian Rule, John Hopkins University Press, Baltimore: 45-70

Pridham, G., 1984, Comparative perspectives on the new Mediterranean democracies: a model of regime transition?, in Pridham, G. (ed.), The New Mediterranean Democracies:regime transition in Spain, Greece and Portugal, Frank Cass, London: 1-29

Rosenau, J., 1966, Pre-theories and theories of foreign policy, in R.B. Farrell (ed.), Approaches to Comparative and International Politics, Northwestern University Press, Evanston

Rosenau, J., 1969, Linkage Politics: essays on the convergence of national and international systems, Free Press, New York

Rosenau, J., 1970, Foreign policy as adaptive behaviour,Comparative Politics, April: 365-87

Rustow, D., 1970, Transitions to democracy: toward a dynamic model, Comparative Politics, April: 337-63

Santamaria, J.(ed.), 1982, Transicion a la Democracia en el Sur de Europa y America Latina, Centro de Investigaciones Sociologicas, Madrid

Schmitter, P., 1985, The consolidation of political democracy in Southern Europe (and Latin America), European University Institute, paper

Tovias, A., 1984, The international context of democratic transition, in G. Pridham (ed.), The New Mediterranean Democracies, Frank Cass, London: 158-71

Wallace, H., 1977, National bulls in the Community china shop, in H. Wallace, W. Wallace, C. Webb (eds.), Policy-Making in the European Community, John Wiley, London

Webb, C., 1983, Theoretical perspectives and problems, in H. Wallace, C. Webb and W. Wallace (eds.), Policy-Making in the European Community, John Wiley, London: 1-41

Whitehead, L., 1986, International aspects of democratisation, in G. O'Donnell, P. Schmitter and L. Whitehead (eds.), <u>Transitions from Authoritarian Rule</u>, John Hopkins University Press, Baltimore: Pt. 3, 3-46

Whitehead, L., 1988, The consolidation of fragile democracies, European Consortium for Political Research (ECPR), paper

Williams, A. (ed), 1984, <u>Southern Europe Transformed</u>, Harper & Row, London

38

```
┌─────────────────────────────────────────────────────────────┐
│                     A P P E N D I X                          │
└─────────────────────────────────────────────────────────────┘
```

THE INTERNATIONAL CONTEXT OF DEMOCRATIC TRANSITION IN
SOUTHERN EUROPE: A COMPARATIVE FRAMEWORK

(A) INTRODUCTION

(Briefly) relevant background patterns and factors:
geopolitical situation; historical and cultural factors;
potential for system 'penetrated-ness'

Nature of democratic transition and scope for external
influences

Identification of different phases: pre-transition
pressures; inauguration of transition; process of
transition; outcome of transition, looking towards
democratic consolidation

(B) INNER-DIRECTED LINKAGES

International Environment(s) during Democratic Transition:

- Time Context/Geopolitical situation: significant
international events

- Phases of Democratic Transition in this respect

- International Economy: socio-economic modernisation
pressures

- International organisations: EC, NATO, IMF

- Bilateral links with other countries: W. Europe, USA,
USSR

Themes: Sources of external influence - political,
diplomatic, economic, moral, covert; democratisation by
international 'incorporation', by 'contagion'; a case of
'confining conditions'

(C) OUTER-DIRECTED LINKAGES/RESPONDING TO INNER-DIRECTED LINKAGES

(i) The Operational Environment

Structures of government in the different phases of democratic transition; how the changing system/distribution of power relates to external linkages

Political uncertainties in democratic transition: problems of government stability under the new democracy; external policy continuity

(ii) Domestic Linkage Actors and 'Crossing the Boundary'

Different elite groups: their motivation, extent to which they developed 'international dimensions' to their strategies in democratic transition or not, their transnational links

Pre-transition phase: role of opposition groups under previous dictatorship and how much dependent on international links

Political elites and political parties: strategies, preferences and options

Economic elites, business community, economic interest groups

Military elites: how their (changing?) position during transition is related to external considerations

Other elites, where relevant, e.g. bureaucratic

Themes: motivation as long- or short-term; political choice - variation in response to international environment, forms of response (penetrative, reactive, emulative)

(iii) Domestic Environment

Existence or not of international cleavage/division of opinion over issues during transition period

Internal cohesion: political opposition

Media/communications; public opinion

Expectations of relationship with the EC

(iv) Brief overall assessment

40

(D) CONCLUSION

Relating the two directions of linkages; national-specific aspects within a comparative perspective
Has the international environment made a significant difference to democratic transition? E.g. effects on nature, intensity or relative importance of transition problems; effect as long- or short-term, direct or indirect
What international pressures have been most conducive to transition? Are these dependent or crucial intervening variables?
Summary re: phases of democratic transition: looking towards democratic consolidation in the light of the international context

[24]

The International Context of Democratic Transition

Alfred Tovias

INTRODUCTION

Many scholars have stressed that the failure of the Second Spanish Republic was largely due to internatonal factors and events not under the control of those who had succeeded initially in performing a peaceful transition from the dictatorship of Primo de Rivera (1923–9) to the republic in 1931. Economic historians have produced clear-cut evidence of the tremendous impact that the world economic crisis had on the Spanish economy, with some years of delay in relation not only to the USA (where it had already started in 1929) but also in relation to other European countries (where it hit by early 1931), notably in Germany where the Depression was crucially instrumental in the collapse of the Weimar Republic.

One could say, so the argument goes, that 'double bad luck' contributed considerably to the end of the Second Spanish Republic. As from 1932, Spain had to confront the inevitable adjustment to a deteriorated world economic situation at a time when domestically the public was expecting economic miracles from the republic. Three or four years later, with a domestic economic crisis still present, political, diplomatic and military developments abroad (e.g. the rise to power of the Popular Front in France, or the invasion of Ethiopia by Italy) were to have an immediate impact on the Spanish domestic political scene. But by that time the experiment was already doomed, for international economic factors played a larger role than international political developments in the failure of the Second Republic.

Up to what point can we draw an historical parallel with the democratic transition that has taken place in Spain, Greece and Portugal since the mid 1970s in a period of economic crisis? If the 'bad luck' theory is right what functioned differently this time, given the relative success of the present democratic experiments? Or if the differences between the two settings are not striking, is the theory therefore irrelevant? In that event, should one resort to an alternative theory?

The focus of this chapter is on international factors with relevant linkages to domestic developments. The discussion follows a chronological approach by periods, and for two reasons the economic calendar is preferred to the diplomatic one: first, because the 'bad luck' thesis mentioned above favours the economic explanation; second, because the three countries being considered fall clearly under the western sphere of influence and have not been subject to any serious east/west competition for their loyalty. Four periods have marked economic developments in the western world:

1. 1945–73: Reconstruction and boom of the western economies.
2. 1973–9: Economic crisis and partial adjustment to the first oil shock.
3. 1979–82: Economic crisis and adjustment to the second oil shock.
4. 1982–?: Recovery?

INTERNATIONAL CONTEXT OF DEMOCRATIC TRANSITION   159

Diplomatic factors will also be taken into consideration, especially as the Middle East during this period became a theatre of increasing confrontation, although they constitute a secondary dimension to the economic explanation.

THE PRE-1973 PERIOD: A STORY OF BOOM AND DIPLOMATIC STABILITY

That the general economic prosperity of the west in the 1960s had a beneficial impact on these three countries is indisputable. In the 1960s and up to 1973, Spain, Portugal and Greece enjoyed higher rates of growth than the Six or the Nine. While in the latter GDP increased in volume on average by an annual rate of 4 to 5 per cent, in the three southern European countries annual growth rates revolved around the 6 to 8 per cent mark.[1] It is commonly agreed that the tourism boom, combined with the absorption by other OECD countries of cheap labour from southern Europe and a boom of direct investment into that area, had a tremendous influence on the balance of payments and the growth rates of the three countries.

The three dictatorships followed this change, but were not responsible for it although, to be sure, they facilitated growth by opening up their economies. In the case of Spain (1959), the government was almost forced to do it to prevent a collapse of the economy and with it possibly of the regime. The OECD boom undoubtedly contributed to the survival of the Spanish and Greek dictatorships. Portugal is a *sui generis* case, in that it still behaved as a colonial power with the economy largely directed towards the colonies. However, as V. Curzon has shown,[2] Portugal was the main beneficiary of EFTA's creation, suggesting that the country was not so closed in the 1960s, as sometimes said, to western economic influence.

Democratic Europe did not counteract actively any of the adaptive policies implemented by the dictatorships. To be sure, some of their opponents in the Benelux countries tried to limit the degree of the EEC's economic co-operation with Franco's Spain by rejecting Spain's economic integration into the EEC beyond the partial preferential agreement formula.[3] There was also the 'freeze' imposed on the EEC association agreement with Greece at the time of the military junta. However, in the two cases, this resistance was economically unimportant. In other words, the liberalisation of the three economies proceeded essentially with the acquiescence of all the OECD countries, and not only of the USA. It is still an open question whether this acquiescence occurred for self-interest reasons or was part of a plan for bringing those three countries to a higher level of economic development, thereby allowing for a smooth transition to a western-type democracy. In the opinion of this author, the first explanation seems the more convincing, for there was no evidence of a debate in Europe or in the USA on the latter theme in the 1960s.

Turning briefly to the strategic front up to the mid-1970s, NATO's southern flank seemed unchallenged. Portugal, Greece and Turkey were fully-fledged members of the Alliance and Spain had been firmly attached to the west by a bilateral agreement with the USA since 1953. US bases in Greece and Turkey controlled the sea lanes in the Aegean, and covered the eastern Mediterranean and the Middle East. Even though by the end of the 1960s and beginning of the

1970s the US Sixth Fleet began to be challenged by the Soviet Eskadra, the stategic implications of this had so far not been far-reaching, since the Suez Canal remained closed.

ECONOMIC AND STRATEGIC CONSEQUENCES OF THE FIRST OIL SHOCK FOR THE THREE COUNTRIES

From the end of 1973, the rapid increase in the price of oil was to have two devastating consequences for the economic situation of the three countries. A direct one came clearly from the fact that Greece, Portugal and Spain were among the most energy-dependent countries in the OECD. According to the International Energy Agency (IEA), Spain's oil imports accounted in 1980 for about 68 per cent of her total primary energy consumption. In 1978, the import of oil represented 28 per cent of total Spanish purchases abroad. The increased oil bill became an economic nightmare precisely for countries which had based their industrialisation strategies on abundant and cheap energy. Indirectly, they were also affected because the OECD entered a recessionary period, which was bound to hit economies that had been opened beforehand precisely in the direction of the OECD countries.

Strategically speaking, the 1973 oil crisis implied that the stakes were higher in the Mediterranean, both for western Europe and for the USA. Security of access to oil has consequently become a first-rank preoccupation, not only because unpredictable states like Algeria and Libya are important oil producers but also as much of Middle East oil moves across the Mediterranean, altogether implying that the prosperity of western Europe could easily be challenged by any aggressive attitude on the part of Mediterranean neighbours.[4] Very soon after October 1973, three governments at least (those of the USA, the UK and West Germany) realised the importance of maintaining pro-western stability in southern Europe at a time when economically this had become more difficult to achieve.

Domestic developments in the Iberian peninsula reinforced this concern. December 1973 saw the assassination in Spain of Admiral Carrero Blanco, who had been appointed by Franco to guarantee the survival of the régime after his own death, and this together with a worsening of the Basque problem created a new uncertainty. Portugal was embroiled in a colonial war which was taking a heavy toll on its economy. It began to be realised that economic prosperity could not be ensured by the current state of affairs under the two dictatorships. Backing them could now possibly provoke strong counter-reactions. Thoughts turned to the question of how to facilitate an orderly transition to democracy, not leaving any void that could be exploited by the Soviet Union. Economically, the danger seemed limited in the short run as far as Spain was concerned, for that country could take foreign loans and try to make the most of its traditionally pro-Arab policies.

In Portugal, however, events developed more quickly than expected. The economy began to decline rapidly after the revolution of April 1974, both because of the repatriation of hundreds of thousands of people from the lost colonies and also because of the world-wide economic crisis. Since Portugal was much poorer and had a lower growth record than Spain or Greece, its credit-worthiness was therefore much less. Beginning in 1974, Portugal's balance of payments, normally in surplus, moved into deficit. The GDP growth rate increased by only 1.1 per cent in 1974 and declined by 4.3 per cent in 1975. Economic destabilisation led to political destabilisation, and there was an attempted leftist coup at the end of 1975. At this stage, West Germany and the EEC backed by the US intervened. In October 1975, the Nine decided to accord extraordinary financial aid of about $200 million from the European Investment Bank and to open discussions for the improvement of the 1972 Portuguese-Community trade agreement. Later on, the loan was increased.[5] The leftist coup did not succeed, but the authorities, still unsure and facing national elections in the spring of 1976, decided to reflate. Given the low level of confidence of foreign borrowers in the ability of the new Portuguese government arising from the 1976 elections to handle the political and economic situation, there followed a second foreign exchange crisis. This time (June 1977) 14 countries decided to act under the leadership of the IMF and provided Portugal with $750 million over 18 months. Germany and the USA provided two-thirds of the total. The results were spectacular, and the balance of payments deficit was eliminated by 1979.[6]

In the case of Greece, the role of the western powers was somewhat different. The dictatorship had collapsed in July 1974 not for economic reasons but because of its foreign and defence policy failures, notably over Cyprus. In other words, the military in power failed in their own field of specialisation, and they suffered accordingly a loss of prestige.[7] The USA and NATO were rightly or wrongly seen as having supported the dictatorship, and as having condoned Turkey's invasion of Cyprus. In protest, Greece under civilian leadership withdrew from the integrated military command of NATO.[8] At the same time, the Greek lobby put pressure on the US president to take some action against Turkey (early in 1975 an arms embargo against Turkey was imposed), while the Turkish government began to speak of considering new stategic options. Thus, in the course of one year the cohesion of the entire southern flank of NATO was called into question, a situation that was to last for five years. Turkey and Greece have always been viewed as being strategically linked, something reinforced by the fact that they are geographically isolated from the rest of NATO. That is, in the case of an attack from their north, each depends on the other for support. By the same token, conflict among the two leads automatically to a cumulative deterioration of the whole southern flank's strategic position.

Not surprisingly, this problem in relation to NATO affected Greek interest in joining the European Community. Prime Minister Karamanlis could point out domestically that the EEC's commission and council of ministers had taken consistently tough positions towards the preceding military junta, such as with the 'freeze' of the 1961 Association Treaty. For both diplomatic and domestic political reasons (in the latter case a wish to buttress the new democratic regime), Karamanlis soon presented Greece's application for EEC membership in June 1975. Only the EEC commission expressed some concern over this, not only in reference to the economic consequences of Greek membership but above all because of its impact on relations with Turkey.[9] Some Greeks even wanted to assign a strategic value to membership. 'Turkey

11

will think twice before attacking an EEC country,' was a Greek statement that frightened the commission, maybe because it was not accustomed to considering strategic questions. After all, the first enlargement had not entailed this kind of consideration. The commission's hesitations were, however, pushed aside in 1976 by the council of ministers, which chose to take a calculated risk given the position of Turkey. The reasoning was the following: politically, the Community had to give a clear yes to Greece and then take care of Turkey's interests by providing further economic help, while delaying the negotiations with Greece as long as possible.

Returning to Spain, Franco's death in November 1975 opened the way for the transition, and this was backed with no hesitation by the west, including the USA. Economic adjustment to the oil shock and the western economic crisis was postponed, as with Greece, because Spain's economy was much healthier than Portugal's. Her reserves were higher, as well as her international credit-worthiness. At the same time, however, regionalist claims, non-existent in the case of Greece or Portugal, had a potentially destabilising influence especially as it could irritate an army that was more inward- than outward-looking. The Spanish army has always been extremely sensitive to any matter affecting the 'unity' of the country. A related question was whether or not the postponement of economic adjustment was necessary in order to ensure a smooth transition to democracy and hence make a military coup less likely even though there was no pattern of direct army involvement in economic and social affairs, as in Portugal. In fact, the postponement of the search for a solution to the economic problems until late in 1977 (Moncloa Pact),[10] four years after the first oil shock, was to have negative consequences. When the second oil shock broke in early 1979, the stabilisation plan had not had time to produce all the desired effects.

For both Portugal and Spain, establishing new EEC links appeared to be a second-rate priority in the first two years of their transitions. To be sure, both countries could not ignore Greece's own application for membership,[11] and this by itself precluded too long a waiting period for dealing with the issue. But neither was there urgency, as in Greece's case, on foreign policy grounds. For the new Iberian democracies, such foreign policy considerations could for the moment be shelved.

Then, at the end of 1975, the scene changed in Portugal. The Socialist Party, which had up to 1974 been anti-EEC, now saw Portugal's membership of the Community as a way of preventing a second leftist coup attempt. The socialist parties in power in Germany and the UK came to the same analysis: while, economically speaking, Portugal was not ready for membership (something stressed particularly by France), EEC membership now appeared as a political necessity. Pre-accession, as suggested by the EEC Commission, was no solution, because the important thing according to Soares was to enter the Community soon and then undergo a long transition period. In this respect, the situation was similar to Greece's. After all, so the argument went, the EEC should be able to absorb the two countries, given the small size of their economies. In other words, the price to be paid by the Community was considered small compared to the overall potential risks from leaving them out, especially in the light of the events of 1975 in Portugal and the 1977 Greek elections. The Portuguese Communist Party consistently drew 15 to 20 per cent of the popular vote, while PASOK obtained in 1977 over 25 per cent of votes in the Greek national elections. Both parties were anti-western, in so far as they postulated withdrawal from NATO, the withdrawal of US bases and non-entry into the EEC.

The context was different in the case of Spain, because her greater economic size meant substantial economic adjustment problems for the Nine after her entry. Moreover, the political costs of leaving Spain out appeared less, for there was at least no danger of destabilisation from the political left, as in Greece or Portugal. The only possible reason for pushing Spain's entry to the EEC was the chance of preventing a rightist coup, but very soon in the debate the way it appeared to some was that there was a certain political risk in having Spain in the Community, precisely because with her size a successful coup could endanger the Community itself in all kinds of ways (by 'infection', by 'paralysis', etc.). After the attempted coup in Spain in February 1981, this pessimistic line of thinking became more outspoken by stressing that Spain must first get her political house in order and then join the Community, not the other way round. It was partly for the same reason that Greece and Portugal persistently tried to show that their case was totally different, for they were trying to enter the Community before Spain and so avoid being part of a general package deal.

Given the Community's basic apathy towards Spain's candidature almost from the beginning, one wonders why the Spanish governments and parties decided to push so hard for entry, as from 1977. Was it because of distrust towards the other ally, the USA, as was the case with Greece? No. Was it to overcome geographical isolation and exclusive military, financial or economic dependence on a major power? Not really. What seems closer to the truth is that the factor of having been absent from world affairs for some time played a role in Spanish post-Franco political thinking. Entry into the EEC could be regarded as part of a general activation of Spain's foreign policy in all directions. It expressed the will to see Spain present in the world and a return to an ambitious diplomatic tradition.[12] A long list of diplomatic initiatives taken between 1976 and 1979 demonstrated this point. During that short period, Spain entered the Council of Europe, re-established diplomatic relations with the USSR after more than 40 years, participated in the Non-Aligned Summit at Havana, became a member of the UN Security Council, won the candidacy for organising in Madrid the Third Session of the European Security Conference (CSCE) to start in 1980, and became an observer at the Organisation of American States and the Andean Pact and a member of the Inter-American Development Bank.

Spanish membership of the EEC was favoured for at least three other major reasons at that time. First, it was perceived as a way of consolidating a recently born democracy. At the very least, membership should give the new Spanish regime an aura of international respectability, in contrast with the image of Franco's Spain. Second, there was the idea of participating in what was perceived in Spain as the 'European adventure' from which she had been separated since its inception. Spaniards have tended to think rather idealistically in terms of the original movement for European unity, without taking sufficient account of the complex and somewhat disappointing reality of the Community. As in Portugal, general ignorance of the actual character of the EEC was widespread.[13] Third, many informed circles have stressed the net economic gains from accession to the EEC. Here they touched on more solid ground. According to recent research by this author,[14] it appears that membership would offer an historical opportunity to develop the great agricultural potential of Spain, thus also achieving a better domestic regional balance. Industrially, integration would imply a redeployment of the Spanish industrial base along the same lines as in other EEC countries as a result of accession; i.e. the development of intra-industry trade with other Community countries as partners. Such a redeployment would make the most of the fact that, being a 'border country' in relation to the EEC, Spain could succeed in the rapid assimilation and improvement of foreign technologies. Membership, however, means adjustment with its inherent costs, but Spain seems well placed in relation to the rest of Europe, given the relative youth of her population, something which facilitates horizontal mobility.[15]

The case of Spain showed how much – as with the other two countries – European, strategic and domestic political considerations were closely linked. This was no surprise in view of international concern over the Mediterranean following the first oil shock of 1973, which had predictably disruptive and potentially destabilising effects on the three countries because their economies were very vulnerable to precisely this kind of development. However, this very concern on the part of western countries expressed through financial assistance and a readiness to involve Greece, Spain and Portugal as partners in European integration was important in mitigating the effects of this event during these crucial formative years of the new democracies.

ECONOMIC AND STRATEGIC IMPLICATIONS OF THE SECOND OIL SHOCK FOR SOUTHERN EUROPE

The revolution in Iran in early 1979 induced a new quantum-jump in the oil price, aggravating the plight of Spain, Portugal and Greece, both directly (by a deterioration in terms of trade) and indirectly (by contracting external demand originating in OECD countries). The oil price reached new heights at the end of 1980, when hostilities between Iraq and Iran opened, leading to a further drop in the supply of oil.

In contrast with the first oil crisis, a postponement this time of economic adjustment to the new situation was much more difficult to achieve. The international financial situation was tighter and many newly industrialising countries, including the three in question, had been accumulating debt since 1973. The deterioration in the economic situation of the three countries was therefore unavoidable, and became a reality sooner rather then later. For example, the non-agricultural annual GDP growth rate in Spain, which was still 4 per cent in the 1974–5 period and 2.2 per cent between 1976 and 1979, dropped to zero per cent on average for the period 1979–81.

From a strategic viewpoint, the fall of the Shah (1979), the crisis in Afghanistan (1979) and the Iran-Iraq war (1980) enhanced the importance of Turkey for the West. Of course, after the first oil shock, Greece, Portugal and

INTERNATIONAL CONTEXT OF DEMOCRATIC TRANSITION   165

Spain had also acquired greater strategic importance than before because of their position in relation to the Mediterranean and the Middle East. However, Turkey ranked that much higher because of its position between the Soviet Union and the Gulf. This change in the Graeco-Turkish strategic balance had a predictable impact on domestic developments in Greece. The government of George Rallis was confronted by an opposition led by PASOK, which asserted that the new developments would be to the detriment of Greece. Moreover, the domestic situation in Turkey during 1979–80 was so chaotic, PASOK argued, that a diversionary attack on Greece was not to be discounted.

Although the pro-western military coup in Turkey in the autumn of 1980 reduced these fears somewhat in Greece (as in the rest of NATO), it was too late for Rallis to redress a domestic situation aggravated by the economic crisis, which ensued after the second oil price shock.[16] EEC membership from January 1981 could not help to solve the Greek economic dilemma. On the contrary, soon after entry imports from the Community increased at a higher rate than exports to it, expanding an already large trade deficit. As expected, PASOK won the parliamentary elections in the autumn of 1981. At first, it looked as if the new government was going to make radical changes in foreign policy, such as withdrawal from EEC and NATO or the closing down of the US bases. PASOK stressed that membership in the Community would obstruct any socialist experiment in the domestic economy. Very soon, however, the government accepted that it was not so much the Community as the domestic economic situation which precluded for the moment any large-scale expansionary programmes. Politically also, Papandreou knew that a referendum on possible withdrawal from the Community could only be initiated by the pro-EEC prime minister Karamanlis according to the constitution. In that situation, it seemed better to stay in the community while maintaining publicly that Greece needed to renegotiate her entry terms, given the economic situation. This strategy worked, for in early 1983 the EEC commission proposed to grant an extra £1.6 billion to Greece and to delay tariff cuts on EEC imports, which were originally scheduled to take place up to 1985.[17]

In relation to NATO, tension grew after PASOK's accession to power in the autumn of 1981. The preceding Rallis government had decided a year before to rejoin NATO's integrated military command, justifying this by saying that only thus could Greece obtain modern equipment and prevent an attack from Turkey. Turkey's new military government had not used its veto against Greece's request, which undoubtedly ameliorated the political atmosphere between the two countries. On becoming prime minister, Papandreou hence found a less conflictive situation than before; although more recently Greece has refused to participate in NATO manoeuvres that would not include some procedures implicitly recognising Greece's sovereignty over disputed areas in the Aegean Sea.[18] Finally, in the summer of 1983, a new agreement was reached between the USA and Greece which foresaw the closure of the four US bases over a period of 17 months starting by 1989. Clearly, the strategy of Papandreou's government is partly angled to satisfying as much as possible the electorate of the Greek left as a whole by displaying some radicalism in foreign affairs. This is related to the need to obtain from the trade unions (which are controlled by the two left parties) some wage restraint and a general moderation over economic and social issues, not to mention electoral competition from the communists. The government knows that it cannot substantially improve the economic situation, whereas there is some room for manoeuvre in foreign affairs.

While the impact of the second oil shock had for Greece both economic and strategic consequences, the economic effects dominated the scene in Portugal. The crisis in western Europe led to increased unemployment among Portuguese foreign workers there and an immediate fall in their remittances sent home. EEC protectionism against labour-intensive products reached new heights and hit Portugal's textile sector heavily. These balance of payments difficulties were compounded by the lack of confidence of foreign investors in the Portuguese economy (including foreign workers). This situation does much to explain the instability of governments in the following years. For instance, in 1983, Mário Soares and his Socialist Party – expelled from office in 1978 – were returned by the electorate to extricate the country from a confidence and financial crisis. The foreign debt had reached more than $14 billion. Soares seemed eager to enter the EEC as soon as possible in order to solve some of Portugal's financial problems. According to his statements in the past, the EEC should replace the IMF in its banker's role, but whether the Community would be prepared to meet this expectation is another matter. In the very short run, the only ready help Portugal can acquire is from the IMF.[19] In October 1983, its board had to approve formally an 18-month standby agreement to lend Portugal $480 million, accompanied by $250 million in special drawing rights. In turn, this package should permit the raising of a further $300 million in syndicated loans. But the package deal involves the cutting of the balance of payments from a record $3.2 billion in 1982 to $1.25 billion in 1984. The medicine is hard to swallow, which probably explains why Soares and his government think that other lenders (e.g. the EEC) might be less rigorous or more generous.

One can draw some parallel between Spain's situation and Portugal's after the second oil shock. The new oil crisis produced a total halt in Spain's economic growth. Unemployment increased rapidly (from a rate of 8.5 per cent in early 1979 to 15.4 per cent in the last quarter of 1981, according to OECD figures), reaching one of the highest levels in the OECD. This threatened the position of the Suarez government, already under pressure from the Basque terrorist ETA. The situation seemed somewhat analogous to that in Turkey, although violence had not yet reached the same levels. Western acceptance of the military takeover in Turkey was taken by a minority in the Spanish army as a sign, together with Reagan's accession to the US presidency, that the moment was appropriate for a similar attempt in Spain. As in Turkey, their primary stated intention was to 'open a parenthesis' in the transition to democracy rather than a simple return to dictatorship, motivated by the desire to stop the devolution process and eliminate terrorism. The economy was of no immediate concern. In other words, those initiating the February 1981 coup knew well that they must count on civilians to redress the economy if they wanted to succeed. Independently of the fact that the coup did not succeed ultimately because of the King's firm refusal to support this attempt, the speculation of the putschists on possible US backing revealed a poor evaluation of the situation, for Turkey after 1979 (and possibly even before) was of much higher importance for NATO than Spain in the east-west strategic context. Moreover, the danger of an anti-western coup or revolution (whether pro-Soviet or Islamic) was not present in Spain.

Democracy was saved, but this event led both government and opposition parties to some clearer thinking over what now appeared to be the most direct threat to the perpetuation of Spanish democracy: the fact that the army was basically the same as the one which had emerged from the Civil War. The solution might come from the country's role in NATO. Entry into the integrated military structure of the Atlantic Alliance would be likely to reorientate the army's attention to external matters rather than domestic politics. Moreover, joint manoeuvres with other more technologically advanced armies and international contacts between army professionals would modify the attitude of isolation among Spanish army personnel, and hence reduce the scope for domestic political misunderstanding and the perpetuation of fantasies. Also, the required modernisation of equipment and improvements in military technology would help to keep the army busy. This thesis was supported by the fact that those officers with more democratic leanings were also the most pro-NATO, not only for the reasons mentioned above but also because it was in their interest to agree with the principle accepted in NATO, but not in their own army, that promotion should depend on ability and not on seniority. Other arguments had been aired before the February 1981 coup to justify Spain's accession to NATO,[20] but they did not weigh much in the sudden position adopted by the governing UCD. For more than the five years it had been in power, the UCD had always stressed the lack of urgency in deciding on this issue.

The Socialist Party (PSOE), the main opposition party at the time, had opposed NATO entry for many different reasons. The party insisted that the army's temptations could be solved by a redeployment of its forces to the periphery of the national territory to guard the borders of the country instead of maintaining an important military presence around the capital, as in Franco's time. Some arguments put against NATO entry have since proved to be unfounded, such as the fear of 'provoking the other block' or of 'harming Spain's relations with the Arabs or the non-aligned world'. Also, the allegedly unbearable economic costs of membership seem to have been exaggerated, if one compares what other middle-sized countries in western Europe are spending on defence. Finally, it is difficult to argue that being a NATO member means 'an increased risk of nuclear destruction to the Spanish people', given that the four US bases in Spain in any case place Spain in the eyes of the potential enemy in the same category as many other NATO countries. From 1981, some circles in the PSOE began to agree with the UCD's arguments mentioned above, in particular that the most pro-NATO army circles are also those closer to the spirit of the constitution. Accordingly, the party's opposition to NATO was replaced by a less intransigent position stressing that Spain had been outside NATO for more than thirty years and that it could continue with this situation; i.e. keeping a bilateral agreement with the USA but without NATO membership.

This more moderate position opened the way for the next step, for should Spain enter NATO against the will of the party (something that happened in June 1982) it could remain absolved of the responsibility of that decision while asserting that 'one thing is not to get into NATO, another is to opt out'. It has since been widely accepted in the circles of the PSOE government elected in 1982 *a posteriori* that the UCD argument about NATO constituting a common cause for the government and the democratic sectors of the army is fully valid. However, party pressure is sufficiently strong to make Felipe Gonzalez settle for an intermediary position, of freezing Spain's integration in NATO's military command, while remaining in the Atlantic Alliance until a referendum on the issue in 1985. Paradoxically, such a solution does not contribute to tackling the army problem.

In conclusion, the second oil shock once again had disruptive effects on the three countries, for the same reason as before, all the more so as this time international financial circumstances were tighter. Furthermore, the diplomatic and strategic situation surrounding the Mediterranean had grown more uncertain. However, this perilous environment ultimately sharpened the sense of commitment among political élites in the three countries to the new democratic regimes and their determination to make a success of them. This was demonstrated by the way in which domestic partisan differences over the issues of NATO and EEC membership receded when this broader question came to the fore.

THE OIL GLUT AND THE OECD'S ECONOMIC RECOVERY AND THEIR POSSIBLE EFFECTS ON DEMOCRATIC CONSOLIDATION IN SOUTHERN EUROPE

The first, and even more so the second, oil shock have had a permanent impact on consumer and investment behaviour in the OECD area. The effects of oil saving and improved efficiency in its use have begun to be felt since the end of 1981. Compounded by the impact of the economic recession on oil demand, an oil glut developed because of the failure of OPEC to adjust its price to the new international economic situation. After more than a year, OPEC was finally obliged to reduce the price of oil from $34 to $29 a barrel. Consequently, the oil bill of the three countries being examined has been very much affected by these developments since 1981, relieving some of the pressure on their balance of payments.

A second favourable economic development has been the recovery in the OECD, following that in the USA. According to EEC figures,[21] the Ten's industrial production rose 0.7 per cent in the first quarter of 1983 in relation to the last quarter of 1982, compared with the rates in the third and fourth quarters in 1982 of – 1.8 and – 1.7 respectively. Moreover, the rate of unemployment has stabilised at 10.7 per cent in the second quarter of 1983, after having increased continuously since 1979, with a decline beginning in the summer of 1983. According to the IMF, the rate of growth of production in industrialised countries should reach 1.5 per cent in 1983 in relation to the preceding year, while increasing to 3 per cent in the second quarter of 1983 in relation to the first. This last rate should be maintained throughout 1984.

INTERNATIONAL CONTEXT OF DEMOCRATIC TRANSITION   169

Such developments are expected to have a substantial and positive impact on the exports of Spain, Portugal and Greece. In other words, economic constraints should hinder domestic politics in these three countries less than before, and give some breathing space to the three new socialist governments, which were voted into power *inter alia* for economic reasons.

There are, however, two caveats to this more optimistic scenario. First, the possibility of yet another oil crisis, given the permanent turmoil in the Middle East, cannot be excluded. Second, a world-wide debt crisis calling into question the present economic recovery is another possibility. A financial crisis in one of the three countries is a risk assessed to be small by the experts. The gravest problem is with Portugal, which in volume terms would be manageable at the international level. Spain would be another matter, but the basic situation there is much healthier.[22]There would, however, be a link between a third oil shock and the international financial situation. A new increase in energy prices would create enormous problems for the three countries for they would have difficulties in raising another time round the funds needed to pay for the increased oil bill, given the fear prevailing in banking circles of a repetition of the last decade when outside funds were used many times to finance current consumption or long-term public investment (like motor roads).

CONCLUSION

The international economic context has certainly not facilitated democratic consolidation in Greece, Spain and Portugal, although it may be said to have contributed to the acceleration of the transition from dictatorship to democracy (in particular in Spain). This was both because of international and European support for the new democratic systems as well as a strong commitment in the three countries to their success. In particular, the possibility offered by the international financial community to these countries to postpone their adjustment to the first oil shock may have been decisive, bearing in mind that such an alternative was totally unavailable, for instance, to the Spanish Republic in the 1930s.

As to the diplomatic situation, there is little doubt that détente in the 1970s eased the transition to and consolidation of democracy. This was notably the case with Greece, for her geostrategic location in relation to the Middle East, the Soviet Union and especially Turkey could have played havoc with any peaceful transition to democracy, had the general environment been one of cold war. Even after the end of détente at the end of that decade, when in any case the new Greek democracy was already established, the changed international setting did not act to the detriment of domestic stability. This was basically because almost simultaneously a military regime acquired power in Turkey, and in order to gain western acceptance it cooled down relations with its neighbour, so contributing to the stabilisation of the whole area.

In short, the international context which from the mid-1970s seemed generally at first sight to be unfavourable to the delicate process of establishing new democracies nevertheless contained various features which made any repetition of history of half a century ago very unlikely. These features were the following:

1. An international economic system fundamentally different from that of the 1930s, with its strong awareness of, and institutional networks for, stabilising the interdependence of national economies.
2. The new strategic importance of the Mediterranean in this period, reinforcing the commitment of other West European countries to democratic stability in Greece, Spain and Portugal.
3. While foreign and domestic policy considerations were closely interlinked in the three cases, these countries were not subject to the kind of international interference deriving from rivalry between hostile political systems, as was notoriously so with Spain in the 1930s.
4. The existence of integrative international organisations like the EEC and NATO which provided some external outlet for domestic political tensions, particularly so far as the political ambitions of the military were concerned.
5. The fact that public discontent with the performance of the economy tended to be channelled within the new democracies, in the sense that it operated against particular governments in office rather than against the political systems as such.
6. The absence of any credible alternative to the democratic model, as discussed by Di Palma in his chapter, was strengthened by the influence on these new democracies of the West European states.

Hence, the lack of any real historical parallel with the 1930s allows one to conclude that the 'bad luck' theory has been vindicated, for during the last decade democratic forces in the three countries have been able to count on a sounder international environment compared with the earlier period in order to move relatively peacefully from dictatorship to democracy.

NOTES

1. See OECD, *Main Economic Indicators*, Paris, OECD, various issues; and *World Bank Atlas*, Washington, various issues.
2. See V. Curzon, *The Essentials of Economic Integration*, (London: Macmillan (for the Trade Policy Research Centre), 1974).
3. See A. Tovias, *Tariff Preferences in Mediterranean Diplomacy* (London: Macmillan (for the Trade Policy Research Centre), 1977), p. 71.
4. J. W. Schneider (ed.), *From Nine to Twelve: Europe's Destiny* (Alphen, Sijthoff and Noordhoff, 1980), p. 121.
5. See N. Van Praag, 'European Political Co-operation and the Southern Periphery' in *The Mediterranean Challenge: I* (Brighton, Sussex: European Papers No. 2, 1978), p. 78.
6. One can find the same kind of western response in the case of Turkey.
7. The failure was much more significant than the one of the Spanish army in the Sahara at the end of 1975, since the Sahara was not in the backyard of Spain, as Cyprus and Turkey are in relation to Greece. Turkey is omnipresent in Greeks' minds.
8. G. Minet *et al.*, *Spain, Greece and Community Politics* (Brighton, Sussex: European Research Centre, 1981), p. 112.
9. Ibid., pp. 100–3, and pp. 134–5.

10. L. Tsoukalis, *The European Community and its Mediterranean Enlargement* (London: G. Allen and Unwin, 1981), p. 83.
11. Greece applied for membership in the EEC in June 1975, while Portugal and Spain applied respectively in March and in June 1977.
12. See G. Minet *et al.*, op. cit., p. 4.
13. On this point, see Tsoukalis, op. cit., pp. 115–21.
14. A. Tovias, 'The Effects of the Second Enlargement of the European Community upon Israel's Economy' in E. Gutmann (ed.), *Israel and the Second Enlargement of the European Community: Political and Economic Aspects* (Jerusalem: The Hebrew University, 1984).
15. On this and related subjects, see J. Aguirre *et al.*, *España Año Cero* (Madrid: Espasa-Calpe, 1982) and J. Donges *et al.*, *The Second Enlargement of the European Community* (Tübingen; JCB Mohr (Paul Siebeck), 1982).
16. The GDP (evaluated at 1975 prices and exchange rates) decreased by 0.6 per cent in 1981 (OECD, *Main Economic Indicators*, April 1983). The crisis was particularly felt in the first five months of 1981, when output of manufacturing industries fell by 3.2 per cent (*Quarterly Economic Review of Greece*, 4th Quarter 1981, The Economist Intelligence Unit).
17. *The Economist*, 2 April 1983 and 23 July 1983.
18. On the Aegean dispute, see G. Rosenthal, *The Mediterranean Basin, Its Political Economy and Changing International Relations* (London: Butterworths Scientific, 1982).
19. *International Herald Tribune*, 3 October 1983, p. 7.
20. For example, the idea that Gibraltar could became a NATO base once Spain is in and therefore blur the issue of sovereignty; or that in the event of an attack on the Canary Islands, Ceuta or Melilla by some African country, Spain could count on NATO's help. The latter is an unproven assumption, since the Alliance covers Europe and not Africa, while Gibraltar has never been so high in the Spanish agenda after 1975 as to make of it a reason to enter NATO.
21. Commission of the European Communities, *The European Economy*, Supplement A, No. 8–9 (August-September 1983).
22. G. de la Dehesa, 'Perspectivas a medio plazo del endeudamiento exterior de España', Paper presented at the VIIth IEA Congress, Madrid, September 1983, p. 19.

[25]

THE INTERNATIONAL CONTEXT OF CONTEMPORARY DEMOCRATIZATION

Philippe C. Schmitter

Since the 25th of April 1974, when a small group of junior army officers overthrew the regime that had been ruling Portugal for over forty years, almost fifty countries have rid themselves of various forms of autocracy. Democratization began in Southern Europe, spread to Latin America during the later 1970s and early 1980s, affected a few countries in Asia, and then, had a massive impact upon Eastern Europe and the Republics of the former Soviet Union in 1989-90. Currently, its momentum has carried to Africa and the Middle East - with less uniform and unequivocal results.

By one mode or another, previous tyrants were overthrown and the event triggered a vast increase in citizen consciousness, a "resurrection of civil society". Expectations soared and typically focused on national as well as personal goals. The People (or, more accurately, their representatives) assembled; they chose

Phillipe Schmitter is a professor of Political Science at Stanford University. The initial version of this paper was prepared while the author was a Fellow at the Center for Advanced Study in the Behavioral Sciences and will be published in a forthcoming volume edited by Laurence Whitehead, Nuffield College.

Acknowledgments: I am grateful for financial support provided by National Science Foundation Grant #BNS-8700864 and for the intellectual stimulus provided by my colleagues at the Center during the 1991-1992 academic year. Participants in the East-South Systems Transformation project, which was supported by a generous grant from the John D. and Catherine T. MacArthur Foundation, also contributed to my understanding of the topic. As has long been the case with my work on democratization, I have benefitted from the encouragement and critical acumen of Terry Karl. Finally, I would like to thank the student editors of the *Stanford Journal of International Affairs* for their detailed comments. They have contributed in no small measure to improving the clarity of my argument. All of the above, needless to say, are absolved from responsibility for the errors and omissions that remain.

Stanford Journal of International Affairs   **Fall/Winter 1993**

new institutions of self-government and embarked on new policies of self-improvement.

For these symbolic and emotional reasons, few political acts seem more auctocthonous than the instauration or restoration of democracy. Admittedly, this description neglects those cases in which foreigners defeat one set of rulers and rules and subsequently impose their preferred type of regime upon the vanquished. However, most of the recent democratizations have not involved war and, even where there was an obvious international military component to the demise of the previous authoritarian regime, foreign occupation of national territory (e.g. Portugal, Greece, Argentina, the Soviet Union) has not followed.

The emergent literature on democratization has, so far, tended to reflect this "nativist" assumption. One of the most confident assertions in the O'Donnell-Schmitter concluding volume to the *Transitions from Authoritarian Rule* project was that "domestic factors play a predominant role in the transition".[1] Not only does this contradict a substantial body of theory that stresses the dependence, interpenetration and even integration increasingly embedded in the contemporary "world system", but it also clashes with an elementary observation of the facts surrounding the transitions that have occurred in Eastern Europe. Would the astonishingly rapid changes in Poland, Hungary, East Germany, Czechoslovakia, Romania and Bulgaria in 1989-90 have even been imaginable, much less gone as far as they did, without a prior change in the hegemonic pretensions of the Soviet Union? Would Honecker not have been able to hang on to power if it had not been for a switch in Hungarian foreign policy that allowed East Germans to transit Hungarian territory to seek exile in the West? And who could have conceived of a regime change in Albania - a polity virtually without a domestic opposition - in the absence of the collapse of the other communist regimes?

Eastern Europe, therefore, encourages us to reconsider the impact of the international context upon regime change. Could it be more significant than was originally thought? Were the early

---

[1] Guillermo O'Donnell & Philippe C. Schmitter, *Transitions from Authoritarian Rule: Prospects for Democracy*, Vol. III, Baltimore: Johns Hopkins University Press, 1986: 19.

2

Contemporary Democratization

transitions to democracy in Southern Europe and Latin America "peculiarly" auctoctonous? Could the transitions that have occurred since in Asia, Eastern Europe and (most tentatively) Africa have been more influenced by their external - regional as well as global - contexts? More specifically, to what extent do variations in these contexts, over time and across countries, impose significantly different constraints or opportunities upon nascent democracies? How, why, and when do they affect their subsequent choice of institutions and policies? What, if any, is the impact of these contextual differences upon the likelihood that these polities will be able to consolidate successfully some form of democracy?

Concepts

Providing answers to these valid and generalizable questions across the large number and dispersed location of recent cases of democratization will not be easy. The international context is a variable that is notoriously difficult to pin down. On the one hand, it is almost by definition **omnipresent** since very few polities in the contemporary world are isolated from its effects. However, its causal impact is often indirect, working in mysterious and unintended ways through ostensibly national agents. On the other hand, while it is usually presented in the **singular**, i.e. *the* international context, its actual incidence varies greatly according to the size, resource base, regional context, geo-strategic location, and alliance structure of the country involved. Existing international relations theory is relatively good at specifying these conditions at the level of nation-states, but much less well equipped in dealing with phenomena at the sub-national or supra-national levels. In the simplified world of "realists", the only actors worth mentioning are nation-states and the only relevant actions consist of their explicit foreign policies: signing treaties; entering into alliances; making diplomatic protests and threats; voting in international bodies; offering or withdrawing economic incentives; and, in the last resort, declaring war and making peace. The complex world of non-state actors (international organizations, human rights groups, private foundations, interest associations, media organizations, transnational firms, partisan *internationales*,

3

Stanford Journal of International Affairs   **Fall/Winter 1993**

networks of dissidents, even private citizens) have to be taken into account and their actions can augment, undermine, even countermand, those of the states to which they are attached. As we shall see, there is reason to suspect that this world "beneath and beyond the nation-state" has played an especially significant role in the international promotion of democracy.

More than any other scholar, Laurence Whitehead has sought systematically to relate what he calls "the international dimension" to the processes of democratization. In addition to upgrading his assessment of its importance since his earlier work in the *Transitions from Authoritarian Rule* project,[2] he recently proposed a three-fold grouping of the external factors that impinge upon contemporary democratizations.[3] Taking his analytical categories of **contagion, control** and **consent** as my point of departure, I propose adding a fourth generic manner through which international actors can influence the outcome: **conditionality**.

Figure One

THE "SUB-CONTEXTS" OF THE INTERNATIONAL CONTEXT

	BASIS FOR ACTION	
NUMBER OF ACTOR	COERCION backed by states	VOLUNTARY supported by private actors
UNILATERAL	CONTROL	CONTAGION
MULTILATERAL	CONDITIONALITY	CONSENT

As Figure One demonstrates, the dimensions that define the property space within which the international context can be

---

2 *Ibid* at 3-46.

3 "The International Dimension of Democratization: A Survey of the Alternatives", paper presented at the XVth Congress of IPSA, Buenos Aires, 21-25 July 1991.

4

Contemporary Democratization

brought to bear are relatively simple, even if their implications are not. On the vertical axis, the key distinction is between **unilateral** processes of international influence/power, in which one actor intentionally or unintentionally affects another, and **multilateral** ones that involve several, often competing, sources of influence/power and typically work through international, organizational channels (rather than purely national ones). The horizontal axis distinguishes between contexts involving at least the threat, if not the exercise, of **coercive authority** and those whose effect depends on **voluntary exchanges.**[4] Crosstabulating these two dimensions produces the four modal sub-contexts.

Whitehead attempts to assess the significance of three of these sub-contexts. **Contagion** (1), the diffusion of experience through "neutral", i.e. non-coercive and often unintentional, channels from one country to another, he finds present throughout most of the history of democratization. **Control** (2), the promotion of democracy by one country in another through explicit policies backed by positive or negative sanctions, he estimates was present in about two-thirds of the 61 cases he considered to be presently democratic. **Consent** (3), emerges in Whitehead's analysis as a more recent category involving a complex set of interactions between international processes and domestic groups that generate new democratic norms and expectations from below. In the extreme, this interactions leads to an irresistible drive to merge with an already existing democracy (e.g. the DDR); in a milder form, it involves the desire to protect democracy within a given country by joining a regional bloc (e.g. Greece, Spain and Portugal in relation to the EC).

Conditionality should be added to the other three as the most recent sub-context for the exercise of international influence. Its hallmark is the deliberate use of coercion, by attaching specific conditions to the distribution of benefits to recipient countries, on the part of multilateral institutions. The *locus classicus* for this kind of behavior in the past was the International Monetary Fund, although democracy was rarely

---

[4] This is usually the exclusive domain of nation-states although some international organizations such as the IMF, the IBRD, and the EBRD have also acquired some of this capability.

5

Stanford Journal of International Affairs   **Fall/Winter 1993**

one of its stipulated conditions, and those that were imposed
were usually kept confidential in order not to offend national
sovereignty (or dignity).   More recently, the European
Community has insisted upon a certain standard of political
behavior as a condition for membership. Its offshoot, the
European Bank for Reconstruction and Development, has been
especially "up front" about imposing very specific political
criteria before loans will be granted. While the practice of
conditionality seems largely confined to Europe, there are some
signs that other regional organizations such as the Organization
of American States, the British Commonwealth, and even the
Organization for African Unity have begun to discuss the issue
of collective security to prevent "unconstitutional" regime
change.

As we turn now to the theoretical domains in which these
factors might be brought to bear, we will try to estimate what (if
any) changes have been occurring in international sub-contexts
as the locus has shifted from Southern Europe to Latin America
to Eastern Europe over the past two decades and a half. We will
be specifically interested in the extent to which these changes
may be promoting or impeding either the transition from
autocracy or the consolidation of democracy.

But how does one conceptualize the dynamic interaction
between the international context of power, influence and
imitation and the varied national cases of democratization?
Existing International Relations theory, with its bland reflections
on "linkage politics", "penetrated systems", "fusion of domestic
and foreign policy", and "interdependence" does not provide
much help. The field of comparative politics, moreover, has
been so mired in an exclusively national approach to political
culture and a predominantly regional approach to comparison
that it has little to offer in the search for international and
interregional generalizations.

As a heuristic device for breaking through this impasse
between sub-disciplines, one could draw on general theories of
social change which suggest four possible **logics of
transformation** in the relationship between formally discrete
levels of political aggregation. The first and most common
approach would adopt a basically functionalist view and interpret
the outcome in terms of a more-or-less passive, unreflexive
adaptation of the national institutions to independent and

Contemporary Democratization

inexorable **trends** at the international level. An alternative mode of interpretation would be more historically contingent and focus on the impact of specific global or regional **events**, such as war, depression or natural catastrophe, upon national regimes. Other theorists have placed primary emphasis on the complex, spatially and temporally structured interaction between national outcomes and assign primary importance to **waves** of international diffusion and imitation. Finally, one can take a genetic perspective and emphasize the ways in which different **stages** of the democratization process at the national level are affected by the international context. These four approaches are not necessarily mutually exclusive. All may eventually contribute to improving our understanding. Each, however, will bring up different variables, generate different hypotheses, and may even lead to different conclusions.

Trends

The most prevalent hypothesis linking the international context to democratization is probably some version of what could be called "inverted Kantianism". Immanuel Kant suggested that "republics" in which governments were accountable to their (restricted) citizenry were likely to promote commerce, in general, and international trade, in particular. The development of these exchanges between countries, in turn, would place restrictions on their aggressive behavior vis-a-vis each other. Once all polities had become "republican", the nature of the international system would shift to "perpetual peace".[5]

History was not very kind to Kant's optimistic scenario. Shortly after he wrote his little pamphlet (1795), one of his republics (France) deprived three others (the Netherlands, Switzerland and Venice) of their independence and distinctive governing form, transforming itself into an Empire and an

---

[5] For a discussion of "Kantianism" in the context of contemporary regime change, see Philippe C. Schmitter, "Change in Regime Type and Progress in International Relations", in E. Adler and B. Crawford eds., *Progress in International Relations*, New York: Columbia University Press, 1991: 89-127.

Stanford Journal of International Affairs   Fall/Winter 1993

Autocracy! Nevertheless, the *doux commerce* thesis, that trade
tends to produce moderate and accommodative behavior in both
individuals and collectivities, persists.[6] In its more recent
versions, however, Kant's causality is inverted. It is argued that
the development of mutual exchanges between citizens in
different polities during a period of protracted peace tends to
produce a demand for republican government. Put in more
contemporary   terms,   increase   in   international
interdependence,   especially   forms   of   "complex
interdependence"   involving   a   wide   range   of   actors
and   exchanges,   leads   to   the   democratization   of
national   political   institutions.   For example, an
assumption of this sort must have underlay Willy Brandt's
Ostpolitik, as well as European resistance to the U.S. *Diktat*
concerning the construction of a gas pipeline from the Soviet
Union.

Only a small step separates this perspective from inverting
the dependency theory that was used so extensively to explain
the demise of democracy and the rise of bureaucratic-
authoritarian regimes in Latin America and elsewhere during the
1960s and 1970s. This point of view would argue that
subsequent   changes   in   the   content   and   balance   of
(inter)dependencies between Center and Periphery had required
countries in the latter to adapt their domestic institutions (at least
formally) during the later 1970s and 1980s to conform to the
new functional requisite of open, free, and competitive politics.

Samuel Huntington has made a quite different, but related
point. While rising interdependence remains the necessary
condition, the sufficient one concerns the distribution of power
within that evolving system of exchanges. Only those countries
that are closely affected by existing democracies will be affected:
"In large measure, the rise and decline of democracy on a global
scale is a function of the rise and decline of the most powerful
democratic states".[7] As we shall see, this perspective mixes
elements of control, i.e. deliberate policy initiatives by the

---

[6] It also antedated Kant's application of it to the international realm. *Cf.*
Albert O. Hirschman, *The Passions and the Interests*, Princeton: Princeton
University Press, 1977.

[7] "Will More Countries Become Democratic?", *Political Science Quarterly*,
Vol. 99, No. 2, Summer 1984: 206-7.

8

Contemporary Democratization

United States, with the effects of contagion, i.e. the example of successful and prosperous democratic polities.

In our previous work on transitions, Guillermo O'Donnell and I firmly rejected all versions of this "trendy" analysis. It seemed to us that the pattern of external exchanges, the stage of capitalist development, the extent of asymmetric dependencies, the role of major powers in general and the United States in particular, varied so much across the countries in Southern Europe and Latin America that it was patently erroneous to interpret democratization as a response to some common trend or trends toward interdependence. For the period we were examining, it was the *decline* not the rise in US power that seemed to open up spaces for political change. As Terry Karl pointed out subsequently with regard to Latin America, it was precisely in those countries where the influence of the United States remained the greatest, the Caribbean and Central America, where the progress toward democracy was the least advanced.[8] Democratization occurred where the option for direct military intervention was limited, as in the Southern Cone of Latin America or the Southern edge of Western Europe, or where its leaders were significantly divided on what course of action to follow, as in the Philippines and Korea. Conversely, democratic political change has not followed from the "benevolent" armed intervention of the US in Panama or Grenada.

In Southern Europe, a specific form of complex, organizationally saturated interdependence between Spain, Portugal and Greece (and, to a lesser extent, Turkey) and the rest of Europe (the European Community in particular) did exert a powerful and positive influence upon the subsequent processes of consolidation of their respective democracies.[9] The impact upon the timing and nature of their varied transitions from autocracy was marginal, but once regime change was underway, the networks of public and private exchange that bound these

[8] "Dilemmas of Democratization in Latin America", *Comparative Politics*, Vol. 23, No. 1, October 1990: 1-21.

[9] This has subsequently been explored in Geoffrey Pridham, "The Politics of the European Community, Transnational Networks and Democratic Transition in Southern Europe" in G. Pridham ed., *Encouraging Democracy: The International Context of Regime Transition in Southern Europe*, Leicester: Leicester University Press, 1991: 212-245.

Stanford Journal of International Affairs   Fall/Winter 1993

countries to the rest of Europe had a profound effect upon the choice of institutions and policies. Ironically, the political weakness, not the strength, of the EC enabled it to play such a role. Moreover, while the EC insists on the democratic *bona fides* of its members, it itself does not meet the minimal criteria for being a democracy. Both these features provide prospective members with greater assurance that they will not simply be outvoted by larger countries that are already members or be directed to by an overweening supra-national bureaucracy.

Subsequent events in Eastern Europe and the Soviet Union have confirmed the above skeptical reflections concerning the generic importance of international trends. These countries were not characterized by high levels of global, or even regional, interdependence. Their membership in COMECON and unconvertible currencies had the effect of both cutting them off from the mainstream of exchanges within the capitalist world economy and restricting their mutual interdependence. Granted that there was some tendency for commercial and personal exchanges to increase with the West and there was the beginning of a mutual recognition process that might have led to closer EC-COMECON relations, it is nonetheless difficult to assign much causal weight to either. Contrary to Huntington's benevolent assumption about the influence of "the most powerful democratic state", democratization in Eastern Europe was triggered (but not caused) by "the most powerful autocratic state".

Only by dialectical inversion is it possible to rescue the trend hypothesis: the very prospect that economic interdependence was increasing rapidly between neighboring countries in Western Europe (especially since the signing of the Single European Act in 1985) could have provided a significant impetus for regime change before the 1992 process would have completed the "Internal Market" and left Eastern European outsiders even further behind.

Furthermore, there is another way of resuscitating the "trend to interdependence" hypothesis that seems particularly appropriate for Eastern Europe and the Soviet Union. The analyst could switch his or her attention from *doux commerce* to *douce communication*. What if it were not the voluntary exchange of goods and services through trade but the unimpeded

10

Contemporary Democratization

transmission of messages through various media that established the basis of interdependence between political systems? Autocracies might still be able to control the physical movement of items and people, but they seem to have lost the capacity to control the flow of information across their borders. Satellite television, "free" radio, video cameras, computer networks, facsimile and xerox machines, and cellular telephones all seem to have ways of getting around national barriers. Moreover, the content of their messages can be specifically tuned to the process of democratization by disseminating images of individual freedom, self-expression, mass collective action, heroic resistance to tyrants, and so forth. The development of regional and global networks for such transmissions seems to underlay much of the contagion and consent in the contemporary international context. It connects societies without the approval or mediation of their governments. With one's neighbors and the world watching, the cost of repression has gone up and, most of all, the potential benefit of resistance has increased manifold. The images are quite clear: East Germans trying to climb the walls of the West German embassy in Prague or crossing the Hungarian-Austrian border in droves, those joyous people astride the Berlin Wall, that lonely man in front of the tanks in Tienamin Square, and Yeltsin haranguing the crowd in front of the Russian Supreme Soviet!

But we should not exaggerate either the reach of this communicative interdependence or its impact upon democratization. Except for the picturesque "street theater" of the Portuguese revolution, the transitions in Southern Europe and Latin America were relatively unaffected by it. Perhaps some regime changes are just less photogenic than others, or mass publics are less interested in what happens in certain parts of the world. In some out-of-the-way places, *vide* Burma and Haiti, the events can be over before the coverage begins. Nor sufficient was media attention to mass protests in the early 1980s sufficient to bring down Pinochet. As the Chinese example demonstrates, even with poignant images and ingenious means of transmission, the formula is not infallible. Power stands as an irreducible component of the international context and coercion remains a resource available to national autocrats. In other terms, contagion and consent alone are likely to be insufficient to bring about democratization - even in conjunction

11

Stanford Journal of International Affairs   Fall/Winter 1993

with favorable domestic forces. Often, regime change will require elements of control and conditionality.

Events

No one would deny that major unforeseen occurrences in the international environment have historically had a significant impact upon regime changes in general, and democratization in particular.[10] Machiavelli's term for the unexpected was *fortuna*, and he confidently assigned 50% of the variance to it. Whatever its proportional contribution in the contemporary setting, the breakup of the multinational states of the Soviet Union and Yugoslavia illustrates that sudden and unexpected events can still trigger major changes at the level of national regimes.

In the past, the most obvious event was defeat in war. The recent Portuguese, Greek and Argentine cases were all affected by unsuccessful efforts by non-democratic rulers at projecting military power beyond their national boundaries, and one could claim that the defeat of the Soviet Union in Afghanistan played a significant role in bringing about the demise of its autocracy.

Second in historical importance has been the change in the international system brought about by decolonization and, in paticular, the interconnected events that followed in the aftermath of World War II. With the surface of the globe now virtually covered by at least nominally sovereign and self-governing states, there does not appear to be much room left for this class of events. Nevertheless, the Soviet Union's (unexpected) willingness to let its Eastern satellites "go it their own way" in 1988-89 was roughly analogous to the breakup of the British, French, Dutch and Belgian colonial empires after 1947, even if it was accomplished in a more mutual and peaceful fashion. The event underlying both defeat in war and decolonization in this case was the dramatic realization by the rulers of the Soviet Union that they could no longer sustain their level of international commitments and retain their status as a major power.

---

[10] *Cf.* Goran Therborn, "The Rule of Capital and the Rise of Democracy", *New Left Review*, No. 103, May/June 1977: 3-41.

12

Contemporary Democratization

It is not yet clear what impact the subsequent collapse of the bi-polar structure of the international system will have upon national consolidations of democracy. In the East, the removal of that overriding tension has been a factor in unleashing repressed demands for self-determination by ethno-linguistic groups. The consequent ambiguity over national boundaries, including the outbreak of civil wars in such places as Moldavia, the Caucasus and Yugoslavia, has inhibited the choice of democratic institutions and even has been exploited to justify the retention of non-democratic ones. In the South, those autocracies that remain in power are facing renewed pressures for regime change. Cuba may be the most vulnerable due to its isolation in the Western Hemisphere, but there are many other autocracies in Africa, Asia and the Middle East which have lost their previous ability to stay in power by playing the major powers off against each other. Conversely, the countries which have been liberated from Soviet domination, those that have avoided descending into ethnic conflict and/or civil war, have been able to call upon a greater degree of international solidarity and financial support than the generous aid of the United States in the reconstruction of the fledgling democracies of Western Europe after World War II.[11]

Above, we have seen that **trends** have worked largely through contagion and consent and have made a significant, but insufficient contribution to democratization. **Events**, by their very nature, are more difficult to predict and their impact has been mediated by processes of control and conditionality that are still underway.

---

[11] The reason for this seems rather obvious and closely linked to the nature of the international system. These "ex-enemies" in Eastern Europe and the Soviet Union occupy a much more salient position in calculations of global security than do the "friendlier", but less strategically located, countries of Latin America, Africa and Asia. The prospect that they can be somehow "pacified" or "normalized" *via* foreign aid, advice and concessions appears to offer much greater and longer term returns on the policy investments of established democracies. Ironically, if successful, this depolarization is likely to decrease the attention and resources devoted to other needy cases of nascent democratization since it will have removed the element of great power rivalry.

13

Stanford Journal of International Affairs   **Fall/Winter 1993**

Waves

Any plotting of the dates when democracies were founded or when they have significantly expanded their practice of citizenship and/or degree of accountability would reveal a strong tendency towards "temporal clustering". There are a few democracies which have followed more idiosyncratic trajectories and timed their changes in seeming disregard for what was happening to their neighbors - the United States, Chile, Uruguay, Great Britain, Switzerland, Sweden, the Netherlands, Belgium, Canada, New Zealand, Australia,[12] - but most of them can be placed in one or another *wave of democratization*.

The first clustering in 1848 was quite spectacular but ephemeral. Most of those affected returned to their previous mode of governance or to an even more autocratic regime in short order. The second major "outbreak" of democracy corresponded to World War One and its aftermath.[13] Not only were new countries carved out of the defunct Austro-Hungarian Empire and the disrupted Russian Empire, but all of them turned initially to democracy.[14] The Weimar Republic replaced the German Reich, for example. Moreover, important extensions of the franchise and inclusions of new parties into government occurred in those Western European polities that were already partially democratic. The third wave came in the aftermath of

---

[12] Even Switzerland, that eldest and most original of democracies, experienced significant changes in its ruling structures during periods that roughly corresponded to "waves of democratization" in neighboring countries: 1849, 1872, 1917-20, 1947.

[13] It is possible to detect a "mini-wave" in the early 1870s which had a lasting effect on such countries as France, Switzerland, Italy, and Denmark, and a more ambiguous one in Germany and Austria-Hungary. The real "subject-matter" of this wave, however, was state-building and state-reorganization with democracy as an almost incidental by-product. *Cf.* Charles Maier, "Lines of Force or Thought: Redefining Authority, Interest and Identity in the Era of High Nationalism", to appear in P. Schmitter ed., *Experimenting with Scale in Western Europe*, New York: Cambridge University Press, forthcoming.

[14] By 1938, however, only one of them persisted in this status: Czechoslovakia. Finland carved itself out of the former Russian Empire, and Norway out of the dual-monarchy with Sweden. Both of these countries remained democratic.

14

Contemporary Democratization

World War II. Not only were numerous occupied democracies liberated to revert to their previous status and new democracies established in Western Germany and Italy, but the process of regime change spread far beyond Europe through the process of decolonization in Asia and Africa. Occupying powers placed democratic institutions in Japan and Korea. In Latin America, numerous dictators frozen in power by the war itself were overthrown.[15]

We are currently in the fourth wave of democratization. It began quite unexpectedly in Portugal on the 25th of April 1974 and does not yet seem to have crested. In comparison to previous waves, it has some peculiar characteristics:

(1) **It has been much more global in its reach.** It began in Southern Europe, spread to Latin America, affected some Asian countries and literally swept through Eastern Europe. Moreover, from Mongolia to Mali, Madagascar and Mexico, important changes are still in the offing. Only the Middle East seems immune, although even there some change has been occurring in Tunisia, Jordan and Kuwait. In Algeria, however, the experiment was abruptly called off when the first competitive elections produced a fundamentalist, opposition victory.

(2) As a consequence of its global nature, **it has affected far more countries and been more thorough in its regional impact.** Some parts of the world that were previously almost uniformly autocratic are now almost equally democratic. Cuba and Serbia stand out in their respective neighborhoods for their unwillingness to change their regimes, however.

(3) **It has, so far, suffered far fewer regressions to autocracy than in the past.** Twenty-seven years after it

---

[15] Most of these postwar democratizations in Latin America were abortive. By the mid-1950s, authoritarian rule has re-established itself almost everywhere, with the exception of Costa Rica. In the late 1950s and early 1960s, there was another, strictly regional, wave which corresponded roughly with Alliance for Progress and led some observers to believe that the United States could effectively control regime outcomes in that part of the world. At one point in 1961, only Paraguay, Nicaragua and Cuba had non-elected governments. Beginning with Honduras and Brazil, the direction of change reversed itself and democracy once again became the exception rather than the norm in the region.

15

Stanford Journal of International Affairs   **Fall/Winter 1993**

began, the only clear reversal has been Haiti. Its initial experiment with free and contested elections of uncertain outcome resulted in a reassertion of military power. The democratic trajectory resumed after a short interlude, but again met with a violent overthrow by elements of the armed forces - the outcome of which is not yet certain. Thailand and Nigeria seem to be rather special cases of persistent oscillation in regime type. It remains to be seen whether the recent *auto-golpe* by Fujimori in Peru will produce a permanent reversal. In Burma and China, strong pressures for democratization surfaced, but were suppressed before an actual change took place.

Observing this "bunching together" of historical and contemporary experiences does not explain their occurrence, however. The most obvious hypothesis is that the waves of democratization are produced by a process of diffusion. **Contagion** is, therefore, the most plausible explanation, especially when no simultaneous external **event** is present that could otherwise explain the coincidence.[16] The successful example of one country's transition establishes it as a "model" to imitate and, once a given region is sufficiently saturated with this mode of political domination, pressure will mount to compel the remaining autocracies to conform to the newly established norm.

This hypothesis is particularly appealing for the explanation of the contemporary, fourth, wave because, on the one hand, the countries affected have not suffered the impact of any common exogenous event such as a world war and, on the other, because the ensuing development of "complex communicative interdependence" provides greater assurance that the mechanisms of diffusion are working. In fact, the latter observation presents a complication in testing for contagion/diffusion. Previously, the main empirical proof for its presence hinged on geographical propinquity. An innovation was supposed to reach nearby units before ones farther away. Hence, the observation that democratization in the current wave began in Southern Europe and then "leap-frogged" to Latin America in the late 1970s and early 1980s, without first affecting countries in North Africa or Eastern Europe that were closer at

---

[16] The fact that two of the four waves coincided with an international war that directly affected all of the democratizing countries reduces considerably the plausibility that diffusion or contagion alone was involved.

16

Contemporary Democratization

hand, would have constituted a disconfirmation. However, when one considers that modern systems of communication are not so spatially bound and may not even be culturally confined, then, the observation is much less damaging. Given the extraordinary "simultaneity" and "omnipresence" of these systems, one can easily understand how its messages are received and responded to in Mongolia before Mali or Mexico.

With this *prima facia* plausibility in mind, we can turn to the development of further hypotheses. For example, the wave notion leads to the likelihood that the relevance of the international context will increase monotonically with each successive instance of democratization. Those coming later in the wave will be more influenced by those that preceded them. They may be unable to learn from mistakes made earlier, but they may also take advantage of "delayed democratization", just as others have argued that "late development" had its advantages.

One of the reasons for this momentum effect in the contemporary context has less to do with contagion than with consent. Each successive case has contributed more and more to the development of formal non-governmental organizations and informal informational networks devoted to promote further democratization (the protection of minorities, monitoring of elections, promotion of human rights, provision of economic advice, and fostering of exchanges among academics and intellectuals). When the first cases of Portugal, Greece, and Spain emerged, this sort of an international infrastructure hardly existed. Indeed, some key lessons were learned from these experiences and subsequently applied elsewhere. By now, there exist an extraordinary variety of international parties, associations, foundations, movements, networks and firms ready to intervene either to promote or to protect democracy. This suggests a second hypothesis: the international context surrounding democratization has shifted from a primary reliance on public, intergovernmental channels of influence towards an increased involvement of private, non-governmental organizations. It is the concrete activity of these agents of consent, rather than the abstract process of contagion, that accounts for the "global reach" of

17

Stanford Journal of International Affairs   **Fall/Winter 1993**

regime change and the fact. so few regressions to autocracy have occurred.

For, however superficially attractive the process of contagion may appear, it rarely bears closer scrutiny. Take, for example, the case of Portugal and Spain. Despite their geographical and cultural proximity and the temporal coincidence of their transitions, it is very implausible to assert that Spain embarked upon its regime change in 1975 **because** of the prior events of 1974 in Portugal. In fact, the Spaniards had long been waiting for the death of Franco which was the specific triggering event - not the Portuguese Revolution. In many ways, they were much better prepared for democratization than their Portuguese neighbors because they began preparing for it much earlier. At most, it could be claimed that Spain learned some negative lessons about what to avoid during the transition and, therefore, had a relatively easier time. Detailed evidence of diffusion from Southern Europe to Latin America or Asia or Eastern Europe would be just as difficult to provide. Of course, Spain (and, more recently, Chile) seemed to have offered a model of successful transition to late-comers and, therefore, encouraged them to venture into uncertain terrain, but this analysis doesn't allow for the claim that Spain actually caused others to change their regime type.

The more persuasive argument for contagion/diffusion lies within specific regional contexts. The unexpected transition in Paraguay seems to have been influenced by the fact that the country was surrounded by nascent democracies, although Chile under Pinochet held out successfully against such pressures during the 1980s. He even dared to use the example of the poor performance of its recently democratized neighbors as an argument for voting "Sí" in the plebiscite that would have placed him in power for another eight years! Pinochet's loss in the plebiscite suggests that Chilean citizens were influenced not just by their own democratic tradition but also by the wave that had engulfed their neighbors.

Eastern Europe may provide the best possible case for contagion, even though the initial impetus for regime change was given by an exogenous event, i.e. the shift in Soviet foreign and defense policy vis-a-vis the region. No one can question the accelerating flow of messages and images that traveled from Poland to Hungary to the DDR to Czechoslovakia to Romania to

18

Contemporary Democratization

Bulgaria and, eventually, to Albania, or the impact that successive declarations of national independence had upon the member republics of the Soviet Union.

This reasoning leads to a third and final sub-hypothesis, namely, that **the most effective international context that can influence the course of democratization has increasingly become ·regional, and not binational or global in scope.** Both the lessons of contagion and the mechanisms of consent seem to function better at that level.[17]

Stages

Democratization proceeds unevenly as changing sets of actors employ different strategies to accomplish different tasks. The process may not always be continuous, gradual, linear, or cumulative, but virtually all attempts to "model" it refer to the presence of stages, phases, or sequences. The most common distinction has been between a shorter, more intense, uncertain and eventful period of transition and a longer, less heroic, more dispersed, and deliberate period of consolidation, the contrast between an initial, exciting "war of movement" and a subsequent, prosaic "war of position".

From this staged or phased notion of regime change emerges one of the most important general hypotheses linking the international context to domestic political outcomes: **regardless of the form (control, contagion, consent, or conditionality) that it takes, external intervention will have a greater and more lasting effect upon the consolidation of democracy than upon the transition to it.**[18] Part of the explanation rests on the likely structure of

---

[17] Extraregional powers seem to have learned this lesson. Most of the US intervention in the delicate early years of the Portuguese transition was channelled through friendly European powers, just as much of the American aid for Eastern Europe is slated to pass thorough the European Bank for Reconstruction and Development.

[18] One could go further and suggest that the relation is parabolic: low during the initial transition, building up to its maximum effect during the consolidation and, subsequently, declining once national political

19

Stanford Journal of International Affairs   **Fall/Winter 1993**

opportunities.   During the first phase, the probability of exercising a marginal influence over the outcome may be greater than when things have calmed down, but the sheer pace of change, coupled in some cases with its unexpectedness, leaves outsiders without the critical information they would need to intervene effectively and without regular channels of influence through which to operate. The rapid pace of internal change tends to outrun the decision-making capacity of most external actors.[19] Moreover, some foreign governments will have been discredited for the "realist" policies they pursued in relation to the previous autocracy; others, whose actions may prove more acceptable within the country, can have difficulty deciding which fractions to support in a context of divided social groups and ephemeral political alliances. To the extent that the transition is related to processes of national liberation and assertiveness, the intromission of foreigners can be especially unwelcome, although, in this period of high uncertainty, weak domestic political forces may be sorely tempted to look for outside support.

The situation changes once consolidation is underway, however. The relevant domestic actors have been reduced in numbers and variety, and their positions and resources are better known. The national borders and identities will have been asserted, if not definitively established.[20] Those foreigners who

---

institutions are functioning "normally" and, hence, capable of asserting both their internal and external sovereignty.

[19] This point should not be exaggerated. When their security relationship appear to be jeopardized, external powers can find overt and, especially, covert means for intervening decisively on very short notice. And they can not only find, but even create almost *de toutes pieces* the domestic interlocutors they need. Italy in the crucial years leading up to the elections of 1948 and Portugal during the very uncertain Spring and Summer of 1975 were cases-in-point where it can be claimed that the outcome in terms of regime type might have been different were it not for the rapid and deliberate intervention of foreign actors. *Cf.* Robert Leonardi, "The International Context of Democratic Transition in Postwar Italy: A Case of Penetration", and Walter C. Opello Jr., "Portugal: A Case Study of International Determinants of Regime Transition", both in G. Pridham ed., *Encouraging Democracy, Supra* note 9 at 62-83, 84-102.

[20] This primordial element of transitional uncertainty, the absence of an accepted delimitation of the territorial and cultural parameters of the "national" political unit, may persist for some time. Indeed, until it is resolved, little or no progress can be made on the more concrete aspects of

20

Contemporary Democratization

find it in their interest to intervene can do so with greater deliberation and selectivity. The potential marginal impact may have diminished, but so has the risk of backing the wrong forces. Moreover, the *modus operandi* will likely move away from covert actions by foreign governments intending to seize upon a "target of opportunity" in order to influence a particular event through specific inducements or sanctions (e.g. trying to encourage an autocrat to step down peacefully[21], or to change the outcome of a founding election[22]) toward more open and long-term attempts, often by non-governmental actors, aimed at supporting sets of institutions (e.g. the encouragement of opposition parties, trade unions independent of state authority or legal organizations ensuring access to justice or protection of civil rights). These external efforts to penetrate domestic civil society (and even to create a regional or global civil society) may have begun when the regime was still autocratic, but they rarely, if ever, seem to have contributed much to its demise. Whether they can do better to enhance the likelihood of consolidation remains to be seen. The evidence from Southern Europe provides encouraging evidence, but one can question its global relevance since the regional context provided a unusually rich and multi-layered set of non-governmental exchanges and a powerful incentive for accepting them (i.e.,not just full and

---

consolidation and foreign intervention remains a highly risky proposition. The most obvious, and obtrusive, external action at the governmental level would be to recognize the contested sovereignty of the pre-existing unit, or that of its previous sub-components. While this issue has not arisen in Southern Europe (with the possible exception of the Basque Country in Spain) or in Latin America, it is very crucial to the role of external powers in several Eastern European cases. The cautious attitude of the EC countries with regard to the Baltic Republics, and their initial refusal to recognize the breakaway republics of Yugoslavia or the other Soviet republics is evidence of how sensitive this issue can be at the level of existing states. In the "irrealist" world of contemporary international relations, this has not, however, prevented private initiatives and non-state actions from promoting the formation of these sub-units, often with considerable success.

[21] The examples of U.S. intervention in Nicaragua to encourage Somoza to step aside peacefully and in the Philippines to depose Marcos offer contrasting evidence as to the efficacy of such efforts.

[22] The Italian elections of 1948 were, perhaps, an extreme example of this sort of intervention and covert US support for a Christian Democratic victory succeeded in making that party the dominant political force until the present day.

Stanford Journal of International Affairs   **Fall/Winter 1993**

formal entry into the European Community, but participation in a
very vibrant and lucrative European civil society).
Democratizers in Latin America have no such prospect, and,
much as those in Eastern Europe may aspire to integrate with the
rest of Europe, the prospect of an immediate positive response is
becoming increasingly remote.

As we have seen above, **conditionality**, especially when
practiced through multi-lateral diplomacy and international
organizations, is the newest weapon in the arsenal of external
forces. Following conditionality strategies, a state will seek the
fulfillment of stipulated political obligations as a prerequisite for
obtaining economic aid, debt relief, most-favored-nation
treatment, access to subsidized credit, or membership in coveted
regional or global organizations. The foreign "conditioners"
should manipulate these incentives, at least in theory, in such a
way as to encourage the natives to sustain the momentum of
their political transformation and help them over specific critical
thresholds: acceptance of existing sovereignties; supervision of
free elections; amnesty for political opponents; adoption of
specific institutions; refusal to allow non-democratic parties into
governing alliances; resistance to military pressures; and
tolerance for partisan rotation in power.[23] Not only can any or
all of these be made "conditional", but domestic politicians may
even welcome this "interference in internal affairs" as an excuse,
arguing that their hands are tied and they must go ahead with
unpopular decisions. Moreover, a judicious application of
conditionality could be useful in the especially difficult context in
which several institutional transformations are simultaneously
clamoring for attention. By providing incentives for tackling
certain issues first - say, holding elections before removing price
controls or privatizing state holdings - the external conditioners
could help to ensure a more orderly transition. This observation
assumes, of course, the following: (1) they have an adequate
theoretical understanding of the situation to enable them to
determine what should precede what, and (2) the external

---

[23] I have seen a reference somewhere to the fact that Turkey even allowed
representatives from the Council of Europe to make unannounced
inspections of local police stations in an effort to convince foreigners that it
was respecting the civil rights of its citizens!

22

Contemporary Democratization

institutions at different levels and functional domains are not pushing different priorities and emitting contradictory signals.[24]

Of course, conditionality in economic and monetary matters has long been a feature of the postwar international context, the International Monetary Fund (IMF) being its most active practitioner. The tying of policy responses to political objectives provides the innovative features of more recent forms of conditionality.[25] Moreover, precisely because of its novelty and its blatant disregard for traditional notions of national sovereignty, there seems to be a propensity for hiding its manifestations behind the facade of multilateral institutions. It seems easier to justify conforming to explicit requests to establish specific political institutions or to perform specific political acts when they come from an international, and especially an appropriately regional, organization than when they are demanded by a single government. This effort at multilateral conditionality began with the very first transition in the current wave, but it has gathered momentum as the focus of regime change shifted from Southern Europe to South America to Asia to Eastern Europe, and, now, to Africa. In part, this may be a reflection that the more recent neo-democracies are more vulnerable in their trading, investment, and indebtedness patterns; in part, it seems to have emerged from an independent process of the accumulation of precedents and organizational capacities at the regional or global levels of the world system.

During a critical phase of the Portuguese transition, an extensive multilateral effort was mounted to ensure that its outcome would conform both to the country's previous alliance

---

[24] For a further discussion of the importance of timing for the process of consolidation, *Cf.* Philippe C. Schmitter, "La Consolidación de las democracias: processos, ritmos, sequencias y tipos", forthcoming in J. R. Montero ed., *Democracia*, Madrid: Siglo XXI. On the "impossibility" of resolving the problem of simultaneous transitions in economic, social and political structures, *cf.* Claus Offe, "Capitalism by Democratic Design? Democratic Theory Facing the Triple Transition in East Central Europe", *Social Research*, Vol. 58, No. 4, Winter 1991: 865-892.

[25] Recently, the IMF found itself embroiled in a controversy over political conditionality when one of its functionaries is (alleged) to have remarked that Brazil would only receive a stabilization loan if it changed its constitution to eliminate a provision guaranteeing individual states a share of federal tax revenues. Victoria Griffith, "Brazil suspends IMF talks in negotiator row", *Financial Times*, July 24, 1991.

23

Stanford Journal of International Affairs   **Fall/Winter 1993**

commitments and to "western" standards of democracy and public policy. This move involved mobilizing the formal institutions of NATO (and Portugal's momentary exclusion from its Nuclear Planning Group), the European Community (with a critically timed emergency loan in the Fall of 1975), and the International Monetary Fund (with massive balance of payments support), as well as a variety of unilateral (and less public) interventions by the United States and the Federal Republic of Germany. According to one well-informed source, even Superpower concertation was brought to bear when President Ford informed Secretary-General Brezhnev at their Vladivostok Meeting that *detente* was off unless the Russians stopped assisting the Portuguese Communist Party in its (apparent) bid for power.[26]

But most expressions of conditionality have been less dramatic and improvised. By far, the most important one for Southern and Eastern Europe remains the firm policy that only democracies are eligible for full membership in the European Community.[27] Needless to say, neither this provision of the Rome Treaty, nor the subsequent Birkelback Report (1962) of the European Parliament defines precisely what operative criteria are involved. Geoffrey Pridham has suggested that these seem to be the following: (1) genuine, free elections; (2) the "right"

---

[26] *Cf.* Tad Szulc, "Lisbon and Washington: Behind the Portuguese Revolution", *Foreign Policy,* 21, 1976: 3-62; also Thomas Bruneau, "As dimensões internacionais da revolução portuguesa: apoios e constrangimentos no estabelecimento de democracia", *Analise Social,* 18, Nos. 72-74, 1982-83: 885-896.

According to another account, Helmut Schmidt, Giscard D'Estaing, and Harold Wilson all discussed Soviet commitments in Portugal with Brezhnev "with a view to trying to get them scaled down". *Cf.* Tony Benn, *Against the Tide: Diaries, 1973-76,* London: Hutchinson, 1989: 423.

[27] To which one should add that even those countries which have previously negotiated some associate status are likely to find it jeopardized if they revert to authoritarian rule. The Greek colonels who seized power in 1967 faced a "freezing" of its developing relationship with the EC (as well as expulsion from the Council of Europe). These were only lifted in September 1974, shortly after their overthrow, and even before the first democratic elections were held.

One should note, however, that several, if not most, of the countries in the Africa, Caribbean and Pacific program of the EC would not qualify as democracies.

24

Contemporary Democratization

electoral results, i.e. a predominance of pro-democratic parties; (3) a reasonably stable government; (4) leadership by a credible (and pro-European) figure; and (5) the inauguration of a liberal democratic constitution.[28] None of the three Southern European applicants were formally admitted to full membership until they had crossed most, if not all, of these hurdles. Their admission, however, fails to describe thier respective democracies as reliably consolidated. Portugal still had significant, "constitutionalized" military intromission in policy-making and unstable minority governments; Spain had a weak governing coalition and even suffered an attempted military coup after entry.

Greece is, perhaps, the country that made most intensive use of EC conditionality to assist its unusually rapid transition and consolidation. Karamanlis anchored his entire strategy upon rapid and full entry into the Community and openly proclaimed that this decision rested on political, not economic, grounds.[29] This effort was no doubt facilitated by the strong role the EC (and the Council of Europe) had taken in opposition to the regime of the Colonels, but it was a policy which did not meet with universal approval in Greece. Moreover, Karamanlis coupled his European ploy with a (temporary) withdrawal from NATO. EC officials and member governments responded quickly by unfreezing the association agreement, sending a flock of visitors and providing emergency aid. They also pressured for a rapid convocation of national elections.[30] In the cases of Portugal and Spain, the responses of both democratizers and integrators concerning full membership were much more hesitant and drawn-out. In the cases of Eastern Europe, in which newly elected presidents and prime ministers placed EC entry at the top of the policy agenda, the lack of enthusiasm, perhaps veiled opposition, of the 12 member states has been increasingly apparent.[31]

---

[28] *Supra* note 9 at 235.

[29] *Ibid.* at 226. Also Susannah Verney and Theodore Couloumbis, "State-International Systems Interaction and the Greek Transition to Democracy in the mid-1970s", *ibid.* at 103-124.

[30] *Supra* note 9, Susannah Verney and Theodore Couloumbis: 117.

[31] The creation of the European Bank for Reconstruction and Development (EBRD) with its quite explicit commitment to conditionality raises the

Stanford Journal of International Affairs   **Fall/Winter 1993**

The extent of the impact of this specific form of conditionality is worth further exploration, even though no similar regional arrangement exists elsewhere in the world to promote the consolidation of democracy. First, EC membership is expected to be permanent in nature and to provide access to an expanding variety of economic and social opportunities far into the future. Second, it is backed up by "complex interdependence", an evolving system of private transnational exchanges at many levels and involving many different types of collective action (parties, interest associations, social movements, subnational governments, etc.). And finally, it engages lengthy, public, multilateral deliberation and is decided unanimously in the Council of Ministers and by an absolute majority in the European Parliament. This requirement enhances the "reputation" or "certification" effect beyond the level attainable *via* unilateral recognition or bilateral exchanges where other criteria (i.e. security calculations) may override the democratic ones.[32]   More than any other international commitment, full EC membership has served to stabilize both political and economic expectations. It does not directly guarantee the consolidation of democracy; it indirectly makes it easier for national actors to agree within a narrower range of rules and practices.

NATO conditionality, for example, has been a good deal less effective. Not only were the authoritarian regimes in Portugal, Greece, and Turkey "members-in-good-standing" of the

---

prospect that the EC may be able to influence the choice, timing and sequence of institutions in Eastern Europe without extending the immediate prospect of full membership. The initial funding is substantial (if far inferior to the sums required), but it is not yet clear how conditionality will be exercised, especially in a body of such heterogenous composition.

Another possibility is that the Community may relax its insistence on the *acquis communautaire*, on all new members accepting the complete accumulation of collective obligations, and create a multi-track system which would contain incentives for partial compliance of Community norms. *Cf.* Philippe C. Schmitter, "Interests, Powers and Functions: Emergent Properties and Unintended Consequences in the European Polity", unpublished paper, Center for Advanced Study in the Behavioral Sciences, April 1992.

[32] The persistent Greek opposition to Turkish membership on grounds other than regime type suggests that such security calculations can interfere with the choice process, although there is no convincing evidence that the other EC members wish to allow Turkey in their ranks.

Contemporary Democratization

alliance, but newly democratized Greece found it expedient to leave the organization for a brief period. Spanish membership in NATO was much more hotly contested domesticately than its EC application, and only narrowly won membership in a national referendum (and, then, only after the Socialist Party changed its position). Nevertheless, several observers have suggested that the engagement of national militaries in NATO, the external security role, the base agreements, and the funds for modernization and professionalization linked to this process, has facilitated the establishment of civilian control over the armed forces in the aftermath of regime change.[33] Again, the absence of such incentives in the functioning of the Rio Treaty in Latin America or after the collapse of the Warsaw Treaty Organization in Eastern Europe points to greater difficulties in these areas. The members of the Organization of American States (OAS) may, however, be breaking new ground with regard to multi-lateral conditionality. At their annual meeting in Santiago in June 1991, the foreign ministers of its 34 member states (momentarily, all representing democratic governments) agreed to meet in emergency session "to adopt any measures deemed appropriate" to restore democracy if one of their number were to be overthrown by non-constitutional means. The coup in Haiti which followed only three months later has provided an almost perfect case for testing their resolve. The OAS did meet in response to the overthrow of Jean-Bertrand Aristide, and voted unanimously to send a high-level mission to Port-au-Prince, as well as to apply comprehensive diplomatic and economic sanctions. There has even been some discussion about threatening the *golpistas* with sending a multinational military force to Haiti, but that stategy's credibility has floundered on the obvious reluctance of member states, the United States, in particular, to commit actual troops and "assets" to such a venture. The continuing uncertainty in that country makes if difficult to assess what the effect of the measures taken to date will be, but for the first time there exists, at least *in embryo*, a system of international collective security that claims to protect countries (specifically, democracies) not only from external military aggression but also from internal political overthrow.

---

[33] *Cf.* Felipe Aguero, "The Assertion of Civilian Supremacy in Post-Authoritarian Contexts: Spain in Comparative Perspective", PhD Dissertation, Duke University, 1991.

27

Stanford Journal of International Affairs   **Fall/Winter 1993**

Was this system to become effective and be extended to other regions of the world, the entire international context of democratization would be radically transformed.

How can we explain this sudden flurry of attention on collective efforts at promoting the consolidation of democracy, especially when previous unilateral or multilateral efforts at making "the world safe for democracy" met with such a lack of success? It is tempting to refer to the standard variables of "interdependence" and "internationalization", perhaps with a side reference to the growing "regionalization" of IGOs and NGOs. Moreover, in certain of these regions, democracy at the national level has become the norm not the exception. While these broad parametric trends and waves, no doubt, contribute something to the desire to impose conditionality, its feasibility would seem to hinge on major changes in the system of global security. The end of the Cold War and, with it, the loss of external support for anti-capitalist and autocratic experiments in development have meant that regime changes no longer threaten the global balance of power. Democratic superpowers, such as the United States or Europe collectively, no longer need fear that the uncertainty of transition will be exploited by the sinister external forces of "world communism" aimed at undermining their security. On the one hand, this observation seems to leave insiders freer than before to choose their own institutions and follow their own policies, but only within the narrower constraints imposed by economic interdependence and international norms. On the other, it leaves outsiders freer to intervene when those norms are transgressed or when the interests of interdependence are violated, especially in those *regimes d'exception* where the effort can be orchestrated multilaterally.

Conclusion

An exploratory article about a process that is still unfinished can have no definitive conclusion. While we have found evidence for all four types of external intervention in democratization at the national (and, occasionally, at the sub-national) level, their importance seems to have shifted over time. Frequency of outright **control** by one state over the regime

28

Contemporary Democratization

outcome in another has declined, although the assimilation of the ex-DDR by the Federal Republic of Germany comes close to being a pure case. **Contagion** from one unit to another was certainly a factor within Eastern Europe and among the former republics of the Soviet Union, but its role elsewhere has been more disputable. To an extent, it may have been replaced by the emergence of multilateral, private networks of **consent** that bring together a variety of actors across state boundaries to influence the choice and eventual consolidation of democratic institutions, although the evidence on these trends is very hard to marshall without detailed case studies. Finally, explicit political **conditionality** has definitely increased to the point that present outcomes in Eastern Europe and the former Soviet Union may well hinge upon it. Whether the pressures from these agents of multilateral compulsion will be sufficient to extend the wave of democratization into the remaining autocracies of Africa, Asia, and the Middle East remains to be seen.

To facilitate further discussion and research, an "inventory" of propositions-*cum*-hypotheses has been appended to this article. They are offered to prospective researchers as inductive generalizations based on a restricted set of cases and period of time, not as confirmed empirical findings or invariant deductive conclusions. For, if there is one overarching lesson to be gleaned from these speculations, it is that the international context for democratization can change rapidly and unexpectedly.

Stanford Journal of International Affairs   **Fall/Winter 1993**

Propositions/Hypotheses

I. All contemporary regime changes are affected to a significant degree by the international political context in which they occur, even if:

A. This context does *not* dictate or determine the timing, type or outcome of the transition process.

B. The impact of the international context is normally mediated through national or sub-national actors and processes.

II. Transitions to democracy are more affected by this context than transitions to autocracy since they involve a greater number and variety of actors with a wider range of public and private contacts to that environment. Moreover, once the transition has begun, even more numerous and novel channels of exchange open up as a sideproduct of the change in regime.

III. The significance of the international context tends to increase over time in the course of a "wave of democratization" because:

A. Those cases coming later will be influenced (positively and negatively) by their predecessors (especially those in the immediate vicinity)

B. As the wave progresses, new international institutions and arrangements will be formed and apply their efforts to those that follow, *ergo*:

1. Over the course of successive democratizations in a wave, the nature of the international context will shift from primarily governmental and public action toward an increasing role for non-governmental and private institutions.

2. Also, there will be a tendency for the mode of action to change from uni-lateral actions toward multi-lateral efforts.

C. As the number of democratizations increases and is, therefore, geographically more dispersed, the role of actors in

30

Contemporary Democratization

the international context will become increasingly explicit, overt rather than covert, and will seek open legitimation, both nationally and internationally.

IV. The most effective context within which external actors can influence democratic processes at the national level is increasingly regional, because:

A. Cultural and geographic propinquity will encourage the formation of denser and tighter networks among neighboring countries.

B. The contemporary patterns of international interdependence, influenced by the formation of common markets, free trade areas and economic blocs, are themselves becoming increasingly regionalized and these multi-lateral efforts indirectly promote the formation of regionally-based NGOs (parties, interest groups, movements) that can play a significant role at the national level.

C. Moreover, where such regional trading and policy-making organizations exist and where they restrict membership to democracies, they alone can have a very significant impact, especially upon the processes of consolidation.

V. Existing democratic states tend to believe that it is in their national interest, as well as national ethos, that other states become democratic, because:

A. Democracies pose less of a security threat to each other.

B. Democracies tend to establish more reliable, extensive and varied trading relationships with each other.

C. Democracies, however, may fail to act upon their intrinsic preference for other democracies when:

1. The cost of actual intervention is excessive.

2. The risk of failure is too great.

3. The concern for possible changes in national security is significant due to:

a. possible defection from an alliance to neutrality

b. possible shift to opposing alliance

31

Stanford Journal of International Affairs   **Fall/Winter 1993**

c. possible change to protectionist or discriminatory economic or social policies that would negatively affect national producers

VI. Transitions toward democracy either occur during or tend to provoke serious crises in a country's international economic relations which, in turn, tends to make the consolidation of democracy more difficult. However:

A. Disillusionment with economic performance, even where severe and involving international complications, does not necessarily doom the regime change to failure, rather:

B. Citizens are **less** likely (in the present international context) to come to believe that an alternative form of political domination (i.e. some form of autocracy) would perform **better** in the international economy and **more** likely to focus their negative evaluation upon the government or party in power than upon the regime-type.

VII. The extent of influence that the international context will have over the processes of regime change varies with:

A. the size of country

B. its geo-strategic location

C. its vulnerability to specific external flows such as:

1. indebtedness payments

2. critical energy or raw material imports

3. easily substitutable or subsidized exports

VIII. The extent of external influence will vary with the stage, moment or sequence of the process of regime change.

A. Its potential marginal impact will be greatest during the transition, but this is when such an influence will be the most difficult to bring to bear effectively.

B. It will be easier and less risky to bring external influence to bear during the consolidation, but this is when the immediate marginal impact will be lower (and less visible).

Contemporary Democratization

IX. The greater the stalemate between internal political forces, the higher the likelihood that one or another of them will be tempted to appeal for external support to break that stalemate, although foreign powers may prove reluctant to get involved in such an indeterminate situation.

X. The more that thé contending internal forces disagree over basic foreign policy objectives, the greater the incentive for foreigners to intervene since the outcome is more likely to produce policy difference that could affect their interests.

XI. In the contemporary international context, the more open and penetrated the national economy and the more complex its interdependencies, the more likely that regime change, once it occurs, will be toward democracy, and the more likely that it will result in the eventual consolidation of democracy. This is **not** to argue:

A. that in an increasingly interdependent world system **all** regime changes will be in the same direction, or

B. that similar levels or degrees of interdependence will **necessarily** produce (and reproduce) similar domestic political institutions.

XII. The presence of a powerful democratic superpower (or powers) in the regional environment of a given country will have less of an impact upon the consolidation of democracy than the presence of a viable, expanding multi-lateral international organization.

XIII. The consolidation of democracy will leave most polities more, rather than less, dependent upon the international context. However:

A. The citizenry of these nascent democracies will be more rather than less inclined to accept the interference of foreign actors in their political (as well as economic and social) existence.

B. Indeed, in certain parts of the world, e.g. Europe, the dispersion and consolidation of democracy opens up the possibility of the formation of a "regional civil society" that may

Stanford Journal of International Affairs   **Fall/Winter 1993**

precede (and eventually precipitate) the formation of a "regional polity" that will institutionalize democracy at a supra-national level. [Even Europe is still far from this outcome (*pace* the neo-functionalists), but its emergence is worth simulating (and, where possible, stimulating)].

Part V
Towards Democratic Consolidation

[26]
THE CONSOLIDATION OF POLITICAL DEMOCRACIES: PROCESSES, RHYTHMS, SEQUENCES AND TYPES

PHILIPPE C. SCHMITTER*

Several countries in Southern Europe, Latin America, Asia, Eastern Europe and Africa have recently 'transited' from authoritarian regimes of varying duration, configuration and repressiveness to some tentative form of political democracy. In retrospect, these transformations in the mode of governance occurred relatively smoothly – even if, at the time, there was a great deal of uncertainty about their outcome. Large-scale loss of life and destruction of property were avoided. Previous power-holders were replaced or deposed with the consent, not to say the enthusiastic support, of the population. Authoritarian rulers – some of whom had endured for years, most of whom seemed so awesome in their coercive capacity, and all of whom were allegedly so necessary for the development and international security of their countries – were exposed in their full incoherence, incompetence, corruption and unpopularity. In most cases, they were removed from office with surprising ease. Not only was physical violence rarely employed, but widespread political mobilization usually took place *after*, not *during*, the demise of the previous regime.

These remarks should by no means be interpreted as belittling the importance of what has been accomplished in, for example: Albania, Argentina, Brazil, Bulgaria, Chile, Czechoslovakia, the Dominican Republic, Ecuador, Greece, Hungary, Paraguay, Peru, Poland, the Philippines, Portugal, South Korea, Spain and Uruguay. Quite the contrary! Behind these 'aggregate' successes in relatively peaceful transformation lies a multitude of individuals and groups that took difficult choices, carried out risky actions and made important sacrifices for the common good. Seen as a sort of 'quasi-movement' which, through international solidarity and diffusion, has affected whole continents or cultural areas, the demise of so many authoritarian regimes and the concomitant rise of so many democratic ones represent a sea-change in political fortune, matched only by that which attended and followed upon the defeat of Fascism and Nazism in the Second World War. In Southern and Eastern Europe and South and Central America, within a short period of time, dictatorships have become the exception rather than the rule. Whether this will remain the case is precisely the subject which concerns us in this essay.

For, having mastered the uncertain transition towards democracy does not guarantee enduring success in sustaining that form of political domination. In the past, such changes have often proved to be ephemeral. Bolivia and Ecuador in Latin America, Turkey in Southern Europe and Thailand in Asia stand out as examples of polities trapped in seemingly unbreakable cycles of authoritarian and democratic rule. Elsewhere, the pendulum may have swung less frequently or regularly between regime-types, but remission via coup to some form of autocracy has occurred in the past and remains a concern in the present. If these polities are to break the 'long wave'

* This is an abbreviated version of Chapters Five and Six of Philippe C. Schmitter's forthcoming book, *Essaying Democracy*.

of authoritarian rule or the 'short cycles' of regime change, they must consolidate the democracies they have so recently acquired. To do so, the new identities, collectivities, rules and resources that have emerged during the transition must be structured and legitimated in such a way that future challenges to their viability will be met, either with the stalwart resistance of a 'democratic (if usually conservative) establishment' or the flexible adaptability of a 'democratic (but hopefully reformist) opposition'.

It hardly seems worthwhile lamenting here the absence of scholarly attention to this problem of democratic consolidation. As Guillermo O'Donnell and I have observed in our recent work on regime transition,[1] modern democratic theory tends to ignore the question of how such regimes come into being and concentrate its attention (with much sophistication) on the issue of how already existing political democracies manage to function and to reproduce themselves over time. This is not to say that a good deal cannot be learned from this literature which might be relevant to understanding the processes of initial consolidation, just that they are not 'problematized' as such in most of what has been written about democracy. Of special potential interest are those theoretical works and empirical monographs which deal with crises – with compressed periods during which some significant and urgent alteration in governance is deemed necessary for the regime to survive. While these analyses of 'reform movements', 'consociational pacts', 'critical elections', 'realigning coalitions', 'social contracts', 'historical compromises' and so forth presume the prior existence of some form of democracy which must be changed as the result of pressures from below or calculations from above, they can be exploited *mutatis mutandis* by students of contemporary regime change to help make better sense of what has to be done to consolidate some form of democracy in the first place.

In defence of previous theorists of democracy, it should be observed that, at a logical and abstract level, the concept of 'democratic consolidation' would seem to be a contradiction in terms. Democracies are never supposed to be fully consolidated. Unique among regime types, they should contain within themselves the potentiality for continuous change and, eventually, self-transformation. By a process of citizen deliberation and majority choice, they can presumably choose to alter their rules and structures. They can even – as happened several times in the history of the Athenian Polis and Roman Republic —democratically decide to become a different kind of regime. Indeed, the very concept of dictatorship evolved out of democratic practice!

This 'theoretical' reflection clashes, however, with our everyday experience of contemporary democracies. Not only do their patterns and norms become *de facto* structured in highly predictable and persistent ways, but considerable effort is expended *de jure* to make it quite difficult to change these structures. Past 'founding' generations write constitutions which attempt to bind subsequent ones to a specific institutional format and set of rights – and they deliberately make these rules difficult to amend. They also draft statutes and codes which make certain kinds of political behaviour punishable, which make difficult (or effectively exclude) the entry of new parties into the electoral arena, which confer monopolistic recognition upon certain associations, and so forth. Of course constitutions can be ignored and laws can be changed in response to pressures from the *demos*, but let us not exaggerate how easily and frequently this can occur in even the most loosely-structured of democracies. As Adam Przeworski has argued,[2] uncertainty may well be a central characteristic of this type of regime, but it is a form of relative uncertainty heavily conditioned by relative certainties. For citizens to tolerate the possibility that unexpected and unspecified persons or groups may occupy or influence particular governing positions in their polity and that these newly-empowered authorities may subsequently pursue different, possibly damaging, courses of action requires not only a great deal of mutual trust ('a civic culture'?), but also significant structural reassurance. Democratic consolidation can be seen as the process (or better, processes) that makes such reassurance possible, and therefore that confirms regular, uncertain and yet circumscribed competition for office and influence. It institutionalizes uncertainty in one subset of political roles and policy arenas, while institutionalizing certainty in others.

Before plunging into the obviously indispensable exercise of defining terms, it may be useful to expose certain assumptions. The first has already been made: namely, that democratic consolidation (DC) poses distinctive problems to political actors and, hence, to those of us who seek to understand (usually retrospectively) what they are doing. This further implies that consolidation is not just a prolongation of the transition from authoritarian rule. To a significant extent, DC involves new actors, new rules, new processes and, perhaps, even new values and resources. This is not to say that everything changes when a polity 'shifts' into DC. Many of the persons and collectivities will be the same, but they will be facing different problems, making different calculations and behaving in different ways. This opens up the possibility (but not, I stress, the inevitability) of contradictions. As O'Donnell and I have stressed in previous work,[3] the conditions which encouraged the demise of authoritarian regimes were not always, and not necessarily, those most appropriate for ensuring a smooth and reliable transition to political democracy. Concordantly, those 'enabling conditions' most conducive to reducing and mastering the uncertainty of this crucial interim period may turn into 'confining conditions', making more difficult the consolidation of what has been accomplished. Moreover, the shift in problem-space may reduce the significance of actors who previously played a central role and enhance that of others who, by prudence or impotence, were marginal to the demise and transition. Revolutions, it has been suggested, have a tendency to 'eat their own children'; more peaceful and less consequential regime changes are likely to 'disown their own parents'.

Even more provocative is the possibility that a sort of epistemological shift occurs at this point. Whereas during the transition, an exaggerated form of political causality tends to predominate in a situation of rapid change, high risk and indeterminate strategic choice, during the consolidation, actors have to 'settle into the trenches' (to use a metaphor from Gramsci). They have to organize their internal structures more predictably, consult their constituencies more regularly, mobilize their resource base more reliably, consider the long-term consequences of their actions more seriously, and generally experience the constraints imposed by deeply-rooted material deficiencies and normative habits much more saliently. In short, causality shifts towards a socioeconomic rationality conditioned by capitalist class relations, longstanding cultural and ethnic cleavages, persistent status conflicts and international antagonisms. The implication of this latter assumption is daunting since it means that we will have to create another model to capture the logic of political change during democratic consolidation – just when we have managed, so tentatively and precariously, to identify a quite differently specified one for democratic transition. Fortunately for what follows, the 'new' model I shall be developing below more closely approximates those that prevail in orthodox political sociology and political economy.

To summarize, *democratic consolidation requires explicit treatment as a theoretical subject and concerted effort as an object of empirical inquiry.* This treatment and effort can be more reliably rooted in previous scholarly work than was the case when we studied the demise of authoritarian regimes and the transition to democratic ones, even if there exists very little literature explicitly on the topic.

Defining Democratic Consolidation

Let us begin with the imagery of Gramsci referred to earlier. Regime transition resembles what he called 'a war of movement' – a strategic context when a wide range of options seems available, when the behaviour of actors is mutually unpredictable and when it appears that great progress may be gained by audacious action. Regime consolidation involves a shift to what he called 'a war of positions'. The actors settle into fixed trenches defined by stable perceptions of interests, confront each other across a broad range of issues, mobilize and organize their respective resource bases, debate under known rules and techniques, and seek to obtain marginal advantages rather than to overwhelm or eliminate each other. The metaphor effectively captures the fundamental distinction between the two processes, though it should not be stretched too far. For one thing, in democracies, the forces engaged in politics do not simply confront each other like two armies in the field; nor are they always struggling for a fixed quantum of benefits. Gramsci's military imagery may be a bit simplistic, but it will serve to get us started on what is a very complex topic.

The genus of social processes of which CoD is a subspecies has been given a number of labels. 'Structuration' is the currently fashionable one, thanks to the growing influence of the work of Anthony Giddens.[4] Routinization, institutionalization and stabilization – not to mention reification – were concepts used earlier to refer to cognate phenomena. The basic idea common to all of these is that social relations can become social structures; that is, patterns of interaction can become so regular in their occurrence, so endowed with meaning, so capable of motivating behaviour that they become autonomous in their internal functioning and resistant to externally induced change. In ordinary parlance, structures are collectivities in which 'the whole is greater than the sum of its parts'. The strategies and norms of individuals within them are constrained by the whole. The actions and goals of the structure are not reducible to those of its component parts.

These notions are rather elementary, and much of the theorizing about them quite abstract and devoid of clear statements from which one could derive discretely researchable propositions. At best, such theorizing could be exploited for a few broad guidelines and orienting hypotheses. For our purposes, this very generic approach has an unfortunate tendency to overlook political action in general and democratic processes in particular. A subtle analyst like Giddens may well insist on the relative freedom of choice which actors enjoy even in highly 'structurated' contexts – on the ambiguity of the rules that bind them and the indeterminacy of the resources that they can bring to bear upon collective decisions – but this is still a long way from conceptualizing the intrinsic competitiveness and dynamic uncertainty of democratic politics. What we need is a more specific definition and theory of structuration/institutionalization/stabilization/routinization that captures precisely these features and explains not only *how* they come to be adopted, but also *why* actors might willingly prefer them.

The consolidation of political democracy involves the structuration of a particular type of regime. Democracies, in turn, come in several different types (a theme to which we shall return below) and exist at various levels, but all presumably share certain characteristics. The ones that interest us here are all *state regimes* in the sense that they are organized at the level of the most comprehensive, 'sovereign', unit of authority and collective choice in the present world system. In our work on transition, O'Donnell and I defined a regime as 'the *ensemble* of patterns, explicit or not, that determines the forms and channels of access to principal governmental positions, the characteristics of the actors who are admitted and excluded from such access, and the resources and strategies that they can use to gain access'[5]. Retrospectively, I would only add to the above that a political regime must also contain specific rules determining how collective decisions are made.

Regime consolidation consists in transforming the accidental arrangements, prudential norms and contingent solutions that emerged in relation to the above issues during the uncertain struggles of the transition into structures, i.e. into relationships that are reliably known, regularly practised and habitually accepted by those persons or collectivities defined as the participants/citizens/subjects of such structures.

The consolidation of democracy (CoD), then, consists of transforming these *ad hoc* patterns into stable structures in such a way that the ensuing forms/channels of access, inclusion/exclusion of actors, resources/strategies for action and rules/norms about decision making conform to a specific standard: 'The guiding principle of democracy is that of citizenship. This involves both the *right* to be treated by fellow human beings as equal with respect to the making of collective choices and the *obligation* of those implementing such choices to be equally accountable and accessible to all members of the polity. Inversely, this principle imposes the *obligation* on the ruled to respect the legitimacy of choices made by deliberation among equals (or their representatives), and the *right* for the rulers to act with authority (and, therefore, to apply coercion when necessary) in order to promote the effectiveness of such choices and to protect the regime from threats to its persistence.[6]

After having made this apodictic statement, O'Donnell and I immediately went on to observe that conformity to such a generic principle and its corollary rights and obligations by no means guarantees that regime structuration will result in a particular or unique set of institutions. Lots of different decision-rules, inclusion formulae, distributions of resources, forms of participation, strategies of influence and so forth can claim to embody the principle of citizenship. Across time and space – not to mention culture and class – opinions have differed over what institutions and rules are to be considered democratic. So have the concrete institutions/rules which have been established in different 'democratic' countries. Given the positive connotation which the term has acquired, each country tends to claim that the way its institution/rules are structured is most democratic. The 'others', especially one's adversaries and competitors, are accused of having some inferior type of democracy or another kind of regime altogether. With the United States such a 'hegemonic' power in some academic disciplines, this has meant that in recent times the particular – not to say, peculiar – configuration of its regime has often been taken for 'the' model of conformity to the citizenship principle. Not so long ago, it was Great Britain, 'the mother of Parliaments', that was regarded as the model.

The implication of the preceding discussion is that *no single set of institutions/rules (and, least of all, no single institution or rule) defines political democracy.* Not even such prominent candidates as majority rule, multi-party competition, territorial representation, 'free and fair' elections, parliamentary sovereignty or a popularly-elected executive can be taken as its distinctive hallmark. This is obviously a serious debility when it comes to measuring CoD. One cannot just seize on some key pattern or 'meta-institution', trace its transformation into a structure and assume that all the rest will covary with it or fall into line after crossing some critical threshold. What must be analysed is an emerging *Gestalt*, a network of relationships involving multiple processes and sites. It may not be difficult to agree on what Robert Dahl[7] has called 'the procedural minimum' without which a possible case of DC could not be said to occur (e.g. secret balloting, universal adult suffrage, regular elections, partisan competition, associational freedom, an accountable executive), but underlying these accomplishments and flowing from them are much more subtle and complex relations which define both the substance and form of nascent democratic regimes.

Let me not be misunderstood: it is important that elections be held, that parties compete with varying chances of winning, that voter preferences be secretly recorded and honestly counted, that associations be free to form, recruit members and exercise influence, that citizens be allowed to contest the policies of their government and hold leaders responsible for their actions. The longer these structures and rules of the 'procedural minimum' exist, the greater the likelihood they will persist. Polities that have had regular elections of uncertain outcome for, say, 40 years are more likely to continue having them in the future than those which have only had them for, say, ten years – and so forth down the line. Therefore it is probably correct, *ceteris paribus*, to assume that Italian democracy is more consolidated than Portuguese or Spanish democracy, although recent events in the former should serve to remind us that even long-persisting regimes can become 'deconsolidated' unless they manage to modify their structure and rules to fit changing parameters.

But even the sheer fact of 'longevity' in such structures and rules is an inadequate base upon which to build an understanding of CoD. For one thing, it fails to tell us much about *why* or *how* they persisted. It just records the fact *ex post*. A more serious accusation is that such an approach privileges one set of democratic institutions (usually political parties and elections) and reifies (not to say, 'fetishizes') their presence at the expense of others. If, as I have argued above, democracy is the application of the principle of citizenship to the making of collective choices, this can be (and has been) put into practice through a wide range of decision rules, eligibility criteria and specific forums. An adequate theory of CoD must be sensitive to such variations in time and space. It must have the capacity at least to monitor, if not to measure, the emerging relationship between diverse institutions of representation (for example, interest associations and social movements – not just political parties) and multiple sites of governance (for example, executive decision making, cabinet formation, 'discretion' in civil and military bureaucracies – not just legislative process). This is what I meant earlier in referring to the need to think in terms of a *Gestalt* or, to use a somewhat less forbidding term, a *network* of exchanges between citizens and their rulers. Most important, the conceptualization of DC must avoid adopting an historically or culturally peculiar *Gestalt* as the standard against which to measure the progress of contemporary nascent democracies. The obvious danger is to consider competition between two centrist 'catch-all' parties as the norm and rotation in exclusive responsibility for governance as the hallmark of successful consolidation, i.e. to apply the US model to the cases of Southern Europe, Latin America and Asia.

Perhaps it is now time to switch to a more visual presentation of the concept of democratic consolidation. Although only a preliminary sketch, Figure 1 has the virtue of displaying succinctly what may be the basic 'shape' of the problem and some of its most distinguishing characteristics. The 'stages' in regime change (the term is advanced cautiously and intentionally stripped of its evolutionary connotations) are not seen as sequential and cumulative occurrences, but as overlapping processes. Certain of their aspects are conceived as happening in the same time frame, presumably in close and interdependent relation to each other. That the stages of demise, transition, consolidation and persistence appear to be of similar length does not imply that they are expected to take the same time to complete. As O'Donnell and I

FIGURE 1

A VISUAL REPRESENTATION OF REGIME CHANGE FROM AUTHORITARIAN RULE TO DEMOCRACY

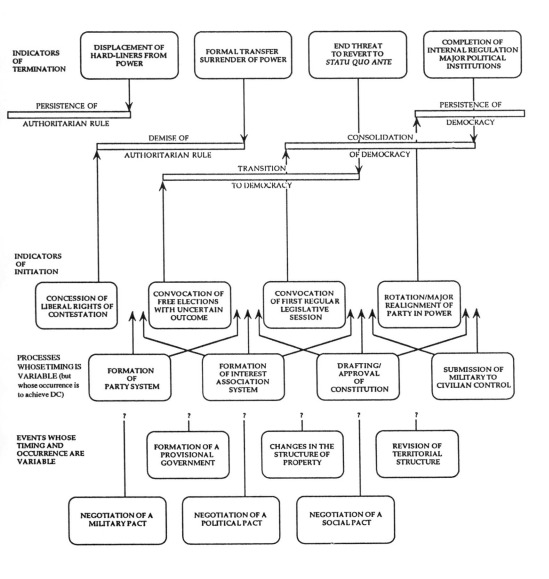

have stressed,[8] demise/transition has varied quite significantly in length and configuration across polities, from being almost instantaneous and conflated in the Portuguese case to being highly drawn-out and differentiated in the Brazilian one. Moreover, these differences are predictably related to the position of key actors during the regime change, e.g. the greater the power of authoritarian incumbents, the more protracted will be the transition.

The Initiation of Legislative Activity

For present purposes, let us concentrate on the segments of Figure 1 which deal with democratic transition, consolidation and persistence. My 'hunch' is that CoD should be conceptualized as starting some time before the transition is over. The convening of the first regular session of a freely and competitively elected legislature can be taken as the most likely generic indicator that it has begun – the *terminus a quo* for detailed empirical inquiry. Of course, the type of ensuing democracy will not necessarily be 'parliamentary'. Indeed, at the formal level, semi-presidential (as well as parliamentary) regimes have emerged in Southern Europe, while the presidential pattern tends to prevail in Latin America. Rather, the assumption is that the con-vocation of a regular legislature is bound to set in motion processes which will eventually define the following: the nature and role of territorial representation, the connection between parties in the electorate and parties in parliament, the extent of party discipline and/or accountability to constituency pressures, the form of executive accountability, the autonomy of state and para-state agencies, the strategies of interest associations, and so forth. Some parliaments may lose out in this definition of power relations. They may become relatively minor actors characterized by highly penetrated and dependent structures which can be manipulated and/or circumvented by other actors. In and by itself, this is not an indicator of the failure – much less the demise – of democracy. As we have stressed above, no single institutional configuration exclusively defines democratic rule. One can lament that fact on a variety of normative grounds, but some parliaments/legislatures are simply weaker than others.[9] This does not make the regimes of which they form part necessarily less democratic – just democratic in a different sense. Basically, then, the formal setting-in-motion of legislative activity will have widespread effects on CoD, given its putative centrality in the political process and the attendant necessity for other institutions to adapt strategically to its presence.

The Stabilization of Partisan and Associational Channels

According to the speculations of Figure 1, the transition is over once the structuration of rep-resentation has somehow been stabilized. In the contemporary setting, this involves two generic channels of access – the *territorial* one usually controlled by parties and the *functional* one usually dominated by interest associations. The two have evolved (and sometimes revolved) historically in rather different rhythms and sequences, so that there should be no presumption that they will stabilize their respective organizational formats, identifications, resource bases and modes of access at the same time. Thus, the exact 'moment' when democratic transition is over may be difficult to assess. Indicators in the territorial-partisan channel may show that a relatively 'steady state' has been attained: party identification is high; recruitment of militants and candidates has been regularized; voter preferences vary within predictable margins; regional differentiations have diminished; defections to another party have become rare. At the same time, indicators in the functional-associational channel may still show a great deal of volatility: membership is erratic; new groups continue to organize while old ones refuse to merge; bargaining arrangements in such areas as industrial relations vary from issue to issue and moment to moment; local and regional variations have yet to converge to a national norm. Of course, one can imagine the inverse scenario in which the party system lags behind the associational one in its structuration, but this seems relatively unlikely. The presence of a fairly uniform set of rules and a central competitive mechanism makes it much easier to structure and then to protect a party system than a more disparate set of interest associations, many of which do not even interact with each other and most of which have quite varied relationships with their members/clients.

Whatever the sequence and difficulty in measuring these indicators of the end of transition, it is important to note that this stabilization of systems of representation occurs during the consolidation of which it is very much a part. For example, the output of initial legislative sessions (as well as the drafting of a new constitution, whenever that happens) will doubtless have a significant impact on the stabilization of party and associational systems. Not only are a number of measures likely to be taken which *directly* affect freedom of association, registration and recognition of organizations, conditions of electoral competition and interest bargaining, etc., but many of the substantive policies likely to be on the agenda (agrarian reform, industrial promotion, social security, revision of the civil service and para-state sector) contain provisions which *indirectly* affect specific channels of representation. For example, the opportunities for political parties to exercise patronage and the availability of subsidies for interest associations may be established during this phase in ways that will subsequently prove very resistant to change.

The Initial Rotation in Power

The next more-or-less predictable event in consolidation may be more controversial and possibly biased by the strong Anglo-Saxon tradition in much of democratic theory. In Figure 1, I have indicated 'rotation or major realignment of party in power' as the crucial threshold. To have added 'coalitional realignment' might have diminished somewhat the 'ethnocentric' tendency of this property to be associated historically with the two-party systems of Great Britain, the United States, Australia and New Zealand. More recently, West Germany, Austria, Norway and Sweden have moved towards rotation in power between social democratic and bourgeois parties or blocs. In Latin America, 'rotativismo' has become a regular practice in Costa Rica and Venezuela. The French Fifth Republic has tried it once and a half. Elsewhere – for example, in Belgium, Denmark, Finland, Italy, the Netherlands and Switzerland – the 'test' of whether democracy has settled into a persistent pattern of contingent consent has been less stringent. Instead of admitting to exclusive governing responsibility some party or bloc that had previously been excluded, the dominant party or coalition has remained in office, but shifted (usually to the Left) to admit some previous outsiders.

The Swiss seem to have been masters of this 'subtle' strategy for persistence: after 43 years of single-party rule by the Freisinnige/Radicaux at the national level, the Catholics were incorporated in 1891 and the Socialists in 1943. Since then, the country has been 'persistently' governed by a 'magic 2-2-2-1 formula' that includes all of the four large parties and excludes only minor ones such as the Communists (Partei der Arbeit/Parti du Travail) with their 2 per cent of the total vote. By the criteria proposed, Italy could be said to have passed its test for persistence either in 1963 when the *apertura a sinistra* brought a different coalitional realignment into power, in 1976 when the more dramatic move was taken to incorporate the Communist Party in a *governo di solidarieta nazionale*, or in 1981 when the Presidency of the Council of Ministers passed from a Catholic to a lay candidate. Of the major contemporary democracies, the only one which has not yet passed this threshold is Japan which has experienced neither partisan rotation in government nor a major realignment in its national ruling coalition. One could argue that the accession to power of the Socialists in the municipality of Tokyo in 1967 signified the beginning of persistence but, given the very restricted powers of that political unit, this would seem to be stretching the point.

The Regulation of Institutions

The termination of the consolidation stage is even more difficult to identify or measure. Figure 1 speculates that this occurs when the internal regulation of major democratic institutions has been accomplished. The specific identity of these institutions would vary according to the type of democracy which had emerged, but everywhere would include competing political parties, voluntary interest associations, a functioning parliament and an accountable national executive. Decentralized administration, federalist states, popular referenda, Ombudsman arrangements, party primaries, proportional representation, an independent judiciary, a directly elected presidency – even schemes for worker participation in management and wage-earner funds – have all been identified as structures which must be consolidated if democracy is to be attained or to persist. Important as they may be in particular cases and periods, it would be unrealistic to expect all of these structures to be institutionalized before a given polity could be considered properly democratic and safely consolidated. Despite strong diffusion effects and a tendency towards convergence, the institutions implementing the citizenship principle remain quite varied in the contemporary period. Some democracies will be consolidated with less 'advanced' political structures than others, just as some will have achieved much less progressive social and economic change than others.

CoD is over when the rules and resources of basic democratic institutions are sufficiently entrenched – sufficiently protected by their own and other vested interests and sufficiently endowed with symbolic significance and normative approval – so as to withstand foreseeable changes in their environments. Parties will rotate in and out of office; coalitions will shift from Right to Left and back again; the business cycle will rise and fall; threats to national security will emerge and disappear; natural disasters will come and go; the Kondratiev waves will ebb and flow – but the regime itself will endure. Central to this conversion of contingent patterns into entrenched structures is the process known in German as *Verrechtlichligung*, i.e. the conversion of practices or norms into laws or regulations which are backed by the authority of the state. This is no magic formula. Constitutions are ratified and subsequently violated; laws are passed and then ignored; regulations are decreed and never applied. Indeed, there is a strong current in Liberal thought which identifies democracy and, specifically, democratic institutions with the absence of such constraints. In this case, political parties are not given (or refuse to acquire) any special legal status; trade unions and business associations do not register as formal associations and entire industrial relations systems run without the help of juridically enforceable sanctions. My hunch is that this is a phenomenon of the past. Contemporary democratic consolidation takes place in an environment saturated with organizations; these require legal status and privilege if they are to command the resources, autonomy and access they need in order to function effectively in the competition for office or influence.

Parliaments and Interest Associations as Sites for Consolidation

At the risk of formalism, I suggest that, normally, CoD can be considered over when the basic democratic institutions of parties, associations, parliament and the executive have acquired a stable *external status* and regulated their *internal structures*. The former tends to precede the latter, in the sense that a particular constitution, code, law or practice first defines the general attributes of an institution, which is then left to its own devices to complete the detailed regulation of its internal processes of recruitment, decision making, resource gathering and so forth.

At the risk of oversimplification, I suggest adopting as a working assumption the idea that parliament will be central to these processes, both in the sense of structuring its own operations and of being called upon (however formalistically) to ratify many of the codes and statutes which will structure the operations of other democratic institutions. In short, just as O'Donnell and I argued that social movements were crucial for determining the outcome of the demise of authoritarian rule and that parties were central to the transition to democracy,[10] I would argue now that parliament and interest associations are critical for consolidating a particular type of democracy.

Since the rhythms and sequences involved are much less well known and more variable than for the processes of demise or transition, I estimate that parliaments will take approximately three full legislative sessions (excluding prematurely dissolved ones) to complete both the structuring of their own rules (standing and temporary committees, seniority in appointments, extent of party discipline, budgetary routine, etc.), and the passing of laws structuring the rules of other institutions (statutes for political parties, regulations for freedom of associations, provisions concerning civil-military relations, codes of industrial relations, etc.). Given an average term of four years, this 'rule of thumb' suggests that CoD will take approximately 12 years. Obviously, the *terminus ad quem* of exceptional cases may vary. Some polities will revert quickly and without much deliberation to the laws/regulations/practices they inherited from their own previous (and usually recent) experience with democracy; others will be so constrained by the conditions of the transition that many relevant decisions will be postponed until such time as the authoritarian 'tutors' of nascent democracy agree to withdraw.

Figure 1 illustrates what I believe to be the basic configuration of the consolidation process and speculates about some of its key processes, thresholds and events. Before refining these observations by distinguishing between differences in points of departure, sequences in timing and so forth, it may be useful to explicate further what is at stake in this analysis of consolidation. Defining it loosely as I have and placing some hypothetical boundaries around its occurrence may help to initiate collaborative work along comparable lines, but fails to penetrate to the heart of the matter.

The Thorny Issue of Legitimacy

At this point, one of the most intractable concepts in the contemporary social sciences must be introduced – namely, *legitimacy*. The patterns converted into structures by consolidation cannot just exist or be protected by law; their *raison d'etre* must be convincingly justified. If they are to persist, they must become valued both by those who act in them and by those who are affected by them. Nothing seems more mysterious or controversial than this social process whereby some institutions come to be accepted as 'natural' or 'valuable' and, hence, capable of attracting loyal support even when the quality of their performance declines.

For a variety of reasons, the issue of legitimacy is especially problematic in democracies, despite the omnipresent use of the concept 'democratic' to justify all kinds of political choices and social action:

1. Democracies extol individual preference and voluntary choice; therefore, the decision to support a given structure is presumably subject to critical and rational calculation in ways denied in more traditional or coercive polities.
2. Democracies are based on the principle of citizenship, i.e. on the imputed equality of all those affected. However, what is normally being legitimated is some structure of inequality which assigns roles, resources or benefits to people differentially.
3. Democracies depend on competition, challenge and relatively free information – all of which tend to undermine the apparent naturalness and desirability of existing institutions by disclosing shortcomings in their performance and by proclaiming the virtues of alternative arrangements.
4. Democracies generate particularly close linkages between groups in civil society and agencies of the state. However, this threatens the operational autonomy of all public institutions and subverts their putative defence of the general or common interest.
5. Democracies encourage the open expression of conflicts of interest within the ruling group. This destroys members' capacity for unified action and, hence, their image as competent governors.
6. If such political dilemmas were not enough, add to them the classic Marxist, socioeconomic contradiction between democracy that distributes citizen rights equally and capitalism that concentrates property rights unequally!

With such a litany of potential difficulties, it would seem highly improbable that nascent democratic patterns could become, or remain, legitimate structures that people would learn to value and defend irrespective of their transient utility.

Eppur si muove! The 'democratic bargain', as Dahl has called it,[11] has not always proved so ephemeral. Positive attitudinal evidence of the legitimacy of democracy is fragile (most survey questions designed to measure this property are irrelevant or volatile), whereas negative behavioural evidence is quite strong: relatively few people in contemporary political democracies are actively trying to replace them with some other system, far less than are trying to undermine contemporary political autocracies. Despite what seems to be a secular trend towards declining respect for all kinds of institutions,[12] the predominant reaction (at least in Western Europe) has been to attempt to improve the fairness of competition within existing democratic structures and to extend the principle of citizenship beyond public institutions – not to abolish the uncertainty of competition altogether or to restrict citizen choice to a narrower sphere of collective action.

The crucial question is: how is legitimacy produced and then reproduced? How can patterns of strategic interaction and alliance that are initially just historical accidents, temporary compromises or second-best solutions be converted into structures that not only survive, but acquire valued symbolic status and the capacity to motivate behaviour in a particular manner? If we could understand this process of 'social alchemy', this way of converting base elements into noble metals, we might gain a very important clue to explaining democratic consolidation. If we could discover its formula 'quasi-experimentally' in our scholarly laboratories, perhaps we could then help to mass-produce it in the polities that preoccupy us.

This topic demands full-scale treatment that cannot possibly be accomplished here. The literature on it is enormous – and inconclusive. I propose to concentrate briefly on two aspects: (i) the *means* whereby legitimation is acquired; and (ii) the *sites* at which it must occur.

The Means of Legitimation

Everyone would seem to agree that learning is the generic method by which legitimacy is acquired. The channel most frequently stressed has been socialization – the more-or-less unconscious inculcation of norms, symbols and identities through basic social institutions such as the family, the peer group and the school. This leads to the hypothesis that legitimation is primarily a function of the passage of time, to be analysed in terms of generations. In an elegant argument, Philip Converse[13] has 'proven' that a new set of party identifications – no doubt a central aspect of some democracies – takes approximately 75 years to acquire. This may not be of much comfort to those trying to ensure continuity over the next few years, but it does have the virtue of inevitability – provided that unforeseen interruptions do not occur.

To the sheer passage of time, other analysts have added the impact of specific events. The idea seems to be that crises of particular intensity (e.g. protracted depression, runaway inflation or cataclysmic war) interrupt the steady inculcation of symbols and identifications, forming a unique and persistent generation of citizens with common experiences and expectations about justice, competence, trust and civic virtue. Indirectly, however, this introduces the possibility that legitimation may not be a purely social process but may contain significant elements of political calculation. A generation of victims of unemployment, inflation or war presumably is formed not just by the event, but by their common opinion of how regimes, governments, parties, associations and so forth performed in response to it. This, in turn, suggests that legitimation will depend upon perceptions of the effectiveness, efficiency and fairness of political institutions in relation to specific 'authoritative allocations'. Our analytical attention is thus shifted from distant horizon to immediate context, from conditioned reflex to learning from experience, from succeeding generations differentially subject to the appeal of particular symbols to competing classes and status groups differentially affected by the impact of concrete policies.

Such a shift in perspective may also allow us to incorporate the important concept of 'relativities' which has been virtually absent from the legitimation literature. The calculation as to whether a given arrangement of offices or group of actors is worthy of 'diffuse support', to use another of David Easton's terms,[14] may depend upon what alternative arrangements or groups are deemed to be available. That hinges, in turn, on what has been learned from past experience with non-democratic rule in one's own polity or on what can be observed from the present performance of other democracies and authoritarian regimes. Put bluntly, the likelihood of legitimation is enhanced – at least in the short run – if preceding dictatorships have left a legacy of incompetence, corruption and violence, and if other democracies in the area are doing reasonably well in coping with problems. Juan Linz has not hesitated to speak of a democratic *ethos* which permeates a given time period and set of countries through international diffusion and which consequently affects the normative/evaluative calculations of almost all actors.[15] Indeed, to the extent that this ethos prevails, the issue of legitimation will centre not on democracy *per se*, but on kinds or types of democracy, i.e. which set of rules, mix of institutions or extent of coverage best exemplifies its core principle of citizenship.

The Site(s) of Legitimation

When it comes to the site to which legitimation is attached, the literature takes an about-face. Social inculcation was stressed over political calculation as a means, but when we turn from *how* to *where*, we find ourselves back exclusively in the realm of the political. It is taken as self-evident that the legitimacy of the political order is located in political institutions. Moreover, in democracies, the site from which consent is extracted and reproduced is quite obvious: it is the *political party* or, more specifically, the competitive system of political parties.[16] If true, this would have the singular virtue of greatly simplifying the task of those who would study democratic consolidation. CoD could be reduced to two core problems which, if successfully resolved, would ensure the legitimacy of a regime: (i) how to structure the party system in such a way that it will produce, as a result of the free expression of individual voter preferences, either an outright winner or a minimum winning coalition capable of forming a stable government that can plausibly claim to rule 'in the name of the people'; (ii) how to ensure that parties not part of this winning majority will remain voluntarily within the established system of electoral competition, respecting the legitimacy of those presently in office, with the prospect of themselves forming a government after assembling a majority? This 'elitist' or 'party' theory of democracy presumes that citizens will bestow legitimacy upon such an arrangement, provided that the identity of those who govern remains contingent upon the people's collective preference as expressed through fair, regular and competitive elections of uncertain outcome.[17] Moreover, its implicit claim is that resolution of the above problems is not merely necessary, but sufficient to ensure legitimacy. No other linkages between citizen and state and no other arrangements among those in power need be taken into account.

In our speculations about the transition process, O'Donnell and I placed a good deal of emphasis on these two mechanisms of government formation and contingent consent.[18] While we were probably right to stress them for that period, I believe it would be a serious mistake to confine analysis to the party-electoral realm in confronting the problems of democratic consolidation. In the first place, this would ignore the range of sites for decision making and representation which have increased enormously in importance in recent decades – *pari passu* with the expansion in the role of the state. The conditions of participation, access, responsiveness and accountability which surround these exchanges between interest associations and administrative agencies have become a significant element in how citizens evaluate the performance of the political order. Indeed, it is through these channels that much of the deliberate effort at legitimation expended by the contemporary welfare state has flowed, rather than through the traditional means of party organization, machine politics, patronage by local notables, etc.

The Need for Pre-political, Hegemonic Consensus

We shall return to these issues when attempting to refine further the concept of democratic consolidation. What I propose to introduce here – and space will restrict me from doing much more than that – is the question of the social basis of government formation and contingent consent. The issue can be put quite succinctly: if citizens consent to be ruled in this manner, must they not already have reached an agreement on certain underlying substantive matters? Does political democracy depend on a prior social compromise or even on a set of compromises? And if so, can this be arrived at by an implicit process whereby individuals conclude that a particular system of ownership of property, strategy of investment, level of employment, distribution of income, right of inheritance and role for the state are somehow 'just' and, therefore, enter into an informal and ongoing pact that respects these parameters and confines politics to other issues or to marginal improvements in the ones listed? Or does it require an explicit 'deal' whereby organized collectivities negotiate on behalf of member interests a formal and time-bound contract which specifies reciprocal rights and obligations in the economic and social realm. Then, and only then, will these classes, sectors, professions, churches, sects, *éthnies* and so forth consent to 'the democratic bargain'?

The answers to these questions are not simply a matter of empirical inquiry. If one assumes that the means for acquiring legitimacy depend upon the gradual inculcation of proper norms and symbols, one will search for evidence of 'civic culture' and 'party identification' as essential components of CoD – and the appropriate survey instruments will no doubt find traces of them. If attention is focused on a more political calculus, one will certainly find evidence that varying social groups perceive the emerging institutions of democracy as differentially capable of satisfying their interests, and calibrate their evaluation of them accordingly. Those capable of mobilizing sufficient collective influence will seek to modify specific rules and arrangements in ways that make them more 'legitimate'. The really powerful ones will seek (and probably be accorded) legal and constitutional guarantees that place their interests and resources beyond the reach of democratic uncertainty. Even powerless groups may end up accepting the new regime simply because alternative forms of domination would be even worse, or because the costs of attaining them would be prohibitive. This is not to say that the mere initiation of democracy is sufficient to ensure its legitimation – even when the contemporary ethos (*Zeitgeist*) seems to favour it – just that the value-adding process may not be as protracted or culturally specific as is sometimes depicted.

The last contrast in perspectives bears much more directly on the role of organized interests in democratic consolidation. If, on the one hand, legitimation required no prior social consensus or compromise, then we could concentrate exclusively on the competition of parties and their efforts to form stable governments. Interest associations (and social movements) might have an effect upon the substantive content of policies, but little or no role to play in the legitimation of the regime itself. If, on the other hand, one accepts the possibility of a necessary social contract effected by the implicit calculations of individuals, then class associations assume somewhat greater importance since such interest calculations may be considerably affected by class ideologies and mobilizations. Nevertheless, these organizations and their patterns of bargaining would not be the central concern in studying CoD. Primary attention would be focused instead on more nebulous and fleeting groups within the dominant class which would first have to unify their competing interests and then impose upon subordinate classes a coherent conception of the economic-social freedoms and guarantees necessary for 'the welfare of all'. The formation of *hegemony*, in other words, becomes the precondition for the successful consolidation of democracy within a capitalist society; formal bargaining between highly structured, competitive class associations is not particularly conducive to creating such a state of affairs. Indeed, until relatively recently, Western polities did not have the capacity to substitute or supplement *social consensus* (based upon a fragile, ideologically mediated, calculation of individuals) with a *social contract* (based on a stable, organizationally mediated, negotiation among associations). Whether this development is sufficiently important to cause us to revise our thinking about the detailed processes of democratic consolidation is just one of the topics we will explore in the following section.

Refining Democratic Consolidation

Before plunging into further complications, let me summarize the above meanderings. Consolidation involves the process of converting patterns into structures, of endowing what are initially fortuitous interactions, episodic arrangements, *ad hoc* solutions, temporary pacts, etc. with sufficient autonomy and value to stand some chance of persisting. Actors respond by adjusting their expectations to this likelihood and come to regard the rules and resources of these emergent structures as acceptable, if not desirable. In consolidating a democracy, the predominant rules will be competition in forming governments and contingency in mobilizing consent, with the predominant (but, I stress, not exclusive) resource for accomplishing both being that of citizenship. In terms of the procedural minimum, this involves civic rights of contestation and association, secret ballots, universal suffrage and 'the rule of law'; in terms of the structural minimum, it involves regular elections, multiple political parties, associational recognition and access, and an accountable executive.

The mere existence of these procedures/structures is, however, insufficient to ensure consolidation. They must be successfully legitimated, i.e. their intrinsic value must come to be appreciated, not just the instrumental benefits they bring. In modern, representative, 'established democracies', high levels of positive identification, ethical approval and participatory enthusiasm are rarely the norm; indeed, they are regarded with some scepticism and are even discouraged. Such values may be very much in evidence and very important during the transition – especially during what O'Donnell and I called 'the popular upsurge'[19] – but what seems to suffice in the longer run are diffuse feelings within the citizenry of the 'naturalness' and 'appropriateness' of their regime. As long as the new rules and institutions are thought to reflect the standards of the times more accurately than conceivable alternatives, or as long as other normatively 'superior' configurations are judged to be too difficult or costly to attain, legitimation is likely to settle in – along with a certain amount of disenchantment (*desencanto*) with what has been accomplished. It may be comforting that this calculus of relative satisfaction leads to more optimistic expectations about consolidation than would be the case if the nascent democracies had to wait decades for the inculcation of a satisfactory 'civic culture' and set of partisan/associational identities (although this same satisficing calculus is what sustained many authoritarian regimes in power long after they 'should' have been overthrown on instrumental or ethical grounds).

Three Levels of Analysis

My operational conclusion from the above is that democratic consolidation can be analysed on three levels. All three can contribute significantly to an understanding of the phenomenon although, for theoretical reasons, they may not all be worth equal emphasis and, for practical reasons, they may not all be incorporated within any given research project.

First, CoD can be measured at *the level of discrete institutions*. What parties, associations, movements, assemblies and executive powers emerge during the transition or are revived from the past? What scale of organization, scope of representation, configuration of interests and number of supporters do they claim – and effectively acquire? What material resources do they manage to capture? What identities and symbols do they appropriate? What rules do they establish to regulate their internal functioning? What strategies of recruitment do they use to attract leaders, militants, followers and professional staff? How different are the 'new' democratic institutions from those that preceded them during the authoritarian period? From this perspective, the accent is on the processes whereby political organizations – public and private – acquire identity and autonomy under the new conditions of freedom, competitiveness and accountability. Let us call this aspect of CoD *group structuration*.

Second, the extent of democratic consolidation can be assessed in terms of *the ways in which these political institutions relate to each other*. What formal rights and obligations are mandated by constitutions, codes, statutes, etc.? What decision rules are adopted *de jure* and applied *de facto* for the making of public policy? What patterns of competition spontaneously emerge and then settle in between parties, between class associations, etc.? What interdependencies become established between the various channels of representation? What structures of hierarchy and accountability develop within the 'apparatus' of public choice? What kinds of coalitions or winning combinations form governments? Here, attention has shifted from the autonomy and identity of singular institutions to networks of power among interdependent or hierarchically ordered institutions. This we could call *(partial) regime structuration*.

Finally and most ambitiously, CoD can be conceived, measured and ultimately evaluated as a process of linking this *Gestalt* of emergent political institutions to the economic and social groups whose support (or at least acquiescence) is crucial to their long-run survival. What linkages form between various private constituencies and public authorities? What guarantees and privileges are extended to such *poderes de hecho* as capital, religious authorities, aristocracies, armed forces, police, ethnic minorities, local communities, secret societies or the civil service to sustain their commitment to the 'democratic bargain'? What social groups are systematically excluded or ignored? What *ententes* exist at the pre-political level which determine the subsequent political agenda? How dependent are regime institutions upon the processes of economic production and accumulation? What strategies of influence are tolerated by public authorities and justified by public discourse? This aspect of 'rooting' the emergent regime in the everyday practices and norms of society could be called *hegemonic structuration*.

Given the Gramscian derivation of the concept, it could be misunderstood to imply that the only relevant problem is to legitimate the unequal ownership of property and distribution of income. Democracies must also cope with other lines of cleavage – of religion, race, language and gender, to name the most obvious – and must somehow justify the disparities in benefits and the violations of minority interests which inevitably ensue from its decisions (and non-decisions) in these areas. Moreover, regardless of the substantive content of the problems they must deal with, modern (i.e. 'indirect' and 'complex') democracies have their own procedural difficulties. They must convince their citizens that existing mechanisms of representation and decision making are appropriately (if not always perfectly) democratic. This may not be an easy task when intermediaries have become increasingly professionalized and bureaucratized, and when the authorities act on the basis of compromises – many worked out in private outside the legislative process. The old slogans of 'majority rule', 'parliamentary sovereignty', 'popular mandate' and 'public deliberation' may carry less and less conviction. This situation is not unusual. Democracy has changed its organizational format and decision rules several times in the past – and belatedly found justification for doing so. Contemporary polities making the transition may have a more difficult time consolidating their new regimes simply because democratic practice has so far outstripped democratic theory, empirical or normative.

No study of democratic consolidation is likely to give equal emphasis to all three of the levels identified above. Group structuration can never be completely ignored for the simple reason that it identifies the *personae* in the post-authoritarian drama, endowing them with sufficient material and symbolic resources to play credible parts under the new rules. While it is certainly an oversimplification to assume that only those players who are organized formally will have a significant role, it would seem difficult to incorporate systematically into a comparative analysis such qualities as the impact of the personalities of leading protagonists (and of the clashes of personality among leading antagonists), the presence of shadowy factions, cliques, *éminences grises*, foreign agents, etc. or the mood swings in public opinion, whether national or international. Even such 'old stand-bys' as Rousseau's inspired *législateur*, the mysterious appeal of a charismatic leader or the more prosaic formation of a political class may prove difficult to script, much less to substantiate convincingly. We may suspect that any or all of these 'extra-organizational' factors will have a part to play in the evolving drama, but at best we are likely to assign them the role of *deus ex machina*, descending providentially and unexpectedly from above to resolve complications that our simpler cast of characters could not deal with.

A Digression on Contemporary Social Movements

To the usual cast of democratizers – political parties, interest associations, parliamentary groups, cabinets, prime ministers and presidents – a new type of organization has to be added. This is 'the social movement', usually mobilized around a single issue or 'passion'. The fact that contemporary consolidation occurs at a moment when the political processes of already-established democracies are having to cope with a variety of these groups, usually led by passionate, well-educated and relatively efficacious minorities, is bound to result in further complication. By diffusion and imitation alone, the new democracies of Southern Europe (as well as Latin America and Asia) will be challenged by movements defending the interests, for example, of consumers, neighbourhoods, women, handicapped persons, renters, nature lovers, pollution sufferers, religious enthusiasts, pacifists and so forth. Moreover, the centralizing, reactionary and exclusive policies of the preceding authoritarian regimes often exacerbated the concerns addressed by these movements. A great deal of pent-up demand genuinely exists for action to deal with such social inequalities. Parties with large territorial constituencies and associations with functionally-defined memberships have difficulty coping with these demands; indeed, they are very likely to be split into factions by some of them. The 'new politics' – with its emphasis on individual expressive action and its resort to unconventional collective behaviour – has already posed serious dilemmas for the established channels of representation in old democracies.[20] Might it not have even more impact on fragile new ones?

How these varied and often highly volatile members of the cast will fit into the drama of consolidating the more traditional institutions of democracy is by no means clear. O'Donnell and I stressed the crucial role of such 'grassroots' movements at a particular moment during the transition, and their rapid decline in significance once elections had been called and parties had moved to centre stage.[21] One assumption is that, during the course of consolidation, their energies and issues are largely coopted by the newly-established parties, class associations and specialized public agencies. This does not mean that social movements disappear. They may either remain as factions or pressure groups within these more-encompassing organizations, or lie dormant as small sects of enthusiasts and professionals capable of mobilizing larger followings when special circumstances or crises arise. In either case, they have not significantly modified the conventional mechanisms of voting and bargaining which to date have defined modern liberal democracies. A more 'optimistic' (and, in my view, unrealistic) scenario is that the fortuitous coincidence of activism in new social movements and regime change to democracy will have a more enduring effect on structuration processes. Not only would these movements forcefully place very divisive issues on the consolidation agenda – thereby making inter-elite and inter-class compromises more difficult to reach – but the sheer presence of such enthusiasm and commitment would compel the emerging regime to establish new means for citizen participation and to tolerate an extensive repertoire of 'unconventional' political behaviours.[22]

Regardless of the eventual outcome, contemporary inquiry into the CoD will have to take some cognizance of the existence and varying strength of these new social movements. It may have no sound theoretical grounds for assessing their probable role but, at a purely practical level, it cannot ignore the fact that the cast involved in group structuration is larger and more varied and, hence, that the patterns of possible competition and coalition are becoming more complex. This all makes the plot upon which regime consolidation is based much more difficult to decipher.

Shifting from Group to Regime Structuration

At the present level of inquiry, further theoretical refinement hardly seems necessary. Political science and sociology are relatively rich in concepts and classifications which can capture emergent differences in group structuration. Deciding which of the many typologies of party organization, party systems and electoral arrangements; of interest associations; of industrial relations systems; of parliamentary procedure, legislative role and committee structure; of administrative format, civil-military relations and chief executive role are best suited may prove difficult (and time consuming), but at least there is an *embarras de choix*.

When one shifts from the level of group to regime structuration, there is no such plethora of alternative conceptualizations available. Ideally, what is needed is a reliable and subtle general typology of democratic regimes, a well-established categorization of the range of variance in patterns or structures that embody to differing degrees and in different ways the principle of citizenship. If one could thereby identify *a priori* which type was emerging from the transition in a given case – either as a first preference or as a second-best compromise – one could presumably understand much better the likelihood of consolidation and the relative importance that interest intermediaries might play in it.

Alas, we lack such a typology[23] – even if there is an awareness among analysts that modern democracy does not emerge from a single mould. As I have argued elsewhere, 'democrats usually have very different institutional arrangements and political practices in mind in their struggle against authoritarian rule. These desired arrangements and practices tend to correspond – not incidentally to the structure of power that democratizing actors consider will best guarantee the defense of their established interests or the acquisition of their coveted ones. In short, actors in the transition do not choose democracy *toute courte*, but some type of democracy – and the version that eventually emerges may well be a compromised hybrid that resembles none of their first premises.'[24]

Frankly, I doubt that one can tackle the problem of regime structuration from such a high level of generality and aggregation, even with the help of multiple sub-types and *ad hoc* categories. If the aim is to guide empirical research, conceptual effort might better be directed towards understanding the interrelationships of specific sets of institutions, towards the structuration of a 'pattern within an, as yet undisclosed, pattern'. It may be neither possible nor useful to search for a single *Gestalt* or overarching network, much less to derive a single typology within which all cases of CoD find an appropriate niche.

At a more modest 'middle-level' of abstraction, one can focus on those sites or processes that link the newly structured institutions of political democracy to each other. Hence, parties and associations (and, to a degree, movements) compete and coalign through different channels of representation in their efforts to gain office and influence policy. Legislative groupings interact with party executives (and sometimes with relatively independent, popularly-elected government executives) to produce stable coalition arrangements that constitute and support governments. Electoral codes, political party self-image, organization and ideology, and distributions of voter preference all combine to produce a pattern of enduring competition. Interest associations and state agencies seek each other out and create institutionalized exchanges that circumvent other channels of representation.

Perhaps instead of trying to grasp the whole and give it a label, we would do better to map out these 'partial regimes', these landmarks in the political process at which two or more types of structured groups come together and, in the course of competing and cooperating with each other, define meta-rules or institutions which make their mutual behaviour more predictable.

The Significance of Constitutionalism

In modern regime transitions, this usually occurs during the drafting and ratifying of a new constitution. How this is accomplished will no doubt affect several, if not all, partial regimes. Not only do such documents lay out an explicit matrix of institutions and a formal distribution of their competencies, but they do so by means of general norms that are supposed to govern behaviour (and establish legitimacy) in a wide range of transactions. Two other general features of 'constitutionalism' are particularly relevant for CoD. First, it seeks to define the future substance, as well as the form, of politics by placing certain social and economic rights (and privileges) beyond the reach of democratic uncertainty. For instance, present-day constitutions may condition absolute guarantees of the sanctity of private property with clauses referring to 'social utility' or the 'public good'. Indeed, the use of such documents (plus affiliated codes and statutes) to reassure powerful minorities that their vital interests will not be violated by a change in regime is still commonplace. Second, to make such reassurances more credible, the new constitutions must effectively bind, not just their drafters, but future generations. Hence, they must resound with permanent ('self-evident') principles, be difficult to amend, and empower specific institutions (a Supreme Court, a Council of State) with an independent capacity to ensure that they are applied.

If 'electoralism' was the panacea of the transition stage,[25] 'constitutionalism' is probably that for democratic consolidation. In both cases, the basic idea is the same: giving a particular form to the resolution of political conflicts will *per se* modify the substance of political demands and alter the strategies of political actors. While such formalisms are not without independent significance, it would be very hazardous —not to say foolish – to focus exclusively on the definition of a comprehensive legal framework delimiting the powers of institutions and the rights of citizens as *the* hallmark of consolidation. For one thing, not all countries undergoing regime change engage in constitutionalism. Some, virtually without deliberation, simply reach back into their democratic past and resuscitate a previous document whose institutional format and definition of rights are taken as given. Most, however, do deliberate explicitly about these matters (often in the form of a special constituent assembly) and produce a new constitution. As I have suggested in Figure 1, the timing of such an occurrence may vary.

What seems particularly significant for CoD is less *what* is contained within the document than *how* it is drafted and ratified. Here, the crucial distinction is between those constitutions that result from a process of extensive compromise and unanimous acceptance, and the more 'audacious' ones that are enacted by a victorious majority over the objections of vehement minorities. Consensual constitutions would seem to have a greater and intentional 'freezing' effect on subsequent content and behaviour,[26] but even dissatisfied minorities may discover that they can live under contested constitutions, provided that the basic rule of contingent consent is respected, i.e. that they can compete fairly for majority support and can confidently expect to form future governments if successful. Moreover, they are likely to learn that modern constitutions – despite their increasing length and detail – cannot cover all eventualities. Lacunae and ambiguities will provide opportunities for developing extra-constitutional arrangements and engaging in unconventional behaviours. 'Flexible interpretation', not to say 'outright disregard', of specific constitutional norms may permit the democratic process to adopt new forms and alter old substances, especially in those polities that have not yet established an independent judiciary.

Constitutionalism as ideology and constitutionalization as process are thus elements in regime structuration, but no more than that. This legal-formal document represents the most ambitious attempt to impose 'a pattern of patterns' upon the emerging configuration of power – and it is doomed to be at least a partial failure. Modern democracies (fortunately) lack the arbitrariness of leadership behaviour and disregard for citizen rights of modern autocracies. From this perspective, they are bound to be more constitutional, but their processes of selection, access, participation, competition, accountability and responsiveness are simply too various and mutable to be definitively codified – much less indefinitely frozen for future generations. Their constitutions may not be 'periodical literature', as one wag apparently described those of Latin America, but neither are they 'holy writ'.

The Variety of Partial Regimes

In fact, as we turn our attention from the whole regime to partial regimes, we discover that it is precisely in the interstices between structured groups and group-systems that constitutional norms are most vague and least prescriptive. For example, very little can be deduced from even the most detailed constitution about how political parties and interest associations will interact to structure the channels of representation, or about how various executive powers and parties in parliament will produce coalitions to form governments.

Nor do such grand documents tell us much about the 'delicate' issue of how civilian governments effectively control the military-police-intelligence agencies of the state. Even the more prosaic matter of how publicly-elected authorities manage to ensure that civilian administrators reliably implement agreed-upon regulations and allocations is difficult to formalize into generally applicable norms. In these and other areas of governance, 'partial regimes' will emerge to convert exceptional contingencies into standard operating routines, formal declarations of principle into informal rules of prudence, temporary pacts into stable compromises – in other words, patterns into structures – during the consolidation phase.

Concentration on this meso-problem of the structuration of partial regimes would seem to offer both the most empirically feasible and the most theoretically strategic level of analysis from which to approach the global problem of democratic consolidation. Such an approach would have to incorporate information about group structuration and, eventually, to deal with the complex issue of hegemonic structuration, but it should deal primarily with topics of its own choosing. In Figure 2, I have attempted to sketch out the property-space involved. As the reader can observe, it is considerable and complex. At the centre of the consolidation process is the arena of *governing authorities*, in keeping with the frequent observation that, in modern democracies, power has shifted from its 'historical' site in parliament towards the presidential or prime ministerial executive. Its internal relations are depicted as involving exchanges with four institutional complexes: *legislative assemblies*; *political parties*; *administrative agencies* (civilian, military and para-state); and *interest associations*. To a partial degree (hence, the dotted hexagon), these relations can be constitutionalized. At the very least, they occur in an environment heavily conditioned (but not strictly determined) by formal prescriptions and regulations. *Grosso modo*, two dimensions define this 'internal regime': a vertical one based on the structure of powers, and a horizontal one based on the process of government formation. Crucial for the first dimension are such traditional political science concepts as unitary/regional/federal/confederal territorial administration and presidential/semi-presidential/parliamentary executive. The second has been less conventionally mapped by the discipline, but seems to be defined by the type of coalition formed (minimal majority/maximal majority/minority), by the principle of inclusion in government (party affiliation/associational support/personal loyalty/technocratic expertise), and by the number of actors involved (single party/dominant party/multi-party/supra-party governments).

In contrast to these *internal relations of authority* and government formation, the five partial regimes depicted in Figure 2 as structuring *the external linkages of democratic institutions with civil society* tend to be more informal. To a degree they are protected by the constitution, but are not prescribed by it in the way internal regimes are. By far the best described of these is the *electoral regime* that links political parties and legislative assemblies through such devices as the nomination and promotion of candidacies, the selection and distribution of winning

FIGURE 2

SKETCH OF THE PROPERTY-SPACE INVOLVED IN THE CONSOLIDATION
OF WHOLE AND PARTIAL REGIMES IN MODERN DEMOCRACIES

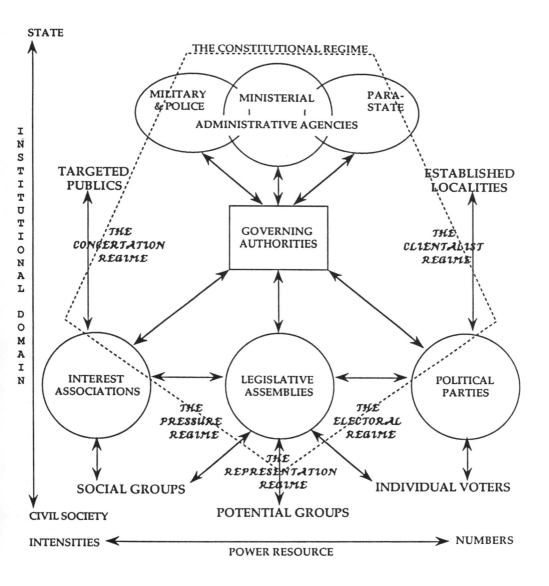

representatives, and the organizing and disciplining of legislators – subject to the outside constraint of voter preference. The *pressure regime* that structures exchanges between parliaments and interest associations has also been extensively described (if inadequately analysed) in the literature on lobbying, candidate financing, 'influence peddling', etc. Its principle external constraint consists of the willingness of members of social groups to contribute voluntarily to collective action. Recent writings on neo-corporatism have served to improve conceptualization of the *concertation regime*, i.e. the ways in which interest associations may (and may not) interact directly with administrative agencies through various mechanisms of policy bargaining and implementation, subject to the willingness of the publics targeted by such policies to behave appropriately. One has to turn to political anthropology or to the more lurid accounts of 'machine politics' to capture the relevant dimensions of patronage, favouritism and 'pork barrel' spending that are involved in the *clientelist regime* that may or may not link particular established localities via political parties to specific agencies of the state. Finally, the *representation regime* links parties and associations to each other in varying degrees of competition and cooperation for member allegiance and financial support. Here, the major outside constraint consists of the possibility that potential groups, dissatisfied with existing representatives and their definitions of interest, will mobilize outside these channels by creating new parties and associations or, as we noted above, by forming new, single-issue, social movements.

It is one of the key (if often implicit) assumptions of modern democratic theory that the legitimacy and, hence, the long-term viability of a given democratic regime depend upon how well these external linkages with civil society function. Unlike previous, purely legal or formal, approaches to democracy that stressed such internal institutional configurations as 'parliamentarism-presidentialism', 'unitarism-federalism', 'separatism of powers-checks and balances', this contemporary 'sociological' perspective asks whether these partial regimes afford satisfactory participation, whether they ensure accountability to citizen preferences, and whether authorities affected by them are accessible and responsive to individuals and groups – without assuming that some single or exemplary configuration of institutions would 'legitimately' resolve all of these problems for all polities.[27]

The property-space of Figure 2 is defined by *institutional domain* on the vertical axis, varying from state to civil society, and by *power resource* on the horizontal one, ranging from the counting of numbers to the weighing of intensities. Seen from this perspective, the overall democratic regime being consolidated in any given case will not only be identified by its internal configuration, but will also be composed of different external regimes or, better, of mixes of external regimes that differ in importance. Some will be more majoritarian, i.e. structured around the principle of primary citizenship based on number of votes mobilized *via* electoral and clientelist regimes in favour of a given candidate or policy; others will be more consociational and, hence, built around expressions of secondary citizenship, i.e. weighted to favour the intensity of preferences of particular minorities *via* the pressure and concertation regimes. Some will be more 'state-centred' in the way they focus partisan and associational demands directly on exchanges with administrative agencies *via* clientelist or concertative channels; others will be more 'societally-centred' in their capacity to resolve conflicts through private exchanges within the representation regime and/or in their insistence that demands from below be channelled through legislative assemblies, referenda or popularly-elected executives *via* group pressure or electoral mobilization.

Shifting from (Partial) Regime to Hegemonic Structuration

There would be little advantage in refining further an approach to the third general level discussed above – that of *hegemonic structuration*. Its accomplishment is notoriously difficult to observe and is measured largely by what does not occur rather than by what does. Hegemony can be 'alleged' whenever certain forms of violence, resistance or struggle do not appear, e.g. whenever resourceful, if contentious, protagonists agree to play by the rules, or whenever subordinates defer without a fight to the wishes or commands of their 'superiors'. Of its two components mentioned above, the first – the cohesion of dominant groups in their political actions and justifications – is often masked in democracies behind a facade of continuous (usually partisan) conflict. Only after the fact can one discern the underlying unity of purpose and function behind competing elite factions. Its second component – the acceptance by subordinate groups of a compromise whereby some are accorded the right to political office (and, usually, to own productive property and to enjoy social privilege) while others receive certain benefits – can be captured by various survey research instruments. Nevertheless, answers to questions about 'regime satisfaction' are notoriously unreliable. Not only are their referents unclear but, as the conditions underlying the social compromise change, so may the evaluations of individuals and groups (unless these attitudes are as deeply rooted in normative socialization as some political psychologists have argued). In democracies, overt elite competition for the formation of governments usually leads to an underestimation of the unity of rulers, while contingent calculations of public opinion tend to overestimate the consent of the ruled. Only when manifestly in demise can we be sure that a regime has failed to legitimate itself by not fitting its rules and institutions to the socially required (if often implicit) compromise between classes, sectors, *éthnies*, religions, genders, generations, etc. While any comprehensive analysis of democratic consolidation – especially a retrospective one – would eventually have to involve some consideration of this problem of hegemony, it does not seem to be a promising place to start. At least, not until we have a much better understanding of the levels of group and regime structuration.

Explaining Democratic Consolidation

The bulk of this essay has been devoted to defining the consolidation of democracy and to refining its multiple components within a more general approach to the problem of regime change. In this conceptual effort to carve out a distinctive space for CoD between uncertain and tumultuous transition and predictable and settled persistence, explanations have only been hinted at. Now it is time to take a (tentative) look at the following question: What factors/conditions/contexts are most favourable to a consolidation of political democracy? Is there one formula for its accomplishment, or are there a multitude of relevant paths? With contemporary democracies so different in their rules and institutions, and historically so different in their timing and sequence, can one even envisage a common explanation for the process(es) of consolidation? Might we not end up with a different explanation for each case? Or just a description of each occurrence? If the latter, we could pass directly to the task of gathering information on the dependent variable outlined above.

It may be most useful to consider certain countries as 'cases' of an analogous nature and therefore subject to similar processes, events, choices, dilemmas and outcomes. Southern

Europe offers the comparativist a particularly promising subset for analysis, given that (except for Italy) four countries in that area moved to democracy at the same time and shared certain common features including geo-strategic location, social and economic structure, position in world markets, historical experience, cultural norms, legal tradition, and so forth. Indeed, the juxtaposition of these two observations suggests the 'strong hypothesis' that a causal relation exists between them, i.e. that 'it is not an accident that' four of these five polities in Southern Europe have only belatedly transited from authoritarian rule to democracy and done so more or less at the same time. What is more, the consolidation of their new forms of political domination seems, so far, to have been generally successful. Turkey is the obvious exception to this generalization, but (conveniently for our hypothesis) it is farthest from the 'contextual communality' of the subset. In any case, despite the overall similarity, variations among the five countries doubtless explain the manifold differences in form and content of the eventual regime outcomes.

The Importance of Contingent Factors

Before plunging into a very tentative and incomplete 'heuristic model', let us first consider three aspects of CoD that precede a causal explanation: *speed, timing* and *sequence*. By speed, I mean quite simply the rapidity with which patterns can be expected to turn into structures. The existing literature tends to be 'glacial'. The formation of stable and enduring democracies is depicted as a very slow process of gradual accretion and slow displacement. Previously subordinate groups are enfranchised or associated only after a long period of resistance and after indicating their willingness to play according to pre-existing rules. Previously dominant ones are gradually marginalized through demographic or social processes or find it expedient to accept new allies. Socialization to new rules and institutions extends over generations.

Needless to say, few polities can support such a delicate and protracted historical process. Analysts who adopt (explicitly or implicitly) such a viewpoint tend to emphasize the fact that rather few of the world's polities have attained, and even fewer have sustained, such an exalted status. For the remaining imprudent and impatient countries, instability and failures of democracy are the expected outcomes.[28]

Ironically, since the *locus classicus* for this perspective has been English democracy, the single most apposite historical monograph on the subject – J.H. Plumb's *The Growth of Political Stability in England*[29] – advances a quite different argument. Plumb states his central thesis quite simply and dramatically: 'the acceptance by society of its political institutions and of those classes of men or officials who control them ... comes quite quickly ... as suddenly as water becomes ice'.[30] He admits that the *possibility* of such an outcome depends on a number of long-term factors (he calls them 'tidal forces'), but argues that contemporaries are usually unaware of what these are. The *actuality* of stability is determined by the actions of conscious and calculating individuals creating new arrangements and organizations in response to quite specific events and challenges. Making the right choices may require 'political genius' but, once in place, they can have a rapid effect on both behaviour ('the rage of party gave way to the pursuit of place') and values (the new practices acquired 'an aura of inevitability' and became 'the object of veneration').

Admittedly, the political stability that Plumb found developing so suddenly in 18th-century England was not exactly democratic. Rather, it took the form of oligarchic parliamentarism as an alternative to popular democracy: 'the evolution of political stability had gone hand in hand with the diminution and close control of the electorate and a more thorough exploitation of patronage, but also with the evolution of single party government and the proscription of a political opposition'.[31] Even if his stimulating essay cannot be exploited directly in building a contemporary heuristic model, his central point about the *speed* of consolidation is worth retaining. Above, I advanced the proposition that the process begins with the first seating of a regular parliament and should be over by the end of its third term, a period of about 12 years on average. That may seem a rather long time to turn 'water into ice' but, by Plumb's calculation, the English took between 40 and 50 years to accomplish the feat definitively! A comprehensive theory of regime change may well conclude that the speed of consolidating autocracies, oligarchies and democracies differs, and that the last may be the slowest of all since they involve a greater number and variety of actors.

In terms of *timing*, one central issue is the occurrence of democratic consolidation in one country relative to the nature of political domination in analogous countries. This tends to be perceived as a 'regional' phenomenon since the appropriateness and desirability of institutions are often restricted to some subset within which interactions and ideas circulate with particular intensity. One can, of course, speak of 'epochs' affecting a large number of countries during which political expectations are noticeably uniform. The decade after World War II was certainly one of these. Many dictatorships frozen into power by the war itself were overthrown in its immediate aftermath, although Portugal and Spain testify to the possibility of successfully resisting such contagious or faddish behaviour. With respect to Western Europe, we may be in such a democratic epoch at the present moment. Not only is there a diffuse expectation that some form of democracy is the natural, the 'civilized', way to rule this part of the world, but there are also regional organizations and networks of solidarity (and subsidization) that support those who promote such an outcome and threaten those who do not. Whether this *Zeitgeist* extends to all regions of the world is not yet clear. It would seem that Africa and the Middle East (excluding Israel and Turkey) have not been subjected to the same internationalized norms and sanctions.

Of special relevance may be the timing of regime change within the same region. The experiences and experiments of precocious neighbours tend to be regarded as lessons – positive and negative – by those following on. Plumb, for example, points out that the English outcome was significantly influenced by the reaction to contemporary French absolutism. English leaders had to compete with the seemingly greater stability and efficiency (not to mention glory) of the French monarchy; at the same time, they sought to avoid the political displacement of the local gentry which this earlier experience had entailed. Analogous learning effects may now be underway within Southern Europe, Latin America and Eastern Europe. Hence, it is claimed that the unexpectedly rapid (and, for a moment, seemingly revolutionary) transition in Portugal helps to explain why the Spaniards moved so cautiously after Franco's death; also that the disappointing results of the nationalization policy of the French socialists taught the Spanish socialists 'what not to do' when they came to power. Inversely, the successive democratizations of Brazil, Uruguay, Peru and Argentina in the early 1980s put pressure on Pinochet's Chile – without much immediate result, other than repeated (but ultimately frustrated) popular mobilizations. Eventually, however, not only Chile but also Paraguay conformed to the new regional norm of popularly accountable government.

But we should be cautious and not assume that just because countries are adjacent and share certain traits – say, in sub-Saharan or North Africa – that they necessarily form a 'region' in the strict sense. Indeed, the historical patterns of colonialism and the contemporary dependencies on capitalism may link individual countries much more closely to extra-regional 'central' powers than to each other, either in terms of socioeconomic exchanges or normative-ideological standards. Often the signals and rewards coming from these remoter *patrons* are much more significant than those coming from next door.

Sequence is the third premise we should discuss briefly before examining the general model. That 'a' happens relative to 'b' and, especially, that 'a' must happen before 'b' can happen are important elements in many dynamic models of social/economic/political change. In Figure 1, a series of overlapping sequences were depicted which defined the beginning and end of successive phases of regime change. It was suggested that there was no necessary or fixed time lag. The change in state regime could be compressed within a few days, as in Portugal, or stretched out over a protracted period, as in Brazil and, later, Chile. In Eastern Europe, the *boutade* circulated that the demise of communism took ten years in Poland, ten months in Hungary and ten days in Czechoslovakia – to which one could add, ten hours in Romania.

Regardless of the variance in overall time frames, a certain 'logical' sequence between the *events* to be accomplished can be posited. Thus, some rights of contestation are normally granted before hard-line protagonists are displaced from power; elections have to be convoked (and held) before a regular legislature can sit, while stabilization of party identifications and group memberships 'should' precede rotation in power. Beyond these presumed sequences (which can, of course, be overturned) come a number of *processes* which are necessary but variable with respect to other 'happenings' during democratization, and *events* that are optional and may not be chosen.

In Figure 1, four *necessary* processes were suggested:

1. the formation of a party system;
2. the formation of an interest associational system;
3. the drafting or revival of a constitution;
4. the submission of the military to civilian control.

When these will occur is significant in determining outcomes, but difficult to predict *a priori*. The party system, for example, may be inherited virtually intact from a previous democratic period and survive continuously (if quietly) during authoritarian rule – or it may have to emerge *ex novo* during the transition after elections have been called. Associational systems are more complicated due to the differential repression of class and sectoral interests, but they too can enter the scene at different moments. Nowadays, all democracies tend to have a written constitution, but some can revive an appropriate one from the past, while others must go through an elaborate process of electing a constituent assembly and drafting a new document. One would think that such assemblies would precede the seating of normal parliaments, but in some cases (e.g. Brazil) the latter get down to business under rules established by the outgoing authoritarian regime before the former are convoked.

Under the tentative rubric '*events whose occurrence is variable*' (and, therefore, whose sequencing is even more unpredictable), Figure 1 offered six categories:

1. the formation of a provisional government;
2. the negotiation of a pact of military extraction from power;
3. the imposition of changes in the structure of property;
4. the negotiation of a pact among political parties;
5. the negotiation of a social pact with the participation of interest associations;
6. the revision of the territorial distribution of authority.

A polity moving from authoritarian rule to political democracy is not generically 'required' to do any of these. They are not intrinsic to the new form of domination, as were the four previous processes. However, if they do occur, and especially where they occur in combination (as, for example, when a provisional government imposes changes in the property structure that could not be decided by a regularly elected parliament), the consequences for CoD will be significant. In previous work, O'Donnell and I have stressed the possible role of pacts – military, political and/or social – as a means to a relatively continuous and peaceful transition from authoritarian rule,[32] but did not insist that they were necessary for the instauration or restauration of democracy. One should nevertheless be sensitive to the possible impact of such events, even if they cannot be incorporated within a single general model.

A Heuristic (and, therefore, Incomplete) Model

The core of the model proposed in Figure 3 is formed by a series of successive transformations of political patterns and structures at the regime level. Put simply, *the primary (but by no means exclusive) determinant of the consolidation of democracy (and type of ensuing democracy) is the mode of transition*. This in turn is strongly influenced by how the previous authoritarian regime was overturned, which is linked to the type of regime it was – and so forth. This central political 'rhythm' of regime succession is sometimes accelerated and sometimes deflected in new directions by *socioeconomic trends* (Plumb's 'tidal forces'), *unexpected events* (war and, more recently, terrorism being the most important), *cyclical disturbances* (e.g. trade depressions, foreign indebtedness, massive unemployment, product obsolescence and, perhaps, 'long waves') and, finally, *shifts at the international level* (in dependencies, allegiances and norms).

The structure of Figure 3 is merely a first approximation and will undoubtedly be modified by future empirical research and conceptual discussion. This is where 'confrontation' between scholars from different areas of the world – South and Central America, East and South Asia, Southern and Eastern Europe in particular – should be especially valuable in establishing the generality of various suppositions and the range of variation in specific conditions.

Some progress has recently been made on the conceptual front, although only further research can confirm whether its descriptions and classifications have put us on the right track. For example, Leonardo Morlino has made an effort to clarify the content of the dependent variable described in Figure 3 as 'type and extent of democratic consolidation'. He proposes three kinds of consolidation based on the leading role played by different actors (by parties, by associa-

FIGURE 3

A HEURISTIC MODEL OF THE FACTORS INFLUENCING THE TYPE/EXTENT OF DEMOCRATIC CONSOLIDATION

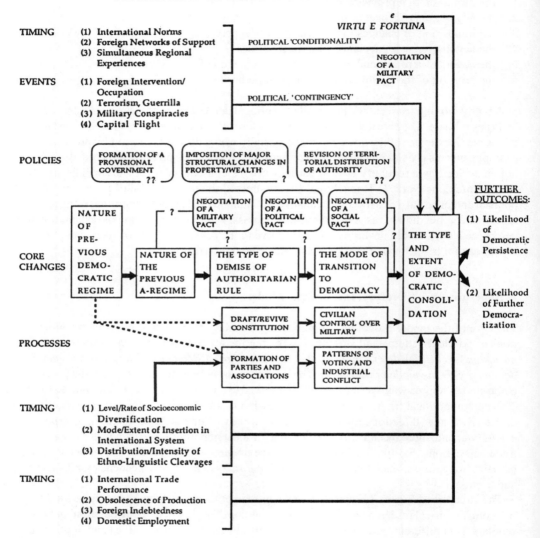

tions and by charismatic leaders) and two 'syndromes' involving different degrees of success in institutionalization (strong/weak).[33]

Terry Karl has developed an interesting typology of 'modes of transition' that could help clarify the contents of that box in Figure 3. Distinguishing on one axis the predominant means employed to effect the transition (physical violence vs. peaceful accommodation) and, on the other, the predominant actors involved (elite-sponsored vs. mass-driven), she generates a fourfold table: (1) *pact* (elite-sponsored accommodation); (2) *imposition* (elite-sponsored violence) which could be further subdivided into foreign and domestic instigators; (3) *reform* (mass-driven accommodation); and (4) *revolution* (mass-driven violence). For the region that interests her most – Central America and the Caribbean – she shows convincingly that all four modes have been tried, but that only pacts and impositions have led to the subsequent consolidation of political democracy, e.g. in the cases of Venezuela and Costa Rica.[34]

In an earlier article, I proposed a fourfold scheme for classifying the different ways in which authoritarian regimes are terminated: (1) a *seizure of power* occurs when an existing dictatorship is violently displaced (usually by coup) by some of its previous protagonists; (2) a *transfer of power* involves handing over executive authority without violence to some of the authoritarian regime's previous beneficiaries or allies; (3) a *surrender of power* happens when power passes peacefully to a new ruling group that was previously excluded; and, finally, (4) an *overthrow of power* is a violent (and usually abrupt) change in regime in which antagonists mobilize and are successful in militarily defeating the authoritarian incumbents. Types (2) and (3) are hypothesized to favour a transition to democracy, usually *via* the concession of reforms in the first case and the negotiation of pacts in the second.[35]

Juan Linz has done pioneering work on typologizing authoritarian regimes (sultanistic/military/bureaucratic military/organic statist/fascist).[36] Guillermo O'Donnell's distinction between traditional- and bureaucratic-authoritarian regimes[37] has been hypothetically linked to different types of authoritarian demise.[38] It could also be useful in explaining probable differences in transition and consolidation paths.

There are also signs of renewed interest in distinguishing different types of democracy. Arend Lijphart's *Democracies*[39] lays out the case for two of them: 'the Westminster model' and 'the consensus model'. Scholars writing in the more legal-formal French tradition of political science have been actively mapping out certain aspects of executive and legislative structures in innovative ways, e.g. Maurice Duverger's work on 'semi-presidentialism'[40] and Jean-Claude Colliard's on 'structured-stabilized parliamentarianism'.[41] Juan Linz has explicitly raised a number of provocative questions about the relative merits of presidential vs. parliamentary vs. semi-presidential structures of executive power for the likelihood of consolidation.[42] Terry Karl and I have proposed a more abstract scheme for classifying the types of democracy that are emerging in Southern and Eastern Europe and in South and Central America.[43]

All this is by way of saying that most of the basic conceptual instruments for describing the successive 'core' transformations in Figure 3 are within our grasp. Whether by so categorizing, juxtaposing and correlating these diachronic transformations we will be able to explain *why* they have occurred is another matter. Getting such general labels to stick on specific historical cases will no doubt present problems of its own. Nevertheless, I am convinced that some such effort at specifying and measuring crucial distinctions in the 'core phases' of regime transformation is needed. At the very least, it will help us to identify major differences and similarities among our countries.

As for the variables suggested under the rubrics *events, timing, trends* and *cycles*, they should be easier to observe, even to measure, once we are convinced that they are relevant to explaining the type or extent of democratic consolidation in particular cases. Knowing (or, better, strongly suspecting) that a certain factor affects the dependent variable is not necessarily the same thing as knowing how it does so or in what direction its effect is felt. For example, the advent of a guerrilla or terrorist movement using violence against an embryonic democracy accused of betraying the ideals of its struggle against the previous authoritarian regime can have a beneficial impact upon consolidation (Venezuela in the early 1960s and, less clearly, Spain in the late 1970s) or can undermine it quite significantly (Argentina after 1973). Some international interventions and even foreign occupations seem to have contributed substantially to a democratic outcome (Italy, West Germany, Japan, Austria); others have left a quite different legacy (Haiti, Nicaragua, the Dominican Republic, Guatemala, South Korea, the Philippines). Where conspiracies by the military or other armed groups to seize power during a consolidation are unsuccessful or disarmed early enough (Portugal in 1974; Spain in 1981; Argentina in 1985), the result may be a rallying around the nascent regime. Otherwise, they may be successful in deposing it (Argentina, Bolivia and Ecuador on numerous occasions; Turkey at regular ten-year intervals; Haiti and Burma, more recently).

Nor can we be certain *a priori* about the impact of the trends indicated in Figure 3. Even that 'favourite' of development theory – economic growth – has been questioned[44] and further examined.[45] Plumb makes the ironic observation that, in 17th-century England, political instability was endemic while social stability was exceptionally high. In the following century, political stability was attained – precisely when social instability had greatly increased. He makes an effort to explain this apparent paradox by suggesting, on the one hand, that socioeconomic experimentation and growth are fostered by the climate of relatively stable expectations produced by a well-established polity and, on the other, that human beings have a certain capacity for expressive action which they may shift from one domain to another – from socioeconomic self-advancement to political self-promotion (and vice-versa) – depending on external, even accidental, incentives.[46] Might not the same sort of dialectical effects be at work in linking a country's 'mode and extent of insertion in the international economic system' to its 'type and extent of democratic consolidation', *pace* the orthodoxy of current 'dependency theory' that postulates a more linear and asymmetric relationship between the two?

As for the trade, product, indebtedness and employment cycles sketched at the bottom of Figure 3, it is a little easier to hypothesize how they relate to CoD. When on the downswing – and especially where they covary to produce a fully-fledged crisis in the business cycle – these factors certainly complicate the consolidation process. Authoritarian regimes typically leave a very difficult economic legacy to their successors;[47] to some extent, however, the timing of consolidation bears a fortuitous relation to these cycles which, after all, are largely determined by other forces. In the case of those mysterious (and, perhaps, mythical) Kondratiev 'long waves', some countries may be lucky enough to democratize on their upswing while others will have to cope with the downswing.

In Figure 3 the attentive reader will find an error variable in the upper right-hand corner labelled *virtù* and *fortuna*. Machiavelli thought that 50 per cent of the variance could be explained by the latter, and also placed a great deal of emphasis on the former. Euphemistically called 'leadership' in some analyses and misleadingly labelled 'charisma' in others, the tendency proposed here is to assign a residual status to the competence, imagination and audacity of individual leaders. Leonardo Morlino has suggested that such leaders may deserve more explicit attention than our structural and collectivist bias has assigned to them. Certainly there have been recent cases (Garcia in Peru, Alfonsin in Argentina, Collor in Brazil, Papandreu in Greece and perhaps Walesa in Poland) where a populistic-plebiscitary component centring on a single person has been very much in evidence.[48] It has become abundantly clear, however, not only that these concentrations of personal power are not conducive to the consolidation of new democratic institutions, but that they seriously undermine existing party structures, executive-legislative relations, systems of interest bargaining, etc.

Finally, Figure 3 suggests that we should ultimately concentrate our attention on explaining two outcomes:

1. the usual 'empirical' one of the probable persistence of whatever type of democracy has emerged; and
2. the more unusual 'normative' one of trying to assess whether consolidation has been accomplished so as to preclude further extensions of the citizenship principle – or whether it increases the probability that equality of rights, obligations and conditions will expand to cover new arenas, issues and institutions.

Tocqueville is famous for his view that democratic equality cannot be granted in some domains and denied in others, that it is an 'irresistible force', a fact 'which a government can claim to regulate, but not to stop'.[49] With hindsight, this *telos* seems less compelling. Unsuspected compatibilities between different forms of equality have been discovered and unanticipated compromises between different interests established.[50] Moreover, the consolidated rules and institutions of political democracy have not infrequently been used to restrict rather than to encourage further extensions of citizenship into economic and social domains. Outcomes in those countries that have recently moved towards democracy should be evaluated not just according to how long these regimes are expected to last, but also how likely they are to diminish existing social inequalities, to tackle the problem of concentrations of private economic power, to be accessible to new political issues and groups and, in general, to extend the realm of civic equality, tolerance and deliberation throughout society. In short, the consolidation of democracy should be understood as representing the *beginning*, not the *end*, of politics.

Notes

1   Guillermo O'Donnell and Philippe C. Schmitter (1986), *Transitions from Authoritarian Rule: Tentative Conclusions about Uncertain Democracies*, Baltimore: Johns Hopkins University Press, pp. 4–5.
2   Adam Przeworski, 'Some Problems in the Study of the Transition to Democracy' in Guillermo O'Donnell and Philippe C. Schmitter (eds) (1986), *Transitions from Authoritarian Rule: Prospects for Democracy*, Vol. III, Baltimore: Johns Hopkins University Press, pp. 57–61.
3   O'Donnell and Schmitter, *op. cit.*
4   Anthony Giddens (1979), *Central Problems in Social Theory*, Berkeley: University of California Press, and *ibidem.* (1984), *The Constitution of Society*, Cambridge: Polity Press.
5   O'Donnell and Schmitter, *op.cit.*, p. 73, fn. 1.
6   *Ibid.*, pp. 7–8. Also Philippe C. Schmitter (1983), 'Democratic Theory and Neocorporatist Practice', Florence: European University Working Paper, No. 74.

7   Robert A. Dahl (1971), *Polyarchy: Participation and Opposition*, New Haven: Yale University Press; *ibidem.*, 'Procedural Democracy' in Peter Laslett and James Fishkin (eds) (1979), *Philosophy, Politics and Society*, fifth series, Oxford: Basil Blackwell, pp. 97–133; and *ibidem.* (1982), *Dilemmas of Pluralist Democracy*, New Haven: Yale University Press.

8   O'Donnell and Schmitter, *op. cit.*, pp. 10 and 65

9   Jean Blondel (1973), *Comparative Legislatures*, Englewood Cliffs: Prentice Hall.

10 O'Donnell and Schmitter, *op. cit.*, pp. 59–60.

11 Robert Dahl (1970), *After the Revolution: Authority in a Good Society*, New Haven: Yale University Press.

12 Samuel Barnes and Max Kaase (1979), *Political Action: Mass Participation in Five Western Democracies*, Beverly Hills: Sage Publications.

13 Philip Converse (1969), 'Of Time and Partisan Stability', *Comparative Political Studies*, **2**, July, pp. 139–71.

14 D. Easton (1965), *A Systems Analysis of Political Life*, New York: Wiley.

15 Juan Linz (1986), 'Il fattore tempo nei mutamenti de regime', *Teoria Politica*, 2 (1), pp. 3–47. *Ibidem.* (1978), 'Some Comparative Thoughts on the Transition to Democracy in Portugal and Spain' in Jorge Braga de Macedo and Simon Serfaty (eds) (1981), *Portugal Since the Revolution: Economic and Political Perspectives*, Boulder: Westview Press.

16 Giuseppe Di Palma (1983), 'Governo dei Partiti e riproducibilita democratica: il dilemma delle nouve democrazie', *Rivista Italiana di Scienze Politica*, **XIII**.

17 This, of course, is the core defining characteristic of the so-called Schumpeterian approach to modern democracy. For the original, see Joseph Schumpeter (1950), *Capitalism, Socialism and Democracy*, 3rd ed., New York: Harper & Row, pp. 269–83; for an extensive critique, see Graham Duncan and Steven Lukes, 'The New Democracy' in S. Lukes (ed.) (1963), *Essays in Social Theory*, London: Macmillan, pp. 30–51 and David Held (1987), *Models of Democracy*, Stanford: Stanford University Press, esp. pp. 143–85.

18 G. O'Donnell and P. Schmitter, *op. cit.*

19 G. O'Donnell and P. Schmitter, *op. cit.*, p. 53.

20 See Samuel Barnes and Max Kaase (1979), *Political Action: Mass Participation in Five Western Democracies*, Beverly Hills: Sage Publications.

21 *Op. cit.*, pp. 26–8.

22 Scott Mainwaring and Eduardo Viola (1984), 'New Social Movements, Political Culture and Democracy: Brazil and Argentina in the 1980's', *Telos*, **61**, pp. 17–52.

23 *Pace* Gabriel Almond (1956), 'Comparative Political Systems', *Journal of Politics*, **16**, August, pp. 391–409 and Arendt Lijphart (1968), 'Typologies of Democratic Systems', *Comparative Political Studies*, April, pp. 3–44.

24 Philippe C. Schmitter (1985), 'Speculations about the Prospective Demise of Authoritarian Rule and Its Possible Consequences (I)', *Revista de Ciencia Politica* (Lisbon), **I** (1), pp. 83–102.

25 Terry Lynn Karl, 'Imposing Consent? Electoralism Versus Democratization in El Salvador' in Paul Drake and Eduardo Silva (1986), *Elections and Democratization in Latin America 1980–1985*, San Diego: Center for Iberian and Latin American Studies, Center for U.S.-Mexican Studies, University of California, pp. 9–36.

26 James Buchanan and Gordon Tullock (1974), *The Calculus of Consent: Logical Foundations of Constitutional Democracy*, Ann Arbor: University of Michigan Press.

27 Philippe C. Schmitter (1983), 'Democratic Theory and Neocorporatist Practice', Florence: European University Working Paper, No. 74, and Philippe C. Schmitter and Terry Lynn Karl (1991) 'What Democracy is ... and is not', *Journal of Democracy*, **III** (3), Summer, pp. 75–88.

28 This viewpoint seems deeply embedded in the North American literature on political development and democratic theory. Two good examples are Samuel B. Huntington (1968), *Political Order in Changing Societies*, New Haven: Yale University Press, and J. Roland Pennock (1979), *Democratic Political Theory*, Princeton: Princeton University Press.

29 J.H. Plumb (1973) *Growth of Political Stability in England 1675–1725*, London: Penguin.

30 *Ibid.*, pp. xvi–xvii.

31 *Ibid.*, p. 172.

32 The original emphasis on *pactos* stems from Terry Karl, 'Petroleum and Political Pacts: The Transition to Democracy in Venezuela', *Latin American Research Review*, **22**, pp. 63–94, but this is picked up and generalized in G. O'Donnell and P. Schmitter, *op. cit.*, pp. 37–47.

33 Leonardo Morlino's initial paper on 'Democratic Consolidation' was discussed at one of the early sessions of the EUI working group on Southern Europe in April 1985. A much revised version appeared in 1992 as 'Consolidamento democratico: definizioni e modelli', *Rivista italiana di scienza politica*, **16**, pp. 83–135.

34 Terry Lynn Karl (1990), 'Dilemmas of Democratization in Latin America', *Comparative Politics*, **23** (1), October, pp. 1–21.

35 Philippe C. Schmitter (1985), 'Speculations about the Prospective Demise of Authoritarian Rule and Its Possible Consequences (I) and (II)', *Revista de Ciencia Politica* (Lisbon), **I** (1), pp. 83–102 and **I** (2), pp. 125–44.

36 Juan J. Linz, 'Totalitarian and Authoritarian Regimes' in Fred Greenstein and Nelson Polby (eds) (1975), *Handbook of Political Science*, Vol. III, Reading: Addison-Wesley, pp. 175–412.

37 Guillermo O'Donnell (1973), *Modernization and Bureaucratic-Authoritarianism*, Berkeley: University of California Institute for International Studies, and *ibidem.* (1978), 'Reflections on the Patterns of Change in the Bureaucratic-Authoritarian State', *Latin American Research Review*, **13** (1), pp. 3–38.

38 G. O'Donnell and P. Schmitter, *op. cit.*

39 Arend Lijphart (1984), *Democracies: Patterns of Majoritarian and Consensus Government in Twenty-One Countries*, New Haven: Yale University Press.

40 Maurice Duverger (1980), 'A New Political System Model: Semi-presidential Government', *European Journal of Political Research*, **8**, pp. 165–87.

41 J. Colliard (1978), *Les Régimes Parlementaires Contemporains*, Paris: Presses de la Foundation nationale des sciences politiques.

42 Juan J. Linz (1990), 'Transitions to Democracy', *The Washington Quarterly*, **13** (3), Summer, pp. 143–64 and Juan J. Linz and Arturo Valenzuela (1994), *The Failure of Presidential Democracy*, Baltimore: Johns Hopkins University Press.

43 Philippe C. Schmitter and Terry Karl, 'The Types of Democracy Emerging in Southern and Eastern Europe and South and Central America' in Peter M.E. Volten (ed.) (1992), *Bound to Change: Consolidating Democracy in East Central Europe*, New York: Institute for EastWest Studies, pp. 42–68.

44 Guillermo O'Donnell (1973), *Modernization and Bureaucratic-Authoritarianism*, Berkeley: University of California Institute for International Studies.

45 David Collier (ed.) (1979), *The New Authoritarianism in Latin America*, Princeton: Princeton University Press, and, Larry Diamond, 'Economic Development and Democracy Reconsidered' in Gary Marks and Larry Diamond (eds) (1992), *Reexamining Democracy: Essays in Honor of Seymour Martin Lipset*, Newbury Park: Sage Publications, pp. 93–139.

46 J. Plumb, *op.cit.*

47 See, for example, John Sheahan, 'Economic Policies and the Prospects for Successful Transition from Authoritarian Rule in Latin America' in Guillermo O'Donnell, Philippe C. Schmitter and Laurence Whitehead (eds) (1986), *Transitions from Authoritarian Rule: Comparative Perspectives*, Baltimore: The Johns Hopkins University Press, pp. 154–67.

48 Leonardo Morlino (1986), 'Consolidamento democratico: alcuni ipotesi esplicativa', *Rivista italiana di scienza politica*, **16**, pp. 197–238.

49 See the discussion of this aspect of Tocqueville's work in James T. Schleifer (1980), *The Making of Tocqueville's 'Democracy in America'*, Chapel Hill: University of North Carolina Press, pp. 263–4.

50 Cf. Adam Przeworski (1991), *Democracy and the Market: Political and Economic Reforms in Eastern Europe and Latin America*, Cambridge: Cambridge University Press.

[27]
DEMOCRATIC CONSOLIDATION: DEFINITION AND MODELS

LEONARDO MORLINO

The Problem

The latter half of the 1970s and the early 1980s witnessed the beginning and partial or complete achievement of democratic installation in countries like Portugal, Spain and Greece in the Mediterranean area; Argentina, Brazil, Uruguay, Ecuador and Bolivia in South America, and Mexico, El Salvador, Guatemala and Honduras in Central America. All these countries have had to confront the problem of consolidating and of ensuring the persistence of their new political structures. This phenomenon is so widespread as to involve about one-third of existing democracies. The issues raised by consolidation have been crucial for such powerful European democracies as France, Italy, Germany and Austria. In a different context, Japan also faced problems of consolidation at the end of the 1940s and the beginning of the 1950s, as did other Latin American countries like Colombia, Costa Rica and Venezuela from the 1960s to the early 1970s. Hence, the phenomenon is not only very relevant at the moment, but was also very important in the recent past.

In this essay, my attention will not focus on those cases in Europe or in the Western world where democratic consolidation was a long and gradual process and where the transition from competitive oligarchy to mass liberal democracy was uninterrupted by authoritarian periods. I do not deny the importance of this theme but have simply chosen a different research perspective. It is useful to note, however, that cases of gradual transition, installation and successive consolidation are the exceptions and not the rule among existing democracies; such cases are confined to certain geo-political areas like Great Britain, the US, Australia and New Zealand, and the small democracies of north-central Europe; these regimes were established earlier and, at times, very much earlier than all the cases considered here. Thus, in this essay I shall analyse (though necessarily rather briefly) the principal problems that confront anyone who is preparing to conduct research on democratic consolidation: a definition of the phenomenon, the identification of common empirical characteristics of the process, together with an indication of the main models of consolidation that the countries mentioned here have followed or could follow.

Until the mid-1980s, consolidation was a term used mainly by historians, with only a few political scientists having attempted to define it.[1] In an article published in 1970, Rustow deals, very briefly, with the phase following installation. However, he does not refer to consolidation, but rather to a period in which people become accustomed to living in a democracy – an 'habituation phase' – which is characterized by the spreading of democratic agreement to other strata of the population and by a clearer process of selecting democratic leaders.[2] Let us not overlook the fact that a large body of literature exists which includes both distinctly theoretical and markedly empirical studies on one or (less frequently) in a group of countries, which is indirectly relevant to the topic analysed here. I refer, above all, to the extensive literature on persistence and stability, on the process of institutionalization and, more generally, to the numerous analyses that address so-called democratic theory. Nor should one overlook the various studies that have been carried out on more specific aspects, such as the structures of intermediation, i.e. parties and interest groups.[3]

A Definition

If we take 'democracy' as an attribute of *consolidation*, a general, empirical definition of the former will suffice. Following a line of thought which can be traced back at least to Kelsen and to the subsequent theoretical developments put forward by Schumpeter and Dahl,[4] democracy is seen as a method or, rather, as a set of rules that allow all citizens to compete and participate. The rules are embodied in structures and procedures which permit the peaceful resolution of conflict and which guarantee political and civil rights (the right to vote, freedom of expression and freedom of the press, freedom to form and join organizations, and so on) to an extent that varies from country to country. These rights, in turn, provide greater opportunity for the defence and affirmation of interests and lead, therefore, to more participation, competition and political equality than existed in the previous authoritarian period. Free, recurring, competitive and fair elections; universal male and female suffrage; the involvement of more than one political party in elections; the existence of various interest organizations and alternative sources of information, and the elective nature of the most important political posts are the minimal indicators of a mass liberal democratic system.

It must also be remembered that these structures and procedures are adopted after a period of authoritarianism. The creation of structures and rules that characterize the installation phase is the result of a *compromise* among the political elite, the institutional actors (such as the army), and the politically relevant and active social actors, about how to achieve a peaceful resolution of conflicts.[5] The essence of this compromise lies in a widespread – but also partial and even implicit – acceptance of the presence of an opposition, of the politicization of the lower socio-economic strata and, above all, of the 'uncertainty'[6] as to which interests will prevail and what the outcome of the decision-making processes will be. That uncertainty is, however, limited by the actual distribution of resources (including organizational resources) which are permitted by the apparatus of civil and political rights and by the institutional rules. On the one hand, therefore, there is relative certainty about the rules of the game, which are decided *a priori*; on the other hand, there is relative uncertainty about the substantial outcomes – the concrete decisions that will be made in parliament and in other arenas. This is exactly the opposite of what happens in authoritarian regimes.[7]

In an industrialized democracy, uncertainty is relative and limited as far as the interests of the social actors who are central to the industrial structure (i.e. the entrepreneurs and workers) are concerned. These actors clearly play a crucial role in the productive structure, with the possibility of entrepreneurs seeking to maximize their profits, and workers using every non-violent means at their disposal to ensure better working conditions and job security. Ultimately, the pursuit of the respective interests of these social actors is guaranteed by the cluster of democratic rights. Here, we have come full circle to the centrality of the rules of the game and of the structures and procedures that derive from them.

To conclude, I define democracy as a set of explicit structures and procedures for the peaceful resolution of conflicts. The relevant political structures are the result of a post-authoritarian agreement-compromise, which may be temporary and casual, but whose substantive outcomes remain relatively uncertain. The authors of and main actors in the agreement-compromise are party elites. These are either autonomous and indirectly, or dependent and directly, tied to the various interests which play a leading role in a variety of decision-making arenas. The general definition given above helps us to differentiate more clearly among cases examined in the present work, not only those like Spain, Greece and others that fall fully within the definition, but also those like Mexico, Guatemala and Portugal which do not totally or immediately conform to it.[8]

At this point, I can begin to define *democratic consolidation* as the process by which the democratic regime is strengthened so as to ensure its persistence and to resist and prevent possible crises.[9] Although to some degree accurate, this definition is almost a tautology. However, let me stress, first, that the concept has to retain the 'engineering' connotation: a wall, for example, is buttressed or 'consolidated'. The definition thus yields two important and not immediately obvious elements. First, we are considering a process that takes a certain amount of time to unfold and which, simultaneously, is the result of complex interrelationships among all the actors involved, i.e., all the institutional and politically relevant social actors with their various strategies, positions, choices and resources, at both the elite and mass levels. In this process, as Rustow maintains, the actors who are readier to adapt to the new institutional context are most likely to have their own choices ratified and protect their own interests.[10]

The second feature is connected to the first: in maintaining that consolidation is a *process*, I am making an explicit choice. More precisely, I am placing particular emphasis, both in the definition and in the ensuing analysis, on the first of the two ways in which this phenomenon can be interpreted. Consolidation can be understood either as a complex process whose outcome is to reinforce or strengthen democratic arrangements, or as the point of arrival or the outcome of this process. It is to this second meaning that one refers in talking of 'consolidated' institutions.

For greater precision let us examine the semantic field to which the concept belongs. I shall consider, first of all, consolidation in relation to the other processes intrinsic to a democratic system. In this regard, let me say that transition, installation, consolidation and persistence or (as the case may be) crisis are not phenomena that necessarily follow one another in a linear fashion.[11] The installation of democracy can lead to consolidation, but also to a crisis of the whole political system. Alternatively, there can be a change of direction during the installation process itself: the case of Portugal between 1975 and 1976 provides an example of a swing of this kind in that a change occurred in the relative strengths of the various civil/military alliances within the regime. Above all, one cannot overlook how the role and importance of each actor, the resources at his disposal and his capacity to make use of them, can change in the course of the confused and eventful years during which the first two processes take place. Consolidation, therefore, is only one of the possible outcomes of installation, though an important one. The crisis, or even collapse, of a democratic regime is due to an inability to consolidate, which in turn is due to the absence or weakness of the democratic actors who should endeavour to defend it. Take, for example, the crisis of the democratic countries in Europe between the two World Wars and in Latin America later on.[12]

Transition, used here in the strict sense, refers to that fluid and confused period when new democratic structures are about to emerge, while some characteristic structures of the old regime continue to exist. Sometimes this phase is concentrated in a few rapid events, such as those that typify a coup d'état. *Installation* is characterized by the formation of new institutions and procedures, as well as by the presence of all the other features intrinsic to a democratic regime as outlined above.

Consolidation, however, has none of this kind of fluidity and 'creativity'. On the contrary, it is not an innovative process but is characterized, rather, by the firm establishment of structures and procedures that are intended to last for a long time. From this perspective, the most important factor in the process is the passage of time. In other words, consolidation is the overall result, which has various internal sequences, of the interrelationship between time and each of the essential elements that together make up the entire political system.

Let me now suggest a definition of consolidation which takes account both of the differences between it and installation and of the time variable: consolidation is the process by which the essential characteristics of the various democratic structures and norms are established and the secondary ones adapted so as to ensure their persistence over time. Time may bring crises, breakdowns and changes, but if this establishment-adaptation has occurred, then there is consolidation. Let me add that establishment-adaptation does not necessarily imply rigidity, but just the specification and firm establishment of structures and procedures which characterize a certain democratic regime.

This, however, is a reductive definition of the consolidation of a democratic regime *stricto sensu*. It is also important to consider the relationships between the regime and civil society. Therefore, where democracy has not been immediately and fully accepted by almost every politically relevant actor, consolidation has a further dimension: acceptance of the structures and norms for the peaceful resolution of conflicts must have become more and more widespread. There will be an ever-increasing awareness of this acceptance, support for institutional compromise, as well as recognition of the value of the formula of 'limited uncertainty'. In a word, there will be a progressive broadening of the legitimation of the regime. It is important to stress that this is a *necessary* aspect of consolidation, though one that may be virtually complete by the end of installation if the regime and the system itself have achieved immediate widespread legitimation.

If a distinction is drawn between consolidation and persistence, other observations become necessary. Thus, there is a form of consolidation that involves the norms and structures of the democratic regime as a whole and their interrelationships; there is also consolidation that involves the broadening of legitimation, which is neither blocked nor overturned by crisis. Whereas the first follows installation and can be considered complete at a certain point,[13] the second, when not immediately achieved, can continue into and be confused with the successive phase of persistence, as the regime and/or the entire political system progressively acquire greater legitimacy. Thus, we can discern two different elements in consolidation, the second of which may be of a much longer duration (though it may also be very short) and can continue into the phase of persistence of the democratic system, overlapping with and compounding the latter process.[14]

Levels of the Process

To sum up, *democratic consolidation* is *the process of establishing and adapting democratic structures and norms that come to be accepted as legitimate by the civil society, in part or in full.* Let me add that this is a variegated and composite process which unfolds in various directions and ends by strengthening those institutions and norms so as to ensure their persistence.

It is *composite and variegated* because the process assumes various forms. It consists of the establishment of political practices, models and patterns of behaviour, which are then repeated over time; it then further articulates the various democratic structures; it involves the progressive adaptation of institutions to the changes that occur as the democratic model – as laid down in the wording of the constitution and by the other fundamental laws of a given country – is concretely implemented; it denotes the process by which some institutions acquire a distinct identity and some degree of autonomy *vis-à-vis* civil society; it consists in a broadening of support for the various democratic institutions which, in the absence of overt challenges to the democratic order, can result either from the simple passage of time and/or from the actual functioning of the institutions. If the regime has acquired widespread legitimacy by the end of installation and if there are no challenges to it, then the passage of time will ensure that democratic consolidation will be further legitimated and strengthened. It should not be forgotten, moreover, that the progressive legitimation or acceptance of both the main and intermediate structures of the regime are essential for the strengthening of those institutions and, therefore, for consolidating the regime. Hence, legitimation is not just an analytically distinct part of the process; it is its very foundation.

The concrete forms that democratic consolidation may assume can be better understood by observing the various directions the process may take. Consolidation can occur at the following levels: (a) democratic structures and procedures; (b) relationships between the structures or, rather, the various powers, as laid down in the countries' legal systems; (c) parties and the party system; (d) interest structures; (e) relationships between intermediation structures and civil society; (f) relationships between intermediation structures and the regime.

With regard to the *structures and procedures that characterize a democratic regime* (such as the government, parliament and administrative structures), consolidation involves the affirmation of definite practices in the decision-making arenas and the perfecting of mechanisms for implementing decisions. There can be problems of adapting the legal system to the needs of the regime as these become clearer, and also problems that arise from the need to adapt, integrate or eliminate the body of law inherited from the preceding non-democratic regime. Although the latter difficulties emerge in the installation phase, they come into focus only during the process of consolidation. Inside parliament, in particular, the urgency of the problems left by the preceding regime and the need to find solutions encourage the formation of patterns in the relationships between the majority and the opposition, in the making of consensual decisions or in the formation of different majorities according to the various problems under discussion.

The acquisition of decision-making capacity and practices also implies the achievement of stable control over resources, including material resources (by means of taxation, for example) so that decisions are not only implemented, but also obeyed. In more concrete terms, this involves the acquisition of a 'serviceable' administration which is autonomous *vis-à-vis* the groups who were dominant in the preceding authoritarian regime. In other words, either the administrative personnel will express their loyalty to the new regime and the new rulers, or there must be 'purges' to ensure that they do so. Another important feature is the possibility that the administration may have to experience a phase of gradual integration-rationalization and adjustment-adaptation immediately after the installation of democracy. Some countries and their new democratic governments may be faced with a serious problem of state-building, or even with the need to provide themselves with the necessary administrative structures for the implementation of decisions. It is precisely in this period, moreover, that a strong interest in the maintenance of the regime should emerge and become established both among the political class and the administrative personnel. This, in itself, should contribute to the success of the consolidation process.

As far as *relationships between the various democratic institutions* or powers are concerned, consolidation will ensure recurrent patterns of behaviour and the stabilization of roles, a certain amount of adaptation of the original constitutional model, the control and containment of conflicts within the democratic rules and, finally, the continued expression of the interests of public agencies through the practices permitted by law (if not expressly contained in the constitution). The last point is particularly important as far as the military are concerned.[15]

The third direction the process can take concerns the territorial forms of interest representation, especially *parties and the party system*. Here consolidation means the strengthening of the organization, including ancillary structures, and the acquisition of a party image and identity which are then modified slowly over time as the party builds up the solid electoral support which is its backbone and base for the interests it represents. At the level of the party system, consolidation also means the firm establishment of competitive patterns which lead to parliamentary alliances and support for the government, to the creation of parties that either represent only certain interests and/or are catch-all and inter-class. It also leads to an occupation of the competitive space which, if the electoral laws remain unchanged, renders the emergence of new movements or parties more difficult in the medium or short run.

If one looks at the functional dimension of *interest representation*, consolidation means the strengthening of party organizations and the crystallizing of their identities (right up to the elite level) so as to communicate, express and represent a variety of interests. The identity of the various collectively organized interests and their capacity to establish channels of communication and to apply pressure, even in situations of competition, are very important aspects. They give the interest groups that are capable of being organized (blue- and white-collar trade unions, associations of entrepreneurs, landowners, small farmers/peasants, traders, artisans and so on) an enormous advantage in forwarding their own aims, enabling them to obtain favourable decisions as readily through the parties as through direct pressure on the formal decision-making bodies in government and parliament. When that advantage is clearly perceived, the groups are encouraged both to organize themselves better and to support the democratic system that enables them to do so.

On the level of *relationships between the various structures of intermediation and civil society*, consolidation can be seen in terms of the acquisition of identity and autonomy with regard to parties, groups and associations. As far as identity is concerned, consolidation serves to reinforce a phenomenon already mentioned in discussing the two previous levels: various social groups adopt positions and decisions which, taken as a whole, contribute to the formation of the identities of parties and of interest groups. This can also lead to their identification with certain parties, unions or other associations. Consolidation also involves the acquisition of a considerable degree of autonomy by all the intermediate structures that occupy the competitive space at various levels; thus these, too, are able to condition and impose their preference on the various groups that form civil society.

The last level of consolidation analysed here – *relationships between the structures of intermediation and the regime* – is of special importance because the phenomena that comprise it are fundamental to the whole process of democratic consolidation. In other words, consolidation on this level 'enables' and *partly* strengthens all the intrinsic aspects of the process at the various other levels mentioned above. Consolidation on this level appears to be linked to the need to legitimize and integrate the various structures of intermediation. This leads to the weakening and, ultimately, to the disappearance of movements, groups and parties which do not support the regime and whose ideology and activity, at a parliamentary level and in relation to civil society, fail to legitimize the regime and the political system as a whole.[16] The acceptance – be it gradual or immediate – by the military of the role laid down for it by the democratic legal system, for instance, involves its acceptance of democratically elected governments. The broadening of legitimation and greater integration are two interconnected factors which free the democratic system from *internal* challenges of a more or less serious nature and guarantee that persistence which is the principal outcome of successful consolidation.[17]

One could also imagine another level – relationships between civil society and the regime which are *not* mediated by any structures. The central problem here is the presence or absence of a widespread belief in the legitimacy of the regime; in other words, the presence or absence of varied unorganized forms of protest, dissatisfaction, alienation, passivity or indifference. These kinds of attitudes can be affected only by government activity and by the structures of intermediation. We are therefore brought back to the levels that have already been considered.

The process of consolidation is successfully concluded when a period of persistence, which can be more or less stable according to the degree of consolidation achieved, is initiated. Thus, the duration of the process should now be explicit and clear. As far as the beginning is concerned, the problem is relatively simple and has been dealt with in the preceding section, albeit in a somewhat different context. Let me add that the process begins as soon as the building or installation of democratic structures has been accomplished in the various sectors. As to the end of the process, this is indefinable. Suffice it to say that a clear end does not exist for two good reasons. First, successful consolidation flows into stable persistence; second, the various aspects of consolidation have different durations. For example, relationships between the various structures of the regime become established in the short term but can, if necessary, be modified at a later day. They commence and are put to the test as soon as the regime begins to 'function', being subject to slow modification as and when various concrete situations arise. The military can pose a somewhat different problem: if the army is not politicized at the end of installation (because of the specific circumstances in which the latter occurred) and if such politicization does not occur in the early years of consolidation, then a pattern of subordination to civil authority is set which may, but very likely will not, be modified in the medium term.

The process of legitimation, which is central to consolidation, can also take place very quickly. However, if consolidation is only partially achieved because anti-regime formations still exist, then legitimation is likely to be extended and expanded over time. In other words, the regime may be accepted immediately by all the politically active forces; alternatively, legitimation may be only partial because anti-democratic formations survive. The latter may be integrated into the democratic process only very slowly, if the regime survives. Moreover, it is very unlikely, except in very particular and exceptional circumstances (e.g. the death of a leader that weakens a specific party), that new anti-regime parties will emerge once the political space has been occupied. If anything, existing but weak anti-regime groups will probably gain strength; this would indicate a failure of consolidation. Thus, if not concluded quickly (and barring a crisis), legitimation goes on for years, overlapping with the phase of persistence.

It would be empirically useful to suggest a reasonable period of time after which the outcome of consolidation could be examined. The European experiences of the post-war period seem to suggest that a decade from the end of the installation of all the principal democratic structures is generally most appropriate. Why a decade? One can answer this question and justify the choice by focusing on the structures and norms of the regime itself. Thus, it can be maintained that consolidation is more or less successfully accomplished when the passage of time no longer has an evident effect on established practices and tested structures and norms. This seems to occur, as far as the cases under consideration are concerned, in the medium term, that is, about 10 to 12 years after installation.

Similarities, Models and Actors

The second question I should like to deal with is more difficult and complicated: is it possible to build models of consolidation that can define the process and actors involved in the various countries? In other words, bearing in mind past experiences (Italy, Germany and Austria in the 1940s) and more recent ones (Colombia, Venezuela and Costa Rica), together with cases in which the process of consolidation is coming to an end (Spain, Portugal and Greece) and others in which it is still in progress, with outcomes as yet unknown (some Latin American countries of more recent democratization), is it possible to identify the various paths taken by consolidation and the ways in which actors are linked to the more specific internal dynamic that emerges after installation?

A first general evaluation of the various cases yields at least two results that are not entirely expected.[18] Concentrating on the numerous past experiences, there are more similarities than differences. Of course, in analysing the actors and processes in greater detail, every case seems to follow a different, individual model. The contrast is thus marked between common and recurrent aspects and the uniqueness of each individual case when examined in greater depth. This does not hold true for other democratic dynamics; for example, an examination of the process of installation immediately reveals wide differences among cases. Secondly, while some general features can be found among cases of recent consolidation, these seem unable to draw useful indications or 'lessons' from the experiences of the past: again the ways in which their varied and specific institutional, social and political features combine seem to lead them in extremely 'individual' and probably unique directions.

It is not possible in this article to review the specific *configurations* of these processes in each of the countries mentioned above. I shall therefore continue my analysis of common features, attempting to indicate possible variations in these and to formulate models of consolidation which are as definitive as possible.

Moreover, in dealing with processes, it seems appropriate to focus my analysis on the actors involved (insofar as they are potential *agents* of consolidation) and on how they can trigger off and intensify the process. One must consider these actors both at the elite level (with relevant inter-elite relationships) and at the mass level, without neglecting the interconnections between civil society, structures of intermediation and the regime. This is an explicit research choice. In fact, we cannot exclude the possibility that consolidation is a side-effect of actions which are not specifically aimed at that objective.

The main and common trait to which all the others may be linked is *the activation, implementation and maintenance of democratic compromise* or, alternatively, the way in which democratic legitimation grows and is maintained and reproduced. The installation of a democracy can be the result of casual events, but for consolidation to take place, 'uncertain compromise' (which was analysed earlier) must be maintained and strengthened; recognition of the opposition and of political equality must become explicit and conscious, not only among the elites; finally, there must be a strong conviction of the need for cooperation among these elites, political or otherwise. This has happened in all the countries in which some form of consolidation, be it only limited and partial, has been achieved. In all of them, political elites who backed the compromise have retained the support of at least a majority of the electorate. The key question therefore becomes: how and by whom can that agreement/compromise among elites and between them and the citizens of the democratic system be maintained and strengthened?

The second common element, closely related to the first and logically and empirically prior to the others, is *respect for legality*. By this expression, I do not refer exclusively to the maintenance of civil order which is important in itself and is related to the growth of legitimation and the levels of mobilization reached during installation and sometimes maintained in the next period. (More specifically, where protest or other forms of civil disorder occurred during consolidation, a gradual decrease in these phenomena is indicative of the success of the processes of legitimation, integration and, therefore, consolidation.) By 'respect for legality', however, I refer to the capacity of governing elites and of their apparatuses to stand as guarantors for the rule of law and for the decisions that have been taken, however approximate or limited this stance may be. It is precisely this factor, in fact, which allows the democratic compromise to function concretely.

If it has roots in the political traditions of the country, then respect for legality may be achieved without great difficulty. Indeed, it can even be seen as a positive legacy from the preceding non-democratic regime. Alternatively, it may come about during installation when the democratic compromise is formed. Finally it can be achieved, though with greater difficulty, at a later date as a result of government policy for the reorganization of the administrative structures so as to gain at least partial control of the coercive arena. At any rate, in all cases of consolidation, the governing authorities must be –and have been – able to ensure obedience to their decisions and, in this way, to guarantee the concrete implementation and strengthening of the democratic compromise for all social groups.

This common and recurrent aspect can be better understood if I refer to a *contrasting* example. The difficulty that some Latin American countries, like Bolivia, have had in achieving consolidation can be explained, among other things, by the existence of a 'weak state', characterized by instability at the highest levels of administration, inadequate formalization of procedures, marked corruption and clientelism, inefficient taxation and confusion as to the hierarchy principle. Alongside these deficiencies are found organized, active and extremely politicized interest groups. It seems obvious that, in such situations, there cannot be consolidation of any type of regime, be it authoritarian or democratic, because the institutions cannot guarantee any agreement or compromise, even one that favours an authoritarian military solution. Respect for legality, be it only limited or partial, is therefore a minimum requisite for consolidation; its creation or maintenance is a basic responsibility of democratic rulers. I used the expression 'prior' above, not just in an analytic,but also in an empirical sense. In fact, this problem was overcome by the end of installation in the various European countries mentioned above, with the partial exception of Greece; to a certain extent this was also true in Latin American countries such as Colombia and Venezuela.

The third common element to be considered is *the neutrality or the neutralization of the military*. Consolidation is possible only if this problem has already been solved, or if policies that will lead to its solution have been accepted. More precisely, in some countries (Italy, Germany, Austria and Costa Rica, for example), the problem was solved in the transition phase since military structures had been destroyed or did not exist (as in Costa Rica). In other cases, when the military structure had lost legitimacy, the solution was prepared during installation by new appointments, substitutions, purges and even trials of military personnel (for example, in Greece or Argentina). In all other cases, even if attempted coups occurred during the period of installation (for example in Spain, Venezuela and Colombia), government leaders implemented policies that satisfied the corporate interests of the military (better pay conditions, modernization of armaments, and so on) or, at any rate, avoided interfering in its internal affairs (such as promotions and the retirement of some military personnel). In other words, the complete success of consolidation implies that the civilian elites initiate a strategy that will lead the military to accept the new political arrangements and then to remain, definitively, in their barracks. This means that the military can, in fact, be part of an initial democratic agreement; later, however, they must be definitively excluded, without allowing the democratic compromise between civilian actors to be modified in the process.

At any rate, an analysis of relevant cases suggests that, where a problem of neutralization exists, these policies, however important, are not definitive. It is even more vital that the functioning and maintenance of the civil democratic compromise at the two levels already mentioned – relationships among elites and between them and the masses – should leave no space or pretext for the military to intervene again. Should such an intervention occur, the existence of a compromise in itself may not be enough to deter certain military elites from supporting the coup. Even where the compromise exists, the process of neutralizing the military can take quite a few years. In Portugal, for example, only in 1986 with the election of a civilian president, the socialist leader Mario Soares (in place of the military leader General Ramalho Eanes), did that neutralization become irreversible.[19]

An analysis of past cases of consolidation shows a wide variation in economic and social factors from country to country so that it is not really viable to propose any generalization along these lines. Nevertheless, elements of this kind that have been 'chased out the door' tend to come in again 'through the window'. Therefore, in all cases of consolidation, even when the public sector is large, it is impossible to overlook how the more or less organized groups of *private entrepreneurs may have their interests guaranteed fully* or, better, may have ample opportunities to protect their interests, either directly through the executive and the legislature (which may have been widely 'penetrated' by the groups), or indirectly via certain parties and party leaders. The classic position of these groups *vis-à-vis* the political arrangements can be defined as *accidentalism* or indifference towards the political institutions, be they authoritarian or democratic. Yet, if previous authoritarian experience has shown that these interests have been subordinated to the institutions of government (as they were, for example, at certain times in Nazi Germany or in Fascist Italy), and if, on the other hand, democratic institutions succeed in guaranteeing order and legality, then these groups are likely to approve this solution and actively support the democratic compromise.

The situation of unions and of small farmer/peasant organizations is somewhat different. In most of the cases analysed, these are closely linked to and dependent on the parties. It is doubtful whether they would even exist in a different political system. For them, therefore (and for the parties to which they are linked), it is simply a case of recognizing that their interests lie in the maintenance and strengthening of the compromise. This, too, is a recurrent element in all cases of consolidation. It must be said, however, that the authoritarian traditions and characteristics of trade unionism in Argentina do not augur well for the prospects of democracy in that country.

The position of the Catholic Church can also be considered one of accidentalism. But, in fact, in the various Catholic countries in which consolidation has occurred and in which it was influential, the Catholic Church supported the democratic solution directly or indirectly through its own organizations and by contributing in a decisive way to the formation of Catholic parties. This has happened, for example, even in Venezuela and Colombia. The involvement of the Catholic Church has, however, become less evident in recent years in more modern and secularized countries like Spain, or even in Portugal, where the Church has been less active in politics since the Second Vatican Council. Although it is not surprising that problems have arisen when issues like divorce and abortion were on the political agenda of some countries in which consolidation was under way, in no case did these problems cause the regime to lose significant legitimacy.

Perhaps, the principal common trait in consolidation is the role of *parties and the party system.* It is quite obvious that parties which are not anti-regime, but democratic because of their ideology, programmes and activity, have a vital interest in the maintenance of the democratic system. One must remember that, under an authoritarian regime, the leaders of these parties would be (and have been) in exile, in gaol or, in any case, in fear of their personal safety, while party organizations would have, at best, a precarious and difficult existence. For leaders and party organizations, therefore, increasing their strength and achieving democratic consolidation are goals that coincide. Moreover, by cooperating, party elites can guarantee the survival of decision-making processes which are important for the various interests they represent. At the same time, they can organize and control participation and legitimation on a mass level and can absorb successive social groups. One should also note how the very mechanism that provides for democratic competition also encourages the parties to increase their organizational strength.[20] Therefore, it comes as no surprise that parties have been central to all recent and less recent cases of consolidation, including those like Portugal where party structures were not the initiators of transition and installation. The only difference is that, in some cases, parties were the only principal agents of consolidation, and in some they were not. I shall return to this aspect later, but at this point further clarifications are necessary.

When I speak of parties in reference to various concrete cases, I am, in fact, also referring to party systems. In many cases, anti-regime or semi-anti-regime parties are formed, but there may also be one or more parties whose elites cooperate (or even agree to limit competition among themselves) for the entire period of consolidation; in so doing, they ostracize and isolate those political actors who are not clearly pro-regime from decision-making processes and from the management of resources, and try to reduce their electoral appeal. Thus, an *internal* system emerges which is supported at least by a large plurality or by a bare absolute majority of the electorate. This system has its own mode of operation with respect to the party system as a whole. It can, indeed, be a single party which manages to capture a majority of seats in parliament and, by taking advantage of the low mobilization of other forces, succeeds in establishing this pattern. A more frequent case is that of the elites of two to five parties who achieve consolidation, albeit weak and partial, by distributing (or even partially alternating) positions of authority in the regime.

With regard to parties, it is also true that the need to increase their organizational strength is directly linked to the level of mobilization and potential participation of civil society established during the preceding phase of installation. If the intervention and mobilization of society have played an important role in installation, then the achievement of any degree of consolidation will require a high level of organizational strength, a clear identity and deep overall rooting of the parties in society. If, on the other hand, the installation phase has been characterized by marked passivity and lack of participation, then even less structured parties can play a pivotal role and the institutions of the regime will not have any great problems of social control. On the whole, our cases show that the process of consolidation tends to be characterized by a decline in participation that is natural, though it can be the result of a deliberate policy of demobilization carried out by the parties themselves through an agreement to limit competition (for several reasons, for example, the fear of a coup d'état).

This picture can be completed by some remarks on the *structures of the regime* or the 'state' from three points of view: institutional arrangements, particularly those that concern relationships between the executive and the legislature, the role of the public sector in the economy, and how policies are implemented. With regard to institutional solutions of a parliamentary or presidential kind, the former offer greater scope for cooperation, negotiation and accommodation and for the penetration of decision-making bodies by interest groups. In this sense, a parliamentary system can be more favourable to consolidation. But, as Venezuela and Colombia show, a presidential system can be equally favourable, on two conditions: (a) that the president's power is limited and conditioned by parliament and parliamentary opposition, and (b) that, either explicitly or implicitly, the alternation of the presidency between the two largest parties is ensured, so that the party system will at least tend to veer towards moderate bi-polarization.[21]

In almost all past cases of consolidation, a public economic sector was formed or retained from the preceding authoritarian regime (for example, in Italy and Spain). The importance of the public sector for the achievement of consolidation is evident: it allows rulers and the parties themselves, through the structures of government, to control and distribute resources to groups who may be more or less organized or to the general population. In this way, the process of legitimation, the strengthening of the democratic compromise and, sometimes, of the parties themselves – which have been identified as the core of the process of consolidation – are clearly encouraged. There are also various other government policies which may overlap and tend in the same direction. These include clientelist policies, the creation and broadening of institutions characteristic of a welfare state, as well as certain substantive policies that ensure the continuing support of social institutions, like the Catholic Church, and of other interest groups.

On the basis of these observations on groups, parties and governmental institutions, and bearing in mind that the two principal directions of consolidation involve, in the first case, the role and presence of certain actors in the decision-making process and, in the second, the achievement and maintenance of legitimation at the elite and mass levels, it is possible to outline two models of consolidation. These represent two poles, which in empirical terms are not very far apart: *consolidation through parties* and *symbiotic consolidation*. Having specified again that the vast majority of less recent cases tend to cluster round the first pole rather than the second, we can try to delineate the two models.

Consolidation Through Parties

This model is characterized, above all, by the progressive organization and expansion of party structures and the party system as a whole, which is then able to control and, if needs be, moderate and integrate all forms of participation. The parties finance themselves with public money as sanctioned by requisite laws. Clear, long-term alignments of parties and social groups are established. Party identities are crystallized and the rules of internal competition among party elites are laid down. Furthermore, party elites play a central role in the decision-making processes, and at the same time they begin gradually occupying the principal positions responsible for administering and distributing resources at local and national levels. Such an 'occupation' may also involve the appointment of party elites to key positions within interest group organizations, and it can go so far as to pass laws or administrative regulations that will form or transform interest groups which may have been poorly organized or not organized at all.[22] In this model, obviously, the unions are also tied to and dependent on the parties. This kind of *party government*, broadly speaking, is compatible with any type of parliamentary or presidential institutional arrangement. We shall see below that a parliamentary system can initially facilitate the penetration by groups of decision-making structures of various kinds. Yet this tendency can be counterbalanced by other factors such as the number of parties, the type of party system and the relationship between legislative and executive branches. In a parliamentary system, in fact, concrete configurations of consolidation are usually closer to the party than to the symbiotic model.

It is possible to achieve consolidation through parties starting from various different traditions and situations. Bearing in mind some European cases, the process of consolidation is more likely to follow this model if the preceding authoritarian (or totalitarian) experience had profoundly altered the social fabric of the country and had succeeded in destroying old, traditional forms of solidarity and organization, particularly if accompanied by considerable socioeconomic transformation. Moreover, if the central actors in installation were the elites and the party organizations, and if the situation was one of high mobilization and initial detachment from the various interests groups – such as the entrepreneurial associations – then the path is fairly linear, characterized by the strengthening of parties, by the process of occupation mentioned above and by progressive demobilization on a mass level. Italy experienced such a process.

Another possible variant is as follows: the parties are not at the centre of the transition, but later become the principal vehicles of installation; from the outset mobilization is low, episodic and limited. In this case, party elites and economic and social elites coincide and overlap at the beginning, but later on the parties take control of the conflict and competition, thus activating the process of occupation – the key element of this model. Spain would seem to be relatively close to this model, whereas a *contrasting* example is the French Fourth Republic. Though the parties in France did not initiate the transition, they did become central to installation. However, the process of occupation was not successful. It was the interest groups that got the upper hand and dominated the political scene in the 1950s. As a result, there was no consolidation in the end, but rather a change of regime, though still in a democratic direction.

In terms of the model discussed here, therefore, different variants can be and have been formed. The principal differentiating factors are as follows: the role of parties (and party elites) during transition and installation; the levels of mobilization of civil society throughout the period under examination; the forms and degrees of strengthening of party organization; the importance of the principal decision-making arenas (within the party structures in their relationships to the groups and/or within parliament and other national and local government institutions); the relationships, in terms of alignments and identification, between parties and civil society; the main patterns of competition within the party system; and, of particular importance, the degree of partisan occupation of governmental structures and interest groups. As far as the success of all the variants of this type of consolidation is concerned, there is a close relationship between the degree of strengthening of party structures and levels of mobilization: a higher level of mobilization will correspond to a greater strengthening (in the various ways indicated above) of the structures of intermediation; on the other hand, a lower degree of mobilization *can* correspond to less organizational strengthening, less clear identification, and so on. In any case, in the absence of studies and material on these specific aspects, a more precise analysis and identification of the different variants would require *ad hoc* case-by-case research. In this paper, it is not possible to go beyond the indications already mentioned.

In outlining this model, my insistence on the centrality of 'occupation' by the parties calls for further clarification. In terms of democratic 'quality', or of the capacity of political systems to give effective expression to the 'preferences of the citizens considered as equals',[23] this kind of consolidation does not establish the best possible institutional systems. In this context, one can understand how, as a result of the will to assert certain 'democratic' values, ideals and principles, a bitter debate on 'partitocrazia', 'occupation of the state' and so on, arose in Italy in the 1950s and has also been voiced in various other countries at different times. This, however, was a 'battle of ideals' which is understandable in the context of an already consolidated democracy precisely because it activates the mechanisms of self-correction that have already been mentioned.

On the empirical level, the fact remains that this model – together with its variations – corresponds closely to the majority of the countries considered here. These are characterized by authoritarian experiences, repeated military interventions and anti- or semi-anti-regime formations, movements and parties; that is, characterized by initial, serious and objective difficulties in consolidation. Moreover, in other cases in which the very first attempt at democratization was successful (i.e. those countries which had not experienced difficult authoritarian periods), analysis must be undertaken on different terms. However, for these cases (i.e. the countries of Northern Europe and the Anglo-Saxon area), too, it is important to remember that the immediate success of the process of consolidation was often due to the decisive role played by parties.

Symbiotic Consolidation

I have called the second model *symbiotic* to emphasize the presence during installation and consolidation of, and the crucial role played in the democratic regime by, the two principal structures of intermediation – parties (and party systems) and interest groups. Both of these achieve the strengthening, the autonomy and all the other characteristics indicated as intrinsic to the consolidation of systems of representation. Furthermore, the competitive mechanisms in democracy give parties room to manoeuvre during the electoral process and further their legitimation at mass level; on the other hand, interest groups manage to organize themselves rapidly and soon succeed in penetrating the principal decision-making structures. While the key process in consolidation through parties is the occupation of government structures and the formation and transformation of groups, in this second model, there is a significant though gradual process of *penetration* by groups of these same structures, although this does not diminish the role reserved for parties in other contexts. The degree of penetration can be ascertained empirically by analysing the following: the role of groups in choosing candidates for elections; the financial contributions given to the parties, over and above public financing; the presence of members of interest associations in parliamentary committees; the activity of parliamentarians affiliated to groups in defending the interests of the latter by means of legislative initiatives or parliamentary questions; and, finally, at the intermediate level, the overlapping of leaders and functionaries from unions and parties.

In such a model, the preceding authoritarian experience would not have been such as to seriously disrupt the social formations within civil society, either because it had little substantial effect (for various reasons) and/or because the country had strong traditions and a real subculture, either Catholic or working-class. In the installation phase, a certain overlap must already have existed between party elites and economic or religious elites, while the unions would have been able to condition the workers' parties without becoming their 'transmission belt'. Installation, then, must have been characterized by low overall mobilization of civil society and by very limited activity on the part of anti-regime movements and groups. In short, from the very beginning, mobilization must have presented fewer problems for the regime.

A strong state tradition with, perhaps, an important public sector is indispensable in this model. Finally, this model can be implemented more easily in a parliamentary system which provides groups with greater opportunities to penetrate and condition the parliamentary process of decision making although, on a hypothetical level, one cannot exclude the possibility that, with a presidential form of government, groups may also succeed in penetrating the decision-making structures in order better to defend their own interests. The concrete case which came closest to this symbiotic model was Austria in the 1940s whereas, as already stated, most other countries are in an intermediate position, or closer to the first model.

In schematic terms, one could hypothesize that the *continuum* (role of parties–role of groups), which is the explicit key dimension in these two models, does not cover the entire range of possibilities in the process of consolidation. There is a *third possibility* that differs, in certain characteristics, from the preceding two. More explicitly, if a charismatic leader, who has succeeded in creating a large mass movement around himself, has played a central role in the phase of transition and, more importantly, in installation, can one call this *charismatic consolidation*? Is it possible that such a leader, by means of his direct relationship with the masses, can succeed in legitimating the entire democratic system or, at any rate, in organizing and structuring his own movement and transforming it into a party which is more or less rooted in civil society? Evidently, behind these questions lies the case of the Fifth Republic in France and of some Latin American countries in which the prospects of consolidation remain remote, with the possible outcome as yet unknown. Although possible, consolidation precipitated by the charisma of a leader must face objective difficulties arising either from the organization and rooting of the party, or from its relationships with various groups. At any rate, in such a case, as well as a general tendency towards the personalization of political life, at least two conditions must prevail: (a) a presidential or a parliamentary system which attributes great importance to the role of the prime minister, to the extent that it places the basic resources for consolidation at the disposal of the leader; (b) a tradition of efficiency in the administrative structures and in government (in the broadest sense of the term), which would give access to the further resources necessary for consolidation.

In any case, consolidation through a charismatic leader is a more specific model than the two outlined above. In fact, if a leader succeeds in effectively forging a well-organized and strong party that leads to a system with one dominant party, then that party becomes the central structure of the regime and consolidation can be said to occur through parties in a way that is very close to the first model. There is a second possibility: the party/ies are able to organize themselves but in a situation of low mobilization. At the same time, groups maintain their positions of strength, their own organizations and their own important role in the democratic system. Such a configuration is obviously closer to the symbiotic model outlined above.

Consolidation Through Groups?

Among the possible models of consolidation I have not considered is an even more extreme hypothesis along the party-group continuum – *consolidation through groups*. In a nutshell, this model would be characterized by strong intermediary groups – including the unions – who would find new and additional space for organization and action in the democratic context, and would penetrate into all levels of government and, also, into weak and badly organized parties. This model has not been important in analysing past cases of consolidation, most of which seemed to follow the pattern of consolidation through parties. Nor does the situation in some Latin American countries facing an immediate problem seem to indicate that consolidation through groups is very likely. This is either because of the contrasts that exist between strong organized groups and weak parties or because, on the whole, the structures of intermediation are, and remain, weak.

These various considerations lead me to suggest that, in the last analysis, only the unions (and not other groups) have a vital interest in democracy. However, sometimes even the unions can support authoritarian solutions, with weak and easily penetrable parties representing so many *handicaps* to consolidation. Furthermore, it is very difficult to maintain and strengthen the democratic compromise in these conditions because of the inevitable degree of radicalization that takes place and because of the difficulty of containing the conflict within the established rules and procedures. Finally, democratic mechanisms – particularly the elections themselves – tend to give space and a role to the parties in a functioning democracy. If all this is correct, then it is not possible to assert that real consolidation can occur with groups as the only agents. In conditions of low mass mobilization, it is more realistic to posit an *unstable maintenance* of the democratic regime, sustained by a sort of negative legitimation based, first, on a collective memory of the past – in other words, memory of a disastrous economic period that coincided with the authoritarian regime, together with the enormous human costs sustained in terms of fear and repression. A second basis is the consideration of the difficulty experienced by the economic elites to protect their own interests with a government that tended to detach itself from interest groups and to establish the 'autonomy of the state'. Time may weaken the collective memory, but it can also move the country gradually towards symbiotic consolidation based on a recognition of the opposition, on an acceptance of the role of lower socioeconomic groups in the democratic process and, ultimately, on an acceptance of the democratic compromise – factors that are all fundamental to the process being examined.

Concluding Remarks

In this analysis of common factors and models of consolidation, I have not considered the impact of international economic or political factors. Based on an examination of the preceding cases, I believe that political and economic factors of international origin can, and indeed do, have an effect on the way democratic installation develops and on the maintenance (without consolidation) of democratic regimes. However, because of the characteristics considered above, the process of consolidation clearly has its own intrinsic and internal mechanisms. Of course it is conceivable that in some cases international factors (in the broad sense of the term) can contribute to a clearer understanding of that process and of its results.

In this essay my goal has been to show the relevance of consolidation to political research and the different directions that deserve to be fully explored. I foresaw taking only the first, preliminary steps in such an endeavour. Thus, I began by suggesting a general definition of the phenomenon with regards to the whole dynamics of the democratic system. This definition was made more specific, first, by the analytical consideration of the different forms and levels that can lead to consolidation and, second, by an illustration in empirical terms of its common features. Finally, I described two main models, giving higher salience to the first, i.e. consolidation through parties.

If the theoretical, or even political, relevance of this new topic is established, with some agreement reached on definitions, common features and possible 'models', then the way forward has been established. In my view, at this point, one should proceed by distinguishing between historical periods and geo-political areas (without losing sight of the comparative perspective), by scrutinizing in closer empirical terms the role and possibilities of intermediation structures (such as parties and groups) in the process of democratic consolidation, and by giving closer attention to the explanatory side. Eventually, this research may suggest more specific models or scenarios according to the different paths of democratic installation and, if necessary, introduce new relevant factors.

Notes

This is a partial version of 'Consolidamento democratico: Definizioni e Modelli', published in *Rivista Italiana di Scienza Politica*, XVI (1986): pp. 197–238.

1   Linz is the author who, in two unpublished works, first dealt with the subject in specific terms. To these let me add an unpublished study by myself which provides a general definition of the phenomenon and attempts a comparison between Italy during the 1940s and Spain in the second half of the 1970s. Finally, one should note the very recent though short analysis of the Spanish case by Santamaria and Maravall. See J.J. Linz, *The Consolidation of Regimes: A Theoretical Problem Approach*, paper delivered at VIIIth World Congress of ISA, Toronto, August 1974; Id., *The*

Transition from Authoritarian Regimes to Democratic Political Systems and the Problems of Consolidation of Political Democracy, paper delivered at IPSA Round Table, Tokyo, March 1982; L. Morlino, *Rules of Democratic Consolidation: Some Comparative Notes about Italy and Spain*, paper delivered at the Conference on 'Contemporary Change in Southern Europe', sponsored by SSRC (USA), Madrid, November 1981; J.M. Maravall e J. Santamaria (1985), 'Crisis del Franquismo, transicion politica y consolidacion de la democracia en Espana', in *Sistema*, nos 68–9, pp. 81–2. More material is available on authoritarian consolidation. For example, some of Stepan's hypotheses on Latin America and, in particular, on Peru, can be seen in this light, as can my own work on the theoretical and historical aspects of the consolidation of the Franco regime in Spain during the 1940s. See A. Stepan (1978), *The State and Society: Peru in Comparative Perspective*, Princeton: Princeton University Press, chap. 3; and L. Morlino (1981), *Dalla Democrazia all'Autoritarismo: Il Caso Spagnolo in Prospettiva Comparata*, Bologna: Il Mulino, chaps. 1 and 6.

2   D.A. Rustow (1970), 'Transitions to Democracy: Toward a Dynamic Model', *Comparative Politics*, II, pp. 358–61.

3   Two clarifications are, however, necessary. First, the vast amount of material is not only heterogeneous, but also contains a variety of approaches and positions. Secondly, this literature does not provide answers of even a superficial nature to the central problems indicated above.

4   For H. Kelsen, see the Italian translation of his collected essays (1955), *La Democrazia*, Bologna: Il Mulino. For J.A. Schumpeter, see (1954), *Capitalism, Socialism and Democracy*, London: Allen and Unwin. For R.A. Dahl, see, for example, (1971) *Poliarchy: Participation and Opposition*, New Haven: Yale University Press; and 'Procedural Democracy' in P. Laslett and J. Fishkin (eds) (1979), *Philosophy, Politics and Society*, Fifth Series, New Haven: Yale University Press.

5   On the conditions for an authoritarian crisis and democratic establishment which focuses on European cases during the 1940s and 1970s, see L. Morlino, 'Democratic Establishments: A Dimensional Analysis' in E. Baloyra (ed.) (1986), *Comparing New Democracies: Dilemmas of Transition and Consolidation in Mediterranean Europe and the Southern Cone*, Boulder: Westview Press. See also introduction and essays in the volume edited by G. O'Donnell, P.C. Schmitter and L. Whitehead, quoted in footnote 6.

6   On this point see A. Przeworski, 'Some Problems in the Study of the Transition to Democracy', in G. O'Donnell, P.C. Schmitter and L. Whitehead (eds) (1986), *Transitions for Authoritarian Rule: Comparative Perspectives*, Baltimore: The Johns Hopkins University Press; Id. (1983), *Democracy and a Contingent Outcome of Conflicts*, paper, Chicago: University of Chicago, June, and also Id. (1985), *Capitalism and Social Democracy*, New York and London: Cambridge University Press, chap. 5.

7   The classic essay on authoritarian regimes is J.J. Linz, 'An Authoritarian Regime: The Case of Spain' in E. Allardt and Y. Littunen (eds) (1964), *Cleavages, Ideologies and Party Systems*, Helsinki: Westermarck Society.

8   Mexico and Guatemala, in fact, are experiencing a greater problem in consolidating the process of liberalization than of democratization. I define *liberalization* as an incomplete, partial acknowledgement and concession from above of civil and political rights; the previous authoritarian elites, especially the military, maintain control of civil society through repression and dissuasion from participation. The minimal indicators and other aspects of democracy (listed above) do not fully apply in these two cases. For instance, uncertainty is very limited by the influence that state officials and, more specifically, the military (who have retained their political role beyond the authoritarian period) have on the outcome of decision-making processes. Similar considerations apply to Portugal, even though the military who carried out the coup d'etat in 1974 and piloted the installation of democracy have played a role which is very different from that of the previous generals who supported the Salazar and Caetano regimes. Furthermore, in Portugal there was an attempt to install a 'radical' and 'socialist' democracy, which is quite different from that described above. However, when the time came to consolidate these institutional arrangements, the crisis began, as did the swing which culminated in the constitutional reform of 1982. At the same time, the process of democratic consolidation was resumed, allowing the regime to conform to the definition suggested above.

9   Here I follow G. Sartori who underscored the need to retain the historical and terminological 'anchoring' of the concepts. See his 'The Tower of Babel' in G. Sartori, F.W. Riggs and H. Teune

(1975), *Tower of Babel: On the Definition and Analysis of Concepts in the Social Sciences*, Pittsburgh: University Center for International Studies.

10 See D.A. Rustow, *Transitions to Democracy*, cit., p. 358.

11 Elsewhere I have clarified in what way and to what extent the first two processes can overlap and thereby complicate the picture from an analytical point of view. See L. Morlino, 'Democrazie' in G. Pasquino (ed.) (1986), *Manuale di Scienza Politica*, Bologna: Il Mulino.

12 The relationships between establishment and consolidation will be further clarified when I deal with the *beginning* of the process and, later, when I formulate a better definition of consolidation.

13 I give a more specific description of the various features of consolidation below.

14 In addition, I should stress that consolidation is neither *structuration* nor *encapsulation*, which concern the phase of establishment. On the second concept, see A. Etzioni (1964), 'On Self-encapsulating Conflicts', *Conflict Resolution*, VIII, pp. 242ff. But consolidation is not even *institutionalization*, a key concept in sociological theory. Starting from Parson's concept, Huntington, more than anyone else, has managed to 'translate' the concept into the political realm. But, in the end, his definition is too general and basically unsatisfactory. According to Huntington (in *Political Order in Changing Societies*, cit., p. 12), institutionalization is 'the process by which organizations and procedures acquire value and stability'. The 'measures' of institutionalization themselves (adaptability-rigidity, complexity-simplicity, autonomy-subordination, coherence-disunity; ibidem, pp. 13–24) are not only criteria that require actual operationalization, but they show reciprocal 'tensions' and strains, if not contradictions. To understand this last consideration better, let us imagine a case of institutionalization characterized by high adaptability and complexity and, at the same time, by strong coherence and autonomy: empirically, this would be an almost impossible outcome. The present study does not intend to examine and resolve the problems of political institutionalization in these processes. The fact remains that the notion of institutionalization raises new difficulties and does not solve some of the most salient ones in the analysis of consolidation. It is therefore more reasonable to concentrate on the latter and to avoid further unnecessary complications by discarding the use of this term altogether.

15 This is a very relevant problem. See below, where I analyse the empirical factors common to past consolidations.

16 However Sartori sees one type of party system – polarized pluralism – as characterized both by anti-system parties and centrifugal competition among parties. See G. Sartori (1976), *Parties and Party System: A Framework for Analysis*, Cambridge: Cambridge University Press, pp. 132–45.

17 I have considered here only the basic aspects of this theme. Legitimacy (and legitimation) is a very large topic which several authors have written on. See L. Morlino (1980) *Come cambiano i regimi politici*, Milano: Angeli, chap. 6 and his bibliography.

18 For the analysis underlying the next few pages, I have relied on countries which I know best because of previous research, including Italy, Spain, Portugal and Greece. For the other countries, my remarks are based on historical works and political science analyses, where these exist. One excellent book is by J.A. Peeler (1985), *Latin American Democracies: Colombia, Costa Rica, Venezuela*, Chapel Hill and London: The University of North Carolina Press.

19 An analysis of policies by which to achieve the 'neutralization' of the army has yet to be made. However, a thoughtful step in that direction is a 1985 paper by A. Stepan and M. Fitzpatrick, *Civil-Military Relations and Democracy: the Role of the Military in the Polity*, written for a project on 'The Role of Political Parties in the Return to Democracy in the Southern Cone', Washington: Woodrow Wilson Center and World Peace Foundation, June. With special, but not exclusive, reference to Brazil, the two authors take into account five research areas: military perceptions of long-term budgetary trends; the military-industrial complex; promotion regulations for generals; possible alternative professional roles for officers, and the role of the military in intelligence. I think that such a problem has to be considered not only with regard to the different ways of wielding legal control over military apparatuses and the other features mentioned in the text, but also with reference to opening up military structures and bringing them nearer to civil society.

20 Several authors would consider parties as possible pillars of the process identified here as consolidation. Among others, see, for example, S.P. Huntington, *Political Order in Changing Societies*, cit., p. 461.

21 The topic deserves more careful discussion. I shall return to it in a forthcoming essay devoted to an analysis of the conditions for consolidation.
22 Relationships between parties and groups have not been analysed in depth. Among authors who have considered the topic see: J. Meynaud (1962), *Nouvelles Etudes sur les Groupes de Pression en France*, Paris: Presses de la F.N.S.P., pp. 123–7; M. Duverger (1972), *Party Politics and Pressure Groups*, London: Nelson, pp. 117 ff.; on parties and unions in Europe and other areas, see K. Von Beyme (1980), *Challenge to Power*, London and Beverly Hills: Sage Publications, pp. 237–56.
23 R.A. Dahl, *Poliarchy, Participation and Opposition*, cit., p.3.

[28]

Political Actors, Linkages and Interactions: Democratic Consolidation in Southern Europe

Geoffrey Pridham

While it is assumed that the new regimes in Spain, Greece and Portugal are fully liberal democratic, the question of their consolidation remains to be assessed. Although this raises problems about the nature of that process, focusing on the role of political parties provides a crucial means for determining the extent to which democratic consolidation has been achieved so far and for identifying any problems here. This is done by constructing a comparative approach based on three relationships: parties with the state; inter-party relationships; and, parties with society. In applying this approach to the three cases, it is hypothesised that regime consolidation may well proceed at variable paces at the different levels.

A growing assumption in the literature on the new democracies of Mediterranean Europe (Spain, Greece and Portugal) is that they have at last conformed to the type of liberal democracy common throughout Western Europe. In fact, the term 'new' is perhaps for this very reason no longer applicable. This assumption about the outcome of regime change, which began a decade and a half ago, is tantamount to saying that, the transition to democracy having been accomplished, these countries have long embarked on the subsequent process of democratic consolidation or have even virtually achieved it.

Such an assumption begs, however, several questions; first, there are different types of liberal democracy institutionally, politically and culturally, so that testing for regime change outcomes requires some differentiation; and, second, the process of consolidation itself is rather more complicated and distinctly lengthier than the preceding phase of democratic transition, suggesting with the new democracies there that if only for reasons of time the former has not yet been completed.

This problem has, furthermore, been aggravated by the dearth of theory about democratic consolidation as a concept and a framework.[1] At least, the few attempts addressed to solving this problem have differed about both the components and the time-scale of the consolidation process. One may even speak of theorising about regime consolidation as being either minimalist or maximalist. However, the purpose of this article is not to re-think consolidation theories as such but rather to focus, less ambitiously, on a particular albeit central feature of democratic consolidation, using comparative perspectives and utilising where relevant to present theoretical work on the subject. That is, examining the role, behaviour and performance of political actors should focus our attention on the dynamics of the consolidation process, and therefore highlight key problems relating to it. The analysis here will, given their crucial role in European liberal democracies, look above all at the contribution of political parties to the outcome of regime change and its consolidation.

'Linkages' are generally understood to refer to the mechanisms or channels of communication between citizens and the state. As one recent study of linkages points out, 'The political party is the one agency that can claim to have as its very *raison d'être* the creation of an entire linkage chain, a chain of connections that runs from the voters through the candidates and the electoral process to the officials of government'.[2] Kay Lawson identifies four main categories of such linkages here: participatory, electoral, clientelistic and directive or controlling[3], and comments: 'All the functions political scientists have identified (a) as normally necessary for the continued operation of a social system, and (b) as being performed in whole or in part by politics must be performed in the context of an interactive connection'. She notes that participation, leadership recruitment, allocation of resources, the creation and propagation of values, the control of behaviour (through the control of force and/or through educative communication) all require the creation of connections between different levels of aggregation, but this may apply to different kinds of political not to mention social actors like interest or pressure groups.[4]

While Lawson refers to systems which are evidently established, the idea of 'linkages' may be suitably incorporated in an approach to regime consolidation. In short, concentrating on political actors and party systems in particular remains an essential way of assessing not only the quality of a liberal democracy but also its progress towards and achievement of consolidation. They may, for instance, reflect on both the positive and negative tendencies in that process. According to Bingham Powell, 'The dynamics of the party system may either inhibit or exacerbate turmoil and violence; the strategies and commitments of party leaders can be critical for the support of the democratic regime in time of crisis'.[5] For instance, there may conceivably be differences between them over what constitute desirable attributes in a democratic system, and indeed also about questions of system maintenance.[6] Moreover, if such differences between political parties run out of control in the presumably sensitive first stage of democratic consolidation, this may make the consolidation process vulnerable to inversion such as by encouraging demands for military intervention.[7]

This in turn reminds us that the linkages between parties and other political actors (i.e. interest groups, business, the military, different movements, the media, also key individual figures) may also be crucial to the outcome of regime change as well as the standard linkage function performed by parties as an intermediary between the new system and the public. In this sense, one can only agree with Whitehead's comment that democratic consolidation 'requires an iterative process of confidence-building' among different strategic sectors and that 'it is misleading to think of the process as one in which a single bloc of "true democrats"

DEMOCRATIC CONSOLIDATION IN SOUTHERN EUROPE   105

imposes their blueprint on the rest of society'.[8] One recalls recent
comparative literature reflecting sceptically on the general importance
of political parties in Western democracies and giving renewed emphasis
to alternative organisations to parties.[9] At the same time, turning to these
Southern European democracies, it is already clear they are much closer
to the party democracy than to the rational-efficient model of liberal
democracy,[10] manifestly evident in post-war Italy but also increasingly
so in the other three cases of Spain, Greece and Portugal. Indeed, with
the latter, post-authoritarian political development has often been marked
by the weakness or absence of politically autonomous interest groups and
movements – not to mention the media – although this is perhaps less true
of Spain than the other countries.

POLITICAL ACTORS IN LIBERAL DEMOCRACIES: LOOKING TOWARDS
CONSOLIDATION

It is thus important to approach the question of democratic consolidation
through an analysis of party systems and not merely of individual parties
in the countries concerned. Parties are collectively crucial as political and
organisational linkage mechanisms between state and society.

As the growing literature on parties in the new Southern European
democracies itself strongly suggests, there is an unmistakable (and really
obvious) relationship between the consolidation of their party systems
and their system consolidation altogether. In fact, a principal reason
why Southern European democracies have been distinctly more successful
at consolidating themselves than their Latin American counterparts has
precisely been the more advanced state of political organisations and civil
society in the former.[11] And in Eastern Europe it is already clear that
political parties are crucial actors in the transitions to liberal democracy
from Communist state systems and as a guarantee of the new political
pluralism. Clearly, then, the two parallel processes of consolidation – of
the party system and of liberal democracy – interact in some decisive way;
and, conceivably, this interaction may be either mutually reinforcing and
hence positive, or the opposite where democratic consolidation may either
be delayed or even self-destruct.

National variation may, however, complicate such an argument. The case
of Spain, for instance, appears at first to challenge this hypothesis. As Bar
wrote (1984):

> The limitation of the role of the party system as an active subject in
> the political system and the consequent presence within the latter
> of other determining forces of great importance . . . the King, the
> armed forces, the police, the bureaucracy and the Church, together
> with other social groups, have maintained autonomous roles, and
> their strength has been decisive when it came to determining the
> functioning of a political system characterised by weak parties, lacking
> both internal consolidation and stable bonds with their electorates.

He notes this is partly due to the conditions under which the transition to democracy took place in Spain, 'a transition in which a whole set of different forces converged as active elements'.[12]

Whether, however, this also holds for democratic consolidation there is a somewhat different matter, given new problems have to be faced in this process and the significance of some actors may change. As Pasquino has suggested, the main point of distinction between democratic transition and consolidation, from the instrumental angle, is that the latter is a party-dominated process while the former is not necessarily that.[13] Portugal is of course a pertinent example of this distinction, bearing in mind the role of the progressive military in the transition after 1974. In Spain, too, this distinction is also applicable but, before further discussing specific cases, it is necessary to define democratic consolidation and the role in it of parties and other actors.

Broadly speaking, democratic consolidation both confirms the outcome of transition but also involves new tasks in the securing of regime change. As Whitehead has written:

> The hall-mark of this process will be that the many uncertainties of the transition period are progressively diminished as the new assumptions and procedures become better known and understood, and more widely accepted. The new regime becomes institutionalised, its framework of open and competitive political expression becomes internalised, and thus in large measure the preceding uncertainties and insecurities are overcome.

According to him, it is unlikely that such a process can ever be fully accomplished in less than a generation. Thus, 'What should concern us [meanwhile] . . . is not so much the factors assuring a full consolidation of democracy, but the conditions necessary to keep the intervening process on track'.[14] Notably, there is a widening range of political actors who assume democratic conduct on the part of their adversaries; a deepening of the commitment of most actors to the mutually negotiated democratic framework; and thus an interactive sequence 'akin to a round of tariff cuts or arms reduction'. This is combined with a process of 'socialising' the population at large into acceptance of democratic norms. In other words, there is an overall process of legitimation of the new system in both élite and popular systems.

More specifically, regime consolidation is rather less exclusive to the role of élites than transition, placing more attention on the evolving relationship between the new system and society. Although that may depend on whether the pressures for transition have been more top-down than bottom-up. Democratic consolidation requires more than the establishment and confirmation of the new political structures. It also entails some 'rooting' of the system in society, where political parties are the obvious and probably crucial agents. According to Huntington, they provide the wider organisational instrument for a modernised society requiring a stable balance between participation and institutionalisation: a strong party system expands participation through the system, preempts or diverts anomic or revolutionary political activity and moderates participation of newly mobilised groups so as not to disrupt the system.[15]

It becomes clear, then, that the division of regime transition theories into functionalist approaches (emphasising the impact of environmental factors, in particular the level of socio-economic development) and genetic approaches (stressing the scope for political choice) is less relevant when turning to the broader and deeper process of consolidation, if only because it is important there to consider both political and socio-economic levels in conjunction more so than in transition. Consolidation is in this sense qualitiatively different from transition, and is not merely an elongation of the latter. As Schmitter has noted, democratic consolidation involves new actors, new rules, new processes and, perhaps, even new values and resources, although this is not to say that everything changes when a polity 'shifts' into that process.

> Many of the persons and collectivities will be the same, but they will be facing different problems, making different calculations and behaving in different ways . . . Moreover, the shift in problem-space may reduce the significance of actors who previously played a central role and enhance that of others who by prudence or impotence were marginal to the demise and transition.[16]

Another definitional problem of consolidation has concerned its dia-chronic dimension. It is generally important to assess patterns of political change from pre-transition through the stages of transition leading up to and encompassing consolidation, with considerable scope here for national variation. Just as the circumstances of pre-transition may help to determine the actual mode of transition and hence influence its course, so that in turn may well influence the process of consolidation and conceivably too its duration, notwithstanding the above-mentioned difference between consolidation and transition. If there is any point of agreement between different versions of the time span of consolidation, it must be that a successful case shows diminishing probability of a reversal, and that therefore its first decade is the most crucial. Hence, this suggests that the time for a study of the contribution of parties and other political actors to democratic consolidation is now opportune, if we broadly say that the 1980s represent this first decade following transition in Spain, Greece and Portugal in the latter half of the 1970s.

The starting and end points of consolidation remain very unclear in the theoretical literature. However, distinguishing it from, on the one hand, the transition process but also especially, on the other hand, general problems of system change and stability in established democracies, it becomes more possible to delimit the consolidation process.[17] Thus, it may be said that transition ends not merely once the constitution is in place, but also once the system begins to function with a popularly elected government. In other words, the élites begin to work the system and to adjust accordingly. This opens the way for gradually removing systemic uncertainties, and so the 'shift' occurs to consolidation. If the support given to the new system during transition is instrumental and even opportunistic on the part of some political circles, then consolidation witnesses the progressive replacement of 'functional democrats' by 'cultural democrats' at the élite level. This is similar to Rustow's point that the habituation or end phase of transition witnesses 'a double process of Darwinian selectivity' among parties competing electorally and among politicians vying for leadership within them.[18] A commonly recognised test of progress here is a peaceful or basically uncontested transfer of power between parties in government and opposition, with the implication that serious 'anti-system' tendencies have disappeared.

Clearly, too, consolidation is on course when potential challenges or threats to the new system from non-political actors diminish and eventually fade. We make a distinction here between those political actors likely to be democratising agents (interest associations and movements as well as parties) and other political actors associated with the previous authoritarian regime (the military and possibly to some extent the Church), whose affiliation to a young democracy may be subject to doubt. In other words, it is required of the latter – which we may call ex-authoritarian political actors – that they should precisely cease to be political actors under the new democracy, especially in the case of the military which should submit themselves to civil control. Other possible political actors – or rather, associations or organisations exercising a degree of political influence – may not fall easily into one or other category, for example business and bureaucracies and their links with the previous regime. However, political parties may perform an indirect democratising role such as through special links with them or, in the case of bureaucracies, political control over the machinery of the state.

While one side of the process may therefore be called 'negative consolidation', i.e. the effective removal of the prospects for system alternatives, what ultimately secures its achievement is the ongoing development of 'positive consolidation'. As already seen, this is crucial at the élite level, but our attention here is particularly directed towards the mass level. Obviously, this must mean that the new system gradually acquires legitimacy. But this is not separate from the élite level, for the interaction between both levels must be decisive in that effective government performance has systemic consequences – it stores up credit for the new system – and this certainly points to an important contribution by political parties. Democratic consolidation may therefore be in sight of achievement when government performance is no longer systemically crucial and merely reflects on the standing of the party or parties in power. Finally, democratic consolidation may be said to have been achieved when there is evidence that the political culture is being 'remade' in a system-supportive direction, thus removing the last of the uncertainties remaining from the transition period.

It is difficult to state any precise time when consolidation is completed, although there is a preference here for a longer rather than shorter time-scale. Certainly, it takes distinctly longer than transition, since consolidation is a much broader and deeper development. Its final point is bound to be rather variable nationally, but it is most relevant to judge that by how much the principal criteria are satisfied contemporaneously or consecutively. This argument for differentiation may be taken further, for it is possible to speak of different levels of the consolidation process. Elaborating in effect on the two basic levels identified so far, Morlino lists the following: democratic structures and procedures which adapt and develop decisional practices; relationships between the structures, in particular over conflict management; the development of parties and the party system; interest structures; relationships between intermediation structures and civil society; and, relationships between intermediation structures and the regime.[19]

Our hypothesis is that consolidation usually proceeds at variant paces at the different levels, and that one may therefore speak of partial consolidation during intermediate stages of the process. But what is evident from Morlino's levels is that the role of parties is pertinent to virtually all of them to a greater or lesser extent, although there is clearly also scope for influence by other kinds of political actors.

POLITICAL PARTIES AND DEMOCRATIC CONSOLIDATION: DEVELOPING A COMPARATIVE APPROACH

From the foregoing, it is evident that any approach to the role of political parties in democratic consolidation has to be three-dimensional. Noting again that parties are crucial linkages between élite and mass levels, it is important also to examine separately their performance in relation to both state and society. Given, too, that any analysis of this subject has to focus not merely on individual parties but also party systems as a whole, it follows that a further dimension of inter-party relationships has to be included. This provides a basic outline for a comparative framework, but it is necessary to fill this out by identifying relevant variables in the light of theoretical perspectives.

According to Morlino:

> Consolidation through parties is characterised, above all, by the progressive organisation and expansion of the party structures and the party system as a whole, which is then able to control and, if needs be, moderate and integrate all forms of participation . . . Clear, long-term alignments between parties and social groups are established. Identities and the rules of internal competition among the party elites are formed. Furthermore – and this is one of the most important aspects – not only do party elites play a central part in the decision-making processes, but the parties gradually occupy the principal administrative roles and the various positions in the administration and in distributing resources at local and national level. . . .[20]

He goes on to argue – again, in parallel with the consolidation process in general – that pre-transition developments may well have a determining influence: that 'The process of consolidation is more likely to follow this model if the preceding authoritarian or, indeed, totalitarian experience had profound effects on the social fabric of the country and succeeded in destroying old, traditional forms of solidarity and organisation, particularly if the system did, simultaneously, undergo considerable socio-economic transformation'.[21] This alludes of course to post-authoritarian parties as possible modernising agents and the conditions which favour this. Paradoxically, too, it may be said that the dictatorship experience – especially if it has taken a totalitarian form – may itself facilitate subsequent 'penetration' of the system by democratic parties through the very precedent of extensive party control. Taking the three new democracies, significant differences deserve mention: on the one hand, the dictatorships in Portugal and Spain lasted much longer and became more institutionalised than the Colonels' regime in Greece; on the other hand, modernisation pressures had started in Spain a decade before Franco's departure – with some influence on individual political forces there – and well ahead of that process in Greece and Portugal.

Further paralleling previous discussion of regime consolidation, we can extrapolate from theories of transition for approaching the role of parties in the consolidation process. In doing so, it is important to observe that parties and party systems are pertinent to both the genetic and the functionalist theories of regime change. On the first count, they provide usually the most powerful political actors and are invariably seen as strategic vehicles. For instance, Rustow sees three elements at work in the final 'habituation phase' of transition (which may be seen as overlapping with early consolidation), all involving the role of parties in different ways: politicians and citizens learn from the successful resolution of some issues to place their faith in new rules and apply them to new issues; experience with democratic techniques and competitive recruitment confirms politicians in their democratic practices and beliefs; and, the population becomes fitted into the new structure by the forging of effective links of party organisation.[22] On the second count, parties obviously present an important linkage with and channel for the impact of socio-economic determinants on political change.

Many functions of political parties in transition are evidently carried over into the consolidation phase, but how does this square with the argument that the latter is qualitatively different? What therefore happens to the role of parties when the 'shift' to consolidation occurs?

First, in so far as consolidation requires the progressive removal of basic uncertainties present in transition, the attitudes, strategies and behaviour of parties must carry great weight. The most difficult case is where one or more parties represent or are associated with systemic alternatives (as in post-1974 Portugal), for then democratic consolidation must entail either their removal or change of strategy, or at least their neutralisation or isolation. Some parties may be carriers of ideas linked with opposite sides of the political divide under the previous authoritarian regime. However, some willingness and effort to overcome their own past, by 'burying the hatchet', is clearly necessary for consolidation to proceed, as notably happened in Spain after Franco. This may be achieved by means of a leadership (perhaps also generational) change, or by adaptation on the part of standing leaders and élites; but, whatever method, this amounts to an important aspect of the 'shift' from transition to consolidation. While the basis for such a compromise is laid during transition, democratic consolidation involves its continual testing and confirmation, particularly if it has been the outcome of some kind of truce.

Second, there is the direct relationship of parties with the new democratic state and their role as its advocate. Here, the situation involving parties and the need for the military's retraction from politics may well be a crucial and possibly sensitive matter at the time transition gives way to consolidation. The relationship between parties and the armed forces may either derive from the former's governmental role in the new democracy (as in Greece after 1975), or it may rely on an intermediary (notably, a non-party political head of state, as in Spain and Portugal at this time). Alternatively, this relationship may be effected by behavioural patterns on either side or events that highlight potentially divisive issues.

Thus, the legalisation of the Communist Party in Spain in 1977 – shortly before the first post-Franco parliamentary election – was commonly seen as a test-case of the military's attitude then. The uncontested decision on this indicated progress in the transition, although the attempted coup four years later questioned whether transition in this respect had been accomplished and the 'shift' to consolidation had occurred. It was more likely that the consequences of this event, in discrediting the reactionary military, secured that 'shift' by reducing the probability of a repeated challenge to civil rule. And it was on this that the new PSOE government capitalised for pursuing its policy of military reform, conceivably its single most important contribution to the consolidation process. Portugal, on the other hand, represents a rather different case, for here a radical group in the military instigated the 1974 revolution. It was a shift to the moderate left military (following the failed November 1975 coup) which enhanced the chances of liberal democracy. Thus, the parties initially played more of a secondary role in the transition; but from the 1976 Constitution onwards we see them emerging as more central actors, this being confirmed by the 1982 constitutional revision which removed the military from the institutional structure.

Third, taking the relationship with the state from a systemic to a more functional level, political parties assume both a more visible and more regular role in consolidation through their contribution to the 'material constitution'. By this is meant the way in which parties, acting individually and collectively, give substance to constitutional rules and thus confirm and enlarge on the formal outcome of transition. Parties thus perform an important legitimising function in the crucial transfer of loyalties to the new regime by exercising decisional authority and expressing social diversity and possibly dissent. Of course, individually their possibilities for a consolidating role usually differ at this point, since some are likely to be in government and others in opposition. The departure from a transitional grand coalition (as in post-war Italy) or its informal version (*consenso* in post-Franco Spain) may also mark the 'shift' to consolidation. The quality of government-opposition relations may then reflect in some way on the consolidation process. This is only likely to raise serious problems if the political pact that marked transition contains an element of a truce with some basic underlying differences still unresolved. The obvious indicator of this problem is the existence of 'anti-system' parties or those suspected of harbouring 'anti-system' intentions.

Fourth, the relationship of political parties with society identifies various other ways in which they may act as agents of democratic consolidation. This is particularly important as it focuses attention on deeper levels at which consolidation has ultimately to be achieved. In a broader sense, parties may promote liberal democracy in different ways, notably through interest optimalisation, and as instruments of popular control and of civic orientation.[23] Apart from structuring the vote, parties also play a part in defining issues in either sectoral or cross-sectoral ways, while they may or may not establish special or other links with interest groups.

As to the direct impact on democratic consolidation of parties *qua* social actors, there are several possibilities to consider. If there are certain special interests fostering a doubtful or ambiguous attitude towards the new democracy, then it is conceivable their links with pro-democratic parties might well help to reduce such problems and encourage their willingness to give democracy a try.[24] This suggests a special role here for parties of the centre-right in the case of Southern Europe. As to parties' capacity for popular control and civic orientation after authoritarianism, much also depends on how much civil society has developed, or been allowed to develop, before the onset of democratisation. This in turn may delimit the scope for parties to emerge as socio-political actors or not. Here one observes a significant difference between the Portuguese and the Spanish and Greek cases, for with the first parties had a difficult inheritance to overcome because of the lack of traditions of political mobilisation.[25] In Spain, social modernisation in the 1960s helped to pave the way for new or revived political organisations; and in Greece the brevity of the Colonels' regime suggested more of an interruption in patterns of political mobilisation.

Finally, as perhaps the ultimate test of democratic consolidation, the question of the legitimation of democracy is one where parties may perform a decisive service. Political actors are invariably in a position to facilitate legitimation of a new regime through their active support and setting an example through competent and impressive government performance. On the other hand, at some stage, we run up against basic limitations to the role here of political parties in new, not to mention established, democracies; but it is nevertheless clear there is considerable scope for their impact on democratic consolidation whatever facet of their relationship with society is examined.

It is also evident from this discussion that we have to beware of overrating the role of parties in regime consolidation, and therefore of raising expectations of this too far. A firm distinction has to be drawn between the special dictates of the consolidation process and the normal requirements of parties in liberal democracies.

POLITICAL PARTIES AND THE ACHIEVEMENT OF DEMOCRATIC
CONSOLIDATION IN SOUTHERN EUROPE

By measuring in turn the components of consolidation, and in relating
them, it becomes possible to examine the dynamics of that process through
the kind of interactive connection described by Lawson at the start of this
article. As shown earlier, there are different levels of this process; and
these may be grouped under the three relationships of parties with the
state, between themselves and with society. Focusing on party systems
allows us to pursue these systematically, given the importance of parties
as intermediary structures.

At the same time, this approach also allows for assessing linkages
between parties and other political actors. To illustrate this, we may
say with respect to the relationship with the state that parties may be
more effective whether system-supportive or 'anti-system' when precisely
they are able to draw on allied resources such as movements, interests or
even social institutions (such as the post-war DC with the Catholic Church
in Italy) or traditional institutions (the PCP and the radical military).
With the second relationship, it is likely that consensual or alternatively
conflictual patterns of inter-party relations will affect the attitudes and
maybe the behaviour of other actors; while the common theme to look
for in the linkage between parties and social actors is whether this is
one of dominance or not, and how that determines progress towards
consolidation.

Applying this approach to the three cases identifies some broad differences in the rate of consolidation between the institutional and society
levels. In Spain, the parties have developed more successfully as institutional than as social actors, so that consolidation has occurred sooner and
more effectively at state rather than society level. This distinction is also to
some extent true in the other two cases, such as Portugal where parties have
neglected their societal function owing partly to their élitism but also to the
virtual absence of traditions of political mobilisation.[26] At this point, it is
useful to turn directly to the three relationships in turn to summarise more
exactly the outcomes so far of the consolidation process and the role here
of parties and other political actors.

Relationship with the state

A first and perhaps obvious variable must be the respective parties'
handling of and attitude towards the constitutional settlement. While
this settlement is an outcome of democratic transition, its remaining an
issue of any significance or even controversy may be held as prima facie
evidence of slow consolidation and maybe of delay in embarking on it.
Here, the three countries offer diverse and in some ways contrasting
examples.

In Portugal, there have been several phases of constitutional revision
– another one recently completed – suggesting slow consolidation in that
country, although that of the early 1980s was based on cross-party support

and involved the formal end to the military's role in the policy process. This may be read as a sign that consolidation was at last under way. Spain was the most straightforward case in this respect. The political consensus on the constitutional settlement (except over the regional question) meant that here the 'shift' to consolidation was relatively uncomplicated. The transitional consensus was replaced by government rivalry, but this was accepted as 'normal' because of wide agreement on the rules of the game. Significantly, there has been no move for constitutional revision in Spain, although the exception of the regional question inhibited the consolidation process and can be said to have partially slowed it down. In Greece, there was controversy from the beginning over the Constitution since it had not been formulated on the basis of consensus. This may, however, have been finally resolved by Pasok's revision of presidential powers in 1985–86, subsequently accepted by the conservative opposition.

Applying the criterion of 'anti-system' parties is not quite so simple. The term itself is definitionally more complex than is often recognised, meaning that identification is not always straightforward. For instance, the PCE could be seen as having been 'defeated' (its electoral deterioration from 1982) rather than 'isolated' in Spanish politics, but in any case its participation in *consenso* during transition argues against its being called 'anti-system'. The Portuguese and Greek Communist Parties are more evidently 'anti-system', but they have remained largely isolated. On the political right, the Alianza Popular is an instance of a party with direct links with the previous regime (most visibly, Fraga, its leader, was one of Franco's ministers), but its own credibility problem has been rooted in this very fact as the recent attempt to refound it once more shows. In Portugal, despite the 1974 revolution, a sizeable minority of public opinion continued to regard favourably the previous authoritarian experience;[27] but – an important point – no political force there has sought to mobilise this opinion, so it has not in effect presented a serious challenge to the prospects for democratic consolidation.

The existence of 'anti-system' parties has a further consequence for democratic consolidation in that it is likely to make alternation in power difficult if not impossible, as the virtually classic example of post-war Italy has demonstrated. Here, on the other hand, the three new democracies emerge more positively on these grounds. The changes of power in 1981–82 in Greece and Spain were hailed as historic with the popular election of Socialist governments, and that only six or seven years after the end of authoritarianism. Undoubtedly, alternation in power based on (a shift in) popular support and remaining uncontested by not only rival parties but also other political actors must be the ultimate test of confidence in the rules of the game. By this account, consolidation in the three new democracies should be a much less lengthy process compared with post-war Italy, although it does not follow the same is also true of other levels of consolidation. For instance, the alternation in power in 1982 in Spain was accompanied by the complete collapse of the previous governing party, the UCD, underlining that there were other difficulties present in consolidating the that party system at the societal level.

DEMOCRATIC CONSOLIDATION IN SOUTHERN EUROPE   115

Inter-Party Relationships

The concern here is, broadly speaking, rather more with the actual dynamics of the party system, and how developments encourage political behaviour promotive of consolidation. One may group relevant themes of inter-party relationships into how far party strategies are transmitted into alliance behaviour, coalitional or political; the location of parties in the ideological spectrum, and whether these are stable and also conducive to centripetal or centrifugal patterns; and, finally, whether political competition has had broadly positive or negative repercussions for the consolidation process.

The 'shift' to consolidation may be marked by the abandonment of formal pactism as a transitional phenomenon, although this change may be followed by an element of pactism in substantial terms, i.e. there remains an underlying consensus on basic matters of policy or certain ones, confirming implicitly if not explicitly the spirit as well as the letter of the constitutional settlement. One can see this in Spain, as a tendency for national solidarity surfaced between the main national parties over the military threat and also over the difficulties of the regional question. In Greece, such 'substantial' pactism was less evident for some time, although convergence over some areas of policy – such as economic and external – by the later 1980s indicated this. Indeed, the conservative/Communist and grand coalitions in 1989–90, although interim and brief, highlighted this new development and were symbolic of a reduction in the historical left/right cleavage to perhaps 'normal' proportions.

Party locations in the ideological spectrum have thus caused some concern in the new democracies, such as in Greece but also Portugal, where party orientations have remained rather unpredictable, although by and large the dynamics of inter-party relationships there have tended to be centripetal rather than centrifugal. The same is also true of Spain, with the exception of some regionalist parties that have been fundamentalist in their opposition. Following from this, political competition has had positive more than negative repercussions for consolidation in the three new democracies as a whole.

Parties and Society

In a formal sense, these democracies have progressed well towards democratic consolidation here. They have undergone an abundance of elections during the first decade and more since the end of authoritarianism. But in terms of the quality of the society relationship, the new systems have met several difficulties in achieving that aim.

Eventually, it is assumed, partisan diversity starts to crystallise and party identification to take root. On these grounds, there is a stark contrast between post-Fascist Italy and the new democracies. In the former case, party affiliation soon pervaded Italian public life, while organisationally the respective parties established a dominant hold over interest groups and social actors. Are we therefore in the latter case looking at a lengthier process of consolidation at this level; or is it a matter of different historical circumstances affecting the possibilities for party identification? There are possible reasons for both scenarios. In Spain, the parties have certainly tended to develop far more as institutional than as social actors,[28] partly because of historical patterns, also because their élites devoted more attention to the first role in managing the transition and that seems to have had some effects on later party development. However, the environmental context also matters. The 1970s and 1980s are a period in which party identification is relatively in decline in European liberal democracies, including even Italy. Moreover, the media play a more central role than ever before as a rival linkage between the system and society, a phenomenon also evident in Spain, Greece and Portugal.

This suggests two possible consequences: parties need to rely less exclusively on party organisations for influencing society; and, in line with media habits, they may seek to personalise strongly their appeals. The prominence of political figures like Gonzalez and Papandreou, not to mention earlier Karamanlis and even Suarez, underlines this. The first consequence may well explain the determination of parties in all these countries to control the media, which at times has been a question of sharp controversy. Also, in several cases – notably, the political parties in Spain – the low level of party membership points to this same effect. In Portugal, the newness of most of the parties – excepting the PCP – has helped to explain their lack of organisational rootedness. In Greece, on the other hand, the parties – particularly Pasok – have tended to dominate social links. One may say that the underdevelopment of civil society there has facilitated this, although there are signs recently of this beginning to change. While noting cross-national differences, it is at least equally relevant to bear in mind party-political differences within countries; but, as a whole, there have been significant limits to the 'structuration' of the party-society relationship.

CONCLUSION

The principal lesson of this survey therefore is that progress towards democratic consolidation should not be measured with respect to certain isolated variables, such as the mere existence of 'anti-system' parties or weak associational networks among partisan supporters. Any analysis has – obviously – to be systemic. Thus, democratic consolidation has to be approached in a multi-dimensional or multi-level way, so as not only to accommodate cross-national variation but also to evaluate the actual or relative importance of individual variables in a given country. Above all, any assessment of movement towards democratic consolidation has to look at interactions between the different levels discussed above, in the sense posited by Lawson in the introduction of this article. In an imperfect world, it is probable that any national case of democratic consolidation will proceed at a different pace between the different levels examined above, but also remain deficient in some respects. In general, though, we can say that the new democracies are now well 'on track' towards democratic consolidation, and that many of the uncertainties of a decade ago have been erased.

DEMOCRATIC CONSOLIDATION IN SOUTHERN EUROPE   117

NOTES

This is an abbreviated and further developed version of the author's 'Southern European Democracies on the Road to Consolidation: A Comparative Assessment of the Role of Political Parties', Chapter 1 in G. Pridham (ed.), *Securing Democracy: Political Parties and Democratic Consolidation in Southern Europe* (London: Routledge, 1990). It was originally presented as a paper at the conference on 'Problems of Democratic Consolidation: Spain and the New Europe', at the Werner Reimers Foundation, Bad Homburg, West Germany, July 1989.

1. P. Schmitter, 'The Consolidation of Political Democracy in Southern Europe (and Latin America)', European University Institute, conference paper for project on organised interests and democratic consolidation, 1985, p. 3
2. K. Lawson, 'When Linkage Fails' in K. Lawson and Peter Merkl (eds.), *When Parties Fail: Emerging Alternative Organisations* (Princeton: Princeton University Press, 1988), p. 16.
3. Ibid, pp. 16–17.
4. Ibid, p. 15.
5. G. Bingham Powell, *Contemporary Democracies* (Cambridge, MA: Harvard University Press, 1982), p. 7.
6. J-E. Lane and S. Ersson, *Politics and Society in Western Europe* (London: Sage, 1987), p. 97.
7. Bingham Powell, op. cit., p. 173.
8. L. Whitehead, 'The Consolidation of Fragile Democracies', ECPR paper 1988, p. 40.
9. Cf. Alan Ware, *Citizens, Parties and the State* (Oxford: Polity Press, 1987), pp. 218–20.
10. William E. Wright (ed.), *A Comparative Study of Party Organisation* (Columbus: Charles Merrill, 1971).
11. G. O'Donnell, P. Schmitter and L. Whitehead (eds.), *Transitions from Authoritarian Rule* (Baltimore: John Hopkins University Press, 1986), pp. 7–8.
12. A. Bar, 'The Emerging Spanish Party System' in *West European Politics*, October 1984, Vol. 7, No. 4, p. 134.
13. G. Pasquino, 'Party Elites and Democratic Consolidation', Chapter 2 in Pridham (ed.), *Securing Democracy*.
14. Whitehead, op. cit., pp. 6–8.
15. S. Huntington, *Political Order in Changing Societies* (New Haven: Yale University Press, 1968), chapter 7.
16. Schmitter, op. cit., pp. 5–6.
17. Pridham, Chapter 1 in Pridham (ed.), *Securing Democracy*.
18. D. Rustow, 'Transitions to Democracy', in *Comparative Politics*, April 1970, p. 358.
19. L. Morlino, 'Consolidamento democratico: definizione e modelli' in *Rivista Italiana di Scienza Politica*, Vol. xvi, No. 2 (August 1986), p. 216.
20. Ibid, pp. 25–6.
21. Ibid, p. 26.
22. Rustow, op.cit., p. 360.
23. Ware, op.cit., pp. 23–27.
24. Cf. Whitehead, op. cit., pp. 18, 22.
25. K. Gladdish, 'Portugal: An Open Verdict', Chapter 5 in Pridham (ed.), *Securing Democracy*.
26. Ibid, pp. 119–21.
27. Ibid, pp. 121–2.
28. R. Gillespie, 'Regime Consolidation in Spain', Chapter 6 in ibid.

[29]

The Consolidation of Democracy and Representation of Social Groups

PHILLIPPE C. SCHMITTER
Stanford University

To the neophyte graduate student at the University of California, Berkeley in the early 1960s, attending Seymour Martin Lipset's course on political sociology (Sociology 290) was a revelation. The big "comparative" questions—development and democracy, class conflict and political change, nation-building and state formation, national trajectories and international trends, public opinion and public policy—were there, and they all got a serious hearing. Lipset handled each with awe-inspiring erudition and that heterodoxical blend of behavioral, structural, and cultural factors that is his hallmark. I remember references to incidents of working-class history in obscure towns I had never heard of, to parties, unions, and movements over a century-long span, to scholars—living and dead—from almost every continent, and to books written in Finnish and Swedish, not to mention German, French, and Italian!

As one of the requirements for that course, I wrote a review of an article that Lipset had published only a few years previously: "Party Systems and the Representation of Social Groups" (Lipset, 1960). This has not proven to be one of his more cited works. Indeed, I wonder if anyone else has been similarly influenced by it.[1] The review I wrote then has long since been lost in one move or another, and I cannot even recall how the author reacted to my effort. What I do remember is that reading and criticizing this particular article not only provided me with several important themes that appeared in my subsequent doctoral dissertation (Schmitter, 1971), but sent me on a lifetime trajectory of research.

The lessons I drew from it at the time may not seem so surprising today, but in the atmosphere of triumphant "behavioralism" and "functionalism" that then prevailed in the social sciences they were decidedly unorthodox:

Author's Note: *The author is indebted to Brad Wilcox and Sharon Pressner for research assistance.*

AMERICAN BEHAVIORAL SCIENTIST, Vol. 35 No. 4/5, March/June 1992 422-449
© 1992 Sage Publications, Inc.

- Political processes cannot be reduced to the preferences or behaviors of individuals but are conditioned by group actions and interactions.
- These groups—their solidarities and their conflicts—make independent contributions to determining political outcomes.
- "Representation" is the key (but not the exclusive) relationship between such groups and the making of authoritative decisions.
- This relationship is increasingly structured through specialized, "legally constituted" organizations with identifiable and reproducible boundaries. Together, they form distinctive subsystems within the polity.
- These representative organizations have a relative autonomy and an operative logic of their own that cannot be reduced either to the preferences of individuals or to the solidarities of groups that compose them. In Lipset's terms, they were neither just "a means for political adjustment" among conflicting social groups nor merely "an instrument of manipulation" by dominant authorities.
- However, the formal institutions of government—their procedures and substantive policies—can have a significant and enduring effect upon groups and the organizations that represent them. In other words, public policy is not a mere epiphenomenon produced by previously formed group interests, even less by independently established individual preferences.

What I disagreed with in the article was its main empirical conclusion, namely, that "parties are by far the most important part of the representative structure in complex democratic societies" (Lipset, 1960, p. 53). Perhaps my objection was due to the fact that I had come to Berkeley from Switzerland (admittedly, an implausible explanation given my total lack of attention to Swiss politics when I was a student at the University of Geneva). In that country, parties were hardly capable of dominating—certainly not monopolizing—the representation of social groups. Even in the United States, it seemed obvious to me that much of the "action" was bypassing its two-party system and electoral process altogether.

So, I was convinced by Lipset's plea for the importance of social groups and the autonomy of representation processes, but I drew the perverse conclusion that this implied looking elsewhere—not at political parties but at what were then called "pressure" or "interest groups"—on the hunch that this was where the linkage between social groups and public authorities would increasingly be channeled.

After a research trajectory that has taken me to several countries and continents, involving a lengthy effort at refining and adapting the categories used to analyze how interest associations structure the representation of social groups, I am now prepared to return to that initial disagreement with Lipset and to focus it on what may well be the most significant issue for contemporary political science: *How can democracy be consolidated in the aftermath of the transition from autocratic rule?* What are the respective roles of such intermediaries as political parties, interest associations, and social movements in this highly complex (and, in most cases, still undecided) process? To what extent do different ways of structuring and governing the process of representation determine what the outcome will be?

THE CONSOLIDATION OF DEMOCRACY

Intuitively, the notion of consolidating democracy seems rather obvious. After a period of considerable uncertainty and unknown duration during which the previous autocracy "transits" to some other form of political domination, it becomes necessary to transform its improvisations into stable rules and alliances under which actors can compete and cooperate on predictable terms. From a "war of movement" in which many have high expectations (and some have great fears) about the magnitude of change, the democratic struggle should settle into a "war of positions" along established lines of cleavage for mutually agreed-on advantage (Gramsci, 1971, pp. 108-110, 229-239). *Consolidation could be defined as the process of transforming the accidental arrangements, prudential norms, and contingent solutions that have emerged during the transition into relations of cooperation and competition that are reliably known, regularly practiced, and voluntarily accepted by those persons or collectivities (i.e., politicians and citizens) that participate in democratic governance.* If consolidation sets in, the democratic regime will have institutionalized uncertainty in certain roles and policy areas,[2] but it will also have reassured its citizens that the competition to occupy office and/or to exercise influence will be fair and circumscribed to a predictable range of outcomes. Modern, representative, political democracy rests on this "bounded uncertainty" and the "contingent consent" of actors to respect the outcomes it produces (Schmitter & Karl, 1991).

Leaving aside the difficulties inherent in distinguishing the two stages and in measuring their duration and effect, it should be noted that the insistence on transition and consolidation that one can find in so much of the contemporary discussion of democratization represents an important, if often implicit, theoretical option (O'Donnell & Schmitter, 1986). It involves a rejection of the previously widespread notion that democracy was a functional requisite or an ethical imperative. Neither the level of economic development, the stage of capitalist accumulation, nor the hegemony of the bourgeoisie can automatically guarantee the advent, much less the persistence, of democracy. Nor is this regime outcome the inevitable product of some previously attained level of "civilization," literacy, educational attainment or distinctive political culture. This is not to deny that affluence, a relatively equal distribution of wealth, an internationally competitive economy, a well-schooled population, a large middle-class, and a willingness to tolerate diversity, to trust adversaries, and to settle conflicts by compromise are not advantageous; it is just that democracy still has to be chosen, implemented and perpetuated by "agents," real live political actors with their distinctive interests, passions, memories, and—why not?—*fortuna* and *virtù*. No doubt, they will be constrained by the above developmental and cultural factors, but there is still plenty of room for making right or wrong choices. Even the most inauspicious setting can still give rise to an attempt to democratize, vide Haiti, Mongolia, Benin, and Albania—and, who knows, some of them may succeed —vide India, Costa Rica, Bolivia, Portugal, and Papua-New Guinea, none of which seemed to stand much of a chance when they began changing regimes.

It is the focus on these strategic interactions that distinguishes much present-day theorizing on democratization from earlier work that stressed functional requisites or cultural imperatives.[3] The ensuing years taught a bitter lesson as many relatively highly developed and "civilized" countries descended into autocracy. Moreover, some of the recent democratizers are simultaneously facing acute problems of adjusting to international economic competition and accommodating to internal cultural diversity—and they have (not yet) regressed to the status quo ante.

Let us not, however, be misled by all this emphasis on choice and voluntaristic action. *The core of the consolidation dilemma lies in coming up with a set of institutions that politicians can agree on and that citizens are willing to support.* Arriving at a stable solution, especially in the climate of exaggerated expectations that tends to characterize the transition, is no easy matter. Not only are the choices *intrinsically conflictual*—with different parties of politicians preferring rules that will ensure their own reelection or eventual access to power and different groups of citizens wanting rules that will ensure the accountability of their professional agents—but they are *extrinsically consequential.* Once they are translated via electoral uncertainty into governments that begin to produce public policies, they will affect rates of economic growth, willingness to invest, competitiveness in foreign markets, distributions of income and wealth, access to education, perceptions of cultural deprivation, racial balance, and even national identity. To a certain extent, these substantive matters are anticipated by actors and incorporated in the compromises they make with regard to procedures, but there is lots of room for error and unintended consequence. In the short run, the consolidation of democracy depends on actors' and citizens' ability to come up with a solution to their intrinsic conflicts over rules; in the long run, it will depend on the extrinsic impact that policies made under these rules will have on social groups. Here is where the "objective realities" of levels of development, positions in the world economy, conflicts over sectoral product and distributions of welfare, and the "subjective preferences" of classes, generations, genders, ethnic types, status groups, and situses reenter the picture with a vengeance. Given the likelihood that some time must elapse before the new rules of cooperation and competition produce observable results, it seems safe to assume that the process of consolidation will be a great deal lengthier than that of transition.

NOTIONS OF PARTIAL
REGIMES AND TYPES OF DEMOCRACY

It may also be a more differentiated and variegated process, for modern democracy is a very complex set of institutions involving multiple channels of representation and sites for authoritative decision making. Citizenship, its most distinctive property, is not confined to voting periodically in elections. It also can be exercised by influencing the selection of candidates, joining associations or movements, petitioning authorities, engaging in "unconventional" protests, and so forth. Nor is the accountability of authorities only guaranteed through the traditional mechanisms of territorial constituency and legislative process. Much of it can circumvent these partisan mechanisms and focus directly through functional channels and bargaining processes on elected or appointed officials within the state apparatus.

If this were not the case, the process of consolidation would be much simpler—and I would readily concede Lipset's point that "parties are by far the most important part of the representative structure." All one would have to do would be to focus on the formation of a party system sufficiently anchored in citizen perceptions, an electoral mechanism reliable (and acceptable) enough to produce winning candidates, and an institutional arrangement for ensuring that decisions binding on the public would be held accountable to its properly elected representatives. Much of the recent literature does exactly this, with considerable confidence and erudition (Pridham, 1990).

My hunch is that this may be inadequate. Either it ignores the very substantial changes that have taken place in the nature and role of parties in well-established Western democracies or it anachronistically presumes that parties in today's neodemocracies will have to go through all the stages and perform all the functions of their predecessors. I believe it is preferable to assume that today's citizens—even in polities that have long suffered under authoritarian rule—have quite different organizational skills, are less likely to identify so closely with partisan symbols or ideologies, and defend a much

more variegated set of interests. Moreover, the new regimes are emerging in
an international environment virtually saturated with different models of
successful collective action. All this may not preclude a hegemonic role for
parties in the representation of social groups, but it does suggest that they
will be facing more competition from interest associations and social movements than their predecessors and that we should revise our thinking about
democratization accordingly.

First, *what if modern democracy were conceptualized, not as "a regime,"
but as a composite of "partial regimes," each of which was institutionalized
around distinctive sites for the representation of social groups and the
resolution of their ensuing conflicts?* Parties, associations, movements, localities and various *clientele* would compete and coalesce through these
different channels in efforts to capture office and influence policy. Authorities
with different functions and at different levels of aggregation would interact
with these representatives and could legitimately claim accountability to
different citizen interests (and passions).

Constitutions, of course, are an effort to establish a single, overarching set
of "metarules" that would render these partial regimes coherent by assigning
specific tasks to each and enforcing some hierarchical relation among them,
but such formal documents are rarely successful in delineating and controlling all these relations. The process of convoking a constituent assembly,
producing an acceptable draft constitution, and ratifying it by vote and/or
plebiscite undoubtedly represents a significant moment in democratic consolidation,[4] but many partial regimes will be left undefined, for it is precisely
in the interstices between different types of representatives that constitutional
norms are most vague and least prescriptive.[5] Imagine trying to deduce from
even the most detailed of constitutions (and they are becoming more detailed)
how parties, associations and movements will interact to influence policies,
or trying to discern how capital and labor will bargain over income shares
under the new metarules.

If political democracy is not a regime but a composite of regimes, then
the appropriate strategy for studying its consolidation would be disaggrega-
tion. Not only is this theoretically desirable; it also makes the effort more
empirically feasible. In Figure 1, I have attempted to sketch out the property
space that would be involved and to suggest some of the specific partial
regimes that are likely to emerge. On the vertical axis, the space is defined
in terms of the institutional domain of action, ranging from authoritatively
defined *state agencies* to *self-constituted units of civil society.* Horizontally,
the variance concerns the power resources that actors can bring to bear on
the emerging political process: *numbers* in the case of those relying primarily
on the counting of individual votes; *intensities* for those that are based on

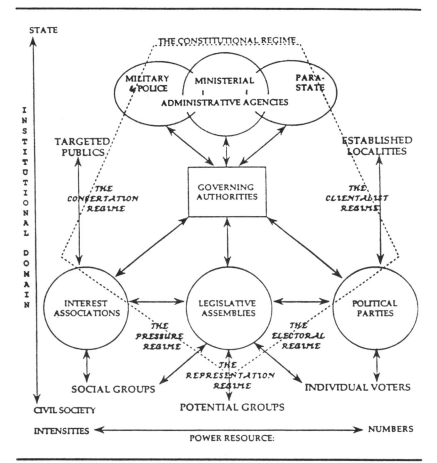

Figure 1: Sketch of the Porperty Space Involved in the Consolidation of Whole and Partial Regimes in Modern Democracies

weighing the contribution of particular groups of citizens. Competing theories and models of democracy— liberal versus statist, majoritarian versus consociational, unitary versus federal, presidential versus parliamentary— have long argued the merits of particular locations in Figure 1. In my view, all are potentially democratic (provided they respect the overarching principle of citizenship and the procedural minima of civil rights, fair elections, free associability, etc.).

Second, *what if it were not "democracy" but "democracies" that are being consolidated?* Beyond some common threshold of basic procedures that must be respected[6] lies a great deal of divergence in concrete rules and practices. These types of democracy are the result of different (but relatively stable) combinations of what I have already termed partial regimes. No single format or set of institutions embodies modern democracy—even if, at a given moment in time, some particular country may seem to represent "best practice." Instead, there is an array of possible combinations, and the dilemma of those who would consolidate democracy is to pick the one among many that satisfies both the short-term interests of politicians and the longer-run expectations of citizens.

If so, *the challenging question facing political scientists becomes not whether autocracy will be succeeded by democracy but by what type of democracy?* It could be argued that in the contemporary period (or at least since April 25, 1974 when the Portuguese "Revolution of the Carnations" launched the current wave), most polities are condemned to be democratic. The absence of a plausible alternative to some form of popularly accountable government means that those autocracies that resist (e.g., Burma, China, Cuba, Vietnam, Indonesia, Kenya, and most of the Middle East) must expend an increasing proportion of their resources in sustaining themselves in power—without much prospect for long-run success.

This "condemnation," however, does not ensure that all those that enter into a transition will succeed in consolidating a democratic regime. Some will regress to autocracy, probably in rather short order, vide Haiti and Burma. More are likely to get stuck in a sort of purgatory. They will persist as "unconsolidated democracies" where the procedural minimum will be respected, but politicians and representatives will prove incapable of agreeing on a viable set of rules for limiting uncertainty and ensuring contingent consent. Argentina and the Philippines are prominent examples of this outcome, and its specter is haunting Eastern Europe.

Third, *what if the outcome of democratization were dependent, not so much on the presence or absence of certain prerequisites or on the virtues or vices of certain persons, but on the sequence with which certain processes occurred?* There are a number of rather concrete tasks to be accomplished during a change in regime: Elections have to be convoked and held; parties, associations, and movements formed or revived; chief executives elected or chosen; ministerial and administrative positions filled or eliminated; collective bargaining arrangements created and institutionalized; constitutions drafted and adopted; legislatures elected and organized, and so forth.[7] My hunch is that the role of different representative organizations and, with it, the type of democracy that will emerge, is determined to a significant degree by the timing and sequence of accomplishing these tasks.[8] A sensible rule of thumb would be that those arrangements that get consolidated first should have a greater and more persistent effect on those coming later. This would normally imply an advantage for political parties, because it is the convocation of so-called "founding elections" that typically links liberalization to democratization and serves to accelerate the process of transition (O'Donnell & Schmitter, 1986, pp. 57-64).

THE PARADOX OF ASSOCIABILITY

Modern democracies tend to emerge as compromises. Their protagonists (not all of whom are "democrats") prefer very different institutions and practices that, not coincidentally, tend to correspond to the arrangements of power that they believe will best defend their interests or advance their ideals in the future. In the initial uncertainty of the transition, however, no dominant group may emerge that can impose its "format" and what comes out is likely to be a hybrid—a second best solution—that resembles no one's first preference.[9]

In this competitive process to define future rules and practices, interest associations and social movements are likely to find themselves in a paradoxical situation. Not infrequently, they will have been more tolerated by the *ancien régime* than political parties, especially if they concentrated on the representation of relatively localized or circumscribed interests.[10] The defections of key professional and business groups often serve to challenge the "indispensability" of authoritarian rulers, just as the declarations of human rights movements discredit their legitimacy. Once the transition has begun, these and other organizations are usually swept up in what Guillermo O'Donnell and I have called "the resurgence of civil society" (O'Donnell & Schmitter, 1986, p. 48). This unexpected mobilization can be a crucial factor in driving the authoritarian rulers beyond their hesitant and limited measures of liberalization toward full-scale democratization.

These initial organizational advantages when combined with a particularly strategic location in the system of production or administration can be translated into a genuine, if momentary, power advantage. In fact, associations representing important class, sectoral, and professional interests may be even victimized by their capacity to disrupt or nullify actions taken by the new democratic rulers.[11] Not only will this be interpreted as extracting unfair rewards for "some" at a time when the rhetoric focuses on the rewards for "all," but the disruption of social peace their actions inevitably provoke can also be seen as encouraging a coup by hardliners already convinced that the transition has gone too far. The pressure on these "functional" organizations not to make opportunistic use of their power during the transition is likely to be great.

For more loosely organized, topically focused "attitudinal" movements, the difficulties are of another nature. Many of their objectives may have been satisfied by the demise of autocracy itself. Others seem too specialized to provide general guidelines for the design of subsequent institutions. Whatever their role in bringing down the ancien regime (and it has varied a great deal), social movements depend on massive amounts of voluntary labor and personal enthusiasm, which are difficult to sustain over time and to focus on the minutiae of consolidation. Sporadic interventions may still be mounted— around the founding elections, the convocation of constituent assemblies, eventual coup attempts, and so on—but the role of these organizations seems inexorably to decline with the definition of stable rules and practices, at least until they are revived by another wave of protest (Tarrow, 1991).

Let us, therefore, concentrate our attention on those permanent associations that specialize in protecting or promoting class, sectoral, or professional interests and try to discern the conditions under which they might intrude on the putative monopoly of political parties in the representation of social groups. As we have speculated above, they can rarely be expected to play a sustained role during the transition, even if their momentary influence can be quite significant. They may also experience a good deal of difficulty in adapting to the rules of the game that emerge out of the consolidation period.

First, interest associations tend to be displaced from the center of political life and public visibility by political parties once elections have been announced, if their outcome appears to be uncertain and it seems safe to run for office. The former are organized along functional lines and can rarely adapt to compete in territorial constituencies. Moreover, their programs and symbols are too specialized to appeal to wider publics.[12] Despite the fact that they rarely play much of a role in initiating the transition, parties do have access to those symbols and programs of general identification and may even draw resources and personnel away from preexisting (and less persecuted) associations and movements once the prospect of "founding elections" is in sight. The dynamics of electoral competition will compel party strategists to appeal to wider and more heterogeneous publics (especially where districts are relatively large and the electoral system less than perfectly proportional), and they may even have to deny their dependence on the very "special interests" that helped them get started. Territorial constituencies impose a different logic of competition and cooperation than functional constituencies. Interest associations will try the best they can to penetrate, even to colonize, these partisan units, but the imperative of assembling numbers and the rhetoric of appealing to the public interest work against their success—at least until longer-run needs for financial resources and specialized information can assert themselves.[13]

Rather, the inverse is more likely to occur during the transition and early consolidation periods. Political parties will seek to penetrate and colonize interest associations. Where they are very successful, the result will be a set of partisan subcultures: *Lager* or *familles spirituelles* in which communities of differing color—"red, black, white, orange"—will confront each other and demand the exclusive affiliation of their members. Where they are only partially successful, they can leave behind a set of interest associations split internally into competing party factions or fragmented into competing units of representation. In either case, the sum total is likely to have less members and financial resources than in the more favorable outcome where class, sectoral and professional organizations manage to retain their respective unity and, hence, their monopolistic location in the emergent system of interest politics.

These tendencies toward fragmentation and/or competitiveness may, in some cases, be further exacerbated by emergent difficulties in responding to regionally or locally based challenges. The highly centralized nature of authoritarian regimes typically leaves an accumulated heritage of frustration in peripheral areas—all the more so when these are ethnically, linguistically, or culturally distinctive. Transition toward a new configuration of public offices may bring out simultaneous demands for a new configuration of territorial authority. These tensions are also likely to affect the unity of political parties, but the creation of regional representative bodies with their own party systems may absorb much of their impact. Because the core issues of economic management and social policy that most affect class, sectoral, and professional associations tend to remain firmly in the hands of central authorities, regionalism can bring little more than symbolic satisfactions to these interests. Effective influence requires a capacity to respond and negotiate at the national level, but resurgent peripheral identities may be hard to ignore (and difficult to gauge) in the relative uncertainty of the transition.

Finally, interest associations seem to face rather special problems of "resource extraction" during the democratization process. The new basis for both joining and contributing to them is (presumably) *voluntarism*. Invariably, the new constitutions enshrine freedom of association among their fundamental rights. Some may even guarantee *Negativekoalitionsfreiheit*, or freedom *from* having to join any specific association. This implies an end to exclusive state recognition and compulsory contributions. Willing individuals from different social classes, economic sectors, and professional categories must come forward to support their respective associations in a situation where lots of other claims are being made on their time and money. One does not have to be a strict devotee of Mancur Olson's *Logic of Collective Action* (1965) to recognize that once the "uncalculated" enthusiasm of participating in the mobilizational phase of regime change is over, the temptation to free-ride on the effort of others is likely to settle in.

One can hypothesize, therefore, that the more the departing autocracy was characterized by extensive state corporatism or monistic control by the governing party, the greater will be the probable difficulty of adjusting to voluntarism and "official" indifference. Admittedly, there exist ample possibilities for granting informally to groups what constitutional freedom of association formally denies them. The complex provisions of a labor code, social security, and labor court systems, and the operation of assorted advisory commissions, not to mention the (often surreptitious) concession of outright subsidies, can help to overcome the limitations of voluntary associability. In some instances, the resource problem may center on the ownership of certain physical assets and the control over certain monopolistic services that associations acquired under authoritarian auspices. Whatever the case, the *patrimoine* from the defunct regime will be a major potential source of group struggle and an important determinant of the resources available to newly "liberated" interest associations. One of the murkiest areas of their operation during the transition and early consolidation is finance. Regardless of the formula that is eventually applied—retention of monopolistic privileges, distribution of the patrimoine, subsidization by government in power (or by other *inconfessable* sources, domestic or foreign)—the adjustment to new conditions of membership should weaken the role of organized business, labor, and agriculture during the interim. Once these problems are resolved, however, their respective associations may come to play a role in defining what type of democracy will consolidate itself.

For the reasons sketched above, my hunch is that such class, sectoral, and professional associations will *not* be a major factor in determining whether democracy as a general mode of domination will succeed authoritarian rule and persist for the near future; rather, their (delayed) impact will be significant in determining what *type* of democracy will eventually be consolidated. In the longer run, this will affect the distribution of benefits that is likely to set in, the formula of legitimation that is likely to be employed, and the level of citizen satisfaction that is likely to prevail. Another way of putting it is that the *quality of democracy*, rather than its quantity and duration, will vary with the emergent properties of associability (Schmitter, 1991). Organized class, sectoral, and professional interests can have an impact on the consolidation process, but it is going to take some time before the full extent of this becomes evident.

The strongest case for their long-run significance comes from the literature on societal or neocorporatism.[14] Liberal thought had long suggested that political order rested on an implicit social contract between individuals and their rulers. "Rational choice Marxists" added the notion that a compromise between classes was necessary if "capitalist democracy" were to survive.[15] Neither (at least initially) paid much attention to the associations that actually aggregated the interests at stake into diverse categories and engaged in the negotiation of explicit agreements—liberals presumably because these organizations were expected to behave no differently than individuals; Marxists because classes *an sich* were supposed to be objectively capable of imposing their logic of conflict over whatever "class fractions" had emerged *für sich*.

The corporatist perspective that flourished during the 1970s and 1980s focused specifically on historical differences in the way these organizations had emerged and how they continued to affect contemporary economic performance, mainly across the advanced industrial countries. It suggested that formalized and centralized intermediation, primarily (but not exclusively) through associations representing class, sectoral, and professional interests, had become an important characteristic of some (but not all) modern political democracies. Moreover, the social contracts/class compromises negotiated under corporatist auspices seemed not only to have a significant impact on rates of inflation, levels of unemployment, and fiscal equilibria, but to contribute to the "governability" of the polity (Bruno and Sachs, 1985; Cameron, 1984; Paloheimo, 1984; Schmidt, 1982; Schmitter, 1981; Schott, 1985; Wilensky and Turner, 1987).

The reasons for this were to be found not in the normative dilemma of ensuring obligation or in the functional imperatives for reproducing capitalism but in such contingent factors as the organizational response to previous social conflicts, the impact of war, and, most of all, the development of the modern welfare state with its Keynesian policy agenda. Once public officials intervened heavily and diversely in the macromanagement of the economy, they found themselves increasingly dependent on organized interests for the information and compliance needed to make their policies work. Associations, meanwhile, sought to shake off the limits of liberal, voluntary collective action by acquiring state recognition, centralized monopoly representation, licensing authority, guaranteed access, and other characteristics that would enhance their membership and resources.

In the well-established democracies of Northern Europe, these developments occurred piecemeal and without explicit ideological justification, even if the predominant Social Democratic parties of the region did stress the generic necessity for reformism and class compromise. Elsewhere, neo-corporatist arrangements either survived from precapitalist practices or emerged pragmatically to solve specific postwar crises. In other words, their legitimacy was questionable—and not just because they resembled previous attempts by authoritarian rulers such as Mussolini, Franco, Salazar, Vargas, and Peron to impose such structures from above during the 1930s and 1940s. To this day, the connection between corporatism and democracy remains "essentially contested" (Schmitter, 1983).

It is, therefore, all the more ironic that the theme should emerge so insistently in discussions of the consolidation of neodemocracies. Here we are faced with a case of international diffusion. The Spaniards were clearly inspired by the relative success of such arrangements in northern and central Europe during the 1960s and 1970s. Their *Pacto de Moncloa* and its successors, in turn, encouraged others to attempt to forge an explicit macrolevel agreement between peak or sectoral associations representing capital and labor in the aftermath of authoritarian rule. While the record outside of Spain has, so far, not been encouraging and one can even question whether the various Spanish pacts from 1975 to 1984 really had much of an impact on controlling key economic parameters, the potential political effects can be very significant. The very image of representatives from such a wide diversity of interests signing such an accord—in the Spanish case, with the added blessing of the king—can serve to reduce uncertainty about substantive outcomes and "reciprocally legitimate" both the negotiating organizations and the government officials that brought them together.[16] In this case, neocorporatism will have switched from being a "consumer" of legitimacy already well-established in state institutions to being a "producer" of it in democratic institutions that are just emerging. What an irony that just as corporatism seems to be dying (or, better, moribund) in the old democracies (Schmitter, 1989), it should be revived in the new ones!

The corporatist "growth industry" of the past two decades has, however, had some impact on the rapidly evolving discussion of types of democracy. Traditionally, these were delineated either according to formal constitutional/institutional criteria or the nature of their party systems. More recently, analysts have used variation in the structure of interest associations to generate new types (Lange & Meadwell, 1985), or have explored the relationship between the variation in the pluralist-corporatist dimension and the more conventional distinctions (Lijphart & Crepaz, 1991). While it is my conviction that these are steps in the right direction that should improve our understanding of the consolidation of democracy, I would like to enter a dissenting note. One of the reasons for the shifting fate of corporatist arrangements in advanced industrial countries has been the changing nature of their working class and, with it, the changing role of trade unions. To the extent that most of the discussion and virtually all of the measurement of corporatism has focused on certain properties of the union movement—concentration, monopoly, density of membership, hierarchic structures, official recognition, guaranteed access, and so on—this may prove misleading, especially in countries where urban, regularly employed, unionized workers are a small, relatively privileged (and usually diminishing) proportion of the total work force. Granted that they may still be sufficiently well-located strategically to bring production to a halt (and they may also be concentrated in sectors of state employment where they are politically well-protected from the consequences of their actions), nevertheless, one should not assume that their consent is necessary for corporatism to work. It may be possible to work out "bipartite" deals between capital and the state that could have similar effects or to bring in associations representing the self-employed, professionals, service employees, consumers, housewives, even various marginal groups from the underground economy to give agreements a "popular" component. Admittedly, this will be a lot messier than the classic tripartite formula, but in places like Latin America where wages are already at a subsistence level and constitute a small percentage of national income, where overmanning and unemployment exist side by side, and where the policy thrust is toward privatization, it may be a feasible alternative. In Eastern Europe, "classic" blue-collar workers are a much more significant proportion of the population, but their ranks are rapidly shrinking and their organizations are in disarray. Who is to say that associations representing emergent "political capitalists," shareholders in privatized enterprises, professionals, farmers, and various petit bourgeois interests will not play a more important role than trade unions in whatever social contracting takes place?

With these heretical thoughts in mind, let us now turn to the issue of how to capture these emergent properties during the difficult period of consolidation.

THE EMERGENT PROPERTIES OF ASSOCIATIONS

In response to the opportunities (and threats) of democratization, individual associations are likely to have to change significantly in their internal structures and operative practices. Some will make every effort to retain the organizational advantages they enjoyed under the previous autocracy; others will seize on the chance of establishing a new relationship with their members and inserting themselves independently into the policy process. Here, there is a deep-seated irony, because *those social groups that are in greatest need of collective action (i.e., those with numerous, dispersed, and relatively impoverished individuals as potential members) are the least likely to be successful in attracting these members on a rational and voluntary basis.* The small, concentrated, and privileged groups should have less difficulty in generating resources under democratic conditions. Not only do they need them less (their members may have adequate resources to act individually), but they were usually the privileged interlocutors and beneficiaries of the previous autocracy. Left to its own devices, then, the new "liberal" associability could produce a systematically skewed overrepresentation of dominant class, sectoral, and professional interests. Subordinate groups have, of course, the new resource of voting between competing parties to pursue their general interests, but they may have to rely on the state recognition, licensing, and subsidization characteristic of the ancien régime to participate effectively in the democratic game when it comes to advancing their more particular interests. The practical temptations of neocorporatism, in other words, may outweigh the ideological attractions of pluralism.

First, let us turn briefly to some properties of individual, direct membership organizations representing the interests of business, labor, and agriculture that may change with the advent of democracy: number, member density, and representational domain.

NUMBER

Theoretically, this should be unlimited under the newly acquired twin freedoms of association and petition. As James Madison put it so bitterly in *The Federalist Papers*, No. 10: "The most frivolous and fanciful distinctions have been sufficient to kindle their unfriendly passions and excite their most violent conflicts." Indeed, his pluralist formula was designed to increase the potential number by multiplying the levels of authority around which they could form, as well as placing no barriers to their continual fragmentation. Several factors, however, may either raise the threshold of association formation for specific social groups, or restrict access to bargaining arenas by those that do manage to get organized. Here is where public policies, either held over from the previous regime or created anew under the new democratic regime, can be expected to play a crucial role. Linked to this basic condition are subsidiary questions of whether the associations are new or merely rebaptized versions of previous ones, whether their formation is spontaneous or sponsored (and, if so, by whom), and whether they tend to emerge early or late in the process of transition.

MEMBER DENSITY

According to liberal democratic theory, the proportion of those eligible to join and contribute to this form of collective action who actually do so is supposed to be determined only by the rational and independent calculation of individual capitalists, workers, and agriculturists. In fact, the usual social and economic "filtering mechanisms" are often supplemented by deliberate public and private actions. This leads to the murky area of outside sponsorship by political parties,[17] statutory obligations by state agencies (vide chamber systems for capitalists and agriculturists, closed shops, and union taxes for workers), and even more subtle forms of fiscal discrimination, licensing, export certification, subsidized services, and outright coercion—all of which can bind various social and economic categories to their respective units of representation in ways they do not freely choose but which have been accepted as compatible with democratic practice.

REPRESENTATIONAL DOMAIN

According to the usual canons of democracy, interest associations (old or new) should be able to determine by themselves whom they wish to represent. They set the limits on whom they attempt to recruit as members and what they purport to speak for. Rarely, however, is this the case. Under state corporatist auspices—the usual Southern European and Latin American inheritance from authoritarian rule—these domains were specified by law or administrative regulation. Interests had to be organized by economic sector or professional specialization, to have adopted a given territorial format, to have restricted themselves to a certain level of interaction, and to perform a prescribed set of tasks. Conversely, certain domains and activities were proscribed, as were specific political, ideological, or cultural affiliations. These are organizational "habits" that may decay slowly, even when the original measures are revoked.[18]

Whatever the inheritance and the inertia, countries are likely to vary considerably in the way in which interest domains are defined. Two dimensions seem especially crucial for future democratic practice: the *degree of specialization* into functional (e.g., product, sector, or class), territorial (e.g., local, provincial, or national) and task (e.g., trade vs. employer associations, unions oriented toward militant action vs. those oriented toward the provision of services) domains, and the *extent of discrimination* according to individual member characteristics, such as size of firm, level of skills, public-private status, religious belief, ethnicity, party affiliation, and so forth.

Summarizing this "bundle" of characteristics relative to individual associations, the two emergent properties that seem to make the most difference for the consolidation of different types of democracy could be called "strategic capacity" (Pizzorno, 1977) and "encompassingness" (Olson, 1965): Are these newly created or recently renovated organizations sufficiently resourceful and autonomous to be able to define and sustain a course of action over the long run that is neither linked exclusively to the immediate preferences of their members nor dependent on the policies of parties and agencies external to their domain? If this is the case, how broad a category of represented interests can be covered by any given organization or coordinated by peak associations through hierarchical arrangements?

Where polities acquire class, sectoral, or professional associations with both strategic capacity and encompassing scope, these associations play a more significant role in the consolidation process than where a great multiplicity of narrowly specialized and overlapping organizations emerge with close dependencies on their members and/or interlocutors. Pluralist associations, in other words, weaken the role of interest intermediaries; corporatist ones strengthen it. This difference also affects the probability of establishing stable partial regimes and, hence, the type of democratic regime. For example, the chance of creating viable *concertation regimes*, the kind of regime that links associations directly with each other and/or to state agencies, seems contingent on the development of strategic capacity and encompassingness. Furthermore, once this linking is initiated, it will tend to encourage "participant associations" to acquire even more autonomy from members and party interlocutors and to extend their scope to bring wider and wider interest domains under their control. At the extreme, the neodemocracy could become populated with a series of "private interest governments" in sensitive policy areas (Streeck & Schmitter, 1984), with profound consequences for political parties, local clienteles, and the legislative process, as well as for the overall governability of the political order (Schmitter, 1981).

THE EMERGENT PROPERTIES OF ASSOCIATIONAL SYSTEMS

The second set of emergent characteristics refers to what one may loosely term the *system of interest intermediation*. The impact of organized interests on the type of democracy cannot be assessed by merely adding together the associations present in a given polity but must also take into account the properties that emerge from their competitive and cooperative interaction. To keep the discussion focused, let us again concentrate on just the three most salient dimensions.

The first is *coverage*. Which social groups are organized into wider networks of collective action, which operate strictly on their own, and which are completely left out? My decision to privilege class, sectoral, and professional associations already implies a biased assessment that these, among all the varied types of interest groups, are likely to make the most crucial decisions with regard to partial regime consolidation and, eventually, the type of democracy. In the narrow sense, the issue is whether identifiable segments

or factions of these interests ("potential groups" in the pluralist jargon) fail
to organize—or do so to a degree appreciably less than would appear
possible. Is this due to the persistence of repressive measures (e.g., prohibi-
tions on the unionization of civil servants or the organization of shop floor
units of worker representation), to a strategic calculation that their interests
would be better promoted/defended through other means of collective action
(e.g., political parties, informal collusion, or clientelistic connections), or to
a structural incapacity to act under the new conditions of voluntarism and
competitiveness? Granted, it may be difficult to assess counterfactually the
presence of interest categories that "exist but do not act" and to reconstruct
the logic that leads conscious and active groups to be satisfied through one
mode rather than another of representation, but a comprehensive assessment
of the coverage of emergent interest systems requires at least some effort in
this direction, if only because of the hypothesis that democracies will face
serious problems of legitimacy and governability if they exclude (or simply
ignore) such potentially active social groups.

The problem is exacerbated when one shifts from this narrow class and
sectoral focus to the much broader question of the coverage of "other"
interests (not to mention passions), specifically, those people who are poor,
aged, sick, unemployed, illiterate, dwelling in slums, foreigners deprived of
decent treatment, natives suffering from ethnic, linguistic, or sexual discrimination, anxious about environmental degradation, concerned about world
peace or the rights of animals, *e cosi via*. Here, there can be no initial
presumption that collective action will take the rather limited and specialized
form of associability. Their demands may be better addressed via political
parties (if they are voters), religious institutions (if they are believers), local
governments (if they are spatially concentrated), or state agencies (if they are
designated clients). They can also form their own social movements, with
both an agenda and a means of action that may not be compatible with the
more narrowly constrained scope of interest organizations. No empirical
study could possibly cover all forms of actual and potential interest and their
corresponding organizations. For Southern Europe, it can be argued that
functionally based interest associations will be more significant in the consolidation process than, say, social movements[19] and, subsequently, will
contribute more to defining the type of regime that will emerge (Tarrow,
1991). This cannot, however, become a license to ignore completely the role
of organizations and institutions representing those "other interests," if only
because they will affect to some degree the number, member density, and
domains, as well as the coverage, of class, sectoral, and professional associations.

The second emergent property is *monopoly*. The advent of democracy
should encourage competition among associations for members, for re-

sources, and for recognition by, as well as access to, authorities. It does not, however, make it imperative or unavoidable. The usual assumption is that the previous authoritarian regime—if it did not suppress associability altogether for specific groups—compelled them to act within a singular, monopolistic, state-recognized (and often state-controlled) organization. Whether this situation persists after that regime has fallen seems to be contingent on political factors that assert themselves during the transition and that can have a lasting effect. By far the most salient, especially with regard to trade unions, is the emergent structure of competition among political parties. Rivalry between communists, socialists, and, occasionally, Christian Democrats over worker affiliation often antedates the demise of authoritarian rule, but it may be only after electoral politics has been restored that it can become sufficiently salient to split more or less unitary workers' movements—as has happened in Italy, Spain, and Portugal. Business associations have historically been less organizationally affected by partisan divisions—even when their members voted for competing parties—but they have sometimes been fragmented by linguistic or religious differences. Far more divisive for them has been the conflict of interest between small, medium and large enterprises—analogous to the difficulties of containing white- and blue-collar workers within the same peak association or of working out "nonraiding agreements" between unions representing differing skill levels. As mentioned above, regionalism and "micronationalism" has also led to situations of competition for members or access.

Whatever the source, the emergent postauthoritarian system will possess varying degrees of "monopoly power" in the representation of interests—and this will be crucial for the formation of partial regimes. Oftentimes, this will prove difficult to assess for the simple reason that associations may appear to have defined their domains in ways that imply competition while in practice coming to less obtrusive arrangements under which they agree not to try to lure away each other's members or to share key resources and even leaders or to engage in a subtle division of labor vis-à-vis potential interlocutors. For example, capitalists in northern and central European countries are organized into separate hierarchies of trade and employer associations that seem to be competing for member allegiance and political access. On closer examination (and despite some past conflicts), this turns out to be a quite stable division of labor that lends considerable flexibility and "redundant capacity" to that class's defense of its interests.

The third system property is *coordination*. Single associations tend to have a limited span of control and capacity for managing interest diversity. The age-old quest for "one big union" has gone unfulfilled for workers, although capitalists and farmers have sometimes come closer to that goal. In order to represent more comprehensive categories, the usual technique has been to create "associations of associations." These peak organizations (*Spitzenverbände* is the incomparable German phrase) may attempt to coordinate the behavior of entities within a single sector (e.g., the entire chemical industry), a whole branch of production (e.g., all of industry) or the class as a whole (all capitalists, workers, or farmers irrespective of branch or sector). They may cover a locality, a province or region, a national state, or even a supranational unit such as the European Community. Their success in effectively incorporating all relevant groups and forging a unity of action among them also varies from very incomplete and loose confederal arrangements, in which members retain their financial and political autonomy and are moved to common action only by exhortation or the personal authority of leaders, to highly centralized and hierarchic bodies with superior resources and even a capacity to discipline all class or sectoral interests that refuse to follow an agreed-on policy line.

Such a high coordinative capacity is not attained without struggle or, at least, never without significant threats to the interests at stake. This is obviously easier to do where the scope is purely local and the sector quite narrow, for at these levels the mutual effects of small numbers and close social interaction can be brought to bear. To accomplish such feats on a national and class basis requires much greater effort. Normally, it comes only after the building blocks, the direct membership local and sectoral associations, have been created,[20] but this tends to make the subsequent subordination of the latter more difficult. Perhaps the heritage of centralization from the immediately preceding state corporatist experience may facilitate such an outcome in Southern Europe. The extraordinary success of the Spanish Confederation of Employers (CEOE) at the peak of Spanish business suggests this (Aguilar, 1983; Perez-Diaz, 1985; Rijen, 1985), but the example of next-door Portugal shows that exactly the contrary can follow. The latter has two competing national industrial associations with little or no power to coordinate the behavior of their members, much less to speak for those (numerous) sectors of business that do not fall within the purview of either.

If strategic capacity and encompassingness were the two composite, emergent properties of individual associations that seemed most relevant, the two that best define the nature of interorganizational systems of interest intermediation are *class governance* and *congruence*.

Class governance is the capacity to commit a comprehensive social category (e.g., all owners of productive property, workers in all industries, self-employed in all sectors) to a common and long-term course of action *and* to be able to assure that those bound by such a policy do indeed comply with it. Theoretically, this could be accomplished by a political party, although the logic of continuous electoral competition tends to undermine this for manual workers—and parties have almost never performed this function for capitalists.[21] In practical and contemporary terms, if class governance is to become a property of civil society and the political order, it is a set of interest associations (or even a single peak association) that will have to do the job.

Congruence refers to the extent to which the coverage, monopoly status, and coordinative capacity of one class or sector are similar to others. One could postulate an underlying trend in this direction, especially between clusters of associations that represent conflicting interests. Nevertheless, in historical terms, some may take the lead in experimenting with (and, occasionally, borrowing from abroad) novel forms of self-organization that subsequently diffuse to their opponents or imitators. Given the high uncertainty of the transition period, incongruence would seem a rather normal state and the question would be whether this tends to diminish during the course of democratic consolidation. Several cases suggest that these differences in timing and structural context may institutionalize initial incongruence across classes and sectors. Japan, for example, has not been an easy case to classify since its location shifts considerably depending on whether it is being scored for its workers (close to the syndicalist pole), its capitalists (close to the societal or neocorporatist position) or its agriculture (close to state corporatism). Switzerland is another—if not so extreme—case of incongruence, with labor much less centrally coordinated and monopolistically organized than capital. Elsewhere, the class and sectoral disparities are less marked, but Austria, Sweden and Norway stand out as models of congruence. Everywhere—even in such otherwise competitive and uncoordinated (i.e., pluralist) systems as in the United States and Canada—agriculture seems to find a distinctively corporatist way of organizing itself!

Together, class governance and congruence (where they are present) play a major role with respect to the partial regimes outlined in Figure 1. "Concertation" (direct-link) arrangements—bilateral or trilateral—are difficult to run without them. Agreements cannot be enforced, and parity in representation becomes illusory. The representation regime—the division of labor between associations, parties, and movements—seems to rest on a particularly close networking between the former two and an exclusion of the latter from effective exchanges. Finally, the pressure regime becomes less relevant, because most of the interaction takes place directly with involved state agencies. Parliament is only brought in when changes in fiscal legislation, welfare measures, and so forth are required in order to seal social contracts drawn up elsewhere. All this is very sketchy, but it should serve to illustrate how these two emergent system properties—as well as those of coverage, monopoly, and coordination that lie behind them—can become (but do not necessarily become) significant factors in determining what type of democracy is going to consolidate itself.

A TENTATIVE CONCLUSION

Nothing in this essay proves that "parties are (no longer) the most important part of the representative structure in complex democratic societies." Rather, on the contrary, these territorially based, symbolically laden and electorally oriented organizations seem to have a considerable initial advantage in the process of consolidation. Whether they will succeed in converting it into a permanent hegemony within whatever type of democracy eventually manages to implant itself remains to be seen. Since it was in Southern Europe (Portugal, Greece, and Spain) that the current wave of democratization began in the mid-1970s and it is there that the processes of consolidation are furthest advanced, these should be the countries that can teach us the most about what (if any) changes have occurred in the respective roles of parties, associations, and movements.

Whatever the evidence should prove, the generic point should remain valid. The label *democracy* hides a continuous evolution in rules and practices and an extraordinary diversity of institutions. Just because the world is being swept on an unprecedented scale by the demise of autocratic regimes (themselves of considerable diversity) does not mean that their successors will necessarily follow the paths taken by the democracies that have gone before them. Not only are these neodemocrats likely to try to "jump stages" in an effort to emulate what they regard as the best practices of their most successful forerunners, but they may even come up with novel arrangements of their own.

It seems highly unlikely that they will be able to do without what has long been the hallmark of modern political democracy, namely, its dependence on the indirect representation, rather than the direct participation, of citizens (Bobbio, 1978). They may, however, be able to produce a different mix of the forms that modern representation can take and, in so doing, consolidate a type of democracy that will be more appropriate to the distinctive cleavages and conflicts of their respective societies. This is not to suggest that "democracy by political parties" is about to be replaced with "democracy by interest associations" or, even less, "democracy by social movements." Those pundits in the past who predicted that function would supplant territory as the basis of representation, or that the legislative process would be gradually displaced by tripartite bargaining between capital, labor, and the state, or that identification with party would wither in comparison to mobilization through social movements, were all proven wrong. If nothing else, they should have learned that representation between social groups and public agencies is not a zero-sum matter. It is a capacious realm in which there is room for movement in several directions, as well as for the simultaneous presence of different forms. Whether the leaders of today's neodemocracies, assailed on all sides by social, economic, and cultural conflicts, will have the imagination and the courage to experiment with these forms and to expand the realm of representation remains to be seen.

NOTES

1. A revised, abbreviated, and presumably more widely circulated version was published as Chapter 9 in Lipset (1963).

2. For this emphasis on uncertainty as "the" characteristic of democracy, see Przeworski (1986, pp. 57-61).

3. The *locus classicus*, of course, is Seymour Martin Lipset (1959a, 1959b). It should be noted that in his recent work, the level of economic development is described not as a requisite but as one among several "facilitating and obstructing factors" (Diamond, Linz & Lipset, 1990, pp. 9-14).

4. However, in some cases this experience can be avoided by pulling off the shelf a venerable constitution from the past, as was the case for Argentina and Uruguay during their recent transitions.

5. For a fascinating argument that it is often the "silences" and "abeyances" of constitutions —their unwritten components—that are most significant, see Foley (1989).

6. The standard list of "minimal procedures" can be found in Dahl (1982). For a revised version, see Schmitter and Karl (1991).

7. There will, of course, be infinitely more to be accomplished if the change in political regime is accompanied by a simultaneous transformation in the distribution of wealth, the institutions of private property, the nature of civil-military relations, or the territorial basis of state authority. Where such "simultaneity" occurs (as in Eastern Europe and the Soviet Union), the potential complexity of timing and sequence increases exponentially.

8. It should be noted that timing and sequence have two distinct points of reference: first, with regard to the accomplishment of these tasks in other polities undergoing regime change in the same "wave of democratization," and second, with regard to when and how these tasks are handled within the country itself. Normally, we would assume the latter to be more significant, because so many functional interdependencies are involved, but under contemporary circumstances, communication across national units has become so frequent that the diffusion effects may be quite powerful. Moreover, there now exist a large number of organizations, national and international, specifically dedicated to spreading lessons about the most appropriate type of institutional response.

9. This was the central insight of a long-forgotten and now frequently cited article by Rustow (1960). I have expanded on this, with a great deal of help from Machiavelli, in Schmitter (1985a, 1985b).

10. The most common scenario is one in which the previous authoritarian regime exercised severe and systematic control over parties and politicians representing working-class constituencies but left trade unions and their leaders relatively free to build their own organizations and defend specific clienteles, often in the shadow of the official corporatist system. Spain fits this pattern during the last decades of the Franco regime more closely than do Greece or Portugal. See Zufieur (1985).

11. This is all the more likely in situations where the previous regime has banned or controlled tightly the activities of so-called "peak associations" that might be capable of coordinating the broad demands of whole classes. The type of associational behavior that emerges during the transition is, therefore, likely to be fragmented, uneven, and localistic, making it all the easier to discredit on grounds of "particularism."

12. The "superiority" of parties in organizing for electoral competition will be all the greater where the duration of authoritarian rule has been brief and the leaders, symbols, and ideologies of former parties can be readily appropriated once the transition begins. Greek parties, according to this line of reasoning, had a considerable advantage over those of Spain, Portugal, and Italy.

13. Juan Linz (1983), speaking of Spain, has put the point well, if cryptically: "Politics takes precedence over interests." In the past when manual workers formed a larger proportion of the potential citizenry, trade unions might have been in a stronger strategic position in the event of regime change. The British Labour Party seems a unique instance when unions took the lead in organizing a party, but that was not a case of change in the type of regime. Indeed, the recent successes of socialist parties in Southern Europe (France, Greece, Spain) have been gained in the absence of, rather than because of, these parties having a strong link with the trade union movement.

14. The literature is enormous and varied. For a guide to its complexities and controversies, see Cawson (1986) or Williamson (1989).

15. See, especially, Przeworski (1980) and Przeworski and Wallerstein (1982). In subsequent work, especially that of Wallerstein, the organizational structure of representation is taken into account, but class actors are always treated dichotomously as "capital" and "labor."

16. The Spanish experience with *pactos economico-sociales* has been examined from a variety of perspectives. See, especially, Perez-Diaz (1987) and Roca (1987), also Foweracker (1987), Martinez-Allier and Roca (1987-1988) and Espina (1991). In Latin America, there has been much more discussion than actual experience with these agreements. See Grossi and dos Santos (1982), Pareja (1984-1985), Delich (1985), Lechner (1985), Flisfisch (1986), dos Santos (1988). For an overview by an outsider, see Cella (1990). The most impressive example, outside of Spain, has been Uruguay. See Rial (1985) and Mieres (1985). The least impressive example has been Argentina (and not for lack of trying). See Cavarozzi, de Riz, and Feldman (1986), Portantiero (1987), and Acuna and Golbert (1988).

17. Cf. Lapalombara (1964, p. 306), where this relationship is given the label *parentela*.

18. That this "decay" may be very slow and that surviving associations, especially trade unions, may struggle to retain the status (and resources) that they were guaranteed under state corporatism is especially well illustrated in Southern Europe by the Greek case after 1974.

19. However, the Basque nationalists and, more particularly, its armed militant component, the ETA, is clearly an exception that proves the rule.

20. To my knowledge, there has been only one case—Norway—in which the formation of comprehensive national class associations of business and labor largely preceded that of their respective, more specialized or localized member associations. Norway retains one of the most centralized and hierarchically structured interest systems in Western Europe.

21. A recent study of the peak association of French business (Weber, 1986) was entitled *Le Parti des Patrons: Le CNPF 1946-1986*. Its main theme is that precisely because capitalists in

France lacked reliable and significant access to political parties, they were compelled to rely so heavily on the CNPF for the defense of their class interests.

REFERENCES

Acuna, C., & Golbert, L. (1988). *Los empresarios y sus organizaciones: Actitudes y reacciones en relacion al Plan Austral y su interacción con el mercado de trabajo (Mimeograph).* Buenos Aires: CEDES.

Aguilar S. (1983). El associacionismo empresarial en la transicion postfranquista. *Papers, 24,* 53-85.

Bobbio, N. (1978). Are there alternatives to representative democracy? *Telos, 35,* 17-30.

Bruno, M., & Sachs, J. (1985). *Economics of worldwide stagflation.* Cambridge, MA: Harvard University Press.

Cameron, D. R. (1984). Social democracy, corporatism, labour quiescence and the representation of economic interest in advanced capitalist society. In J. H. Goldthorpe (Ed.), *Order and conflict in contemporary capitalism policy, power and order: The persistence of economic problems in capitalist states.* New Haven, CT: Yale University Press.

Cavarozzi, M., de Riz, L., & Feldman, V. (1986). *Concertacion, estado y sindicatos en la Argentina contemporanea* (Mimeograph). Buenos Aires: CEDES.

Cawson, A. (1986). *Corporatism and political theory.* Oxford: Blackwell.

Cella, G. P. (1990). Debolezze del pluralimo in America Latina: Quali possibilta per la concertazzione sociale. *Stato e Mercato, 28,* 3-27.

Dahl, R. (1982). *Dilemmas of pluralist democracy.* New Haven, CT: Yale University Press.

Delich, F. (1985). Pacto corporativo, democracia y clase obrera. In *Los limites de la democracia.* Buenos Aires: CLACSO.

Diamond, L., Linz, J. J., & Lipset, S. M. (Eds.). (1990). *Politics in developing countries: Comparing experiences with democracy.* Boulder, CO: Lynne Reimer.

dos Santos, M. R. (1988). *Pacts in the crisis: A reflection on the construction of democracy in Latin America.* Paper presented at the Conference on the Micro-Foundations of Democracy, University of Chicago.

Espina, A. (Ed.). (1991). *Concertación social, neocorporatismo y democracia.* Madrid: Ministerio de Trabajo y Seguridad Social.

Flisfisch, A. (1986). Reflexiones algo obicuas sobre el tema de la concertación. *Desarrollo Economic, 26,* 3-19.

Foley, M. (1989). *The Silence of constitutions: Gaps, "abeyances" and political temperament in the maintenance of government.* London: Routledge.

Foweracker, J. (1987). Corporatist strategies and the transition to democracy in Spain. *Comparative Politics, 20,* 57-72.

Gramsci, A. (1971). *Selections from the prison notebooks* (Q. Hoare & G. N. Smith, Eds./Trans.). New York: International Publishers.

Grossi, M., & dos Santos, M. R. (1982). La concertacion social: Una perspectiva sobre instrumentos de regulacion economico-social en procesos de redemocratizacion. *Critica y Utopia, 9,* 127-147.

Lange, P., & Meadwell, H. (1985). Typologies of democratic systems: From political inputs to political economy. In H. Wiarda (Ed.), *New directions in comparative politics.* Boulder, CO: Westview.

Lapalombara, J. (1964). *Interest groups in Italian politics.* Princeton, NJ: Princeton University Press.

448 AMERICAN BEHAVIORAL SCIENTIST

Lechner, N. (1985). *Pacto social en los processos de democratizacion: La experiencia latino-american.* Santiago: FLACSO.

Lijphart, A., & Crepaz, M. L. (1991). Corporatism and consensus democracy in eighteen countries: Conceptual and empirical linkages. *British Journal of Political Science, 21,* 235-246.

Linz, J. J. (1983). *Transition to democracy: A comparative perspective.* Paper presented at the Conference on Transition to Democracy, San Jose, Costa Rica.

Lipset, M. S. (1959a). *Political man: The social bases of politics.* Baltimore, MD: Johns Hopkins University Press.

Lipset, M. S. (1959b). Some social requisites of democracy: Economic development and political legitimacy. *American Political Science Review, 53,* 69-105.

Lipset, M. S. (1960). Party systems and the representation of social groups. *Archives européennes de sociologie, 1,* 50-85.

Lipset, M. S. (1963). *The first new nation.* New York: Basic Books.

Martinez-Allier, J., & Roca, J. (1987-1988). Spain after Franco: From corporatist ideology to corporatist reality. In P. Mattick, Jr. (Ed.), *International Journal of Political Economy, 17* [Special Issue].

Mieres, P. (1985). Concertación en Uruguay: expectativas elevadas y consensos escasos. *Cuadernos del CLAEH, 36,* 29-44.

O'Donnell, G., & Schmitter, P. C. (1986). *Transitions from authoritarian rule: Tentative conclusions about uncertain democracies.* Baltimore, MD: Johns Hopkins University Press.

Olson, M. (1965). *Logic of collective action.* Cambridge, MA: Harvard University Press.

Paloheimo, H. (1984). Distributive struggle, corporatist power structures and economic policy of the 1970s in developed capitalist countries. In H. Paloheimo (Ed.), *Politics in the era of corporatism and planning.* Helsinki: Finnish Political Science Association.

Pareja, C. (1984-1985). Las instancias de concertación: Sus presupuestos, sus modalidades y su articulación con las formas clásicas de democracia representativa. *Cuadernos del CLAEH, 32.*

Perez-Diaz, V. (1985). Los empresários y la clase política. *Papeles de la Economia Española, 22,* 2-37.

Perez-Diaz, V. (1987). Economic policies and social pacts in Spain during the transition. In L. Scholten (Ed.), *Political stability and neo-corporatism.* London: Sage.

Pizzorno, A. (1977). Scambio politico e identità colletiva nel conflitto di classe. In C. Crouch & A. Pizzorno, A. (Eds.). *Conflitti in Europa: Lotte di classe, sindacati e stato dopo il '68.* Milano: Etas Libri.

Portantiero, J. C. (1987). La transición entre la confrontación y el acuerdo. In J. Nun & J. C. Portantiero (Eds.), *Ensayos sobre la transición democrática en al Argentina.* Buenos Aires: Puntosur.

Pridham, G. (Ed.). (1990). *Securing democracy: Political parties and democratic consolidation in Southern Europe.* London: Routledge.

Przeworski, A. (1980). Material bases of consent: Economics and politics in a hegemonic system. In M. Zeitlin (Ed.), *Political power and social theory,* Vol. 1. Geenwich, CT: JAI.

Przeworski, A. (1986). Some problems in the study of the transition to democracy. In G. O'Donnell, P. C. Schmitter, & L. Whitehead (Eds.), *Transitions from authoritarian rule.* Baltimore, MD: Johns Hopkins University Press.

Przeworski, A., & Wallerstein, M. (1982). The structure of class conflict in democratic capitalist societies. *American Political Science Review, 76,* 215-238.

Rial, J. (1985). *Concertación y governabildad, proyecto, acuerdo político y pacto social: La reciente experiencia uruguaya* (Mimeograph). Montevideo: Seminario de Síntesis, Subprograma Concertación Social en Processos de Democratización.

Rijen, H. (1985). La CEOE como organización. *Papeles de la Economia Española*, 22, 115-121.

Roca, J. (1987). Neo-corporatism in post-Franco Spain. In I. Scholten (Ed.), *Political stability and neo-corporatism*. London: Sage.

Rustow, D. (1960). Transitions to democracy. *Comparative Politics*, 2, 337-363.

Schmidt, M. (1982). Does corporatism matter? Economic crisis and rates of unemployment in capitalist democracies in the 1970s. In G. Lehmbruch & P. C. Schmitter (Eds.), *Patterns of corporatist policy-making*. Beverly Hills, CA: Sage.

Schmitter, P. C. (1971). *Interest conflict and political change in Brazil*. Stanford, CA: Stanford University Press.

Schmitter, P. C. (1981). Interest intermediation and regime governability in contemporary Western Europe and North America. In S. Berger (Ed.), *Organizing interests in Western Europe*. Cambridge: Cambridge University Press.

Schmitter, P. C. (1983). Democratic theory and neo-corporatist practice. *Social Research*, 50, 885-928.

Schmitter, P. C. (1985a). Speculations about the prospective demise of authoritarian rule and its possible consequences: I. *Revista de Ciencia Politica*, 1, 83-102.

Schmitter, P. C. (1985b). Speculations about the prospective demise of authoritarian rule and its possible consequences: II. *Revista de Ciencia Politica*, 1, 125-144.

Schmitter, P. C. (1989). Corporatism is dead! Long live corporatism! *Government and Opposition*, 24, 54-73.

Schmitter, P. C. (1991). *Public opinion and the quality of democracy in Portugal*. Paper presented at the Coloquio sobre Sociedade Valores Culturais e Desenvolvimento, Fundação Luso-Americana para o Desenvolvimento.

Schmitter, P. C., & Karl, T. (1991). What democracy is ... and is not. *Journal of Democracy*, 2, 75-88.

Schott, K. (1985). *Policy power and order: The persistence of economic problems in capitalist states*. New Haven, CT: Yale University Press.

Streeck, W., & Schmitter, P. C. (Eds.). (1984). *Private interest government*. London: Sage.

Tarrow, S. (1991). *Transitions to democracy as waves of mobilization with applications to Southern Europe*. Paper presented at the SSRC Subcommittee on Southern Europe, Delphi, Greece.

Weber, H. (1986). *Le parti des patrons: Le CNPF 1946-1986*. Paris: Seuil.

Wilensky, H., & Turner, L. (1987). *Democratic corporatism and policy linkages: The interdependence of industrial, labor market, incomes and social policies in eight countries*. Berkeley, CA: Institute for International Studies.

Williamson, P. J. (1989). *Corporatism in perspective: An introductory guide to corporatist theory*. London: Sage.

Zufleur, J. M. (1985). El sindicalismo español en la transición y la crisis. *Papeles de la Economia Española*, 22, 286-317.

Name Index